Computer Animation
Complete

Computer Animation
Complete
All-in-One: Learn Motion Capture,
Characteristic, Point-Based, and
Maya Winning Techniques

Rick Parent, David S. Ebert, David A. D. Gould, Markus Gross, Chris

Kazmier, Richard Keiser, Charles J Lumsden, Alberto Menache,

Matthias MÜller-Fischer, F. Kenton Musgrave, Mark Pauly, Darwyn

Peachey, Ken Perlin, Hanspeter Pfister, Jason Sharpe, Martin

Wicke, Mark R. Wilkins, Nicholas Woolridge, Steven Worley

ELSEVIER

AMSTERDAM • BOSTON • HEIDELBERG • LONDON
NEW YORK • OXFORD • PARIS • SAN DIEGO
SAN FRANCISCO • SINGAPORE • SYDNEY • TOKYO

Morgan Kaufmann Publishers is an imprint of Elsevier

MORGAN KAUFMANN PUBLISHERS

Morgan Kaufmann Publishers is an imprint of Elsevier.
30 Corporate Drive, Suite 400,
Burlington, MA 01803, USA

This book is printed on acid-free paper.

Chapters 1, 2, 5, 7, were originally published in *Computer Animation*, by Rick Parent.

Chapters 3, 4, and online Bonus Chapter 14, were originally published in *Understanding Motion Capture for Computer Animation and Video Games*, by Alberto Menache.

Chapter 6 was originally published in *Texturing and Modeling: A Procedural Approach*, by David Ebert, F. Kenton Musgrave, Darwyn Peachey, Ken Perlin, and Steven Worley.

Chapter 8 was originally published in *In Silico*, by Jason Sharpe, Charles J. Lumsden, and Nicholas Woolridge.

Chapter 9 was originally published in *Point-Based Graphics*, by Makus Gross and Hanspeter Pfister

Chapters 10, 12, 13, and online Bonus Chapter 15, were originally published in *MEL Scripting for Maya Animators*, by Mark R. Wilkins and Chris Kazmier.

Chapter 11 was originally published in *Complete Maya Programming Vol.I*, by David A. D. Gould.

Library of Congress Cataloging-in-Publication Data
Computer animation complete: all-in-one: learn motion capture, characteristic, point-based, and Maya winning techniques/Rick Parent ... [et al.].
    p. cm.
Includes bibliographical references and index.
ISBN 978-0-12-375078-5 (pbk. : alk. paper)
1. Computer animation. 2. Maya (Computer file) I. Parent, Rick.
TR897.7.C65 2010
006.6'96--dc22

2009017063

British Library Cataloguing-in-Publication Data
A catalogue record for this book is available from the British Library.

ISBN: 978-0-12-375078-5

For information on all Morgan Kaufmann publications,
visit our Web site at *www.mkp.com* or *www.elsevierdirect.com*

Printed in the United States of America.
09 10 11 12 13   5 4 3 2 1

Typeset by: diacriTech, Chennai, India

Contents

PART II   MOTION CAPTURE TECHNIQUES

PART IV OTHER METHODS

BONUS CHAPTERS

Contributing Authors

Rick Parent (Chapters 1, 2, 5, and 7) is a professor in the Computer Science and Engineering Department of Ohio State University (OSU). As a graduate student, Rick worked at the Computer Graphics Research Group (CGRG) at OSU under the direction of Charles Csuri. In 1977, he received his PhD from the Computer and Information Science (CIS) Department, majoring in artificial intelligence. For the next three years, he worked at CGRG first as a research associate and then as associate director. In 1980, he cofounded and was president of The Computer Animation Company. In 1985, he joined the faculty of the CIS Department (now the Department of Computer Science and Engineering) at Ohio State. Rick's research interests include various aspects of computer animation with special focus on animation of the human figure. Currently, he is working on facial animation and on using model-based techniques to track human figures in video. He is also author of *Computer Animation*, published by Elsevier, 2007.

David S. Ebert (Chapter 6) is an associate professor in the School of Electrical and Computer Engineering at Purdue University. He received his PhD in computer and information science from The Ohio State University in 1991. His research interests are scientific, medical, and information visualization; computer graphics; animation; and procedural techniques. Dr. Ebert performs research in volume rendering, nonphotorealistic visualization, minimally immersive visualization, realistic rendering, modeling natural phenomena, procedural texturing, modeling, animation, and volumetric display software. He has also been very active in the graphics community, teaching courses, presenting papers, chairing the ACM SIGGRAPH '97 Sketches program, cochairing the IEEE Visualization '98 and '99 Papers program, serving on the ACM SIGGRAPH Executive Committee, and serving as editor in chief for IEEE *Transactions on Visualization and Computer Graphics*. He is also coauthor of *Texturing and Modeling: A Procedural Approach*, published by Elsevier, 2002.

David A. D. Gould (Chapter 11) has over a decade of experience in the computer graphics industry and has pursued the dual paths of programmer and artist. This rare ability to combine both the technical and artistic has won him many awards and credits. He has played a key role in the development of an eclectic mix of technology, including an award-winning laser rendering system for Pangolin. He developed software for controlling the Kuper motion-control rig, as well as the Monkey stop-motion puppet. He personally developed Illustrate!, the market leading toon and technical illustration renderer. This renderer is used by NASA, British Aerospace, Walt Disney Imagineering, and Sony Pictures Entertainment, among others.

David's career has spanned a wide variety of companies and continents. In Paris, he supervised the production of 3D stereoscopic scientific films, including the award-winning film, *Inside the Cell*. In London, he developed a patented facial animation system. Further broadening his experiences, he worked in New York in the postproduction industry, where he contributed to many high-profile commercials.

While at Walt Disney Feature Animation, Los Angeles, David developed cutting-edge animation and modeling technology for use in the production of their animated feature films. He diversified further by joining Exluna, Berkeley, the software company founded by former Pixar rendering researchers, including Larry Gritz. While there, he played an active role in the design and development of Entropy, the RenderMan-compatible renderer, as well as other products. David continued his rendering development efforts while at NVIDIA, in Santa Clara, California, by aiding in the design of their future 3D graphics chips. He has since joined Weta Digital, New Zealand, to work on the *Lord of the Rings* film trilogy. His varied roles in production, including shader development, lighting, and CG effects, reflects his broad range of talents. He is also author of *Complete Maya Programming*, published by Elsevier, 2002.

Markus Gross (Chapter 9) is a professor of computer science, chair of the institute of computational science, and director of the Computer Graphics Laboratory of the Swiss Federal Institute of Technology (ETH) in Zurich. His research interests include point-based graphics, physically based modeling, multiresolution analysis, and virtual reality. He has published more than 130 scientific papers on computer graphics and scientific visualization, and he authored the book *Visual Computing*, Springer, 1994. He holds various patents on core graphics technologies. Gross has taught courses at major graphics conferences including ACM SIGGRAPH, IEEE Visualization, and Eurographics. He serves as a member of international program committees of many graphics conferences and on the editorial board of various scientific journals. Gross was a papers cochair of the IEEE Visualization '99, the Eurographics 2000, and the IEEE Visualization 2002 conferences. He was chair of the papers committee of ACM SIGGRAPH 2005. Gross received a master of science in electrical and computer engineering and a PhD in computer graphics and image analysis, both from the University of Saarbrucken, Germany. From 1990 to 1994, Gross worked for the Computer Graphics Center in Darmstadt, where he established and directed the Visual Computing Group. He is a senior member of IEEE, a member of the IEEE Computer Society, a member of ACM and ACM SIGGRAPH, and a member of the Eurographics Association. From 2002 to 2006 he was a member of the ETH research commission. Gross serves in board positions of a number of international research institutes, societies, and government organizations. He is chair of the technical advisory committee of Ageia Corporation. Gross cofounded Cyfex AG, NovodexAG, and LiberoVisionAG. He is also coeditor of *Point-Based Graphics*, published by Elsevier, 2007.

Chris Kazmier (Chapters 10, 12, and 13) is a senior technical director at Sony Pictures Imageworks, where he creates computer-generated effects for live-action films. He has worked on projects ranging from *The Haunted Mansion* to Sony's first all 3D feature animation *Open Season*. Previously, Chris worked at DreamWorks on *Sinbad* and at PDI/DreamWorks on the Intel Aliens ad campaign. Credits also include Fox Animation Studio's *Titan AE* and *Anastasia*. He is also coauthor of *MEL Scripting for Maya Animators*, published by Elsevier, 2005.

Richard Keiser (Chapter 9) is a research associate and PhD student at the Computer Science Department of ETH Zurich, Switzerland. He holds a master's degree in computer science and specializes in physics-based animations using particles and deformable point-based surface modeling. He is also a contributor to *Point-Based Graphics*, published by Elsevier, 2007.

Charles J Lumsden (Chapter 8) is professor of medicine at the University of Toronto. Trained as a theoretical physicist, he studies the mathematical logic behind illnesses such as Alzheimer's disease and cancer. He and his students have explored and championed a variety of 3D graphics software as aids to biomedical discovery, including top-tier commercial tools such as Maya and MEL. He is also coauthor of *In Silico*, published by Elsevier, 2008.

Alberto Menache (Chapters 3 and 4) founded Three Space Imagery, Inc. (TSi), a computer graphics and video game developer, in Los Angeles, where he and his team developed proprietary software for motion capture usage in animation. After selling his software to Motion Analysis Corporation, Menache moved on to Pacific Data Images, a computer graphics industry leader, where he is the lead character technical director at the commercial and film effects division. His latest production credits include the film *Forces of Nature*, commercials for SEGA, Circle K and Pillsbury, the award-winning music video for TLC's "Waterfalls," and dozens of video games, including *Dark Ridge*, *Messiah*, and *Soul Blade*. He is also author of *Understanding Motion Capture for Computer Animation and Video Games*, published by Elsevier, 1999.

Matthias Müller-Fischer (Chapter 9) received his PhD on atomistic simulation of dense polymer systems in 1999 from ETH Zurich and changed fields to macroscopic physically based simulations during his postdoc 1999–2001 with the MIT Computer Graphics Group. In 2002, he cofounded NovodeX, now a subsidiary of AGEIA Inc., the company developing the world's first Physics Processing Unit (PPU) for games. He currently works for AGEIA as a principal software engineer responsible for the development of hardware accelerated simulation software for real-time effects such as fluids, cloth, and rigid body animation. He is also a contributor to *Point-Based Graphics*, published by Elsevier, 2007.

F. Kenton Musgrave (Chapter 6), also known as "Doc Mojo," is a computer artist and computer graphics researcher with a worldwide reputation. Dr. Musgrave lectures internationally on fractals, computer graphics and the visual arts, and his own computer graphics research. He has developed digital effects for such films as *Titanic* and *Apollo 13*. His images have been widely published and exhibited at international venues, including the Lincoln Center and the Guggenheim Museum in New York City. Dr. Musgrave spent six years in the mathematics department at Yale University working with Benoit Mandelbrot, the inventor of fractal geometry, who credited Musgrave with being "the first true fractal-based artist." He is a founding member of the Algorist school of algorithmic artists and CEO/CTO of Pandromeda, Inc., whose planet-building software product, *Mojo World*, is the pinnacle of his research. Musgrave has served as director of advanced 3D research at MetaCreations, principal software engineer at Digital Domain, senior scientist at Bethesda Softworks, and assistant professor at George Washington University. Musgrave received his PhD in computer science from Yale University and his MS and BA in computer science from the University of California at Santa Cruz. He is also coauthor of *Texturing and Modeling: A Procedural Approach*, published by Elsevier, 2002.

Mark Pauly (Chapter 9) is an assistant professor at the computer science department of ETH Zurich, Switzerland, since April 2005. From August 2003 to March 2005, he was a postdoctoral scholar at Stanford University, where he also held a position as visiting assistant professor during the summer of 2005. He received his PhD degree (with highest distinction) in 2003 from ETH Zurich and his MS degree (with honors) in computer science in 1999 from the Technical University of Kaiserslautern, Germany. His research interests include geometry processing, multiscale shape modeling and analysis, physics-based animation, and computational geometry. He is also a contributor to *Point-Based Graphics*, published by Elsevier, 2007.

Darwyn Peachey (Chapter 6) is a technical supervisor at Pixar Animation Studios in Emeryville, California. He has worked at Pixar since 1988 as a developer of rendering and animation software, as a senior technology manager, and as a member of the technical crew on the *Toy Story* films, *Ratatouille*, and *Up*. Peachey studied at the University of Saskatchewan in Canada, where he received bachelor's and master's degrees in computer science. He is a member of the Visual Effects Society and the ACM, and has served on several technical program committees for SIGGRAPH and other conferences, and on the editorial board of the *Journal of Graphics Tools.* His published papers include work in computer graphics and artificial intelligence, and he was one of the recipients of a 1993 Academy Award for the RenderMan rendering package. He is also coauthor of *Texturing and Modeling: A Procedural Approach*, published by Elsevier, 2002.

Ken Perlin (Chapter 6) is a professor in the computer science department and the director of the Media Research Laboratory and Center for Advanced Technology at New York University (NYU). Dr. Perlin's research interests include graphics, animation, and multimedia. In 2002, he received the New York City Mayor's Award for Excellence in Science and Technology and the Sokol Award for Outstanding Science Faculty at NYU. In 1997, he won an Academy Award for Technical Achievement from the Academy of Motion Picture Arts and Sciences for his *noise* and *turbulence* procedural texturing techniques, which are widely used in feature films and television. In 1991, he received a Presidential Young Investigator Award from the National Science Foundation. Dr. Perlin received his PhD in computer science from New York University in 1986 and a BA in theoretical mathematics from Harvard University in 1979. He was head of software development at R/GREENBERG Associates in New York, from 1984 to 1987. Prior to that he was the system architect for computer-generated animation at Mathematical Applications

Group, Inc. *TRON* was the first movie in which Ken Perlin's name appeared in the credits. He has served on the board of directors of the New York chapter of ACM/SIGGRAPH and currently serves on the board of directors of the New York Software Industry Association. He is also coauthor of *Texturing and Modeling: A Procedural Approach*, published by Elsevier, 2002.

Hanspeter Pfister (Chapter 9) is associate director and senior research scientist at MERL Mitsubishi Electric Research Laboratories in Cambridge, Massachusetts. He is the chief architect of VolumePro, Mitsubishi Electric's real-time volume rendering hardware for PCs. His research interests include computer graphics, scientific visualization, and graphics architectures. His work spans a range of topics, including point-based graphics, appearance modeling and acquisition, computational photography, 3D television, and face modeling. Hanspeter Pfister received his PhD in computer science in 1996 from the State University of New York at Stony Brook. He received his MS in Electrical Engineering from the Swiss Federal Institute of Technology (ETH) Zurich, Switzerland, in 1991. Dr. Pfister has taught courses at major graphics conferences including SIGGRAPH, IEEE Visualization, and Eurographics. He has been teaching introductory and advanced graphics courses at the Harvard Extension School since 1999. He is associate editor of the IEEE Transactions on Visualization and Computer Graphics (TVCG), chair of the IEEE Visualization and Graphics Technical Committee (VGTC), and has served as a member of international program committees of major graphics conferences. Dr. Pfister was the general chair of the IEEE Visualization 2002 conference. He is senior member of the IEEE, and member of ACM, ACM SIGGRAPH, the IEEE Computer Society, and the Eurographics Association. He is also coeditor of *Point-Based Graphics*, published by Elsevier, 2007.

Jason Sharpe (Chapter 8) is a cofounder of the award-winning AXS Biomedical Animation Studio in Toronto. Trained in mechanical engineering at Queen's University, fine arts at Emily Carr Institute of Art and Design and biomedical communications at the University of Toronto, he has worked on a wide range of Maya-based 3D animation projects for research, education, and entertainment. He is also coauthor of *In Silico*, published by Elsevier, 2008.

Martin Wicke (Chapter 9) was born in 1979 and studied computer science at the University of Kaiserslautern, Germany. He currently works as a research associate and PhD student at the Computer Graphics Laboratory at ETH Zurich, Switzerland. His main research interests are physics-based modeling and animation. He is also a contributor to *Point-Based Graphics*, published by Elsevier, 2007.

Mark R. Wilkins (Chapter 10, 12, and 13) is a generalist technical director at Rhythm & Hues Studios in the Commercials Division. He previously worked at DreamWorks Animation, developing production pipelines for effects and character animation, and at Walt Disney Feature Animation as software engineer and scene setup supervisor. He has contributed to a number of films, including *Dinosaur, Minority Report, Over the Hedge, The Golden Compass*, and *Fast & Furious.*

Mark holds a degree in physics from Harvey Mudd College. He is also coauthor of *MEL Scripting for Maya Animators,* published by Elsevier, 2005.

Nicholas Woolridge (Chapter 8) is associate professor of Biomedical Communications at the University of Toronto and has played a major role in the development of the visualization design field in the university's renowned master's degree in biomedical communications program. His current research focuses on the optimization of visual media for medical research and education. He is also coauthor of *In Silico*, published by Elsevier, 2008.

Steven Worley (Chapter 6) has focused his research in computer graphics on appearance and rendering models. His early work on algorithmic textures led to new antialiasing and efficiency adaptations to classical algorithms. In 1996, he introduced the concept of the cellular texturing basis function, which has been widely adopted by most commercial rendering packages. His extensive collaboration with many professional studios has led to the creation of a wide variety of 3D tools. Most recently, his tools for rendering hair and fur have been widely adopted and used in film, TV, and game development. His company, Worley Laboratories (http://www.worley.com), publishes plug-in tools for various 3D packages. He is also coauthor of *Texturing and Modeling: A Procedural Approach*, published by Elsevier, 2002.

Introduction to Computer Animation

Introduction

1

Rick Parent

CHAPTER CONTENTS

Computer animation, for many people, is synonymous with big-screen events such as *Star Wars, Toy Story,* and *Titanic.* But not all, or arguably even most, computer animation is done in Hollywood. It is not unusual for Saturday morning cartoons to be entirely computer generated. Computer games take advantage of state-of-the-art computer graphics techniques and have become a major motivating force driving research in computer animation. Real-time performance-driven computer animation

3

has appeared at SIGGRAPH[1] and on *Sesame Street*. Desktop computer animation is now possible at a reasonable cost. Computer animation on the web is routine. Digital simulators for training pilots, SWAT teams, and nuclear reactor operators are commonplace. The distinguishing characteristics of these various venues are the cost, the image quality desired, and the amount and type of interaction allowed. This book does not address the issues concerned with a particular venue, but it does present algorithms and techniques used to do computer animation in all of them.

Computer animation, as used here, refers to any computer-based computation used in producing images intended to create the perception of motion. The emphasis in this book is on algorithms and techniques that process three-dimensional graphical data. In general, any value that can be changed can be animated. An object's position and orientation are obvious candidates for animation, but all the following can be animated as well: the object's shape, its shading parameters, its texture coordinates, the light source parameters, and the camera parameters.

In considering computer animation techniques, there are basically three general approaches to motion control. The first is *artistic animation* in which the animator has the prime responsibility for crafting the motion. The foundation of artistic animation is interpolation. The second is *data-driven animation*, in which live motion is digitized and then mapped onto graphical objects. The primary technology for data-driven animation is referred to as *motion capture*. The third is *procedural animation,* in which there is a computational model that is used to control the motion. Usually, this is in the form of setting initial conditions for some type of physical or behavioral simulation.

To set the context for computer animation, it is important to understand its heritage, its history, and certain relevant concepts. The rest of this chapter discusses motion perception, the technical evolution of animation, animation production, and notable works in computer animation. It provides a grounding in computer animation as a field of endeavor.

1.1 PERCEPTION

A picture can quickly convey a large amount of information because the human visual system is a sophisticated information processor. It follows, then, that moving images have the potential to convey even more information in a short time. Indeed, the human visual system has evolved to provide for survival in an ever-changing world; it is designed to notice and interpret movement.

It is widely recognized that a series of images, when displayed in rapid succession, are perceived by an observer as a single moving image. This is possible because the eye–brain complex has the ability, under sufficient viewing conditions and within certain playback rates, to create a sensation of continuous imagery from such

---

[1]SIGGRAPH is the Association for Computing Machinery's (ACM) Special Interest Group on Computer Graphics. The ACM is the main professional group for computer scientists.

a sequence of still images. A commonly held view is that this experience is due to *persistence of vision*, whereby the eye retains a visual imprint of an image for a brief instant once the stimulus is removed. It is argued that these imprints, called *positive afterimages* of the individual stills, fill in the gaps between the images to produce the perception of a continuously changing image. Peter Roget (of Thesaurus fame) presented the idea of impressions of light being retained on the retina in 1824 [1]. But persistence of vision is not the same as perception of motion. Rotating a white-light source fast enough will create the impression of a stationary white ring. Although this effect can be attributed to persistence of vision, the result is static. The sequential illumination of a group of lights typical of a movie theater marquee produces the illusion of a lighted object circling the signage. Motion is perceived, yet persistence of vision does not appear to be involved because no individual images are present. Recently, the causality of the (physiological) persistence of vision mechanism has been called into question and the perception of motion has been attributed to a (psychological) mechanism known as the *phi phenomenon*; the apparent motion is referred to as *beta motion* [2–4].

Whatever the underlying mechanism is, the result is that in both film and video, a sequence of images can be displayed at rates fast enough to fool the eye into interpreting it as continuous imagery. When the perception of continuous imagery fails to be created, the display is said to *flicker*. In this case, the animation appears as a rapid sequence of still images to the eye–brain complex. Depending on conditions such as room lighting and viewing distance, the rate at which individual images must be played back in order to maintain the perception of continuous imagery varies. This rate is referred to as the *critical flicker frequency* [5].

While perception of motion addresses the lower limits for establishing the perception of continuous imagery, there are also upper limits to what the eye can perceive. The receptors in the eye continually sample light in the environment. The limitations on motion perception are determined, in part, by the reaction time of those sensors and by other mechanical limitations such as blinking and tracking. If an object moves too quickly with respect to the viewer, then the receptors in the eye will not be able to respond fast enough for the brain to distinguish sharply defined, individual detail; *motion blur* results [6]. In a sequence of still images, motion blur is produced by a combination of the object's speed and the time interval over which the scene is sampled. In a still camera, a fast-moving object will not blur if the shutter speed is fast enough relative to the object's speed. In computer graphics, motion blur will never result if the scene is sampled at a precise instant in time; to compute motion blur, the scene needs to be sampled over an interval of time or manipulated to appear as though it were [7,8]. If motion blur is not calculated, then images of a fast-moving object can appear disjointed, similar to live action viewed with a strobe light. This effect is often referred to as *strobing*. In hand-drawn animation, fast-moving objects are typically stretched in the direction of travel so that the object's images in adjacent frames overlap [9], reducing the strobing effect.

As reflected in the discussion above, there are actually two rates that are of concern. One is the *playback* or *refresh* rate – the number of images per second displayed in the viewing process. The other is the *sampling* or *update* rate – the number of different images that occur per second. The playback rate is the rate related to flicker. The sampling rate determines how jerky the motion appears. For example, a television signal conforming to the National Television Standards Committee (NTSC) format displays images at a rate of roughly 30 fps,[2] but because it is *interlaced*,[3] fields are played at 60 fps to prevent flicker under normal viewing conditions [10]. In some programs (e.g. some Saturday morning cartoons), there may be only six different images per second, with each image repeatedly displayed five times. Often, lip-sync animation is drawn *on twos* (every other frame) because drawing it *on ones* (animating it in every frame) makes it appear too hectic. Film is typically shown in movie theatres at playback rates of 24 fps (in the United States) but, in order to reduce the flicker, each frame is actually displayed twice (*double-shuttered*) to obtain an effective refresh rate of 48 fps. On the other hand, because an NTSC television signal is interlaced, smoother motion can be produced by sampling the scene every sixtieth of a second even though the complete frames are only played back at 30 fps [5]. Computer displays are typically progressive scan (*noninterlaced*) devices with refresh rates above 70 fps [10].

1.2 THE HERITAGE OF ANIMATION

In the most general sense, *animate*[4] means "give life to" and includes live-action puppetry such as that found on *Sesame Street* and the use of electromechanical devices to move puppets, i.e. *animatronics*. History is replete with attempts to bring stuff to life. This history is a combination of myth, deception, entertainment, science, and medicine. Many of the references to animation are in the form of stories about conjuring a life force into some humanoid form: from Pygmalion to Prometheus to Wagner's Homunculus in Goethe's Faust to Shelley's Dr. Frankenstein. Some of the history is about trying to create mechanical devices that mimic certain human activity: from Jacque Vaucanson's mechanical flute player, drummer, and defecating duck in the 1730s to Wolfgang von Kempelen's chess player in 1769, to Pierre Jaquet-Droz's writing automaton of 1774, to the electromechanical humanoid robots popular today. The early mechanisms from the 1700s and 1800s were set in the milieu of scientific debate over the mechanistic nature of the human body (e.g. *L'Homme Machine*, translated as *Man a Machine*,

---

[2]More accurately, the format for broadcast television system, established by the National Television Standards Committee (NTSC), specifies a frame rate of 29.97 fps [48].

[3]An *interlaced* display is one in which a frame is divided into two *fields*. Each field consists of either the odd or even numbered scanlines. The odd and even fields are displayed in alternate scans of the display device [5].

[4]A more restricted definition of *animation*, also found in the literature, requires the use of a sequence of stills to create the visual impression of motion. The restricted definition does not admit techniques such as animatronics or shadow puppets under the rubric *animation*.

was written by Julien Offray de La Mettrie in 1747 and was quite controversial). This activity in humanoid mechanical devices was propelled by a confluence of talents contributed by magicians, clock makers, philosophers, scientists, artists, anatomists, glove makers, and surgeons (see Gaby Wood's book for an entertaining survey on the quest for mechanical life [11]). Here, however, the focus is on devices that use a sequence of individual still images to create the effect of a single moving image because these devices have a closer relationship to hand-drawn animation.

1.2.1 Early Devices

Persistence of vision and the ability to interpret a series of stills as a moving image were actively investigated in the 1800s [12], well before the film camera was invented. The recognition and subsequent investigation of this effect led to a variety of devices intended as parlor toys [13,14]. Perhaps the simplest of these early devices is the *Thaumatrope,* a flat disk with images drawn on both sides that has two strings connected opposite each other on the rim of the disk (see Fig. 1.1). The disk can be quickly flipped back and forth by twirling the strings. When flipped rapidly enough, the two images appear to be superimposed. The classic example uses the image of a bird on one side and the image of a birdcage on the other; the rotating disk visually

FIGURE 1.1

A Thaumatrope.

places the bird inside the birdcage. An equally primitive technique is the *flip book,* a tablet of paper with an individual drawing on each page. When the pages are flipped rapidly, the viewer has the impression of motion.

One of the most well known early animation devices is the *Zoetrope* or *wheel of life*. The Zoetrope has a short, fat cylinder that rotates on its axis of symmetry. Around the inside of the cylinder is a sequence of drawings, each one slightly different from the ones next to it. The cylinder has long vertical slits cut into its side between each adjacent pair of images so that when it is spun on its axis each slit allows the eye to see the image on the opposite wall of the cylinder (see Fig. 1.2). The sequence of slits passing in front of the eye as the cylinder is spun on its axis presents a sequence of images to the eye, creating the illusion of motion.

Related gizmos that use a rotating mechanism to present a sequence of stills to the viewer are the *Phenakistoscope* and the *Praxinoscope*. The Phenakistoscope also uses a series of rotating slots to present a sequence of images to the viewer by positioning two disks rotating in unison on an axis; one disk has slits and the other contains images facing the slits. One sights along the axis of rotation, so the slits pass in front of the eye, which can thus view a sequence of images from the other disk. The Praxinoscope uses a cylindrical arrangement of rotating mirrors inside a large cylinder of images facing the mirrors. The mirrors are angled, thus reflecting an observer's view of the images.

Just before the turn of the century, the moving image began making its way on stage. The *Magic Lantern* (an image projector powered by candle or lamp) and shadow puppets became popular theater entertainment [15]. On the educational front, Etienne-Jules Marey [16] and Eadweard Muybridge [17,18] investigated the motions of humans and animals. To show image sequences during his lectures, Muybridge invented the *Zoopraxinoscope,* a projection device also based on

FIGURE 1.2

A Zoetrope.

rotating slotted disks. Then, in 1891, the seed of a revolution was planted: Thomas Edison invented the motion picture viewer (the *Kinetograph*), giving birth to a new industry [14].

1.2.2 **The Early Days of Conventional Animation**

Animation in America exploded in the twentieth century in the form of filming hand-drawn, two-dimensional images (referred to here also as *conventional* or *traditional* animation). Studying the early days of conventional animation is interesting in itself [14,19–21], but the purpose of this overview is to provide an appreciation of the technological advances that drove the progress of animation during the early years.

Following Edison's kinetoscope, there were several rapid developments in film technology. One of the most notable developments was that of the motion picture projector by the Lumiere brothers, Auguste and Louis, in France. They are credited with the first public screening of film on December 28, 1895. They called their device the *Cinematograph*. It could both project and develop film. They used it to film everyday events including a train coming into a train station; this footage, when shown to the audience, sent everyone scrambling for cover. It was also used for aerial photography (years before the airplane took to the skies).

The earliest use of a camera to make lifeless things appear to move occurred in 1896 by Georges Méliès. Méliès used simple camera tricks such as multiple exposures and stop-motion techniques to make objects appear, disappear, and change shape [22,23]. His best known trick film is *A Trip to the Moon* (1902). One of the earliest pioneers in film animation was J. Stuart Blackton, an American who actually animated "smoke" in a scene in 1900 (special effects) and is credited with creating the first animated cartoon, *Humorous Phases of Funny Faces* (1906), by drawing and erasing on a chalkboard between takes. Emile Cohl, a Frenchman, produced several vignettes including *Fantasmagorie* (1908) that is considered to be the first fully-animated film ever made. The American Winsor McCay is the first celebrated animator, best known for his works *Little Nemo* (1911) and *Gertie the Dinosaur* (1914). McCay is considered by many to have produced the first popular animations [19].

Like many of the early animators, McCay was an accomplished newspaper cartoonist. He redrew each complete image on rice paper mounted on cardboard and then filmed them individually. He was also the first to experiment with color in animation. Much of his early work was incorporated into vaudeville acts in which he "interacted" with an animated character on a screen. Similarly, early cartoons often incorporated live action with animated characters. To appreciate the impact of such a popular entertainment format, keep in mind the relative naïveté of audiences at the time; they had no idea how film worked, much less what hand-drawn animation was. It was, indeed, magic.

The first major technical developments in the animation process can be traced to the efforts of John Bray, one of the first to recognize that patenting aspects of the animation process would result in a competitive advantage [19]. Starting in 1910, his work laid the foundation for conventional animation as it exists today. Earl Hurd, who joined forces with Bray in 1914, patented the use of translucent *cels*[5] in the compositing of multiple layers of drawings into a final image and also patented grayscale drawings as opposed to black-and-white. Later developments by Bray and others enhanced the overlay idea to include a peg system for registration and the drawing of the background on long sheets of paper so that *panning* (translating the camera parallel to the plane of the background) could be performed more easily. Out of Bray's studio came Max Fleischer (Betty Boop), Paul Terry (Terrytoons), George Stallings (Tom and Jerry), and Walter Lantz (Woody Woodpecker). In 1915, Fleischer patented *rotoscoping* (drawing images on cells by tracing over previously recorded live action). Several years later, in 1920, Bray experimented with color in the short *The Debut of Thomas Cat.*

While the technology was advancing, animation as an art form was still struggling. The first animated character with an identifiable personality was Felix the Cat, drawn by Otto Messmer of Pat Sullivan's studio [19]. Felix was the most popular and most financially successful cartoon of the mid-1920s. In the late 1920s, however, new forces had to be reckoned with: sound and Walt Disney.

1.2.3 Disney

Walt Disney was, of course, the overpowering force in the history of conventional animation. Not only did his studio contribute several technical innovations, but Disney, more than anyone else, advanced animation as an art form [21]. Disney's innovations in animation technology included the use of a storyboard to review the story and pencil sketches to review motion. In addition, he pioneered sound and color in animation (although he was not the first to use color). Disney also studied live-action sequences to create more realistic motion in his films. When he used sound for the first time in *Steamboat Willie* (1928), he gained an advantage over his competitors.

One of the most significant technical innovations of the Disney studio was development of the multiplane camera (see Fig. 1.3) [19,20]. The multiplane camera consists of a camera mounted above multiple planes, each of which holds an animation cell. Each of the planes can move in six directions (right, left, up, down, in, out), and the camera can move closer and farther away (see Fig. 1.4).

Multiplane camera animation is more powerful than one might think. By moving the camera closer to the planes while the planes are used to move foreground images out to the sides, a more effective zoom can be performed. Moving multiple planes at different rates can produce the *parallax effect,* which is the visual effect of closer objects apparently moving faster across the field of view (fov) than objects farther away as an observer's view pans across an environment. This is very effective

---

[5]*Cel* is short for *celluloid*, which was the original material used in making the translucent layers. Currently, cels are made from acetate.

FIGURE 1.3

Disney multiplane camera that allows independent movement of two-dimensional planes creating effects such as parallax (© Disney Enterprises, Inc.).

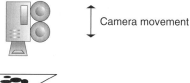

Camera movement

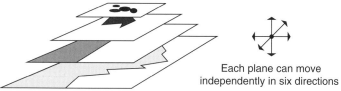

Each plane can move independently in six directions

FIGURE 1.4

Directional range of the multiplane camera, inside of which the image is optically composited.

in creating the illusion of depth and an enhanced sensation of three dimensions. Keeping the camera lens open during movement can produce several additional effects: figures can be extruded into shapes of higher dimension; depth cues can be incorporated into an image by blurring the figures on more distant cels; and motion blur can be produced.

With regard to the art of animation, Disney perfected the ability to impart unique, endearing personalities in his characters, such as those exemplified in Mickey Mouse, Pluto, Goofy, the Three Little Pigs, and the Seven Dwarfs [20,21]. He promoted the idea that the mind of the character was the driving force of the action and that a key to believable animated motion was the analysis of real-life motion. He also developed mood pieces, for example, *Skeleton Dance* (1929) and *Fantasia* (1940).

1.2.4 Contributions of Others

The 1930s saw the proliferation of animation studios, among them Fleischer, Iwerks, Van Beuren, Universal Pictures, Paramount, MGM, and Warner Brothers. The technological advances that are of concern here were mostly complete by this period. The differences between, and contributions of, the various studios have to do more with the artistic aspects of animation than with the technology involved in producing animation [19]. Many of the notable animators in these studios were graduates of Disney's or Bray's studio. Among the most recognizable names are Ub Iwerks, George Stallings, Max Fleischer, Bill Nolan, Chuck Jones, Paul Terry, and Walter Lantz.

1.2.5 Other Media for Animation

The rich heritage of hand-drawn animation in the United States makes it natural to consider it the precursor to computer animation, which also has strong roots in the United States. However, computer animation has a close relationship to other animation techniques as well.

A close comparison can be made between computer animation and some of the stop-motion techniques, such as clay and puppet animation. Typically, in three-dimensional computer animation, one of the first steps is the object modeling process. The models are then manipulated to create the three-dimensional scenes that are rendered to produce the images of the animation. In much the same way, clay and puppet stop-motion animation use three-dimensional figures that are built and then animated in separate, well-defined stages [13]. Once the physical, three-dimensional figures are created, they are used to lay out a three-dimensional environment. A camera is positioned to view the environment and record an image. One or more of the figures are manipulated and the camera may be repositioned. The camera records another image of the scene. The figures are manipulated again, another image is taken of the scene, and the process is repeated to produce the animated sequence.

Willis O'Brien of *King Kong* fame is generally considered the dean of this type of stop-motion animation. His understudy, who went on to create an impressive body of work in his own right, was Ray Harryhausen (*Mighty Joe Young, Jason and the*

Argonauts, and many more). More recent impressive examples of three-dimensional stop-motion animation are Nick Park's *Wallace and Gromit* series and Tim Burton projects such as *The Nightmare Before Christmas, James and the Giant Peach,* and *Corpse Bride.*

Because of computer animation's close association with video technology, it has also been associated with video art, which depends largely on the analog manipulation of the video signal in producing effects such as colorization and warping [24]. Because creating video art is inherently a two-dimensional process, the relationship is viewed mainly in the context of computer animation postproduction techniques. Even this connection has faded because the popularity of recording computer animation by digital means has eliminated most analog processing.

1.2.6 Principles of Animation

To study various techniques and algorithms used in computer animation, it is useful to first understand their relationship to the animation principles used in hand-drawn animation. In an article by Lasseter [25], the principles of animation, articulated by some of the original Disney animators [21], are related to techniques commonly used in computer animation. The principles are *squash and stretch, timing, secondary action, slow in and slow out, arcs, follow through/overlapping action, exaggeration, appeal, anticipation, staging, solid drawing,* and *straight ahead and pose to pose.* Lasseter is a conventionally trained animator who worked at Disney before going to Pixar. At Pixar, he was responsible for many celebrated computer animations including *Tin Toy* that, in 1989, was the first computer animation to win an Academy Award. Although Lasseter discusses each principle in terms of how it might be implemented using computer animation techniques, the principles are organized here according to the type of motion quality they contribute to in a significant way. Because several principles relate to multiple qualities, some principles appear under more than one heading.

1.2.6.1 Simulating Physics

Squash and stretch, timing, secondary action, slow in and slow out, and arcs establish the physical basis of objects in the scene. A given object possesses some degree of rigidity and should appear to have some amount of mass. This is reflected in the distortion (squash and stretch) of its shape during an action, especially a collision. The animation must support these notions consistently for a given object throughout the animation. Timing has to do with how actions are spaced according to the weight, size, and personality of an object or character and, in part, with the physics of movement as well as the artistic aspects of the animation. Secondary action supports the main action, possibly supplying physically based reactions to an action that just occurred. Slow in and slow out and arcs are concerned with how things move through space. Objects slow in and slow out of poses. When speaking of the actions involved, objects are said to ease in and ease out. Such speed variations model inertia, friction, and viscosity. Objects, because of the physical laws of nature such as gravity, usually move not in straight lines but rather in arcs.

1.2.6.2 Designing Aesthetically Pleasing Actions

Exaggeration, appeal, solid drawing, and follow through/overlapping action are principles that address the aesthetic design of an action or action sequence. Often, the animator needs to exaggerate a motion, so it cannot be missed or so it makes a point (Tex Avery is well known for this type of conventional animation). To keep the audience's attention, the animator needs to make it enjoyable to watch (appeal). In addition, actions should flow into one another (follow through/overlapping action) to make the entire shot appear to continually evolve instead of looking like disjointed movements. Solid drawing refers to making the character look pliable and not stiff or wooden, and squash and stretch can be used to exaggerate motion and to create flowing action. Secondary actions and timing considerations also play a role in designing motion.

1.2.6.3 Effectively Presenting Action

Anticipation and staging concern how an action is presented to the audience. Anticipation dictates that an upcoming action is set up so that the audience knows it (or something) is coming. Staging expands on this notion of presenting an action so that it is not missed by the audience. Timing is also involved in effective presentation to the extent that an action has to be given the appropriate duration for the intended effect to reach the audience. Secondary action and exaggeration can also be used to create an effective presentation of an action.

1.2.6.4 Production Technique

Straight ahead versus pose to pose concerns how a motion is created. Straight ahead refers to progressing from a starting point and developing the motion continually along the way. Physically based animation could be considered a form of this. Pose to pose, the typical approach in conventional animation, refers to identifying keyframes and then interpolating intermediate frames.

1.2.7 Principles of Filmmaking

Basic principles of filmmaking are worth reviewing in order to get a sense of how effective imagery is constructed. Several of the basic principles are listed below although more complete references should be consulted by the interested reader (e.g. [26]). Some of the following are guidelines that should be followed in composing a single image; others are options of how to present the action.

1.2.7.1 Three-Point Lighting

There is a standard set of three lights that are used to illuminate the central figure in a scene. These are the key light, the fill light, and the rim light. The key light is often positioned up and to the side of the camera, pointing directly at the central figure. This focuses the observer's attention on what's important. The rim light is positioned behind the central figure and serves to highlight the rim thus outlining the figure which makes the figure stand out from the background. The

(a) Key Light   (b) Fill Light   (c) Rim Light   (d) All Lights

FIGURE 1.5

Three-point lighting example. (a) Key light: a single spot light is placed at 45° from the top-right of the frame. This light has the highest intensity in the set up and is responsible for the cast shadows of the objects. (b) Fill light: a blue fill light from the front and right of the object is used to illuminate the dark areas created by the key light. This light is less intense and does not cast shadows or highlights on the objects. (c) Rim light: multiple lights are placed opposite to the direction of the key light. They highlight the edges, which are otherwise in shadow. These highlights help separate the objects from the background as well as from other overlapping objects in the scene. (d) All lights: this is the final lighting set up – a combination of key, fill, and rim lights. The scene is rendered with ray tracing, generating reflections on selective surfaces (Images courtesy of Sucheta Bhatawadekar, ACCAD).

fill light is a flood light typically positioned below the camera that fills the figure with a soft light bringing out other details in the figure's appearance. See Fig. 1.5 for an example.

1.2.7.2 180° Rule

When filming a line of action, for example the conversation between two figures, it is common to show each figure in isolation during the action. The camera is positioned in front of a figure but a little off to the side. The 180° rule states that when showing the two figures, one after the other, in isolation, the camera should stay on the same side of the line of action. Thus, the camera's orientation should stay within the 180° that is on one side of the line between the figures.

1.2.7.3 Rule of Thirds

The rule of thirds says that the interesting places to place an object in an image is at the one-third along the way, side-to-side, up-and-down, or both. In particular, don't center your subject in the image and don't put your subject at the edge of the image.

1.2.7.4 Types of Shots

Types of camera shots are categorized based on the distance from the camera to the subject and the angle at which the shot is taken. The distance-based shots are *extreme long range, long range, medium range,* or *bust shot, close-up, extreme close-up.* Which type of shot to use depends on the amount and location of detail that is to be shown and how much environmental context is to be included in the shot.

A *low-angle shot*, meaning the camera is low shooting up at the subject, imparts a feeling of power or dominance to the subject. Conversely, a *high-angle shot*, in which the camera shoots down on the subject, presents a feeling that the subject is insignificant or subordinate.

1.2.7.5 Tilt

Tilting the camera (rotating the camera about its view direction) can convey a sense of urgency, strangeness, or fear to the shot.

1.2.7.6 Framing

Framing refers to allowing enough room in the image for the action being captured. In a relatively static view, allow enough room so the subject doesn't fill the frame (unless there is a reason to do so). Allow enough room for motion. If your subject is walking, frame the motion so there is room in front of the subject, so the subject does not appear to be walking out of the frame.

1.2.7.7 Focus the Viewer's Attention

Draw the viewer's attention to what's important in the image. Use color, lighting, movement, focus, etc. to direct the attention of the viewer to what you want the viewer to see. For example, the eye will naturally follow converging lines, the gaze of figures in the image, a progression from dark to light or dark to bright, and an identifiable path in the image.

1.3 ANIMATION PRODUCTION

Although producing a final animated film is not the subject of this book, the production process merits some discussion in order to establish the context in which an animator works. It is useful for technical animators to have some familiarity with how a piece of animation is broken into parts and how a finished piece is produced. Much of this is taken directly from conventional animation and is directly applicable to any type of animation.

A piece of animation is usually discussed using a four-level hierarchy, although the specific naming convention for the levels may vary.[6] Here, the overall animation – the entire project – is referred to as the *production*. Typically, productions are broken into major parts referred to as *sequences*. A sequence is a major episode and is usually identified by an associated staging area; a production usually consists of one to a dozen sequences. A sequence is broken down into one or more *shots*; each *shot* is the recording of the action from a single point of view. A shot is broken down into the individual *frames* of film. A frame is a single recorded image. This results in the hierarchy shown in Fig. 1.6.

---

[6]Live-action film tends to use a five-level hierarchy: film, sequence, scene, shot, and frame [49]. Here, the terminology that is often used in feature-length computer animation is presented.

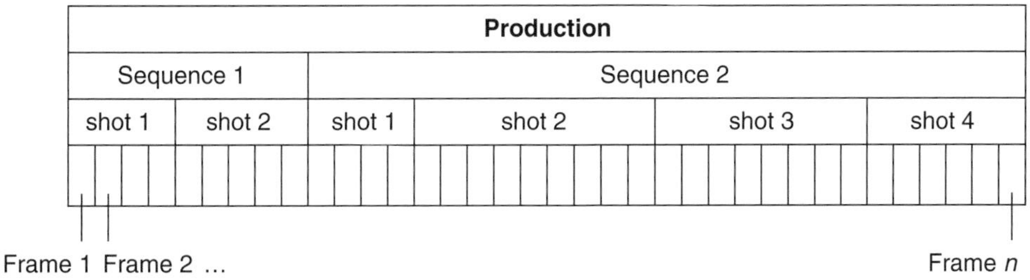

Production					
Sequence 1		Sequence 2			
shot 1	shot 2	shot 1	shot 2	shot 3	shot 4

Frame 1 Frame 2 ...   Frame *n*

FIGURE 1.6

Sample hierarchy of a simple animation production.

Several steps are required to successfully plan and carry out the production of a piece of animation [13,20]. Animation is a trial-and-error process that involves feedback from one step to previous steps and usually demands several iterations through multiple steps at various times. Even so, the production of animation typically follows a standard pattern. First, a *preliminary story* is decided on, including a *script*. A *storyboard* is developed that lays out the action scenes by sketching representative frames. The frames are often accompanied by text that sketches out the action taking place. This is used to present, review, and critique the action, as well as to examine character development.

A *model sheet* is developed that consists of a number of drawings for each figure in various poses and is used to ensure that each figure's appearance is consistent as it is repeatedly drawn during the animation process. The *exposure sheet* records information for each frame such as sound track cues, camera moves, and compositing elements. The *route sheet* records the statistics and responsibility for each scene.

An *animatic,* or *story reel,* may be produced in which the storyboard frames are recorded, each for as long as the sequence it represents, thus creating a rough review of the timing. Often, a *scratch track*, or *rough sound track*, is built at the same time the storyboard is being developed and is included in the animatic. Once the storyboard has been decided on (see Fig. 1.7), the *detailed story* is worked out to identify the actions in more detail. Keyframes (also known as *extremes*) are then identified and produced by master animators to aid in confirmation of timing, character development, and image quality. Associate and assistant animators are responsible for producing the frames between the keys; this is called *inbetweening. Test shots,* short sequences rendered in full color, are used to test the rendering and motions. To completely check the motion, a *pencil test* may be shot, which is a full-motion rendering of an extended sequence using low-quality images such as pencil sketches. Problems identified in the test shots and pencil tests may require reworking of the keyframes, detailed story, or even the storyboard.

Inking refers to the process of transferring the penciled frames to cels. *Opaquing,* also called *painting,* is the application of color to these cels.

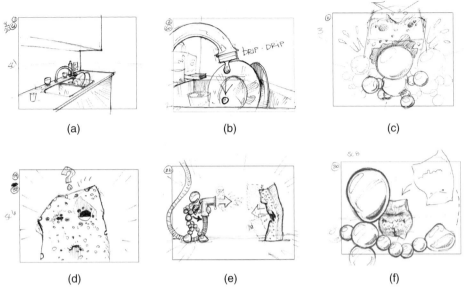

(a)   (b)   (c)

(d)   (e)   (f)

FIGURE 1.7

Sample panels from a storyboard. (a) Establishing shot: overview of the background introduces the place where the action takes place; (b) extreme close-up: the action is shown in detail helping the viewer to get familiar with the main characters and objects; (c) low angle: the camera position and the action happen in the same camera direction increasing the dramatic feeling of the scene; (d) point of view (POV): shows the viewer what the character would be seeing, which helps to better understand the reaction to the action; (e) wide shot: shows the whole action making the viewer understand the motivation, the action, and the consequences all at once; and (f) over the shoulder (OTS): the camera looks to one character, or action, from just behind and over the shoulder of another character to get the viewer involved with the action (Images courtesy of Beth Albright and Iuri Lioi).

1.3.1 Sound

Sound is an integral part of almost all animation, whether it's hand-drawn, computer-based, or stop-motion [13,19]. Up through the 1920s, the early "silent films" were played in theaters with live mood music accompaniment. That changed as sound-recording technology was developed for film and, later, for video.

Audio recording techniques had been around for 30 years by the time moving images were first recorded on film. It took another 30 years to develop techniques for playing a sound track in sync with recorded action. Since then, various formats have been developed for film sound tracks. Most formats record the audio on the same medium that records the images. In most of the various formats for film for example, audio is recorded along the side of the images or between the sprocket holes, in one to six tracks. Early formats used either optical or magnetic analog tracks for sound, but more recent formats digitally print the sound track on the film. By recording the audio on the same stock as the film, the timing between the imagery and the audio is physically enforced by the structure of the recording technology. In some formats, a separate medium, such as a CD, is used to hold the audio. This allows more audio to be recorded but creates a synchronization issue during playback. In the case of video, audio tracks are recorded alongside the tracks used to encode the video signal.

In the early film and video formats, audio was recorded as a low bandwidth analog signal resulting in very low-quality sound. Today's film and video technology acknowledges the importance of sound and provides multiple, high-quality digital audio tracks. Sound has four roles in a production: voice, body sounds, special effects, and background music.

In live action, voice is recorded with the action because of timing considerations while most of the other sounds are added in a postprocessing phase. In animation, voices are recorded first and the animation made to sync with it. In addition, recording visuals of the voice talent during the audio recording can be used to guide the animators as they create the facial expressions and body language that accompanies the speech.

Nonspeech sounds made by the actors, such as rustling of clothes, foot steps, and objects being handled, are called *body sounds*. The recorded body sounds are usually replaced by synthesized sounds, called *foley*, for purposes of artistic control. These synthesized sounds must be synced with the motions of the actors. The people responsible for creating these sounds are called *foley artists*.

Special effects, such as door slams and the revving of car engines must also be synced with the action but with a lesser precision than voice and foley sounds.

Recording background and mood music can be added after the fact and usually require no precise timing with the action. All the sounds other than voice are added after the live action or animation is recorded.

1.4 COMPUTER ANIMATION PRODUCTION

Computer animation production has borrowed most of the ideas from conventional animation production, including the use of a storyboard, test shots, and pencil testing. The storyboard has translated directly to computer animation production although it may be done online. It still holds the same functional place in the animation process and is an important component in planning animation. The use of keyframes, and interpolating between them, has become a fundamental technique in computer animation.

While computer animation has borrowed the production approaches of conventional animation, there are significant differences between how computer animation and conventional animation create an individual frame of the animation. In computer animation, there is usually a strict distinction among creating the models; creating a layout of the models including camera positioning and lighting; specifying the motion of the models, lights, and camera; and the rendering process applied to those models. This allows for reusing models and lighting setups. In conventional animation, all these processes happen simultaneously as each drawing is created, the only exception being the possible reuse of backgrounds, for example, with the multilayer approach.

The two main evaluation tools of conventional animation, test shots and pencil tests, have counterparts in computer animation. A speed/quality trade-off can be made in several stages of creating a frame of computer animation: model building, lighting, motion control, and rendering. By using high-quality techniques in only one or two of these stages, that aspect of the presentation can be quickly checked in a cost-effective manner. A test shot in computer animation is produced by a high-quality rendering of a highly detailed model to see a single frame, a short sequence of frames of the final product, or every nth frame of a longer sequence from the final animation. The equivalent of a pencil test can be performed by simplifying the sophistication of the models used, by using low-quality and/or low-resolution renderings, by eliminating all but the most important lights, or by using simplified motion.

Often, it is useful to have several representations of each model available at varying levels of detail. For example, placeholder cubes can be rendered to present the gross motion of rigid bodies in space and to see spatial and temporal relationships among objects. "Solids of revolution" objects (objects created by rotating a silhouette edge at certain intervals around an axis and then defining planar surfaces to fill the space between these silhouette slices) lend themselves quite well to multiple levels of detail for a given model based on the number of slices used. Texture maps and displacement maps can be disabled until the final renderings.

To simplify motion, articulated figures[7] can be kept in key poses as they navigate through an environment in order to avoid interpolation or inverse kinematics. Collision detection and response can be selectively "turned off" when not central to the effect created by the sequence. Complex effects such as smoke and water can be removed or represented by simple geometric shapes during testing.

Many aspects of the rendering can be selectively turned on or off to provide great flexibility in giving the animator clues to the finished product's quality without committing to the full computations required in the final presentation. Often, the resulting animation can be computed in real time for very effective motion testing before committing to a full anti-aliased, transparent, texture-mapped rendering. Wire-frame rendering of objects can sometimes provide sufficient visual cues to be used in testing. Shadows, smooth shading, texture maps, environmental maps, specular reflection, and solid texturing are options the animator can use for a given run of the rendering program.

Even in finished pieces of commercial animation, it is common practice to take computational shortcuts when they do not affect the quality of the final product. For example, the animator can select which objects can shadow which other objects in

---

[7]*Articulated figures* are models consisting of rigid segments usually connected together in a tree-like structure; the connections are either revolute or prismatic joints, allowing a segment to rotate or translate relative to the segment it's connected to.

the scene. In addition to being a compositional issue, selective shadowing saves time over a more robust approach in which every object can shadow every other object. In animation, environmental mapping is commonly used instead of ray tracing; photorealistic rendering is typically avoided.

Computer animation is well suited for producing the equivalent of test shots and pencil tests. In fact, because the quality of the separate stages of computer animation can be independently controlled, it can be argued to be even better suited for these evaluation techniques than conventional animation.

1.4.1 Computer Animation Production Tasks

While motion control is the primary subject of this book, it is worth noting that motion control is only one aspect of the effort required to produce computer animation. The other tasks (and the other talents) that are integral to the final product should not be overlooked. As previously mentioned, producing quality animation is a trial-and-error iterative process wherein performing one task may require rethinking one or more previously completed tasks. Even so, these tasks can be laid out in an approximate chronological order according to the way they are typically encountered. The order presented here summarizes an article that describes the system used to produce Pixar's *Toy Story* [27] (see Fig. 1.8).

The *Story Department* translates the verbal into the visual. The screenplay enters the Story Department, the storyboard is developed, and the story reel leaves. It goes to the Art Department.

The *Art Department*, working from the storyboard, creates the designs and color studies for the film, including detailed model descriptions and lighting scenarios. The Art Department develops a consistent look to be used in the imagery. This look guides the Modeling, Layout, and Shading Departments.

The *Modeling Department* creates the characters and the world in which they live. Every brick and stick to appear in the film must be handcrafted. Often, figures with jointed appendages, or other models with characteristic motion, are created as parameterized models. Parameters that control standard movements of the figure are defined. This facilitates the ability of animators to *stay on the model,* ensuring that the animation remains consistent with the concept of the model. The models are given to Layout and Shading.

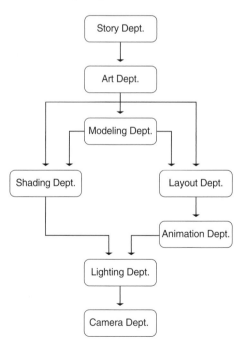

FIGURE 1.8

Computer animation production pipeline.

On one path between the Modeling Department and Lighting Department lies the *Shading Department*. Shading must translate the attributes of the object that relate to its visual appearance into texture maps, displacement shaders, and lighting models. Relevant attributes include the material the object is made of, its age, and its condition. Much of the effective appearance of an object comes not from its shape but from shading – the visual qualities of its surface.

On the other path between Modeling and Lighting lies the *Layout Department*, followed by the Animation Department. Layout is responsible for taking the film from two dimensions to three dimensions. To ensure good flow, Layout implements proper *staging* (designing the space for the action to take place in) and *blocking* (planning out the general movements of the actors and camera). This guides the Animation Department.

Working from audio, the story, and the blocking and staging produced by Layout, the *Animation Department* is responsible for bringing the characters to life. As mentioned above, complex figures are often parameterized by the Model Department so that a character's basic movements (e.g. smile, taking a step) have already been defined. Animation uses these motions as well as creating the subtler gestures and movements necessary for the "actor" to effectively carry out the scene.

The *Lighting Department* assigns to each sequence a team that has responsibility for translating the Art Department's vision into digital reality. At this point, the animation and camera placement have been done. Key lights are set to establish the basic lighting environment. Subtler lighting particular to an individual shot refines this in order to establish the correct mood and bring focus to the action.

The *Camera Department* is responsible for actually rendering the frames. During *Toy Story*, Pixar used a dedicated array of hundreds of processors called the *render farm*. The term *render farm* is now commonly used to refer to any such collection of processors for image rendering.

1.4.2 Digital Editing

A revolution swept the film and video industries in the 1990s: the digital representation of images. Even if computer graphics and digital effects are not a consideration in the production process, it has become commonplace to store program elements in digital form instead of using the analog film and videotape formats. Digital representations have the advantage of being able to be copied with no image degradation. So, even if the material was originally recorded using analog means, it is often cost-effective to transcribe the images to digital image store. And, of course, once the material is in digital form, digital manipulation of the images is a natural capability to incorporate in any system.

1.4.2.1 In the Old Days...

The most useful and fundamental digital image manipulation capability is that of editing sequences of images together to create a new presentation. Originally, film sequences were edited together by physically cutting and splicing tape. This is an

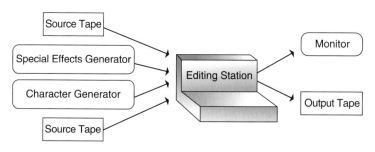

FIGURE 1.9

Linear editing system.

example of *nonlinear editing,* in which sequences can be inserted in any order at any time to assemble the final presentation. However, splicing is a time-consuming process, and making changes in the presentation or trying different alternatives can place a heavy burden on the stock material as well.

Electronic editing[8] allows one to manipulate images as electronic signals rather than use a physical process. The standard configuration uses two source videotape players, a switching box, and an output videotape recorder (see Fig. 1.9). The two source tapes are searched to locate the initial desired sequence; the tape deck on which it is found is selected for recording on the output deck, and the sequence is recorded. The tapes are then searched to locate the next segment, the deck is selected for output, and it is recorded on the output tape. This continues until the new composite sequence has been created on the output tape. The use of two source tapes allows multiple sources to be more easily integrated into the final program. Other analog effects can be incorporated into the output sequence at the switcher by using a *character generator* (text overlays) and/or a *special effects generator* (wipes, fades, etc.). Because the output is assembled in a sequence order, this is referred to as *linear editing.* The linear assembly of the output is considered the main drawback of this technique. Electronic editing also has the drawback that the material is copied in the editing process, introducing some image degradation. Because the output tape is commonly used to master the tapes that are sent out to be viewed, these tapes are already third generation. Another drawback is the amount of wear on the source material as the source tapes are repeatedly played and rewound as the next desired sequence is searched for. If different output versions are required (called *versioning*), the source material will be subjected to even more wear and tear because the source material has to undergo more handling as it is processed for multiple purposes.

---

[8]To simplify the discussion and make it more relevant to the capabilities of the personal computer, the discussion here focuses on video editing, although much of it is directly applicable to digital film editing, except that film standards require much higher resolution and therefore more expensive equipment.

Often, to facilitate the final assemblage of the output sequence and avoid excessive wear of the original source material, copies of the source material are used in a pre-processing stage in which the final edits are determined. This is called *off-line editing*. The result of this stage is an *edit decision list* (EDL), which is a final list of the edits that need to be made to assemble the final piece. The EDL is then passed to the *online editing* stage, which uses the original source material to make the edits and create the finished piece. This process is referred to as *conforming*.

To keep track of edit locations, control track pulses can be incorporated onto the tape used to assemble the 30-fps NTSC video signal. Simple editing systems count the pulses; this is called *control track editing*. However, the continual shuffling of the tape back and forth during the play and rewind of the editing process can result in the editing unit losing count of the pulses. This is something the operator must be aware of and take into account. In addition, because the edit counts are relative to the current tape location, the edit locations are lost when the editing station is turned off.

The Society of Motion Picture and Television Engineers (SMPTE) time code is an absolute eight-digit tag on each frame in the form of HHMMSSFF, where HH is the hour, MM is the minute, SS is the second, and FF is the frame number. This tag is calculated from the beginning of the sequence. This allows an editing station to record the absolute frame number for an edit and then store the edit location in a file that can be retrieved for later use.

The process described so far is *assemble editing*. *Insert editing* is possible if a control signal is first laid down on the output tape. Then sequences can be inserted anywhere on the tape in forming the final sequence. This provides some nonlinear editing capability, but it is still not possible to easily lengthen or shorten a sequence without repositioning other sequences on the tape to compensate for the change.

1.4.2.2 Digital Online Nonlinear Editing

To incorporate a more flexible nonlinear approach, fully digital editing systems have become more accessible [28–30]. These can be systems dedicated to editing, or they can be software systems that run on standard computers. Analog tape may still be used as the source material and for the final product, but everything between is digitally represented and controlled[9] (see Fig. 1.10).

After a sequence has been digitized, an icon representing it can be dragged onto a timeline provided by the editing system. Sequences can be placed relative to one another; they can be repeated, cut short, overlapped with other sequences, combined with transition effects, and mixed with other effects. A simplified example of such a timeline is shown in Fig. 1.11.

The positioning of the elements in the timeline is conceptual only; typically the data in the digital image store are not actually copied or moved. The output sequence can be played back in real time if the disk random access and graphics

---

[9]It is interesting to note that the whole process from recording to projection can now be done digitally.

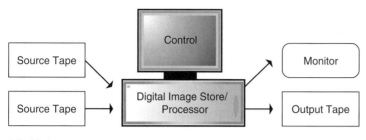

FIGURE 1.10

Online nonlinear editing system.

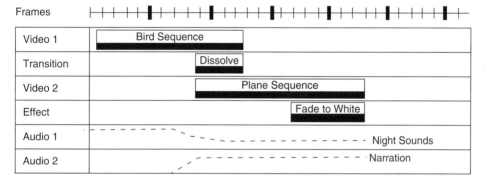

FIGURE 1.11

Simplified example of a timeline used for nonlinear digital editing.

display are fast enough to fetch and compile the separate tracks on the fly. In the case of overlapping sequences with transitions, either the digital store must support the access of multiple tracks simultaneously, so a transition can be constructed on the fly, or the transition sequence needs to be precomputed (sometimes referred to as *rendering*) and explicitly stored for access during playback. When the sequence is finalized, it can be assembled and stored digitally or recorded on video. Whatever the case, the flexibility of this approach with the ability to change edits and try alternatives without generational degradation make nonlinear digital editing systems very powerful.

1.4.3 Digital Video

As the cost of computer memory decreases and processor speeds increase, the capture, compression, storage, and playback of digital video have become more prevalent [31,32]. This has several important ramifications. First, desktop animation has become inexpensive enough to be within the reach of the consumer. Second, in the film industry, it has meant that compositing is no longer optical. Optically compositing each element in a film meant another pass of the negative through an optical film printer, which meant additional degradation of image quality. With the advent of digital compositing, the limit on the number of composited elements is removed. Third, once films are routinely stored digitally, digital techniques can be used for wire removal and to apply special effects. These digital techniques have become the bread and butter of computer graphics in the film industry.

When one works with digital video, there are several issues that need to be addressed to determine the cost, speed, storage requirements, and overall quality of the resulting system. Compression techniques can be used to conserve space, but some compression compromises the quality of the image and the speed of compression/ decompression may restrict a particular technique's suitability for a given application. During video capture, any image compression must operate in real time. Formats used for storage and playback can be encoded off-line, but the decoding must support real-time playback. Video resolution, video frame rates, and full-color imagery require that 27 MB/s be supported for video playback.[10] An hour of uncompressed video requires just under 100 GB of storage.[11] There are several digital video formats used by different manufacturers of video equipment for various applications; these formats include D1, D2, D3, D5, miniDV, DVC, Digital8, MPEG, and digital Betacam. Better signal quality can be attained with the use of component instead of composite signals. Discussion of these and other issues related to digital video is beyond the scope of this book.

1.4.4 Digital Audio

Audio is just as important to computer animation as it is to traditional animation. Over the years, audio technology, like image technology, has gone digital. Early audio recordings used an electromechanical stylus to etch representations of the signal into wax drums or plastic platters. Later, the signal was used to modulate the magnetization of some type of ferromagnetic material on plastic tape. Digital audio has since taken over. Digital audio has the same advantages as digital imagery when it comes to duplicating and editing. Digital audio can be copied, cut and pasted, transitioned, and looped over without any degradation in signal quality – a distinct advantage over the analog counterpart. The sound capability in personal computers has dramatically improved over the years so that now high-quality sound capability is standard. As with digital imagery, there are file formats and compression standards to consider when dealing with digital audio. In addition, there is a standard for digitally controlling musical devices.

1.4.4.1 Digital Musical Device Control

Musical Instrument Digital Interface (MIDI) is a standard developed in 1983 to control musical instruments without being tied to any one instrument in particular. MIDI commands are keynote commands to musical devices and are intended to

---

[10] 640 pixels/scanline × 480 scanlines/frame × 3 bytes/pixel × 30 fps = 27 630 000 bytes/s.
[11] 27 630 000 bytes/s × 3600 s/h = 99 468 000 000 bytes/h.

represent a musical performance. Mostly, the commands take the form of "note x on" and "note x off" where x is any of the standard musical notes. There are also control commands to set pitch, loudness, etc. Some devices can also send out MIDI commands as they are played in order to record the performance as keys are depressed and released. MIDI supports up to 16 channels and devices can be daisy-chained so that, for example, a device can be set up to respond only to a particular track.

1.4.4.2 Digital Audio Sampling

Sounds are pressure waves of air. In audio recording, the pressure waves are converted to some representation of the waveform. When it is recorded digitally, the wave is sampled at certain intervals – the sampling rate – with a certain number of bits per sample – the sample size – using a certain number of tracks. The sampling rate determines the highest frequency, called the Nyquist frequency, that can accurately be reconstructed. A voice signal can be sampled at a much lower rate than CD-quality music because the highest frequency of a voice signal is much lower than the highest frequency that might occur in a piece of music. The number of bits per sample determines how much distortion there is in the recorded signal. The number of tracks is how many independent signals comprise the music – one for mono, two for stereo, more for various "surround sound" recordings or for later editing. A voice signal and AM radio are sampled at approximately 10 K samples per second with 8 bits per sample using one track. CD-quality music is sampled at 44.1 K samples per second with 16 bits per sample using two tracks.

Similar to digital imagery, the digital recording can then be compressed for more efficient storage and transmission. The compression can be done irrespective of its contents, but if the compression uses the fact that the file contains sounds, then it is considered to be perceptually based.

1.5 A BRIEF HISTORY OF COMPUTER ANIMATION

1.5.1 Early Activity (pre-1980)

The earliest computer animation of the late 1960s and early 1970s was produced by a mix of researchers in university labs and individual visionary artists [33–35]. At the time, raster displays driven by frame buffers were just being developed and digital output to television was still in the experimental stage. The displays in use were primarily storage tubes and refresh vector displays. Storage tubes retain an image indefinitely because of internal circuitry that continuously streams electrons to the display. However, because the image cannot be easily modified, storage tubes were used mainly to draw complex static models. Vector (calligraphic) displays use a display list of line- and arc-drawing instructions that an internal processor uses to repeatedly draw an image that would otherwise quickly fade on the screen. Vector displays can draw moving images by carefully changing the display list between refreshes. These displays were popular for interactive design tasks.

During this time period, static images were often recorded onto film by placing a camera in front of the display and recording an image of vectors on the screen. In this way, shaded images could be produced by opening the shutter of the film camera and essentially scan converting the elements (e.g. polygons) by drawing closely spaced horizontal vectors to fill the figure; after scan conversion was completed, the shutter was closed to terminate the image recording. The intensity of the image could be regulated by using the intensity control of the vector display or by controlling other aspects of the image recording such as by varying the density of the vectors. An image of a single color was generated by placing a colored filter in front of the camera lens. A full-color image could be produced by breaking the image into its red, green, and blue components and triple-exposing the film with each exposure using the corresponding colored filter. This same approach could be used to produce animation as long as the motion camera was capable of single-frame recording. Single-frame recording required precise frame registration, usually available only in expensive film equipment. Animated sequences could be colored by triple-exposing the entire film. A programmer or animator was fortunate if both the camera and the filters could be controlled by computer.

The earliest research in computer graphics and animation occurred at MIT in 1963 when Ivan Sutherland developed an interactive constraint satisfaction system on a vector refresh display [36]. The user could construct an assembly of lines by specifying constraints between the various graphical elements. If one of the graphical elements moved, the system calculated the reaction of other elements to this manipulation based on satisfying the specified constraints. By interactively manipulating one of the graphical elements, the user could produce complex motion in the rest of the assembly. Later, at the University of Utah, Sutherland helped David Evans establish the first significant research program in computer graphics and animation.

As early as the early 1960s, computer animation was produced as artistic expression. The early artistic animators in this period included Ken Knowlton, Lillian Schwartz, S. Van Der Beek, John Whitney, Sr., and A.M. Noll. Typical artistic animations consisted of animated abstract line drawings displayed on vector refresh displays. Chuck Csuri, an artist at Ohio State University, produced pieces such as *Hummingbird* (1967) that were more representational.

In the early 1970s, computer animation in university research labs became more widespread. Computer graphics, as well as computer animation, received an important impetus through government funding at the University of Utah [37]. As a result, Utah produced several ground-breaking works in animation: an animated hand and face by Ed Catmull (*Hand/Face,* 1972); a walking and talking human figure by Barry Wessler (*Not Just Reality,* 1973); and a talking face by Fred Parke (*Talking Face,* 1974). Although the imagery was extremely primitive by today's standards, the presentations of lip-synced facial animation and linked-appendage figure animation were impressive demonstrations well ahead of their time.

In 1972, Chuck Csuri founded the Computer Graphics Research Group (CGRG) at Ohio State with the focus of bringing computer technology to bear on creating animation [38]. Tom DeFanti produced the Graphics Symbiosis System (GRASS) in the early 1970s that scripted interactive control of animated objects on a vector display device. Later in the 1970s, CGRG produced animations using a real-time video playback system developed at North Carolina State University under the direction of John Staudhammer. Software developed at CGRG compressed frames of animation and stored them to disk. During playback, the compressed digital frames were retrieved from the disk and piped to the special-purpose hardware, which took the digital information, decompressed it on the fly, and converted it into a video signal for display on a standard television. The animation was driven by the ANIMA II language [39]. In the mid-1980s, Julian Gomez developed TWIXT [40], a track-based keyframe animation system.

In 1973, the first computer-language-based keyframe animation system, ANTICS, was developed by Alan Kitching at the Atlas Computer Laboratory under the auspices of the Royal College of Art in the United Kingdom [41,42]. ANTICS is a Fortran software package specifically designed for animators and graphic designers. It is a two-dimensional system that provides capabilities analogous to traditional cel animation.

In the mid-1970s, Norm Badler at the University of Pennsylvania conducted investigations into posing a human figure. He developed a constraint system to move the figure from one pose to another. He has continued this research and established the Center for Human Modeling and Simulation at the University of Pennsylvania. *Jack* is a software package developed at the center that supports the positioning and animation of anthropometrically valid human figures in a virtual world [43].

In the late 1970s, the New York Institute of Technology (NYIT) produced several computer animation systems, thanks to individuals such as Ed Catmull and Alvy Ray Smith [33]. At the end of the 1970s, NYIT embarked on an ambitious project to produce a wholly computer-generated feature film using three-dimensional computer animation, titled *The Works*. While the project was never completed, excerpts were shown at several SIGGRAPH conferences as progress was made. The excerpts demonstrated high-quality rendering, jointed figures, and interacting objects. The system used at NYIT was BBOP, a three-dimensional keyframe figure animation system [44].

In 1974, the first computer animation nominated for an Academy Award, *Hunger*, was produced by Rene Jodoin; it was directed and animated by Peter Foldes. This piece used a 2½ D system that depended heavily on object shape modification and line interpolation techniques [45]. The system was developed by Nestor Burtnyk and Marceli Wein at the National Research Council of Canada in conjunction with the National Film Board of Canada. *Hunger* was the first animated story using computer animation.

In the early 1980s, Daniel Thalmann and Nadia Magnenat-Thalmann started work in computer animation at the University of Montreal [33]. Over the years, their labs have produced several impressive animations, including *Dream Flight* (1982, N. Magnenat-Thalmann, D. Thalmann, P. Bergeron), *Tony de Peltrie* (1985, P. Bergeron), and *Rendez-vous à Montréal* (1987, N. Magnenat-Thalmann and D. Thalmann).

Others who advanced computer animation during the period were Ed Emshwiller at NYIT, who demonstrated moving texture maps in *Sunstone* (1979); Jim Blinn, who produced the *Voyager* flyby animations at the Jet Propulsion Laboratory (1979); Don Greenberg, who used architectural walk-throughs of the Cornell University campus (1971); and Nelson Max at the Education Development Center, who animated space-filling curves (1972).

Commercial efforts at computer animation first occurred in the late 1960s with Lee Harrison's SCANIMATE system based on analog computing technology [46]. Digital technology soon took over and the mid- to late 1970s saw the first serious hints of commercial three-dimensional digital computer animation. Tom DeFanti developed the GRASS at Ohio State University (1976), a derivative of which was used in the computer graphics sequences of the first *Star Wars* film (1977). In addition to *Star Wars*, films such as *Future World* (1976), *Alien* (1979), and *Looker*[12] (1981) began to incorporate simple computer animation as examples of advanced technology. This was an exciting time for those in the research labs wondering if computer animation would ever see the light of day. One of the earliest companies to use three-dimensional computer animation was the Mathematical Application Group Inc. (MAGI), which used a ray-casting algorithm to provide scientific visualizations. MAGI also adapted its technique to produce early commercials for television.

1.5.2 The Middle Years (The 1980s)

The 1980s saw a more serious move by entrepreneurs into commercial animation. Computer hardware advanced significantly with the introduction of the VAX computer in the 1970s and the IBM PC at the beginning of the 1980s. Hardware z-buffers were produced by companies such as Raster Tech and Ikonas; Silicon Graphics was formed; and flight simulators based on digital technology were taking off because of efforts by the Evans and Sutherland Corporation. These hardware developments were making the promise of cost-effective computer animation to venture capitalists. At the same time, graphics software was getting more sophisticated: Turner Whitted introduced anti-aliased ray tracing (*The Compleat Angler*, 1980); Loren Carpenter produced a flyby of fractal terrain (*Vol Libre*, 1980); and Nelson Max produced several films about molecules as well as one of the first films animating waves (*Carla's Island,* 1981). Companies such as Alias, Wavefront, and TDI were starting to produce sophisticated software tools making advanced rendering and animation available off-the-shelf for the first time.

Animation houses specializing in three-dimensional computer animation started to appear. Television commercials, initially in the form of flying logos, provided a profitable area where companies could hone their skills. Demo reels appeared at SIGGRAPH produced by the first wave of computer graphics companies such as Information International Inc. (III, or triple-I), Digital Effects, MAGI, Robert Abel and Associates, and Real Time Design (ZGRASS).

---

[12]The film *Looker* is interesting as an early commentary on the potential use of digital actors in the entertainment industry.

The first four of these companies combined to produce the digital imagery in Disney's *TRON* (1982), which was a landmark movie in its (relatively) extensive use of a computer-generated environment in which graphical objects were animated. Previously, the predominant use of computer graphics in movies had been to show a monitor (or simulated projection) of something that was supposed to be a computer graphics display (*Futureworld,* 1976; *Star Wars,* 1977; *Alien,* 1979; *Looker,* 1981). Still, in *TRON,* the computer-generated imagery was not meant to simulate reality; the action takes place inside a computer, so a computer-generated look was consistent with the story line.

At the same time that computer graphics was starting to find its way into the movies it was becoming a more popular tool for generating television commercials. As a result, more computer graphics companies surfaced, including Digital Pictures, Image West, Cranston-Csuri Productions, Pacific Data Images, Lucasfilm, Marks and Marks, Digital Productions, and Omnibus Computer Graphics.

Most early use of synthetic imagery in movies was incorporated with the intent that it would appear as if computer generated. The other use of computer animation during this period was to "do animation." That is, the animations were meant not to fool the eye into thinking that what was being seen was real but rather to replace the look and feel of two-dimensional conventional animation with that of three-dimensional computer animation. Of special note are the award-winning animations produced by Lucasfilm and, later, by Pixar:

> *The Adventures of André and Wally B.* (1984): first computer animation demonstrating motion blur.
> *Luxo Jr.* (1986): nominated for an Academy Award.
> *Red's Dream* (1987).
> *Tin Toy* (1988): first computer animation to win an Academy Award.
> *Knick Knack* (1989).
> *Geri's Game* (1997): Academy Award winner.

These early animations paved the way for three-dimensional computer animation to be accepted as an art form. They were among the first fully computer-generated three-dimensional animations to be taken seriously as animations, irrespective of the technique involved. Another early piece of three-dimensional animation, which integrated computer graphics with conventional animation, was *Technological Threat* (1988). This was one of three films nominated for an Academy Award as an animated short in 1989; *Tin Toy* came out the victor.

One of the early uses of computer graphics in film was to model and animate spacecraft. Working in (virtual) outer space with spacecraft has the advantages of simple illumination models, a relatively bare environment, and relatively simple animation of rigid bodies. In addition, spacecraft are usually modeled by relatively simple geometry – as is the surrounding environment (planets) – when in flight. *The Last Starfighter* (1984, Digital Productions) used computer animation instead of building models for special effects; the computer used, the Cray X-MP, even appeared in the movie credits. The action takes place in space as well as on planets; computer graphics was used for the scenes in space, and physical models were used for the scenes on a planet. Approximately 20 minutes of computer graphics is used in the movie. While it is not hard to tell when the movie switches between graphical and physical models, this was the first time graphics was used as an extensive part of a live-action film in which the graphics were supposed to look realistic (i.e. *special effects*).

1.5.3 Animation Comes of Age (The mid-1980s and beyond)

As modeling, rendering, and animation became more sophisticated and the hardware became faster and inexpensive, quality computer graphics began to spread to the Internet, television commercials, computer games, and stand-alone game units. In film, computer graphics helps to bring alien creatures to life. Synthetic alien creatures, while they should appear to be real, do not have to match specific audience expectations. *Young Sherlock Holmes* (1986, ILM) was the first to place a synthetic character in a live-action feature film. An articulated stained glass window comes to life and is made part of the live action. The light sources and movements of the camera in the live action had to be mimicked in the synthetic environment, and images from the live action were made to refract through the synthetic stained glass. In *The Abyss* (1989, ILM), computer graphics is used to create an alien creature that appears to be made from water. Other notable films in which synthetic alien creatures are used are *Terminator II* (1991, ILM), *Casper* (1995, ILM), *Species* (1995, Boss Film Studios), and *Men in Black* (1997, ILM).

A significant advance in the use of computer graphics for the movies came about because of the revolution in cheap digital technology, which allowed film sequences to be stored digitally. Once the film is stored digitally, it is in a form suitable for digital special effects processing, digital compositing, and the addition of synthetic elements. For example, computer graphics can be used to remove the mechanical supports of a prop or to introduce digital explosions or laser blasts. For the most part, this resides in the two-dimensional realm and thus is not the focus of this book. However, with the advent of digital techniques for two-dimensional compositing, sequences are more routinely available in digital representations, making them amenable to a variety of digital postprocessing techniques. The first digital bluescreen matte extraction was in *Willow* (1988, ILM). The first digital wire removal was in *Howard the Duck* (1986, ILM). In *True Lies* (1994, Digital Domain), digital techniques inserted atmospheric distortion to show engine heat. In *Forrest Gump* (1994, ILM), computer graphics inserted a ping-pong ball in a sequence showing an extremely fast action game, inserted a new character into old film footage, and enabled the illusion of a double amputee as played by a completely able actor. In *Babe* (1995, Rhythm & Hues), computer graphics was used to move the mouths of animals and fill in the background uncovered by the movement. In *Interview with a Vampire* (1994, Digital Domain), computer graphics were used to curl the hair of a woman during her transformation into a vampire. In this case, some of the effect was created using three-dimensional graphics, which were then integrated into the scene by two-dimensional techniques.

A popular graphical technique for special effects is the use of particle systems. One of the earliest examples is in *Star Trek II: The Wrath of Khan* (1982, Lucasfilm), in which a wall of fire sweeps over the surface of a planet. Although by today's standards the wall of fire is not very convincing, it was an important step in the use of computer graphics in movies. Particle systems are also used in *Lawnmower Man* (1992, Angel Studios, Xaos), in which a character disintegrates into a swirl of small spheres. The modeling of a comet's tail in the opening sequence of the television series *Star Trek: Deep Space Nine* (1993) is a more recent example of a particle system. In a much more ambitious and effective application, *Twister* (1996, ILM) uses particle systems to simulate a tornado.

More challenging is the use of computer graphics to create realistic models of creatures with which the audience is intimately familiar. *Jurassic Park* (1993, ILM) is the first example of a movie that completely integrates computer graphics characters (dinosaurs) of which the audience has fairly specific expectations. Of course, there is still some leeway here because the audience does not have precise knowledge of how dinosaurs look. *Jumanji* (1995, ILM) takes on the ultimate task of modeling creatures for which the audience has precise expectations: various jungle animals. Most of the action is fast and blurry, so the audience does not have time to dwell on the synthetic creatures visually, but the result is very effective. To a lesser extent, *Batman Returns* (1995, PDI) does the same thing by providing "stunt doubles" of Batman in a few scenes. The scenes are quick and the stunt double is viewed from a distance, but it was the first example of a full computer graphics stunt double in a movie. More recently, the Spider-Man movies (2002–present, Sony) make extensive use of synthetic stunt doubles. The use of synthetic stunt doubles in film is now commonplace.

Computer graphics shows much potential for managing the complexity in crowd scenes. PDI used computer graphics to create large crowds in the *Bud Bowl* commercials of the mid-1980s. In feature films, crowd scenes include the wildebeest scene in *The Lion King* (1994, Disney), the alien charge in *Starship Troopers* (1997, Tippet Studio), synthetic figures populating the deck of the ship in *Titanic* (1998, ILM), and the Star Wars films (1977–2005, Lucasfilm).

A holy grail of computer animation is to produce a synthetic human character indistinguishable from a real person. Early examples of animations using "synthetic actors" are *Tony de Peltrie* (1985, P. Bergeron), *Rendez-vous à Montréal* (1987, N. Magnenat-Thalmann and D. Thalmann), *Sextone for President* (1989, Kleiser-Walziac Construction Company), and *Don't Touch Me* (1989, Kleiser-Walziac Construction Company). However, it is obvious to viewers that these animations are computer generated. Recent advances in illumination models and texturing have produced human figures that are much more realistic and have been incorporated into otherwise live-action films.

Synthetic actors have progressed from being distantly viewed stunt doubles and passengers on a boat to assuming central roles in various movies: the dragon in *Dragonheart* (1996, Tippett Studio, ILM); the Jello-like main character in *Flubber* (1997, ILM); the aliens in *Mars Attacks* (1996, ILM); and the ghosts in *Casper* (1995, ILM).

The first fully articulated humanoid synthetic actor integral to a movie was the character Jar-Jar Binks in *Star Wars: Episode I* (1999, ILM). More recently, Gollum in the *Lord of the Rings: The Return of the King* (2004, New Line Cinema[13]) has displayed actor-like visual qualities as well as the personality of a live actor not demonstrated before in computer-generated characters.

Currently, movies that push the state of the art in digital effects are being produced yearly. Most notable among these are the other movies from the *Lord of the Rings* series (*Lord of the Rings*: *The Fellowship of the Ring*, 2001; *Lord of the Rings: The Two Towers*, 2003, New Line Cinema) and The Matrix series (*The Matrix*, 1999; *The Matrix Reloaded*, 2003; *The Matrix Revolutions*, 2003, Groucho II Film Partnership). *Final Fantasy: The Spirits Within* (2001, Chris Lee Productions) is noteworthy as the most aggressive attempt so far to use synthetic characters to portray realistic people in a film.

Of course, one use of computer animation is simply to "do animation"; computer graphics is used to produce animated pieces that are essentially three-dimensional cartoons that would otherwise be done by more traditional means. The animation does not attempt to fool the viewer into thinking anything is real; it is meant simply to entertain. The film *Hunger* falls into this category, as do the Lucasfilm/Pixar animations. *Toy Story* is the first full-length, fully computer-generated three-dimensional animated feature film. Other feature-length three-dimensional cartoons soon emerged, such as *Antz* (1998, PDI), *A Bug's Life* (1998, Pixar), *Toy Story 2* (1999, Pixar), *Shrek* (2001, PDI), and *Shrek 2* (2004, PDI). In 2002, *Shrek* won the first-ever Academy Award for Best Animated Feature.

Many animations of this type have been made for television. In an episode of *The Simpsons* (1995, PDI), Homer steps into a synthetic world and turns into a three-dimensional computer-generated character. There have been popular television commercials involving computer animation, too many to mention at this point. Many Saturday morning cartoons are now produced using three-dimensional computer animation. Because many images are generated to produce an animation, the rendering used in computer-animated weekly cartoons tends to be computationally efficient.

An example of rendering at the other extreme is *Bunny* (1999, Blue Sky Productions), which received an Academy Award for animated short. *Bunny* uses high-quality rendering in its imagery, including ray tracing and radiosity, as does *Ice Age* (2002, Blue Sky Productions). *The Incredibles* (2004, Disney/Pixar), which garnered another Academy Award for Pixar, included hair animation, subsurface scattering for illuminating skin, cloth animation, and skin-deforming muscle models. *Polar Express* (2004, Warner Bros.) pushed the envelop of motion capture technology to capture full body and face motion in animating this children's story.

---

[13]For brevity, only the first production company itemized on the Internet Movie Database Web site (http://www.imdb.com) is given for the *Lord of the Rings movies, The Matrix* movies, and *Final Fantasy*.

Computer animation is now well-established as a (some would say the) principal medium for "doing animation." Indeed, at the time of this writing, both *Jurassic Park* and *Shrek 2* are on the top ten list of all-time worldwide box office grossing movies [47].

Three-dimensional computer graphics is also playing an increasing role in the production of conventional hand-drawn animation. Computer animation has been used to model three-dimensional elements in hand-drawn environments. The previously mentioned *Technological Threat* (1988) is an early animation that combined computer-animated characters with hand-drawn characters to produce an entertaining commentary on the use of technology. Three-dimensional environments were constructed for conventionally animated figures in *Beauty and the Beast* (1991, Disney) and *Tarzan* (1999, Disney); three-dimensional synthetic objects, such as the chariots, were animated in conventionally drawn environments in *Prince of Egypt* (1998, Dreamworks). Because photorealism is not the objective, the rendering in such animation is done to blend with the relatively simple rendering of hand-drawn animation.

Finally, morphing, even though it is a two-dimensional animation technique, should be mentioned because of its use in some films and its high impact in television commercials. This is essentially a two-dimensional procedure that warps control points (or feature lines) of one image into the control points (feature lines) of another image while the images themselves are blended. In *Star Trek IV: The Voyage Home* (1986, ILM), one of the first commercial morphs occurred in the back-in-time dream sequence. In *Willow* (1988, ILM), a series of morphs changes one animal into another. This technique is also used very effectively in *Terminator II* (1991, ILM). In the early 1990s, PDI promoted the use of morphing in various productions. Michael Jackson's music video *Black and White,* in which people's faces morph into other faces, did much to popularize the technique. In a Plymouth Voyager commercial (1991, PDI), the previous year's car bodies and interiors morph into the new models, and in an Exxon commercial (1992, PDI), a car changes into a tiger. Morphing remains a useful and popular technique.

1.6 CHAPTER SUMMARY

Computer graphics and computer animation have created a revolution in visual effects and animation production. Advances are still being made and new digital techniques are finding a receptive audience. Yet there is more potential to be realized as players in the entertainment industry demand their own special look and each company tries to establish a competitive edge in the imagery it produces. Computer animation has come a long way since the days of Ivan Sutherland and the University of Utah. Viewed in the context of the historical development of animation, the use of digital technology is indeed both a big and an important step. With the advent of low-cost computing and desktop video, animation is now within reach of more people than ever. It remains to be seen how the limits of the technology will be pushed as new and interesting ways to create moving images are explored.

REFERENCES

[1] P. Roget, Explanation of an optical deception in the appearance of the spokes of a wheel seen through vertical apertures, Philos. Trans. R. Soc. Lond. 115 (1825) (presented in 1824) 131–140.

[2] J. Anderson, B. Anderson, The myth of persistence of vision revisited, J. Film Video 45 (1993) 3–12.

[3] J. Anderson, B. Fisher, The myth of persistence of vision, J. Univ. Film Assoc. XXX (1978) 3–8.

[4] W.H. Ehrenstein, Basics of seeing motion, Arq. Bras. Oftalmol. 66 (2003) 44–53.

[5] Conrac Corp., Raster Graphics Handbook, Van Nostrand Reinhold, New York, 1985.

[6] J. Cutting, Perception with an Eye for Motion, MIT Press, Cambridge, MA., 1986.

[7] J. Korein, N. Badler, Temporal anti-aliasing in computer generated animation, Comput. Graph. 17 (1983) 377–388 (Proceedings of SIGGRAPH 83, July 1983, Detroit, MI).

[8] M. Potmesil, I. Chadkravarty, Modeling motion blur in computer generated images, Comput. Graph. 17 (1983) 389–400 (Proceedings of SIGGRAPH 83, July 1983, Detroit, MI).

[9] R. Williams, The Animator's Survival Kit, Faber and Faber, New York, 2002.

[10] C. Poynton, Digital Video and HDTV Algorithms and Interfaces, Morgan-Kaufmann, San-Francisco, CA., 2003.

[11] G. Wood, Living Dolls—A Magical History of the Quest for Mechanical Life, Faber and Faber Limited, London, 2002.

[12] P. Burns, The complete history of the discovery of cinematography, http://www.-precinemahistory.net/introduction.htm, 2000.

[13] K. Laybourne, The Animation Book: A Complete Guide to Animated Filmmaking—from Flip-Books to Sound Cartoons to 3-D Animation, Three Rivers Press, New York, 1998.

[14] C. Solomon, The History of Animation: Enchanted Drawings, Wings Books, New York, 1994.

[15] R. Balzer, Optical Amusements: Magic Lanterns and Other Transforming Images; A Catalog of Popular Entertainments, Richard Balzer, 1987.

[16] E. Marey, Animal Mechanism: A Treatise on Terrestrial and Aerial Locomotion, Appleton and Co., New York, 1874.

[17] E. Muybridge, Animals in Motion, Dover Publications, New York, 1957.

[18] E. Muybridge, The Human Figure in Motion, Dover Publications, New York, 1955.

[19] L. Maltin, Of Mice and Magic: A History of American Animated Cartoons, Penguin Books, New York, 1987.

[20] B. Thomas, Disney's Art of Animation from Mickey Mouse to "Beauty and the Beast," Hyperion, New York, 1991.

[21] F. Thomas, O. Johnson, The Illusion of Life, Hyperion, New York, 1981.

[22] M. Hunt, Cinema: 100 years of the moving image, http://www.angelfire.com/vt/mhunt/cinema.html, 2000.

[23] Wabash College Theater, Georges méliès, http://www.wabash.edu/depart/theater/THAR4/Melies.htm, 2000.

[24] D. Davis, Art and the Future: A History/Prophecy of the Collaboration Between Science, Technology, and Art, Praeger Publishers, New York, 1973.

[25] J. Lasseter, Principles of traditional animation applied to 3D computer animation, Comput. Graph. 21 (1987) 35–44 (Proceedings of SIGGRAPH 87, July 1987, Anaheim, CA, M.C. Stone, (Ed.)).

[26] J. Mascelli, The Five C's of Cinematography, Cine/Grafic Publications, Hollywood, CA., 1965.

[27] M. Henne, H. Hickel, E. Johnson, S. Konishi, The making of Toy Story (1996) 463–468 (Proceedings of Comp Con 96, February 25–28, 1996, San Jose, CA).

[28] M. Horton, C. Mumby, S. Owen, B. Pank, D. Peters, Quantel on-line, Non-linear Editing, http://www.quantel.com/editingbook/index.html, 2000.

[29] B. Pryor, Opus communications, VIDEOFAQ#1: what the heck is 'non-linear' editing anyway?" http://www.opuskc.com/vf1.html, 2000.

[30] R. Whittaker, Linear and non-linear editing, http://www.internetcampus.com/tvp056.htm, 2000.

[31] Synthetic Aperture, Synthetic aperture, http://www.synthetic-ap.com/tips/index.html, 2000.

[32] Tribeca Technologies, LLC, white paper: the history of video, http://www.tribecatech.com/histvide.htm, 2000.

[33] N. Magnenat-Thalmann, D. Thalmann, Computer Animation: Theory and Practice, Springer-Verlag, New York, 1985.

[34] N. Magnenat-Thalmann, D. Thalmann, New Trends in Animation and Visualization, John Wiley & Sons, New York, 1991.

[35] H. Siegel, An overview of computer animation & modelling, Comput. Animation 87 (1987) 27–37 (Proceedings of the Conference Held at Computer Graphics, October 1987, London).

[36] I. Sutherland, SKETCHPAD: a man-machine graphical communication system, Ph.D. dissertation, MIT, 1963.

[37] Geometric Design and Computation, GDC: history, http://www.cs.utah.edu/gdc/history, 2006.

[38] Csurivison Ltd., The digital fine art history of charles csuri, http://www.csuri.com/charles-csuri/art-history-0_0.php, 2006.

[39] R. Hackathorn, Anima II: a 3-D color animation system, Comput. Graph. 11 (1977) 54–64 (Proceedings of SIGGRAPH 77, July 1977, San Jose, CA, J. George, (Ed.)).

[40] E.J. Tajchman, The incredible electronic machine, Videography (1977) 22–24.

[41] A. Kitching, Computer animation—some new ANTICS, Br. Kinematography Sound Television (1973) 372–386.

[42] A. Kitching, The antics computer animation system, http://www.chilton-computing.org.uk/acl/applications/graphics/p003.htm, 2005.

[43] The Center for Human Modeling and Simulation, Welcome to human modeling and simulation, http://www.cis.upenn.edu~hms/home.html, 2006.

[44] G. Stern, Bbop: a program for 3-dimensional animation, Nicograph 83 (1983) 403–404.

[45] N. Burtnyk, M. Wein, Computer animation of free form images, Proceedings of the 2nd Annual Conference on Computer Graphics and Interactive Techniques, SIGGRAPH 75 (Bowling Green, Ohio, June 25–27, 1975) pp. 78–80. ACM Press, New York.

[46] D. Sieg, Welcome to the scanimate site—history of computer animation—early analog computers, http://scanimate.net, 2004.

[47] Box Office Mojo, All time worldwide box office grosses, http://www.boxofficemojo.com/alltime/world, 2006.

[48] The Museum of Broadcast Communications, Standards, http://www.museum.tv/archives/etv/S/htmlS/standards/standards.htm.

[49] D. Coynik, Film: Real to Reel, McDougal, Littell, Evanston, IL, 1976.

Technical Background

2

Rick Parent

CHAPTER CONTENTS

This chapter is divided into two sections. The first serves as a quick review of the basics of the computer graphics display pipeline and discusses potential sources of error when dealing with graphical data. It is assumed that the reader has already been exposed to transformation matrices, homogeneous coordinates, and the display pipeline, including the perspective transformation; this section concisely reviews these topics and the second section covers various orientation representations.

2.1 SPACES AND TRANSFORMATIONS

Much of computer graphics and computer animation involves transforming data (e.g. [1,2]). Object data are transformed from a defining space into a world space in order to build a synthetic environment. Object data are transformed as a function of time in order to produce animation. Finally, object data are transformed in order to view the object on a screen. The workhorse transformational representation of graphics is the 4×4 transformation matrix, which can be used to represent combinations of three-dimensional rotations, translations, and scales.

A coordinate space can be defined by using either a left- or a right-handed coordinate system (see Fig. 2.1). Left-handed coordinate systems have the x-, y-, and z-coordinate axes aligned as the thumb, index finger, and middle finger of the left hand are arranged when held at right angles to each other in a natural pose: extending the thumb out to the side of the hand, extending the index finger coplanar with the palm, and extending the middle finger perpendicular to the palm. The right-handed coordinate system is organized similarly with respect to the right hand. These configurations are inherently different; there is no series of pure rotations that transforms a left-handed configuration of axes into a right-handed configuration. Which configuration to use is a matter of convention. It makes no difference as long as everyone knows and understands the implications. Another arbitrary convention is the axis to use as the up vector. Some application areas assume that the y-axis is "up." Other applications assume that the z-axis is "up." As with handedness, it makes no difference as long as everyone is aware of the assumption being made.

This section first reviews the transformational spaces through which object data pass as they are massaged into a form suitable for display. Then, the use of homogeneous representations of points and the 4×4 transformation matrix representation of three-dimensional rotation, translation, and scale are reviewed. Next come discussions of representing arbitrary position and orientation by a series of matrices, representing compound transformations in a matrix, and extracting a series of basic transformations from a compound matrix. The display pipeline is then described in terms of the transformation matrices used to effect it; the discussion is focused on transforming a point in space. In the case of transforming vectors, the computation is slightly different. This section concludes with a discussion of error considerations, including orthonormalization of a rigid transformation matrix. Unless stated otherwise, space is assumed to be three dimensional.

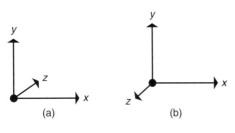

FIGURE 2.1

(A) Left-handed coordinate system: the z-axis goes into the page to form a left-handed coordinate system. (B) Right-handed coordinate systems: the z-axis comes out of the page to form a right-handed coordinate system.

2.1.1 **The Display Pipeline**

The *display pipeline* refers to the transformation of object data from its original defining space through a series of intermediate spaces until its final mapping onto the screen. The object data are transformed into different spaces in order to efficiently compute illumination, clip the data to the view volume, and perform the perspective transformation. This section reviews these spaces, their properties, the transformations that map data from one space to the next, and the parameters used to specify the transformations. The names used for these spaces vary from text to text, so they will be reviewed here to establish a consistent naming convention. Clipping, while an important process that eliminates lines and parts of lines that are not within the viewable space, is not relevant to motion control and therefore is not covered.

The space in which an object is originally defined is referred to as *object space*. The data in object space are usually centered around the origin and often are created to lie within some limited standard range such as −1 to +1. The object, as defined by its data points (which are also referred to as its *vertices*), is transformed, usually by a series of rotations, translations, and scales, into *world space*, the space in which objects are assembled to create the environment to be viewed. Object space and world space are commonly right-handed spaces.

World space is also the space in which light sources and the observer are placed. For purposes of this discussion, *observer position* is used synonymously and interchangeably with *camera position* and *eye position*. The observer parameters include its *position* and its *orientation*. The orientation is fully specified by the *view direction* and the *up vector*. There are various ways to specify these orientation vectors. Sometimes the view direction is specified by giving a *center of interest* (COI), in which case the view direction is the vector from the observer or eye position (EYE) to the center of interest. The eye position is also known as the *look-from point*, and the center of interest is also known as the *look-to point*. The default orientation of "straight up" is defined as the observer's up vector being perpendicular to the view direction and in the plane defined by the view direction and the global y-axis.

A rotation away from this up direction will effect a tilt of the observer's head.

In order to efficiently project the data onto a view plane, the data must be defined relative to the camera, in a camera-centric coordinate system (u, v, w); the v-axis is the observer's y-axis, or *up vector*, and the w-axis is the observer's z-axis, or *view vector*. The u-axis completes the local coordinate system of the observer. For this discussion, a left-handed coordinate system for the camera is assumed. These vectors can be computed in the right-handed world space by first taking the cross product of the view direction vector and the y-axis, forming the u-vector, and then taking the cross product of the u-vector and the view direction vector [Eq. (2.1)].

$$
\begin{aligned}
w &= \text{COI} - \text{EYE} \quad \text{view direction vector} \\
u &= w \times (0,\ 1,\ 0) \quad \text{cross product with } y\text{-axis}
\end{aligned}
\qquad (2.1)
$$

After computing these vectors, they should be normalized in order to form a unit coordinate system at the eye position. A world space data point can be defined in this coordinate system by, for example, taking the dot product of the vector from the eye to the data point with each of the three coordinate system vectors.

Head-tilt information can be provided in one of two ways. It can be given by specifying an angle deviation from the straight-up direction. In this case, a head-tilt rotation matrix can be formed and incorporated in the world-to-eye-space transformation or can be applied directly to the observer's default u-vector and v-vector.

Alternatively, head-tilt information can be given by specifying an up-direction vector. The user-supplied up-direction vector is typically not required to be perpendicular to the view direction as that would require too much work on the part of the user. Instead, the vector supplied by the user, together with the view direction vector, defines the plane in which the up vector lies. The difference between the user-supplied up-direction vector and the up vector is that the up vector by definition is perpendicular to the view direction vector. The computation of the up vector is the same as that outlined in Eq. (2.1), with the user-supplied up-direction vector, UP, replacing the y-axis [Eq. (2.2)].

$$w = \text{COI} - \text{EYE} \quad \text{view direction vector}$$
$$u = w \times UP \qquad \text{cross product with user's up vector} \tag{2.2}$$

Care must be taken when using a default up vector. Defined as perpendicular to the view vector and in the plane of the view vector and global y-axis, it is undefined for straight-up and straight-down views. These situations must be dealt with as special cases or simply avoided. In addition to the undefined cases, some observer motions can result in unanticipated effects. For example, the default head-up orientation means that if the observer has a fixed center of interest and the observer's position arcs directly over the center of interest, then just before and just after being directly overhead, the observer's up vector will instantaneously rotate by up to 180° (see Fig. 2.2).

In addition to the observer's position and orientation, the fov has to be specified to fully define a viewable volume of world space. This includes an *angle of view* (or the equally useful *half angle of view*), *hither clipping distance*, and *yon clipping distance* (sometimes the terms *near* and *far* are used instead of *hither* and *yon*). The fov information is used to set up the *perspective projection*.

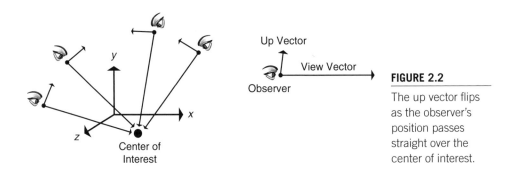

Up Vector

View Vector

Observer

Center of Interest

FIGURE 2.2

The up vector flips as the observer's position passes straight over the center of interest.

The view specification discussed above is somewhat simplified. Other view specifications use an additional vector to indicate the orientation of the projection plane, allow an arbitrary viewport to be specified on the plane of projection that is not symmetrical about the view direction to allow for off-center projections, and allow for a parallel projection. The reader should refer to standard graphics texts such as the one by Foley et al. [1] for in-depth discussion of such view specifications.

The visible area of world space is formed by the observer position, view direction, angle of view, hither clipping distance, and yon clipping distance (Fig. 2.3). These define the *view frustum*, the six-sided volume of world space containing data that need to be considered for display.

In preparation for the perspective transformation, the data points defining the objects are usually transformed from world space to *eye space*. In *eye space*, the observer is positioned along the z-axis with the line of sight made to coincide with the z-axis. This allows the depth of a point, and therefore perspective scaling, to be dependent only on the point's z-coordinate. The exact position of the observer along the z-axis and whether the eye space coordinate system is left-handed or right-handed vary from text to text. For this discussion, the observer is positioned at the origin looking down the positive z-axis in left-handed space. In eye space as in world space, lines of sight emanate from the observer position and diverge as they expand into the visible view frustum, whose shape is often referred to as a *truncated pyramid*.

The *perspective transformation* transforms the objects' data points from eye space to *image space*. The perspective transformation can be considered as taking the observer back to negative infinity in z and, in doing so, makes the lines of sight parallel to each other and to the (eye space) z-axis. The pyramid-shaped view frustum becomes a rectangular solid, or cuboid, whose opposite sides are parallel. Thus, points that are farther away from the observer in eye space have their x- and y-coordinates scaled down more than points that are closer to the observer. This is sometimes referred to as *perspective foreshortening*. Visible extents in image space are usually standardized into the -1 to $+1$ range in x and y and from 0 to 1 in z (although in some texts, visible z is mapped into the -1 to $+1$ range). Image space points are then scaled and translated (and possibly rotated) into *screen space* by mapping the visible ranges in x and y

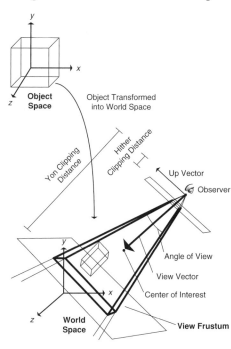

FIGURE 2.3

Object- to world-space transformation and the view frustum in world space.

(−1 to +1) into ranges that coincide with the viewing area defined in the coordinate system of the window or screen; the z-coordinates can be left alone. The resulting series of spaces is shown in Fig. 2.4.

Ray casting (ray tracing without generating secondary rays) differs from the above sequence of transformations in that the act of tracing rays from the observer's position out into world space implicitly accomplishes the perspective transformation. If the rays are constructed in world space based on pixel coordinates of a virtual frame buffer positioned in front of the observer, then the progression through spaces for ray casting reduces to the transformations shown in Fig. 2.5. Alternatively, data can

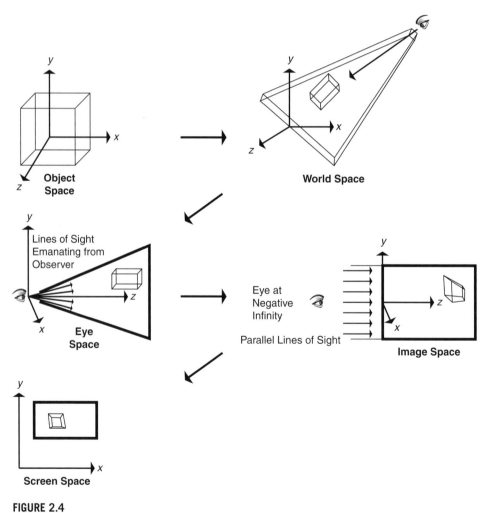

FIGURE 2.4

Display pipeline showing transformation between spaces.

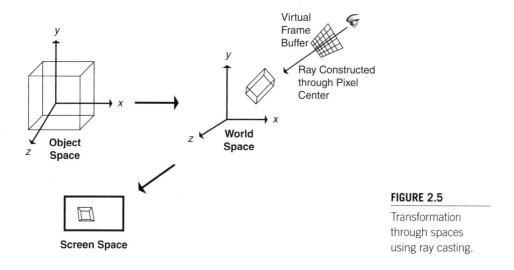

FIGURE 2.5

Transformation through spaces using ray casting.

be transformed to eye space and, through a virtual frame buffer, the rays can be formed in eye space.

In any case, animation is typically produced by one or more of the following: modifying the position and orientation of objects in world space over time, modifying the shape of objects over time, modifying display attributes of objects over time, transforming the observer position and orientation in world space over time, or some combination of these transformations.

2.1.2 Homogeneous Coordinates and the Transformation Matrix

Computer graphics often uses a *homogeneous representation* of a point in space. This means that a three-dimensional point is represented by a four-element vector.[1] The coordinates of the represented point are determined by dividing the fourth component into the first three [Eq. (2.3)].

$$\left(\frac{x}{w}, \frac{y}{w}, \frac{z}{w}\right) = [x, y, z, w] \tag{2.3}$$

Typically, when transforming a point in world space, the fourth component will be one. This means a point in space has a very simple homogeneous representation [Eq. (2.4)].

$$(x, y, z) = [x, y, z, 1] \tag{2.4}$$

The basic transformations of rotate, translate, and scale can be kept in 4×4 transformation matrices. The 4×4 matrix is the smallest matrix that can represent all of

---

[1]Note the potential source of confusion in the use of the term *vector* to mean (1) a direction in space or (2) a $1 \times n$ or $n \times 1$ matrix. The context in which vector is used should make its meaning clear.

the basic transformations. Because it is a square matrix, it has the potential for having a computable inverse, which is important for texture mapping and illumination calculations. In the case of rotation, translation, and nonzero scale transformations, the matrix always has a computable inverse. It can be multiplied with other transformation matrices to produce compound transformations while still maintaining 4×4-ness. The 4×4 identity matrix has zeros everywhere except along its diagonal; the diagonal elements all equal one [Eq. (2.5)].

$$
\begin{bmatrix} x \\ y \\ z \\ 1 \end{bmatrix} = \begin{bmatrix} 1 & 0 & 0 & 0 \\ 0 & 1 & 0 & 0 \\ 0 & 0 & 1 & 0 \\ 0 & 0 & 0 & 1 \end{bmatrix} \begin{bmatrix} x \\ y \\ z \\ 1 \end{bmatrix}
\tag{2.5}
$$

Typically in the literature, a point is represented as a 4×1 column matrix (also known as a *column vector*) and is transformed by multiplying by a 4×4 matrix on the left (also known as *premultiplying* the column vector by the matrix), as shown in Eq. (2.5) in the case of the identity matrix. However, some texts use a 1×4 matrix (also known as a *row vector*) to represent a point and transform it by multiplying it by a matrix on its right (*postmultiplying*). For example, postmultiplying a point by the identity transformation would appear as in Eq. (2.6).

$$
\begin{bmatrix} x & y & z & 1 \end{bmatrix} = \begin{bmatrix} x & y & z & 1 \end{bmatrix} \begin{bmatrix} 1 & 0 & 0 & 0 \\ 0 & 1 & 0 & 0 \\ 0 & 0 & 1 & 0 \\ 0 & 0 & 0 & 1 \end{bmatrix}
\tag{2.6}
$$

Because the conventions are equivalent, it is immaterial which is used as long as consistency is maintained. The 4×4 transformation matrix used in one of the notations is the transpose of the 4×4 transformation matrix used in the other notation.

2.1.3 Compound Transformation: Concatenating Transformation Matrices

One of the main advantages of representing transformations as square matrices is that they can be multiplied together, called *concatenating*, to produce a compound transformation. This enables a series of transformations, M_i, to be premultiplied so that a single compound transformation matrix, M, can be applied to a point P [see Eq. (2.7)]. This is especially useful (i.e. computationally efficient) when applying the same series of transformations to a multitude of points. Note that matrix multiplication is associative $((AB)C = A(BC))$ but not commutative $(AB \neq BA)$.

$$
\begin{aligned}
P' &= M_1 M_2 M_3 M_4 M_5 M_6 P \\
M &= M_1 M_2 M_3 M_4 M_5 M_6 \\
P' &= MP
\end{aligned}
\tag{2.7}
$$

When using the convention of postmultiplying a point represented by a row vector by the same series of transformations used when premultiplying a column vector, the matrices will appear in reverse order in addition to being the transpose of the matrices used in the premultiplication. Equation (2.8) shows the same computation as Eq. (2.7), except in Eq. (2.8), a row vector is postmultiplied by the transformation matrices. The matrices in Eq. (2.8) are the same as those in Eq. (2.7) but are now transposed and in reverse order. The transformed point is the same in both equations, with the exception that it appears as a column vector in Eq. (2.7) and as a row vector in Eq. (2.8).

$$
\begin{aligned}
P'^T &= P^T M_6^T M_5^T M_4^T M_3^T M_2^T M_1^T \\
M^T &= M_6^T M_5^T M_4^T M_3^T M_2^T M_1^T \\
P'^T &= P^T M^T
\end{aligned}
\tag{2.8}
$$

2.1.4 Basic Transformations

For now, only the basic transformations rotate, translate, and scale (uniform as well as nonuniform) will be considered. These transformations, and any combination of these, are *affine transformations* [3]. It should be noted that the transformation matrices are the same whether the space is left-handed or right-handed. The perspective transformation is discussed later. Restricting discussion to the basic transformations allows the fourth element of each point vector to be assigned the value 1 and the last row of the transformation matrix to be assigned the value [0 0 0 1] [Eq. (2.9)].

$$
\begin{bmatrix} x' \\ y' \\ z' \\ 1 \end{bmatrix} =
\begin{bmatrix} a & b & c & d \\ e & f & g & h \\ i & j & k & m \\ 0 & 0 & 0 & 1 \end{bmatrix}
\begin{bmatrix} x \\ y \\ z \\ 1 \end{bmatrix}
\tag{2.9}
$$

The x, y, and z translation values of the transformation are the first three values of the fourth column [d, h, and m in Eq. (2.9)]. The upper left 3×3 submatrix represents rotation and scaling. Setting the upper left 3×3 submatrix to an identity transformation and specifying only translation produces Eq. (2.10).

$$
\begin{bmatrix} x + t_x \\ y + t_y \\ z + t_z \\ 1 \end{bmatrix} =
\begin{bmatrix} 1 & 0 & 0 & t_x \\ 0 & 1 & 0 & t_y \\ 0 & 0 & 1 & t_z \\ 0 & 0 & 0 & 1 \end{bmatrix}
\begin{bmatrix} x \\ y \\ z \\ 1 \end{bmatrix}
\tag{2.10}
$$

A transformation consisting of only uniform scale is represented by the identity matrix with a scale factor, S, replacing the first three elements along the diagonal [a, f, and k in Eq. (2.9)]. Nonuniform scale allows for independent scale factors to be applied to the x-, y-, and z-coordinates of a point and is formed by placing S_x, S_y, and S_z along the diagonal as shown in Eq. (2.11).

$$\begin{bmatrix} S_x x \\ S_y y \\ S_z z \\ 1 \end{bmatrix} = \begin{bmatrix} S_x & 0 & 0 & 0 \\ 0 & S_y & 0 & 0 \\ 0 & 0 & S_z & 0 \\ 0 & 0 & 0 & 1 \end{bmatrix} \begin{bmatrix} x \\ y \\ z \\ 1 \end{bmatrix} \tag{2.11}$$

Uniform scale can also be represented by setting the lowest rightmost value to $1/S$, as in Eq. (2.12). In the homogeneous representation, the coordinates of the point represented are determined by dividing the first three elements of the vector by the fourth, thus scaling up the values by the scale factor S. This technique invalidates the assumption that the only time the lowest rightmost element is not one is during perspective and therefore should be used with care or avoided altogether.

$$\begin{bmatrix} S_x \\ S_y \\ S_z \\ 1 \end{bmatrix} = \begin{bmatrix} x \\ y \\ z \\ \frac{1}{S} \end{bmatrix} = \begin{bmatrix} 1 & 0 & 0 & 0 \\ 0 & 1 & 0 & 0 \\ 0 & 0 & 1 & 0 \\ 0 & 0 & 0 & \frac{1}{S} \end{bmatrix} \begin{bmatrix} x \\ y \\ z \\ 1 \end{bmatrix} \tag{2.12}$$

Values to represent rotation are set in the upper left 3×3 submatrix [a, b, c, e, f, g, i, j, and k of Eq. (2.9)]. Rotation matrices around the x-axis, y-axis, and z-axis are shown in Eqs. (2.13)–(2.15), respectively. In a right-handed coordinate system, a positive angle of rotation produces a counterclockwise rotation as viewed from the positive end of the axis looking toward the origin (the right-hand rule). In a left-handed (right-handed) coordinate system, a positive angle of rotation produces a clockwise (counterclockwise) rotation as viewed from the positive end of an axis. This can be remembered by noting that when pointing the thumb of the left (right) hand in the direction of the positive axis, the fingers wrap clockwise (counterclockwise) around the closed hand when viewed from a position on the positive axis (the thumb).

$$\begin{bmatrix} x' \\ y' \\ z' \\ 1 \end{bmatrix} = \begin{bmatrix} 1 & 0 & 0 & 0 \\ 0 & \cos\theta & -\sin\theta & 0 \\ 0 & \sin\theta & \cos\theta & 0 \\ 0 & 0 & 0 & 1 \end{bmatrix} \begin{bmatrix} x \\ y \\ z \\ 1 \end{bmatrix} \tag{2.13}$$

$$\begin{bmatrix} x' \\ y' \\ z' \\ 1 \end{bmatrix} = \begin{bmatrix} \cos\theta & 0 & \sin\theta & 0 \\ 0 & 1 & 0 & 0 \\ -\sin\theta & 0 & \cos\theta & 0 \\ 0 & 0 & 0 & 1 \end{bmatrix} \begin{bmatrix} x \\ y \\ z \\ 1 \end{bmatrix} \tag{2.14}$$

$$\begin{bmatrix} x' \\ y' \\ z' \\ 1 \end{bmatrix} = \begin{bmatrix} \cos\theta & -\sin\theta & 0 & 0 \\ \sin\theta & \cos\theta & 0 & 0 \\ 0 & 0 & 1 & 0 \\ 0 & 0 & 0 & 1 \end{bmatrix} \begin{bmatrix} x \\ y \\ z \\ 1 \end{bmatrix} \tag{2.15}$$

Combinations of rotations and translations are usually referred to as *rigid transformations* because distance is preserved and the spatial extent of the object does not change; only its position and orientation in space are changed. *Similarity transformations* also allow uniform scale in addition to rotation and translation. These transformations preserve the object's intrinsic properties[2] (e.g. dihedral angles[3]) and relative distances but not absolute distances. Nonuniform scale, however, is usually not considered a similarity transformation because object properties such as dihedral angles are changed. A *shear* transformation is a combination of rotation and nonuniform scale and creates columns (rows) that might not be orthogonal to each other. Any combination of rotations, translations, and (uniform or nonuniform) scales still retains the last row of three zeros followed by a one. Notice that any affine transformation can be represented by a multiplicative 3×3 matrix (representing rotations, scales, and shears) followed by an additive three-element vector (translation).

2.1.5 Representing an Arbitrary Orientation

Rigid transformations (consisting of only rotations and translations) are very useful for moving objects around a scene without disturbing their geometry. These rigid transformations can be represented by a (possibly compound) rotation followed by a translation. The rotation transformation represents the object's orientation relative to its definition in object space. This section considers various ways to represent an object's orientation.

2.1.5.1 Fixed-Angle Representation
One way to represent an orientation is as a series of rotations around the principal axes (the *fixed-angle representation*). In order to illustrate the relationship between orientation and a fixed order of rotations around the principal axes, consider the problem of determining the transformations that would produce a given geometric configuration. For example, consider an aircraft is originally defined at the origin of a right-handed coordinate system with its nose pointed down the *z*-axis and its up vector in the positive *y*-axis direction (i.e. its object space representation). Now, imagine that the objective is to position the aircraft in world space so that its center is at (20, −10, 35), its nose is oriented toward the point (23, −14, 40), and its up vector is pointed in the general direction of the *y*-axis (or, mathematically, so that its up vector lies in the plane defined by the aircraft's center, the point the plane is oriented toward, and the global *y*-axis) (see Fig. 2.6).

The task is to determine the series of transformations that takes the aircraft from its original object space definition to its desired position and orientation in world space. This series of transformations will be one or more rotations about the principal axes followed by a translation of (20, −10, 35). The rotations will transform the

---

[2]An object's intrinsic properties are those that are measured irrespective of an external coordinate system.
[3]The dihedral angle is the interior angle between adjacent polygons measured at the common edge.

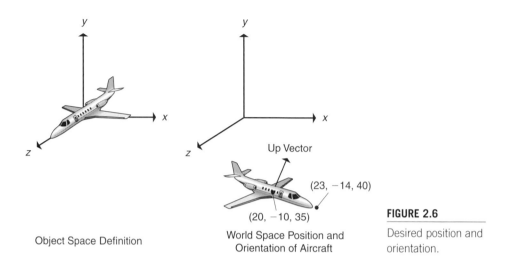

Object Space Definition

World Space Position and
Orientation of Aircraft

Up Vector

$(23, -14, 40)$

$(20, -10, 35)$

FIGURE 2.6

Desired position and
orientation.

aircraft to an orientation so that, with its center at the origin, its nose is oriented toward $(23 - 20, -14 + 10, 40 - 35) = (3, -4, 5)$; this will be referred to as the aircraft's orientation vector.

In general, any such orientation can be effected by a rotation about the z-axis to tilt the object, followed by a rotation about the x-axis to tip the nose up or down, followed by a rotation about the y-axis to swing the plane around to point to the correct direction. This sequence is not unique; others could be constructed as well.

In this particular example, there is no tilt necessary because the desired up vector is already in the plane of the y-axis and orientation vector. We need to determine the x-axis rotation that will dip the nose down the right amount and the y-axis rotation that will swing it around the right amount. We do this by looking at the transformations needed to take the orientation vector from its initial direction in object space aligned with the z-axis so that it aligns with the desired orientation vector.

The transformation that takes the aircraft into the desired orientation can be determined by determining the sines and cosines necessary for the x-axis and y-axis rotation matrices. Note that the length of the orientation vector is $\sqrt{3^2 + (-4)^2 + 5^2} = \sqrt{50}$. In first considering the x-axis rotation, initially position the orientation vector along the z-axis so that its endpoint is at $(0, 0, \sqrt{50})$. The x-axis rotation must rotate the endpoint of the orientation vector so that it is -4 in y. By the Pythagorean Rule, the z-coordinate of the endpoint would then be $\sqrt{50 - 4^2} = \sqrt{34}$ after the rotation. The sines and cosines can be read from the triangle formed by the rotated orientation vector, the vertical line segment that extends from the end of the orientation vector up to intersect the x-z plane, and the line segment from that intersection point to the origin (Fig. 2.7). Observing that a positive x-axis rotation will rotate the orientation vector down in y, we have $\sin \psi = 4/\sqrt{50}$ and $\cos \psi \sqrt{34}/\sqrt{50}$. The x-axis rotation matrix looks like this:

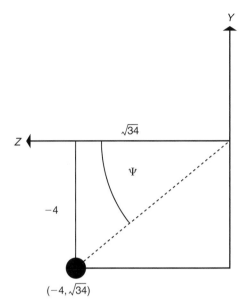

FIGURE 2.7

Projection of desired orientation vector onto y-z plane.

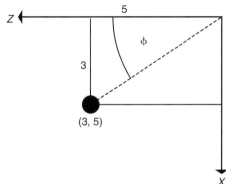

FIGURE 2.8

Projection of desired orientation vector onto x-z plane.

$$R_x = \begin{bmatrix} 1 & 0 & 0 \\ 0 & \cos\psi & -\sin\psi \\ 0 & \sin\psi & \cos\psi \end{bmatrix} = \begin{bmatrix} 1 & 0 & 0 \\ 0 & \dfrac{\sqrt{34}}{\sqrt{50}} & \dfrac{-4}{\sqrt{50}} \\ 0 & \dfrac{4}{\sqrt{50}} & \dfrac{\sqrt{34}}{\sqrt{50}} \end{bmatrix} = \begin{bmatrix} 1 & 0 & 0 \\ 0 & \dfrac{\sqrt{17}}{5} & \dfrac{-2\sqrt{2}}{5} \\ 0 & \dfrac{2\sqrt{2}}{5} & \dfrac{\sqrt{17}}{5} \end{bmatrix} \qquad (2.16)$$

After the pitch rotation has been applied, a y-axis rotation is required to spin the aircraft around (yaw) to its desired orientation. The sine and cosine of the y-axis rotation can be determined by looking at the projection of the desired orientation vector in the x-z plane. This projection is (3, 0, 5). Thus, a positive y-axis rotation with $\sin\phi = 3/\sqrt{34}$ and $\cos\phi = 5/\sqrt{34}$ is required (Fig. 2.8). The y-axis rotation matrix looks like this:

$$R_y = \begin{bmatrix} \cos\phi & 0 & \sin\phi \\ 0 & 1 & 0 \\ -\sin\phi & 0 & \cos\phi \end{bmatrix} = \begin{bmatrix} \dfrac{5}{\sqrt{34}} & 0 & \dfrac{3}{\sqrt{34}} \\ 0 & 1 & 0 \\ \dfrac{-3}{\sqrt{34}} & 0 & \dfrac{5}{\sqrt{34}} \end{bmatrix} \qquad (2.17)$$

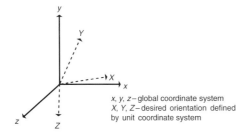

FIGURE 2.9

Global coordinate system and unit coordinate system to be transformed.

x, y, z–global coordinate system
X, Y, Z–desired orientation defined by unit coordinate system

The final transformation of a point P would be $P' = R_x R_y P$.

An alternative way to represent a transformation to a desired orientation is to construct what is known as the *matrix of direction cosines*. Consider transforming a copy of the global coordinate system so that it coincides with a desired orientation defined by a unit coordinate system (see Fig. 2.9). To construct this matrix, note that the transformation matrix, M, should do the following: map a unit x-axis vector into the X-axis of the desired orientation, map a unit y-axis vector into the Y-axis of the desired orientation, and map a unit z-axis vector into the Z-axis of the desired orientation [see Eq. (2.18)]. These three mappings can be assembled into one matrix expression that defines the matrix M [Eq. (2.19)].

$$X = Mx \qquad Y = My \qquad Z = Mz$$
$$\begin{bmatrix} X_x \\ X_y \\ X_z \end{bmatrix} = M \begin{bmatrix} 1 \\ 0 \\ 0 \end{bmatrix} \quad \begin{bmatrix} Y_x \\ Y_y \\ Y_z \end{bmatrix} = M \begin{bmatrix} 0 \\ 1 \\ 0 \end{bmatrix} \quad \begin{bmatrix} Z_x \\ Z_y \\ Z_z \end{bmatrix} = M \begin{bmatrix} 0 \\ 0 \\ 1 \end{bmatrix} \qquad (2.18)$$

$$\begin{bmatrix} X_x & Y_x & Z_x \\ X_y & Y_y & Z_y \\ X_z & Y_z & Z_z \end{bmatrix} = M \begin{bmatrix} 1 & 0 & 0 \\ 0 & 1 & 0 \\ 0 & 0 & 1 \end{bmatrix} = M \qquad (2.19)$$

Since a unit x-vector (y-vector, z-vector) multiplied by a transformation matrix will replicate the values in the first (second, third) column of the transformation matrix, the columns of the transformation matrix can be filled with the coordinates of the desired transformed coordinate system. Thus, the first column of the transformation matrix becomes the desired X-axis as described by its x-, y-, and z-coordinates in the global space, call it u; the second column becomes the desired Y-axis, call it v; and the third column becomes the desired Z-axis, call it w [Eq. (2.20)]. The name *matrix of direction cosines* is derived from the fact that the coordinates of a desired axis in terms of the global coordinate system are the cosines of the angles made by the desired axis with each of the global axes.

In the example of transforming the aircraft, the desired Z-axis is the desired orientation vector, $w = [3, -4, 5]$. With the assumption that there is no longitudinal rotation (roll), the desired X-axis can be formed by taking the cross product of the original y-axis and the desired Z-axis, $u = [5, 0, -3]$. The desired Y-axis can then be formed by taking the cross product of the desired Z-axis and the desired X-axis,

$v = [12, 34, 20]$. Each of these is normalized by dividing by its length to form unit vectors. This results in the following matrix, which is the same matrix formed by multiplying the y-rotation matrix, R_y, by the x-rotation matrix, R_x.

$$M = [u^T, v^T, w^T] = \begin{bmatrix} \dfrac{5}{\sqrt{34}} & \dfrac{6}{5\sqrt{17}} & \dfrac{3}{5\sqrt{2}} \\[2mm] 0 & \dfrac{\sqrt{17}}{5} & -2\dfrac{\sqrt{2}}{5} \\[2mm] -\dfrac{3}{\sqrt{34}} & \dfrac{2}{\sqrt{17}} & \dfrac{1}{\sqrt{2}} \end{bmatrix} = R_y R_x \qquad (2.20)$$

2.1.6 Extracting Transformations from a Matrix

For a compound transformation matrix that represents a series of rotations and translations, a set of individual transformations can be extracted from the matrix, which, when multiplied together, produce the original compound transformation matrix. Notice that the series of transformations to produce a compound transformation is not unique, so there is no guarantee that the series of transformations so extracted will be exactly the ones that produced the compound transformation (unless something is known about the process that produced the compound matrix).

An arbitrary rigid transformation can easily be formed by up to three rotations about the principal axes (or one compound rotation represented by the direction cosine matrix) followed by a translation.

The last row of a 4×4 transformation matrix, if the matrix does not include a perspective transformation, will have zero in the first three entries and one as the fourth entry (ignoring the use of that element to represent uniform scale). As shown in Eq. (2.21), the first three elements of the last column of the matrix, A_{14}, A_{24}, and A_{34}, represent a translation. The upper left 3×3 submatrix of the original 4×4 matrix can be viewed as the definition of the transformed unit coordinate system. It can be decomposed into three rotations around principal axes by arbitrarily choosing an ordered sequence of three axes (such as x followed by y followed by z). By using the projection of the transformed unit coordinate system to determine the sines and cosines, the appropriate rotation matrices can be formed in much the same way that transformations were determined in Section 2.1.5.

$$\begin{bmatrix} x' \\ y' \\ z' \\ 1 \end{bmatrix} = \begin{bmatrix} A_{11} & A_{12} & A_{13} & A_{14} \\ A_{21} & A_{22} & A_{23} & A_{24} \\ A_{31} & A_{32} & A_{33} & A_{34} \\ 0 & 0 & 0 & 1 \end{bmatrix} \begin{bmatrix} x \\ y \\ z \\ 1 \end{bmatrix} \qquad (2.21)$$

If the compound transformation matrix includes a uniform scale factor, the rows of the 3×3 submatrix will form orthogonal vectors of uniform length. The length will be the scale factor, which, when followed by the rotations and translations, forms the decomposition of the compound transformation. If the rows of the 3×3 submatrix form orthogonal vectors of unequal length, then their lengths represent nonuniform scale factors that precede any rotations.

2.1.7 Description of Transformations in the Display Pipeline

Now that the basic transformations have been discussed in some detail, the previously described transformations of the display pipeline can be explained in terms of concatenations of the basic transformations. It should be noted that the descriptions of eye space and the corresponding perspective transformation are not unique. They vary among the introductory graphics texts depending on where the observer is placed along the z-axis to define eye space, whether the eye space coordinate system is left-handed or right-handed, exactly what information is required from the user in describing the perspective transformation, and the range of visible z-values in image space. While functionally equivalent, the various approaches produce transformation matrices that differ in the values of the individual elements.

2.1.7.1 Object Space to World Space Transformation

In a simple implementation, the transformation of an object from its object space into world space is a series of rotations, translations, and scales (i.e. an affine transformation) that are specified by the user (either by explicit numeric input or by some interactive technique) to place a transformed copy of the object data into a world space data structure. In some systems, the user is required to specify this transformation in terms of a predefined order of basic transformations such as scale, rotation around the x-axis, rotation around the y-axis, rotation around the z-axis, and translation. In other systems, the user may be able to specify an arbitrarily ordered sequence of basic transformations. In either case, the series of transformations are compounded into a single object space to world space transformation matrix.

The object space to world space transformation is usually the transformation that is modified over time to produce motion. In more complex animation systems, this transformation may include manipulations of arbitrary complexity not suitable for representation in a matrix, such as nonlinear shape deformations.

2.1.7.2 World Space to Eye Space Transformation

In preparation for the perspective transformation, a rigid transformation is performed on all of the object data in world space. The transformation is designed so that, in eye space, the observer is positioned at the origin, the view vector aligns with the positive z-axis in left-handed space, and the up vector aligns with the positive y-axis. The transformation is formed as a series of basic transformations.

First, the data are translated so that the observer is moved to the origin. Then, the observer's coordinate system (view vector, up vector, and the third vector required to complete a left-handed coordinate system) is transformed by up to three rotations so as to align the view vector with the global negative z-axis and the up vector with the global y-axis. Finally, the z-axis is flipped by negating the z-coordinate. All of the individual transformations can be represented by 4×4 transformation matrices, which are multiplied together to produce a single, compound, world space to eye space transformation matrix. This transformation prepares the data for the perspective transformation by putting it in a form in which the perspective divide is simply dividing by a point's z-coordinate.

2.1.7.3 Perspective Matrix Multiply

The perspective matrix multiplication is the first part of the perspective transformation. The fundamental computation being performed by the perspective transformation is that of dividing the x- and y-coordinates by their z-coordinate and normalizing the visible range in x and y to $[-1, +1]$. This is accomplished by using a homogeneous representation of a point and, as a result of the perspective matrix multiplication, producing a representation in which the fourth element is $Z_e \tan\phi$. Z_e is the point's z-coordinate in eye space and ϕ is the half angle of view. The z-coordinate is transformed so that planarity is preserved and the visible range in z is mapped into $[0, +1]$. (These ranges are arbitrary and can be set to anything by appropriately forming the perspective matrix. For example, sometimes the visible range in z is set to $[-1, +1]$.) In addition, the aspect ratio of the viewport can be used in the matrix to modify either the x or y half angle of view so that no distortion results in the viewed data.

2.1.7.4 Perspective Divide

Each point produced by the perspective matrix multiplication has a nonunitary fourth component that represents the perspective divide by z. Dividing each point by its fourth component completes the perspective transformation. This is considered a separate step from the perspective matrix multiply because a commonly used clipping procedure operates on the homogeneous representation of points produced by the perspective matrix multiplication but before perspective divide.

2.1.7.5 Image to Screen Space Mapping

The result of the perspective transformation (the perspective matrix multiply followed by perspective divide) maps visible elements into the range of -1 to $+1$ ($[-1, +1]$) in x and y. This range is now mapped into the user-specified viewing area of the screen-based pixel coordinate system. This is a simple linear transformation represented by a scale and a translation and thus can be easily represented in a 4×4 transformation matrix.

Clipping, removing data that are outside the view frustum, can be implemented in a variety of ways. It is computationally simpler if clipping is performed after the world space to eye space transformation. It is important to perform clipping in z before perspective divide, to prevent divide by zero, and to avoid projecting objects behind the observer onto the picture plane. However, the details of clipping are not relevant to the discussion here. Interested readers should refer to one of the standard computer graphics texts (e.g. [1]) for the details of clipping procedures.

2.1.8 Error Considerations

2.1.8.1 Accumulated Round-Off Error

Once the object space to world space transformation matrix has been formed for an object, the object is transformed into world space by simply multiplying all of the object's object space points by the transformation matrix. When an object's position and orientation are animated, its points will be repeatedly transformed over time – as a function of time. One way to do this is to repeatedly modify the object's world space points. However, incremental transformation of world space points can lead to the accumulation of round-off errors. For this reason, it is almost always better to modify the transformation from object to world space and reapply the transformation to the object space points rather than to repeatedly transform the world space coordinates. To further transform an object that already has a transformation matrix associated with it, one simply has to form a transformation matrix and premultiply it by the existing transformation matrix to produce a new one. However, round-off errors can also accumulate when one repeatedly modifies a transformation matrix. The best way is to build the transformation matrix anew each time it is to be applied.

An affine transformation matrix can be viewed as a 3×3 rotation/scale submatrix followed by a translation. Most of the error accumulation occurs because of the operations resulting from multiplying the x-, y-, and z-coordinates of the point by the 3×3 submatrix. Therefore, the following round-off error example will focus on the errors that accumulate as a result of rotations.

Consider the case of the moon orbiting the earth. For the sake of simplicity, the assumption is that the center of the earth is at the origin, and initially, the moon data are defined with the moon's center at the origin. The moon data are first transformed to an initial position relative to the earth, for example $(r, 0, 0)$ (see Fig. 2.10). There are three approaches that could be taken to animate the rotation of the moon around the earth, and these will be used to illustrate various effects of round-off error.

The first approach is, for each frame of the animation, to apply a delta z-axis transformation matrix to the moon's points, in which each delta represents the angle

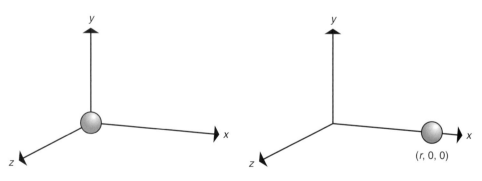

FIGURE 2.10

Translation of moon to its initial position on the x-axis.

it moves in one frame time (see Fig. 2.11). Round-off errors will accumulate in the world space object points. Points that began as coplanar will no longer be coplanar. This can have undesirable effects, especially in display algorithms that linearly interpolate values to render a surface.

The second approach is, for each frame, to incrementally modify the transformation matrix that takes the object space points into the world space positions. In the example of the moon, the transformation matrix is initialized with the x-axis translation matrix. For each frame, a delta z-axis transformation matrix multiplies the current transformation matrix and then that resultant matrix is applied to the moon's object space points (see Fig. 2.12). Round-off error will accumulate in the transformation matrix. Over time, the matrix will deviate from representing a rigid transformation. Shearing effects will begin to creep into the transformation and angles will cease to be preserved. While a square may begin to look like something other than a square, coplanarity will be preserved (because any matrix multiplication is, by definition, a linear transformation that preserves planarity) so that rendering results will not be compromised.

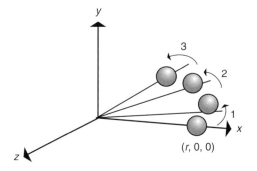

```
for each point P of the moon {
    P· = P
}
R_dz = y-axis rotation of 5 degrees
repeat until (done) {
    for each point P· of the moon {
        P· = R_dz*P·
    }
    record a frame of the animation
}
```

FIGURE 2.11

Rotation by applying incremental rotation matrices to points.

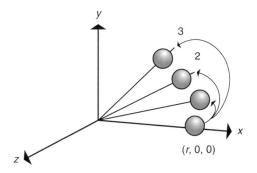

```
R = identity matrix
R_dz = z-axis rotation of 5 degrees
repeat until (done) {
    for each point P of the moon {
        P' = R*P
    }
    record a frame of the animation
    R = R*R_dz
}
```

FIGURE 2.12

Rotation by incrementally updating the rotation matrix.

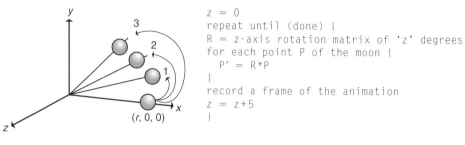

```
z = 0
repeat until (done) {
  R = z-axis rotation matrix of 'z' degrees
  for each point P of the moon {
    P' = R*P
  }
  record a frame of the animation
  z = z+5
}
```

FIGURE 2.13

Rotation by forming the rotation matrix anew for each frame.

The third approach is to add the delta value to an accumulating angle variable and then build the z-axis rotation matrix from that angle parameter. This would then be multiplied with the x-axis translation matrix, and the resultant matrix would be applied to the original moon points in object space (see Fig. 2.13). In this case, any round-off error will accumulate in the angle variable so that, over time, it may begin to deviate from what is desired. This may have unwanted effects when one tries to coordinate motions, but the transformation matrix, which is built anew every frame, will not accumulate any errors itself. The transformation will always represent a valid rigid transformation with both planarity and angles being preserved.

2.1.8.2 Orthonormalization

The rows of a matrix that represent a rigid transformation are perpendicular to each other and are of unit length (orthonormal). The same can be said of the matrix columns. If values in a rigid transformation matrix have accumulated errors, then the rows cease to be orthonormal and the matrix ceases to represent a rigid transformation; it will have the effect of introducing shear into the transformation. However, if it is known that the matrix is supposed to represent a rigid transformation, it can be massaged back into a rigid transformation matrix.

A rigid transformation matrix has an upper 3×3 submatrix with specific properties: the rows (columns) are unit vectors orthogonal to each other. A simple procedure to reformulate the transformation matrix to represent a rigid transformation is to take the first row (column) and normalize it. Take the second row (column), compute the cross product of this row (column) and the first row (column), normalize it, and place it in the third row (column). Take the cross product of the third row (column) and the first row (column) and put it in the second row (column) (see Fig. 2.14). Notice that this does not necessarily produce the correct transformation; it merely forces the matrix to represent a rigid transformation. The error has just been shifted around so that the columns of the matrix are orthonormal and the error may be less noticeable.

If the transformation might contain a uniform scale, then take the length of one of the rows, or the average length of the three rows, and, instead of normal-

The original unit orthogonal vectors have ceased to be orthogonal to each other due to repeated transformations.

Step 1: Normalize one of the vectors.

Step 2:
Form vector perpendicular (orthogonal) to the vector just normalized and to one of the other two original vectors by taking the cross product of the two. Normalize it.

Step 3:
Form the final orthogonal vector by taking the cross product of the two just generated.

FIGURE 2.14

Orthonormalization of a set of three vectors.

izing the vectors by the steps described above, make them equal to this length. If the transformation might include nonuniform scale, then the difference between shear and error accumulation cannot be determined unless something more is known about the transformations represented. For example, if it is known that nonuniform scale was applied before any rotation (i.e. no shear), then Gram-Schmidt Orthonormalization [4] can be performed, without the normalization step, to force orthogonality among the vectors. Gram-Schmidt processes the vectors in any order. To process a vector, project it onto each previously processed vector. Subtract the projections from the vector currently being processed, then process the next vector. When all vectors have been processed, they are orthogonal to each other.

2.1.8.3 Considerations of Scale

When constructing a large database (e.g. flight simulator), there may be such variations in the magnitude of various measures as to create precision problems. For example, you may require detail on the order of a fraction of an inch for some objects, while the entire database may span thousands of miles. The scale of values would range from to 10^{-1} inches to 5000 miles $\cdot$ 5280 feet/mile $\cdot$ 12 inches/foot $= 3.168 \cdot 10^8$ inches. This exceeds the precision of 32-bit single-precision representations. Using double-precision will help eliminate the problem. However, using double-precision representations may also increase storage space requirements and decrease the speed of the computations. Alternatively, subdividing the database into local data, such as airports in the example of a flight simulator, and switching between these localized databases might provide an acceptable solution.

2.2 ORIENTATION REPRESENTATION

A common issue that arises in computer animation is deciding the best way to represent the position and orientation of an object in space and how to interpolate the represented transformations over time to produce motion. A typical scenario is one in which the user specifies an object in two transformed states, and the computer is used to interpolate intermediate states, thus producing animated keyframe motion. Another scenario is when an object is to undergo two or more successive transformations and it would be efficient to concatenate these transformations into a single representation before applying it to a multitude of object vertices. This section discusses possible orientation representations and identifies strengths and weaknesses. In this discussion, it is assumed that the final transformation applied to the object is a result of rotations and translations only, so that there is no scaling involved, nonuniform or otherwise; that is, the transformations considered are *rigid body*.

The first obvious choice for representing the orientation and position of an object is by a 4×4 transformation matrix. For example, a user may specify a series of rotations and translations to apply to an object. This series of transformations is compiled into 4×4 matrices and is multiplied together to produce a compound 4×4 transformation matrix. In such a matrix, the upper left 3×3 submatrix represents a rotation to apply to the object, while the first three elements of the fourth column represent the translation (assuming points are represented by column vectors that are premultiplied by the transformation matrix). No matter how the 4×4 transformation matrix was formed (no matter in what order the transformations were given by the user, such as rotate about x, translate, rotate about x, rotate about y, translate, rotate about y), the final 4×4 transformation matrix produced by multiplying all of the individual transformation matrices in the specified order will result in a matrix that specifies the final position of the object by a 3×3 rotation matrix followed by a translation. The conclusion is that the rotation can be interpolated independently from the translation. (For now, consider that the interpolations are linear, although higher-order interpolations are possible.)

Consider two such transformations that the user has specified as key states with the intention of generating intermediate transformations by interpolation. While it should be obvious that interpolating the translations is straightforward, it is not at all clear how to go about interpolating the rotations. In fact, it is the objective of this discussion to show that interpolation of orientations is not nearly as straightforward as interpolation of translation. A property of 3×3 rotation matrices is that the rows and columns are orthonormal (unit length and perpendicular to each other). Simple linear interpolation between the nine pairs of numbers that make up the two 3×3 rotation matrices to be interpolated will not produce intermediate 3×3 matrices that are orthonormal and are therefore not rigid body rotations. It should be easy to see that interpolating from a rotation of $+90°$ about the y-axis to a rotation of $-90°$ about the y-axis results in intermediate transformations that are nonsense (Fig. 2.15).

So, direct interpolation of transformation matrices is not acceptable. There are alternative representations that are more useful than transformation matrices in

$$\begin{bmatrix} 0 & 0 & 1 \\ 0 & 1 & 0 \\ -1 & 0 & 0 \end{bmatrix}$$

Positive 90-degree y-axis rotation

$$\begin{bmatrix} 0 & 0 & -1 \\ 0 & 1 & 0 \\ 1 & 0 & 0 \end{bmatrix}$$

Negative 90-degree y-axis rotation

$$\begin{bmatrix} 0 & 0 & 0 \\ 0 & 1 & 0 \\ 0 & 0 & 0 \end{bmatrix}$$

Interpolated matrix halfway between the orientation representations above

FIGURE 2.15

Direct interpolation of transformation matrix values can result in nonsense transformations.

performing such interpolations including fixed angle, Euler angle, axis angle, quaternions, and exponential maps.

2.2.1 **Fixed-Angle Representation**

A *fixed-angle* representation[4] really refers to "angles used to rotate about fixed axes." A fixed order of three rotations is implied, such as x-y-z. This means that orientation is given by a set of three ordered parameters that represent three ordered rotations about fixed axes: first around x, then around y, and then around z. There are many possible orderings of the rotations, and, in fact, it is not necessary to use all three coordinate axes. For example, x-y-x is a feasible set of rotations. The only orderings that do not make sense are those in which an axis immediately follows itself, such as in x-x-y. In any case, the main point is that the orientation of an object is given by three angles, such as (10, 45, 90). In this example, the orientation represented is obtained by rotating the object first about the x-axis by 10°, then about the y-axis by 45°, and then about the z-axis by 90°. In Fig. 2.16, the aircraft is shown in its initial orientation and in the orientation represented by the fixed point values of (10, 45, 90).

The following notation will be used to represent such a sequence of rotations: $R_z(90)R_y(45)R_x(10)$ (in this text, transformations are implemented by premultiplying column vectors by transformation matrices; thus, the rotation matrices appear in right to left order).

From this orientation, changing the x-axis rotation value, which is applied first to the data points, will make the aircraft's nose dip either more or less in the y-z plane. Changing the y-axis rotation will change the amount the aircraft, which has been rotated around the x-axis, rotates out of the y-z plane. Changing the z-axis rotation value, the rotation applied last, will change how much the twice-rotated aircraft will rotate about the z-axis.

---

[4]Terms referring to rotational representations are not used consistently in the literature.

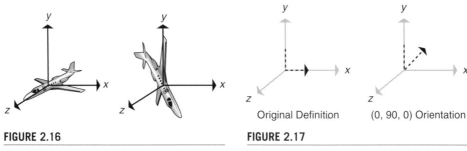

FIGURE 2.16

Fixed-angle representation.

FIGURE 2.17

Fixed-angle representation of (0, 90, 0).

The problem when using this scheme is that two of the axes of rotation can effectively line up on top of each other when an object can rotate freely in space (or around a 3° of freedom[5] joint). Consider an object in an orientation represented by (0, 90, 0), as shown in Fig. 2.17. Examine the effect a slight change in the first and third parametric values has on the object in that orientation. A slight change of the third parameter will rotate the object slightly about the global z-axis because that is the rotation applied last to the data points. However, note that the effect of a slight change of the first parameter, which rotates the original data points around the x-axis, will also have the effect of rotating the transformed object slightly about the z-axis (Fig. 2.18). This effect results because the 90-degree y-axis rotation has essentially made the first axis of rotation align with the third axis of rotation. The effect is called *gimbal lock*. From the orientation (0, 90, 0), the object can no longer be rotated about the global x-axis by a small change in its orientation representation. Actually, the representation that will perform an incremental rotation about the x-axis from the (0, 90, 0) orientation is (90, 90 + ε, 90), which is not very intuitive.

The cause of this problem can often make interpolation between key positions problematic. Consider the key orientations (0, 90, 0) and (90, 45, 90), as shown in Fig. 2.19. The second orientation is a 45-degree x-axis rotation from the first position. However, as discussed above, the object can no longer directly rotate about the x-axis from the first key orientation because of the 90-degree y-axis rotation. Direct interpolation of the key orientation representations would produce (45, 67.5, 45) as the halfway orientation, which is very different from the (90, 22.5, 90) orientation that is desired (desired because that is the representation of the orientation that is intuitively halfway between the two given orientations). The result is that the object will swing out of the y-z plane during the interpolation, which is not the behavior one would expect.

In its favor, the fixed-angle representation is compact, fairly intuitive, and easy to work with because the implied operations correspond to what we know how to

---

[5]The *degrees of freedom* (DOFs) that an object possesses is the number of independent variables that have to be specified to completely locate that object (and all of its parts).

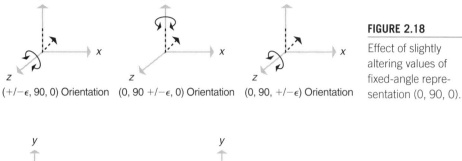

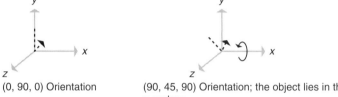

($+/-\epsilon$, 90, 0) Orientation   (0, 90 $+/-\epsilon$, 0) Orientation   (0, 90, $+/-\epsilon$) Orientation

FIGURE 2.18

Effect of slightly altering values of fixed-angle representation (0, 90, 0).

(0, 90, 0) Orientation

(90, 45, 90) Orientation; the object lies in the y-z plane

FIGURE 2.19

Example orientations to interpolate.

do mathematically – rotate data around the global axes. However, it is often not the most desirable representation to use because of the gimbal lock problem.

2.2.2 Euler Angle Representation

In an *Euler angle* representation, the axes of rotation are the axes of the local coordinate system that rotate with the object, as opposed to the fixed global axes. A typical example of using Euler angles is found in the roll, pitch, and yaw of an aircraft (Fig. 2.20).

As with the fixed-angle representation, the Euler angle representation can use any of various orderings of three axes of rotation as its representation scheme. Consider a Euler angle representation that uses an x-y-z ordering and is specified as (α, β, γ). The x-axis rotation, represented by the transformation matrix $R_x(\alpha)$, is followed by the y-axis rotation, represented by the transformation matrix $R_y(\beta)$, around the y-axis of the local, rotated coordinate system. Using a prime symbol to represent rotation about a rotated frame and remembering that points are represented as column vectors and are premultiplied by transformation matrices, one achieves a result of $R_y{}'(\beta)R_x(\alpha)$. Using global axis rotation matrices to implement the transformations, the y-axis rotation around the rotated frame can be effected by $R_x(\alpha)R_y(\beta)R_x(-\alpha)$. Thus, the result after the first two rotations is shown in Eq. (2.22).

$$R_y{}'(\beta)R_x(\alpha) = R_x(\alpha)R_y(\beta)R_x(-\alpha)R_x(\alpha) = R_x(\alpha)R_y(\beta) \qquad (2.22)$$

The third rotation, $R_z(\gamma)$, is around the now twice-rotated frame. This rotation can be effected by undoing the previous rotations with $R_x(-\alpha)$ followed by $R_y(-\beta)$, then rotating around the global z-axis by $R_z(\gamma)$, and then reapplying the previous

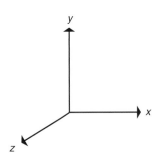

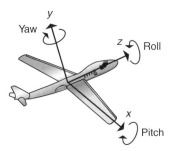

Global coordinate system

Local coordinate system
attached to object

FIGURE 2.20

Euler angle
representation.

rotations. Putting all three rotations together, and using a double prime to denote rotation about a twice-rotated frame, results in Eq. (2.23).

$$R_z''(\gamma)R_y'(\beta)R_x(\alpha) = R_x(\alpha)R_y(\beta)R_z(\gamma)R_y(-\beta)R_x(-\alpha)R_x(\alpha)R_y(\beta)$$
$$= R_x(\alpha)R_y(\beta)R_z(\gamma)$$

(2.23)

Thus, this system of Euler angles is precisely equivalent to the fixed-angle system in reverse order. This is true for any system of Euler angles. For example, *z-y-x* Euler angles are equivalent to *x-y-z* fixed angles. Therefore, the Euler angle representation has exactly the same advantages and disadvantages (i.e. gimbal lock) as those of the fixed-angle representation.

2.2.3 Angle and Axis Representation

In the mid-1700s, Leonhard Euler showed that one orientation can be derived from another by a single rotation about an axis. This is known as the *Euler Rotation Theorem* [5]. Thus, any orientation can be represented by three numbers: two for the axis, such as longitude and latitude, and one for the angle (Fig. 2.21). The axis can also be represented (somewhat inefficiently) by a three-dimensional vector. This can be a useful representation. Interpolation between representations (A_1, θ_1) and (A_2, θ_2) can be implemented by interpolating the axes of rotation and the angles separately (Fig. 2.22). An intermediate axis can be determined by rotating one axis partway toward the other. The axis for this rotation is formed by taking the cross product of two axes, A_1 and A_2. The angle between the two axes is determined by taking the inverse cosine of the dot product of normalized versions of the axes. An interpolant, k, can then be used to form an intermediate axis and angle pair. Note that the axis-angle representation does not lend itself to easily concatenating a series of rotations. However, the information contained in this representation can be put in a form in which these operations are easily implemented: quaternions.

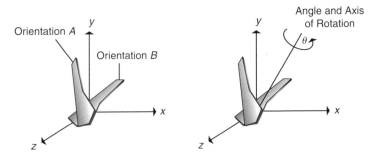

FIGURE 2.21

Euler's rotation theo-
rem implies that for
any two orientations
of an object, one can
be produced from
the other by a single
rotation about an
arbitrary axis.

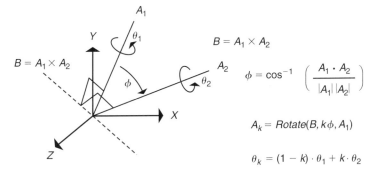

$$B = A_1 \times A_2$$

$$\phi = \cos^{-1}\left(\frac{A_1 \cdot A_2}{|A_1||A_2|}\right)$$

$$A_k = Rotate(B, k\phi, A_1)$$

$$\theta_k = (1 - k) \cdot \theta_1 + k \cdot \theta_2$$

FIGURE 2.22

Interpolating axis-
angle representa-
tions of (A_1, θ_1) and
(A_2, θ_2) by k to get
(A_k, θ_k): Rotate(x, y,
z) rotates z around x
by y degrees.

2.2.4 Quaternion Representation

As shown, the representations above have drawbacks when interpolating intermediate orientations when an object or joint has three degrees of rotational freedom.
A better approach is to use *quaternions* to represent orientation [6]. A quaternion is
a four-tuple of real numbers, [s, x, y, z] or, equivalently, [s, v], consisting of a scalar,
s, and a three-dimensional vector, v.

The quaternion is an alternative to the axis and angle representation in that it
contains the same information in a different, but mathematically convenient, form.
Importantly, it is in a form that can be interpolated as well as used in concatenating
a series of rotations into a single representation. The axis and angle information of a
quaternion can be viewed as an orientation of an object relative to its initial object
space definition, or it can be considered as the representation of a rotation to apply to
an object definition. In the former view, being able to interpolate between represented
orientations is important in generating keyframe animation. In the latter view, concatenating a series of rotations into a simple representation is a common and useful operation to perform to apply a single, compound transformation to an object definition.

2.2.4.1 Basic Quaternion Math

Before interpolation can be explained, some basic quaternion math must be understood. In the equations that follow, a bullet operator represents dot product and "×"
denotes cross product. *Quaternion addition* is simply the four-tuple addition of

quaternion representations, $[s_1, v_1] + [s_2, v_2] = [s_1 + s_2, v_1 + v_2]$. *Quaternion multiplication* is defined as Eq. (2.24). Notice that quaternion multiplication is associative, $(q_1 q_2)q_3 = q_1(q_2 q_3)$, but is not commutative, $q_1 q_2 \neq q_2 q_1$.

$$[s_1, v_1][s_2, v_2] = [s_1 s_2 - v_1 \cdot v_2, s_1 v_2 + s_2 v_1 + v_1 \times v_2] \tag{2.24}$$

A point in space, v, or, equivalently, the vector from the origin to the point, is represented as $[0, v]$. It is easy to see that quaternion multiplication of two orthogonal vectors ($v_1 \cdot v_2 = 0$) computes the cross product of those vectors [Eq. (2.25)].

$$[0, v_1][0, v_2] = [0, v_1 \times v_2] \text{ iff } v_1 \cdot v_2 = 0 \tag{2.25}$$

The quaternion $[1, (0, 0, 0)]$ is the *multiplicative identity;* that is,

$$[s, v][1 (0, 0, 0)][s, v] \tag{2.26}$$

The *inverse of a quaternion,* $[s, v]^{-1}$, is obtained by negating its vector part and dividing both parts by the magnitude squared (the sum of the squares of the four components), as shown in Eq. (2.27).

$$q^{-1} = (1 / \|q\|)^2 [s, -v]$$
$$\text{where } \|q\| = \sqrt{s^2 + x^2 + y^2 + z^2} \tag{2.27}$$

Multiplication of a quaternion, q, by its inverse, q^{-1}, results in the multiplicative identity $[1, (0, 0, 0)]$. A unit-length quaternion (also referred to here as a *unit quaternion*), $\hat{q}$, is created by dividing each of the four components by the square root of the sum of the squares of those components [Eq. (2.28)].

$$\hat{q} = q / (\|q\|) \tag{2.28}$$

2.2.4.2 Representing Rotations Using Quaternions

A rotation is represented in a quaternion form by encoding axis-angle information. Equation (2.29) shows a unit quaternion representation of a rotation of an angle, θ, about a unit axis of rotation (x, y, z).

$$\text{QuatRot}(\theta, (x, y, z)) = q = [\cos(\theta/2), \sin(\theta/2)(x, y, z)] \tag{2.29}$$

Notice that rotating some angle around an axis is the same as rotating the negative angle around the negated axis. In quaternions, this is manifested by the fact that a quaternion, $q = [s, v]$, and its negation, $-q = [-s, -v]$, represent the same rotation. The two negatives in this case cancel each other out and produce the same rotation. In Eq. (2.30), the quaternion q represents a rotation of θ about a unit axis of rotation (x, y, z).

$$
\begin{aligned}
-q &= \left[-\cos(\theta/2),(-\sin(\theta/2))(x,\,y,\,z)\right] \\
&= \left[\cos(180-\theta/2),(-\sin(-\theta/2))(-(x,\,y,\,z))\right] \\
&= \left[\cos((360-\theta)/2),\,\sin((360-\theta)/2)(-(x,\,y,\,z))\right] \qquad (2.30) \\
&= \mathrm{QuatRot}(360-\theta,-(x,\,y,\,z)) = \mathrm{QuatRot}(-\theta,-(x,\,y,\,z)) \\
&= \mathrm{QuatRot}(\theta,(x,\,y,\,z))
\end{aligned}
$$

2.2.4.3 Rotating Vectors Using Quaternions

To rotate a vector, v, using quaternion math, represent the vector as $[0,\,v]$ and represent the rotation by a quaternion, q. The vector is rotated according to Eq. (2.31).

$$
v' = \mathrm{Rot}_q(v) = qvq^{-1} \qquad (2.31)
$$

A series of rotations can be concatenated into a single representation by quaternion multiplication. Consider a rotation represented by a quaternion p followed by a rotation represented by a quaternion q on a vector, v [Eq. (2.32)].

$$
\begin{aligned}
\mathrm{Rot}_q\big(\mathrm{Rot}_p(v)\big) &= q(pvp^{-1})q^{-1} \\
&= \big((qp)v(qp)^{-1}\big) \qquad (2.32) \\
&= \mathrm{Rot}_{qp}(v)
\end{aligned}
$$

The inverse of a quaternion represents rotation about the same axis by the same amount but in the reverse direction. Equation (2.33) shows that rotating a vector by a quaternion q followed by rotating the result by the inverse of that same quaternion produces the original vector.

$$
\mathrm{Rot}_{q^{-1}}\big(\mathrm{Rot}_q(v)\big) = q^{-1}(qvp^{-1})q = v \qquad (2.33)
$$

Also, notice that in performing rotation, qvq^{-1}, all effects of magnitude are divided out due to the multiplication by the inverse of the quaternion. Thus, any scalar multiple of a quaternion represents the same rotation as the corresponding unit quaternion (similar to how the homogeneous representation of points is scale-invariant).

2.2.5 Exponential Map Representation

Exponential maps, similar to quaternions, represent an orientation as an axis of rotation and an associated angle of rotation as a single vector [7]. The direction of the vector is the axis of rotation and the magnitude is amount of rotation. In addition, a zero rotation is assigned to the zero vector, making the representation continuous at the origin. Notice that an exponential map uses three parameters instead of quaternion's four. The main advantage is that it has well-formed derivatives. These are important, for example, when dealing with angular velocity. This representation does have some drawbacks. Similar to Euler angles, it has singularities. However, in practice, these can be avoided. It is difficult to concatenate rotations and is best done by converting to rotation matrices.

2.3 CHAPTER SUMMARY

Linear transformations represented by 4×4 matrices are a fundamental operation in computer graphics and animation. Understanding their use, how to manipulate them, and how to control round-off error is an important first step in mastering graphics and animation techniques.

There are several orientation representations to choose from. The most robust representation of orientation is quaternions, but fixed angle, Euler angle, and axis-angle are more intuitive and easier to implement. Fixed angles and Euler angles suffer from gimbal lock and axis-angle is not easy to composite, but they are useful in some situations. Exponential maps also do not concatenate well but offer some advantages when working with derivatives of orientation.

REFERENCES

[1] J. Foley, A. van Dam, S. Feiner, J. Hughes, Computer Graphics: Principles and Practice, second ed., Addison-Wesley, New York, 1990.

[2] A. Watt, M. Watt, Advanced Animation and Rendering Techniques, Addison-Wesley, New York, 1992.

[3] M. Mortenson, Geometric Modeling, John Wiley & Sons, New York, 1997.

[4] G. Strong, Linear Algebra and Its Applications, Academic Press, New York, 1980.

[5] J. Craig, Robotics, Addison-Wesley, New York, 1989.

[6] K. Shoemake, Animating rotation with quaternion curves, Comput. Graph. 19, (1985) 143–152 (Proceedings of SIGGRAPH 85, August 1985, San Francisco, CA, B.A. Barsky (Ed.)).

[7] F. S. Grassia, Practical parameterization of rotations using the exponential map, J. Graph. Tools 3 (1998).

Motion Capture Techniques

Motion Capture Primer

3

Alberto Menache

CHAPTER CONTENTS

3.1 MOTION CAPTURE AND PERFORMANCE ANIMATION

Motion capture is the process of recording a live motion event and translating it into usable mathematical terms by tracking a number of key points in space over time and combining them to obtain a single three-dimensional (3D) representation of the performance. In brief, it is the technology that enables the process of translating a live performance into a digital performance. The captured subject could be anything that exists in the real world and has motion; the key points are the areas that best represent the motion of the subject's different moving parts. These points should be pivot points or connections between rigid parts of the subject. For a human, for example, some of the key points are the joints that act as pivot points and connections for the bones. The location of each of these points is identified by one or more sensors, markers, or potentiometers that are placed on the subject and that serve, in one way or another, as conduits of information to the main collection device. From now on, when speaking generally about these, I will refer to them as *markers*.

Performance animation is not the same as motion capture, although many people use the two terms interchangeably. While motion capture pertains to the technology used to collect the motion, performance animation refers to the actual performance that is used to bring a character to life, regardless of the technology used. To obtain it, one must go through the whole process of motion capture and then map the resulting data onto a 3D character. In short, motion capture is the collection of data that represents motion, whereas performance animation is the final product of a character driven by a performer.

There are different ways of capturing motion. Some systems use cameras that digitize different views of the performance, which are then used to put together the position of key points, each represented by one or more reflective markers. Others use electromagnetic fields or ultrasound to track a group of sensors. Mechanical systems based on linked structures or armatures that use potentiometers to determine the rotation of each link are also available. Combinations of two or more of these technologies exist, and newer technologies are also being tested, all aiming for one result: real-time tracking of an unlimited number of key points with no space limitations at the highest frequency possible with the smallest margin of error. This is the Holy Grail of motion capture and probably the mission statement of every motion capture hardware manufacturer's research department. I later discuss how each of the current technologies falls short in this respect.

3.2 HISTORY OF PERFORMANCE ANIMATION IN THE ENTERTAINMENT FIELD

3.2.1 The Rotoscope

Motion capture in the entertainment field is the descendent of *rotoscoping*, a technique still used by some traditional animation studios to copy realistic motion from film footage onto cartoon characters.

The rotoscope device was invented and patented by cartoonist Max Fleischer in 1915, with the intent of automating the production of cartoon films. The device projected live-action film, a frame at a time, onto a light table, allowing cartoonists to trace the frame's image onto paper. The first cartoon character ever to be rotoscoped was Koko the Clown. Fleischer's brother, Dave, acted out Koko's movements in a clown suit. Fleischer wanted to use Koko to convince the big studios to use the new process for their cartoon projects. The sale was difficult because it had taken Fleischer about a year to produce the initial one-minute cartoon using the technique, so he couldn't market it as a mass production tool. Eventually, Fleischer realized that rotoscoping would be a viable technique only for certain shots that required realistic motion.

Walt Disney Studios used some rotoscoping in 1937 to create the motion of human characters in *Snow White*. Snow White herself and the Prince were partially rotoscoped. The decision to use rotoscoping wasn't a matter of cost, but of realistic human motion. In fact, *Snow White* went tremendously over budget due to the complexity of the animation.

Rotoscoping has been adopted over the years by many cartoon studios, but few actually admit using it because many people in the animation industry consider it cheating and a desecration of the art of animation.

A two-dimensional (2D) approach, rotoscoping was designed for traditional, hand-drawn cartoons. The advent of 3D animation brought about the birth of a new, 3D way of rotoscoping. Hence, motion capture.

3.2.2 Brilliance

Some of the current motion capture technologies have been around for decades, being used in different applications for medical and military purposes. Motion capture in computer graphics was first used in the late 1970s and early 1980s in the form of research projects at schools such as Simon Fraser University, Massachusetts Institute of Technology, and New York Institute of Technology, but it was used in actual production only in the mid-1980s.

In late 1984, Robert Abel appeared on a talk show and was asked if he would soon be able to counterfeit people digitally. "We are a long ways from that," he replied. "We haven't even figured out human motion, which is the basis, and that's a year away." A week and a half later, Abel received a visit on a Friday afternoon from a creative director from Ketchum, a prominent advertising agency. The visitor brought six drawings of a very sexy woman made out of chrome. She was to have Kathleen Turner's voice and would be the spokesperson for the National Canned Food Information Council, an association formed by Heinz, Del Monte, Campbell's, and a number of big players that sold canned food. They felt they had to make a powerful statement because the idea of buying food in cans was becoming obsolete, so they wanted to do something really different and outrageous, and they wanted it to air during the Super Bowl in January 1985. "Can you do it?" asked the client. "You're certainly here a lot earlier than I would have planned," replied Abel and he asked the client to wait until the end of the weekend for an answer.

At that time, most computer graphics consisted of moving logos, landscapes, and other hard objects, and Robert Abel and Associates had already become a player in that market, along with MAGI, Triple-I (Information International, Inc.), John Whitney's Digital Productions, and Pacific Data Images (PDI), all of which had their own proprietary software, because at that time there was almost no off-the-shelf animation software and whatever was available was still in its infancy. Abel's software was initially based on bits and pieces from Bell Labs, Evans and Sutherland, JPL, and other places, and was augmented over time by his group.

The next step would be to animate a digital character. "For storytelling, which was really our goal, we had to have human characters," recalls Abel, "because nobody better than a human character is able to convey emotion and story. We come from a long line of storytellers that go back maybe 35 000 years, and although the forms may change from cave paintings to digitally made motion pictures, it's still the same thing, it's the passing on of stories." Creating the first animated digital character would open a Pandora's box of many new challenges, such as creating realistic skin, hair, and expression. But first they had to deal with the motion.

Abel and his team decided to lock the doors and not leave the building until Monday morning. If by then they didn't have the solution figured out, they would have to pass on the project. Robert Abel and Associates' background in shooting miniatures with motion control cameras since the late 1960s and early 1970s was the key to the solution. They knew that the answer to their problem would have to do with motion and control, except this time it would be human motion. Keyframe character animation was not an option at the time, so they decided to find a way to track the motions of a woman acting the part of the character. It made sense to shoot the woman with several cameras from different points of view and then use this footage to create a motion algorithm.

Seven people worked throughout the weekend. "Several of us got into our underwear," recalls Abel. "We got black adhesive dots and we put them on our bodies and we would photograph each other with Polaroid cameras and then we would lay out these Polaroids so we could see how they changed from angle to angle." They continued this slow deductive reasoning process until Sunday at 3:00 AM, when they decided that it would take a few weeks to digitize all the motion. It would be close, but they felt that they could do the job in the eight-week schedule that the client had established.

Among the people involved in this project besides Bob Abel were Bill Kovacs and Roy Hall, who later became cofounders of Wavefront Technologies; Frank Vitz, now head of software at Kleiser–Walczak Construction Company; Con Pederson, cofounder of Metrolight Studios a few years later; Randy Roberts, who directed the project and is now a commercial director at Rhythm and Hues; Richard Hollander, recently president of Blue Sky/VIFX and now head of the feature film division at Rhythm and Hues; Neil Eskuri, currently visual effects director at Disney; Charlie Gibson, Oscar-winning special effects supervisor for *Babe*; and John Hughes, who later became cofounder and president of Rhythm and Hues.

They found a woman who was very pretty and graceful and had been a dancer and a model. They had decided that motion on 18 hinge points would be necessary to achieve the desired result, so with black magic markers, they put black dots on each of her 18 joints. A stool with a 360° axis of rotation in the middle was assembled so that the model could sit and perform the moves without obstacles. The team photographed her from multiple points of view and then managed to import the images to SGI Iris 1000 systems. These workstations appeared in early 1984 and were the first model produced by Silicon Graphics. They were then able to analyze the difference in measurement between pairs of joints (for example, the elbow and the wrist) for each point of view and to combine them to come up with a series of algorithms that would ultimately be used to animate the digital character. This process was done on a frame-by-frame basis and took four and a half weeks.

At the same time, the wire-frame model was built in separate sections, all rigid parts. The motion algorithms were applied to all the combined moving parts, and the animation was output as a vector graphic. "We then had to deal with the basic issue of wrapping her body in chrome," says Abel. "Of course, there is no way in the world we could do ray-tracing to real reflective chrome the way those guys do it at SIGGRAPH, with those multimillion dollar supercomputers. We had VAX 750s, which were early DEC computers." This problem was solved by Charlie Gibson, who figured out a way of texture mapping the body so that when it moved, the map would animate following the topology of the body. Today, we call this a reflection map.

The last challenge was to render the final spot, all 30 seconds of it, in the two weeks that they had left. "The good and the bad news is this," Abel announced. "We don't nearly have the horse power, but the VAX 750 is a staple of almost every university, laboratory, and engineering place in the country." They ended up using 60 additional VAX 750s around the country, from Florida to Alaska to Hawaii, and even a few places in Canada. The final spot, "Brilliance," was rendered and pieced together about two days before the delivery date. It is now known by most people in the industry as "Sexy Robot."

3.2.3 Pacific Data Images

PDI is the oldest operating computer animation studio, and it played a big part in the history of performance animation. Founded in 1980 in Sunnyvale, California, by Carl Rosendahl, and later joined by Richard Chuang and Glenn Entis, it wasn't until eight years later that the studio would produce its first project using some kind of human tracking technology.

Over the years, PDI used different types of tracking devices that fit particular project needs, ranging from custom-built electromechanical devices to electromagnetic and optical tracking systems, but it wasn't PDI's intention to specialize in motion capture. "We use technology where it is appropriate," says Richard Chuang. "We are not a one-technique company; our goal is not to be a master of any one thing, just be good at a lot of them."

3.2.3.1 The Jim Henson Hour

In 1988, PDI, now located in Palo Alto, California, began collaboration with Jim Henson and Associates to create a computer-generated character for *The Jim Henson Hour*. Henson had already done some tests with a digital character at Digital Productions and had been holding the idea until the technology was mature enough to produce the result he wanted. Graham Walters, now a technical supervisor at Pixar, was the technical lead for PDI on the project.

The character was called Waldo C. Graphic. "One of the criteria on the project was that they wanted to be able to perform the character live when they were videotaping the TV show," recalls Carl Rosendahl. "It didn't mean that the final render needed to be live; they had to be able to record him live because of the spontaneity of the performance and such." Figure 3.1 is a photograph of the taping of *The Jim Henson Hour*.

Henson already had been doing some work with wireless telemetric robotics to animate characters for shots in which there was no way of controlling them directly, such as for a scene in *The Muppet Movie* in which Kermit is riding a bicycle and the audience sees the whole character in frame with his head moving around and singing a song. "It was a robot Kermit, and Jim had this foam Kermit head with some potentiometers on

FIGURE 3.1

Taping *The Jim Henson Hour* (Photo courtesy of Rex Grignon).

it that transmitted a radio signal to the robot on the bike," says Rosendahl. That device, shown in Fig. 3.2, was used for the Waldo C. Graphic character, with some modifications. PDI built a mechanical arm to record the position of the character in space. Instead of the radio link, the robot had a direct hardware link to one of PDI's Silicon Graphics systems. A control box with buttons allowed them to do eye blinks.

"All the videotape recording was done in Toronto, so we moved all the equipment up there and basically got it to work live on the set," says Rosendahl, "so that we took a feed of the video camera and then comped in Waldo on top of it, and that's what the performance would look like, even though the video was recording the final image without Waldo in there, but the performers would look at the one with the rough-version Waldo."

Steve Whitmire, who is now in charge of bringing Kermit the Frog to life, was the puppeteer operating the device. "Essentially, it was a puppet, something that the puppeteer was familiar with at the end," recalls Rex Grignon, supervising animator at PDI. "He could put his hand in this and just fly it anywhere in the space within that region." During the show, the puppeteer's motion data were read in and interpreted to control Waldo on the screen as a low-resolution version. "We modeled a 50-polygon version of Waldo," says Grignon. "It was all within screen space. The

FIGURE 3.2

Steve Whitmire (L) and Rex Grignon operating the device used to control Waldo C. Graphic (Photo courtesy of Rex Grignon).

puppeteers, when doing a normal puppet, would have their hand in the puppet, and they'd be looking down at a monitor, so they'd be able to gauge their performance, so they were absolutely used to this." The new technique had the added benefit that the puppeteer could bring the puppet down and not worry about hiding from the camera.

Grignon was in charge of recording the motion. "As we started a performance I'd essentially start the system recording, do the blinks, and when the director said cut, I'd cut and I'd save that take in a similar language to what they were using on the show," says Grignon. They kept track of the takes that Henson liked, because they needed to ensure that the data stayed in sync with the rest of the characters in the show. This was necessary so that after the editing of the show, PDI could use the data matching the chosen takes to produce the animation.

The device generated some interference, but although the character tended to jump and pop around, it looked pretty good for the live session. After the recording session, the data would be sent *via* phone line to the PDI studio, then located in Sunnyvale, California, and a PDI team would massage it to eliminate all the noise and add the necessary secondary animation, such as the belly wiggle. The team would also add several costume changes that required transitions, such as scenes in which the character turned into other objects (for example, a book or an electric saw), and would render the final high-resolution character.

They were doing one episode a week with about one minute of the Waldo character. "We'd go up on the weekend, we'd shoot the show on Monday, we'd send the tape back on Tuesday, and then Michelle Choi, who was here, would basically render the tape. We'd come back, we'd all work on this for about five days rendering a minute of stuff and adding any extra props and extra animation," recalls Grignon. "We lived here, we just lived here. We slept here every night."

"I still think this is one of the best uses of motion capture," notes Grignon, "You can take advantage of the puppeteer's skills, because these guys are masters. It's just amazing seeing them put their hand in a puppet and it just comes to life. I just remember Graham and I, both were just continually astounded with the subtleties that these guys could bring to these characters."

Waldo C. Graphic was brought back to life by PDI in 1991 for the *MuppetVision 3D* movie, still being shown at Disney's Hollywood Studios in Orlando, Florida.

3.2.3.2 Exoskeleton

In 1988, PDI commissioned Rick Lazzarini's The Creature Shop to build a Waldo device for the upper body and head. They called this mechanical device an "exoskeleton"; it was based on optical potentiometers on each joint (see Fig. 3.3). "It took us two passes to get one that really worked well," recalls Carl Rosendahl. "Analog parts are too noisy," notes Richard Chuang. The second version had digital parts.

The second exoskeleton was used for the Barry Levinson movie *Toys*, in a sequence for which PDI had to create an X-ray view of an ongoing meeting. "Jamie

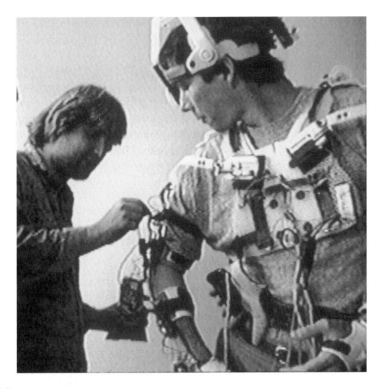

FIGURE 3.3

Dixon wearing the Pacific Data Images (PDI) exoskeleton as Graham Walters makes adjustments during a shoot for Toys (Photo courtesy of PDI).

Dixon, who was our lead guy in the LA office, was the effects supervisor, and he actually was the one who did the performing," says Rosendahl. "And because there were multiple characters, he actually did it in multiple passes." Rosendahl also recalls that there were some glitches in the data that had to be cleaned up after the performance, but usable data were available in a reasonable amount of time. *Toys* was the first motion picture in which a digital character was successfully created using motion capture.

PDI later used a Flock of Birds, an electromagnetic device manufactured by Ascension Technology Corporation, on several projects in their Los Angeles office. One of them was a bit called "The Late Jackie Lenny" for a Comedy Central pilot in which a skeleton was a talk show host and would interview live comics or do a stand-up act.

For all the projects involving that device, PDI fabricated accessories to help hold the sensors in place and make the capture experience easier on the performer. Most of these were based on Velcro strips, but the head sensor was placed on top of a baseball cap so that when the performer took off the cap, the character would look like it had taken off its head. The device had some problems with interference. For example, the studio was located on the third floor of a three-story building, and the air conditioning equipment was located on the roof, right above the stage. When the air conditioning kicked on while the device was being used, the characters on screen would sway up and down.

3.2.4 deGraf/Wahrman

Brad deGraf experimented with performance animation while working at Digital Productions, using Jim Henson's Waldo device. After Digital Productions was purchased by Omnibus, Brad left and joined forces with Michael Wahrman, also from Digital Productions, and founded deGraf/Wahrman Production Company.

In 1988, Silicon Graphics contracted the services of deGraf/Wahrman to create a demonstration piece for their new four-dimensional (4D) models. The piece was an interactive animation called *Mike the Talking Head*, which was showcased at SIGGRAPH '88. For the first time, an animated character was able to interact with the audience. The controls that animated the character in real time were operated by a puppeteer during the conference. deGraf/Wahrman's proprietary software was used to create an interface between the controls and the rendering engine and to produce interpolated instances of the character's geometry. The new Silicon Graphics 4D workstation had the horsepower to render the character in real time.

When deGraf and Wahrman dissolved their partnership, Brad joined Colossal Pictures and started rewriting the performance animation software. In 1993, he developed "Moxy," a character for the Cartoon Network that was operated in real time using an electromagnetic tracker. In 1994, he founded Protozoa, a spin-off from Colossal's performance animation studio. His focus has been on real-time performance animation solutions, including software and character development for different media, including television and the Web. ALIVE, Protozoa's proprietary performance animation software, supports multiple input devices, including motion capture systems, joysticks, and MIDI controllers. It also outputs to different formats, including live television and the World Wide Web *via* Virtual Reality Modeling Language (VRML).

3.2.5 Kleiser–Walczak Construction Company

In 1986, Jeff Kleiser began experimenting with motion capture while he was at Omnibus Computer Graphics. "We used the optical system from Motion Analysis in Santa Rosa, California, to encode martial arts movement for use in a test for Marvel Comics," recalls Kleiser. "Results were disappointing due to the alpha code we were working with."

In 1987, after Omnibus closed, Kleiser joined forces with Diana Walczak, who had been sculpting human bodies, and founded Kleiser–Walczak Construction Company. Their specialty would be to build and animate computer-generated actors or *Synthespians.*

"After creating our first Synthespian, Nestor Sextone in 1988, we got together with Frank Vitz and went back to Motion Analysis to capture motion for our second digital actor, Dozo, in creating the film *Don't Touch Me*, in 1989," says Kleiser. "We were only able to get about 30 seconds of usable motion capture, and we had to recycle it to fill the 3.5 minutes of the song we had written." Vitz had been working with Robert Abel and Associates and had some motion capture experience, as he had been part of the team that created "Brilliance."

Over the years, Kleiser–Walczak has created digital actors for special venue, commercial, and feature film projects. They created dancing water people for the Doug Trumbull stereoscopic ride In Search of the Obelisk, located inside the Luxor Hotel in Las Vegas. Using a Flock of Birds electromagnetic system by Ascension Technology Corporation, they also created digital stunt doubles for Sylvester Stallone, Rob Schneider, and others for the film *Judge Dredd*. In their most recent use of motion capture, Kleiser–Walczak produced "Trophomotion," a commercial spot for Stardox athletic braces in which two basketball trophies come to life. They used a combination of keyframe animation and motion capture, which they achieved with an optical system manufactured by Adaptive Optics in Cambridge, Massachusetts.

Their latest project is computer imagery for The Amazing Adventures of Spider-man, a ride for Universal Studios' Islands of Adventure, in Orlando, Florida. "We tested mocap [motion capture] for this project, but it quickly became clear that superhero characters need to have super-human motion, and that keyframe animation gave us the look and flexibility we wanted," says Kleiser. "All the animation in the project was therefore done with keyframe animation."

3.2.6 Homer and Associates

In the early 1990s, projects utilizing motion capture in computer graphics were starting to become part of actual production work, so companies whose main business was based on this technology started to surface. Medialab, Mr. Film, Windlight Studios, SimGraphics, and Brad deGraf at Colossal Pictures concentrated their efforts on real-time applications that included character development and puppeteering, while Biovision, TSi, and Acclaim embraced the nonreal-time technology for the up-and-coming video game market. At the same time, commercial production using the now traditional motion capture techniques was initiated by Homer and Associates.

3.2.6.1 Party Hardy

Although Homer and Associates had already created a shot for the film *The Lawnmower Man* in 1991 using motion capture, they produced their initial entry in the advertising market in 1992: "Party Hardy," a spot promoting the Pennsylvania Lottery. It consisted of an animated crowd of lottery tickets at a costume party. The spot was especially challenging because it had to have humanoid motion and facial expressions, and each ticket had to be different. There also had to be a feeling of interaction among the characters.

Peter Conn, president and founder of Homer and Associates, decided to use a camera-based system to collect the motions for the spot. The system used was an Elite Motion Analyzer, a system manufactured by Bioengineering Technology Systems (BTS) in Italy primarily for medical and industrial applications, and provided by SuperFluo, a company dedicated to bringing these medical systems to the entertainment industry. SuperFluo added custom software geared to computer animation to the already existing configuration.

The spot was directed by Michael Kory, who also performed the motions for all the characters. For the body motions, markers were placed on human-size foam rectangles, shown in Fig. 3.4, which Kory held while acting. The facial motions were also performed by Kory using the Elite system but this time using smaller markers placed in specific areas of his face. The captured facial motion was used to help interpolate between facial shapes that were built by Kory.

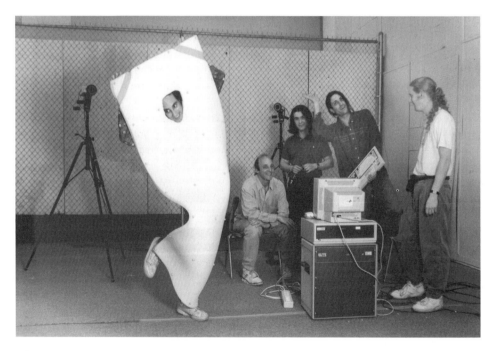

FIGURE 3.4

The Homer and Associates team with the Bioengineering Technology Systems (BTS) motion capture system for the Pennsylvania Lottery commercial "Party Hardy": (left to right) Michael Kory, director (behind foam); Peter Conn, producer; Francesco Chiarini (Superfluo, motion capture specialist); Umberto Lazzari (Superfluo, motion capture specialist); John Adamczyk, technical director (Photo courtesy of Homer and Associates).

"Party Hardy" is a good example of a project in which motion capture was used to collect data from an object or character puppeteered by a performer, as opposed to data collected from the actual performer's body.

3.2.6.2 Steam

Peter Gabriel's music video "Steam" was a coproduction between Colossal Pictures and Homer and Associates. The video was produced in 1992 and was directed by Stephen Johnson, director of other award-winning Peter Gabriel videos, including "Big Time."

"There was a period of several months when we were actively working with Brad deGraf and Stephen Johnson," recalls Peter Conn, president of Homer and Associates. "[Stephen Johnson] had a fertile imagination and an equally formidable lack of decisiveness and reality orientation. I remember that every meeting we had about what the video would include always involved going through dozens of story-boards of very elaborate effects. Although the beginning of the song was precisely worked out bar by bar, we never ever got through even half the song. There were dozens of elaborate concepts, which he seemed to want in the video. Since he was having inability to downsize the scope, he would fly to London or Senegal to get Peter's input. When he came back, there was never any consensus, just more and more concepts and ideas. A lot would have been almost achievable had the months of prep been actual production, but by the time the video was officially green-lighted there was no more than four weeks or so left to do everything. Motion capture was always specified as the great technique that would somehow make it all possible."

The motions would be collected using the same BTS optical system used on "Party Hardy." "By the time Peter Gabriel showed up for the motion capture sessions, the SuperFluo guys, Umberto Lazzari and Francesco Chiarini, had set up in our usual place, the large abandoned white storage room in the basement of the adjacent build-ing," says Conn.

They spent two days capturing motion data from Peter Gabriel and a dancer. About 150 different movements were collected. "Peter had one rule for the room: no spectators," recalls Conn. "When the playback rolled, everyone had to dance and get into the music. He liked so much doing the motion samplings that he refused to quit. Knowing that we had only time left to animate a few scenes, it was way over the top, but hey, it was Peter Gabriel and we were getting data."

In the end, there were only a couple of shots in which captured motion data were used. The longest shot was one in which Peter was supposed to be made of ice, with dancing fire girls alongside. "He was to melt then reemerge as water," says Conn. Michael Kory animated the scene and Scott Kilburn wrote the particle soft-ware, which was based on Homer's proprietary code that had been written by John Adamczyk for *The Lawnmower Man*.

A crew of eight undertook the task of putting together the shots in a short period of time, while the director was in London. "Memorable moments included a confer-ence call after they had seen a test over in the U.K.," says Conn. "Stephen was upset because he said that he had wanted the girls 'not on fire' but 'of fire.' We didn't really know what he meant, but we kept adding more particles. Then after the scene was delivered, he was still upset. It turned out that the girls weren't voluptuous enough, so we took the models and pulled the breasts out an ungodly much and then rendered just some breast fire and comped it on."

The other scene with captured motion data was the "Garden of Eden," in which both Gabriel and the dancer turn into digital characters after walking through an imaginary plane. "Actually, Brad [deGraf] did a great mocap piece with Peter Gabriel as a puppet but for some reason it never made the final cut," recalls Conn. "Despite the multitudinous mistakes and us knowing what it could have been given more time, the video went on to win some major awards, like the Grammy for Video of the Year in 1993," he notes.

Other notable motion capture works involving Homer and Associates include shots from the film *The Lawnmower Man* and music videos such as Vince Neil's "Sister of Pain" and TLC's "Waterfalls," produced for Atomix with motion data from TSi.

3.3 TYPES OF MOTION CAPTURE

Human motion capture systems are classified as outside-in, inside-out, and inside-in systems. These names are indicative of where the capture sources and sensors are placed.

- An *outside-in system* uses external sensors to collect data from sources placed on the body. Examples of such systems are camera-based tracking devices, in which the cameras are the sensors and the reflective markers are the sources.

- *Inside-out systems* have sensors placed on the body that collect external sources. Electromagnetic systems, whose sensors move in an externally generated electromagnetic field, are examples of inside-out systems.

- *Inside-in systems* have their sources and sensors placed on the body. Examples of these devices are electromechanical suits, in which the sensors are potentiometers or powered goniometers and the sources are the actual joints inside the body.

The principal technologies used today that represent these categories are optical, electromagnetic, and electromechanical human tracking systems.

3.3.1 Optical Motion Capture Systems

Optical motion capture is a very accurate method of capturing certain motions when using a state-of-the-art system. It is not a real-time process – at least not yet; immediate feedback is not possible on the target character, but an almost real-time stick-figure visual aid is now possible. Data acquired optically require extensive postprocessing to become usable.

A typical optical motion capture system is based on a single computer that controls the input of several digital charge-coupled device (CCD) cameras. CCDs are light-sensitive devices that use an array of photoelectric cells (also called *pixels*) to capture light, and then measure the intensity of the light for each of the cells, creating a digital representation of the image. A CCD camera contains an array of pixels that can vary in resolution from as low as 128×128 to as high as 4096×4096 or even greater.

Obviously, the higher the resolution, the better, but there are other trade-offs. The samples-per-second rate, or frame rate, has to be fast enough for capturing the nuances of very fast motions. In most cases, 512 samples per second are more than enough. By today's standards, a CCD camera with a resolution of 4096×4096 would be able to produce less than 1 fps, but this is changing very quickly. Another important feature is shutter synchronization, by which the camera's shutter speed can be synchronized with external sources, such as the light-emitting diodes (LEDs) with which optical motion capture cameras are usually outfitted.

The number of cameras employed is usually no less than four and no more than 32, and they capture the position of reflective markers at speeds anywhere between 30 and 1000 samples per second. The cameras are normally fitted with their own light sources that create a directional reflection from the markers, which are generally spheres covered with a material such as Scotch-Brite tape. Infrared light sources are preferred because they create less visual distortion for the user. The marker spheres can vary from a few millimeters in diameter, for small-area captures, to a couple of inches. The Vicon 8 system, shown in Fig. 3.5, is an example of a state-of-the-art optical system that can accommodate up to 24 cameras.

Most optical systems are manufactured for medical applications; as such, they lack many features that are important to computer graphics applications. The Vicon 8 system is the first system designed with computer graphics in mind. Until very recently, optical motion capture systems were unable to support SMPTE time code, a time stamp used by most film and television applications. Even if you videotaped your capture session, there was no easy way to match the video to the actual motion data. Having time code in the motion data allows you to edit the motion files, as you would do with live-action video, and properly plan the association of the characters with background plates. Another very useful new feature of the Vicon 8 is the fact that reference video of the session can be synchronized, or *genlocked*, with the actual data collection. In addition to video genlock, the Vicon 8 software can shoot AVI movie files at the same time as it captures. These movies are great references for data postprocessing and application.

The optical system must be calibrated by having all the cameras track an object with known dimensions that the software can recognize, such as a cube or a wand with reflective markers. By combining the views from all cameras with the known dimensions of the object, the exact position of each camera in space can be calculated. If a camera is bumped even slightly, a new calibration must be performed. It is a good idea to recalibrate the system after every few minutes of capture, since any kind of motion or vibration can shift the position of a camera, especially if the studio is located on unstable ground.

At least two views are needed to track a single point's 3D position, and extra cameras are necessary to maintain a direct line of sight from at least two cameras to every marker. That doesn't mean that more cameras are better, because each additional camera increases postprocessing time. There are other methods for minimizing occlusions

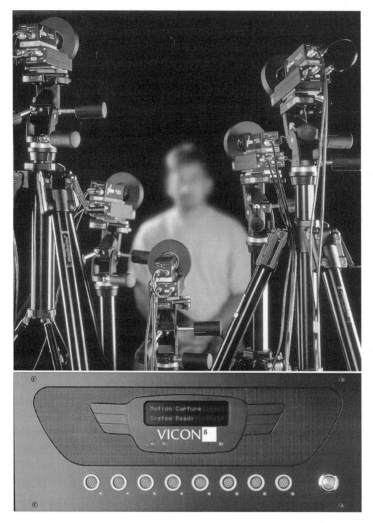

FIGURE 3.5

The Vicon 8 optical motion capture system (Photo courtesy of Vicon Motion Systems).

that are implemented in software and used during postprocessing. The most time- and cost-effective solution is different for every case, depending on the type, speed, and length of the motion, as well as on the volume of capture and the available light. Figure 3.6 shows a performance being filmed on an optical motion capture stage.

Once the camera views are digitized into the computer, it is time for the postprocessing to begin. The first step is for the software to try to produce a clean playback of only the markers. Different image processing methods are used to minimize the noise and isolate the markers, separating them from the rest of the environment. The most basic approach is to separate all the groups of pixels that exceed a predetermined luminosity threshold. If the software is intelligent enough, it will use adjacent frames to help solve

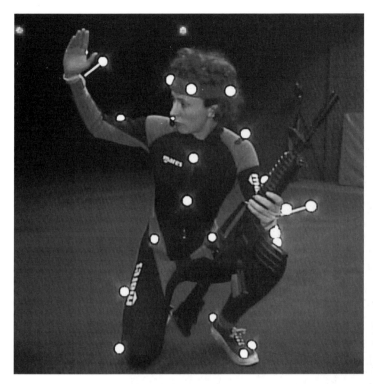

FIGURE 3.6

A performance in an optical motion capture stage (Photo courtesy of Vicon Motion Systems).

any particular frame. The system operator has control over many variables that will help in this process, such as specifying the minimum and maximum lines expected per marker so the software can ignore anything smaller or bigger than these values.

The second step is to determine the 2D coordinates of each marker for each camera view. These data will later be used in combination with the camera coordinates and the rest of the camera views to obtain the 3D coordinates of each marker.

The third step is to actually identify each marker throughout a sequence. This stage requires the most operator assistance, since the initial assignment of each marker has to be recorded manually. After this assignment, the software tries to resolve the rest of the sequence until it loses track of a marker due to occlusion or crossover, at which point the operator must reassign the markers in question and continue the computation. This process continues until the whole sequence is resolved, and a file containing positional data for all markers is saved.

The file produced by this process contains a sequence of marker global positions over time, which means that only each marker's Cartesian (x, y, and z) coordinates are listed per frame and no hierarchy or limb rotations are included. It is possible to use this file for computer animation, but a more extensive setup is required inside the animation software in order to resolve the final deformation skeleton to be used. Experienced technical directors can benefit by using this file's data, because it allows more control over what can be done in a character setup. For the average user, however, the data should be processed further, at least to the point of including a skeletal hierarchy with limb rotations. Systems such as the Vicon 8 include data editing systems that allow the user to produce the rotational hierarchical data before importing it to animation software. Figure 3.7 shows a sample screen of the Vicon Mobius hierarchical motion editor that is shipped with the Vicon 8 optical motion capture system.

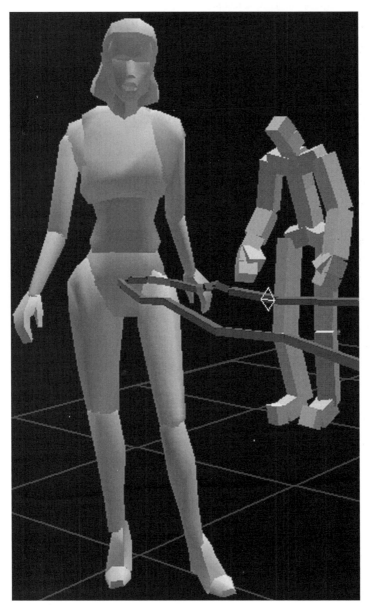

FIGURE 3.7

The Vicon Mobius hierarchical motion editor (Photo courtesy of Vicon Motion Systems).

3.3.1.1 Advantages of Optical Systems

- Optical data are extremely accurate in most cases.
- A larger number of markers can be used.
- It is easy to change marker configurations.
- It is possible to obtain approximations to internal skeletons by using groups of markers.
- Performers are not constrained by cables.
- Optical systems allow for a larger performance area than most other systems.
- Optical systems have a higher frequency of capture, resulting in more samples per second.

3.3.1.2 Disadvantages of Optical Systems

- Optical data require extensive postprocessing.
- The hardware is expensive, costing between $100 000 and $250 000.
- Optical systems cannot capture motions when markers are occluded for a long period of time.
- Capture must be carried out in a controlled environment, away from yellow light and reflective noise.

3.3.2 Electromagnetic Trackers

Electromagnetic motion capture systems are part of the six degrees of freedom electromagnetic measurement systems' family and consist of an array of receivers that measure their spatial relationship to a nearby transmitter. These receivers or sensors are placed on the body and are connected to an electronic control unit, in most cases by individual cables.

Also called magnetic trackers, these systems emerged from the technology used in military aircraft for helmet-mounted displays (HMDs). With HMDs, a pilot can acquire a target by locating it visually through a reticle located on the visor. A sensor on the helmet is used to track the pilot's head position and orientation.

A typical magnetic tracker consists of a transmitter, 11–18 sensors, an electronic control unit, and software. A state-of-the-art magnetic tracker can have up to 90 sensors and is capable of capturing up to 144 samples per second. The cost ranges from $5000 to $150 000, considerably less than optical systems. To take advantage of the real-time capabilities of a magnetic tracker, it must be connected to a powerful computer system that is capable of rendering a great number of polygons in real time. Depending on the needs of a particular project, the cost of this computer system alone could exceed the cost of the magnetic tracker.

The transmitter generates a low-frequency electromagnetic field that is detected by the receivers and input into an electronic control unit, where it is filtered and amplified. Then it is sent to a central computer, where the software resolves each sensor's position in x, y, and z Cartesian coordinates and orientation (yaw, pitch, and roll). These data are piped into another algorithm that, in most cases, will convert each sensor's global orientation and position into one hierarchical chain with only one position and multiple rotations, which can then be streamed into animation software. Sometimes this conversion happens inside the animation software itself.

The whole process is not truly real time, but it is close, depending on the amount of filtering, amplifying, and postprocessing, and the speed of the connection between the control unit and the host computer. Slow and congested Ethernet connections can slow this process down considerably. Magnetic trackers have a specification called *latency*, which indicates the amount of time elapsed between the data collection and the display of the resulting performance. This specification can vary from a few milliseconds to a few seconds.

Magnetic trackers such as the Flock of Birds by Ascension Technology Corporation use direct current (DC) electromagnetic fields, whereas others, such as the Polhemus ULTRATRAK PRO (Fig. 3.8), use alternating current (AC) fields. Both of these technologies have different problems associated with metallic conductivity. AC trackers are very sensitive to aluminum, copper, and carbon steel, but not as sensitive to stainless steel or iron, whereas DC trackers have problems with ferrous metals, such as iron and steel, but not with aluminum and copper.

FIGURE 3.8

The Polhemus ULTRATRAK PRO system (Photo courtesy of Polhemus).

Many of these conductivity problems are caused by the induction of a current in the metal that creates a new electromagnetic field that interferes with the original field emitted by the tracker. These new fields are called *eddy currents*. Some magnetic trackers use special algorithms to compensate for these distortions by mapping the capture area, but these calibrations only work with static, predefined problem areas such as metallic structures in buildings. In most cases, it is better to avoid any high-conductivity metals near the capture area. This limitation makes the magnetic tracker difficult to transport to different stages or sets.

The fact that a magnetic tracker can provide position as well as orientation data means that it requires less markers than its optical counterpart; however, it also means that internal skeleton data will not be calculated. This limitation is acceptable in many cases, since these kinds of trackers are normally used for real-time purposes and it is possible to calibrate the character setup to compensate for this deficiency by using joint offset measurements.

Magnetic trackers in the entertainment industry are used mostly for real-time applications such as live television, live performances, and location-based or Internet virtual reality implementations. Many times they are used in combination with other puppeteering devices. A performer can author the body motions of a character with the magnetic tracker while someone else is performing the facial expressions and lip-syncing using a face tracker or a data glove. At the same time, a puppeteer can be animating the character's eyes using a simple mouse.

Magnetic trackers are also used on nonreal-time applications in which immediate feedback on a character is required. Nonentertainment-related applications include the already mentioned military applications plus simulations for various industries such as aerospace, medicine, and education. Figure 3.9 shows a performer wearing an electromagnetic tracker.

3.3.2.1 Advantages of Magnetic Trackers

- Real-time data output can provide immediate feedback.
- Position and orientation data are available without postprocessing.
- Magnetic trackers are less expensive than optical systems, costing between $5000 and $150 000.
- The sensors are never occluded.
- It is possible to capture multiple performers interacting simultaneously with multiple setups.

3.3.2.2 Disadvantages of Magnetic Trackers

- The tracker's sensitivity to metal can result in irregular output.
- Performers are constrained by cables in most cases.
- Magnetic trackers have a lower sampling rate than some optical systems.
- The capture area is smaller than is possible with optical systems.
- It is difficult to change marker configurations.

FIGURE 3.9

Polhemus ActionTRAK electromagnetic tracker (Photo courtesy of Polhemus).

3.3.3 Electromechanical Suits

The electromechanical motion capture suit is a group of structures linked by potentiometers or similar angular measurement devices located at the major human joint locations; it is driven by a human body's actions.

Potentiometers are components that have been used for many years in the electronics industry, in applications such as volume controls on old radios. A slider moving along a resistor element in the potentiometer produces a variable voltage-potential reading, depending on what percentage of the total resistance is applied to the input voltage. The potentiometers used for motion capture suits and armatures are much more complex versions of the old radio volume knob; they are sometimes called *analog* or *digital angular sensors.*

One big drawback of electromechanical systems based on potentiometers is their inability to measure global translations. In most cases, an electromagnetic sensor is added to the configuration to solve this problem, but that subjects the setup to the same disadvantages as the electromagnetic systems, such as sensitivity

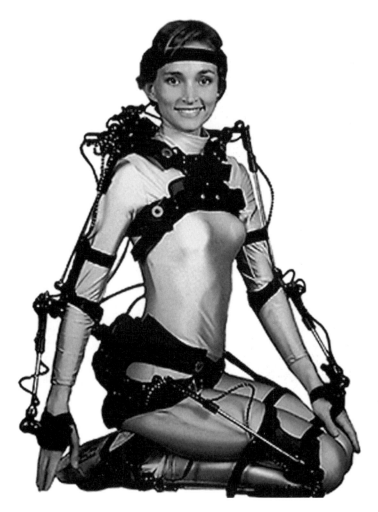

FIGURE 3.10

The Analogus Gypsy 2.5 electromechanical suit (Feb. 1999, ID8 Media, San Francisco, California).

to nearby metals. In addition, the design of most of these devices is based on the assumption that most human bones are connected by simple hinge joints, so they don't account for nonstandard rotations that are common to human joints, such as in the shoulder complex or the lower arm. Of course, this can actually be a benefit if the mechanical setup of a particular digital character calls for such types of constraints.

A good example of an electromechanical suit is the Gypsy 2.5 Motion Capture System, by Analogus, shown in Fig. 3.10.

3.3.3.1 Advantages of Electromechanical Body Suits

- The range of capture can be very large.
- Electromechanical suits are less expensive than optical and magnetic systems.
- The suit is portable.
- Real-time data collection is possible.
- Data are inexpensive to capture.
- The sensors are never occluded.
- It is possible to capture multiple performers simultaneously with multiple setups.

3.3.3.2 Disadvantages of Electromechanical Body Suits

- The systems have a low sampling rate.
- They are obtrusive due to the amount of hardware.
- The systems apply constraints on human joints.
- The configuration of sensors is fixed.
- Most systems do not calculate global translations without a magnetic sensor.

3.3.4 Digital Armatures

Digital armatures can be classified into two types: (1) keyframing or stop-motion armatures and (2) real-time or puppeteering armatures. Like the mechanical suit, both types consist of a series of rigid modules connected by joints whose rotations are measured by potentiometers or angular sensors. The sensors are usually analog devices, but they are called "digital" because the resulting readings are converted to digital signals to be processed by the computer system. These armatures are typically modular in order to accommodate different character designs.

Keyframing armatures were initially used to help stop-motion animators animate digital characters; they are not really considered motion capture systems because they are not driven by a live performer. I mention them because most commercially available armatures can also be used as real-time armatures. Some proprietary armatures are dual-purpose, such as a device initially called the Dinosaur Input Device (DID), which was devised by Craig Hayes at Tippett Studio in Berkeley, California. The name was conceived because this unit was used to animate some of the digital dinosaurs in *Jurassic Park*. Later, the device was used to animate the bugs in *Starship Troopers*. It is now called the Digital Input Device (Fig. 3.11).

The basic concept behind keyframing armatures is that the animator poses the device manually to generate each keyframe in the animation. The character in the animation software is set up with a mechanical structure equivalent to the armature's. By pressing a key, the animator uses the computer to record the armature's pose into the digital character for a particular frame in time. This is done *via* a driver program that connects the device, typically plugged into a serial port, to the animation software. Once all the key poses are recorded, the software treats them as regular keyframes that might have been created with the software by itself.

FIGURE 3.11

Digital Input Device designer Craig Hayes and the Raptor Digital Input Device puppet. *Jurassic Park* 1992–1993 (Photo courtesy of Tippett Studio).

Puppeteering armatures are very similar to keyframing armatures, except the motion is captured in real time as performed by one or more puppeteers. An example of such a setup is the proprietary armature developed by Boss Film Studios to capture the motion of Sil, the alien character that H.R. Giger designed for the film *Species*.

There are not many commercially available armatures, so most production companies have had to design their own. A commercially available example of a digital armature is the Monkey 2 by Digital Image Design in New York City (Fig. 3.12). This unit can be used as both a keyframe and real-time armature. It is modular, so it can be assembled in different joint configurations. The first-generation Monkey had a fixed configuration, which made it unusable for any nonhumanoid applications. The typical cost for a 39-joint Monkey 2 setup is approximately $15 000, which includes all the necessary parts as well as driver software for most well-known animation packages. The device plugs into an RS-232 serial port.

3.3.4.1 Advantages of Digital Armatures

- Digital armatures are easy to use for multiple characters animated using stop motion.
- Setup for different character types is easy.

FIGURE 3.12

The Monkey 2 armature (Photo courtesy of Digital Image Design).

- The cost is low.
- Armatures are good digital input devices for stop-motion animators.
- Data are available immediately.

3.3.4.2 Disadvantages of Digital Armatures

- Global translations are usually not captured.
- In most armatures, all the joints are hinge joints.
- Real-time armatures have low sampling rates compared with optical and magnetic systems.

3.3.5 **Other Motion Capture Systems**

3.3.5.1 The Waldo

The Waldo is a telemetric device that imitates the motions of whatever it is controlling. It was named after Waldo Farthingwaite Jones, a fictional disabled scientist in Robert A. Heinlein's 1942 short story "Waldo" who invents a device that allows him to act beyond his biomechanical possibilities. Telemetry is by definition the transmission of measurements; consequently, the Waldo transmits measurements of the motion of joints and other body parts to a mimicking device. There are many kinds of Waldos, controlled by different body parts, such as the head, arms, or legs, or even the body as a whole. Their main applications in entertainment are the control of digital or animatronic characters.

The name "Waldo" is rumored to have been first used at NASA to name an early telemetry device, and it was used for years as a generic name for such machines. It is now a trademark of The Character Shop, a company that specializes in animatronic characters. Figure 3.13 shows different kinds of Waldos manufactured by The Character Shop. The Jim Henson Creature Shop uses a device of this genre called the Henson Performance Control System to bring their animatronic or digital creatures to life.

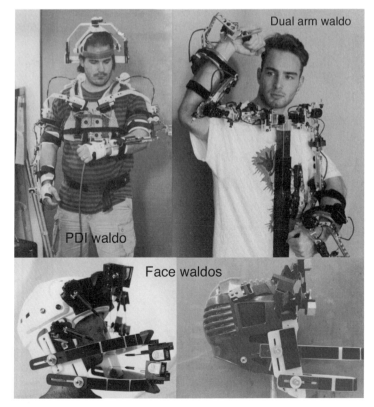

Dual arm waldo

PDI waldo

Face waldos

FIGURE 3.13

Different types of Waldos manufactured by The Character Shop (Photos courtesy of Rick Lazzarini/The Character Shop).

3.3.5.2 Small Body Part Trackers

To capture the motion of small body parts, special trackers are needed, because full-body tracking devices lack the necessary resolution. However, there are some exceptions. For example, it is practically impossible to track facial movements and movement of fingers with an electromagnetic tracker because the sensors are bigger than the locations where they need to be placed. It is possible to handle such situations with optical trackers in some cases.

There are several mechanical and optical devices for capturing facial motion. The most popular are the real-time optical face trackers, consisting of a camera that is placed in a structure attached to the performer's head, so that it moves with the performer. The device captures the motion of small markers placed in different areas of the face. Unfortunately, these are 2D devices that cannot capture certain motions such as puckering of the lips, so the data are all in one plane and are not very realistic. Three-dimensional facial motion data can be captured with an optical system using two or three cameras, yielding a much better result, but not in real time.

For hand motions, there are several types of gloves that have small form-factor technologies, such as the CyberGlove, the DataGlove, and the PowerGlove. The CyberGlove (Fig. 3.14) is manufactured by Virtual Technologies, Inc. (VTI). It has been available since 1991 and uses VTI's patented piezoresistive bend-sensing technology. It

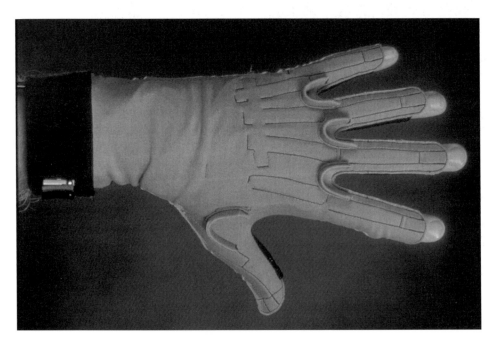

FIGURE 3.14

The VTI CyberGlove (Photo courtesy of Virtual Technologies, Inc., http://www.virtex.com).

is available in 18- and 22-sensor models at prices ranging from approximately $9500 to $14000 for a single glove. The 18-sensor model measures most finger rotations, abduction (the angle between adjacent fingers), thumb crossover, palm arch, and wrist rotations. The 22-sensor model adds a sensor for the distal joint of the index, middle, ring, and pinkie fingers. The sensors can capture a minimum rotation of 0.5° and can work at up to about 110 samples per second. Like many other similar devices, it requires a third-party device in order to measure global positioning and orientation.

The DataGlove, shown in Fig. 3.15, has been around since 1987. It was manufactured by VPL Research, but the company's technical assets and patents were acquired by Sun Microsystems in February 1998, so the fate of DataGlove support and future availability is uncertain at this time. It is based on fiber-optic sensors placed along the back of the fingers. As fingers rotate, the fibers are bent and their transmitted light is attenuated. The strength of the light is turned into a signal that can be measured by the processor to calculate the rotation of the fingers. Most DataGlove models have 10 sensors that measure the rotations of each of the two upper joints of the fingers. Some versions also have measurements for abduction. It can measure a minimum of 1° at up to 60 samples per second.

FIGURE 3.15

The VPL DataGlove (Photo courtesy of Zak Zaidman).

The Mattel PowerGlove was introduced in 1989 as an add-on controller for the Nintendo Entertainment System and has similar technology to that of the DataGlove. In fact, the PowerGlove was conceived as a low-cost alternative to the DataGlove. It was initially called Z-Glove by VPL Research, which later licensed it to Abrams Gentile Entertainment (AGE), the company that manufactured it for Mattel.

The difference that makes the PowerGlove's cost so much lower than the DataGlove's is in the components. The optic fibers were replaced with less expensive conductive ink that is used as a resistor whose impedance variations indicate degrees of flexion. The global position and orientation are measured *via* ultrasonic pulses that are emitted from a few locations on the glove. The time taken for these pulses to reach the receivers is used to calculate in a very loose way the position and orientation of the glove. In fact, the glove emitters always have to be pointing at the receivers, which limits its range of motion. The PowerGlove only measures flexion of the thumb and three fingers, at a much lower resolution than the DataGlove.

The PowerGlove became very popular as an inexpensive virtual reality input device, mainly because its cost was around $100. It was sold as a peripheral device for the Nintendo game console and it had no standard interface. Thus, there was no easy way to connect it to anything else. When the popularity of the device became apparent, interfaces to use it with an IBM-compatible PC or an Apple Macintosh started to surface, released by AGE, third-party manufacturers, or people experimenting with the device. A very popular interface device among "garage virtual reality" enthusiasts is the Menelli Box, a public-domain interface design that helps transmit the PowerGlove's signals to an RS-232 port.

3.4 APPLICATIONS OF MOTION CAPTURE

Most motion capture equipment was developed with applications other than entertainment in mind. Such devices have been used for many years before becoming viable tools for 3D computer graphics.

The main markets that benefit from motion capture are medicine, sports, entertainment, and law, but there are smaller markets that are also taking advantage of the technology. For example, motion capture equipment is used to help design ergonomic environments. In addition, it is used for automobile safety tests: the motion of crash test dummies is captured and analyzed.

3.4.1 Medicine

In clinical circles, motion capture is called 3D biological measuring or 3D analysis. It is used to generate biomechanical data to be used for gait analysis and several orthopedic applications, such as joint mechanics, analysis of the spine, prosthetic design, and sports medicine.

There have been a great number of studies of gait performed with patients of all ages and conditions. The first ones were made by Etienne Jules Marey and Eadweard Muybridge in the late 1800s using photographic equipment.

Muybridge's studies started when he was hired by Leland Stanford, governor of California, to study the movement of his race horses in order to prove that all four hooves left the ground simultaneously at a given point during gallop. In 1876, Muybridge succeeded by photographing a galloping horse using 24 cameras (Fig. 3.16). He then continued his studies of human and animal motion for many years. His paper on the subject, "Animal Locomotion," was published in 1884 and is still one of the most complete studies in the area.

A professor of natural history, Etienne Marey used only one camera to study movement, as opposed to the multiple-camera configuration used by Muybridge. Even though they met in 1881, Marey and Muybridge followed separate paths in their research. Studies continued in this fashion for a century, but until the introduction of optical motion capture systems in the 1970s, the research yielded almost no benefits.

Gait analysis is useful in medicine because it accurately separates all the different mechanisms that are used during the multiple phases of a walk cycle in a way that makes it easy to detect certain abnormalities and changes. For example, gait analysis helps to measure any degree of change in conditions such as arthritis or strokes. It is also used along with other tests to determine treatment for certain pathological conditions that affect the way we walk, such as cerebral palsy. Rehabilitation by gait training is used for patients with pelvis, knee, or ankle problems.

FIGURE 3.16

Muybridge's galloping horse photographs (Photo courtesy of Eadweard Muybridge Collection, Kingston Museum).

3.4.2 Sports

Sports analysis is a major application of motion capture. Three-dimensional data are being used extensively to improve the performance of athletes in sports such as golf, tennis, gymnastics, and even swimming by studying the performance of professionals and dissecting and classifying the different components of the movement. As motion capture technology improves to the point at which undisturbed data collection are possible, the potential uses will become even greater in this field.

There are a few motion capture studios across the country dedicated exclusively to the analysis of sports, especially golf. For a few hundred dollars, any golfer can have his or her swing analyzed or compared with the swing of a professional golfer. Visualization software allows the studios to study the athlete's motions to find any problem areas.

The market for sports analysis is mostly amateur sports enthusiasts, but professionals look for help as well. Biovision, a company that operates three sports analysis studios across the country, claims to have helped professional golfer John Daly to find a problem related to opposite movements of his hips and shoulders that happened for one-tenth of a second during his swing.

The benefit of using motion capture rather than videotape for this kind of sports application is that motion capture yields a 3D representation of the motion that can be examined from any possible angle. A second important advantage is that at the normal speed a videotape records (30 fps), most fast-paced motions are not fully captured. Since motion capture is capable of recording at higher frequencies than regular video, much more of the motion is recorded.

3.4.3 The Entertainment Industry

The entertainment industry is the fastest growing segment of the market for motion capture; although not yet the largest, it certainly is the segment with the highest profile. Of the different entertainment applications, the use of motion capture in video games is currently the most widespread and the most well accepted and understood. Television and feature film applications of motion capture are still an experimental market.

3.4.3.1 Video Games

Motion capture is used on almost every video game that involves human motion. The video game industry was the first segment of entertainment to embrace motion capture as a viable tool for character motion. It started doing so at a time when the motion capture hardware and software was still producing low-quality results at a high, but not extreme, cost. Even though the use of motion capture in entertainment started in television and film, those markets still remain resistant to widespread use of the tool, whereas the computer game segment has adopted it as the primary source of capturing human motion.

As recently as a few years ago, it was impossible to produce a game with character animation of sufficient quality to require the skill of a character animator. The hardware simply lacked the horsepower to render the images onto the screen at a desirable frame rate. When motion capture came into the picture, it was still in its infancy as a motion generation tool, but it was cost-effective and had more quality than any game that used real-time rendering could take advantage of. The data were usually good enough and didn't require any further tweaking for the kind of games that used it. As game engines become faster, motion capture is also maturing. It remains a cost-effective solution for these kinds of projects, but it now requires some massaging to make it look as good as possible. Eventually, the quality of the motion required for real-time video games will be equal to that of any other linear project.

3.4.3.2 Television

The use of performance animation in animated TV shows is a small market that is growing slowly and has met with several obstacles. The main problem is that motion capture has been used primarily as a cost-cutting tool, resulting in an unexpected quality trade-off. Shows that used performance animation in the past have usually not included a budget for modifying the animation beyond the performance. An example of a show with this problem is *The Real Adventures of Jonny Quest*, in which only a few minutes per show contain any kind of computer animation.

Other cartoon shows have been successful in using performance animation in their entirety. Most of these shows have been produced by the company that is actually collecting the motion, and the motion is captured in real time in most cases, so there are no surprises in what the quality of the final animation will be. Companies that have succeeded in producing these kinds of shows are Medialab, with *Donkey Kong Country*, and Modern Cartoons, with *Jay-Jay the Jet Plane*.

Commercials are still a very small part of the performance animation market. Because they are short projects, it is difficult to establish a pipeline for motion capture data that will only be used for a couple of shots. Specific shots that require a particular person's motion are what drives this market, such as the "Virtual Andre" spot that Digital Domain produced for Nike, which featured a digital version of Andre Agassi.

Music videos have benefited from motion capture since the early 1990s. Homer and Associates produced computer graphics based on performance animation for music videos by Peter Gabriel, Vince Neil, and TLC. More recently, two Bjork music videos have been produced using motion capture, one by Rhythm and Hues and another by Digital Domain.

3.4.3.3 Feature Films

The main applications of motion capture in live-action feature films are digital extras, digital stunts, and digital crowds. Digital extras are background human characters that for one reason or another have to be digitally generated. An example of such a case is a shot of the ship in the feature film *Titanic* as it leaves port. A live shot like this would be filmed with a helicopter and a lot of extras walking on deck, but since the actual ship did not exist, a miniature ship was shot, using a motion control camera. Because of the size of the shot, filming real people in green screen to composite over the ship would have been impossible, so the only solution was to create digital extras. The shot was produced at Digital Domain.

Digital stunts are actions that either are not humanly possible or that need to be seen on screen performed by a person other than the stuntperson. After a stunt is captured, it can only be enhanced to a certain level before the realistic motion is lost; thus, if a stunt is not humanly possible, it is best to hand it to a good character animator who specializes in realistic motion. Another kind of digital stunt involves applying motion data from a stuntperson to a digital version of a known actor. An example of such a stunt is the sky-surfing sequence in *Batman and Robin*, for which sky-surfers' stunts were captured by PDI and applied to digital versions of George Clooney's Batman and Chris O'Donnell's Robin.

Motion capture is a good tool to use for digital crowd scenes in which no interactions between characters occur. A perfect scenario would be a crowded stadium where some kind of sport is being played. A computer-generated crowd could be procedurally animated by first capturing different versions of each crowd reaction. As the game proceeds, the crowd may go into a cheering frenzy, or be bored, or angry. When one of the teams playing the sport scores, part of the crowd will be angry, others will be excited, and some will be ambivalent. A percentage of the crowd would be animated by using randomly selected angry cycles, another group would be animated by the cheering cycles, and the rest by the ambivalent cycles. An example of a sequence using multiple digital characters and motion capture is the group of crowd scenes at the end of *The Borrowers*, produced by The Moving Picture Company.

3.4.4 Law

Motion capture is applied in law to produce reconstructive videos of events. These videos are used as evidence in trials to aid the jury in understanding a witness's opinion about a particular order of events. According to a study conducted by the American Bar Association, this kind of evidence is much more effective with jurors than any other demonstrative evidence.

An example of an effective use of motion capture in the legal context is the video produced by Failure Analysis to recreate the events of the murder of Nicole Brown Simpson and Ronald Goldman during the O.J. Simpson trial. The video wasn't actually used as evidence in the trial, but it serves as an example of the kind of animation that could be used in a court of law.

To be admissible, the animation must be very plain, without any complex lighting, texture mapping, or detailed models, and, like any other evidence, it must meet the local and federal rules of evidence. In most cases, it has to be accompanied by supporting testimony from the animation creators, during either trial or deposition. Many animation companies specialize in all aspects of evidence animation, from its preparation to the presentation in court.

The Motion Data

4

Alberto Menache

CHAPTER CONTENTS

4.1 MOTION DATA TYPES AND FORMATS

Depending on the system you are using, you will have to deal with several different motion data file formats. Real-time systems usually generate a stream of data that can be used directly in the animation software with the help of special plug-ins. Optical systems' data is not generated in real time, so it cannot be streamed into the animation software; instead, it is imported from a data file. Packages such as Softimage, Maya, and 3D Studio Max include converters that allow you to import data files in several file formats, but when performing character setup, it is important to know what data items these files contain. None of these file formats has any information pertaining to the deformation of the character's surfaces; rather, the information pertains to the mechanical aspects of rigid segments. All deformations are specific to the animation software being used.

Optical systems' data files go through a few stages before becoming final. As the data is collected, a video stream file is created for each of the system's cameras, containing the raw images captured. This is termed *raw data*. These files, in combination with a file containing the calibration of the stage, are used to track the three-dimensional data. The second stage is the file generated after tracking, which contains the Cartesian coordinates of each of the markers. The data in this file is called *global translation data*; it represents the position of each marker in reference to the world

105

origin, without including any hierarchy or skeleton definition. I will refer to this type of file as *translational* because it contains no rotations, only translations of independent points in space.

A translational file can be used for performance animation, but there are other levels of simplification, such as files that contain data based on segments or limbs rather than points. Two data types meet this description: the hierarchical segment translation and rotation and the global segment translation and rotation. Both are based on a definition of a skeleton to be used for driving the motion of the character and are created by combining the points in the translational file. In the hierarchical rotational file, primarily the root point has rotations and translations, and the rest have only initial local translations that define the position and length of each segment, plus a stream of local rotations. The file also contains a set of scale channels that represent the variation in length of each segment. This is necessary because the segments are not exactly rigid since the markers have to be placed over skin or clothes. The scale channel also helps in the determination of data accuracy. The global rotational file contains translations, rotations, and scale channels for each independent segment; there are no dependencies between the segments.

Rotational files are generally easier to use than translational files because most of the work in setting up a skeleton has already been done for you; however, translational files allow you to create better and more complicated character setups. Experienced users should work mostly with translational data. In addition, because translational files contain no rotations, they are less prone to common problems associated with Euler angle transformations. Figure 4.1 shows a set of curves that represent marker coordinates in a translational file. The data is smooth and does not include any sudden jumps or perturbations.

The primary data file format in use for optical motion capture today is the Acclaim .amc and .asf combination. Other file types available are the Biovision .bva and .bvh files and the Motion Analysis .trc and .htr formats. Many companies have special file formats that fit their particular needs. At TSi, for example, we had the .tsi file, a binary file that was well suited for fast random access, an essential item in video games and data editing tools. Some of the file types mentioned here are rotational and others translational; they're all delimited by tabs. I will later explain each one in detail.

Bringing these files into animation software is not always as easy as it seems. Often, the file has to be prepared with certain restrictions based on the particular program into which it is being imported. The most common restriction has to do with world space. Some animation programs consider XY as the front plane, whereas others use XZ. Another common difference among off-the-shelf animation software packages is the order of transformations and the order of rotations. Most animation programs have a hard-coded order of transformations. Others have a hard-coded order of rotations, and the data file must be prepared accordingly. It is not enough to change the definitions in the file – the data must be recalculated as well. One more item to consider is the base position: some programs require their initial skeleton's zero pose to be aligned in a certain way. In addition, the segment scale specified in some files is totally ignored when the data is imported into some animation programs. Other restrictions include naming conventions and units. Translational data is the easiest type to import: since no hierarchy, rotation, or scale channels are present, most of the restrictions are not applicable. The downside of importing translational

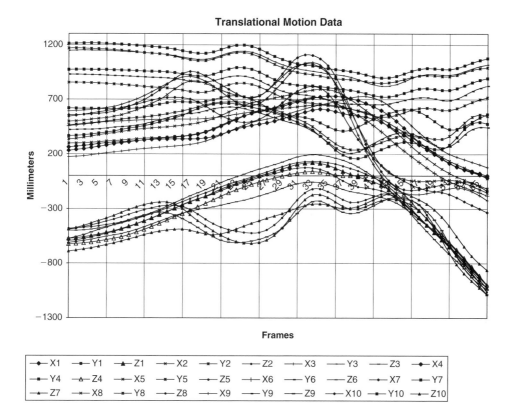

FIGURE 4.1

Translational data chart.

data is that the character setup is much more involved; on the other hand, you have better control over what you want to do with the setup.

4.1.1 **The Acclaim File Format**

The Acclaim file format was developed by Acclaim and Biomechanics for Acclaim's proprietary optical motion capture system. The file format is the most comprehensive of all mainstream formats and is supported by a large majority of commercial animation applications, such as Maya, Alias, Softimage, 3D Studio Max, Nichimen, Prisms, and Houdini. Optical motion capture systems such as the Vicon 8 support the Acclaim format as their primary format.

The format is based on a combination of two files, *Acclaim skeleton format*, or *.asf*, and *Acclaim motion capture*, or *.amc*. The former deals with the definition of a hierarchy of rigid segments, or skeleton, whereas the latter contains the actual data associated with the skeleton. Multiple .amc files can be associated with a single .asf file, which can be beneficial for complicated character setups. Acclaim files can contain translational or rotational data although rotational is the most commonly used.

4.1.2 The .asf File

The .asf file is much more than just a definition of hierarchy. It contains all the information pertaining to the mechanical function of the skeleton, including units, multipliers, degrees of freedom, limits, and documentation. The only item not included in this file is the data itself, although the file does include the initial pose or base position that is used for character setup. All the data in the associated .amc files is relative to the base position specified.

The .asf file is divided in eight sections identified by the following keywords preceded by a colon: version, name, units, documentation, root, bonedata, hierarchy, and skin, as shown in the following code extract.

```
# AST/ASF file generated using VICON BodyLanguage  ←—— Comments are preceded by a pound sign and
#  ————————————                                        are ignored.  They can be anywhere in the file
:version 1.10  ←———————————————————————— File format version
:name VICON  ←————————————————————————— Name of the skeleton
:units  ←——————————————————————————————— Heading for units section
    mass 1.0  ←——————————————————————————————— Multipliers for mass and length
    length 0.45  ←
    angle deg  ←————————————————————————— Angles specified in degrees or radians
:documentation  ←——————————————————————— Specific documentation is included here
       .ast/.asf automatically generated from VICON data using
       VICON BodyBuilder and BodyLanguage model BRILLIANT.MOD
:root  ←———————————————————————————————— Root node information
    order TX TY TZ RX RY RZ  ←———————————————— Order of transformations for root
    axis XYZ  ←———————————————————————————— Order of orientation rotations
    position 0 0 0  ←——————————————————————— Position relative to world axis
    orientation 0 0 0  ←——————————————————— Orientation rotations (in order specified)
:bonedata  ←———————————————————————————— Definitions for all bones relative to root
    begin  ←——————————————————————————————— Begin bone definition
        id 1  ←—————————————————————————————— Bone id (optional)
        name lowerback  ←—————————————————————— Bone name
        direction 0 1 0  ←————————————————————— Bone's direction vector
        length 2.07313  ←————————————————————— Bone length
        axis 0 0 -5.3486 e-035  XYZ  ←————————— Global orientation of axis and its order of
                                                 initial rotations
        dof rx ry rz  ←——————————————————————— Degrees of freedom allowed and order of
                                                 transformations (tx ty tz rx ry rz l)
        limits (-inf inf)  ←                     Limits for each degree of freedom
               (-inf inf)                      ← specified (inf = infinity)
               (-inf inf)  ←
        bodymass 3.0  ←——————————————————————— Mass of the bone
        cofmass 1.0  ←———————————————————————— Center of mass along the bone
    end  ←—————————————————————————————— End of bone definition
    begin
        id 2
        name lfemur
        direction 0.34202 -0.939693 0
        length 6.88435
        axis 0 0 20  XYZ
        dof rx ry rz
```

```
        limits (-160.0 20.0)
              (-70.0 70.0)
              (-60.0 70.0)
   end
   begin
      id 3
      name ltibia          ◄─────────────────── Subsequent bone definitions
      direction 0.34202 -0.939693 0
      length 7.02085
      axis 0 0 20  XYZ
      dof rx
      limits (-10.0 170.0)
   end
   .
   .
   .
begin
    id 30
    name rthumb
    direction -0.707107 -6.34892e-011 0.707107
    length 1.17742
    axis -90 -45 -2.85299e-015  XYZ
    dof rx rz
    limits (-45.0 45.0)
          (-45.0 45.0)
   end

:hierarchy                              ── Parent
   begin                                   Children
     root lhipjoint rhipjoint lowerback
     lhipjoint lfemur
     lfemur ltibia
     ltibia lfoot
     lfoot ltoes
     rhipjoint rfemur
     rfemur rtibia
     rtibia rfoot
     rfoot rtoes
     lowerback upperback
     upperback thorax
     thorax lowerneck lclavicle rclavicle   ── Hierarchy definition
     Hierarchy definition
     upperneck head
     lclavicle lhumerus
     lhumerus lradius
     lradius lwrist
     lwrist lhand lthumb
     lhand lfingers
     rclavicle rhumerus
     rhumerus rradius
     rradius rwrist
     rwrist rhand rthumb
     rhand rfingers
   end
```

```
:skin <filename>
      <filename>
        .
        .
        .
```

List of 3D models that fit this skeleton (optional)

The `units` section contains three fields: `mass`, `length`, and `angle`. The `mass` field is a multiplier for segment mass, but it is usually ignored by animation software. `length` is a multiplier for the bone's length. The `angle` field specifies whether the orientation data is given in degrees or radians.

The entire hierarchy is relative to the position and orientation of the root, which has an order of transformations as well as a separate axis order that defines its initial orientation. The bone definitions, however, are specified in global space: the direction vector and axis are not relative to the root but to the world axis.

The `dof` field is the specification of the allowed degrees of freedom for the particular segment, which can be any or all of `tx`, `ty`, `tz`, `rx`, `ry`, `rz`, and `l`. The `l` field is a translation value along the segment's length. A variation in this field's data indicates that the segment is not rigid. These variations can be used in the animation to stretch and compress the character's skin, but they should be reasonably low. The `dof` tokens are optional and can be specified in any order, which will define the order of transformations for the segment.

In many cases, all translations are omitted from the child segments, except when the file contains only translational data. In such a file, the degrees of freedom for length and rotation would be omitted. I don't recommend omitting any of the rotational degrees of freedom in a rotational file even if a bone, such as the elbow, is supposed to be unable to rotate toward a certain orientation because the joints are never totally confined.

The `limits` are used to constrain the motion of a particular degree of freedom and are specified in the same order as the dof tokens, in pairs of minimum and maximum values. The .amc file in most systems is generated within these limits. One should not constrain motion data unless it is absolutely necessary. Most cases where constraining is used include real-time nonlinear video game applications, but there are other cases in which it may be desirable.

Many of the fields in the .asf file are used differently by different software, and some fields are used for special purposes by a particular program. The optional `skin` section, for example, can be used by animation software to load one or more specific models. `bodymass` and `cofmass` are fields used by some systems to calculate certain segment's dynamic characteristics that can be used to implement alternate procedures, such as hair and clothing. The norm is that if a field is not recognized, it is ignored. Preparing an .asf file for importation into some animation software requires special planning. For example, some programs require a different order of rotations or have a differently oriented world axis, which has to be taken into account before creating the .asf and .amc files.

4.1.3 **The .amc File**

The .amc file contains the actual motion data stream. All the data in this file is relative to the definitions in the .asf file, and the fields are sequenced in the same order as the dof field in the .asf file.

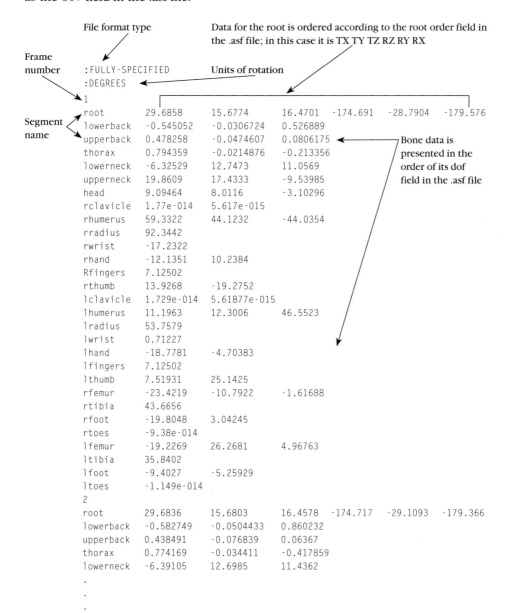

File format type

Data for the root is ordered according to the root order field in the .asf file; in this case it is TX TY TZ RZ RY RX

Frame number

Units of rotation

Segment name

Bone data is presented in the order of its dof field in the .asf file

```
:FULLY-SPECIFIED
:DEGREES
1
root        29.6858     15.6774     16.4701   -174.691   -28.7904   -179.576
lowerback   -0.545052   -0.0306724  0.526889
upperback   0.478258    -0.0474607  0.0806175
thorax      0.794359    -0.0214876  -0.213356
lowerneck   -6.32529    12.7473     11.0569
upperneck   19.8609     17.4333     -9.53985
head        9.09464     8.0116      -3.10296
rclavicle   1.77e-014   5.617e-015
rhumerus    59.3322     44.1232     -44.0354
rradius     92.3442
rwrist      -17.2322
rhand       -12.1351    10.2384
Rfingers    7.12502
rthumb      13.9268     -19.2752
lclavicle   1.729e-014  5.61877e-015
lhumerus    11.1963     12.3006     46.5523
lradius     53.7579
lwrist      0.71227
lhand       -18.7781    -4.70383
lfingers    7.12502
lthumb      7.51931     25.1425
rfemur      -23.4219    -10.7922    -1.61688
rtibia      43.6656
rfoot       -19.8048    3.04245
rtoes       -9.38e-014
lfemur      -19.2269    26.2681     4.96763
ltibia      35.8402
lfoot       -9.4027     -5.25929
ltoes       -1.149e-014
2
root        29.6836     15.6803     16.4578   -174.717   -29.1093   -179.366
lowerback   -0.582749   -0.0504433  0.860232
upperback   0.438491    -0.076839   0.06367
thorax      0.774169    -0.034411   -0.417859
lowerneck   -6.39105    12.6985     11.4362
.
.
.
```

A clear advantage of the Acclaim file over other formats is that each of the bones or segments can have a different order of transformations, whereas other formats specify an order of rotations that applies to all segments and assume that translations occur before rotations. Furthermore, the Acclaim format can contain translational and global rotational data as well as hierarchical rotational data without the need for changing file formats.

4.1.4 The .bva File Format

The .bva file format was created by Biovision, a group of optical motion capture studios specializing in sports analysis and animation. This type of file is very simple because it lists all nine possible transformations without allowing for any changes in order. Each segment's transformations are absolute or relative only to the world axis, so no hierarchy is necessary. No header is present, only clusters of lines that denote each segment, with the motion data laid out in columns that represent each transformation.

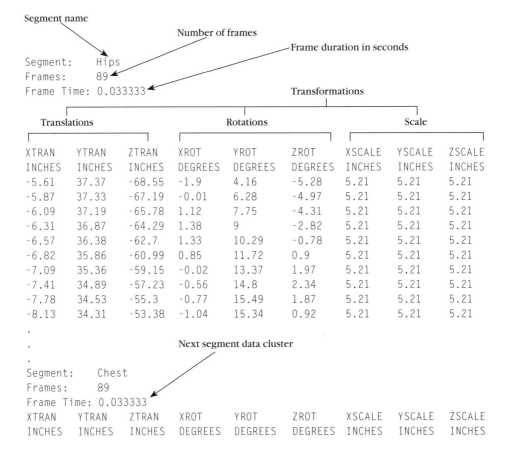

```
-5.13    42.56    -68.73   56.54    -5.13    -17.92   18.65    18.65    18.65
-5.42    42.52    -67.19   56.25    -2.18    -18.19   18.65    18.65    18.65
-5.7     42.38    -65.67   56.35    0.83     -17.96   18.65    18.65    18.65
-6.06    42.07    -64.16   56.56    4.4      -17.85   18.65    18.65    18.65
-6.5     41.59    -62.58   56.71    8.37     -17.71   18.65    18.65    18.65
-6.9     41.07    -60.91   57.1     11.9     -16.74   18.65    18.65    18.65
-7.27    40.57    -59.15   57.75    14.3     -14.58   18.65    18.65    18.65
-7.63    40.1     -57.28   58.54    15.15    -11.2    18.65    18.65    18.65
-7.95    39.74    -55.37   59.55    13.54    -6.65    18.65    18.65    18.65
-8.21    39.51    -53.47   60.61    9.2      -1.15    18.65    18.65    18.65
.
.
.
```

In addition to the transformations, each cluster contains a segment name, the number of frames, and the frame duration in seconds. In the given example, each frame has a duration of 0.033333 s, which means that the data is supposed to be played back at 30 fps.

The scale transformations in the example are all equal for each segment, which means that the segment is rigid throughout the entire data stream.

Having three scale transformations is redundant because only one is required to specify the length of the segment. Note that the example contains equal values for each of the three scale values so that the target animation software can use the one it prefers.

4.1.5 The .bvh File Format

The .bvh file, another Biovision format, is more widely supported than the .bva format. 3D Studio Max and Nichimen, among others, are able to import this file type. The main difference between the .bvh and the .bva files is that the former includes a hierarchy. The file is divided into two major sections: hierarchy and motion. The hierarchy section includes all necessary definitions to create a skeleton in animation software. The motion section contains the data stream.

The hierarchy is defined within blocks of braces. Within each node's braces are defined all of its children, which have their own subblocks.

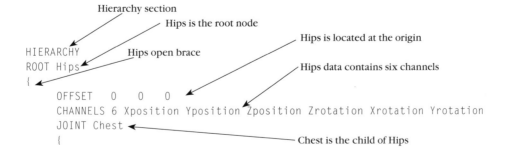

```
OFFSET    0    5.21     0
CHANNELS 3 Zrotation Xrotation Yrotation
JOINT Neck  ◄─────────────────── Neck is the child of Chest
{
    OFFSET    0    18.65    0
    CHANNELS 3 Zrotation Xrotation Yrotation
    JOINT Head
    {                              ┌── Offset translation is relative to parent
        OFFSET    0    5.45    0  ◄┘
        CHANNELS 3 Zrotation Xrotation Yrotation
        End Site
        {
            OFFSET    0    3.87    0 ◄
        }
    }
}                              ─── LeftCollar is the child of Chest
JOINT LeftCollar  ◄
{
    OFFSET    1.12    16.23    1.87
    CHANNELS 3 Zrotation Xrotation Yrotation
    JOINT LeftUpArm
    {
        OFFSET    5.54    0    0
        CHANNELS 3 Zrotation Xrotation Yrotation
        JOINT LeftLowArm
        {
            OFFSET    0    -11.96    0
            CHANNELS 3 Zrotation Xrotation Yrotation
            JOINT LeftHand
            {
                OFFSET    0    -9.93    0
                CHANNELS 3 Zrotation Xrotation Yrotation
                End Site
                {
                    OFFSET    0    -7    0
                }
            }
        }
    }
}
JOINT RightCollar
{
    OFFSET    -1.12    16.23    1.87
    CHANNELS 3 Zrotation Xrotation Yrotation
    JOINT RightUpArm
    {
        OFFSET    -6.07    0    0
        CHANNELS 3 Zrotation Xrotation Yrotation
```

```
                JOINT RightLowArm
                {
                    OFFSET    0  -11.82   0
                    CHANNELS 3 Zrotation Xrotation Yrotation
                    JOINT RightHand
                    {
                        OFFSET    0  -10.65   0
                        CHANNELS 3 Zrotation Xrotation Yrotation
                        End Site
                        {
                            OFFSET    0    -7   0
                        }
                    }
                }
            }
        }
    }
JOINT LeftUpLeg
{
    OFFSET    3.91  0    0
    CHANNELS 3 Zrotation Xrotation Yrotation
    JOINT LeftLowLeg
    {
        OFFSET    0    -18.34   0
        CHANNELS 3 Zrotation Xrotation Yrotation
        JOINT LeftFoot
        {
            OFFSET    0    -17.37   0
            CHANNELS 3 Zrotation Xrotation Yrotation
            End Site
            {
                OFFSET    0    -3.46   0
            }
        }
    }
}
JOINT RightUpLeg
{
    OFFSET    -3.91   0    0
    CHANNELS 3 Zrotation Xrotation Yrotation
    JOINT RightLowLeg
    {
        OFFSET    0    -17.63   0
        CHANNELS 3 Zrotation Xrotation Yrotation
        JOINT RightFoot
        {
            OFFSET    0    -17.14   0
            CHANNELS 3 Zrotation Xrotation Yrotation
            End Site
```

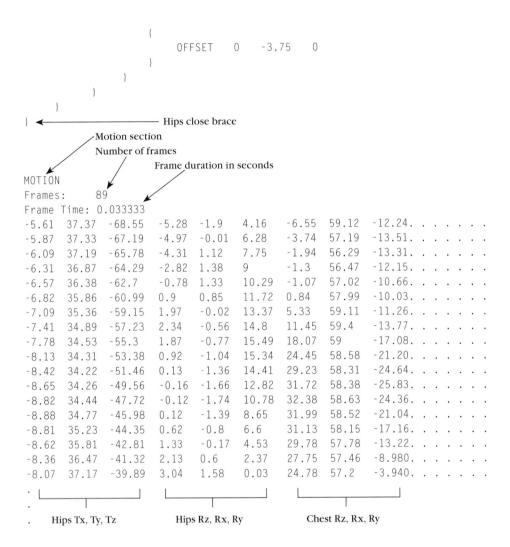

```
                                {
                                        OFFSET    0    -3.75    0
                                }
                            }
                        }
                    }
        } ◄─────────────────────── Hips close brace
                        Motion section
                        Number of frames
                            Frame duration in seconds
        MOTION
        Frames:      89
        Frame Time: 0.033333
        -5.61  37.37  -68.55   -5.28  -1.9    4.16    -6.55  59.12  -12.24. . . . . . .
        -5.87  37.33  -67.19   -4.97  -0.01   6.28    -3.74  57.19  -13.51. . . . . . .
        -6.09  37.19  -65.78   -4.31   1.12   7.75    -1.94  56.29  -13.31. . . . . . .
        -6.31  36.87  -64.29   -2.82   1.38   9       -1.3   56.47  -12.15. . . . . . .
        -6.57  36.38  -62.7    -0.78   1.33  10.29    -1.07  57.02  -10.66. . . . . . .
        -6.82  35.86  -60.99    0.9    0.85  11.72     0.84  57.99  -10.03. . . . . . .
        -7.09  35.36  -59.15    1.97  -0.02  13.37     5.33  59.11  -11.26. . . . . . .
        -7.41  34.89  -57.23    2.34  -0.56  14.8     11.45  59.4   -13.77. . . . . . .
        -7.78  34.53  -55.3     1.87  -0.77  15.49    18.07  59     -17.08. . . . . . .
        -8.13  34.31  -53.38    0.92  -1.04  15.34    24.45  58.58  -21.20. . . . . . .
        -8.42  34.22  -51.46    0.13  -1.36  14.41    29.23  58.31  -24.64. . . . . . .
        -8.65  34.26  -49.56   -0.16  -1.66  12.82    31.72  58.38  -25.83. . . . . . .
        -8.82  34.44  -47.72   -0.12  -1.74  10.78    32.38  58.63  -24.36. . . . . . .
        -8.88  34.77  -45.98    0.12  -1.39   8.65    31.99  58.52  -21.04. . . . . . .
        -8.81  35.23  -44.35    0.62  -0.8    6.6     31.13  58.15  -17.16. . . . . . .
        -8.62  35.81  -42.81    1.33  -0.17   4.53    29.78  57.78  -13.22. . . . . . .
        -8.36  36.47  -41.32    2.13   0.6    2.37    27.75  57.46  -8.980. . . . . . .
        -8.07  37.17  -39.89    3.04   1.58   0.03    24.78  57.2   -3.940. . . . . . .
        .  └──────────────┘   └──────────────┘   └──────────────┘
        .         ┬                  ┬                  ┬
        .    Hips Tx, Ty, Tz     Hips Rz, Rx, Ry      Chest Rz, Rx, Ry
```

Each node has an offset field that defines its translation relative to its immediate parent node, except for the root, where the offset is absolute. In the given example, the node Chest is located 5.21 units in the y direction from its parent, Hips. The offset order is always *XYZ* and no orientation is specified. These values also help define the length of the parent segment, but only in the case in which there are no siblings in different locations. There is no assumption in the hierarchy section about the initial orientation of any node, including the root, which leaves it open for interpretation by the animation software. The .bvh file has to be prepared with this in mind.

The brace blocks located at the deepest levels of the chain, called End Site, contain only an Offset field. This offset value defines the length of the last segment in each particular chain.

The `Channels` field serves two purposes. It defines the allowed transformations for each segment in particular, and it defines the order of occurrence of the transformations. Usually, only the root has any kind of translations, and no scale is used, so all segments are assumed to be rigid. The rest of the segments contain only rotations most of the time. The omission of a scale field makes it difficult to assess each segment's approximation to rigidity, a good measure of margin of error for captured motion data. It is only visually that one can estimate whether the motion is distorted due to marker misplacement or tracking errors.

The `Motion` section is laid out by column per channel in the order defined by the hierarchy section. The first fields define the number of frames and the time per frame. In the example, there are 89 frames that last 0.033333 s each. Each of the following lines contains a frame of animation for each of the channels defined in the hierarchy section, arranged in the same order. The number of these lines is equal to the number of frames specified.

4.1.6 The .trc File Format

The .trc file is generated by Motion Analysis optical motion capture systems and contains translational data. The first part of the file is a header with global information, such as the sample rates of the data in the file and the data at the time of capture, the number of frames and markers, the measure units, and the file path.

The following file header not only shows the current state of the data but also that of the original data captured. The data was originally collected at 60 samples per second and the first file generated had 600 frames, or 10 s. The final file was sampled down to 30 samples per second and shortened to 55 frames for a resulting total of 1.83 s. This information is useful in case one needs more data for this particular motion; you know that you can always go back to the original file.

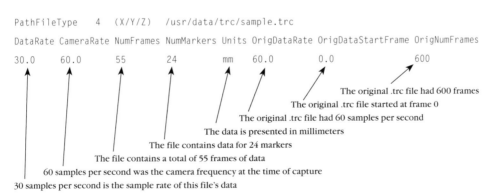

```
PathFileType    4   (X/Y/Z)   /usr/data/trc/sample.trc
DataRate CameraRate NumFrames NumMarkers Units OrigDataRate OrigDataStartFrame OrigNumFrames
30.0      60.0        55        24        mm     60.0           0.0                 600
```

The original .trc file had 600 frames
The original .trc file started at frame 0
The original .trc file had 60 samples per second
The data is presented in millimeters
The file contains data for 24 markers
The file contains a total of 55 frames of data
60 samples per second was the camera frequency at the time of capture
30 samples per second is the sample rate of this file's data

Immediately after the header is the data section. It is organized in columns, the first two being the frame number and the elapsed time, followed by the X, Y, and Z coordinates for each of the markers. The sample file has a total of 74 columns, but only a small portion of it is displayed here due to space limitations.

Frame number

Elapsed time from original data in seconds

Markers

X, Y, and Z coordinates for each marker

Frame#Time	HeadTop			HeadLeft		
	X1	Y1	Z1	X2	Y2	Z2. . . . .
1 0.817	230.93735	1208.98096	-574.76648	334.8299	1166.96545	-594.16943. . . . . . .
2 0.85	240.0072	1210.76257	-569.7652	340.59796	1167.55347	-589.94135. . . . . . .
3 0.883	247.31165	1213.39099	-561.43689	350.31845	1165.92798	-577.86694. . . . . . .
4 0.917	256.81323	1214.14697	-550.07343	361.84949	1163.37598	-562.20605. . . . . . .
5 0.95	268.03162	1213.01514	-536.69348	372.88889	1160.41479	-546.67401. . . . . . .
6 0.983	279.90372	1209.90393	-521.5434	383.58591	1156.65479	-529.50519. . . . . . .
7 1.017	291.30228	1205.90015	-505.01001	393.53964	1152.14868	-511.16791. . . . . . .
8 1.05	300.8645	1201.92969	-486.47925	403.14886	1147.81055	-492.53708. . . . . . .
9 1.083	310.15146	1197.76892	-464.68546	413.05984	1141.46301	-470.33188. . . . . . .
10 1.117	319.0394	1193.06042	-440.80731	423.74298	1132.39136	-441.99075. . . . . . .
11 1.15	327.33527	1187.74207	-415.48169	431.36893	1126.23242	-415.71805. . . . . . .
12 1.183	335.61041	1182.35669	-387.25925	435.79279	1121.53906	-389.98529. . . . . . .
13 1.217	342.04376	1176.35315	-357.57205	441.3559	1115.30664	-361.85596. . . . . . .
14 1.25	346.83585	1168.34473	-328.24915	447.29584	1106.78125	-331.64551. . . . . . .
15 1.283	352.17249	1157.34167	-298.41638	453.83853	1093.90649	-299.004. . . . .
16 1.317	359.34326	1143.95654	-267.88205	462.08264	1076.38452	-264.96805. . . . . . .
17 1.35	367.59335	1130.49084	-239.15077	471.05423	1061.25952	-235.97731. . . . . . .
18 1.383	380.05081	1120.76318	-213.7711	483.44202	1052.48083	-212.00629. . . . . . .
19 1.417	399.8569	1120.18323	-187.46774	501.26627	1053.41492	-190.12701. . . . . . .
20 1.45	424.87695	1132.76147	-156.1911	523.26544	1068.0321	-167.37 . . . .
21 1.483	453.22705	1155.68127	-123.87888	551.185	1091.57129	-138.01402. . . . . . .
22 1.517	484.33765	1179.08362	-95.45136	583.29871	1114.5094	-109.01964. . . . . . .
23 1.55	516.72577	1193.46533	-71.39763	614.81665	1127.37964	-84.13749 . . . .
24 1.583	546.89313	1195.06714	-47.64498	643.01587	1127.25989	-61.68094 . . . .
25 1.617	571.77026	1183.40857	-23.64239	666.65216	1113.55811	-38.76169 . . . .
26 1.65	590.37518	1159.01172	-2.46658	685.62512	1087.17603	-14.94808 . . . .
27 1.683	604.61987	1126.01575	17.18866	700.51947	1053.99719	4.73558 . . . .
28 1.717	618.47876	1092.82764	38.93685	712.78497	1020.67932	21.58421 . . . .
29 1.75	635.88593	1064.63171	61.72252	725.93372	990.01843	40.35942 . . . .
30 1.783	656.48572	1042.42273	84.18129	741.39056	964.52283	57.84112 . . . .
31 1.817	676.87695	1026.60754	103.41233	757.79572	946.63202	69.60565 . . . .
32 1.85	694.78033	1015.62036	115.42829	772.42316	935.22876	74.00996 . . . .
33 1.883	710.32184	1005.88342	119.15073	784.44037	925.51843	71.607 . . . .
34 1.917	721.96924	994.08282	112.42614	790.62396	913.33234	58.56801 . . . .
35 1.95	729.18774	981.94446	94.91256	787.341	900.19971	32.36996 . . . .
36 1.983	728.96234	972.63641	69.04857	771.02301	890.52222	-4.78092 . . . .
37 2.017	720.39075	965.42316	40.12129	740.43433	885.24048	-44.97452 . . . .
38 2.05	706.97437	956.35742	13.84147	698.77313	881.125	-78.80532 . . . .
39 2.083	689.16138	942.43048	-8.84137	650.47784	874.30579	-100.69447. . . . . . .
40 2.117	664.60425	924.6507	-30.82248	599.46606	864.21606	-110.90468. . . . . . .
41 2.15	633.25525	907.31055	-54.29322	548.83063	854.13361	-119.71699. . . . . . .
42 2.183	597.2608	896.60681	-84.46886	500.12531	848.90173	-136.10138. . . . . . .
43 2.217	554.41614	898.05011	-127.57875	450.83124	852.71204	-164.01965. . . . . . .
44 2.25	500.37473	912.37244	-183.38701	395.72012	865.45477	-204.66075. . . . . . .
45 2.283	437.23184	935.49677	-246.46567	333.65088	883.71863	-257.9906 . . . .

```
46  2.317  372.21469  959.72858  -313.86023  270.37036  902.46088  -318.92545. . . . . . .
47  2.35   310.91772  977.48767  -382.59006  211.77318  916.40338  -380.58499. . . . . . .
48  2.383  255.18663  984.98004  -451.91742  157.638    921.98083  -444.11844. . . . . . .
49  2.417  204.3597   982.39105  -520.44476  107.93311  917.8783   -509.36462. . . . . . .
50  2.45   158.57669  976.11462  -585.55585  63.39154   910.49255  -573.0976 . . . . . . .
51  2.483  117.98418  975.84723  -650.65942  24.49508   910.52509  -638.02075. . . . . . .
52  2.517  84.24587   987.77338  -720.19849  -8.76104   923.41449  -707.52234. . . . . . .
53  2.55   60.78411   1009.94342 -793.19592  -36.3148   946.66852  -779.4585 . . . . . . .
54  2.583  42.29954   1036.10669 -868.96185  -62.06355  970.36346  -853.00854. . . . . . .
55  2.617  22.16514   1058.95776 -947.20618  -88.7204   984.33331  -926.72235. . . . . . .
```

Notice that the elapsed time in the sample file starts at .817 s. That means that the first portion of the original 60-samples-per-second file was cropped after frame 49. If you wanted to go back to the original file, you have all the information necessary to relocate the segment you want.

4.1.7 **The .htr File Format**

The .htr file is generated by the Motion Analysis optical motion capture system and contains rotational and translational data and scale channels per marker. It is divided into four parts: the header, the segment hierarchy definitions, the base position, and the data stream.

This sample .htr file was converted from the .trc file in the previous section and has 55 frames as well. It has only 24 segments in order to simplify the analysis. Let's first look at the header portion:

```
#Created by TSi Motion Capture Translator on Tue May  7 11:01:18 1996
#Hierarchical Translation and Rotation (.htr) file
[Header]
FileType htr              ◄──────────── File and data type
DataType HTRS◄──────────── For version control use
FileVersion 1 ◄──────────── Number of rigid segments or bones
NumSegments 14 ◄──────────── Total number of frames
NumFrames 55 ◄──────────── Data sample rate
DataFrameRate 30◄──────────── Rotation order for each segment
EulerRotationOrder ZYX◄──────────── Units at which translations are presented
CalibrationUnits mm  ◄──────────── Units at which rotations are presented
RotationUnits Degrees◄──────────── Height axis
GlobalAxisofGravity Y◄──────────── Axis aligned with segment length
BoneLengthAxis Y◄──────────── Factor by which data has been scaled
ScaleFactor 1.000000 ◄────────────
```

The Euler rotation order is important because each segment's orientation is obtained by three successive rotations in a particular sequence. The decision as to what order of rotations will be used must be reached before generating the .htr file.

The choice depends largely on the animation software to be used because some off-the-shelf animation programs have a hard-coded default rotation order that cannot be modified by the user.

Other parameters relevant to this type of file are the axis that points in the direction of gravity and the one that points in the length direction of a segment. These are also subject to the animation software defaults. As shown in Fig. 4.2, most packages consider Y as the gravity axis, but some use Z. The axis that corresponds to the bone length is Y in most cases, as seen in Fig. 4.3.

The translational data and segment lengths can be scaled to conform to a certain environment size. The ScaleFactor field is used to keep track of this modification. This factor pertains to all the data, not to particular segments.

Following the header is the hierarchy and segment definition section, which is where all the segment names and parental links are defined. All segments are listed in the first column; their parents are listed in the second column. If a segment is listed as *global*, it has no parent. It is possible to list all segments as global, resulting in a stream of global segment rotational data. If a hierarchy is defined, the data falls under the hierarchical segment rotational category. In this case, there has to be at least one segment marked as global. Figure 4.4 is a graphic representation of the following hierarchy.

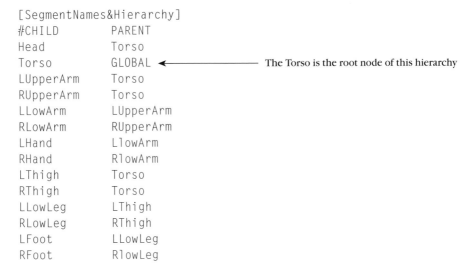

```
[SegmentNames&Hierarchy]
#CHILD          PARENT
Head            Torso
Torso           GLOBAL  ◄────────────── The Torso is the root node of this hierarchy
LUpperArm       Torso
RUpperArm       Torso
LLowArm         LUpperArm
RLowArm         RUpperArm
LHand           LlowArm
RHand           RlowArm
LThigh          Torso
RThigh          Torso
LLowLeg         LThigh
RLowLeg         RThigh
LFoot           LLowLeg
RFoot           RlowLeg
```

The next section in the .htr file (see the following code) defines the base position. During the motion capture session, a file with the neutral pose is captured. A frame in that file is selected to represent the closest pose to the digital character model. This frame will become the common base position and will be embedded in the body of all .htr files as they are generated. The base position is also the initial skeleton of the character in the animation software, so by using a common one for all .htr files, only one character setup is necessary. All motion transformations in the .htr file are relative to this base position. Thus, if all translations and rotations are zeroed out,

FIGURE 4.2

Global axis of gravity.

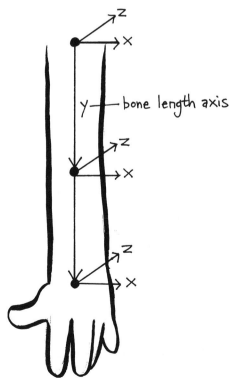

FIGURE 4.3

Bone length axis.

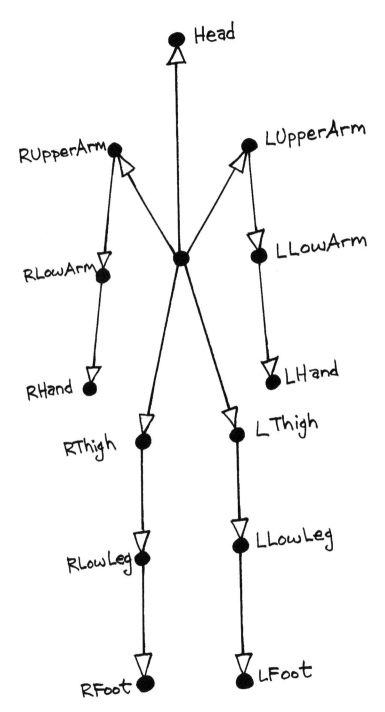

FIGURE 4.4

Representation of the hierarchy of the sample file.

the skeleton will return to this pose. If the base position is changed, all the data in the file must be recomputed. You should not set up your character unless you have already imported a base-position file into your animation software. It is possible to avoid this if you can write software to recalculate the data for a predetermined base position based on your character setup.

Position of the segment joint
Rotation of the segment
Length of the segment toward the direction specified by BoneLengthAxis

[BasePosition] #SegmentName	Tx,	Ty,	Tz,	Rx,	Ry,	Rz,	BoneLength
Head	0.000000	431.23397	-0.000053	-9.986019	3.761429	3.400506	280.064167
Torso	275.22095	506.79619	288.57797	2.376954	1.443789	-0.355906	431.233965
LUpperArm	156.87617	386.75287	-3.185811	-175.5559	3.333388	32.855909	304.366044
RUpperArm	-155.4525	372.40142	-7.013619	-67.02254	-80.17111	-152.5459	298.021147
LLowArm	-0.000001	304.36605	0.000000	-33.04495	-40.31584	30.437916	203.737662
RLowArm	0.000000	298.02114	0.000000	7.865308	20.230543	-22.0888	219.662102
LHand	0.000045	203.73765	0.000000	-10.28575	-0.006313	0.564050	85.290146
RHand	-0.000034	219.66210	0.000000	-6.072895	0.253441	-8.168635	82.679801
LThigh	97.146641	-52.36968	26.442271	5.630001	2.513765	-175.8221	429.857263
RThigh	-99.16115	-56.27259	16.734767	3.840584	2.445667	175.9028	435.858359
LLowLeg	0.000000	429.85727	-0.000007	-21.21125	-10.18572	-0.322527	467.848511
RLowLeg	0.000000	435.85837	0.000002	-21.01293	12.252749	2.709794	450.882350
LFoot	0.000000	467.84850	0.000003	105.25284	0.000000	0.000000	207.073423
RFoot	0.000000	450.88235	-0.000023	104.01143	0.000000	0.000000	227.807044

The translation and rotation values of a segment are relative to its parent. Notice how the value of Ty for the head is almost equal to the torso's bone length. That means that the head is almost exactly at the end of the torso's segment, and we know that the head is the torso's child. Also, notice how the torso's Tx and Tz values are much higher than all the others are. This is because the torso is the only global segment – its transformations are all relative to the world axis, whereas the transformations of all other segments are relative to their direct parents. The only value that is not relative is the bone length.

The fourth section of the .htr file is the data itself. It is divided into subsections per segment, each line representing a frame number.

Frame number
Translations relative to base position
Rotations relative to base position
Scale factor

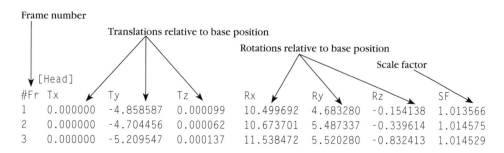

[Head] #Fr	Tx	Ty	Tz	Rx	Ry	Rz	SF
1	0.000000	-4.858587	0.000099	10.499692	4.683280	-0.154138	1.013566
2	0.000000	-4.704456	0.000062	10.673701	5.487337	-0.339614	1.014575
3	0.000000	-5.209547	0.000137	11.538472	5.520280	-0.832413	1.014529

```
4   0.000000   -5.944353   -0.000067   12.095569   5.352387   -1.547831   1.015056
5   0.000000   -5.811870   -0.000099   12.113773   5.297226   -2.093981   1.014358
6   0.000000   -5.177482   -0.000032   12.020602   4.992712   -2.545206   1.014178
7   0.000000   -5.068451    0.000082   12.188824   4.664569   -3.514527   1.014793
8   0.000000   -4.903581    0.000022   12.427092   4.548636   -4.889447   1.017025
9   0.000000   -5.314583   -0.000142   12.031311   4.223691   -5.832687   1.016775
10  0.000000   -6.237838   -0.000062   11.218972   3.141907   -6.143721   1.013859
.
.

.
```

[Torso]

#Fr	Tx	Ty	Tz	Rx	Ry	Rz	SF
1	0.256104	-4.690031	-901.21180	3.419065	11.191740	1.183391	0.988733
2	6.268514	-4.833825	-899.39510	3.633979	9.386523	1.177484	0.989091
3	12.662476	-4.319671	-898.89568	4.130778	7.166818	1.362676	0.987919
4	20.360730	-3.851736	-898.68094	5.012617	5.342751	1.549584	0.986215
5	28.105710	-4.242471	-897.52817	6.094990	4.100763	1.545525	0.986523
6	33.560872	-5.928574	-892.96085	7.047348	3.505319	1.296721	0.987994
7	38.214739	-7.738103	-887.69563	7.983385	3.506861	1.311696	0.988247
8	43.544279	-9.604294	-882.33720	9.022912	3.708099	1.677518	0.988629
9	48.072781	-10.739373	-875.16154	10.465145	3.904763	1.771565	0.987676
10	50.492413	-11.234768	-864.79241	12.111266	4.148431	1.412131	0.985535

```
.
.

.
```

[LUpperArm]

#Fr	Tx	Ty	Tz	Rx	Ry	Rz	SF
1	1.286490	0.963057	0.574860	-7.653392	44.051043	8.626731	1.005609
2	2.559994	1.111917	0.151302	-7.338404	43.176098	9.013981	1.010282
3	4.056162	-0.641842	-0.707999	-7.043097	41.024858	9.262136	1.014424
4	4.616618	-2.865766	-1.335355	-7.426399	38.204100	9.111665	1.015329
5	4.444702	-3.268960	-1.380717	-8.580342	36.165418	8.315740	1.015126
6	4.286494	-2.383443	-1.185014	-9.953407	35.276832	6.634077	1.016061
7	2.765563	-2.713288	-1.117306	-12.110188	34.826341	3.701319	1.020946
8	0.416213	-3.832802	-1.007864	-14.591061	33.521631	0.304836	1.027364
9	-0.619820	-4.311412	-0.618119	-16.499243	30.467864	-2.514869	1.028296
10	-1.814847	-3.660805	-0.214309	-17.731646	27.028367	-5.659754	1.027257

```
.
.

.
```

[RUpperArm]

#Fr	Tx	Ty	Tz	Rx	Ry	Rz	SF
1	-0.628667	-10.007628	-0.789967	22.216529	-20.359719	-8.588245	1.024184
2	-2.122022	-9.640057	-0.377274	22.541990	-20.343501	-9.684186	1.020901
3	-4.127241	-8.594386	0.464602	22.742894	-20.373516	-11.309095	1.016075
4	-5.090433	-7.676922	1.081377	22.469946	-19.966937	-12.619528	1.013768
5	-4.973729	-7.047965	1.126349	22.183319	-19.175667	-13.327397	1.011921

6	-4.703499	-6.747547	0.936658	21.930873	-19.265821	-12.519854	1.012378
7	-3.171071	-6.455877	0.873939	21.246082	-19.429001	-10.699060	1.015006
8	-0.836609	-5.405571	0.770152	20.195218	-18.945001	-9.169760	1.016727
9	0.397692	-5.898392	0.380475	19.195593	-18.120445	-8.334362	1.018571
10	1.899746	-8.523217	-0.021126	18.050606	-17.667981	-7.758186	1.024040

.
.
.

[LLowArm]

#Fr	Tx	Ty	Tz	Rx	Ry	Rz	SF
1	0.000003	1.707023	0.000000	-17.836864	-2.427292	8.876852	0.994353
2	-0.000002	3.129388	0.000000	-19.191384	-1.679347	10.090833	0.980333
3	0.000004	4.390150	0.000000	-21.031146	-0.105618	11.730428	0.975999
4	0.000003	4.665619	0.000000	-22.703322	1.634425	13.370107	0.978072
5	-0.000007	4.603944	0.000000	-24.137978	2.738765	14.980390	0.972584
6	0.000010	4.888471	0.000000	-26.076666	3.162832	17.149450	0.961580
7	0.000000	6.375176	0.000000	-27.982561	3.193934	19.458814	0.954579
8	-0.000004	8.328783	0.000000	-29.160452	2.733712	21.585777	0.961696
9	0.000009	8.612477	0.000000	-29.531369	2.209042	23.412567	0.975206
10	-0.000006	8.296200	0.000000	-29.638691	2.200138	24.648625	0.979509

.
.
.

[RLowArm]

#Fr	Tx	Ty	Tz	Rx	Ry	Rz	SF
1	0.000000	7.207338	0.000000	4.077527	4.779736	-9.261399	0.997339
2	0.000000	6.228889	0.000000	3.718802	4.740024	-8.438207	1.001040
3	0.000000	4.790671	0.000000	3.249446	4.777283	-7.330081	1.002267
4	0.000000	4.103032	0.000000	2.757547	5.175765	-6.211417	0.998304
5	0.000000	3.552562	0.000000	2.311264	4.783585	-5.304502	0.995057
6	0.000000	3.688861	0.000000	2.874347	3.508883	-6.663122	1.002753
7	0.000000	4.472061	0.000000	3.777142	2.759954	-8.812203	1.008979
8	0.000000	4.985092	0.000000	4.036366	4.543184	-9.327195	0.999816
9	0.000000	5.534443	0.000000	4.044032	7.539941	-9.130649	0.981114
10	0.000000	7.164408	0.000000	4.499946	8.880659	-10.043492	0.962622

.
.
.

[LHand]

#Fr	Tx	Ty	Tz	Rx	Ry	Rz	SF
1	-0.000015	-1.150439	0.000000	8.243739	1.486729	-8.919611	1.043678
2	-0.000061	-4.006916	0.000000	8.754663	1.456218	-8.584533	1.055827
3	-0.000006	-4.889940	0.000000	9.829340	1.418586	-7.960398	1.055248
4	-0.000081	-4.467616	0.000000	10.936380	1.245752	-6.496042	1.035544
5	-0.000014	-5.585692	0.000000	11.011182	1.099799	-5.658061	1.030126
6	-0.000035	-7.827684	0.000000	11.076282	1.267397	-6.592873	1.040425
7	-0.000027	-9.253875	0.000000	10.745705	1.561329	-8.369294	1.049638

8	-0.000061	-7.804008	0.000000	7.959112	1.591583	-9.831184	1.046414
9	-0.000031	-5.051480	0.000000	5.722562	1.411336	-10.370656	1.032841
10	-0.000107	-4.174827	0.000000	4.688785	1.273762	-10.227041	1.029007

.

.

[RHand]

#Fr	Tx	Ty	Tz	Rx	Ry	Rz	SF
1	-0.000008	-0.584451	0.000000	-2.948995	-0.370179	2.644674	1.019734
2	0.000077	0.228431	0.000000	-4.240219	-0.165327	0.509767	1.019569
3	0.000107	0.498062	0.000000	-4.668479	-0.048645	-0.048041	1.011510
4	0.000072	-0.372647	0.000000	-4.733414	-0.023255	1.129299	0.992169
5	0.000021	-1.085705	0.000000	-5.367082	0.051834	2.634300	0.981505
6	0.000023	0.604676	0.000000	-7.631311	0.208044	3.920976	0.984171
7	0.000043	1.972392	0.000000	-9.173343	0.277757	4.768445	0.994198
8	0.000017	-0.040381	0.000000	-7.029188	0.082563	4.287978	1.007134
9	0.000066	-4.148576	0.000000	-2.578875	-0.163798	4.247556	1.016898
10	0.000056	-8.210634	0.000000	2.125026	-0.614249	5.558822	1.025910

.

.

.

[LThigh]

#Fr	Tx	Ty	Tz	Rx	Ry	Rz	SF
1	-1.948971	-5.743679	1.216170	4.584717	-1.803198	-2.301923	1.028563
2	-0.819284	-5.643427	-1.622541	4.615649	-3.503848	-2.869945	1.030591
3	0.158322	-5.891428	-5.515270	5.094698	-5.986699	-3.830506	1.033867
4	-0.692296	-6.019829	-7.226451	5.927294	-7.332279	-4.776852	1.038741
5	-2.293193	-5.962193	-6.119729	6.874762	-7.096426	-5.249797	1.042618
6	-2.342179	-5.886886	-4.811534	7.378632	-6.509944	-5.284106	1.041001
7	-2.065793	-5.799062	-3.707482	7.864546	-5.981563	-5.689823	1.038133
8	-3.800748	-5.834549	-1.233139	8.284303	-4.674531	-6.110074	1.036010
9	-5.134686	-5.948454	2.060023	8.993702	-3.019969	-6.024278	1.036358
10	-4.070278	-5.600185	3.463773	9.976612	-2.572359	-5.753804	1.037939

.

.

.

[RThigh]

#Fr	Tx	Ty	Tz	Rx	Ry	Rz	SF
1	1.917365	3.396889	4.574878	3.263076	-1.041816	0.892310	1.022364
2	1.460515	3.232908	7.627397	3.558135	-2.758124	0.611140	1.021666
3	1.254415	3.206850	12.467492	4.524791	-5.219322	-0.051084	1.023668
4	1.992551	2.845752	15.895479	6.201461	-6.483182	-0.951123	1.025984
5	2.868044	2.121395	16.976760	8.234925	-6.081634	-1.490023	1.026711
6	2.570853	1.448601	17.569256	10.236563	-5.317917	-1.403521	1.025387
7	1.385562	0.769813	18.910872	13.008264	-4.511639	-1.841973	1.022732
8	0.920314	0.211667	19.865216	17.074544	-2.596840	-2.962349	1.019291
9	0.256353	-0.208364	21.005662	22.052302	-0.184869	-3.433113	1.018606
10	-1.015619	-0.821060	23.861019	26.525253	0.857900	-3.166014	1.015690

.
.
.

[LLowLeg]

#Fr	Tx	Ty	Tz	Rx	Ry	Rz	SF
1	0.000000	12.277876	-0.000005	-9.310979	3.958743	2.994572	0.987525
2	0.000000	13.149770	0.000005	-9.350337	3.621027	3.505744	0.986619
3	0.000000	14.557776	0.000005	-9.343923	3.591080	4.326684	0.985922
4	0.000000	16.652874	0.000008	-9.397132	3.228173	4.814963	0.983453
5	0.000000	18.319480	0.000012	-9.767744	2.445292	4.794431	0.980062
6	0.000000	17.624747	0.000016	-9.847268	2.552874	4.845590	0.977428
7	0.000000	16.391952	0.000001	-9.706737	2.869017	5.127302	0.976938
8	0.000000	15.479248	0.000014	-9.485002	2.161337	4.660242	0.976370
9	0.000000	15.628608	0.000009	-9.413728	1.386960	3.896389	0.975466
10	0.000000	16.308507	0.000013	-9.479881	2.118380	4.032616	0.978753

.
.
.

[RLowLeg]

#Fr	Tx	Ty	Tz	Rx	Ry	Rz	SF
1	0.000000	9.747725	-0.000003	-1.969391	2.713994	-0.256803	0.964314
2	0.000000	9.443244	-0.000004	-2.309806	2.925325	-0.349927	0.965662
3	0.000000	10.315879	-0.000002	-3.293559	3.200043	-0.279514	0.966694
4	0.000000	11.325171	0.000000	-4.596793	2.633765	-0.463029	0.967041
5	0.000000	11.642023	-0.000002	-6.360722	1.133664	-1.235632	0.968146
6	0.000000	11.065212	-0.000002	-8.939798	0.143144	-2.253221	0.970705
7	0.000000	9.908082	-0.000001	-13.063365	0.262553	-2.668486	0.972029
8	0.000000	8.408095	-0.000001	-19.404992	0.503464	-2.941691	0.970976
9	0.000000	8.109777	-0.000001	-26.918280	-0.086212	-3.564932	0.969294
10	0.000000	6.838414	-0.000001	-33.084023	-0.002488	-4.141806	0.969350

.
.
.

[LFoot]

#Fr	Tx	Ty	Tz	Rx	Ry	Rz	SF
1	0.000000	5.836589	-0.000075	6.849172	0.000000	0.000000	1.014277
2	0.000000	-6.260494	-0.000031	7.131442	0.000000	0.000000	1.007809
3	0.000000	-6.586196	-0.000045	7.382423	0.000000	0.000000	1.008357
4	0.000000	-7.741686	0.000070	7.669603	0.000000	0.000000	1.013625
5	0.000000	-9.328047	-0.000074	8.037170	0.000000	0.000000	1.017301
6	0.000000	-10.560292	-0.000021	8.281682	0.000000	0.000000	1.020076
7	0.000000	-10.789751	0.000048	8.494574	0.000000	0.000000	1.022273
8	0.000000	-11.055420	-0.000067	8.699128	0.000000	0.000000	1.020523
9	0.000000	-11.478071	0.000051	9.061934	0.000000	0.000000	1.016536
10	0.000000	-9.940176	-0.000067	9.780009	0.000000	0.000000	1.017310

.
.
.

```
[RFoot]
#Fr Tx         Ty          Tz          Rx         Ry         Rz         SF
1   0.000000   -16.090285  -0.000007   0.854710   0.000000   0.000000   0.991550
2   0.000000   -15.482314  0.000083    1.151425   0.000000   0.000000   0.990986
3   0.000000   -15.017190  0.000111    1.753048   0.000000   0.000000   0.996231
4   0.000000   -14.860747  -0.000018   2.355142   0.000000   0.000000   0.997485
5   0.000000   -14.362526  -0.000003   2.974844   0.000000   0.000000   0.996350
6   0.000000   -13.208670  0.000027    3.658937   0.000000   0.000000   0.993913
7   0.000000   -12.611719  0.000000    3.844048   0.000000   0.000000   0.986665
8   0.000000   -13.086514  0.000060    2.895532   0.000000   0.000000   0.976994
9   0.000000   -13.844775  -0.000034   1.293673   0.000000   0.000000   0.975546
10  0.000000   -13.819476  -0.000009   0.294280   0.000000   0.000000   0.983843
.
.

.
[EndOfFile]
```

The SF column in the .htr file is a scale of the particular segment along the axis indicated by BoneLengthAxis. This number represents deviations in the length of the bone caused by the sliding of the skin over the bone. This number must always be very close to 1; otherwise, it indicates a faulty marker location or perhaps a marker placed over loose clothing. If the number is very close to 1 throughout the whole data stream, you may ignore it or approximate it to 1.0, thus assuming that the segment is rigid.

Figure 4.5 is a chart of the segment length scale for the sample file. In this particular case, the scale factor cannot be ignored completely because some values exceed the acceptable rigidity deviation. The LHand segment, for example, has a peak deviation of almost 30%. In a situation like this, it may be necessary to recalculate the .htr file using a different combination of markers. If that doesn't work, the motion may have to be recaptured. The acceptable deviation depends on each particular motion, but it should not exceed 10% in any case.

4.2 WRITING A MOTION CAPTURE TRANSLATOR

Most animation programs support at least one motion capture format, but if your application is proprietary, you may have to write your own. The language and platform are not relevant to this discussion, but I will use the C language to illustrate the programming steps. I also present the code in a sequential as opposed to modular way, since I believe the continuity aids in understanding the logic. If you decide to write your own translator, you may want to use more functions and subroutines, a much recommended programming practice.

As a case study, I use the .htr format as the input file and the Acclaim format as the output file. I chose Acclaim as the output format because it is the most complicated one, I have already explained it in detail and it is the closest to what an animation file format would look like.

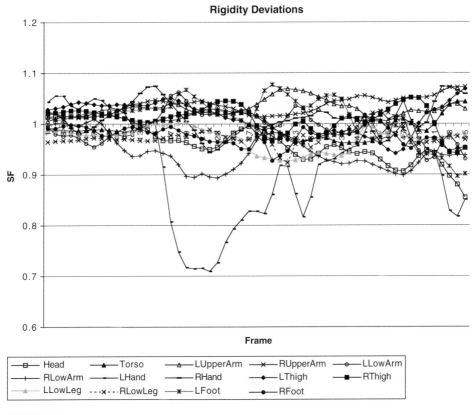

FIGURE 4.5

Segment length scale.

The first step in creating a translator is to define a buffer that will hold all the data of both the input and output files. The .htr file buffer looks like this:

```
/* Hierarchy pairs */
struct htrSegmentHierarchy {
    char *child;                    /* child segment  */
    char *parent;                   /* parent segment */
};
/* Base position structure */
struct htrBasePosition {
    char *name;                     /* segment name   */
    double tx;                      /* initial values */
    double ty;
    double tz;
```

```
        double rx;
        double ry;
        double rz;
        double boneLength;
};
/* Frame data */
struct htrFrame {
        int frameNo;                    /* frame number      */
        double tx;                      /* transformations        */
        double ty;
        double tz;
        double rx;
        double ry;
        double rz;
        double SF;                      /* segment scale factor */
};
/* Segment data */
struct htrSegmentData {
        char *segmentName;              /* segment name */
        struct htrFrame *frame;         /* frame data     */
};
/* .htr format wrapper struct */
struct htrFormat {
        char *fileType;                 /* file type                 */
        char *dataType;                 /* data type                 */
        int fileVersion;                /* file version              */
        int numSegments;                /* number of segments        */
        int numFrames;                  /* total number of frames    */
        int dataFrameRate;              /* frame rate                */
        char *eulerRotationOrder;       /* global order of rotations */
        char *calibrationUnits;         /* units of translation      */
        char *rotationUnits;            /* units of rotation         */
        char *globalAxisofGravity;      /* global up axis            */
        char *boneLengthAxis;           /* axis along bone           */
        float scaleFactor;              /* global scale factor       */
        struct htrSegmentHierarchy *childParent;  /* hierarchy       */
        struct htrBasePosition *basePosition;     /* base position */
        struct htrSegmentData *segmentData;       /* segment data   */
};
/* .htr data buffer */
struct htrFormat htrFile;
```

htrFile, a variable of type struct hrtFormat, will end up containing the entire data in the .htr file. The first 12 variables in struct hrtFormat correspond to the .htr file's header section. childParent is a buffer that will hold all the child-parent pairs as defined in the SegmentNames&Hierarchy section. This buffer is of the previously defined type struct htrSegmentNamesandHierarchy, which will hold both child and parent strings. basePosition will contain all the data in the BasePosition section. It is of type struct htrBasePosition, where the segment and initial transformations are defined. Finally, segmentData, of type struct htrFrame, will hold the motion data.

The output file is actually a combination of both .asf and .amc files; its structure can be defined as follows:

```
/* This structure will hold each dof's limit pairs */
struct acclaimBoneLimits {
    double minMax[2];         /* min/max values (0 if infinity)  */
    int infinity[2];          /* infinity flag (1 if infinity)   */
};
/* Segment's bone data section */
struct acclaimBoneData {
    int id;                             /* segment id            */
    char *name;                         /* segment name          */
    float direction[3];                 /* direction vector      */
    double length;                      /* segment length        */
    double axis[3];                     /* global orientation    */
    char axisOrder[5];                  /* order of r for above  */
    char dof[20];                       /* dof tokens            */
    int dofNumber;                      /* number of dof tokens  */
    struct acclaimBoneLimits *limits;   /* limits defined above  */
    float bodyMass;                     /* body mass             */
    float cofMass;                      /* center of mass        */
};
/* Hierarchy section */
struct acclaimHierarchy {
    char *parent;                       /* parent segment */
    char children[MAXLINE];             /* child segments */
};
/* Skin section */
struct acclaimSkin {
    char *skinFile;                     /* skin file name */
};
/* Motion data section in the .amc file */
struct acclaimMotionData {
    char *segment;                      /* segment name    */
    double tx;                          /* transformations */
    double ty;
    double tz;
```

```
        double rx;
        double ry;
        double rz;
        double l;
};
/* Frame data */
struct acclaimFrameData {
        int frame;                              /* frame number */
        struct acclaimMotionData *motionData;   /* segment data */
};
/* Acclaim format wrapper struct */
struct acclaimFormat {
        char* version;                          /* file version      */
        char *name;                             /* skeleton name     */
        float unitsMass;                        /* mass multiplier   */
        float unitsLength;                      /* length multiplier */
        char unitsAngle[5];                     /* angles (deg/rad)  */
        char *documentation;                    /* notes             */
        char rootOrder[20];                     /* root's xform order */
        char rootAxis[5];                       /* initial rot. order */
        double rootPosition[3];                 /* initial position  */
        double rootOrientation[3];              /* initial rotation  */
        struct acclaimBoneData *boneData;       /* segments' data    */
        struct acclaimHierarchy *hierarchy;     /* hierarchy pairs   */
        struct acclaimSkin *skin;               /* skin files        */
        struct acclaimFrameData *frameData;     /* frame data        */
};
/* Acclaim data buffer */
struct acclaimFormat acclaimFile;
```

acclaimFile will hold all the data in the .asf and .amc files. It is of type struct acclaimFormat. The bone information will be located in boneData, and hierarchy will hold all the parent–child relationships. frameData will contain all the data from the .amc file. Notice in the definition of struct acclaimBoneData that the integer variable dofNumber doesn't actually come from the .asf file. It will contain the number of degrees of freedom available for each particular segment so that the dof line will be parsed only once per segment. Another special-purpose variable is the infinity integer inside the definition of struct acclaimBoneLimits, which, as its name says, will hold a flag to indicate infinity. struct acclaimHierarchy will hold the hierarchy data in pairs of parent and child, as opposed to the way in which the .asf file holds it (i.e. with a parent and all of its children in the same line). If the parent has several children, more than one pair will be generated.

If you compare the definitions above with the actual file structures as explained in the previous section, you will find that most of the variable and type names are very close to those in the files themselves. You will also find that the structures above contain more information than will be used in the conversion from .htr to Acclaim, but including this information in the data structure is a good practice in case you need it in the future.

The next step is to start reading the information from the .htr file into the data bufffer. Assuming a file is available and its name has already been processed by the program and placed in the string htrFileName, we proceed to open the file and then process the header section.

```
#define MAXLINE 500         /* Max length of a line of text   */
#define MAXTOKENS 50        /* Max number of tokens per line  */
#define DELIMIT " \t\n"     /* Characters separating tokens   */
#define XYZ 1               /* Order of rotations             */
#define XZY 2               /* Order of rotations             */
#define ZXY 3               /* Order of rotations             */
#define ZYX 4               /* Order of rotations             */
#define YXZ 5               /* Order of rotations             */
#define YZX 6               /* Order of rotations             */
int found;                  /* Boolean variable              */
int value;                  /* Return value                  */
int htrRotOrder;            /* htr order of rotations        */
int numTokens;              /* Number of tokens per line     */
int numParents;             /* Number of parent nodes        */
int numBones;               /* Number of segments            */
int numFrames;              /* Number of frames              */
int i, j, k;                /* Counters                      */
FILE *htrFileHandle;        /* Handle to .htr file           */
char *htrFileName;          /* The .htr file name            */
FILE *asfFileHandle;        /* Handle to .asf file           */
char *asfFileName;          /* The .asf file name            */
FILE *amcFileHandle;        /* Handle to .amc file           */
char *amcFileName;          /* The .amc file name            */
char textLine[MAXLINE];     /* Buffer will hold a line of text */
char *genStr;               /* Generic string                */
char *token[MAXTOKENS];     /* Token buffer                  */

/* Process arguments and other initializations */
/* Open .htr file */
htrFileHandle = fopen(htrFileName, "r");
if (!htrFileHandle) {
    fprintf(stderr, "\nError: Unable to open %s \n", htrFileName);
    exit();
    }
```

```
/* Find the header section */
found = 0;
while (!found && fgets(textLine, MAXLINE, htrFileHandle)) {
    if (strncmp("[Header]", textLine, strlen("[Header]")) == 0)
    found = 1;
    }
if (!found) {
    fprintf(stderr, "\nError: Unable to find 'Header'\n");
    exit();
    }

/* Start reading header data */

/* fileType */
/* Get a line of text */
found = 0;
value = 1;
while (!found && value) {
    value = fgets(textLine, MAXLINE, htrFileHandle);

    /* Skip if comment or newline */
    if (textLine[0] == '\n' !! textLine[0] == '#')
        found = 0;
    else
        if (value)
            found = 1;
    }
if (!found) {
    fprintf(stderr, "\nError: Premature end of file\n");
    exit();
    }

/* Parse line */
numTokens = 0;
token[numTokens++] = strtok(textLine, DELIMIT);
while (token[numTokens-1])
    token[numTokens++] = strtok(NULL, DELIMIT);
numTokens -= 1;

/* Make sure we got two tokens */
if (numTokens != 2) {
    fprintf(stderr, "\nError: Invalid 'fileType'\n");
    exit();
    }
```

```
/* Allocate memory and save fileType into buffer */
htrFile->fileType =
      (char *)malloc((strlen(token[1])+1)*sizeof(char));
strcpy(htrFile->fileType, token[1]);


/* dataType */
/* Get a line of text */
found = 0;
value = 1;
while (!found && value) {
      value = fgets(textLine, MAXLINE, htrFileHandle);

      /* Skip if comment or newline */
      if (textLine[0] == '\n' !! textLine[0] == '#')
          found = 0;
      else
          if (value)
                found = 1;
      }
if (!found) {
      fprintf(stderr, "\nError: Premature end of file\n");
      exit();
      }


/* Parse line */
numTokens = 0;
token[numTokens++] = strtok(textLine, DELIMIT);
while (token[numTokens-1])
      token[numTokens++] = strtok(NULL, DELIMIT);
numTokens -= 1;


/* Make sure we got two tokens */
if (numTokens != 2) {
      fprintf(stderr, "\nError: Invalid 'dataType'\n");
      exit();
      }


/* Allocate memory and save dataType into buffer */
htrFile->dataType =
      (char *)malloc((strlen(token[1])+1)*sizeof(char));
strcpy(htrFile->dataType, token[1]);


/* fileVersion */
/* Get a line of text */
```

```
found = 0;
value = 1;
while (!found && value) {
      value = fgets(textLine, MAXLINE, htrFileHandle);

      /* Skip if comment or newline */
      if (textLine[0] == '\n' !! textLine[0] == '#')
          found = 0;
      else
          if (value)
              found = 1;
      }
if (!found) {
      fprintf(stderr, "\nError: Premature end of file\n");
      exit();
      }

/* Parse line */
numTokens = 0;
token[numTokens++] = strtok(textLine, DELIMIT);
while (token[numTokens-1])
      token[numTokens++] = strtok(NULL, DELIMIT);
numTokens -= 1;

/* Make sure we got two tokens */
if (numTokens != 2) {
      fprintf(stderr, "\nError: Invalid 'fileVersion'\n");
      exit();
      }

/* Save fileVersion into buffer */
htrFile->fileVersion = atoi(token[1]);

/* numSegments */
/* Get a line of text */
found = 0;
value = 1;
while (!found && value) {
      value = fgets(textLine, MAXLINE, htrFileHandle);

      /* Skip if comment or newline */
      if (textLine[0] == '\n' !! textLine[0] == '#')
          found = 0;
```

```
        else
            if (value)
                found = 1;
    }
if (!found) {
    fprintf(stderr, "\nError: Premature end of file\n");
    exit();
    }

/* Parse line */
numTokens = 0;
token[numTokens++] = strtok(textLine, DELIMIT);
while (token[numTokens-1])
    token[numTokens++] = strtok(NULL, DELIMIT);
numTokens -= 1;

/* Make sure we got two tokens */
if (numTokens != 2) {
    fprintf(stderr, "\nError: Invalid 'numSegments'\n");
    exit();
    }

/* Save numSegments into buffer */
htrFile->numSegments = atoi(token[1]);

/* numFrames */
/* Get a line of text */
found = 0;
value = 1;
while (!found && value) {
    value = fgets(textLine, MAXLINE, htrFileHandle);

    /* Skip if comment or newline */
    if (textLine[0] == '\n' !! textLine[0] == '#')
        found = 0;
    else
        if (value)
            found = 1;
    }
if (!found) {
    fprintf(stderr, "\nError: Premature end of file\n");
    exit();
    }
```

```c
/* Parse line */
numTokens = 0;
token[numTokens++] = strtok(textLine, DELIMIT);
while (token[numTokens-1])
     token[numTokens++] = strtok(NULL, DELIMIT);
numTokens -= 1;

/* Make sure we got two tokens */
if (numTokens != 2) {
    fprintf(stderr, "\nError: Invalid 'numFrames'\n");
    exit();
    }

/* Save numFrames into buffer */
htrFile->numFrames = atoi(token[1]);

/* dataFrameRate */
/* Get a line of text */
found = 0;
value = 1;
while (!found && value) {
     value = fgets(textLine, MAXLINE, htrFileHandle);

     /* Skip if comment or newline */
     if (textLine[0] == '\n' !! textLine[0] == '#')
         found = 0;
     else
         if (value)
              found = 1;
     }
if (!found) {
    fprintf(stderr, "\nError: Premature end of file\n");
    exit();
    }

/* Parse line */
numTokens = 0;
token[numTokens++] = strtok(textLine, DELIMIT);
while (token[numTokens-1])
     token[numTokens++] = strtok(NULL, DELIMIT);
numTokens -= 1;

/* Make sure we got two tokens */
if (numTokens != 2) {
```

```c
        fprintf(stderr, "\nError: Invalid 'dataFrameRate'\n");
        exit();
        }

/* Save dataFrameRate into buffer */
htrFile->dataFrameRate = atoi(token[1]);

/* eulerRotationOrder */
/* Get a line of text */
found = 0;
value = 1;
while (!found && value) {
    value = fgets(textLine, MAXLINE, htrFileHandle);

    /* Skip if comment or newline */
    if (textLine[0] == '\n' !! textLine[0] == '#')
        found = 0;
    else
        if (value)
            found = 1;
    }
if (!found) {
    fprintf(stderr, "\nError: Premature end of file\n");
    exit();
    }

/* Parse line */
numTokens = 0;
token[numTokens++] = strtok(textLine, DELIMIT);
while (token[numTokens-1])
    token[numTokens++] = strtok(NULL, DELIMIT);
numTokens -= 1;

/* Make sure we got two tokens */
if (numTokens != 2) {
    fprintf(stderr, "\nError: Invalid 'eulerRotationOrder'\n");
    exit();
    }

/* Allocate memory and save eulerRotationOrder into buffer */
htrFile->eulerRotationOrder =
    (char *)malloc((strlen(token[1])+1)*sizeof(char));
strcpy(htrFile->eulerRotationOrder, token[1]);
```

```c
/* calibrationUnits */
/* Get a line of text */
found = 0;
value = 1;
while (!found && value) {
     value = fgets(textLine, MAXLINE, htrFileHandle);

     /* Skip if comment or newline */
     if (textLine[0] == '\n' !! textLine[0] == '#')
          found = 0;
     else
          if (value)
               found = 1;
     }
if (!found) {
     fprintf(stderr, "\nError: Premature end of file\n");
     exit();
     }

/* Parse line */
numTokens = 0;
token[numTokens++] = strtok(textLine, DELIMIT);
while (token[numTokens-1])
     token[numTokens++] = strtok(NULL, DELIMIT);
numTokens -= 1;

/* Make sure we got two tokens */
if (numTokens != 2) {
     fprintf(stderr, "\nError: Invalid 'calibrationUnits'\n");
     exit();
     }

/* Allocate memory and save calibrationUnits into buffer */
htrFile->calibrationUnits =
     (char *)malloc((strlen(token[1])+1)*sizeof(char));
strcpy(htrFile->calibrationUnits, token[1]);

/* rotationUnits */
/* Get a line of text */
found = 0;
value = 1;
while (!found && value) {
     value = fgets(textLine, MAXLINE, htrFileHandle);
```

```
        /* Skip if comment or newline */
        if (textLine[0] == '\n' !! textLine[0] == '#')
            found = 0;
        else
            if (value)
                found = 1;
    }
if (!found) {
    fprintf(stderr, "\nError: Premature end of file\n");
    exit();
    }
/* Parse line */
numTokens = 0;
token[numTokens++] = strtok(textLine, DELIMIT);
while (token[numTokens-1])
    token[numTokens++] = strtok(NULL, DELIMIT);
numTokens -= 1;

/* Make sure we got two tokens */
if (numTokens != 2) {
    fprintf(stderr, "\nError: Invalid 'rotationUnits'\n");
    exit();
    }

/* Allocate memory and save rotationUnits into buffer */
htrFile->rotationUnits =
    (char *)malloc((strlen(token[1])+1)*sizeof(char));
strcpy(htrFile->rotationUnits, token[1]);

/* globalAxisofGravity */
/* Get a line of text */
found = 0;
value = 1;
while (!found && value) {
    value = fgets(textLine, MAXLINE, htrFileHandle);

    /* Skip if comment or newline */
    if (textLine[0] == '\n' !! textLine[0] == '#')
        found = 0;
    else
        if (value)
                found = 1;
    }
```

```
    if (!found) {
        fprintf(stderr, "\nError: Premature end of file\n");
        exit();
        }

    /* Parse line */
    numTokens = 0;
    token[numTokens++] = strtok(textLine, DELIMIT);
    while (token[numTokens-1])
        token[numTokens++] = strtok(NULL, DELIMIT);
    numTokens -= 1;

    /* Make sure we got two tokens */
    if (numTokens != 2) {
        fprintf(stderr, "\nError: Invalid 'globalAxisofGravity'\n");
        exit();
        }

    /* Allocate memory and save globalAxisofGravity into buffer */
    htrFile->globalAxisofGravity =
        (char *)malloc((strlen(token[1])+1)*sizeof(char));
    strcpy(htrFile->globalAxisofGravity, token[1]);

    /* boneLengthAxis */
    /* Get a line of text */
    found = 0;
    value = 1;
    while (!found && value) {
        value = fgets(textLine, MAXLINE, htrFileHandle);

        /* Skip if comment or newline */
        if (textLine[0] == '\n' !! textLine[0] == '#')
            found = 0;
        else
            if (value)
                found = 1;
        }
    if (!found) {
        fprintf(stderr, "\nError: Premature end of file\n");
        exit();
        }

    /* Parse line */
    numTokens = 0;
    token[numTokens++] = strtok(textLine, DELIMIT);
```

```c
while (token[numTokens-1])
    token[numTokens++] = strtok(NULL, DELIMIT);
numTokens -= 1;

/* Make sure we got two tokens */
if (numTokens != 2) {
    fprintf(stderr, "\nError: Invalid 'boneLengthAxis'\n");
    exit();
    }

/* Allocate memory and save boneLengthAxis into buffer */
htrFile->boneLengthAxis =
    (char *)malloc((strlen(token[1])+1)*sizeof(char));
strcpy(htrFile->boneLengthAxis, token[1]);

/* scaleFactor */
/* Get a line of text */
found = 0;
value = 1;
while (!found && value) {
    value = fgets(textLine, MAXLINE, htrFileHandle);

    /* Skip if comment or newline */
    if (textLine[0] == '\n' !! textLine[0] == '#')
        found = 0;
    else
        if (value)
            found = 1;
    }
if (!found) {
    fprintf(stderr, "\nError: Premature end of file\n");
    exit();
    }

/* Parse line */
numTokens = 0;
token[numTokens++] = strtok(textLine, DELIMIT);
while (token[numTokens-1])
    token[numTokens++] = strtok(NULL, DELIMIT);
numTokens -= 1;

/* Make sure we got two tokens */
if (numTokens != 2) {
    fprintf(stderr, "\nError: Invalid 'scaleFactor'\n");
    exit();
    }
```

```
/* Save scaleFactor into buffer */
htrFile->scaleFactor = atof(token[1]);
```

Now we proceed to load the SegmentNames&Hierarchy section into the buffer. The next step after finding the section is to allocate memory for the branch that will hold this data. We can do this now because we already have loaded the number of segments that we need to process.

```
/* Find the SegmentNames&Hierarchy section */
found = 0;
while (!found && fgets(textLine, MAXLINE, htrFileHandle)) {
     if (strncmp("[SegmentNames&Hierarchy]", textLine,
         strlen("[SegmentNames&Hierarchy]")) == 0)
     found = 1;
     }
if (!found) {
     fprintf(stderr,
         "\nError: Unable to find 'SegmentNames&Hierarchy' \n");
     exit();
     }

/* Allocate memory based on number of segments */
htrFile->childParent = (struct htrSegmentHierarchy *)
     malloc(htrFile->numSegments *
     sizeof(struct htrSegmentHierarchy));

/* Start reading SegmentNames&Hierarchy data */
for (i=0; i < htrFile->numSegments; i++) {

     /* Get a line of text */
     found = 0;
     value = 1;
     while (!found && value) {
         value = fgets(textLine, MAXLINE, htrFileHandle);

         /* Skip if comment or newline */
         if (textLine[0] == '\n' !! textLine[0] == '#')
             found = 0;
         else
             if (value)
                 found = 1;
         }
     if (!found) {
         fprintf(stderr, "\nError: Premature end of file\n");
```

```
        exit();
        }

/* Parse line */
numTokens = 0;
token[numTokens++] = strtok(textLine, DELIMIT);
while (token[numTokens-1])
    token[numTokens++] = strtok(NULL, DELIMIT);
numTokens -= 1;

/* Make sure we got two tokens */
if (numTokens != 2) {
    fprintf(stderr, "\nError: Invalid hierarchy\n");
    exit();
    }

/* Allocate memory and save hierarchy pair into buffer */
htrFile->childParent[i].child =
    (char *)malloc((strlen(token[0])+1)*sizeof(char));
strcpy(htrFile->childParent[i].child, token[0]);
htrFile->childParent[i].parent =
    (char *)malloc((strlen(token[1])+1)*sizeof(char));
strcpy(htrFile->childParent[i].parent, token[1]);
}
```

We continue with the BasePosition section. We are now looking for eight tokens per line that represent the segment name, all six transformations, and the bone length.

```
/* Find the BasePosition section */
found = 0;
while (!found && fgets(textLine, MAXLINE, htrFileHandle)) {
    if (strncmp("[BasePosition]", textLine,
        strlen("[BasePosition]")) == 0)
    found = 1;
    }
if (!found) {
    fprintf(stderr,
        "\nError: Unable to find 'BasePosition' \n");
    exit();
    }

/* Allocate memory based on number of segments */
htrFile->basePosition = (struct htrBasePosition *)
    malloc(htrFile->numSegments *
```

```
          sizeof(struct htrBasePosition));

/* Start reading BasePosition data */
for (i=0; i < htrFile->numSegments; i++) {

     /* Get a line of text */
     found = 0;
     value = 1;
     while (!found && value) {
          value = fgets(textLine, MAXLINE, htrFileHandle);

          /* Skip if comment or newline */
          if (textLine[0] == '\n' !! textLine[0] == '#')
               found = 0;
          else
               if (value)
                    found = 1;
          }
     if (!found) {
          fprintf(stderr, "\nError: Premature end of file\n");
          exit();
          }

     /* Parse line */
     numTokens = 0;
     token[numTokens++] = strtok(textLine, DELIMIT);
     while (token[numTokens-1])
          token[numTokens++] = strtok(NULL, DELIMIT);
     numTokens -= 1;

     /* Make sure we got eight tokens */
     if (numTokens != 8) {
          fprintf(stderr, "\nError: Invalid base position\n");
          exit();
          }

     /* Allocate space and save Baseposition line into buffer */
     htrFile->basePosition[i].name =
          (char *)malloc((strlen(token[0])+1)*sizeof(char));
     strcpy(htrFile->basePosition[i].name, token[0]);
     htrFile->basePosition[i].tx = atof(token[1]);
     htrFile->basePosition[i].ty = atof(token[2]);
     htrFile->basePosition[i].tz = atof(token[3]);
     htrFile->basePosition[i].rx = atof(token[4]);
```

```
    htrFile->basePosition[i].ry = atof(token[5]);
    htrFile->basePosition[i].rz = atof(token[6]);
    htrFile->basePosition[i].boneLength = atof(token[7]);
    }
```

The last step in loading the .htr file is the processing of the actual segment data. It also consists of eight tokens, but there is one set of data per frame for each segment. We must allocate space for htrFile->segmentData based on the number of segments and for htrFile->segmentData->frame based on the number of frames.

```
/* Process SegmentData section */
/* Allocate memory based on number of segments */
htrFile->segmentData = (struct htrSegmentData *)
     malloc(htrFile->numSegments *
     sizeof(struct htrSegmentData));

/* Start reading SegmentData data */
for (i=0; i < htrFile->numSegments; i++) {

     /* Get a line of text */
     found = 0;
     value = 1;
     while (!found && value) {
          value = fgets(textLine, MAXLINE, htrFileHandle);

          /* Skip if comment or newline */
          if (textLine[0] == '\n' !! textLine[0] == '#')
               found = 0;
          else
               if (value)
                    found = 1;
          }
     if (!found) {
          fprintf(stderr, "\nError: Premature end of file\n");
          exit();
          }

     /* Look for segment name */
     if (genStr = strrchr(textLine, ']'))
          genStr[0] = '\0';

     /* Allocate space for segment name and save w/o brackets */
     htrFile->segmentData[i].segmentName = (char *)
```

```
            malloc((strlen(textLine)-1) * sizeof(char));
    strcpy(htrFile->segmentData[i].segmentName, textLine+1);

    /* Allocate space for frame data based on number of frames */
    htrFile->segmentData[i].frame = (struct htrFrame *)
        malloc(htrFile->numFrames * sizeof(struct htrFrame));

    /* Start gathering the segment's data */
    for (j=0; j < htrFile->numFrames; j++) {

        /* Get a line of text */
        found = 0;
        value = 1;
        while (!found && value) {
            value = fgets(textLine, MAXLINE, htrFileHandle);

            /* Skip if comment or newline */
            if (textLine[0] == '\n' !! textLine[0] == '#')
                found = 0;
            else
                if (value)
                    found = 1;
        }
        if (!found) {
            fprintf(stderr, "\nError: Premature end of file\n");
            exit();
        }

        /* Parse line */
        numTokens = 0;
        token[numTokens++] = strtok(textLine, DELIMIT);
        while (token[numTokens-1])
            token[numTokens++] = strtok(NULL, DELIMIT);
        numTokens -= 1;

        /* Make sure we got eight tokens */
        if (numTokens != 8) {
            fprintf(stderr, "\nError: Invalid frame data\n");
            exit();
        }

        /* Save data line into buffer */
        htrFile->segmentData[i].frame[j].frameNo = atoi(token[0]);
        htrFile->segmentData[i].frame[j].tx = atof(token[1]);
        htrFile->segmentData[i].frame[j].ty = atof(token[2]);
        htrFile->segmentData[i].frame[j].tz = atof(token[3]);
```

```
            htrFile->segmentData[i].frame[j].rx = atof(token[4]);
            htrFile->segmentData[i].frame[j].ry = atof(token[5]);
            htrFile->segmentData[i].frame[j].rz = atof(token[6]);
            htrFile->segmentData[i].frame[j].SF = atof(token[7]);
            }
    }

/* Close .htr file */
fclose(htrFileHandle);
```

All the .htr's file data has now been loaded into memory. At this point, we will start porting the data into the Acclaim format buffer. One could write the data straight into the .asf and .amc files, but moving it first into the buffer will help illustrate this operation in case you decide to write a converter from Acclaim to any other format in the future. If you end up writing a more complicated application in which you can port data between several formats, you could perhaps have a different kind of generic buffer that could save data from any of the file formats. This buffer could be designed in a way that would facilitate other operations as well.

```
/* Start writing data into Acclaim buffer */

/* Allocate space and write version number */
acclaimFile->version = (char *)
      malloc((strlen("1.10")) * sizeof(char));
strcpy(acclaimFile->version, "1.10");

/* Get .htr file name without extension to use as skeleton name */
strcpy(textLine, htrFileName);
if (genStr = strrchr(textLine, '.'))
      genStr[0] = '\0';

/* Allocate space and write skeleton name */
/* You can use any user-defined name here */
acclaimFile->name = (char *)
      malloc((strlen(textLine)) * sizeof(char));
strcpy(acclaimFile->name, textLine);

/* Write unitsMass default value since it is not included in .htr */
acclaimFile->unitsMass = 1.0;

/* Write unitsLength from .htr scaleFactor */
acclaimFile->unitsLength = htrFile->scaleFactor;

/* Write unitsAngle based on .htr rotationUnits */
if (htrFile->rotationUnits[0] == 'R' ||
```

```
        htrFile->rotationUnits[0] == 'r')
        strcpy(acclaimFile->unitsAngle, "rad");
else
        strcpy(acclaimFile->unitsAngle, "deg");

/* Allocate space and write notes as needed */
strcpy(textLine, "Created from htr data");
acclaimFile->documentation = (char *)
        malloc((strlen(textLine)) * sizeof(char));
strcpy(acclaimFile->documentation, textLine);
```

Now let's write the :root section. The order of transformations in the .htr file always includes translations first and then rotations, followed by scale. Because of this, we will assume all translations occur before all other transformations, and thus we will include code only to process different rotation arrangements. We also save a predefined rotation-order value in htrRotOrder that we will use later, since the .htr file uses a single order of rotations across the board (unlike the Acclaim format, in which each segment can have a different one).

```
/* We now write the root's xform order and axis        */
/* from eulerRotationOrder. We assume translations     */
/* first because .htr always assumes translations first */
if (strcmp(htrFile->eulerRotationOrder, "XYZ")) {
        strcpy(acclaimFile->rootOrder, "tx ty tz rx ry rz");
        strcpy(acclaimFile->rootAxis, "xyz");
        htrRotOrder = XYZ;
        }
else
        if (strcmp(htrFile->eulerRotationOrder, "XZY")) {
            strcpy(acclaimFile->rootOrder, "tx ty tz rx rz ry");
            strcpy(acclaimFile->rootAxis, "xzy");
            htrRotOrder = XZY;
            }
        else
            if (strcmp(htrFile->eulerRotationOrder, "ZXY")) {
                strcpy(acclaimFile->rootOrder, "tx ty tz rz rx ry");
                strcpy(acclaimFile->rootAxis, "zxy");
                htrRotOrder = ZXY;
                }
            else
                if (strcmp(htrFile->eulerRotationOrder, "ZYX")) {
                    strcpy(acclaimFile->rootOrder,
                        "tx ty tz rz ry rx");
                    strcpy(acclaimFile->rootAxis, "zyx");
```

```
                        htrRotOrder = ZYX;
                        }
                else
                    if (strcmp(htrFile->eulerRotationOrder, "YXZ")){
                        strcpy(acclaimFile->rootOrder,
                            "tx ty tz ry rx rz");
                        strcpy(acclaimFile->rootAxis, "yxz");
                        htrRotOrder = YXZ;
                        }
                    else
                        if (strcmp(htrFile->eulerRotationOrder, "YZX"))
                            {
                            strcpy(acclaimFile->rootOrder,
                                "tx ty tz ry rz rx");
                            strcpy(acclaimFile->rootAxis, "yzx");
                            htrRotOrder = YZX;
                            }
```

The .htr file uses an actual segment as the parent of all the hierarchies. In the Acclaim format, we will move the hierarchy one step down, leaving the .htr's parent node as a child of the root node; the root node is left at the origin at all times. This is very useful because you can use the root to add a transformation offset to the whole tree if desired. One could also do this at the animation software level by adding a parent node, but if you are dealing with a great number of motions, it is better to offset all the motion data files.

```
/* Assume by default that the root bone is the        */
/* parent of all hierarchy in the .htr file and that it */
/* is located at the origin                           */
acclaimFile->rootPosition[0] = 0.0;
acclaimFile->rootPosition[1] = 0.0;
acclaimFile->rootPosition[2] = 0.0;
acclaimFile->rootOrientation[0] = 0.0;
acclaimFile->rootOrientation[1] = 0.0;
acclaimFile->rootOrientation[2] = 0.0;
```

Next, we start saving the bonedata section. We assume that all segments are initially located at the origin and that the length axis is pointing in the globalAxis-ofGravity direction. Some variation in this section can exist between animation software packages because not all of them use this assumption for the initial position of bones. A more elaborate translator should include switches to deal with these software peculiarities.

```
/* Allocate memory for boned ata based on number of segments */
acclaimFile->boneData = (struct acclaimBoneData *)
    malloc(htrFile->numSegments * sizeof(struct acclaimBoneData));
```

```
/* Start writing bone data based on base position section */
for (i=0; i < htrFile->numSegments; i++) {

        /* Use i for id # */
        acclaimFile->boneData[i].id = i+1;

        /* Bone name */
        acclaimFile->boneData[i].name = (char *)
            malloc((strlen(htrFile->basePosition[i].name)) *
            sizeof(char));
        strcpy(acclaimFile->boneData.name,
            htrFile->basePosition[i].name);

        /* Write direction vector using globalAxisofGravity   */
        /* The .htr assumption is that all bones' initial      */
        /* length vector is pointing toward the up axis        */
        acclaimFile->boneData[i].direction[0] = 0.0;
        acclaimFile->boneData[i].direction[1] = 0.0;
        acclaimFile->boneData[i].direction[2] = 0.0;
        switch (htrFile->globalAxisofGravity[0])
        {
        case 'X':
            acclaimFile->boneData[i].direction[0] = 1.0;
            break;
        case 'Y':
            acclaimFile->boneData[i].direction[1] = 1.0;
            break;
        case 'Z':
            acclaimFile->boneData[i].direction[2] = 1.0;
            break;
        }

        /* Segment length */
        acclaimFile->boneData[i].length =
            htrFile->basePosition[i].boneLength;
```

Even though the Acclaim format has the ability to select which transformations are available per segment, we have to include them all because the .htr file includes all seven transformations for each of the segments. The limits are also left open because these are not supported by the .htr format.

```
        /* process axis and dof order */
        /* using htrRotBone           */
        switch(htrRotBone)
```

```
{
case XYZ:
     acclaimFile->boneData[i].axis[0] =
          htrFile->basePosition[i].rx;
     acclaimFile->boneData[i].axis[1] =
          htrFile->basePosition[i].ry;
     acclaimFile->boneData[i].axis[2] =
          htrFile->basePosition[i].rz;
     strcpy(acclaimFile->boneData[i].axisOrder, "xyz");
     strcpy(acclaimFile->boneData[i].dof,
          "tx ty tz rx ry rz l");
     break;
case XZY:
     acclaimFile->boneData[i].axis[0] =
          htrFile->basePosition[i].rx;
     acclaimFile->boneData[i].axis[1] =
          htrFile->basePosition[i].rz;
     acclaimFile->boneData[i].axis[2] =
          htrFile->basePosition[i].ry;
     strcpy(acclaimFile->boneData[i].axisOrder, "xzy");
     strcpy(acclaimFile->boneData[i].dof,
          "tx ty tz rx rz ry l");
     break;
case YXZ:
     acclaimFile->boneData[i].axis[0] =
          htrFile->basePosition[i].ry;
     acclaimFile->boneData[i].axis[1] =
          htrFile->basePosition[i].rx;
     acclaimFile->boneData[i].axis[2] =
          htrFile->basePosition[i].rz;
     strcpy(acclaimFile->boneData[i].axisOrder, "yxz");
     strcpy(acclaimFile->boneData[i].dof,
          "tx ty tz ry rx rz l");
     break;
case YZX:
     acclaimFile->boneData[i].axis[0] =
          htrFile->basePosition[i].ry;
     acclaimFile->boneData[i].axis[1] =
          htrFile->basePosition[i].rz;
     acclaimFile->boneData[i].axis[2] =
          htrFile->basePosition[i].rx;
     strcpy(acclaimFile->boneData[i].axisOrder, "yzx");
     strcpy(acclaimFile->boneData[i].dof,
          "tx ty tz ry rz rx l");
```

```
            break;
        case ZXY:
            acclaimFile->boneData[i].axis[0] =
                htrFile->basePosition[i].rz;
            acclaimFile->boneData[i].axis[1] =
                htrFile->basePosition[i].rx;
            acclaimFile->boneData[i].axis[2] =
                htrFile->basePosition[i].ry;
            strcpy(acclaimFile->boneData[i].axisOrder, "zxy");
            strcpy(acclaimFile->boneData[i].dof,
                "tx ty tz rz rx ry l");
            break;
        case ZYX:
            acclaimFile->boneData[i].axis[0] =
                htrFile->basePosition[i].rz;
            acclaimFile->boneData[i].axis[1] =
                htrFile->basePosition[i].ry;
            acclaimFile->boneData[i].axis[2] =
                htrFile->basePosition[i].rx;
            strcpy(acclaimFile->boneData[i].axisOrder, "zyx");
            strcpy(acclaimFile->boneData[i].dof,
                "tx ty tz rz ry rx l");
            break;
    }

    /* Because all data is included in .htr file, dof# = 7 */
    acclaimFile->bonedata[i].dofNumber = 7;

    /* Allocate space for 7 limits */
    acclaimFile->boneData[i].limits = (struct acclaimBoneLimits *)
        malloc(acclaimFile->boneData[i].dofNumber *
        sizeof(struct acclaimBoneLimits));

    /* All limits in this particular conversion are open */
    for (j=0; j < htrFile->numFrames; j++) {
        acclaimFile->boneData[i].limits[j].minMax[0] = 0;
        acclaimFile->boneData[i].limits[j].minMax[1] = 0;
        acclaimFile->boneData[i].limits[j].infinity[0] = 1;
        acclaimFile->boneData[i].limits[j].infinity[1] = 1;
        }

    /* bodyMass and cofMass are not used by .htr file */
    acclaimFile->boneData[i].bodyMass = 1.0;
    acclaimFile->boneData[i].cofMass = 1.0;
    }
```

The hierarchy section in the .asf file is quite different from that in the .htr file. The .asf file lists a parent first, followed by all its children in the same line, whereas the .htr file lists each child first, followed by its parent. The number of lines in the hierarchy section of the .htr file is equal to the number of segments, whereas in the .asf file, it is equal to the number of nodes that have children (not counting the root node). Thus, before starting to save the hierarchy in the Acclaim buffer, we must find out how many segments have children.

```
/* Start processing hierarchy */
/* Find out how many bones have children */
numParents = 0;
for (i=0; i < htrFile->numSegments; i++) {
    for (j=0; j < htrFile->numSegments; j++) {
        if (strcmp(htrFile->childParent[i].child,
            htrFile->childParent[j].parent)) {
            numParents++;
            j = htrFile->numSegments;
            }
        }
    }

/* Allocate space for hierarchy based on number of parents */
acclaimFile->hierarchy = (struct acclaimHierarchy *)
    malloc((numParents + 1) * sizeof(struct acclaimHierarchy));

/* Start reading .htr file's hierarchy section */
/* Allocate space and save root */
acclaimFile->hierarchy[0].parent = (char *)
    malloc((strlen("root")) * sizeof(char));
strcpy(acclaimFile->hierarchy[0].parent, "root");

/* Find nodes with GLOBAL parent */
for (i=0; i < htrFile->numSegments; i++) {

    /* If GLOBAL is found, add child to list */
    if (strcmp(htrFile->childParent[i].parent, "GLOBAL")) {
        strcat(acclaimFile->hierarchy[0].children,
            htrFile->childParent[i].child);

        /* Add a blank space after child string */
        acclaimFile->hierarchy[0].children[strlen(
            acclaimFile->hierarchy[0].children)] = ' ';
        }
    }
```

```c
/* Remove last space */
acclaimFile->hierarchy[0].children[strlen(
    acclaimFile->hierarchy[0].children)-1] = '\0';

/* Process rest of parent and child nodes */
k = 1;
for (i=0; i < htrFile->numSegments; i++) {
    found = 0;
    for (j=0; j < htrFile->numSegments; j++) {

        /* Find all children of node i */
        if (strcmp(htrFile->childParent[i].child,
            htrFile->childParent[j].parent)) {

            /* If first one, allocate space and save parent */
            if (!found) {
                acclaimFile->hierarchy[k].parent = (char *)
                        malloc((strlen(htrFile->childParent[j].parent))
                        * sizeof(char));
                strcpy(acclaimFile->hierarchy[k].parent,
                htrFile->childParent[j].parent);
                found = 1;
            }

            /* Cat child's name */
            strcat(acclaimFile->hierarchy[k].children,
                htrFile->childParent[j].child);

            /* Add a blank space after child string */
            acclaimFile->hierarchy[k].children[strlen(
                acclaimFile->hierarchy[k].children)] = ' ';
        }
    }

    /* Remove last space */
    if (found) {
        acclaimFile->hierarchy[k].children[strlen(
            acclaimFile->hierarchy[k].children)-1] = '\0';

        /* Update parent number counter */
        k++;
    }
}
```

```
/* I skip the skin section as it is not  */
/* supported by .htr or most animation   */
/* packages                              */
```

Now start saving the data stream. We will not worry yet about the order of transformations. These will be dealt with when we write the .amc file. The l channel in the .amc data is not the same as the SF channel in the .htr file and it must be converted before saving. SF is a scaling factor or a multiplier for the initial segment length, whereas l is a translation. This means that an SF value of 1 is equivalent to an l value of 0. To convert the scaling factor to a translation, we multiply the initial length by the scaling factor and then subtract the segment length, obtaining the difference in length between the initial length and the length for the frame in question.

```
/* Process motion data stream */
/* Allocate space for data stream based on number of frames */
acclaimFile->frameData = (struct acclaimFrameData *)
    malloc(htrFile->numFrames * sizeof(struct acclaimFrameData));

/* Start processing frames */
for (i=0; i < htrFile->numFrames; i++) {

    /* Write frame number (start at 1 by default) */
    acclaimFile->frameData[i].frame = i+1;

    /* Allocate space for segment data, including root */
    acclaimFile->frameData[i].motionData =
        (struct acclaimMotionData *)
        malloc((htrFile->numSegments+1) *
        sizeof(struct acclaimMotionData));

    /* Write root segment (default at origin) */
    acclaimFile->frameData[i].motionData[0].tx = 0;
    acclaimFile->frameData[i].motionData[0].ty = 0;
    acclaimFile->frameData[i].motionData[0].tz = 0;
    acclaimFile->frameData[i].motionData[0].rx = 0;
    acclaimFile->frameData[i].motionData[0].ry = 0;
    acclaimFile->frameData[i].motionData[0].rz = 0;
    acclaimFile->frameData[i].motionData[0].l = 0;

    /* Allocate memory and write segment name */
    acclaimFile->frameData[i].motionData[0].segment = (char *)
        malloc(strlen("root") * sizeof(char));
    strcpy(acclaimFile->frameData[i].motionData[0].segment,
        "root");
```

```
        /* Read other segment data for this frame */
        for (j=1; j <= htrFile->numSegments; j++) {

            /* Write segment data */
            acclaimFile->frameData[i].motionData[j].tx =
                htrFile->segmentData[j-1].frame[i].tx;
            acclaimFile->frameData[i].motionData[j].ty =
                htrFile->segmentData[j-1].frame[i].ty;
            acclaimFile->frameData[i].motionData[j].tz =
                htrFile->segmentData[j-1].frame[i].tz;
            acclaimFile->frameData[i].motionData[j].rx =
                htrFile->segmentData[j-1].frame[i].rx;
            acclaimFile->frameData[i].motionData[j].ry =
                htrFile->segmentData[j-1].frame[i].ry;
            acclaimFile->frameData[i].motionData[j].rz =
                htrFile->segmentData[j-1].frame[i].rz;

            /* Calculate bone translation deviation using */
            /* .htr's SF and bone length                  */
            acclaimFile->frameData[i].motionData[j].l =
                acclaimFile->boneData[j-1].length -
                (htrFile->segmentData[j-1].frame[i].SF *
                acclaimFile->boneData[j-1].length);

            /* Allocate memory and write segment name */
            acclaimFile->frameData[i].motionData[j].segment = (char *)
                malloc(strlen(htrFile->segmentData[j-1].segmentName) *
                sizeof(char));
            strcpy(acclaimFile->frameData[i].motionData[j].segment,
                htrFile->segmentData[j-1].segmentName);
        }
    }

/* Save number of segments and frames for later use */
numBones = htrFile->numSegments;
numFrames = htrFile->numFrames;
```

We have now saved all the data in the .htr file into the Acclaim buffer. The next step is to write the actual .asf and .amc files. The number of segments was saved in a variable named numBones and the number of frames in a variable named numFrames because the Acclaim format does not include fields for these values.

```
/* Open .asf file */
asfFileHandle = fopen(asfFileName, "w");
if (!asfFileHandle) {
```

```
        fprintf(stderr,"\nError: Unable to open %s \n", asfFileName);
        exit();
        }

/* version */
fprintf(asfFileHandle, ":version %s\n", acclaimFile->version);

/* name */
fprintf(asfFileHandle, ":name %s\n", acclaimFile->name);

/* units section */
fprintf(asfFileHandle, " mass %f\n", acclaimFile->unitsMass);
fprintf(asfFileHandle, " length %f\n", acclaimFile->unitsLength);
fprintf(asfFileHandle, " angle %s\n", acclaimFile->unitsAngle);

/* documentation */
fprintf(asfFileHandle, ":documentation\n");
fprintf(asfFileHandle,      "%s\n", acclaimFile->documentation);

/* doot section */
fprintf(asfFileHandle, ":root\n");
fprintf(asfFileHandle, " order %s\n", acclaimFile->rootOrder);
fprintf(asfFileHandle, " axis %s\n", acclaimFile->rootAxis);
fprintf(asfFileHandle, " position %d %d %d\n",
     acclaimFile->rootPosition[0],
     acclaimFile->rootPosition[1],
     acclaimFile->rootPosition[2]);
fprintf(asfFileHandle, " orientation %d %d %d\n",
     acclaimFile->rootOrientation[0],
     acclaimFile->rootOrientation[1],
     acclaimFile->rootOrientation[2]);

/* bonedata section */
fprintf(asfFileHandle,":bonedata\n");
for (i=0; i < numBones; i++) {
     fprintf(asfFileHandle, " begin\n");
     fprintf(asfFileHandle, "     id %d\n",
         acclaimFile->boneData[i].id);
     fprintf(asfFileHandle, "     name %s\n",
         acclaimFile->boneData[i].name);
     fprintf(asfFileHandle, "     direction %f %f %f\n",
         acclaimFile->boneData[i].direction[0],
         acclaimFile->boneData[i].direction[1],
         acclaimFile->boneData[i].direction[2]);
```

```
     fprintf(asfFileHandle, "          length %d\n",
         acclaimFile->boneData[i].length);
     fprintf(asfFileHandle, "     axis %d %d %d %s\n",
         acclaimFile->boneData[i].axis[0],
         acclaimFile->boneData[i].axis[1],
         acclaimFile->boneData[i].axis[2],
         acclaimFile->boneData[i].axisOrder);
     fprintf(asfFileHandle, "     dof %s\n",
         acclaimFile->boneData[i].dof);

     /* Write limits */
     fprintf(asfFileHandle, "     limits");
     for (j=0; j < acclaimFile->bonedata[i].dofNumber; j++) {
         if (acclaimFile->bonedata[i].limits.infinity[0])
             fprintf(asfFileHandle,"(-inf");
         else
             fprintf(asfFileHandle,"(%d",
                 acclaimFile->boneData[i].limits.minMax[0]);
         if (acclaimFile->bonedata[i].limits.infinity[1])
             fprintf(asfFileHandle," inf)\n");
         else
             fprintf(asfFileHandle," %d)\n",
                 acclaimFile->boneData[i].limits.minMax[1]);
     }
     fprintf(asfFileHandle," end\n");
     }

/* hierarchy */
fprintf(asfFileHandle, ":hierarchy\n");
fprintf(asfFileHandle," begin\n");
for (i=0; i < numParents; i++)
     fprintf(asfFileHandle," %s %s\n",
         acclaimFile->hierarchy[i].parent,
         acclaimFile->hierarchy[i].children);

/* If there were skin file data, you would write it at this point */

/* Close .asf file */
fclose(asfFileHandle);
```

As we write the motion data, we must deal with the order of transformations per segment. We will use the dof field to determine the order per segment.

```
/* Frame data */
/* Open .amc file */
```

```
amcFileHandle = fopen(amcFileName, "w");
if (!amcFileHandle) {
    fprintf(stderr, "\nError: Unable to open %s \n", amcFileName);
    exit();
    }

/* File type */
fprintf(amcFileHandle, ":FULLY-SPECIFIED\n");
if (strcmp(acclaimFile->unitsAngle, "deg"))
    fprintf(amcFileHandle, ":DEGREES\n");
else
    fprintf(amcFileHandle, ":RADIANS\n");

/* Start frame loop */
for (i=0; i < numFrames; i++) {

    /* Frame number */
    fprintf(amcFileHandle, %d\n",
        acclaimFile->frameData[i].frame);

    /* Process root (at origin by default) */
    fprintf(amcFileHandle,
        "root 0.0, 0.0, 0.0, 0.0, 0.0, 0.0, 0.0");

    /* Write bone data for this frame */
    for (j=1; j <= numBones; j++) {

        /* Bone name */
        fprintf(amcFileHandle, "%s",
            acclaimFile->frameData[i].motionData[j].segment);

        /* Process dof tokens */
        numTokens = 0;
        token[numTokens++] =
            strtok(acclaimFile->boneData[j-1].dof, DELIMIT);
        while (token[numTokens-1])
            token[numTokens++] = strtok(NULL, DELIMIT);
        numTokens -= 1;

        /* Write data to file in the order defined by dof */
        for (k=0; k < numTokens; k++) {
            switch(token[k][0]) {
                case 'l':
                    fprintf(amcFileHandle, " %d",
```

```
                              acclaimfile->frameData[i].
                              motionData.1);
                    break;
            case 't':
                    switch(token[k][1]) {
                            case 'x':
                            fprintf(amcFileHandle," %d",
                                    acclaimFile->frameData[i].
                                    motionData[j].tx);
                            break;
                    case 'y':
                            fprintf(amcFileHandle," %d",
                                    acclaimFile->frameData[i].
                                    motionData[j].ty);
                            break;
                    case 'z':
                            fprintf(amcFileHandle," %d",
                                    acclaimFile->frameData[i].
                                    motionData[j].tz);
                            break;
                    }
        case 'r':
            switch(token[k][1]) {
                    case 'x':
                            fprintf(amcFileHandle," %d",
                                    acclaimFile->frameData[i].
                                    motionData[j].rx);
                            break;
                    case 'y':
                            fprintf(amcFileHandle," %d",
                                    acclaimFile->frameData[i].
                                    motionData[j].ry);
                            break;
                    case 'z':
                            fprintf(amcFileHandle," %d",
                                    acclaimFile->frameData[i].
                                    motionData[j].rz);
                            break;
                    }
            }
        }
```

```
        fprintf(amcFileHandle, "\n");
        }
    }

/* Close .amc file */
fclose(amcFileHandle);

/* Clean memory here if you need to */
```

Animating Substances

Animating Facial Features

5

Rick Parent

CHAPTER CONTENTS

Realistic facial animation is one of the most difficult tasks that a computer animator can be asked to do. Human faces are familiar to us all. Facial motion adheres to an underlying, well-defined structure but is idiosyncratic. A face has a single mechanical articulator but has a flexible covering capable of subtle expression and rapid, complex, lip movements during speech.

The face is an important component in modeling a figure because it is the main instrument for communication and for defining a figure's mood and personality. Animation of speech is especially demanding because of the requirement for audio synchronization (and, therefore, is often referred to as *lip-sync animation*). In addition, a good facial model should be capable of geometrically representing a specific person (called *conformation* by Parke [26], *static* by others, e.g. [30]).

Facial models can be used for cartooning, for realistic character animation, for telecommunications to reduce bandwidth, and for human-computer interaction (HCI). In cartooning, facial animation has to be able to convey expression and personality, often exaggerated. In realistic character animation, the geometry and movement of the face must adhere to the constraints of realistic human anatomy. Telecommunications and HCI have the added requirement that the facial model and motion must be computationally efficient. In some applications, the model must correspond closely to a specific target individual.

In addition to the issues addressed by other animation tasks, facial animation often has the constraint of precise timing with respect to an audio track during lip-synching and some expressions. Despite its name, lip-synching involves more than just the lips; the rigid articulation of the jaw and the muscle deformation of the tongue must also be considered.

5.1 THE HUMAN FACE

5.1.1 Anatomic Structure

The human face has an underlying skeletal structure and one main skeletal articulatory component – the jaw. In addition to the jaw, the other rigid articulatory components are the eyes.

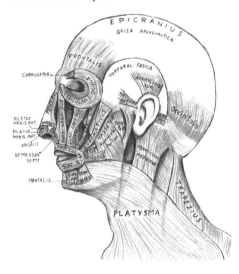

FIGURE 5.1

Muscles of the face and head [32] (Image courtesy of Arun Somasundaram).

The surface of the skull is covered with muscles, most of which (at least indirectly) connect areas of the skin to positions on the skull. These muscles tug on the skin to create movement, often recognizable as expressions. Features of the skin include eyelids, mouth, and eyebrows. The skin has various expressive wrinkles such as forehead and mouth.

As with the rest of the body, muscles are the driving force (Fig. 5.1). However, unlike the rest of the body, the muscles mainly move the skin into interesting positions, producing recognizable lip and skin configurations and, in speech, modify the sounds emanating from the labial opening. In particular, the muscles around the mouth are extremely flexible and capable of producing a variety of shapes and subtle movements. A muscle

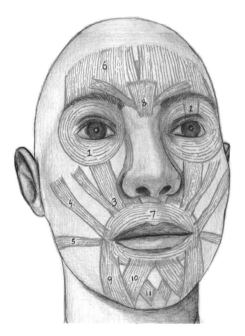

FIGURE 5.2

Muscles of the face that are significant in speech and linguistic facial expressions [32] (Image courtesy of Arun Somasundaram).

of particular importance is the orbicularis oris (muscle number 7 in Fig. 5.2), which wraps around the mouth and is connected to several muscles that are connected to the skull.

5.1.2 The Facial Action Coding System (FACS)

The FACS is the result of research conducted by the psychologists Ekman and Friesen [15] with the objective of deconstructing all facial expressions into a set of basic facial movements. These movements, called action units (AUs), when considered in combinations, can be used to describe all facial expressions.

Forty-six AUs are identified in the study, and they provide a clinical basis from which to build a facial animation system. Examples of AUs are brow lowerer, inner brow raiser, wink, cheek raiser, upper lip raiser, and jaw drop. See Fig. 5.3 for an example of diagrammed AUs. Given the AUs, an animator can build a facial model that is parameterized according to the motions of the AUs. A facial animation system can be built by giving a user access to a set of variables that are in one-to-one correspondence with the AUs. A parametric value controls the amount of the facial motion that results from the associated AU. By setting a variable for each AU, the user can generate all the facial expressions analyzed by Ekman and Friesen. By using the value of the variables to interpolate the degree to which the motion is realized and by interpolating their value over time, the user can then animate the facial model. By combining the AUs in nonstandard ways, the user can also generate many truly strange expressions.

While this work is impressive and is certainly relevant to facial animation, two of its characteristics should be noted before it is used as a basis for such a system. First, the FACS is meant to be descriptive of a static expression, not generative. The FACS is not time based, and facial movements are analyzed only relative to a neutral pose. This means that the AUs were not designed to animate a facial model in all the ways that an animator may want control. Second, the FACS describes facial expressions, not speech. The movements for forming individual phonemes, the basic units of speech, were not specifically incorporated into the system. While the AUs provide a good start for describing the basic motions that must be in a facial animation system, they were never intended for this purpose.

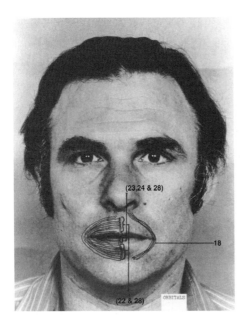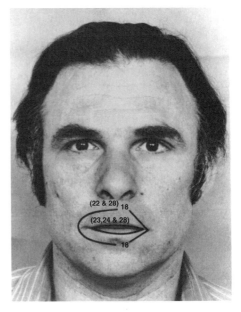

FIGURE 5.3

Three action units of the lower face [15].

5.2 FACIAL MODELS

Depending on the objective of the animation, there are various ways to model the human face. As with all animation, trade-offs include realism and computational complexity.

If a cartoon type of animation is desired, a simple geometric shape for the head (such as a sphere) coupled with the use of animated texture maps often suffices for facial animation. The eyes and mouth can be animated using a series of texture maps applied to a simple head shape (see Fig. 5.4). The nose and ears may be part of the head geometry, or, simpler still, they may be incorporated into the texture map.

Stylized models of the head may also be used that mimic the basic mechanical motions of the human face, using only a pivot jaw and rotating spheres for eyeballs. Eyelids can be skin-colored hemispheres that rotate to enclose the visible portion of the eyeball. The mouth can be a separate geometry positioned on the surface of the face geometry, and it can be animated independently or sequentially replaced in its entirety by a series of mouth shapes to simulate motion of deformable lips (see Fig. 5.5). These approaches are analogous to techniques used in conventional hand-drawn and stop-motion animation.

For more realistic facial animation, more complex facial models are used whose surface geometry more closely corresponds to that of a real face. And the animation of these models is correspondingly more complex. For an excellent in-depth presentation of facial animation, see Parke and Waters [27]. An overview is given here.

FIGURE 5.4

Texture-mapped facial animation from *Getting into Art* (Copyright 1990 David S. Ebert [12]).

The first problem confronting an animator in facial animation is creating the geometry of the facial model to make it suitable for animation. This in itself can be very difficult. Facial animation models vary widely, from simple geometry to anatomy based. Generally, the complexity is dictated by the intended use. When deciding on the construction of the model, important factors are geometry data acquisition method, motion control and corresponding data acquisition method, rendering quality, and motion quality. The first factor concerns the method by which the actual geometry of the subject's or character's head is obtained. The second factor concerns the method by which the data describing changes to the geometry are obtained. The quality of the rendered image with respect to smoothness and surface attributes is the third concern. The final concern is the corresponding quality of the computed motion.

The model can be discussed in terms of its static properties and its dynamic properties. The statics deal with the geometry of the model in its neutral form, while the dynamics deal with the deformation of the geometry of the model during animation. Facial models are either polygonal or higher order. Polygonal models are used most often for their simplicity (e.g. [26,27,34,35]); splines are chosen when a smooth surface is desired.

Polygonal models are relatively easy to create and can be deformed easily. However, the smoothness of the surface is directly related to the complexity of the model, and

FIGURE 5.5

Simple facial model using rigid components for animation (Image courtesy of John Parent).

polygonal models are visually inferior to other methods of modeling the facial surface. Currently, data acquisition methods only sample the surface, producing discrete data, and surface fitting techniques are subsequently applied.

Spline models typically use bicubic, quadrilateral surface patches, such as Bezier or B-spline, to represent the face. While surface patches offer the advantage of low data complexity in comparison to polygonal techniques when generating smooth surfaces, they have several disadvantages when it comes to modeling an object such as the human face. With standard surface patch technology, a rectangular grid of control points is used to model the entire object. As a result, it is difficult to maintain low data complexity while incorporating small details and sharp localized features, because entire rows and/or entire columns of control information must be modified. Thus, a small addition to one local area of the surface to better represent a facial feature means that information has to be added across the entire surface.

Hierarchical B-splines, introduced by Forsey and Bartels [18], are a mechanism by which local detail can be added to a B-spline surface while avoiding the global modifications required by standard B-splines. Finer resolution control points are carefully laid over the coarser surface while continuity is carefully maintained. In this way, local detail can be added to a surface. The organization is hierarchical, so finer and finer detail can be added. The detail is defined relative to the coarser surface so that editing can take place at any level.

5.2.1 Creating a Continuous Surface Model

Creating a model of a human head from scratch is not easy. Not only must the correct shape be generated, but when facial animation is the objective, the geometric elements (vertices, edges) must be placed appropriately so that the motion of the surface can be controlled precisely. If the model is dense in the number of geometric elements used, then the placement becomes less of a concern, but in relatively low-resolution models it can be an issue. Of course, one approach is to use an interactive system and let the user construct the model. This is useful when

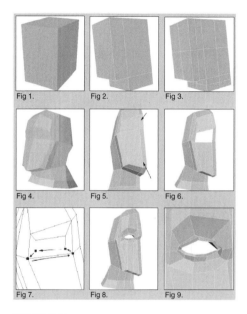

Fig 1.   Fig 2.   Fig 3.

Fig 4.   Fig 5.   Fig 6.

Fig 7.   Fig 8.   Fig 9.

FIGURE 5.6

Early stages in facial modeling using subdivision surfaces [29].

the model to be constructed is a fanciful creature or a caricature or must meet some aesthetic design criteria. While this approach gives an artist the most freedom in creating a model, it requires the most skill. There are three approaches used to construct a model: refining from a low-resolution model, modifying a high-resolution simple shape, and designing the surface out from high-resolution areas.

Subdivision surfaces (e.g. [11]) use a polygonal control mesh that is refined, in the limit, to a smooth surface. The refinement can be terminated at an intermediate resolution, rendered as a polygonal mesh, vertices adjusted, and then refined again. In this manner, the designer can make changes to the general shape of the head at relatively low resolution. Figure 5.6 shows the initial stages of a subdivision-based facial design [29]. Subdivision surfaces have the advantage of being able to create local complexity without global complexity. They provide an easy-to-use, intuitive interface for developing new models, and provisions for discontinuity of arbitrary order can be accommodated [11]. However, they are difficult to interpolate to a specific data set, which makes modeling a specific face problematic.

Alternatively, the designer may start with a relatively high-resolution simple shape such as a sphere. The designer pushes and pulls on the surface to form the general features of the face and refines areas as necessary to form the face [19] (see Fig. 5.7).

Another alternative is to build the surface out from the expressive regions of the face – the mouth and eyes. This approach can be used to ensure that these regions are flexible enough to support the intended animation. See Fig. 5.8 for an example of an initial surface design [31].

Besides the interactive design approach, there are two main methods for creating facial models: digitization using some physical reference and modification of an existing model. The former is useful when the model of a particular person is desired; the latter is useful when animation control is already built into a generic model.

As with any model, a physical sculpture of the desired object can be generated with clay, wood, or plaster and then digitized most often using a mechanical or a magnetic digitizing device. A two-dimensional surface-based coordinate grid can be drawn on the physical model, and the polygons can be digitized on a polygon-by-polygon basis. Postprocessing can identify unique vertices, and a polygonal mesh

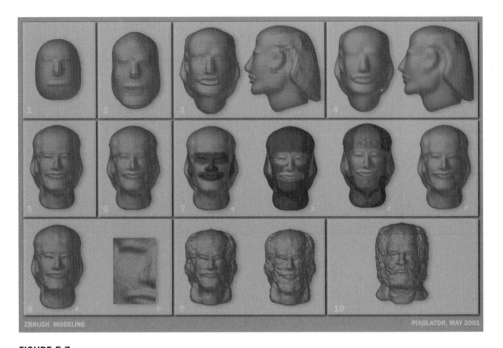

FIGURE 5.7

Facial design by pushing and pulling surface of high-resolution sphere-like shape [19].

can be easily generated. The digitization process can be fairly labor intensive when large numbers of polygons are involved, which makes using an actual person's face a bit problematic. If a model is used, this approach still requires some artistic talent to generate the physical model, but it is easy to implement at a relatively low cost if small mechanical digitizers are used.

Laser scanners use a laser to calculate distance to a model surface and can create very accurate models. They have the advantage of being able to directly digitize a person's face. The scanners sample the surface at regular intervals to create an unorganized set of surface points. The facial model can be constructed in a variety of ways. Polygonal models are most commonly generated. Scanners have the added advantage of being able to capture color information that can be used to generate a texture map. This is particularly important with facial animation: a texture map can often cover flaws in the model and motion. Laser scanners also have drawbacks: they are expensive, bulky, and require a physical model.

Muraki [24] presents a method for fitting a blobby model (implicitly defined surface formed by summed, spherical density functions) to range data by minimizing an energy function that measures the difference between the isosurface and the range data. By splitting primitives and modifying parameters, the user can refine the isosurface to improve the fit.

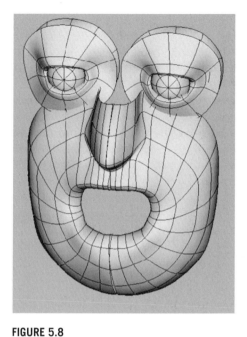

FIGURE 5.8

Facial design by initially defining the eyes and mouth region [31].

Models can also be generated from photographs. This has the advantage of not requiring the presence of the physical model once the photograph has been taken, and it has applications for video conferencing and compression. While most of the photographic approaches modify an existing model by locating feature points, a common method of generating a model from scratch is to take front and side images of a face on which grid lines have been drawn (Fig. 5.9). Point correspondences can be established between the two images either interactively or by locating common features automatically, and the grid in three-space can be reconstructed. Symmetry is usually assumed for the face, so only one side view is needed and only half of the front view is considered.

Modifying an existing model is a popular technique for generating a face model. Of course, someone had to first generate a generic model. But once this

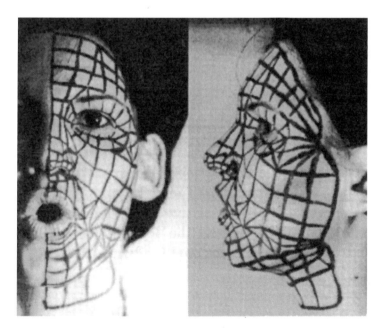

FIGURE 5.9

Photographs from which a face may be digitized [27].

is done, if it is created as a parameterized model and the parameters were well designed, the model can be used to try to match a particular face, to design a face, or to generate a family of faces. In addition, the animation controls can be built into the model so that they require little or no modification of the generic model for particular instances.

One of the most often used approaches to facial animation employs a parameterized model originally created by Parke [25, 26]. The parameters for his model of the human face are divided into two categories: *conformational* and *expressive*. The conformational parameters are those that distinguish one individual's head and face from another's. The expressive parameters are those concerned with animation of an individual's face; these are discussed later. There are 22 conformational parameters in Parke's model. Again, symmetry between the sides of the face is assumed. Five parameters control the shape of the forehead, cheekbone, cheek hollow, chin, and neck. There are 13 scale distances between facial features[1]: head x, y, z; chin to mouth and chin to eye; eye to forehead; eye x and y; widths of the jaw, cheeks, nose bridge, and nostril. Five parameters translate features of the face: chin in x and z; end of nose x and z; eyebrow z. Even these are not enough to generate all possible faces although they can be used to generate a wide variety.

Parke's model was not developed based on any anatomical principles but from the intuitions from artistic renderings of the human face. Facial anthropomorphic statistics and proportions can be used to constrain the facial surface to generate realistic geometries of a human head [10]. Variational techniques can then be used to create realistic facial geometry from a deformed prototype that fits the constraints. This approach is useful for generating heads for a crowd scene or a background character. It may also be useful as a possible starting point for some other character; however, the result will be influenced heavily by the prototype used.

The MPEG-4 standard proposes tools for efficient encoding of multimedia scenes. It includes a set of facial definition parameters (FDPs) [17] that are devoted mainly to facial animation for purposes of video teleconferencing. Figure 5.10 shows the feature points defined by the standard. Once the model is defined in this way, it can be animated by an associated set of facial animation parameters (FAPs) [16], also defined in the MPEG-4 standard. MPEG-4 defines 68 FAPs. The FAPs control rigid rotation of the head, eyeballs, eyelids, and mandible. Other low-level parameters indicate the translation of a corresponding feature point, with respect to its position in the neutral face, along one of the coordinate axes [9].

One other interesting approach to generating a model of a face from a generic model is fitting it to images in a video sequence [10]. While not a technique developed for animation applications, it is useful for generating a model of a face of a specific individual. A parameterized model of a face is set up in a three-dimensional viewing configuration closely matching that of the camera that produced the video images.

---

[1]In Parke's model, the z-axis is up, the x-axis is oriented from the back of the head toward the front, and the y-axis is from the middle of the head out to the left side.

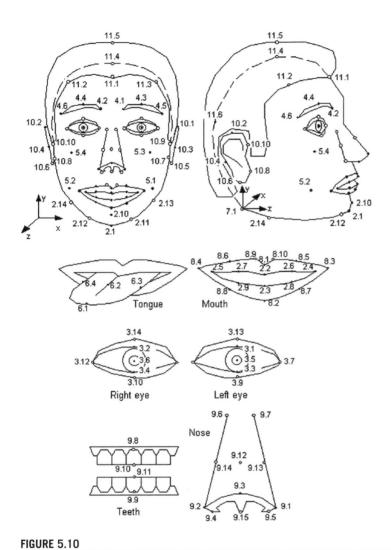

FIGURE 5.10

Feature points corresponding to the MPEG-4 FDP [17].

Feature points are located on the image of the face in the video and are also located on the three-dimensional synthetic model. Camera parameters and face model parameters are then modified to more closely match the video by using the pseudo-inverse of the Jacobian. (The Jacobian is the matrix of partial derivatives that relates changes in parameters to changes in measurements.) By computing the difference in the measurements between the feature points in the image and the projected feature points from the synthetic setup, the pseudoinverse of the Jacobian indicates how to change the parametric values to reduce the measurement differences.

5.2.2 **Textures**

Texture maps are very important in facial animation. Most objects created by computer graphics techniques have a plastic or metallic look, which, in the case of facial animation, seriously detracts from the believability of the image. Texture maps can give a facial model a much more organic look and can give the observer more visual cues when interacting with the images. The texture map can be taken directly from a person's head; however, it must be registered with the geometry. The lighting situation during digitization of the texture must also be considered.

Laser scanners are capable of collecting information on intensity as well as depth, resulting in a high-resolution surface with a matching high-resolution texture. However, once the face deforms, the texture no longer matches exactly. Since the scanner revolves around the model, the texture resolution is evenly spread over the head. However, places are missed where the head is self-occluding (at the ears and maybe the chin) and at the top of the head.

Texture maps can also be created from photographs by simply combining top and side views using pixel blending where the textures overlap [1]. Lighting effects must be taken into consideration, and because the model is not captured in the same process as the texture map, registration with a model is an issue. Using a sequence of images from a video can improve the process.

5.3 **ANIMATING THE FACE**

Attempts to animate the face raise the questions: What are the primitive motions of the face? And how many degrees of freedom (DOFs) are there in the face?

5.3.1 **Parameterized Models**

As introduced in the discussion of the FACS, parameterizing the facial model according to primitive actions and then controlling the values of the parameters over time is one of the most common ways to implement facial animation. Abstractly, any possible or imaginable facial contortion can be considered as a point in an n-dimensional space of all possible facial poses. Any parameterization of a space should have complete coverage and be easy to use. Complete coverage means that the space reachable by (linear) combinations of the parameters includes all (at least most) of the interesting points in that space. Of course, the definition of the word *interesting* may vary from application to application, so a generally useful parameterization includes as much of the space as possible. For a parameterization to be easy to use, the set of parameters should be as small as possible, the effect of each parameter should be independent of the effect of any other parameter, and the effect of each parameter should be intuitive. Of course, in something as complex as facial animation, attaining all of these objectives is probably not possible, so determining appropriate trade-offs is an important activity in designing a parameterization. Animation brings an additional requirement to the table: the animator should be able to generate

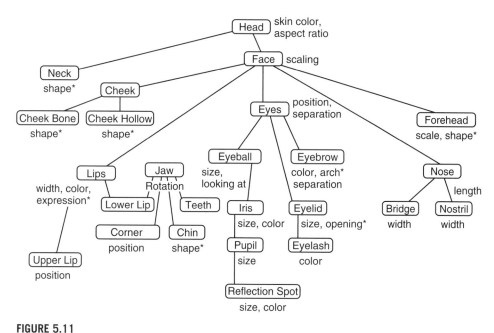

FIGURE 5.11

Parke model; * indicates interpolated parameters [27].

common, important, or interesting motions through the space by manipulating one or just a few parameters.

The most popular parameterized facial model is credited to Parke [25–27] and has already been discussed in terms of creating facial models based on the so-called *conformational parameters* of a generic facial model. In addition to the conformational parameters, there are *expression parameters*. Examples of expression parameters are upper-lip position, eye gaze, jaw rotation, and eyebrow separation. Figure 5.11 shows a diagram of the parameter set with the (interpolated) expression parameters identified. Most of the parameters are concerned with the eyes and the mouth, where most facial expression takes place. With something as complex as the face, it is usually not possible to animate interesting expressions with a single parameter. Experience with the parameter set is necessary for understanding the relationship between a parameter and the facial model. Higher-level abstractions can be used to aid in animating common motions.

5.3.2 Blend Shapes

The simplest approach to facial animation is to define a set of key poses, also called *blend shapes*. For a set of examples, see Fig. 5.12. Facial animation is produced by selecting two of the key poses and interpolating between the positions of their corresponding vertices in the two poses.

BLEND SHAPES for FACIAL ANIMATION

FIGURE 5.12

Blend shapes of a character (character design by Chris Oatley; rig design by Cara Christeson; character modeling and posing by Daniel Guinn).

This restricts the available motions to be the interpolation from one key pose to another. To generalize this a bit more, a weighted sum of two or more key poses can be used in which the weights sum to one. Each vertex position is then computed as a linear combination of its corresponding position in each of the poses whose weight is nonzero. This can be used to produce facial poses not directly represented by the keys. However, this is still fairly restrictive because the various parts of the facial model are not individually controllable by the animator. The animation is still restricted to those poses represented as a linear combination of the keys. If the animator allows for a wide variety of facial motions, the key poses quickly increase to an unmanageable number.

5.3.3 Muscle Models

Parametric models encode geometric displacement of the skin in terms of an arbitrary parametric value. Muscle-based models (e.g. Fig. 5.13) are more sophisticated, although there is a wide variation in the reliance on a physical basis for the models. There are typically three types of muscles that need to be modeled for the face: linear, sheet, and sphincter. The *linear muscle* is a muscle that contracts and pulls one point (the *point of insertion*) toward another (the *point of attachment*). The *sheet muscle* acts as a parallel array of muscles and has a line of attachment at each of its two ends rather than a single point of attachment as in the linear model. The sphincter muscle contracts a loop of muscle. It can be thought of as contracting radially toward an imaginary center. The user, either directly or indirectly, specifies muscle activity to which the facial model reacts. Three aspects differentiate one muscle-based model from another: the geometry of the muscle–skin arrangement, the skin model used, and the muscle model used.

The main distinguishing feature in the geometric arrangement of the muscles is whether they are modeled on the surface of the face or whether they are attached to a structural layer beneath the skin (e.g. bone). The former case is simpler in that only the surface model of the face is needed for the animation system (Fig. 5.14). The latter case is more anatomically correct and thus promises more accurate results, but it requires much more geometric structure in the model and is therefore much more difficult to construct (Fig. 5.15).

FIGURE 5.13

Example muscles for facial animation [32] (Image courtesy of Arun Somasun-daram).

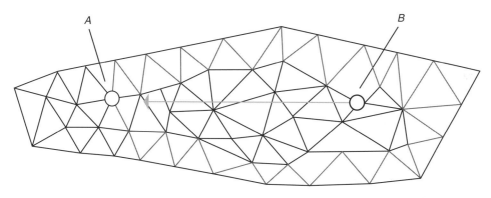

FIGURE 5.14

Part of the surface geometry of the face showing the point of attachment (*A*) and the point of insertion (*B*) of a linear muscle; point *B* is pulled toward point *A*.

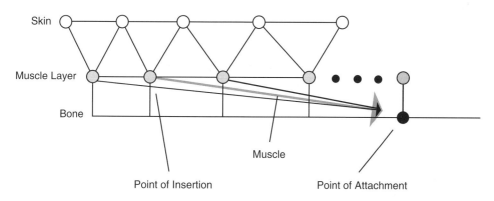

FIGURE 5.15

Cross section of the trilayer muscle as presented by Parke and Waters [27]; the muscle only directly affects nodes in the muscle layer.

The model used for the skin will dictate how the area around the point of insertion of a (linear) muscle reacts when that muscle is activated; the point of insertion will move an amount determined by the muscle. How the deformation propagates along the skin as a result of that muscle determines how rubbery or how plastic the surface will appear. The simplest model to use is based on geometric distance from the point and deviation from the muscle vector. For example, the effect of the muscle may attenuate based on the distance a given point is from the point of insertion and on the angle of deviation from the displacement vector of the insertion point. See Fig. 5.16 for sample calculations. A slightly more sophisticated skin model might model each edge of the skin geometry as a spring and control the propagation of the deformation based on spring constants. The insertion point is moved by the action of the muscle, and this displacement creates restoring forces in the springs attached to the insertion point, which moves the adjacent vertices, which in turn moves the vertices attached to them, and so on (see Fig. 5.17). The more complicated Voight model treats the skin as a viscoelastic element by combining a spring and a damper in parallel (Fig. 5.18). The movement induced by the spring is damped as a function of the change in length of the edge.

The muscle model determines the function used to compute the contraction of the muscle. The alternatives for the muscle model are similar to those for the skin, with the distinction that the muscles are active elements, whereas the skin is

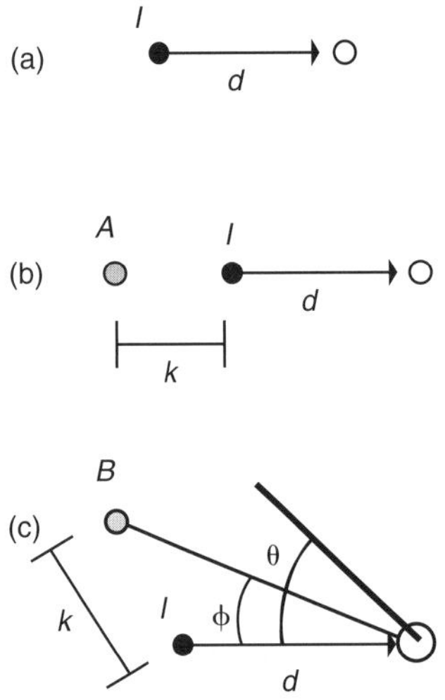

(a) $\qquad d_0 = d$

(b)
$$d_k = d \cdot \frac{\left(\cos\left(\frac{k}{R} \cdot \pi\right) + 1.0\right)}{2.0} \qquad 0 \le k \le R$$
$$= 0 \qquad \text{otherwise}$$

(c)
$$d_{k\phi} = \left(d \cdot \frac{\left(\cos\left(\frac{k}{R} \cdot \pi\right) + 1.0\right)}{2.0}\right) \cdot \left(\frac{\left(\sin\left(\frac{\phi}{\theta} \cdot \pi\right) + 1.0\right)}{2.0}\right) \qquad 0 \le \phi \le \theta$$
$$= 0 \qquad \text{otherwise}$$

FIGURE 5.16

Sample attenuation: (A) insertion point I is moved d by muscle; (B) point A is moved d_k based on linear distance from the insertion point; and (C) point B is moved d_k based on the linear distance and the deviation from the insertion point displacement vector.

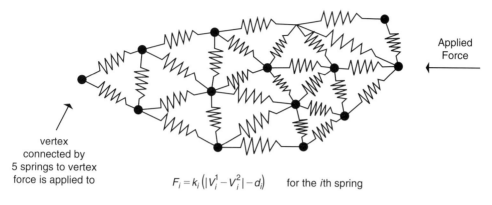

$$F_i = k_i \left(|V_i^1 - V_i^2| - d_i \right) \qquad \text{for the } i\text{th spring}$$

FIGURE 5.17

Spring mesh as skin model; the displacement of the insertion point propagates through the mesh according to the forces imparted by the springs.

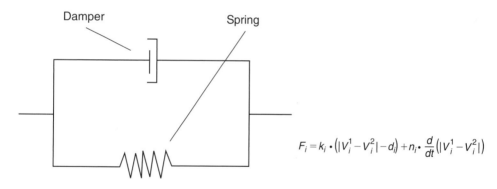

$$F_i = k_i \cdot \left(|V_i^1 - V_i^2| - d_i \right) + n_i \cdot \frac{d}{dt} \left(|V_i^1 - V_i^2| \right)$$

FIGURE 5.18

Voight viscoelastic model; the motion induced by the spring forces is damped; variables k and n are spring and damper constants, respectively; d_i is the rest length for the spring.

composed of passive elements. Using a linear muscle as an example, the displacement of the insertion point is produced as a result of muscle activation. Simple models for the muscle will simply specify a displacement of the insertion point based on activation amount. Because, in the case of the orbicularis oris, muscles are attached to other muscles, care must be taken in determining the skin displacement when both muscles are activated.

More physically accurate muscle models will compute the effect of muscular forces. The simplest dynamic model uses a spring to represent the muscle. Activating the muscle results in a change in its rest length so as to induce a force at the point of insertion. More sophisticated muscle models include damping effects. A muscle model developed by clinical observation is shown in Fig. 5.19. However, spring-based facial muscles often result in a computationally expensive approach and giggling of the skin can be difficult to control.

5.3.4 Expressions

Facial expressions are a powerful means of communication and are the basis for most facial animation. Any facial animation system will provide for a basic set of expressions. A commonly used set is happy, angry, sad, fear, disgust, and surprise (Fig. 5.20).

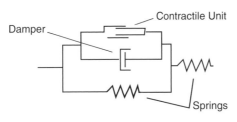

FIGURE 5.19

Hill's model for the muscle.

5.3.5 Summary

A wide range of approaches can be used to model and animate the face. Which to use depends greatly on how realistic the result is meant to be and what kind of control the animator is provided. Results vary from cartoon faces to parameterized surface models

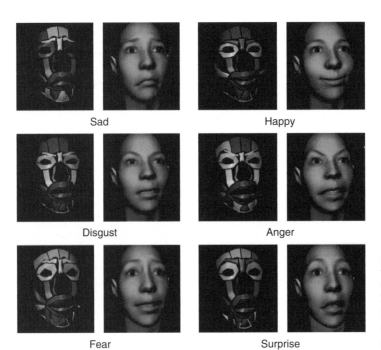

Sad Happy

Disgust Anger

Fear Surprise

FIGURE 5.20

A basic set of facial expressions [32] (Image courtesy of Arun Somasundaram).

to skull–muscle–skin simulations. Realistic facial animation remains one of the interesting challenges in computer animation.

5.4 LIP-SYNC ANIMATION

5.4.1 Articulators of Speech

Speech is a complex process and not even completely understood by linguists. Involved in the production of speech are the lungs, the vocal folds, the velum, lips, teeth, and tongue. These articulators of speech constitute the *vocal tract* (see Fig. 5.21). The lungs produce the primary air flow necessary for sound production. Sound is a sensation produced by vibrations transmitted through air. The various sounds of speech are produced primarily by controlling the frequency, amplitude, and duration of these vibrations. Vibrations are generated either by the vocal folds in the throat or by the tongue in the oral cavity, or by lips. When vibration is produced by the vocal folds, the sound is called *voiced*. For example, the "th" sound in "then" is voiced, whereas the "th" of "thin" is not voiced. The sound travels up into either nasal cavity (e.g. "n") or oral cavity depending on the configuration of the velum. In the oral cavity, the sound is modified by the configuration of the lips, jaw, and tongue with certain frequencies resonating in the cavity. In addition, the

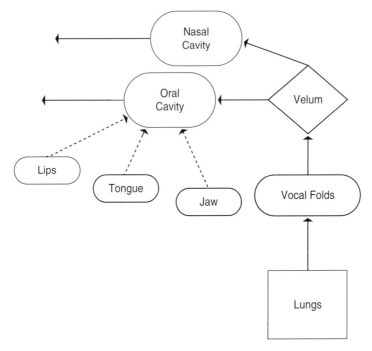

FIGURE 5.21

Schematic of air flow through the vocal tract. Lungs produce air flow. Vocal folds may vibrate. Velum deflects air flow to either nasal cavity or oral cavity. Harmonics of vibrations initiated by vocal folds may be reinforced in oral cavity depending on its configuration; vibrations may be initiated in oral cavity by lips or tongue. Dashed lines show agents that modify oral cavity configuration.

tongue and lips can vibrate by either partially obstructing the air flow or completely stopping and then releasing it. If the air flow is relatively unrestricted, then the sound is considered a vowel, otherwise it is a consonant. If the air flow is completely stopped and then released (e.g. "t," "d"), then it is referred to as a *stop*. If the air flow is partially restricted creating a vibration (e.g. "f," "th"), then it is referred to as a *fricative*.

The fundamental frequency of a sound is referred to as F0 and is present in voiced sounds [23]. Frequencies induced by the speech cavities, called *formants*, are referred to as F1, F2, ... in the order of their amplitudes. The fundamental frequency and formants are arguably the most important concepts in processing speech.

While most of this activity is interior and therefore not directly observable, it can produce motion in the skin that may be important in some animation. Certainly, it is important to correctly animate the lips and the surrounding area of the face. Animating the tongue is also usually of some importance.

Some information can be gleaned from a time–amplitude graph of the sound, but more informative is a time–frequency graph with amplitude encoded using color. Using these *spectrographs*, trained professionals can determine the basic sounds of the speech.

5.4.2 Phonemes

In trying to understand speech and how a person produces it, a common approach is to break it down into a simple set of constituent, atomic sound segments. The most commonly used segments are called *phonemes*. Although the specific number of phonemes varies from source to source, there are generally considered to be around 42 phonemes.

The corresponding facial poses that produce these sounds are referred to as *visemes*. Visemes that are similar enough can be combined into a single unique viseme and the resulting set of facial poses can be used, for example, as blend shapes for a simple type of lip-sync animation.

However, the sounds and the associated lip movements are much more complex than can be represented by simply interpolating between static poses. Within the context of speech, a phoneme is manifested as variations of the basic sound. These variations of a phoneme are called *allophones* and the mechanism producing the variations is referred to as *coarticulation*. While the precise mechanism of coarticulation is a subject for debate, the basic reason for it is that the ideal sounds are slurred together as phonemes are strung one after the other. Similarly, the visemes of visual speech are modified by the context of the speech in which they occur. The speed at which speech is produced and the physical limitations of the speech articulators result in an inability to attain ideal pronunciation. This slurs the visemes together and, in turn, slurs the phonemes. The computation of this slurring is the subject of research.

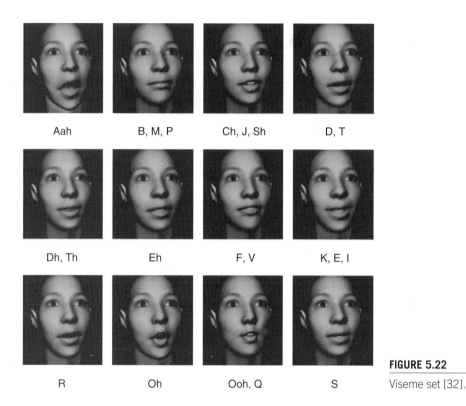

| Aah | B, M, P | Ch, J, Sh | D, T |

| Dh, Th | Eh | F, V | K, E, I |

| R | Oh | Ooh, Q | S |

FIGURE 5.22

Viseme set [32].

5.4.3 Coarticulation

One of the complicating factors in automatically producing realistic (both audial and visual) lip-sync animation is the effect that one phoneme has on adjacent phonemes. Adjacent phonemes affect the motion of the speech articulators as they form the sound for a phoneme. The resulting subtle change in sound of the phoneme produces what is referred to as an allophone of the phoneme. This effect is known as *coarticulation*. Lack of coarticulation is one of the main reasons that lip-sync animation using blend shapes appears unrealistic. While there have been various strategies proposed in the literature to compute the effects of coarticulation, Cohen and Massaro [8] have used weighting functions, called *dominance functions*, to perform a priority-based blend of adjacent phonemes. King and Parent [20] have modified and extended the idea to animating song. Pelechaud et al. [28] cluster phonemes based on deformability and use a look-ahead procedure that applies forward and backward coarticulation rules. Other approaches include the use of constraints [14], physics [2, 32], rules [6], and syllables [21]. None have proven to be a completely satisfying solution for automatically producing realistic audiovisual speech.

5.4.4 Prosody

Another complicating factor to realistic lip-sync animation is changing neutral speech to reflect emotional stress. Such stress is referred to as *prosody*. Affects of prosody include changing the duration, pitch, and amplitude of words or phrases of an utterance. This is an active area of research, e.g. [4–6,13,22].

5.5 CHAPTER SUMMARY

The human figure is an interesting and complex form. It has a uniform structure but contains infinite variety. As an articulated rigid structure, it contains many DOFs, but its surface is deformable. Modeling and animating hair in any detail is also enormously complex. Moreover, the constant collision and sliding of cloth on the surface of the body represents significant computational complexity.

One of the things that make human motion so challenging is that no single motion can be identified as correct human motion. Human motion varies from individual to individual for a number of reasons, but it is still recognizable as reasonable human motion, and slight variations can seem odd or awkward. Research in computer animation is just starting to delve into the nuances of human motion. Many of these nuances vary from person to person but, at the same time, are very consistent for a particular person, for a particular ethnic group, for a particular age group, for a particular weight group, for a particular emotional state, and so on. Computer animation is only beginning to analyze, record, and synthesize these important qualities of movement. Most of the work has focused on modeling changes in motion resulting from an individual's emotional state (e.g. [3,7]).

REFERENCES

[1] T. Akimoto, Y. Suenaga, Three-dimensional facial model creation using generic model and front and side view of face, IEICE Trans. Inf. Syst. E75-D (1992) 191–197.

[2] I. Albrecht, J. Haber, H.-P. Seidel, Speech synchronization for physics-based facial-animation, Proceedings of WSCG, pp. 9–16, February 2002.

[3] K. Amaya, A. Bruderlin, T. Calvert, Emotion from motion. in: W.A. Davis, R. Bartels (Eds.), Graphics Interface '96, Canadian Human-Computer Communications Society, 1996, pp. 222–229. ISBN 0-9695338-5-3.

[4] M. Byun, N. Badler, Facemote: qualitative parametric modifiers for facial animations, Proceedings of the ACM SIGGRAPH Symposium on Computer Animation, pp. 65–71, 2002.

[5] Y. Cao, P. Faloutsos, F. Pighin, Unsupervised learning for speech motion editing, Proceedings of ACM SIGGRAPH/Eurographics Symposium on Computer Animation, pp. 225–231, 2003.

[6] J. Cassell, C. Pelachaud, N. Badler, M. Steedman, B. Achorn, W. Becket, B. Douville, S. Prevost, M. Stone, Animated conversation: rule-based generation of facial expression, gesture and spoken intonation for multiple conversational agents. Proceedings of ACM SIGGRAPH, pp. 413–420, 1994.

[7] D. Chi, M. Costa, L. Zhao, N. Badler, The EMOTE model for effort and shape, in: K. Akeley (Ed.), Computer Graphics, Annual Conference Series (Proceedings of SIGGRAPH 2000), ACM Press/ACM SIGGRAPH/Addison-Wesley Longman, 2000, pp. 173–182. ISBN 1-58113-208-5.

[8] M. Cohen, D. Massaro, Modeling coarticulation in synthetic visual speech, in: Models and Techniques in Computer Animation, Springer-Verlag, Tokyo, 1993.

[9] COVEN, http://coven.lancs.ac.uk/mpeg4/index.html, January 2001.

[10] D. DeCarlo, D. Metaxas, M. Stone, An anthropometric face model using variational techniques, in: M. Cohen, (Ed.), Computer Graphics, Annual Conference Series (Proceedings of SIGGRAPH 98, July 1998, Orlando, Florida), Addison-Wesley, 1998, pp. 67–74. ISBN 0-89791-999-8.

[11] T. DeRose, M. Kass, T. Truong, Subdivision surfaces for character animation, in: M. Cohen (Ed.), Computer Graphics, Annual Conference Series (Proceedings of SIGGRAPH 98, July 1998, Orlando, Florida), Addison-Wesley, 1998, pp. 85–94. ISBN 0-89791-999-8.

[12] D. Ebert, J. Ebert, K. Boyer, Getting into Art (animation), CIS Department, Ohio State University, May 1990.

[13] J. Edge, S. Maddock, Expressive visual speech using geometric muscle functions, Proceedings of Eurographics UK Chapter Annual Conference (EGUK), pp. 11–18, 2001.

[14] J. Edge, S. Maddock, Constraint-based synthesis of visual speech, Conference Abstracts and Applications of SIGGRAPH, 2004.

[15] P. Ekman, W. Friesen, Facial Action Coding System, Consulting Psychologists Press, Palo Alto, California, 1978.

[16] FAP Specifications, http://www-dsp.com.dist.unige.it/~pok/RESEARCH/MPEGfapspec.htm, January 2001.

[17] FDP Specifications, http://www-dsp.com.dist.unige.it/~pok/RESEARCH/MPEGfdpspec.htm, January 2001.

[18] D. Forsey, R. Bartels, Hierarchical B-spline refinement, Comput. Graph. 22 (1988) 205–212 (Proceedings of SIGGRAPH 88, August 1988, Atlanta, GA, J. Dill (Ed.)).

[19] International Computer, Three-dimensional tutorials: Pixologic ZBrush: Head modeling part 1, http://www.3dlinks.com/oldsite/tutorials_ZOldHead.cfm, August 2006.

[20] S. King, R. Parent, Animating song, Comput. Animat. Virtual Worlds 15 (2004) 53–61.

[21] S. Kshirsagar, N. Magnenat-Thalmann, Visyllable based speech animation, Proc. Eurograph. 22 (2003) 631–639.

[22] S. Kshirsagar, T. Molet, N. Magnenat-Thalmann, Principle components of expressive speech animation, in: Computer Graphics International, IEEE Computer Society, 2001, pp. 38–44.

[23] S. Lemmetty, Review of Speech Synthesis Technology, M.S. Thesis, Helsinki University, 1999 (http://www.acoustics.hut.fi/publications/files/theses/lemmetty_mst/).

[24] S. Muraki, Volumetric shape description of range data using Blobby Model, Comput. Graph. 25 (1991) 227–235 (Proceedings of SIGGRAPH 91, July 1991, Las Vegas, NV, T.W. Sederberg (Ed.)). ISBN 0-201-56291-X.

[25] F. Parke, Computer-generated animation of faces, Proceedings of the ACM Annual Conference, August 1972.

[26] F. Parke, A Parametric Model for Human Faces, Ph.D. dissertation, University of Utah, 1974.

[27] F. Parke, K. Waters, Computer Facial Animation, A.K. Peters, Wellesley, Massachusetts, 1996. ISBN 1-56881-014-8.

[28] C. Pelachaud, N. Badler, M. Steedman, Generating facial expressions for speech, Cogn Sci 20(1) (1996) 1–46.

[29] P. Ratner, Subdivision modeling of a human, http://www.highend3d.com/maya/ tutorials/-modeling/polygon/189.html, August 2006.

[30] M. Rydfalk, CANDIDE: a parameterized face, Technical Report LiTH-ISY-I-0866, Linköping University, Sweden, 1987.

[31] F. Silas, FrankSilas.com Face Tutorial, http://www.franksilas.com/FaceTutorial.htm, August 2006.

[32] A. Somasundaram, A facial animation model for expressive audio-visual speech, Ph.D. dissertation, Ohio State University, 2006.

[33] K. Waters, A muscle model for animating three-dimensional facial expressions, Proc. SIGGRAPH 21 (1987) 17–24.

[34] K. Waters, A physical model of facial tissue and muscle articulation derived from computer tomography data, SPIE Vis. Biomed. Comput. 1808 (1992) 574–583.

[35] K. Waters, D. Terzopoulos, Modeling and animating faces using scanned data, J. Vis. Comput. Animat. 2 (1991) 123–128.

Animating Solid Spaces

David S. Ebert

CHAPTER CONTENTS

This chapter discusses animating gases and other procedurally defined solid spaces. There are several ways that solid spaces can be animated. This chapter will consider two approaches:

1. Changing the solid space over time
2. Moving the point being rendered through the solid space

The first approach has time as a parameter that changes the definition of the space over time, a very natural and obvious way to animate procedural techniques. With this approach, time has to be considered in the design of the procedure, and the procedure evolves with time. Procedures that change the space to simulate growth, evolution, or aging are common examples of this approach. A related technique creates the

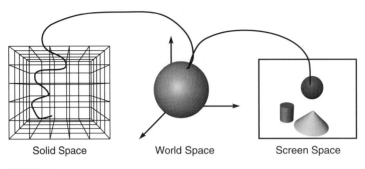

Solid Space   World Space   Screen Space

FIGURE 6.1

Moving a screen space point through the solid space.

procedure in a four-dimensional space, with time as the fourth dimension, such as a 4D noise function.

The second approach does not actually change the solid space but moves the point in the volume or object over time through the space, in effect procedurally warping or perturbing the space. Moving the fixed three-dimensional screen space point along a path over time through the solid space before evaluating the turbulence function animates the gas (solid texture, hypertexture). Each three-dimensional screen space point is inversely mapped back to world space. From world space, it is mapped into the gas and turbulence space through the use of simple affine transformations. Finally, it is moved through the turbulence space over time to create the movement. Therefore, the path direction will have the reverse visual effect. For example, a *downward* path applied to the screen space point will show the texture or volume object *rising*. Figure 6.1 illustrates this process.

Both of these techniques can be applied to solid texturing, gases, and hypertextures. After a brief discussion of animation paths, the application of these two techniques to solid texturing is discussed, followed by an exploration of the way they are used for gas animation and hypertextures, including liquids. Finally, the chapter concludes with a discussion of an additional procedural animation technique, particle systems.

6.1 ANIMATION PATHS

This chapter will describe various ways of creating animation paths for movement through the solid space. For many examples, I will use a helical (spiral) path. There are two reasons for using helical paths. First, most gases do not move along a linear path. Turbulence, convection, wind, and so on change the path movement. From my observations, smoke, steam, and fog tend to swirl while moving in a given direction. A helical path can capture this general sense of motion. Second, helical paths are very simple to calculate. The calculation involves rotation around the axis of the helix (direction of motion) and movement along the axis. To create the rotation, the sine and cosine functions are used. The angle for these functions is based on the frame number to produce the rotation over time. The rate of rotation can be controlled by taking the frame number modulo a constant. Linear motion, again based on the frame number, will be used to create the movement along the axis.

The code segment below creates a helical path that rotates about the axis once every 100 frames. The speed of movement along the axis is controlled by the variable `linear_speed`.

```
theta = (frame_number%100)*(2*M_PI/100);
path.x = cos(theta);
path.y = sin(theta);
path.z = theta*linear_speed;
```

One final point will clarify the procedures given in this chapter. To get smooth transitions between values and smooth acceleration and deceleration, *ease-in* and *ease-out* procedures are used. These are the standard routines used by animators to stop a moving object from jumping instantaneously from a speed of 0 to a constant velocity. One simple implementation of these functions assumes a sine curve for the acceleration and integrates this curve over one-half of its period.

6.2 ANIMATING SOLID TEXTURES

This section will show how the previous two animation approaches can be used for solid texturing. Applying these techniques to color solid texturing will be discussed first, followed by solid-textured transparency.

A marble procedure will be used as an example of color solid texture animation. The following simple marble procedure is based on Perlin's `marble` function (Perlin 1985).

```
rgb_td marble(xyz_td pnt)
{
  float y;
  y = pnt.y + 3.0*turbulence(pnt, .0125);
  y = sin(y*M_PI);
  return (marble_color(y));
}
rgb_td marble_color(float x)
{
  rgb_td clr;
  x = sqrt(x+1.0)*.7071;
  clr.g = .30 + .8*x;
  x = sqrt(x);
  clr.r = .30 + .6*x;
  clr.b = .60 + .4*x;
  return (clr);
}
```

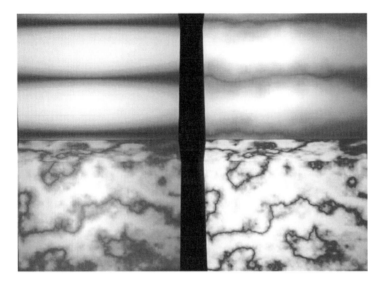

FIGURE 6.2

Marble forming. The images show the banded material heating, deforming, then cooling and solidifying (Copyright © 1992 David S. Ebert).

This procedure applies a sine function to the turbulence of the point. The resulting value is then mapped to the color. The results achievable by this procedure can be seen in Fig. 6.2 (lower right).

6.2.1 Marble Forming

The application of the previous two animation approaches to this function has very different effects. When the first approach is used, changing the solid space over time, the formation of marble from banded rock can be achieved. Marble is formed from the turbulent mixing of different bands of rock. To simulate this process, initially no turbulence is added to the point; therefore, the sine function determines the color. Basing the color on the sine function produces banded material. As the frame number increases, the amount of turbulence added to the point is increased, deforming the bands into the marble vein pattern. The resulting procedure is the following:

```
rgb_td marble_forming(xyz_td pnt, int frame_num, int
                      start_frame, int end_frame)
 {
 float x, turb_percent, displacement;

 if(frame_num < start_frame)
```

```
    {turb_percent=0;
     displacement=0;
     }
   else if (frame_num >= end_frame)
   {turb_percent=1;
    displacement=3;
    }
   else
   {turb_percent = ((float)(frame_num-start_frame))/
                    (end_frame-start_frame);
     displacement = 3*turb_percent;
    }
x = pnt.x + turb_percent*3.0*turbulence(pnt, .0125)-
    displacement;
x = sin(x*M_PI);
return (marble_color(x));
}
```

The displacement value in this procedure is used to stop the entire texture from moving. Without the displacement value, the entire banded pattern moves horizontally to the left of the image, instead of the veins forming in place.

This procedure produces the desired effect, but the realism of the results can be increased by a few small changes. First, ease-in and ease-out of the rate of adding turbulence will give more natural motion. Second, the color of the marble can be changed to simulate heating before and during the deformation and to simulate cooling after the deformation. The marble color is blended with a "glowing" marble color to simulate the heating and cooling. (Even though this may not be physically accurate, it produces a nice effect.) This can be achieved by the following procedure:

```
rgb_td marble_forming2(xyz_td pnt, int frame_num, int start_frame,
                    int end_frame, int heat_length)
 {
  float x, turb_percent, displacement, glow_percent;
  rgb_td m_color;
  if(frame_num < (start_frame-heat_length/2) 1½
    frame_num > end_frame+heat_length/2)
     glow_percent=0;
  else if (frame_num < start_frame + heat_length/2)
     glow_percent= 1.0 - ease( ((start_frame+heat_length/2-
                        frame_num)/ heat_length),0.4, 0.6);
  else if (frame_num > end_frame-heat_length/2)
     glow_percent = ease( ((frame_num-(end_frame-
                    heat_length/2))/heat_length),0.4, 0.6);
```

```
                else
        glow_percent=1.0;

   if(frame_num < start_frame)
     { turb_percent=0; displacement=0;
     }
   else if (frame_num >= end_frame)
     { turb_percent=1; displacement=3;
     }
   else
     { turb_percent= ((float)(frame_num-start_frame))/
                     (end_frame-start_frame);
       turb_percent=ease(turb_percent, 0.3, 0.7);
       displacement = 3*turb_percent;
     }
   x = pnt.y + turb_percent*3.0*turbulence(pnt, .0125) -displacement;
   x = sin(x*M_PI);
   m_color=marble_color(x);
   glow_percent= .5* glow_percent;
   m_color.r= glow_percent*(1.0)+ (1-glow_percent)*m_color.r;
   m_color.g= glow_percent*(0.4)+ (1-glow_percent)*m_color.g;
   m_color.b= glow_percent*(0.8)+ (1-glow_percent)*m_color.b;
   return(m_color);
 }
```

The resulting images can be seen in Fig. 6.2. This figure shows four images of the change in the marble from banded rock (upper left image) to the final marbled rock (lower right image). Of course, the resulting sequence would be even more realistic if the material actually deformed, instead of the color simply changing. This effect will be described in the "Animating Hypertextures" section.

6.2.2 Marble Moving

A different effect can be achieved by the second animation approach, moving the point through the solid space. Any path can be used for movement through the marble space. A simple, obvious choice would be a linear path. Another choice, which produces very ethereal patterns in the material, is to use a turbulent path. The procedure below uses yet another choice for the path. This procedure moves the point along a horizontal helical path before evaluating the turbulence function, producing the effect of the marble pattern moving through the object. The helical path provides a more interesting result than the linear path but does not change the general marble patterns, as does using a turbulent path through the turbulence space. This technique can be used to determine the portion of marble from which to "cut" the object in order to achieve the most pleasing vein patterns.

(You are in essence moving the object through a three-dimensional volume of marble.)

```
rgb_td moving_marble(xyz_td pnt, int frame_num)
 {
 float       x, tmp, tmp2;
 static float down, theta, sin_theta, cos_theta;
 xyz_td      hel_path, direction;
 static int  calcd=1;

 if(calcd)
    { theta=(frame_num%SWIRL_FRAMES)*SWIRL_AMOUNT;//swirling
      cos_theta = RAD1 * cos(theta) + 0.5;
      sin_theta = RAD2 * sin(theta) - 2.0;
      down = (float)frame_num*DOWN_AMOUNT+2.0;
      calcd=0;
    }
  tmp = fast_noise(pnt); //add some randomness
  tmp2 = tmp*1.75;
//calculate the helical path
  hel_path.y = cos_theta + tmp;
  hel_path.x = (-down) + tmp2;
  hel_path.z = sin_theta - tmp2;
  XYZ_ADD(direction, pnt, hel_path);
  x = pnt.y + 3.0*turbulence(direction, .0125);
  x = sin(x*M_PI);
  return (marble_color(x));
 }
```

In this procedure, `SWIRL_FRAMES` and `SWIRL_AMOUNT` determine the number of frames for one complete rotation of the helical path. By choosing `SWIRL_FRAMES` = 126 and `SWIRL_AMOUNT` = $2\pi/126$, the path swirls every 126 frames. `DOWN_AMOUNT` controls the speed of the downward movement along the helical path. A reasonable speed for downward movement for a unit-sized object is to use `DOWN_AMOUNT` = 0.0095. `RAD1` and `RAD2` are the y and z radii of the helical path.

6.2.3 Animating Solid-Textured Transparency

This section describes the use of the second solid space animation technique, moving the point through the solid space, for animating solid-textured transparency.

This animation technique is the one that I originally used for animating gases and is still the main technique that I use for gases. The results of this technique applied to solid-textured transparency can be seen in [1]. The `fog` procedure given next is similar in its animation approach to the earlier `moving_marble` procedure. It produces fog moving through the surface of an object and can be used as a surface-based approach to simulate fog or clouds. Again in this procedure, a downward helical path is used for the movement through the space, which produces an upward swirling to the gas movement.

```
void fog(xyz_td pnt, float *transp, int frame_num)
{
 float tmp;
 xyz_td direction,cyl;
 double theta;
 pnt.x += 2.0 +turbulence(pnt, .1);
 tmp = noise_it(pnt);
 pnt.y += 4+tmp; pnt.z += -2 - tmp;
theta =(frame_num%SWIRL_FRAMES)*SWIRL_AMOUNT;
 cyl.x =RAD1 * cos(theta); cyl.z =RAD2 * sin(theta);
 direction.x = pnt.x + cyl.x;
 direction.y = pnt.y - frame_num*DOWN_AMOUNT;
 direction.z = pnt.z + cyl.z;
 *transp = turbulence(direction, .015);
 *transp = (1.0 -(*transp)*(*transp)*.275);
 *transp =(*transp)*(*transp)*(*transp);
}
```

An image showing this procedure applied to a cube can be seen in Fig. 6.3. The values used for this image can be found in Table 6.1.

FIGURE 6.3

Solid-textured transparency-based fog (Copyright © 1994 David S. Ebert).

Table 6.1 Values for Fog Procedure

Parameters	Value
DOWN_AMOUNT	0.0095
SWIRL_FRAMES	126
SWIRL_AMOUNT	$2\pi/126$
RAD1	0.12
RAD2	0.08

FIGURE 6.4

A scene from *Once a Pawn a Foggy Knight* ... showing solid-textured transparency used to simulate fog (Copyright © 1989 David S. Ebert).

Another example of the use of solid-textured transparency animation can be seen in Fig. 6.4, which contains a still from an animation entitled *Once a Pawn a Foggy Knight* ... [1]. In this scene, three planes are positioned to give a two-dimensional approximation of three-dimensional fog. One plane is in front of the scene, one plane is approximately in the middle, and the final plane is behind all the objects in the scene.

This technique is similar to Gardner's technique for producing images of clouds [2], except that it uses turbulence to control the transparency instead of Fourier synthesis. As with any surface-based approach to modeling gases, including Gardner's, this technique cannot produce three-dimensional volumes of fog or accurate shadowing from the fog.

6.3 ANIMATION OF GASEOUS VOLUMES

As described in the previous section, animation technique 2, moving the point through the solid space, is the technique that I use to animate gases. This technique will be used in all the examples in this section. Moving each fixed three-dimensional screen space point along a path over time through the solid space before evaluating the turbulence function creates the gas movement. First, each three-dimensional screen space point is inversely mapped back to world space. Second, it is mapped from world space into the gas and turbulence space through the use of simple affine transformations. Finally, it is moved through the turbulence space over time to create the movement of the gas. Therefore, the path direction will have the reverse visual effect. For example, a downward path applied to the screen space point will cause the gas to rise.

This gas animation technique can be considered to be the inverse of particle systems because each point in three-dimensional screen space is moved through the gas space to see which portion of the gas occupies the current location in screen space. The main advantage of this approach over particle systems is that extremely large geometric databases of particles are not required to get realistic images. The complexity is always controlled by the number of screen space points in which the gas is potentially visible.

Several interesting animation effects can be achieved through the use of helical paths for movement through the solid space. These helical path effects will be described first, followed by the use of three-dimensional tables for controlling the gas movement. Finally, several additional primitives for creating gas animation will be presented.

6.3.1 Helical Path Effects

Helical paths can be used to create several different animation effects for gases. In this chapter, three examples of helical path effects will be presented: steam rising from a teacup, rolling fog, and a rising column of smoke.

6.3.1.1 Steam Rising from a Teacup

Convincing animations of steam rising from the teacup can be produced by the addition of helical paths for motion. Each point in the volume is moved downward along a helical path to produce the steam rising and swirling in the opposite direction. This animation technique is the same technique that was used in the `moving_marble` procedure.

```
void steam_moving(xyz_td pnt, xyz_td pnt_world, float *density,
                  float *parms, vol_td vol)
{
```

```
*** float noise_amt,turb, dist_sq, density_max, offset2, theta, dist;
    static float pow_table[POW_TABLE_SIZE], ramp[RAMP_SIZE],
                offset[OFFSET_SIZE];
    extern int frame_num;
    xyz_td direction, diff;
    int i, indx;
    static int calcd=1;
*** static float down, cos_theta, sin_theta;

    if(calcd)
      { calcd=0;
      // determine how to move point through space(helical path)
***    theta =(frame_num%SWIRL_FRAMES)*SWIRL;
***    down = (float)frame_num*DOWN*3.0 +4.0;
***    cos_theta = RAD1*cos(theta) +2.0;
***    sin_theta = RAD2*sin(theta) -2.0;
       for(i=POW_TABLE_SIZE-1; i>=0; i--)
           pow_table[i] =(float)pow(((double)(i))/(POW_TABLE_SIZE-1)*
                        parms[1]* 2.0,(double)parms[2]);
       make_tables(ramp);
       }
    // move the point along the helical path
*** noise_amt = fast_noise(pnt);
*** direction.x = pnt.x + cos_theta + noise_amt;
*** direction.y = pnt.y - down + noise_amt;
*** direction.z = pnt.z +sin_theta + noise_amt;
    turb =fast_turbulence(direction);
    *density = pow_table[(int)(turb*0.5*(POW_TABLE_SIZE-1))];
    // determine distance from center of the slab ^2.
    XYZ_SUB(diff,vol.shape.center, pnt_world);
    dist_sq = DOT_XYZ(diff,diff) ;
    density_max = dist_sq*vol.shape.inv_rad_sq.y;
    indx = (int)((pnt.x+pnt.y+pnt.z)*100) & (OFFSET_SIZE -1);
    density_max += parms[3]*offset[indx];
    if(density_max >= .25) //ramp off if > 25% from center
      { // get table index 0:RAMP_SIZE-1
      i = (density_max -.25)*4/3*RAMP_SIZE;
      i=MIN(i,RAMP_SIZE-1);
      density_max = ramp[i];
      *density *=density_max;
      }
    // ramp it off vertically
    dist = pnt_world.y - vol.shape.center.y;
    if(dist > 0.0)
```

```
{ dist = (dist +offset[indx]*.1)*vol.shape.inv_rad.y;
if(dist > .05)
  { offset2 = (dist -.05)*1.111111;
    offset2 = 1 - (exp(offset2)-1.0)71.718282;
    offset2*=parms[1];
    *density *= offset2;
  }
}
}
```

The lines that have changed from the earlier `steam_slab1` procedure are marked with three asterisks (***). This procedure creates upward swirling movement in the gas, which swirls around 360° every `SWIRL_FRAMES` frame. Noise is applied to the path to make it appear more random. The parameters `RAD1` and `RAD2` determine the elliptical shape of the swirling path. Additional variables in this procedure are the angle of rotation about the helical path (`theta`), the frame number (`frame_num`), the cosine of the angle of rotation (`cos_theta`), the sine of the angle of rotation (`sin_theta`), the amount to move along the helical axis (`down`), a noise amount to add to the path (`noise_amt`), and the new location of the point after movement along the path (`direction`).

The downward helical path through the gas space produces the effect of the gas rising and swirling in the opposite direction.

For more realistic steam motion, a simulation of air currents is helpful. Adding turbulence to the helical path can approximate this, where the amount of turbulence added is proportional to the height above the teacup. (This assumes that no turbulence is added at the surface.)

6.3.1.2 Fog Animation

The next example of helical path effects is the creation of rolling fog. For this animation, a horizontal helical path will be used to create the swirling motion of the fog to the right of the scene. From examining the following `volume_fog_animation` procedure, it is clear that this procedure uses the same animation technique as the earlier `steam_moving` procedure: move each point along a helical path before evaluating the turbulence function. The value returned by the turbulence function is again multiplied by a density scalar factor, `parms[1]`, and raised to a power, `parms[2]`. As in the previous procedures, a precomputed table of density values raised to a power is used to speed calculation. A more complete description of the use of helical paths for producing fog animation can be found in [3].

```
void volume_fog_animation(xyz_td pnt, xyz_td pnt_world, float
                          *density, float *parms, vol_td vol)
{
 float noise_amt, turb;
 extern int frame_num;
```

```
xyz_td direction;
int indx;
static float pow_table[POW_TABLE_SIZE];
int i;
static int calcd=1;
static float down, cos_theta, sin_theta, theta;
if(calcd)
  {
  down = (float)frame_num*SPEED*1.5 +2.0;
  theta =(frame_num%SWIRL_FRAMES)*SWIRL_AMOUNT;//get swirlingeffect
  cos_theta = cos(theta)*.1 + 0.5; //use a radius of .1
  sin_theta = sin(theta)*.14 - 2.0; //use a radius of .14
  calcd=0;
  for(i=POW_TABLE_SIZE-1; i>=0; i--)
    {
    pow_table[i]=(float)pow(((double)(i))/(POW_TABLE_SIZE-1)*
            parms[1]*4.0,(double)parms[2]);
    }
  }
// make it move horizontally & add some noise to the movement
noise_amt = fast_noise(pnt);
direction.x = pnt.x - down + noise_amt*1.5;
direction.y = pnt.y + cos_theta +noise_amt;
direction.z = pnt.z + sin_theta -noise_amt*1.5;
// base the turbulence on the new point
turb =fast_turbulence(direction);
*density = pow_table[(int)((turb*turb)*(.25*(POW_TABLE_SIZE-1)))];
// make sure density isn't greater than 1
if(*density >1)
  *density=1;
}
```

As in the fog and steam_moving procedures, the volume_fog_animation procedure uses the same values for SWIRL_FRAMES (126) and SWIRL_AMOUNT ($2\pi/126$). SPEED controls the rate of horizontal movement, and the value I use to produce gently rolling fog is 0.012. The results achievable by this procedure can be seen in Fig. 6.5, which is a still from an animation entitled *Getting into Art* [4]. For this image, parms[1] = 0.22 and parms[2] = 4.0.

6.3.1.3 Smoke Rising

The final example of helical path effects is the animation of the smoke_stream procedure given earlier to create a single column of smoke. Two different helical paths are used to produce the swirling column of smoke. This smoke_stream

FIGURE 6.5

A scene from *Getting into Art*, showing volume-rendered fog animation created by horizontal helical paths (Copyright © 1990 David S. Ebert).

procedure already used a helical path to displace each point to get a more convincing column of smoke. We will now modify this helical path to make it a downward helical path based on the frame number, creating the rising column of smoke. The second helical path will actually displace the center point of the cylinder, producing a swirling cylinder of smoke. This second helical path will swirl at a different rate than the first. The same input parameter values can be used for this procedure. The following is the procedure that is the result of these modifications.

```
// *********************************************************
// Rising_smoke_stream
// *********************************************************
// parms[1] = maximum density value - density scaling factor
// parms[2] = height for 0 density (end of ramping it off)
// parms[3] = height to start adding turbulence
// parms[4] = height (length) for maximum turbulence
// parms[5] = height to start ramping off density
// parms[6] = center.y
// parms[7] = speed for rising
// parms[8] = radius
// parms[9] = max radius of swirling
// *********************************************************
void rising_smoke_stream(xyz_td pnt,float *density, float
                         *parms, xyz_td pnt_world, vol_td *vol)
```

```
{
 float dist_sq;
 extern float offset[OFFSET_SIZE];
 extern int frame_num;
 static int calcd=1;
 static float down, cos_theta2, sin_theta2;
 xyz_td hel_path, center, diff, direction2;
 double ease(), turb_amount, theta_swirl, cos_theta, sin_theta;
 static xyz_td bottom;
 static double rad_sq, max_turb_length, radius, big_radius,
               st_d_ramp, d_ramp_length, end_d_ramp, down3,
               inv_max_turb_length, cos_theta3, sin_theta3;
 double        height, fast_turb, t_ease, path_turb, rad_sq2;

 if(calcd)
   {
     bottom.x = 0; bottom.z = 0;
     bottom.y = parms[6];
     radius = parms[8];
     big_radius = parms[9];
     rad_sq = radius*radius;
     max_turb_length = parms[4];
     inv_max_turb_length = 1/max_turb_length;
     st_d_ramp = parms[5];
     st_d_ramp =MIN(st_d_ramp, end_d_ramp);
     end_d_ramp = parms[2];
     d_ramp_length = end_d_ramp - st_d_ramp;
     //calculate rotation about the helix axis based on frame_number
***  theta_swirl=(frame_num%SWIRL_FRAMES_SMOKE)*SWIRL_SMOKE; // swirling
***  cos_theta = cos(theta_swirl);
***  sin_theta = sin(theta_swirl);
***  down = (float)(frame_num)*DOWN_SMOKE*.75 * parms[7];
     // Calculate sine and cosine of the different radii of the
     // two helical paths
***  cos_theta2 = .01*cos_theta;
***  sin_theta2 = .0075*sin_theta;
***  cos_theta3 = cos_theta2*2.25;
***  sin_theta3 = sin_theta2*4.5;
***  down3 = down*2.25;
     calcd = 0;
   }
 height = pnt_world.y - bottom.y + fast_noise(pnt)*radius;
 // We don't want smoke below the bottom of the column
 if(height < 0)
   {*density = 0; return;}
```

```
  height -= parms[3];
  if (height < 0.0)
    height = 0.0;
  // calculate the eased turbulence, taking into account the
  // value may be greater than 1, which ease won't handle.
  t_ease = height* inv_max_turb_length;
  if(t_ease > 1.0)
    { t_ease =((int)(t_ease))+ease((t_ease-((int)t_ease)), .001,.999);
      if( t_ease > 2.5) t_ease = 2.5;
    }
  else
    t_ease = ease(t_ease, .5, .999);
  // move point along the helical path before evaluating turbulence
*** pnt.x += cos_theta3;
*** pnt.y -= down3;
*** pnt.z += sin_theta3;
  fast_turb = fast_turbulence_three(pnt);
  turb_amount = (fast_turb -0.875)* (.2 + .8*t_ease);
  path_turb = fast_turb*(.2 + .8*t_ease);
  // add turbulence to the height & see if it is above the top
  height += 0.1*turb_amount;
  if(height > end_d_ramp)
    { *density = 0; return; }
  //increase the radius of the column as the smoke rises
  if(height <= 0)
    rad_sq2 = rad_sq*.25;
  else if (height <= end_d_ramp)
    {
      rad_sq2 = (.5 +.5*(ease( height/(1.75*end_d_ramp),.5, .5)))*radius;
      rad_sq2 *= rad_sq2;
    }
  else
    rad_sq2 = rad_sq;
  //
  // move along a helical path plus add the ability to use tables
  //
  // calculate the path based on the unperturbed flow: helical path
  //
*** hel_path.x = cos_theta2 *(1+path_turb)*(1+t_ease*.1)*
      (1+cos((pnt_world.y+down*.5)*M_PI*2)*.11) + big_radius*path_turb;
*** hel_path.z = sin_theta2 * (1+path_turb)*(1+ t_ease*.1)*
      (1+sin((pnt_world.y +down*.5)*M_PI*2)*.085) + .03*path_turb;
*** hel_path.y = (- down) - path_turb;
  XYZ_ADD(direction2, pnt_world, hel_path);
  // adjusting center point for ramping off density based on the
```

```
  // turbulence of the moved point
turb_amount *= big_radius;
center.x = bottom.x - turb_amount;
center.z = bottom.z + .75*turb_amount;
  // calculate the radial distance from the center and ramp
  // off the density based on this distance squared.
diff.x = center.x - direction2.x;
diff.z = center.z - direction2.z;
dist_sq = diff.x*diff.x + diff.z*diff.z;
if(dist_sq > rad_sq2)
    {*density = 0; return;}
*density = (1-dist_sq/rad_sq2 + fast_turb*.05)* parms[1];
if(height > st_d_ramp)
    *density *= (1-ease( (height - st_d_ramp)/(d_ramp_length),
                         .5 , .5));
}
```

The statements that have been changed from the smoke_stream procedure are marked with three asterisks (***). As can be seen, the main changes are in calculating and using two helical paths based on the frame number. One path displaces the center of the cylinder, and the point being rendered is moved along the other path. After trials with only one helical path, it becomes clear that two helical paths give a better effect. Figure 6.6 shows the results of this rising_smoke_stream procedure. This figure contains three images from an animation of rising smoke.

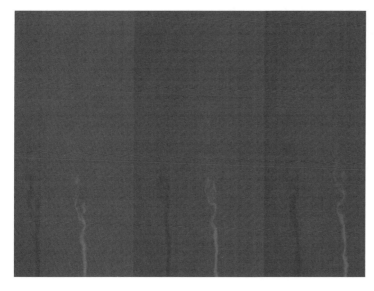

FIGURE 6.6

Rising column of smoke animation. Images are every 30 frames (Copyright © 1994 David S. Ebert).

6.4 THREE-DIMENSIONAL TABLES

As shown above, a wide variety of effects can be achieved through the use of helical paths. These aforementioned procedures require the same type of path to be used for movement throughout the entire volume of gas. Obviously, more complex motion can be achieved by having different path motions for different locations within the gas. A three-dimensional table specifying different procedures for different locations within the volume is a good, flexible solution for creating complex motion in this manner.

The use of three-dimensional tables (solid spaces) to control the animation of the gases is an extension of my previous use of solid spaces in which three-dimensional tables were used for volume shadowing effects [3].

The three-dimensional tables are handled in the following manner: the table surrounds the gas volume in world space, and values are stored at each of the lattice points in the table (see Fig. 6.7). These values represent the calculated values for that specific location in the volume. To determine the values for other locations in the volume, the eight table entries forming the parallelepiped surrounding the point are interpolated. For speed in accessing the table values, I currently require table dimensions to be powers of two and actually store the three-dimensional table as a one-dimensional array. This restriction allows the use of simple bit-shifting operations in determining the array index. These tables could be extended to have nonuniform spacing between table entries within each dimension, creating an octree-like structure; however, this would greatly increase the time necessary to access values from the table, as this fast bit-shifting approach could no longer be used. Table dimensions are commonly of the order of $64 \times 64 \times 64$ or $128 \times 64 \times 32$.

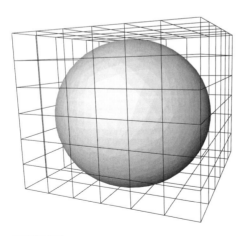

FIGURE 6.7

Three-dimensional table surrounding a sphere.

I use two types of tables for controlling the motion of the gases: vector field tables and functional flow field tables. The vector field tables store direction vectors, density scaling factors, and other information for their use at each point in the lattice. Therefore, these tables are suited for visualizing computational fluid dynamics simulations or using external programs for controlling the gas motion. The vector field tables will not be described in this chapter. A thorough description of their use and merits can be found in [5]. This chapter concentrates on the use of functional flow field tables for animation control.

The functional flow field and vector field tables are incorporated into the volume density functions for controlling the shape and movement of the gas. Each volume density function has a default path and velocity for the gas movement. First, the default path and velocity are calculated; second, the vector field tables are evaluated; and finally, functions that calculate direction vectors, density scaling factors, and so on from the functional flow field tables are applied. The default path vector, the vector from the vector field table, and the vector from the flow field function are combined to produce the new path for the movement through the gas space.

6.4.1 Accessing the Table Entries

When values are accessed from these tables during rendering, the location of the sample point within the table is determined. As mentioned earlier, this point will lie within a parallelepiped formed by the eight table entries that surround the point. The values at these eight points are interpolated to determine the final value. The location within the table is determined by first mapping the three-dimensional screen space point back into world space. The following formula is then used to find the location of the point within the table:

```
ptable.x = (point.x-table_start.x) * table_inv_step.x
ptable.y = (point.y-table_start.y) * table_inv_step.y
ptable.z = (point.z-table_start.z) * table_inv_step.z
```

`ptable` is the location of the point within the three-dimensional table, which is determined from `point`, the location of the point in world space. `table_start` is the location in world space of the starting table entry, and `table_inv_step` is the inverse of the step size between table elements in each dimension. Once the location within the table is determined, the values corresponding to the eight surrounding table entries are then interpolated (trilinear interpolation should suffice).

6.4.2 Functional Flow Field Tables

Functional flow field tables are a valuable tool for choreographing gas animation. These tables define, for each region of the gas, which functions to evaluate to control the gas movement. Each flow field table entry can contain either one specific function to evaluate or a list of functions to evaluate to determine the path for the gas motion (path through the gas space). For each function, a file is specified that contains the type of function and parameters for that function. The functions evaluated by the flow field tables return the following information:

- Direction vector
- Density scaling value
- Percentage of vector to use
- Velocity

The advantage of using flow field functions is that they can provide infinite detail in the motion of the gas. They are not stored at a fixed resolution but are evaluated for each point that is volume rendered. The disadvantage is that the functions are much more expensive to evaluate than simply interpolating values from the vector field table.

The "percentage of vector to use" value in the previous list is used to provide a smooth transition between control of the gas movement by the flow field functions, the vector field tables, and the default path of the gas. This value is also used to allow a smooth transition between control of the gas by different flow field functions. This value will decrease as the distance from the center of control of a given flow field function increases.

6.4.3 Functional Flow Field Functions

Two powerful types of functions for controlling the movement of the gases are attractors/repulsors and vortex functions. Repulsors are the *exact* opposite of attractors, so only attractors will be described here. To create a repulsor from an attractor, simply negate the direction vector.

All the following procedures will take as input the location of the point in the solid space (pnt) and a structure containing parameters for each instance of the function (ff). These procedures will return a density scaling factor (density_scaling), the direction vector for movement through the gas space (direction), the percentage of this vector to use in determining the motion through the gas space (percent_to_use), and a velocity scaling factor (velocity). The density_scaling parameter allows these procedures to decrease or increase the gas density as it moves through a region of space. The velocity parameter similarly allows these procedures to change the velocity of the gas as it moves through a region of space. The most important parameters, however, are the direction and percent_to_use parameters, which are used to determine the path motion through the solid space.

6.4.3.1 Attractors

Attractors are primitive functions that can provide a wide range of effects. Figure 6.8 shows several frames of an attractor whose attraction increases in strength over time. Each attractor has a minimum and maximum attraction value. In this figure, the interpolation varies over time between the minimum and maximum attraction values of the attractor. By animating the location and strength of an attractor, many different effects can be achieved. Effects such as a breeze blowing (see Fig. 6.9) and the wake of a moving object are easy to create. Spherical attractors create paths radially away from the center of attraction (as stated previously, path movement needs to be in the opposite direction of the desired visual effect). The following is an example of a simple spherical attractor function:

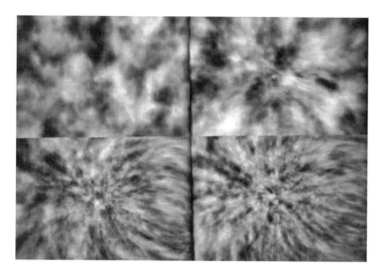

FIGURE 6.8

Effect of a spherical
attractor increasing
over time. Images
are every 45 frames.
The top-left image
has 0 attraction.
The lower right
image has the
maximum attraction
(Copyright © 1992
David S. Ebert).

FIGURE 6.9

An increasing breeze
blowing toward
the right created
by an attractor
(Copyright © 1991
David S. Ebert).

```
void spherical_attractor(xyz_td point, flow_func_td ff, xyz_td
                         *direction, float *density_scaling,
                         float *velocity, float *percent_to_use)
{
float dist, d2;
// calculate distance & direction from center of attractor
XYZ_SUB(*direction, point, ff.center);
dist=sqrt(DOT_XYZ(*direction,*direction));
```

```
// set the density scaling and the velocity to 1
*density_scaling=1.0;
*velocity=1.0;
// calculate the falloff factor (cosine)
if(dist > ff.distance)
   *percent_to_use=0;
else if (dist < ff.falloff_start)
   *percent_to_use=1.0;
else
  { d2 =(dist-ff.falloff_start)/(ff.distance-
                              ff.falloff_start);
 *percent_to_use = (cos(d2*M_PI)+1.0)*.5;
   }
}
```

The flow_func_td structure contains parameters for each instance of the spherical attractor. The parameters include the center of the attractor (ff.center), the effective distance of attraction (ff.distance), and the location to begin the falloff from the attractor path to the default path (ff.falloff_start). This function ramps the use of the attractor path from ff.falloff_start to ff.distance. A cosine function is used for a smooth transition between the path defined by the attractor and the default path of the gas.

6.4.3.2 *Extensions of Spherical Attractors*

Variations on this simple spherical attractor include moving attractors, angle-limited attractors, attractors with variable maximum attraction, nonspherical attractors, and of course, combinations of any or all of these types.

One variation on the preceding spherical attractor procedure is to animate the location of the center of attraction. This allows for dynamic animation control of the gas. Another useful variation is angle-limited attractors. As opposed to having the range of the attraction being 360°, an axis and an angle for the range of attraction can be specified. This can be implemented in a manner very similar to angle-limited light sources and can be animated over time. These two variations can be combined to produce interesting effects. For example, an angle-limited attractor following the movement of the object can create a wake from a moving object. This attractor will cause the gas behind the object to be displaced and pulled in the direction of the moving object. The minimum and maximum attraction of the attractor can also be animated over time to produce nice effects as seen in Figs 6.8 and 6.9. Figure 6.8 shows an attractor increasing in strength over time, and Fig. 6.9 shows a breeze blowing the steam rising from a teacup. As will be described later, the breeze is simulated with an animated attractor.

The geometry of the attraction can be not only spherical but also planar or linear. A linear attractor can be used for creating the flow of a gas along a wall, as will be explained later.

6.4.3.3 Spiral Vortex Functions

Vortex functions have a variety of uses, from simulating actual physical vortices to creating interesting disturbances in flow patterns as an approximation of turbulent flow. The procedures described are not attempts at a physical simulation of vortices – an extremely complex procedure requiring large amounts of supercomputer time for approximation models.

One vortex function is based on the simple 2D polar coordinate function

$$r = \theta$$

which translates into three-dimensional coordinates as

$$x = \theta \times \cos(\theta)$$
$$y = \theta \times \sin(\theta)$$

The third dimension is normally linear movement over time along the third axis. To animate this function, θ is based on the frame number. To increase the vortex action, a scalar multiplier for the sine and cosine terms based on the distance from the vortex's axis is added. This polar equation alone produces swirling motion; however, more convincing vortices can be created by the modifications described below, which base the angle of rotation on both the frame number and the distance from the center of the vortex. The resulting vortex procedure is the following:

```
void calc_vortex(xyz_td *pt, flow_func_td *ff, xyz_td *direction,
    float *velocity, float *percent_to_use, int frame_num)
 {
 static tran_mat_td mat={0,0,0,0,0,0,0,0,0,0,0,0,0,0,0,0};
 xyz_td       dir, pt2, diff;
 float        theta, dist, d2, dist2;
 float        cos_theta, sin_theta, compl_cos, ratio_mult;
 // calculate distance from center of vortex
XYZ_SUB(diff,(*pt), ff->center);
dist = sqrt(DOT_XYZ(diff,diff));
 dist2 = dist/ff->distance;
 // calculate angle of rotation about the axis
 theta = (ff->parms[0]*(1+.001*(frame_num)))/
        (pow((.1+dist2*.9), ff->parms[1]));
  // calculate matrix for rotating about the cylinder's axis
 calc_rot_mat(theta, ff->axis, mat);
transform_XYZ((long)1,mat,pt,&pt2);
 XYZ_SUB(dir,pt2,(*pt));
 direction->x = dir.x;
 direction->y = dir.y;
```

```
  direction->z = dir.z;
  // Have the maximum strength increase from frame parms[4] to
  // parms[5] to a maximum of parms[2]
  if(frame_num < ff->parms[4])
    ratio_mult = 0;
  else if (frame_num <= ff->parms[5])
    ratio_mult = (frame_num - ff->parms[4])/
              (ff->parms[5] - ff->parms[4])* ff ->parms[2];
  else
    ratio_mult = ff->parms[2];
    //calculate the falloff factor
  if(dist > ff->distance)
     { *percent_to_use = 0;
      *velocity = 1;
     }
  else if (dist < ff->falloff_start)
     { *percent_to_use = 1.0 *ratio_mult;
      // calc velocity
      *velocity = 1.0+(1.0 - (dist/ff->falloff_start));
     }
  else
     { d2 = (dist-ff->falloff_start)/(ff->distance -
                                   ff->falloff_start);
      *percent_to_use = (cos(d2*M_PI)+1.0)*.5*ratio_mult;
      *velocity = 1.0+(1.0 - (dist/ff->falloff_start));
     }
}
```

This procedure uses the earlier polar function in combination with suggestions from Karl Sims [6] to produce the vortex motion. For these vortices, both the frame number and the relative distance of the point from the center (or axis) of rotation determine the angle of rotation about the axis. The direction vector is then the vector difference of the transformed point and the original point. The calc_vortex procedure also allows the animation of the strength of the vortex action.

A third type of vortex function is based on the conservation of angular momentum: $r * q = constant,$ where r is the distance from the center of the vortex. This formula can be used in the earlier vortex procedure to calculate the angle of rotation about the axis of the vortex: $\theta = (time * constant)/r.$ The angular momentum will be conserved, producing more realistic motion.

An example of the effects achievable by the previous vortex procedure can be seen in Fig. 6.10. Animating the location of these vortices produces interesting effects, especially when coordinating their movement with the movement of objects in the scene, such as a swirling wake created by an object moving through the gas.

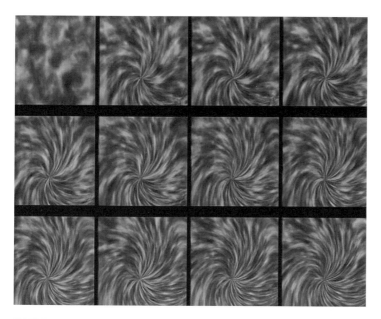

FIGURE 6.10

Spiral vortex. Images are every 21 frames. The top-left image is the default motion of the gas. The remaining images show the effects of the spiral vortex (Copyright © 1994 David S. Ebert).

6.4.4 Combinations of Functions

The real power of flow field functions is the ability to combine these primitive functions to control the gas movement through different volumes of space. The combination of flow field functions provides very interesting and complex gas motion. Two examples of the combination of flow field functions, wind blowing and flow into a hole, are presented next to illustrate the power of this technique.

6.4.4.1 Wind Effects

The first complex gas motion example is wind blowing the steam rising from a teacup. A spherical attractor is used to create the wind effect. Figure 6.9 shows frames of an animation of a breeze blowing the steam from the left of the image. To produce this effect, an attractor was placed to the upper right of the teacup and the strength of attraction was increased over time. The maximum attraction was only 30%, producing a light breeze. An increase in the maximum attraction would simulate an increase in the strength of the wind. The top-left image shows the steam rising vertically with no effect of the wind. The sequence of images (top right image to bottom right image) shows the effect on the steam as the breeze starts blowing toward the right of the image. This is a simple combination of helical motion with an attractor. Notice how the volume of the steam, as well as the motion of the individual plumes, is "blown" toward the upper right. This effect was created by moving the center of the volume point for the ramping of the density over time. The *x*-value of the center point is increased based on the height from the cup and the frame number. By changing the spherical_attractor flow function and the steam_moving procedure given earlier, the blowing effect can be implemented. The following is the addition needed to the spherical_attractor procedure:

```
// ************************************************
// Move the Volume of the Steam
// Shifting is based on the height above the cup
// (parms[6]->parms[7]) and the frame range for increasing
// the strength of the attractor. This is from ratio_mult
// that is calculated above in calc_vortex.
// ************************************************
// Have the maximum strength increase from frame parms[4] to
// parms[5] to a maximum of parms[2]
if(frame_num < ff->parms[4])
   ratio_mult = 0;
else if (frame_num <= ff->parms[5])
   ratio_mult = (frame_num - ff->parms[4])/
    (ff->parms[5] - ff->parms[4]) * ff->parms[2];
if(point.y < ff->parms[6])
    x_disp = 0;
 else
 {if(point.y <= ff->parms[7])
    d2=COS_ERP((point.y-ff->parms[6])/
              (ff->parms[7]-ff->parms[6]));
   else
    d2 = 0;
    x_disp=(1-d2)*ratio_mult*parms[8]+fast_noise(point)*
           ff->parms[9];
 }
return(x_disp);
```

Table 6.2 clarifies the use of all the parameters. The ratio_mult value for increasing the strength of the attraction is calculated in the same way as in the calc_vortex procedure. The x_disp value needs to be returned to the steam_rising function. This value is then added to the center variable before the density is ramped off. The following addition to the steam_rising procedure will accomplish this:

```
center = vol.shape.center;
center.x += x_disp;
```

Table 6.2 Parameters for wind effects

Variables	Description
`point`	Location of the point in world space
`ff → parms[2]`	Maximum strength of attraction
`ff → parms[4]`	Starting frame for attraction increasing
`ff → parms[5]`	Ending strength for attraction increasing
`ff → parms[6]`	Minimum y-value for steam displacement
`ff → parms[7]`	Maximum y-value for steam displacement
`ff → parms[8]`	Maximum amount of steam displacement
`ff → parms[9]`	Amount of noise to add in

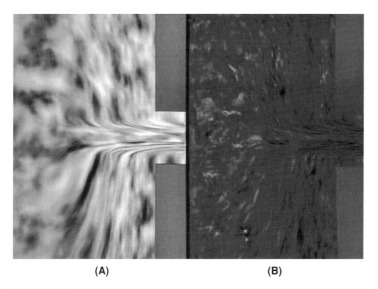

(A)　　　　　　　　　**(B)**

FIGURE 6.11

(A) Gas flowing into a hole in the wall. (B) Liquid flowing into a hole in the wall (Copyright © 1991 David S. Ebert).

6.4.4.2 Flow into a Hole in a Wall

The next example of combining flow field functions constrains the flow into an opening in a wall. The resulting images are shown in Fig. 6.11. Figure 6.11(A) shows gas flowing into an opening in a wall on the right of the image. Figure 6.11(B) shows liquid flowing into the opening. For this example, three types of functions are used. The first function is an angle-limited spherical attractor placed at the center of the hole. This attractor has a range of 180° from the axis of the hole toward the left. The next function is an angle-limited repulsor placed at the same location, again with a range of repulsion of 180° but to the right of the hole. These two functions create the flow into the hole and through the hole. The final type of function creates the tangential flow along the walls. This function can be considered a linear attraction field on the left side of the hole. The line in this case would be through the hole and perpendicular to the wall (horizontal). This attractor has maximum attraction near the wall, with the attraction decreasing as the distance from the wall increases. As can be seen from the flow patterns toward the hole and along the wall in Fig. 6.11, the effect is very convincing. This figure also shows how these techniques can be applied to hypertextures. Figure 6.11(B) is rendered as a hypertexture to simulate a (compressible) liquid flowing into the opening.

6.5 ANIMATING HYPERTEXTURES

All the animation techniques described above can be applied to hypertextures; only the rendering algorithm needs to be changed. The volume density functions that I use for gases are, in reality, hypertexture functions. The difference is that an atmospheric rendering model is used. Therefore, by using a nongaseous model for illumination and for converting densities to opacities, the techniques described above will produce hypertexture animations. An example of this is Fig. 6.11(B). The geometry and motion procedures are the same for both the images in Fig. 6.11.

6.5.1 Volumetric Marble Formation

One other example of hypertexture animation will be explored: simulating marble formation. The addition of hypertexture animation to the solid texture animation discussed earlier will increase the realism of the animation considerably.

One approach is to base the density changes on the color of the marble. Initially, no turbulence will be added to the "fluid": density values will be determined in a manner similar to the marble color values, giving the different bands different densities. Just as in the earlier `marble_forming` procedure, turbulence will be added over time. In the following procedure, these changes are achieved by returning the amount of turbulence, `turb_amount`, from the solid-texture function, `marble_forming`, described earlier. The density is based on the turbulence amount from the solid-texture function. This is then shaped using the power function in a similar manner to the gas functions given before. Finally, a trick by Perlin (subtracting 0.5, multiplying by a scalar, adding 0.5, and limiting the result to the range of 0.2–1.0) is used to form a hard surface more quickly [7]. The result of this function can be seen in Fig. 6.12.

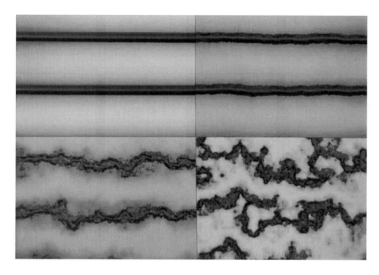

```
//
// parms[1] = maximum density value: density scaling factor
// parms[2] = exponent for density scaling
// parms[3] = x resolution for Perlin's trick (0-640)
// parms[8] = 1/radius of fuzzy area for Perlin's trick(> 1.0)
//
void molten_marble(xyz_td pnt, float *density, float *parms,
                   vol_td vol)
{
 float parms_scalar, turb_amount;
 turb_amount = solid_txt(pnt,vol);
 *density = (pow(turb_amount, parms[2]) )*0.35 +0.65;
 // Introduce harder surface more quickly.
 // parms[3] multiplied by 1/640
 *density *= parms[1];
 parms_scalar = (parms[3]*.0015625)*parms[8];
 *density = (*density-0.5)*parms_scalar +0.5;
 *density = MAX(0.2, MIN(1.0,*density));
}
```

6.6 PARTICLE SYSTEMS: ANOTHER PROCEDURAL ANIMATION TECHNIQUE

As previously mentioned, particle systems are different from the rest of the procedural techniques presented in this book in that their abstraction is in control of the animation and specification of the object. Particle systems were first used in computer graphics by Reeves [8] to model a wall of fire for the movie *Star Trek II: The*

Wrath of Khan. Since particle systems are a volumetric modeling technique, they are most commonly used to represent volumetric natural phenomena such as fire, water, clouds, snow, and rain [8]. *Structured particle systems*, an extension of particle systems, have also been used to model grass and trees [9].

A particle system is defined by both a collection of geometric particles and the algorithms that govern their creation, movement, and death. Each geometric particle has several attributes, including its initial position, velocity, size, color, transparency, shape, and lifetime.

To create an animation of a particle system object, the following are performed at each time step [8]:

- New particles are generated and assigned their attributes.
- Particles that have existed in the system past their lifetime are removed.
- Each remaining particle is moved and transformed by the particle system algorithms as prescribed by their individual attributes.
- These particles are rendered, using special-purpose rendering algorithms, to produce an image of the particle system.

The creation, death, and movement of particles are controlled by stochastic procedures, allowing complex, realistic motion to be created with a few parameters. The creation procedure for particles is controlled by parameters defining either the mean number of particles created at each time step and its variance or the mean number of particles created per unit of screen area at each time step and its variance. These values can be varied over time as well. The actual number of particles created is stochastically determined to be within *mean + variance* and *mean − variance*. The initial color, velocity, size, and transparency are also stochastically determined by mean and variance values. The initial shape of the particle system is defined by an origin, a region about this origin in which new generated particles are placed, angles defining the orientation of the particle system, and the initial direction of movement for the particles.

The movement of particles is also controlled by stochastic procedures (stochastically determined velocity vectors). These procedures move the particles by adding their velocity vector to their position vector. Random variations can be added to the velocity vector at each frame, and acceleration procedures can be incorporated to simulate effects such as gravity, vorticity, conservation of momentum and energy, wind fields, air resistance, attraction, repulsion, turbulence fields, and vortices. The simulation of physically based forces allows realistic motion and complex dynamics to be displayed by the particle system while being controlled by only a few parameters. Besides the movement of particles, their color and transparency can also change dynamically to give more complex effects. The death of particles is controlled very simply by removing particles from the system whose lifetimes have expired or who have strayed more than a given distance from the origin of the particle system.

The Genesis Demo sequence from *Star Trek II: The Wrath of Khan* is an example of the effects achievable by such a particle system. For this effect, a two-level particle system was used to create the wall of fire. The first-level particle system generated concentric, expanding rings of particle systems on the planet's surface. The second-level particle system generated particles at each of these locations, simulating explosions. During the Genesis Demo sequence, the number of particles in the system ranged from several thousand initially to over 750 000 near the end.

Reeves extended the use of particle systems to model fields of grass and forests of trees, calling this new technique structured particle systems [9]. In structured particle systems, the particles are no longer an independent collection of particles but rather form a connected, cohesive three-dimensional object and have many complex relationships among themselves. Each particle represents an element of a tree (e.g. branch, leaf) or part of a blade of grass. These particle systems are, therefore, similar to L-systems and graftals, specifically probabilistic, context-sensitive L-systems. Each particle is similar to a letter in an L-system alphabet, and the procedures governing the generation, movement, and death of particles are similar to the production rules. However, they differ from L-systems in several ways. First, the goal of structured particle systems is to model the visual appearance of whole collections of trees and grass, and not to correctly model the detailed geometry of each plant. Second, they are not concerned with biological correctness or modeling the growth of plants. Structured particle systems construct trees by recursively generating subbranches, with stochastic variations of parameters such as branching angle, thickness, and placement within a value range for each type of tree. Additional stochastic procedures are used for placement of the trees on the terrain, random warping of branches, and bending of branches to simulate tropism. A forest of such trees can, therefore, be specified with a few parameters for distribution of tree species and several parameters defining the mean values and variances for tree height, width, first branch height, length, angle, and thickness of each species.

Both regular particle systems and structured particle systems pose special rendering problems because of the large number of primitives. Regular particle systems have been rendered simply as point light sources (or linear light sources for anti-aliased moving particles) for fire effects, accumulating the contribution of each particle into the frame buffer and compositing the particle system image with the surface-rendered image. No occlusion or interparticle illumination is considered. Structured particle systems are much more difficult to render, and specialized probabilistic rendering algorithms have been developed to render them [9]. Illumination, shadowing, and hidden surface calculations need to be performed for the particles. Since stochastically varying objects are being modeled, approximately correct rendering will provide sufficient realism. Probabilistic and approximate techniques are used to determine the shadowing and illumination of each tree element. The particle's distance into the tree from the light source determines its amount of diffuse shading and probability of having specular highlights. Self-shadowing is simulated by exponentially decreasing the ambient illumination as the particle's distance within the tree increases. External shadowing is also probabilistically calculated to simulate the shadowing of one tree by another tree. For hidden surface calculations, an initial depth sort of all trees and a painter's algorithm are used. Within each tree, again, a painter's algorithm is used, along with a back-to-front bucket sort of all the particles. This will not correctly solve the hidden surface problem in all cases but will give realistic, approximately correct images. Figure 6.13 contains images from

FIGURE 6.13

Examples of probabilistic rendering of structure particle systems from *The Adventures of André and Wally B* (Image courtesy of W. Reeves and R. Blau).

the animation *The Adventures of André & Wally B,* illustrating the power of structured particle systems and probabilistic rendering techniques for structured particle systems.

Efficient rendering of particle systems is still an open active research problem (e.g. [10]). Although particle systems allow complex scenes to be specified with only a few parameters, they sometimes require rather slow, specialized rendering algorithms. Simulation of fluids [11], cloth ([12,13]; Plath 2000), and surface modeling with oriented particle systems [14] are recent, promising extensions of particle systems. Sims [6] demonstrated the suitability of highly parallel computing architectures to particle systems simulation. Particle systems, with their ease of specification and good dynamical control, have great potential when combined with other modeling techniques such as implicit surfaces [15] and volumetric procedural modeling.

Particle systems provide a very nice, powerful animation system for high-level control of complex dynamics and can be combined with many of the procedural techniques described in this book. For instance, turbulence functions are often combined with particle systems.

6.7 CONCLUSION

This chapter described several approaches to animating procedural models and showed several practical examples. The general animation approaches presented can be used with any procedural model or texture.

REFERENCES

[1] D. Ebert, K. Boyer, D. Roble, Once a pawn a foggy knight ... [videotape], SIGGRAPH Video Review, 54, ACM SIGGRAPH, New York, 1989, (Segment 3).

[2] G. Gardner, Visual simulation of clouds, Comput. Graph. 19 (1985) 297–304 (Proceedings of SIGGRAPH '85, B.A. Barsky (Ed.)).

[3] D.S. Ebert, R.E. Parent, Rendering and animation of gaseous phenomena by combining fast volume and scanline a-buffer techniques, Comput. Graph. 24 (1990) 357–366 (Proceedings of SIGGRAPH '90, F. Baskett (Ed.)).

[4] D. Ebert, J. Ebert, K. Boyer, Getting into art [videotape], Department of Computer and Information Science, Ohio State University, 1990.

[5] D.S. Ebert, Solid spaces: a unified approach to describing object attributes, Ph.D. thesis, Ohio State University, 1991.

[6] K. Sims, Particle animation and rendering using data parallel computation, Comput. Graph. 24 (1990) 405–413 (Proceedings of SIGGRAPH '90, F. Baskett (Ed.)).

[7] K. Perlin, A hypertexture tutorial. SIGGRAPH "92: Course Notes 23, 1992.

[8] W.T. Reeves, Particle systems: a technique for modeling a class of fuzzy objects, ACM Trans. Graph. 2 (1983) 91–108.

[9] W.T. Reeves, R. Blau, Approximate and probabilistic algorithms for shading and rendering structured particle systems, Comput. Graph. 19 (1985) 313–322.

[10] O. Etzmuss, B. Eberhardt, M. Hauth, Implicit-explicit schemes for fast animation with particle systems, Comput. Animat. Simul. 2000 (2000) 138–151.

[11] G. Miller, A. Pearce, Globular dynamics: a connected particle system for animating viscous fluids, Comput. Graph. 13 (1989) 305–309.

[12] D.E. Breen, D.H. House, M.J. Wozny, Predicting the drape of woven cloth using interacting particles, Proceedings of SIGGRAPH '94 (1994) 365–372.

[13] D. Baraff, A.P. Witkin, Large steps in cloth simulation, Proceedings of SIGGRAPH '98 (1998) 43–54.

[14] R. Szeliski, D. Tonnesen, Surface modeling with oriented particle systems, Comput. Graph. 26 (1992) 185–194 (Proceedings of SIGGRAPH "92).

[15] A. Witkin, P. Heckbert, Using particles to sample and control implicit surfaces, in: Andrew Glassner (Ed.), Computer Graphics (Proceedings SIGGRAPH "94), 1994, pp. 269–278.

Animating Fluids and Gases

7

Rick Parent

CHAPTER CONTENTS

Among the most difficult graphical objects to model and animate are those that are not defined by a static, rigid, topologically simple structure. Many of these complex forms are found in nature. They present especially difficult challenges for those intent on controlling their motion. In some cases, special models of a specific phenomenon will suffice. We begin the chapter presenting special models for water, clouds, and fire that approximate their behavior under certain conditions. These models identify salient characteristics of the phenomena and attempt to model those characteristics explicitly. Such approaches are useful for a specific appearance or motion, but for a more robust model, a more rigorous scientific approach is needed. As far as a computational science is concerned, all the phenomena mentioned above fall under the classification of *fluids* and computing their motion is called *computational fluid dynamics* (CFD). The basics of CFD are given at the end of this chapter.

Many of the time-varying models described in this chapter represent work that is state of the art. It is not the objective here to cover all aspects of recent research. The basic models are covered, with only brief reference to the more advanced algorithms.

7.1 SPECIFIC FLUID MODELS

Fire, smoke, and clouds are gaseous phenomena that have no well-defined surface to model. They are inherently volumetric models, although surface-based techniques have been applied with limited success. For example, water when relatively still has a well-defined surface; however, water changes its shape as it moves. In the case of ocean waves, features on the water's surface move, but the water itself does not travel. The simple surface topology can become arbitrarily complex when the water becomes turbulent. Splashing, foaming, and breaking waves are complex processes best modeled by particle systems and volumetric techniques, but these techniques are inefficient in nonturbulent situations. In addition, water can travel from one place to another, form streams, split into separate pools, and collect again. In modeling these phenomena for purposes of computer graphics, programmers often make simplifying assumptions in order to limit the computational complexity and model only those features of the physical processes that are important visually in a specific situation.

7.1.1 Models of Water

Water presents a particular challenge for computer animation because its appearance and motion take various forms [13,15,34,41]. Water can be modeled as a still, rigid-looking surface to which ripples can be added as display attributes by perturbing the surface normal as in bump mapping [2]. Alternatively, water can be modeled as a smoothly rolling height field in which time-varying ripples are incorporated into the geometry of the surface [23]. In ocean waves, it is assumed that there is no transport of water even though the waves travel along the surface in forms that vary from sinusoidal to cycloidal[1] [14,30]. Breaking, foaming, and splashing of the waves are added on top of the model in a postprocessing step [14,30]. The transport of water from one location to another adds more computational complexity to the modeling problem [20].

7.1.1.1 Still Waters and Small-Amplitude Waves

The simplest way to model water is merely to assign the color blue to anything below a given height. If the y-axis is "up," then color any pixel blue in which the world space coordinate of the corresponding visible surface has a y-value less than some given constant. This creates the illusion of still water at a consistent "sea level." It is sufficient for placid lakes and puddles of standing water. Equivalently, a flat blue plane perpendicular to the y-axis and at the height of the water can be used to represent the water's surface. These models, of course, do not produce any animation of the water.

---

[1]A *cycloid* is the curve traced out by a point on the perimeter of a rolling disk.

Normal vector perturbation (essentially the approach employed in bump mapping) can be used to simulate the appearance of small-amplitude waves on an otherwise still body of water. To perturb the normal, one or more simple sinusoidal functions are used to modify the direction of the surface's normal vector. The functions are parameterized in terms of a single variable, usually relating to distance from a *source point*. It is not necessarily the case that the wave starts with zero amplitude at the source. When standing waves in a large body of water are modeled, each function usually has a constant amplitude. The wave crests can be linear, in which case all the waves generated by a particular function travel in a uniform direction, or the wave crests can radiate from a single user-specified or randomly generated source point. Linear wave crests tend to form self-replicating patterns when viewed from a distance. For a different effect, radially symmetrical functions that help to break up these global patterns can be used. Radial functions also simulate the effect of a thrown pebble or raindrop hitting the water (Fig. 7.1). The time-varying height for a point at which the wave begins at time zero is a function of the amplitude and wavelength of the wave (Fig. 7.2). Combining the two, Fig. 7.3 shows the height of a point at some distance d from the start of the wave. This is a two-dimensional

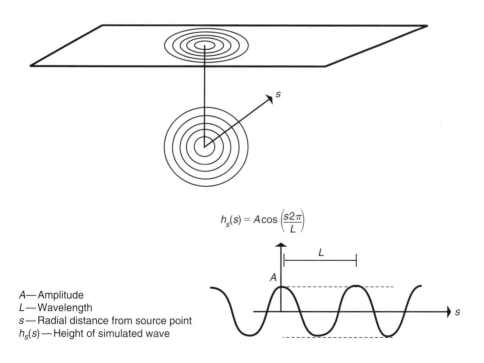

$$h_s(s) = A\cos\left(\frac{s2\pi}{L}\right)$$

A—Amplitude
L—Wavelength
s—Radial distance from source point
$h_s(s)$—Height of simulated wave

FIGURE 7.1

Radially symmetric standing wave.

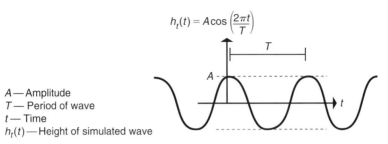

A — Amplitude
T — Period of wave
t — Time
$h_t(t)$ — Height of simulated wave

FIGURE 7.2

Time-varying height of a stationary point.

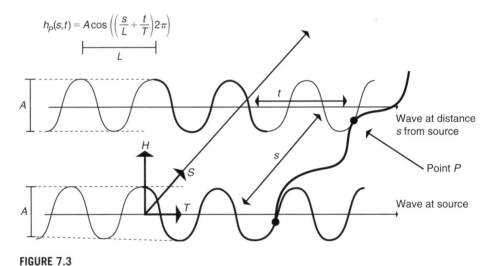

FIGURE 7.3

Time-varying function at point P.

function relative to a point at which the function is zero at time zero. This function can be rotated and translated so that it is positioned and oriented appropriately in world space. Once the height function for a given point is defined, the normal to the point at any instance in time can be determined by computing the tangent vector and forming the vector perpendicular to it (as discussed later and shown in Fig. 7.4). These vectors should then be oriented in world space, so the plane they define contains the direction that the wave is traveling.

Superimposing multiple sinusoidal functions of different amplitude and with various source points (in the radial case) or directions (in the linear case) can generate interesting patterns of overlapping ripples. Typically, the higher the frequency of the

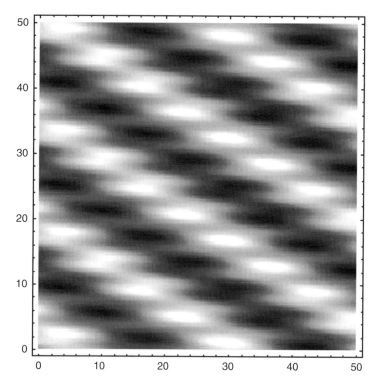

FIGURE 7.4

Superimposed tinear waves of various amptitudes and frequencies.

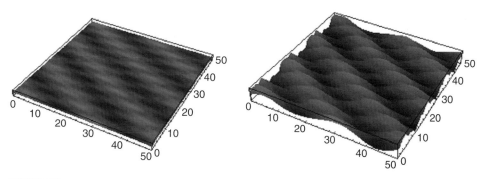

FIGURE 7.5

Normal vector displacement versus height displacement.

wave component, the lower the amplitude (Fig. 7.5). Notice that these do not change the geometry of the surface used to represent the water (e.g. a flat blue plane) but are used only to change the shading properties. Also notice that it must be a time-varying function that propagates the wave along the surface.

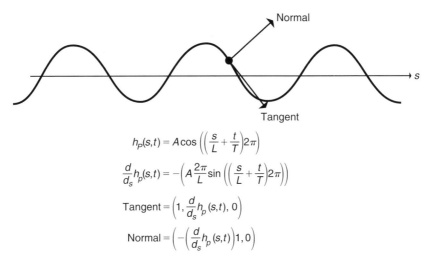

$$h_p(s,t) = A\cos\left(\left(\frac{s}{L}+\frac{t}{T}\right)2\pi\right)$$

$$\frac{d}{d_s}h_p(s,t) = -\left(A\frac{2\pi}{L}\sin\left(\left(\frac{s}{L}+\frac{t}{T}\right)2\pi\right)\right)$$

$$\text{Tangent} = \left(1,\frac{d}{d_s}h_p(s,t),0\right)$$

$$\text{Normal} = \left(-\left(\frac{d}{d_s}h_p(s,t)\right)1,0\right)$$

FIGURE 7.6

Normal vector for two-dimensional wave function.

The same approach used to calculate wave normals can be used to modify the height of the surface (e.g. [23]). A mesh of points can be used to model the surface of the water, and the heights of the individual points can be controlled by the overlapping sinusoidal functions. Either a faceted surface with smooth shading can be used or the points can be the control points of a higher-order surface such as a B-spline surface. The points must be sufficiently dense to sample the height function accurately enough for rendering. Calculating the normals without changing the actual surface creates the illusion of waves on the surface of the water. However, whenever the water meets a protruding surface, like a rock, the lack of surface displacement will be evident. See Fig. 7.6 for a comparison between water surface modeled by normal vector perturbation and a water surface modeled by a height field. An option to reduce the density of mesh points required is to use only the low-frequency, high-amplitude functions to control the height of the surface points and to include the high-frequency, low-amplitude functions to calculate the normals.

7.1.1.2 The Anatomy of Waves

A more sophisticated model must be used to model waves with greater realism, one that incorporates more of the physical effects that produce their appearance and behavior. Waves come in various frequencies, from tidal waves to capillary waves, which are created by wind passing over the surface of the water. The waves collectively called wind waves are those of most interest for visual effects. The sinusoidal form of a simple wave has already been described and is reviewed here in a more appropriate form for the equations that follow. In Eq. (7.1), the function $f(s, t)$

describes the amplitude of the wave in which s is the distance from the source point, t is a point in time, A is the maximum amplitude, C is the propagation speed, and L is the wavelength. The period of the wave, T, is the time it takes for one complete wave to pass a given point. The wavelength, period, and speed are related by the equation $C = L/T$.

$$f(x, t) = A \cos\left(\frac{2\pi\left(s - (Ct)\right)}{L}\right) \tag{7.1}$$

The motion of the wave is different from the motion of the water. The wave travels linearly across the surface of the water while a particle of water moves in nearly a circular orbit (Fig. 7.7). While riding the crest of the wave, the particle will move in the direction of the wave. As the wave passes and the particle drops into the trough between waves, it will travel in the reverse direction. The steepness, S, of the wave is represented by the term H/L, where H is defined as half of the amplitude.

Waves with a small steepness value have basically a sinusoidal shape. As the steepness value increases, the shape of the wave gradually changes into a sharply crested peak with flatter troughs. Mathematically, the shape approaches that of a cycloid.

In an idealized wave, there is no net transport of water. The particle of water completes one orbit in the time it takes for one complete cycle of the wave to pass. The average orbital speed of a particle of water is given by the circumference of the orbit, πH, divided by the time it takes to complete the orbit, T [Eq. (7.2)].

$$Q_{\text{average}} = \frac{\pi H}{T} = \frac{\pi H C}{L} = \pi S C \tag{7.2}$$

If the orbital speed, Q, of the water at the crest exceeds the speed of the wave, C, then the water will spill over the wave, resulting in a breaking wave. Because the average speed, Q, increases as the steepness, S, of the wave increases, this limits the steepness of a nonbreaking wave. The observed steepness of ocean waves, as reported by Peachey [30], is between 0.5 and 1.0.

A common simplification of the full CFD simulation of ocean waves is called the Airy model, and it relates the depth of the water, d, the propagation speed, C, and the wavelength of the wave, L [Eq. (7.3)].

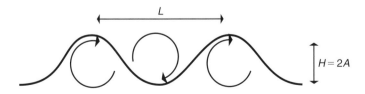

FIGURE 7.7

Circular paths of particles of water subjected to waves.

$$C = \sqrt{\frac{g}{\kappa}\tanh(\kappa d)} = \sqrt{\frac{gL}{2\pi} \cdot \tanh\left(\frac{2\pi d}{L}\right)}$$

$$L = CT$$

(7.3)

In Eq. (7.3), g is the acceleration of a body due to gravity at sea level, 9.81 m/s^2, and $\kappa = 2\pi/L$ is the spatial equivalent of wave frequency. As the depth of the water increases, the function $\tanh(\kappa d)$ tends toward one, so C approaches $gL/2\pi$. As the depth decreases and approaches zero, $\tanh(\kappa d)$ approaches κd, so C approaches $\sqrt{gd}$. Peachey suggests using *deep* to mean $d > L/4$ and *shallow* to mean $d > L/20$.

As a wave approaches the shoreline at an angle, the part of the wave that approaches first will slow down as it encounters a shallower area. The wave will progressively slow down along its length as more of it encounters the shallow area. This will tend to straighten out the wave and is called *wave refraction*.

Interestingly, even though speed (C) and wavelength (L) of the wave are reduced as the wave enters shallow water, the period, T, of the wave remains the same and the amplitude, A (and, equivalently, H), remains the same or increases. As a result, the orbital speed, Q [Eq. (7.2)], of the water remains the same. Because orbital speed remains the same as the speed of the wave decreases, waves tend to break as they approach the shoreline because the speed of the water exceeds the speed of the wave. The breaking of a wave means that water particles break off from the wave surface as they are "thrown forward" beyond the front of the wave.

7.1.1.3 Modeling Ocean Waves

The description of modeling ocean waves presented here follows Peachey [30]. The ocean surface is represented as a height field, $y = f(x, z, t)$, where (x, z) defines the two-dimensional ground plane, t is the time, and y is the height. The wave function f is a sum of various waveforms at different amplitudes [Eq. (7.4)].

$$f(x, z, t) = \sum_{i=1}^{n} A_i W_i(x, z, t)$$

(7.4)

The wave function, W_i, is formed as the composition of two functions: a wave profile, w_i; and a phase function, $\theta_i(x, z, t)$, according to Eq. (7.5). This allows the description of the wave profile and phase function to be addressed separately.

$$W_i(x, z, t) = w_i\left(\text{fraction}\left[\theta_i(x, z, t)\right]\right)$$

(7.5)

Each waveform is described by its period, amplitude, source point, and direction. It is convenient to define each waveform, actually each phase function, as a linear rather than radial wave and to orient it so the wave is perpendicular to the x-axis and originates at the source point. The phase function is then a function only of the x-coordinate and can then be rotated and translated into position in world space.

Equation (7.6) gives the time dependence of the phase function. Thus, if the phase function is known for all points x (assuming the alignment of the waveform along the x-axis), then the phase function can be easily computed at any time at any position. If the depth of water is constant, the Airy model states that the wavelength and speed are also constant. In this case, the aligned phase function is given in Eq. (7.7).

$$\theta_i(x, z, t) = \theta_i(x, z, t_0) - \frac{t - t_0}{T_i} \tag{7.6}$$

$$\theta_i(x, z, t) = \frac{x_i}{L_i} \tag{7.7}$$

However, if the depth of the water is variable, then L_i is a function of depth and θ_i is the integral of the depth-dependent phase-change function from the origin to the point of interest [Eq. (7.8)]. Numerical integration can be used to produce phase values at predetermined grid points. These grid points can be used to interpolate values within grid cells. Peachey [30] successfully uses bilinear interpolation to accomplish this.

$$\theta_i(x, z, t) = \int_0^x \theta_i'(u, z, t)\,du \tag{7.8}$$

The wave profile function, w_i, is a single-value periodic function of the fraction of the phase function [Eq. (7.5)] so that $w_i(u)$ is defined for $0.0 \le u \le 1.0$. The values of the wave profile function range over the interval $[-1, 1]$. The wave profile function is designed so that its value is one at both ends of the interval [Eq. (7.9)].

$$w_i(0.0) = w_i(1.0) = 1.0 \tag{7.9}$$

Linear interpolation can be used to model the changing profile of the wave according to steepness. Steepness (H/L) can be used to blend between a sinusoidal function [Eq. (7.1)] and a cycloid-like function [Eq. (7.10)] designed to resemble a sharp-crested wave profile. In addition, wave asymmetry is introduced as a function of the depth of the water to simulate effects observed in waves as they approach a coastline. The asymmetry interpolant, k, is defined as the ratio between the water depth, d, and deep-water wavelength, L_i [see Eq. (7.11)]. When k is large, the wave profile is handled with no further modification. When k is small, u is raised to a power in order to shift its value toward the low end of the range between zero and one. This has the effect of stretching out the back of the wave and steepening the front of the wave as it approaches the shore.

$$w_i(u) = 8|u - 1/2|^2 - 1 \tag{7.10}$$

$$L_i^{deep} = \frac{gT_i^2}{2\pi}$$

$$k = \frac{d}{L_i^{deep}}$$

(7.11)

As the wave enters very shallow water, the amplitudes of the various wave components are reduced, so the overall amplitude of the wave is kept from exceeding the depth of the water.

Spray and foam resulting from breaking waves and waves hitting obstacles can be simulated using a stochastic but controlled (e.g. Gaussian distribution) particle system. When the speed of the water, $Q_{average}$, exceeds the speed of the wave, C, then water spray leaves the surface of the wave and is thrown forward. Equation (7.2) indicates that this condition happens when $\pi S > 1.0$ or, equivalently, $S > 1.0/\pi$. Breaking waves are observed with steepness values less than this (around 0.1), which indicates that the water probably does not travel at a uniform orbital speed. Instead, the speed of the water at the top of the orbit is faster than at other points in the orbit. Thus, a user-specified spray-threshold steepness value can be used to trigger the particle system. The number of particles generated is based on the difference between the calculated wave steepness and the spray-threshold steepness.

For a wave hitting an obstacle, a particle system can be used to generate spray in the direction of reflection based on the incoming direction of the wave and the normal of the obstacle surface. A small number of particles are generated just before the moment of impact, are increased to a maximum number at the point of impact, and are then decreased as the wave passes the obstacle. As always, stochastic perturbation should be used to control both speed and direction.

For a more complete treatment of modeling height-field displacement-mapped surface for ocean waves using a Fast Fourier Transform description including modeling and rendering underwater environmental effects, the interested reader is directed to the course notes by Tessendorf [38].

7.1.1.4 Finding Its Way Downhill

One of the assumptions used to model ocean waves is that there is no transport of water. However, in many situations, such as a stream of water running downhill, it is useful to model how water travels from one location to another. In situations in which the water can be considered a height field and the motion assumed to be uniform through a vertical column of water, the vertical component of the velocity can be ignored. In such cases, differential equations can be used to simulate a wide range of convincing motion [20]. The *Navier–Stokes* (NS) equations (which describe flow through a volume) can be simplified to model the flow.

To develop the equations in two dimensions, the user parameterizes functions that are in terms of distance x. Let $z = h(x)$ be the height of the water and $z = b(x)$ be the height of the ground at location x. The height of the water is $d(x) = h(x) - b(x)$. If one assumes that motion is uniform through a vertical column of water and that

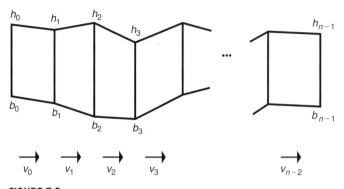

FIGURE 7.8

Discrete two-dimensional representation of height field with water surface h, ground b, and horizontal water velocity v.

$v(x)$ is the velocity of a vertical column of water, then the shallow-water equations are as shown in Eqs. (7.12) and (7.13), where g is the gravitational acceleration (see Fig. 7.8). Equation (7.12) considers the change in velocity of the water and relates its acceleration, the difference in adjacent velocities, and the acceleration due to gravity when adjacent columns of water are at different heights. Equation (7.13) considers the transport of water by relating the temporal change in the height of the vertical column of water with the spatial change in the amount of water moving.

$$\frac{\partial v}{\partial t} + v\frac{\partial v}{\partial x} + g\frac{\partial h}{\partial x} = 0 \tag{7.12}$$

$$\frac{\partial d}{\partial t} + \frac{\partial}{\partial x}(vd) = 0 \tag{7.13}$$

These equations can be further simplified if the assumptions of small fluid velocity and slowly varying depth are used. The former assumption eliminates the second term of Eq. (7.12) while the latter assumption implies that the term d can be removed from inside the derivative in Eq. (7.13). These simplifications result in Eqs. (7.14) and (7.15).

$$\frac{\partial v}{\partial t} + g\frac{\partial h}{\partial x} = 0 \tag{7.14}$$

$$\frac{\partial d}{\partial t} + d\frac{\partial v}{\partial x} = 0 \tag{7.15}$$

Differentiating Eq. (7.14) with respect to x and Eq. (7.15) with respect to t and substituting for the cross derivatives results in Eq. (7.16). This is the one-dimensional wave equation with a wave velocity $\sqrt{gd}$. As Kass and Miller [20] note, this degree of simplification is probably not accurate enough for engineering applications.

$$\frac{\partial^2 h}{\partial t^2} = gd\frac{\partial^2 h}{\partial x^2} \tag{7.16}$$

This partial differential equation is solved using finite differences. The discretization, as used by Kass and Miller, is set up as in Fig. 7.8, with samples of v positioned halfway between the samples of h. The authors report a stable discretization, resulting in Eqs. (7.17) and (7.18). Putting these two equations together results in Eq. (7.19), which is the discrete version of Eq. (7.16).

$$\frac{\partial h_i}{\partial t} = \left(\frac{d_{i-1} + d_i}{2\Delta x}\right)v_{i-1} - \left(\frac{d_i + d_{i+1}}{2\Delta x}\right)v_i \tag{7.17}$$

$$\frac{\partial v_i}{\partial t} = \frac{(-g)(h_{i+1} - h_i)}{\Delta x} \tag{7.18}$$

$$\frac{\partial^2 h_i}{\partial t^2} = -g\left(\frac{d_{i-1} + d_i}{2(\Delta x)^2}\right)(h_i - h_{i-1}) + g\left(\frac{d_i + d_{i+1}}{2(\Delta x)^2}\right)(h_{i+1} - h_i) \tag{7.19}$$

Equation (7.19) states the relationship of the height of the water surface to the height's acceleration in time. This could be solved by using values of h_i to compute the left-hand side and then using this value to update the next time step. As Kass and Miller report, however, this approach diverges quickly because of the sample spacing.

A first-order implicit numerical integration technique is used to provide a stable solution to Eq. (7.19). Numerical integration uses current sample values to approximate derivatives. Explicit methods use approximated derivatives to update the current samples to their new values. Implicit integration techniques find the value whose derivative matches the discrete approximation of the current samples. Implicit techniques typically require more computation per step, but, because they are less likely to diverge significantly from the correct values, larger time steps can be taken, thus producing an overall savings.

Kass and Miller find that a first-order implicit method [Eqs. (7.20), (7.21)] is sufficient for this application. Using these equations to solve for $h(n)$ and substituting Eq. (7.19) for the second derivative $(\ddot{h}(n))$ results in Eq. (7.22).

$$\dot{h}(n) = \frac{h(n) - h(n-1)}{\Delta t} \tag{7.20}$$

$$\ddot{b}(n) = \frac{\dot{b}(n) - \dot{b}(n-1)}{\Delta t} \tag{7.21}$$

$$b_i(n) = 2b_i(n-1) - b_i(n-2) - g(\Delta t)^2 \frac{d_{i-1} + d_i}{2 \cdot \Delta x^2} (b_i(n) - b_{i-1}(n))$$

$$+ g(\Delta t)^2 \frac{d_i + d_{i+1}}{2 \cdot \Delta x^2} (b_{i+1}(n) - b_i(n)) \tag{7.22}$$

Assuming d is constant during the iteration, the next value of b can be calculated from previous values with the symmetric tridiagonal linear system represented by Eqs. (7.23)–(7.25).

$$Ab_i(n) = 2b_i(n-1) + b_i(n-2) \tag{7.23}$$

$$A = \begin{bmatrix} e_0 & f_0 & 0 & 0 & 0 & 0 & 0 \\ f_0 & e_1 & f_1 & 0 & 0 & 0 & 0 \\ 0 & f_1 & e_2 & \cdots & 0 & 0 & 0 \\ 0 & 0 & & & 0 & 0 \\ 0 & 0 & 0 & & e_{n-3} & f_{n-3} & 0 \\ 0 & 0 & 0 & 0 & f_{n-3} & e_{n-2} & f_{n-2} \\ 0 & 0 & 0 & 0 & 0 & f_{n-2} & e_{n-1} \end{bmatrix} \tag{7.24}$$

$$e_0 = 1 + g(\Delta t)^2 \left(\frac{d_0 + d_1}{2(\Delta x)^2} \right)$$

$$e_i = 1 + g(\Delta t)^2 \left(\frac{d_{i-1} + 2d_i + d_{i+1}}{2(\Delta x)^2} \right) \quad (0 < i < n-1)$$

$$e_{n-1} = 1 + g(\Delta t)^2 \left(\frac{d_{n-2} + d_{n-1}}{2(\Delta x)^2} \right) \tag{7.25}$$

$$f_i = -\left(g(\Delta t)^2 \left(\frac{d_i + d_{i+1}}{2(\Delta x)^2} \right) \right)$$

To simulate a viscous fluid, Eq. (7.23) can be modified to incorporate a parameter that controls the viscosity, thus producing Eq. (7.26). The parameter τ ranges between 0 and 1. When $\tau = 0$, Eq. (7.26) reduces to Eq. (7.3).

$$Ab_i(n) = b_i(n-1) + (1-\tau)(b_i(n-1) - b_i(n-2)) \tag{7.26}$$

```
Specify h(t=0), h(t=1), and b
for j=2 ... n
    to simulate sinks and sources, modify appropriate h values
    calculate d from h(j-1) and b; if h_i<b_i, then d_i=0
    use Equation 7.10 (Equation 7.13) to calculate h(j) from h(j-1) and
        h(j-2)
    adjust the values of h to conserve volume (as discussed above)
    if h_i<b_i, set h_i(j) and h_{i-1}(j) to b_i-ε
```

FIGURE 7.9

Two-dimensional algorithm for water transport.

Volume preservation can be compromised when $h_i < b_i$. To compensate for this, search for the connected areas of water ($b_j < b_j$ for $j = i, i + 1,..., i + n$) at each iteration and compute the volume. If the volume changes from the last iteration, then distribute the difference among the elements of that connected region. The algorithm for the two-dimensional case is shown in Fig. 7.9.

Extending the algorithm to the three-dimensional case considers a two-dimensional height field. The computations are done by decoupling the two dimensions of the field. Each iteration is decomposed into two subiterations, one in the x-direction and one in the y-direction.

7.1.1.5 Summary

Animating all the aspects of water is a difficult task because of water's ability not only to change shape but also to change its topology over time. Great strides have been made in animating individual aspects of water such as standing waves, ocean waves, spray, and flowing water. An efficient approach to an integrated model of water remains a challenge.

7.1.2 Models of Clouds (by David Ebert)

Modeling clouds is a very difficult task because of their complex, amorphous, space-filling structure and because even an untrained eye can easily judge the realism of a cloud model. The ubiquitous nature of clouds makes them an important modeling and animation task. This section describes their important visual and physical characteristics, important rendering issues, and several approaches for cloud modeling and animation.

7.1.2.1 Basic Cloud Types and Physics

Clouds are made of visible ice crystals and/or water droplets suspended in air, depending on altitude and, hence, air temperature. Clouds are formed when air rises, its water vapor cooling to the saturation point and condensing. The visible condensed water vapor is what constitutes the cloud [6]. The shape of the cloud varies based on processes that force the air to rise or bubble up (convection, convergence, lifting along frontal boundaries, lifting due to mountains, or orography, Kelvin–Helmholtz shearing, etc.) and the height (and other conditions) at which the cloud forms [6]. Several sources [5,6,18,39] present a very good introduction to clouds and their identification. Clouds formed above 20000 feet (cirrus) are wispy and white in appearance and composed primarily of ice crystals. Clouds formed between 6500 feet and 23000 feet (i.e. altocumulus) are primarily composed of water droplets; they are small and puffy and they collect into groups, sometimes forming waves. Clouds formed below 6500 feet (e.g. stratus, stratocumulus) are again composed primarily of water droplets; they extend over a large area and have a layered or belled appearance. The most characteristic cloud type is the puffy cumulus. Cumulus clouds are normally formed by convection or frontal lifting and can vary from having little vertical height to forming huge vertical towers (cumulonimbus) created by strong convection.

7.1.2.2 Visual Characteristics of and Rendering Issues for Clouds

Clouds have several easily identifiable visual characteristics that must be modeled to produce accurate images and animations. First, clouds have a volumetrically varying amorphous structure with detail at many different scales. Second, cloud formation often results from swirling, bubbling, and turbulent processes that produce characteristic time-varying patterns. Third, clouds have several illumination and shading characteristics that must be accurately rendered to obtain convincing images. Clouds are a three-dimensional medium of small ice and water droplets that absorb, scatter, and reflect light. Illumination models for clouds are classified as low-albedo and high-albedo models. A low-albedo reflectance model assumes that secondary scattering effects are negligible, whereas a high-albedo illumination model calculates the secondary and higher-order scattering effects. For optically thick clouds, such as cumulus, stratus, and cumulonimbus, secondary scattering effects are significant and high-albedo illumination models (e.g. [1,19,22,26,33]) should be used. Detailed descriptions of implementing a low-albedo illumination algorithm can be found in several sources [10,19]. Simulation of wavelength-dependent scattering is also important for creating correct atmospheric dispersion effects for sunrise and sunset scenes (see Fig. 7.10 for a rendering of sunset illumination). Self-shadowing of clouds and cloud shadowing on landscapes are also important for creating realistic images of cloud scenes and landscapes. Correct cloud shadowing requires volumetric shadowing techniques to create accurate images, which can be very expensive

FIGURE 7.10

An example of cirrus and cirrostratus clouds at sunset (Copyright 1998 David S. Ebert).

when volumetric ray tracing is used. A much faster alternative is to use volumetric shadow tables [9,10,19].

7.1.2.3 Early Approaches to Cloud Modeling

Modeling clouds in computer graphics has been a challenge for more than 20 years [7]. Many early approaches used semitransparent surfaces to produce convincing images of clouds [16,17,40]. Voss [40] has used fractal synthesis of parallel plane models to produce images of clouds seen from a distance. Gardner [16,17] has produced convincing images and animations of clouds by using Fourier synthesis to control the transparency of large, hollow ellipsoids. This approach uses groups of ellipsoids to define and animate the general shape of clouds while using procedurally textured transparency to produce the appearance of cloud detail.

A similar approach has been taken by Kluyskens [21] to produce clouds in Alias/Wavefront's Maya™ animation systems. He uses randomized, overlapping spheres to define the general cloud shape. A solid *cloud texture* is then used to color the cloud and to control the transparency of the spheres. Finally, Kluyskens increases the transparency of the spheres near their edges so that the defining shape is not noticeable.

7.1.2.4 Volumetric Cloud Modeling

Although surface-based techniques can produce realistic images of clouds viewed from a distance, these cloud models are hollow and do not allow the user to seamlessly enter, travel through, and inspect their interior. Volumetric density-based models must be used to capture the three-dimensional structure of a cloud.

FIGURE 7.11

An example of a cumulus cloud (Copyright 1997 David S. Ebert).

Kajiya [19] produced the first volumetric cloud model in computer graphics. Stam and Fiume [35] and Foster and Metaxas [12] have produced convincing volumetric models of smoke and steam but have not done substantial work on modeling clouds.

Neyret [25] has produced some preliminary results of a convective cloud model based on general physical characteristics, such as bubbling and convection processes. This model seems promising for simulating convective clouds; however, it currently uses surfaces (large particles) to model the cloud structure. Extending this approach to volumetric modeling/animation should produce convincing cloud images and animations.

Particle systems [31] are commonly used to simulate the volumetric gases, such as smoke, with convincing results and provide easy animation control. The difficulty with using particle systems for cloud modeling is the massive number of particles that is necessary to simulate realistic clouds.

Several authors have used the idea of volume-rendered implicit functions (e.g. [3]) for volumetric cloud modeling. Nishita, Nakamae, and Dobashi [26] have concentrated on illumination effects and have used volume-rendered implicits as a basic cloud model in their work on multiple scattering illumination models. Stam [35–37] has also used volumetric blobbies to create his models of smoke and clouds. Ebert [8,9] has used volumetric implicits combined with particle systems and procedural detail to simulate the formation and geometry of volumetric clouds. This approach uses implicits to provide a natural way of specifying and animating the global structure of the cloud while using more traditional procedural techniques to model the detailed structure. The implicits are controlled by a modified particle system that incorporates simple simulations of cloud formation dynamics. Example images created by this technique can be seen in Figs. 7.10 and 7.11.

7.1.2.5 *Example Volumetric Cloud Modeling System*

Ebert's cloud modeling and animation approach uses procedural abstraction of detail to allow the designer to control and animate objects at a high level. Its inherent procedural nature provides flexibility, data amplification, abstraction of detail, and ease of parametric control. Abstraction of detail and data amplification are necessary to make the modeling and animation of complex volumetric phenomena, such as clouds, tractable. It would be impractical for an animator to specify and control the detailed three-dimensional density of a cloud model. This system does not use a physics-based approach because it is computationally prohibitive and nonintuitive for many animators and modelers. Setting and animating correct physics parameters for condensation temperature, temperature and pressure gradients, and so on is a time-consuming, detailed task. This model was developed to allow the modeler and the animator to work at a much higher level and does not restrict the animator by the laws of physics. Since a procedure is evaluated to determine the object's density, any advanced modeling technique, simple physics simulation, mathematical function, or artistic algorithm can be included in the model.

As mentioned earlier, this volumetric cloud model uses a two-level hierarchy: the cloud macrostructure and the cloud microstructure. These are modeled by implicit functions and turbulent volume densities, respectively. The basic structure of the cloud model combines these two components to determine the final density of the cloud.

The cloud's microstructure is created by using procedural *noise* and *turbulence* functions. This allows the procedural simulation of natural detail to the level needed. Simple mathematical functions are added to allow shaping of the density distributions and control over the sharpness of the density falloff.

Implicit functions work well to model the cloud macrostructure because of their ease of specification and their smoothly blending density distributions. The user simply specifies the location, type, and weight of the implicit primitives to create the overall cloud shape. Any implicit primitive, including spheres, cylinders, ellipsoids, and skeletal implicits, can be used to model the cloud macrostructure. Since these are volume rendered as a semitransparent medium, the whole volumetric field function is being rendered compared to implicit surface rendering, where only a small range of values of the field are used to create the objects.

The implicit density functions are primitive based: they are defined by summed, weighted, parameterized, primitive implicit surfaces. A simple example of the implicit formulation of a sphere centered at the point *center* with radius r is $F(x, y, z) = (x - center.x)^2 + (y - center.y)^2 + (z - center.z)^2 - r^2 = 0$.

The real power of implicit functions is the smooth blending of the density fields from separate primitive sources. A standard cubic function [42] is often used as the density (blending) function for the implicit primitives [Eq. (7.27)]. In Eq. (7.28), r is the distance from the primitive. This density function is cubic in the distance squared, and its value ranges from 1, when $r = 0$ (within the primitive), to 0 at $r = R$. This density function has several advantages. First, its value drops off quickly to zero (at the distance R), reducing the number of primitives that must be considered in creating the final surface. Second, it has zero derivatives at $r = 0$ and $r = R$ and is symmetrical about the contour value 0.5, providing for smooth blends between primitives. The final implicit density value is then the weighted sum of the density field values of each primitive [Eq. (7.28)]. Variable w_i is the weight of the ith primitive, and q is the closest point on element i from p.

$$F(r) = -\frac{4}{9}\frac{r^6}{R^6} + \frac{17}{9}\frac{r^4}{R^4} - \frac{22}{9}\frac{r^2}{R^2} + 1 \qquad (7.27)$$

$$D(p) = \sum_i w_i F(|p - q|) \qquad (7.28)$$

To create nonsolid implicit primitives, the animator procedurally alters the location of the point before evaluating the blending functions. This alteration can be the product of the procedure and the implicit function and/or a warping of the implicit space. These techniques are combined into a simple cloud model as shown in the high-level description below.

```
volumetric_procedural_implicit_function(pnt, blend, pixel_size)
    perturbed_point = procedurally alter pnt using noise and turbulence
    density1 = implicit_function(perturbed_point)
    density2 = turbulence(pnt, pixel_size)
    blend = blend * density1 + (1 - blend) * density2
    density = shape the resulting blend based on user controls for
      wispiness and denseness (e.g., use pow and exponential function)
      return(density)
```

The density from the implicit primitives is combined with a pure turbulence-based density using a user-specified blend (60–80% gives good results). The blending of the two densities allows the creation of clouds that range from those entirely determined by the implicit function density to those entirely determined by the procedural turbulence function. When the clouds are completely determined by the implicit functions, they tend to look more like cotton balls. The addition of the procedural alteration and turbulence is what gives them their naturalistic look.

7.1.2.6 Cumulus Clouds

Cumulus clouds are very common and can be easily simulated using spherical or elliptical implicit primitives. Figure 7.11 shows the type of result that can be achieved by using nine implicit spheres to model a cumulus cloud. The animator or modeler simply positions the implicit spheres to produce the general cloud structure. Procedural modification then alters the density distribution to create the detailed wisps. The algorithm used to create the clouds in Fig. 7.11 follows.

```
cumulus(pnt, density, parms, pnt_w, vol)
    xyz_td pnt;                /* location of point in cloud space */
    xyz_td pnt_w;              /* location of point in world space */
    float *density,*parms;
    vol_td vol;
{
    float turbulence();        /* turbulence function */
    float noise();             /* noise function */
    float metaball_evaluate(); /* function for evaluating the metaball
                                  primitives*/
        float mdens,           /* metaball density value */
        turb,                  /* turbulence amount */
        noise_value;           /* noise value */
    xyz_td path;               /* path for swirling the point */
    extern int frame_num;
    static int ncalcd = 1;
    static float sin_theta_cloud, cos_theta_cloud, theta,
        path_x, path_y, path_z, scalar_x, scalar_y, scalar_z;

    /* calculate values that only depend on the frame number once per
       frame */
    if(ncalcd) {
        ncalcd = 0;
        /* create gentle swirling in the cloud */
        theta = (frame_num%600)*.01047196;    /* swirling effect */
        cos_theta_cloud = cos(theta);
        sin_theta_cloud = sin(theta);
        path_x = sin_theta_cloud*.005*frame_num;
        path_y = .01215*(float)frame_num;
        path_z = sin_theta_cloud*.0035*frame_num;
        scalar_x = (.5+(float)frame_num*0.010);
        scalar_z = (float)frame_num*.0073;
    }

    /* Add some noise to the point's location */
    noise_value = noise(pnt);           /* Use noise function */
    pnt.x -= path_x - noise_value*scalar_x;
    pnt.y  = pnt.y - path_y + .5*noise_value;
    pnt.z += path_z - noise_value*scalar_z;

    /* Perturb the location of the point before evaluating the implicit
       primitives. */
    turb = turbulence(pnt);
    turb_amount = parms[4]*turb;
    pnt_w.x += turb_amount;
```

```
    pnt_w.y -= turb_amount;
    pnt_w.z += turb_amount;

    mdens = (float)metaball_evaluate((double)pnt_w.x, (double)pnt_w.y,
                                     (double)pnt_w.z, (vol.metaball));

    *density = parms[1]*(parms[3]*mdens + (1.0 - parms[3])*turb*mdens);
    *density = pow(*density,(double)parms[2]);
}
```

parms[3] is the blending function value between implicit (metaball) density and the product of the turbulence density and the implicit density. This method of blending ensures that the entire cloud density is a product of the implicit field values, preventing cloud pieces from occurring outside the defining primitives. Using a large *parms*[3] generates clouds that are mainly defined by their implicit primitives and are, therefore, "smoother" and less turbulent. *parms*[1] is a density scaling factor; *parms*[2] is the exponent for the *pow*() function; and *parms*[4] controls the amount of turbulence used in displacing the point before evaluation of the implicit primitives. For good images of cumulus clouds, useful values are the following: $0.2 < parms[1] < 0.4$, $parms[2] = 0.5$, $parms[3] = 0.4$, and $parms[4] = 0.7$.

7.1.2.7 Cirrus and Stratus Clouds

Cirrus clouds differ greatly from cumulus clouds in their density, thickness, and falloff. In general, cirrus clouds are thinner, less dense, and wispier. These effects can be created by altering the parameters of the cumulus cloud procedure and also by changing the implicit primitives. The density value parameter for a cirrus cloud is normally chosen as a smaller value and the chosen exponent is larger, producing larger areas of no clouds and a greater number of individual clouds. To create cirrus clouds, the user can simply specify the global shape (envelope) of the clouds with a few implicit primitives, or he/she can specify implicit primitives to determine the location and shape of each cloud. In the former case, the shape of each cloud is controlled mainly by the volumetric procedural function and turbulence simulation, unlike with cumulus clouds, for which the implicit functions are the main shape control. It is also useful to modulate the densities along the direction of the jet stream to produce more natural wisps. This can be created by the user specifying a predominant direction of wind flow and using a turbulent version of this vector in controlling the densities as follows:

```
Cirrus(pnt, density, parms, pnt_w, vol, jet_stream)
    xyz_td pnt;              /* location of point in cloud space */
    xyz_td pnt_w;            /* location of point in world space */
    xyz_td jet_stream;
    float *density,*parms;
    vol_td vol;
```

```
{
   float turbulence();        /* turbulence function */
   float noise();             /* noise function */
   float metaball_evaluate(); /* function for evaluating the metaball
                                    primitives*/
   float mdens,               /* metaball density value */
       turb,                  /* turbulence amount */
       noise_value;           /* noise value */
   xyz_td path;               /* path for swirling the point */
   extern int frame_num;
   static int ncalcd = 1;
   static float sin_theta_cloud, cos_theta_cloud, theta,
         path_x, path_y, path_z, scalar_x, scalar_y, scalar_z;

   /* calculate values that only depend on the frame number once per
      frame */
   if(ncalcd) {
      ncalcd = 0;
      /* create gentle swirling in the cloud */
      theta = (frame_num%600)*01047196;    /* swirling effect */
      cos_theta_cloud = cos(theta);
      sin_theta_cloud = sin(theta);
      path_x = sin_theta_cloud*.005*frame_num;
      path_y = .01215*(float)frame_num;
      path_z = sin_theta_cloud*.0035*frame_num;
      scalar_x = (.5 + (float)frame_num*0.010);
      scalar_z = (float)frame_num*.0073;
   }

   /* Add some noise to the point's location */
   noise_value = noise(pnt);
   pnt.x -= path_x - noise_value*scalar_x;
   pnt.y = pnt.y - path_y + .5*noise_value;
   pnt.z += path_z - noise_value*scalar_z;

   /* Perturb the location of the point before evaluating the implicit
         primitives. */
   turb = turbulence(pnt);
   turb_amount = parms[4]*turb;
   pnt_w.x += turb_amount;
   pnt_w.y -= turb_amount;
   pnt_w.z += turb_amount;

/* make the jet stream turbulent */
   jet_stream.x += .2*turb;
   jet_stream.y += .3*turb;
   jet_stream.z += .25*turb;
```

```
/* warp point along the jet stream vector */
pnt_w = warp(jet_stream, pnt_w);

mdens = (float)metaball_evaluate((double)pnt_w.x, (double)pnt_w.y,
                                 (double)pnt_w.z, (vol.metaball));

*density = parms[1]*(parms[3]*mdens + (1.0 - parms[3])*turb*mdens);
*density = pow(*density,(double)parms[2]);
}
```

An example of a cirrus cloud formation created using these techniques is given in Fig. 7.10.

Stratus clouds can also be modeled by using a few implicits to create the global shape or extent of the stratus layer while using volumetric procedural functions to define the detailed structure of all the clouds within this layer. Stratus cloud layers are normally thicker and less wispy than cirrus clouds. This effect can be created by adjusting the size of the turbulent space (smaller/fewer wisps), using a smaller exponent value (creates more of a cloud layer effect), and increasing the density of the cloud. Some of the more interesting stratus effects, such as a mackerel sky, can be created by using simple mathematical functions to shape the densities.

7.1.2.8 *Animating Volumetric Procedural Clouds*

The volumetric cloud models described above produce nice still images of clouds and also clouds that gently evolve over time. The models can be animated by particle system dynamics with the implicit primitives attached to each particle. Since the implicits are modeling the macrostructure of the cloud while procedural techniques are modeling the microstructure, fewer primitives are needed to achieve complex cloud models. The smooth blending and procedurally generated detail allow complex results with less than a few hundred primitives, a factor of 100–1000 less than needed with traditional particle systems. The user specifies a few initial implicit primitives and dynamics information, such as speed, initial velocity, force function, and lifetime, and the system generates the location, number, size, and type of implicit for each frame. Unlike traditional particle systems, cloud implicit particles never die; they just become dormant.

Any commercial particle animation program, such as Maya™, can also be used to control the dynamics of the cloud particle system. A useful approach for cloud dynamics is to use *qualitative dynamics*: simple simulations of the observed properties and formation of clouds. The underlying physical forces that create a wide range of cloud formations are extremely complex to simulate, computationally expensive, and very restrictive. The incorporation of simple, parameterized rules that simulate observable cloud behavior will produce a powerful cloud animation system. Fig. 7.12(a) shows a graphical user interface (GUI) used to generate and animate a particle system for simulating convective (cumulus) cloud formations based on qualitative dynamics. This Maya GUI controls a MEL™ script that generates the particle system and controls its dynamics. It uses Maya's vortex,

Cloud			
Length (frames)	10		
Maximum particles	200		
Growth rate	50.0		
No of Emitters	1.0		
Emitter Pos XYZ	0.0	0.0	0.0
VortexB Mag	500.0		
VortexB Pos XYZ	0.0	0.0	0.0
VortexT Mag	65.0		
VortexT Pos XYZ	0.0	70.0	0.0
Weight	0.05		
Gravity	10.0		
Turb Mag	4.0		
Turb Freq	0.20		
Turb Pos XYZ	0.0	60.0	0.0
OpacityPPMax	0.70		
GlowPPMax	0.00		
Threshold	0.10		
RadiusPPMax	3.00		
TypeOfCloud at Alt(miles)	Cumulus 0–2		
Surface Temp	0.10		
Humidity	0.10		

☑ Height=SurfTemp/4
☑ Rate=Humidity*SurfTemp

| Stabilizing Height | 45.0 | | |

Grow Cloud

Close

(a) GUI used to control cloud formation

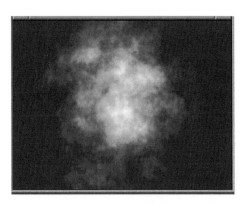

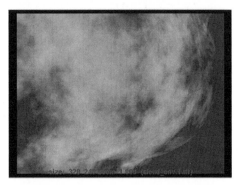

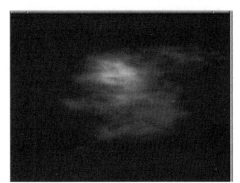

(b) Example clouds

FIGURE 7.12

An example of cloud dynamics GUI and example images created in Maya™ (Copyright 1999 Ruchi Gartha).

airfield, and turbulence fields in its simulation of convection and cloud particle bubbling. Example images from this script can be seen in Fig. 7.12(b). The simulation works as follows. Cloud bubbles are generated on the ground by the user specifying either the area and the humidity level or the placement of a particle emitter and its spread. The bubbles rise due to the force generated by temperature difference, and their weight and the force of gravity affect them. A vortex field is used to simulate the movement of the bubbles in air. At an altitude determined by the surface temperature, the number of dust nuclei at that height, and the humidity content, condensation takes place, so the hot steam cools off and can now be seen as cloud particles. Alternatively, the user can explicitly specify the height at which the stabilization and the aggregation of the bubbles occur to form the cloud. The bubbles are simulated by particles, which have several attributes, such as position, radius, opacity, velocity, and lifetime. When a particle's radius becomes too large, the particle creates child particles and has its radius decreased to conserve matter.

7.1.2.9 Summary

Despite the complexity of the physical processes that form clouds, most of their important visual aspects have been effectively modeled by researchers. However, there are still challenges in terms of providing user control of cloud motion and in improving the fine-grain motion and rendering.

7.1.3 Models of Fire

Fire is a particularly difficult and computationally intensive process to model. It has all the complexities of smoke and clouds and the added complexity of very active internal processes that produce light and motion and create rapidly varying display attributes. Fire exhibits temporally and spatially transient features at a variety of granularies. The underlying process is that of combustion – a rapid chemical process that releases heat (i.e. is *exothermic*) and light accompanied by flame. A common example is that of a wood fire in which the hydrocarbon atoms of the wood fuel join with oxygen atoms to form water vapor, carbon monoxide, and carbon dioxide. As a consequence of the heated gases rising quickly, air is sucked into the combustion area creating turbulence.

Recently, impressive advances have been made in the modeling of fire. At one extreme, the most realistic approaches require sophisticated techniques from CFD and are difficult to control (e.g. [35]). Work has also been performed in simulating the development and spread of fire for purposes of tracking its movement in an environment (e.g. [4,32]). These models tend to be only global, extrinsic representations of the fire's movement and less concerned with the intrinsic motion of the fire itself. Falling somewhere between these two extremes, procedural image generation and

FIGURE 7.13

Image representing fire generated using pixel averaging operations.

particle systems provide visually effective, yet computationally attractive, approaches to fire.

7.1.3.1 Procedurally Generated Image

A particularly simple way to generate the appearance of fire is to procedurally generate a two-dimensional image by coloring pixels suggestive of flames and smoke. The procedure iterates through pixels of an image buffer and sets the palette indices based on the indices of the surrounding pixels [29]. Modifying the pixels top to bottom allows the imagery to progress up the buffer. By using multiple buffers and the alpha (transparency) channel, a limited three-dimensional effect can be achieved. In Fig. 7.13, a color palette filled with hues from red to yellow is used to hold RGB values. The bottom row of the image buffer is randomly initialized with color indices.

7.1.3.2 Particle System Approach

One of the first and most popularly viewed examples of computer-generated fire appears in the movie *Star Trek II: The Wrath of Khan* [28]. In the sequence referred to as the *genesis effect*, an expanding wall of fire spreads out over the surface of the planet from a single point of impact. The simulation is not a completely convincing model of fire although the sequence is effective in the movie. The model uses a two-level hierarchy of particles. The first level of particles is located at the point of impact to simulate the initial blast; the second level consists of concentric rings of particles, timed to progress from the central point outward, forming the wall of fire and explosions.

Each ring of second-level hierarchy consists of a number of individual particle systems that are positioned on the ring and overlap so as to form a continuous ring. The individual particle systems are modeled to look like explosions (Fig. 7.14). The

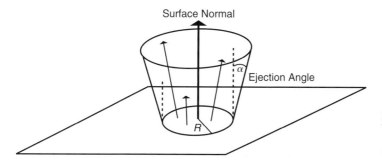

FIGURE 7.14

Explosion-like
particle system.

FIGURE 7.15

Images from a
particle system
simulation of fire.

particles in each one of these particle systems are oriented to fly up and away from
the surface of the planet. The initial position for a particle is randomly chosen from
the circular base of the particle system. The initial direction of travel for each particle is constrained to deviate less than the ejection angle away from the surface
normal. Figure 7.15 shows a simple particle system fire.

7.1.3.3 Other Approaches

Various other approaches have been used in animations with varying levels of
success. Two-dimensional animated texture maps have been used to create the
effect of the upward movement of burning gas, but such models are effective only
when viewed from a specific direction. Using a two-dimensional multiple planes
approach adds some depth to the fire, but viewing directions are still limited. Stam
and Fiume [35] present advection-diffusion equations to evolve both density and
temperature fields. The user controls the simulation by specifying a wind field.

The results are effective, but the foundation mathematics are complicated and the model is difficult to control.

7.1.3.4 Summary

Modeling and animating amorphous phenomena is difficult. Gases are constantly changing shape and lack even a definable surface. Volume graphics holds the most promise for modeling and animating gas, but currently it has computational drawbacks that make such approaches of limited use for animation. A useful and visually accurate model of fire remains the subject of research.

7.2 COMPUTATIONAL FLUID DYNAMICS

Gases and liquids are referred to collectively as *fluids*. The study of ways to compute their behavior is called CFD for short.

Fluids are composed of molecules that are constantly moving. These molecules are constantly colliding with one another and with other objects. The molecular motion transports measurable amounts of fluid properties throughout the fluid. These properties include such things as density, temperature, and momentum. In CFD, the assumption is that the fluid is a continuous medium in the sense that these properties are well defined at infinitely small points of the fluid and that the property values are smoothly varying throughout the fluid. This is called the *continuity assumption* [1].

Modeling gaseous phenomena (smoke, clouds, fire) is particularly challenging because of their ethereal nature. Gas has no definite geometry, no definite topology. Gas is usually treated as *compressible*, meaning that density is spatially variable and computing the changes in density is part of the computational cost. Liquids are usually treated as *incompressible*, which means the density of the material remains constant. In fact, the equations in the previous section, on the transport of water, were derived from the CFD equations.

In a *steady state flow*, the motion attributes (e.g. velocity and acceleration) at any point in space are constant. Particles traveling through a steady state flow can be tracked similarly to how a space curve can be traced out when the derivatives are known. *Vortices*, circular swirls of material, are important features in fluid dynamics. In steady state flow, vortices are attributes of space and are time invariant. In time-varying flows, particles that carry a nonzero vortex strength can travel through the environment and can be used to modify the acceleration of other particles in the system by incorporating a distance-based force.

7.2.1 General Approaches to Modeling Fluids

There are three approaches to modeling gas: grid-based methods (*Eulerian formulations*), particle-based methods (*Lagrangian formulations*), and hybrid methods. The approaches are illustrated here in two dimensions, but the extension to three dimensions should be obvious.

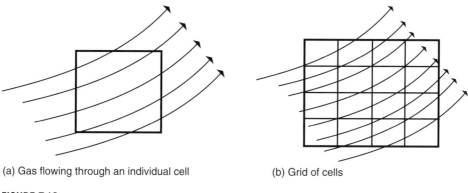

(a) Gas flowing through an individual cell   (b) Grid of cells

FIGURE 7.16

Grid-based method.

7.2.1.1 Grid-Based Method

The grid-based method decomposes space into individual cells, and the flow of the gas into and out of each cell is calculated (Fig. 7.16). In this way, the density of gas in each cell is updated from time step to time step. The density in each cell is used to determine the visibility and illumination of the gas during rendering. Attributes of the gas within a cell, such as velocity, acceleration, and density, can be used to track the gas as it travels from cell to cell.

The flow out of the cell can be computed based on the cell velocity, the size of the cell, and the cell density. The flow into a cell is determined by distributing the densities out of adjacent cells. External forces, such as wind and obstacles, are used to modify the acceleration of the particles within a cell.

The rendering phase uses standard volumetric graphics techniques to produce an image based on the densities projected onto the image plane. Illumination of a cell from a light source through the volume must also be incorporated into the display procedure.

The disadvantage of this approach is that if a static data structure for the cellular decomposition is used, the extent of the interesting space must be identified before the simulation takes place in order to initialize the cells that will be needed during the simulation of the gas phenomena. Alternatively, a dynamic data structure that adapts to the traversal of the gas through space could be used, but this increases overhead.

7.2.1.2 Particle-Based Method

In the particle-based method, particles or globs of gas are tracked as they progress through space, often with a standard particle system approach (Fig. 7.17). The particles can be rendered individually or they can be rendered as spheres of gas with a given density. The advantage of this technique is that it is similar to rigid body

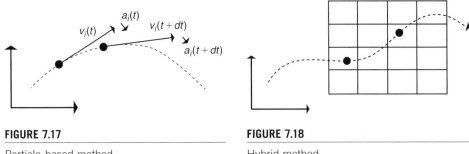

FIGURE 7.17

Particle-based method.

FIGURE 7.18

Hybrid method.

dynamics and therefore the equations are relatively simple and familiar. The equations can be simplified if the rotational dynamics are ignored. In addition, there are no restrictions imposed by the simulation setup as to where the gas may travel. The disadvantage of this approach is that a large number of particles are needed to simulate a dense expansive gas. Particles are assigned masses, and external forces can be easily incorporated by updating particle accelerations and, subsequently, velocities.

7.2.1.3 Hybrid Method

Some models of gas trace particles through a spatial grid. Particles are passed from cell to cell as they traverse the interesting space (Fig. 7.18). The display attributes of individual cells are determined by the number and type of particles contained in the cell at the time of display. The particles are used to carry and distribute attributes through the grid, and then the grid is used to produce the display.

7.2.2 CFD Equations

In developing the CFD calculations, the volume occupied by the fluid is broken up into individual cells that cover the domain to be analyzed. The equations are created by describing what is happening at each cell. Differential equations are produced by taking the cell resolution to the limit and considering differential elements (Fig. 7.19). The basic process for computing fluid dynamics is to:

- discretize the fluid continuum by constructing a grid of cells that, collectively, cover the space occupied by the fluid and at each node (cell) approximate the fluid variables (e.g. density and velocity) and use the approximations to initialize the grid cells;
- create the discrete equations using the approximate values at the cells;
- numerically solve the system of equations to compute new values at the cells using a Newton-like method for the large, sparse system of equations at each time step.

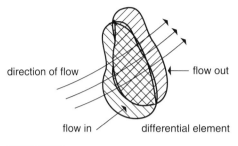

FIGURE 7.19

Differential element used in Navier–Stokes.

The full CFD equations consist of equations that state, in a closed system:

- mass is conserved;
- momentum is conserved;
- energy is conserved.

When expressed as equations, these are the NS equations. The NS equations are nonlinear differential equations. There are various simplifications that can be made in order to make the NS equations more tractable. First, for most graphics applications, energy conservation is ignored. Another common simplification used in graphics is to assume the fluid is nonviscous. These assumptions result in what are called Euler equations [24]. When dealing with liquids (as opposed to a gas), another useful assumption is that the fluid is incompressible, which means that its density does not change. By ignoring energy conservation and viscosity, the Euler equations describing the conservation of mass and conservation of momentum can be readily constructed for a given flow field.

7.2.2.1 Conservation of Mass

Conservation of mass is expressed by the *continuity equation* [11]. The underlying assumption of the conservation of mass is that mass is neither created nor destroyed inside of the fluid. The fluid flows from cell to cell and, if compressible, can become more dense or less dense at various locations. To determine how the total mass inside of a cell is changing, all the sources and sinks in the cell have to be added up. The *divergence* of a flow field describes the strength of the source or sink at a location; the divergence for a field, F, is $\dfrac{\delta F}{\delta x} + \dfrac{\delta F}{\delta y} + \dfrac{\delta F}{\delta z}$. If no mass is created or destroyed inside the cell, then it is reasonable that the total divergence within the cell must be equal to the flow differences across the cell at the x, y, and z boundaries. This is stated by the *Divergence Theorem*: the integral of the flow field's divergence over the volume of the cell is the same as the integral of the flow field over the cell's boundary. So, instead of worrying about all the sources and sinks inside of the cell, all that has to be computed is the flow at the boundaries.

For now, for a given three-dimensional cell, consider only flow in the x-direction. To make the discussion a bit more concrete, assume that the fluid is flowing left to right, as x increases, so that the mass flows into a cell on the left, at x, and out of the cell on the right, at $x + \mathrm{d}x$. In the following equations, ρ is density, p is pressure, A is the area of the face perpendicular to the x-direction, V is the volume of the cell, and the cell dimensions are $\mathrm{d}x$ by $\mathrm{d}y$ by $\mathrm{d}z$. To compute the mass flowing across a surface, multiply the density of the fluid times area of the surface times the velocity component normal to the surface, v_x in this case. The conservation of mass equation states that the rate at which mass changes is equal to the difference between mass flowing into the cell and the mass flowing out of the cell [see Eq. (7.29)].

$$-\frac{d(\rho V)}{dt} = \left(\rho v_x A\right)\big|_{x+dx} - \left(\rho v_x A\right)\big|_x \tag{7.29}$$

Replace the volume, V, and area, A, by their definitions in terms of the cell dimensions [Eq. (7.30)].

$$-\frac{d(\rho dxdydz)}{dt} = \left(\rho v_x dydz\right)\big|_{x+dx} - \left(\rho v_x dydz\right)\big|_x \tag{7.30}$$

Divide through by $dxdydz$ [Eq. (7.31)].

$$-\frac{d(\rho)}{dt} = \left(\frac{\rho v_x}{dx}\right)\bigg|_{x+dx} + -\left(\frac{\rho v_x}{dx}\right)\bigg|_x \tag{7.31}$$

Replace the finite differences by their corresponding differential forms [Eq. (7.32)].

$$-\frac{d(\rho)}{dt} = \frac{\delta(\rho v_x)}{\delta x} \tag{7.32}$$

Finally, include flow in all three directions [Eq. (7.33)].

$$-\frac{d(\rho)}{dt} = \frac{\delta(\rho v_x)}{\delta x} + \frac{\delta(\rho v_y)}{\delta y} + \frac{\delta(\rho v_z)}{\delta z} \tag{7.33}$$

If ∇ is used as the gradient operator, $\nabla F = \left(\frac{\delta F}{\delta x}, \frac{\delta F}{\delta y}, \frac{\delta F}{\delta z}\right)$, then a common notation is to refer to the divergence operator as [Eq. (7.34)].

$$\nabla \cdot F = \frac{\delta F}{\delta x} + \frac{\delta F}{\delta y} + \frac{\delta F}{\delta z} \tag{7.34}$$

Using the divergence operator in Eq. (7.33) produces Eq. (7.35).

$$-\frac{d(\rho)}{dt} = \nabla \cdot (\rho v) \tag{7.35}$$

If the fluid is incompressible, then the density doesn't change. This means that $\frac{d(\rho)}{dt}$ is zero and the constant density can be divided out [Eq. (7.36)].

$$0 = \nabla \cdot v \tag{7.36}$$

7.2.2.2 Conservation of Momentum

The momentum of an object is its mass times its velocity. The momentum of a fluid is its density times the volume of the fluid times the average velocity of the fluid.

A change in momentum $\dfrac{d(mv)}{dt}$ must be induced by a force (e.g. $f = ma = m\dfrac{dv}{dt}$). The force in the cell of a flow field is either a global force, such as gravity, or a change in pressure across the cell, $\dfrac{dp}{dx}$. As noted above, effects of viscosity are commonly ignored in order to simplify the equations; we will also ignore gravity for now.

For a grid cell, the change in momentum is the change of momentum inside the cell plus the difference between the momentum entering the cell and the momentum leaving the cell. The momentum inside the cell is $\rho V v$. The change of momentum inside the cell is $\dfrac{d(\rho V v)}{dt}$.

For now, given a three-dimensional cell, consider flow only in the x-direction. The mass flowing out one surface is density times area of the surface (which will be notated as $p\big|^{\text{surface}}_{\text{location}}$) times velocity in the x-direction, v_x. The momentum out one surface is the mass flowing out the surface times its velocity, $\rho A v_x v$. The force on the cell in the x-direction is the pressure difference across the cell from x to $x + dx$. The force is equal to the negative of the change in momentum [Eq. (7.37)].

$$-\left(p\big|^{A}_{x+dx} - p\big|^{A}_{x}\right) = \frac{d(\rho V v)}{dt} + \left(\left(\rho v_x A\right)v\big|_{x+dx} - \left(\rho v_x A\right)v\big|_{x}\right) \qquad (7.37)$$

Following the steps above in developing the conservation of mass equation by replacing the area, A, with its definition in terms of cell dimensions, $dydz$, replacing the volume, V, with $dxdydz$, dividing through by $dxdydz$ and putting everything in differential form, gives [Eq. (7.38)].

$$-\frac{dp}{dx} = \frac{\delta(\rho v_x v)}{\delta x} + \frac{d(\rho v)}{dt} \qquad (7.38)$$

Now, considering flow in all three directions, and separating out momentum only in the x-direction, produces [Eq. (7.39)].

$$-\frac{dp}{dt} = \frac{\delta(\rho v_x^2)}{\delta x} + \frac{\delta(\rho v_y v_x)}{\delta y} + \frac{\delta(\rho v_z v_x)}{\delta z} + \frac{d(\rho v_x)}{dt} \qquad (7.39)$$

If desired, viscosity and other forces can be added to the pressure differential force on the left-hand side of the equation. Similar equations can be derived for the y and z directions.

7.2.2.3 Solving the Equations

Before solving these equations, boundary conditions must be set up to handle the cells at the limits of the domain. For example, the *Dirichlet boundary condition*, which sets solution values at the boundary cells, is commonly used. The CFD equations, set up for each cell of the grid, produce a sparse set of matrix equations. There are various ways to solve such systems. For example, LU and conjugate gradient solvers are often used. Efficient, accurate methods of solving symmetric and asymmetric sparse matrices, such as these, are the topic of ongoing research. Thankfully in computer animation, believability is more of a concern than accuracy, so approximate techniques often suffice.

7.2.2.4 Stable Fluids

Jos Stam presents a method that solves the full NS equations that is easy to implement and allows real-time user interaction [34]. Although too inaccurate for engineering, it is useful in computer graphics applications. In particular, the procedures are designed to be stable more than accurate while still producing interesting visuals. The procedures operate on a velocity vector field and density field. The velocity field moves the density values around.

7.2.2.5 Density Update

Density values are moved through the density grid assuming a fixed velocity field over the time step. The density equation [Eq. (7.40)] states that density (ρ) changes over time according to density sources (s), the diffusion of the density at some specified rate (κ), and advection according to the velocity field (u).

$$\frac{\partial \rho}{\partial t} = s + \kappa \nabla^2 \rho - (u \cdot \nabla)\rho \qquad (7.40)$$

In implementing stable fluids, density is kept in an array of scalars. The first term, s, is an array of density sources set by user interaction or by the environment. These are used to initialize the new density grid at each time step. The second term diffuses the density from each cell to its adjacent cells. The diffusion of the grid can be solved by relaxation. The third term advects the density according to the velocity field.

To diffuse, each cell is updated by a weighted average of its four neighbors added to the original value. Each neighboring value is multiplied by a, where $a = dt^*diff^*N^*N$, *diff* is a user-supplied parameter and N is the resolution of the grid. This sum is added to the cell's original value and then this sum is divided by $1 + 4^*a$.

To advect, the position is interpolated backward according to the velocity field. In the simplest case, the velocity vector at the particle position is accessed and linearly stepping backward according to the selected time step, making sure to clamp within the grid boundaries. The density is then bilinearly interpolated from nearby values and this interpolated value is used as the density of the position.

7.2.2.6 The Velocity Update

The change of the velocity over time is given by Eq. (7.41) and is due to external forces (f), diffusion of the velocities, and self-advection.

$$\frac{\partial u}{\partial t} = f + \mu \nabla^2 u - (u \cdot \nabla) u \qquad (7.41)$$

The velocity is kept in an array of vectors. The first term, f, adds in external forces from the user or environment. The second term allows for the diffusion of the velocity, and the third term allows the velocity to be carried along by the velocity field.

These equations are implemented by the sequence: add force, advect, diffuse, and project. The projection step is to adjust the density so that mass is preserved.

7.2.2.7 The Simulation

The simulation is conducted by updating the contributions from density forces and external forces, then stepping the velocity field a step in time, taking the density field a step in time, then drawing the density.

7.3 CHAPTER SUMMARY

Most of the techniques discussed in this chapter are still the subject of research efforts. Water, smoke, clouds, and fire share an amorphous nature, which makes them difficult to model and animate. Approaches that incorporate a greater amount of physics have been developed recently for these phenomena. As processing power becomes cheaper, techniques such as CFD become more practical (and more desirable) tools for animating water and gas, but convenient controls for such models have yet to be developed.

REFERENCES

[1] J. Blinn, Light reflection functions for simulation of clouds and dusty surfaces, Comput. Graph. 16 (1982) 21–29 (Proceedings of SIGGRAPH 82, July 1982, Boston, MA).

[2] J. Blinn, Simulation of wrinkled surfaces, Comput. Graph. 12 (1978) 286–292 (Proceedings of SIGGRAPH 78, August 1978, Atlanta, GA).

[3] J. Bloomenthal, C. Bajaj, J. Blinn, M.-P. Cani-Gascuel, A. Rockwood, B. Wyvill, G. Wyvill, Introduction to Implicit Surfaces, Morgan Kaufmann, San Francisco, 1997.

[4] R. Bukowski, C. Sequin, Interactive simulation of fire in virtual building environments, in: T. Whitted (Ed.), Computer Graphics, Annual Conference Series (Proceedings of SIGGRAPH 97, August 1997, Los Angeles, CA), Addison-Wesley, 1997, pp. 35–44. ISBN 0-89791-896-7.

[5] W. Cotton, A. Anthes, Storm and Cloud Dynamics, Academic Press, New York, 1989.

[6] Department of Atmospheric Sciences, University of Illinois, Cloud Catalog, http://covis.atmos.uiuc.edu/guide/clouds/.

[7] W. Dungan Jr., A terrain and cloud computer image generation model, Comput. Graph. 13 (1979) 143–150 (Proceedings of SIGGRAPH 79, August 1979, Chicago, IL).

[8] D. Ebert, Volumetric modeling with implicit functions: a cloud is born, in: Computer Graphics, Annual Conference Series (Visual Proceedings of SIGGRAPH 97, August 1997, Los Angeles, CA), Addison-Wesley, 1997, p. 147.

[9] D. Ebert, K. Musgrave, D. Peachey, K. Perlin, S. Worley, Texturing and Modeling: A Procedural Approach, AP Professional, Cambridge, MA, 1998.

[10] D. Ebert, R. Parent, Rendering and animation of gaseous phenomena by combining fast volume and scanline A-buffer techniques, Comput. Graph. 24 (1990) 357–366 (Proceedings of SIGGRAPH 90, F. Baskett (Ed.), August 1990, Dallas, TX. ISBN 0-201-50933-4).

[11] Engineers Edge, Continuity Equation—Fluid Flow, http://www.engineersedge.com/fluid_flow/continuity_equation.htm, August 2005.

[12] N. Foster, D. Metaxas, Modeling the motion of a hot, turbulent gas, in: T. Whitted (Ed.), Computer Graphics, Annual Conference Series (Proceedings of SIGGRAPH 97, August 1997, Los Angeles, CA), Addison-Wesley, 1997, pp. 181–188. ISBN 0-89791-896-7.

[13] N. Foster, D. Metaxas, Realistic animation of liquids, Graph. Models Image Process. 58 (1996) 471–483.

[14] A. Fournier, W. Reeves, A simple model of ocean waves, Comput. Graph. 20 (1986) 75–84 (Proceedings of SIGGRAPH 86, David C. Evans, Russell J. Athay (Eds.), August 1986, Dallas, TX).

[15] P. Fournier, A. Habibi, P. Poulin, Simulating the flow of liquid droplets, in: K. Booth, A. Fournier (Eds.), Graphics Interface '98, 1998, pp. 133–142. ISBN 0-9695338-6-1.

[16] G. Gardner, Simulation of natural scenes using textured quadric surfaces, Comput. Graph. 18 (1984) 11–20 (Proceedings of SIGGRAPH 84, July 1984, Minneapolis, MI).

[17] G. Gardner, Visual simulation of clouds, Comput. Graph. 19 (1985) 297–303 (Proceedings of SIGGRAPH 85, B.A. Barsky (Ed.), August 1985, San Francisco, Calif.).

[18] R. House, Cloud Dynamics, Academic Press, Orlando, FL, 1993.

[19] J. Kajiya, B. Von Herzen, Ray tracing volume densities, Comput. Graph. 18 (1984) 165–174 (Proceedings of SIGGRAPH 84, July 1984, Minneapolis, MN).

[20] M. Kass, G. Miller, Rapid, stable fluid dynamics for computer graphics, Comput. Graph. 24 (1990) 49–57 (Proceedings of SIGGRAPH 90, Forest Baskett (Ed.), August 1990, Dallas, TX). ISBN 0-201-50933-4.

[21] T. Kluyskens, Making Good Clouds, MAYA based QueenMaya magazine tutorial, http://reality.sgi.com/tkluyskens_aw/txt/tutor6.html.

[22] N. Max, Efficient light propagation for multiple anisotropic volume scattering, in: Fifth-Eurographics Workshop on Rendering, 1994, pp. 87–104 (June 1994, Darmstadt, Germany).

[23] N. Max, Vectorized procedural models for natural terrains: waves and islands in the sunset, Comput. Graph. 15 (1981) 317–324 (Proceedings of SIGGRAPH 81, August 1981, Dallas, TX).

[24] NASA, Euler Equations, http://www.grc.nasa.gov/WWW/K-12/airplane/eulereqs.html. August, 2005.

[25] F. Neyret, Qualitative simulation of convective clouds formation and evolution, in: D. Thalmann, M. van de Panne (Ed.), Eurographics Computer Animation and Simulation '97, (September 1997, Budapest, Hungary), 1997, pp. 113–124. ISBN 3-211-83048-0.

[26] T. Nishita, E. Nakamae, Y. Dobashi, Display of clouds and snow taking into account multiple anisotropic scattering and sky light, in: H. Rushmeier (Ed.), Computer Graphics, Annual Conference Series (Proceedings of SIGGRAPH 96, August 1996, New Orleans, LA), Addison-Wesley, 1996, pp. 379–386. ISBN 0-201-94800-1.

[27] P. Oppenheimer, Real-time design and animation of fractal plants and trees, Comput. Graph. 20 (1986) 55–64 (Proceedings of SIGGRAPH 86, David C. Evans, Russell J. Athay (Ed.), August 1986, Dallas, TX).

[28] Paramount, Star Trek II: The Wrath of Khan (film), June 1982.

[29] A. Parusel, Simple Fire Effect, GameDev.net, http://www.gamedev.net/reference/articles/article222.asp, January, 2007.

[30] D. Peachey, Modeling waves and surf, Comput. Graph. 20 (1986) 65–74 (Proceedings of SIGGRAPH 86, David C. Evans, Russell J. Athay (Ed.), August 1986, Dallas, TX).

[31] W.T. Reeves, Particle systems: a technique for modeling a class of fuzzy objects, ACM Trans. Graph. 2 (1983) 91–108.

[32] H. Rushmeier, A. Hamins, M. Choi, Volume rendering of pool fire data, IEEE Comput. Graph. Appl. 15 (1995) 62–67.

[33] H. Rushmeier, K. Torrance, The zonal method for calculating light intensities in the presence of a participating medium, Comput. Graph. 21 (1987) 293–302 (Proceedings of SIGGRAPH 87, Maureen C. Stone (Ed.), July 1987, Anaheim, CA).

[34] J. Stam, Stable fluids, in: A. Rockwood (Ed.), Computer Graphics, Annual Conference Series (Proceedings of SIGGRAPH 99, August 1999, Los Angeles, CA), Addison-Wesley Longman, 1999, pp. 121–128. ISBN 0-20148-560-5.

[35] J. Stam, E. Fiume, Depicting fire and other gaseous phenomena using diffusion processes, in: Computer Graphics, Annual Conference Series (Proceedings of SIGGRAPH 95, ACM SIGGRAPH, August 1995, Los Angeles, CA), pp. 129–136.

[36] J. Stam, E. Fiume, A multiple-scale stochastic modelling primitive, in: Graphics Interface '91, Canadian Information Processing Society, 1991, pp. 24–31.

[37] J. Stam, E. Fiume, Turbulent wind fields for gaseous phenomena, in: James T. Kajiya (Ed.), Computer Graphics, Annual Conference Series (Proceedings of SIGGRAPH 93, August 1993, Anaheim, CA), 1993, pp. 369–376. ISBN 0-201-58889-7.

[38] J. Tessendorf, Simulating ocean water, in: SIGGRAPH 2002 Course Notes #9 (Simulating Nature: Realistic and Interactive Techniques), ACM Press, 2002.

[39] R. Tricker, The Science of the Clouds, American Elsevier, New York, 1970.

[40] R. Voss, Fourier Synthesis of Gaussian Fractals: 1/f Noises, Landscapes, and Flakes, Tutorial, SIGGRAPH 83, July 1983, Detroit, MI.

[41] H. Weimer, J. Warren, Subdivision schemes for fluid flow, in: A. Rockwood (Ed.), Computer Graphics, Annual Conference Series (Proceedings of SIGGRAPH 99, August 1999, Los Angeles, CA), Addison-Wesley Longman, 1999, pp. 111–120. ISBN 0-20148-560-5.

[42] B. Wyvill, C. McPheeters, G. Wyvill, Data structures for soft objects, Vis. Comput. 2 (1986) 227–234.

Animating Biology

8

Jason Sharpe
Charles J. Lumsden
Nicholas Woolridge

CHAPTER CONTENTS

8.1 INTRODUCTION

To animate is to give life to an otherwise inanimate object [1]. For our purposes in 3D computing, the verb refers to a change over time in a property of a given item, rendered into a succession of still images, or frames. Somehow, our visual system is able to view this succession and create, in our minds, the perception of motion and behavior in the depicted objects. So we will begin this chapter with a brief look at how we see and how we perceive motion in animated images. You'll then meet some of the lexicon and methods of animation and how and why they might be adapted to scientific visualization. A 3D computer animation workflow will be laid out to give us the road map to learning Maya and MEL, placing them in the overall process of 3D animation production.

Since Maya is designed for animation, its effective use follows the workflow you'd find in a professional animation studio. This workflow, which we'll explore in this chapter, applies terminology and conventions that draw (pardon the pun) on modes of practice honed over decades in the ateliers of animation pioneers like Walt Disney and the Fleischer Brothers. These terms and conventions may seem strange, at first, if you are coming to Maya from a science or engineering field. But we hope to show you that there are benefits to the co-option of cinema-oriented animation practices by scientists intent on understanding biological phenomena.

Experienced animators may encounter some familiar topics in this chapter, but will still benefit from the connections drawn between the animator's and the bioscientist's workflow. By the end of this chapter, you should be able to see how animator's techniques can potentially apply to the science discovery process and have a broadened appreciation for the experimental and expressive power of modern digital animation tools.

8.2 ANIMATION AND FILM PERCEPTION

In film and video, there is no motion, there is only a succession of still images, rapidly displayed. Yet, we perceive motion. How is this possible?

8.2.1 Seeing, in Brief

The early "anatomical" stages of vision are fairly well-known; we will sketch them below as means of explaining the raw processing power that vision brings to the world. The sensory impulses originating in the retina are ultimately transformed into a skein of neuronal activity in the brain that presents to our consciousness an integrated picture of the world. This latter process – how biochemical fluxes turn into meaning – is the hard part, and something we can't hope to address here.

Five crucial events make up the initial stages of vision (the structures described below are illustrated in Fig. 8.1):

1. Light originating from the sun or some other source scatters through the environment, bouncing off various objects. A small fraction of this light happens to pass through the pupil of your eye (a distensible hole that varies in diameter between 2 and 6 mm and is analogous to a camera's aperture).

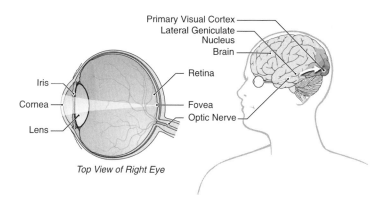

Primary Visual Cortex
Lateral Geniculate Nucleus
Brain
Retina
Iris
Cornea
Fovea
Optic Nerve
Lens

Top View of Right Eye

FIGURE 8.1

The anatomy of vision. Light enters the eye and is focused upon the retina, where it is transduced into electrochemical signals by the photoreceptors. The signals travel via the optic nerve, through the lateral geniculate nucleus, to the primary visual cortex in the occipital lobe of the brain. Here, the signals are rapidly dispatched in a parallel fashion to various processing centers (V1, V2, etc.) where salient features of the scene are extracted, and ultimately integrated into a coherent internal representation of the scene.

2. The light is refracted by the lens in your eye (as well as the cornea and the refractive gels that fill the eyeball) to focus a high-resolution two-dimensional (2D) image on our retina, a complex nine-layered tissue comprised of photoreceptors, blood vessels, and multiple layers of neurons. These neurons form the earliest stage of visual processing: they take the light pattern detected by the photoreceptors and perform various tasks, such as enhancing the contrast at edges and suppressing jittery motion.

3. Impulses derived from the photoreceptors, and modulated by those early neurons, are relayed to the optic nerve. The optic nerve passes through the back of the eye (creating the blind spot), and after passing through the optic chiasm (a "neural traffic interchange" where the left and right visual fields from each eye are united and sent to the appropriate hemisphere), the signals are sent to the lateral geniculate nucleus in the thalamus (a deep brain structure). Early stages of color and motion processing occur here.

4. From the lateral geniculate nucleus, the nerve impulses are passed to an area near the base of the occipital lobe known as V1 (visual area 1). The cortical processing of vision occupies about 40% of the gray matter of our brain and V1 is the first station in that process.

5. From V1, the neural activity is distributed to brain regions V2, V3, V4, V5, and onward. In a feat of massively parallel processing, an astonishing array of features are rapidly extracted from the 2D image received on the retina: edges are detected, objects are separated from the background, depth is assessed through multiple concurrent cues, the direction and magnitude of motion is appraised, faces are recognized, and various salient object features (orientation, size, color, and texture, among others) of the scene are assessed. In addition, remarkable feats of "mental construction" are accomplished, as 3D stereoscopic depth is created from the divergent images originating from each eye, and partially represented (or, in the case of some visual illusions, even nonexistent!) objects are built from fragmentary evidence in the scene.

A **neuron** is a cell type essential to the operation of our nerves and brains. Neurons are electrically excitable and conduct signals from one part of our body to another.

Less than one-fifth of a second has elapsed since the light wave reached the retina at the back of the eye.

In the moments that follow, your brain integrates this initial decoding of the visual scene with other elements of your conscious awareness, calling on the power of your memories, reason, and emotions to interpret it. How astonishing that so much complicated processing occurs so quickly, and with so little deliberate effort!

The fact that vision requires so much active (if unconscious) creation on the part of the viewer helps to explain how we end up imparting so much meaning to cinematic stories; we will see another aspect of the "creative" abilities of visual perception in the next section.

8.2.2 Seeing Motion and Animation

It may be hard to believe, but the nature of motion perception is still under active investigation.

Many film theory textbooks still claim that the basis for motion perception in film is a phenomenon known as persistence of vision, where the image falling on the retina persists biochemically over some interval until it is replaced by succeeding images; this overlap allows the images to blend, retinally, into "motion." While some biochemical truth lies behind this idea – photoreceptors in the eye do continue to signal for some time after the stimulus has passed – the idea of persistence of vision has largely been replaced by a more comprehensive understanding of mechanisms of motion perception [2]. Newer accounts of motion perception call for a more active engagement from the viewer, and rely on multiple, overlapping mechanisms.

Two of those mechanisms – flicker fusion and short-range apparent motion – are worth spending some time on, as they relate rather directly to the standard frame rates that animators use in the production of their films.

Film has a frame rate of 24 frames per second (fps), but each individual frame is actually flashed onto the screen two or three times in succession, leading to a flicker rate of 48–72 Hz (times per second). Why is this? It turns out that in order to present the sensation of viewing a continuously illuminated screen, the projector must flash-on and flash-off rapidly enough to achieve flicker fusion. This is a phenomenon whereby a flickering source of illumination will, at some frequency, fuse into the perception of continuous illumination. If you watch a strobe light flashing at an increasing rate, at some point the discrete flashes will fuse into what seems like a light that is simply "on." The rate required for flicker fusion varies depending on a number of factors (e.g. whether the flicker is present in central or peripheral vision, the brightness of the illumination, the fatigue of the viewer) but is usually in the range of 50–60 Hz for film and television applications.

This helps explain how frame rates for film and video were determined: if each frame of a 24 fps film were shown only once, the image would "strobe" in a way that would make it very difficult to watch, so each frame is projected more than once. In North American video (NTSC), which is nominally 30 fps (actually 29.97 fps), each frame is composed of two interlaced subframes displayed in sequence, leading to a 60-Hz flicker rate.

European (PAL) video is 25 fps, leading to a 50-Hz flicker rate.

Does flicker fusion explain motion perception? No, it simply explains how many projection and display technologies can appear to present a continuous image, rather than one that is strobing. It is worth noting that most newer flat panel display technologies, such as LCDs, do not flicker, since they are continuously illuminated by their backlights. Any digital display, however, has a refresh rate, separate from the potential flicker rate of the display, that is determined by how often the displayed image is updated by the underlying graphics circuitry.

Apparent motion is the term for several distinct phenomena, initially discovered by vision researchers in the early twentieth century, in which certain configurations of rapidly displayed still images could precipitate a perception of motion. Short-range apparent motion requires fine-grained changes between successive images, as is the case with most film and video.

The perceptual mechanisms underlying short-range apparent motion appear to be identical to those active in perceiving real-world motion. Clinical evidence for this comes from the cases of unfortunate individuals who have experienced damage to the part of the brain that allows them to perceive the shape of still objects; these patients cannot recognize, or even see, objects that are not moving. Once an object moves, however, it pops into existence in their perceptual world. Fascinatingly, these individuals can also perceive moving objects in television and film, despite the fact that, of course, they are really seeing a sequence of still images. This demonstrates that, in these subjects, and probably people in general, the mechanisms of film perception are the same as, or very similar to, that of general motion perception.

So, the mystery of film motion perception is starting to yield to scientific study: animated representations of motion are similar enough to real-world stimuli that they engage the same perceptual mechanisms that real-world motion does. Two of those mechanisms – flicker fusion, which in some media makes still images appear as continuous, and short-range apparent motion – help to explain why animation is usually crafted as sequences of 24–30 still images per second, with relatively small differences between individual frames. Later in this chapter, we will look at animation frame rates and in which contexts it might be advisable (or not) to vary them.

8.3 THE ANIMATOR'S WORKFLOW

8.3.1 Story: The Workflow's Driving Force

The animator's workflow (Fig. 8.2) is a time-tested approach to the highly economical depiction of an idea expressed in a finished scene or in the completed film. "Economical" is not used here in a financial sense, but in terms of efficiency: animation is generally so labor intensive – even when powerful computers and software are used – that many benefits accrue to animators who do what they need to, but no more than is necessary; spending weeks diligently animating a scene that is ultimately left out of the film is a painful, costly experience. Thus, the necessity of an organized approach to the animation process. This is a process of experimentation and refinement, and it is very much a part of the computer animator's approach as well, where modern digital tools can somewhat speed the iterations shown in Fig. 8.2.

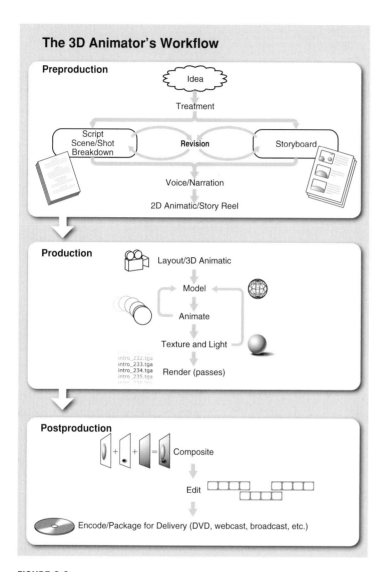

FIGURE 8.2

A typical workflow for computer animation production.

Many scientists experience similar cycles as they refine experimental protocols, improving results and explanatory models (Fig. 8.3). At the heart of science is humanity's yearning to make sense of the world, in a way we are all free to understand and to evaluate in a logical, testable manner. This notion of making sense, of arranging objects and concepts in plausible causal chains, is also at the heart of storytelling.

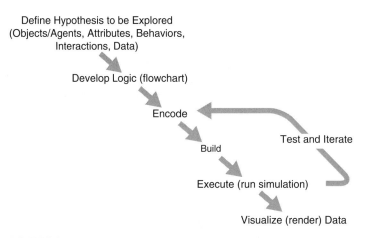

FIGURE 8.3

A typical science animation/simulation workflow. We will be adapting this approach and using it in combination with the traditional animation workflow illustrated in Fig. 8.2.

The broad range of stories – those limited only by the teller's imagination – encompasses a much larger range of possibilities beyond the narratives of reality told by science. Science, of course, is concerned with what is, with actuality and truth. But like the great novels, plays, and myths, important works of fictive cinema – animated and otherwise – also illuminate truth.

Experiencing fictional worlds helps us make sense of human existence, its glory, and its foibles. Filmmaking of the "Hollywood style," for example, is all about telling "readable" stories – the struggles and conflicts of exciting imaginary characters – written, shot, and edited in ways that allow them to be easily interpreted. This ease of interpretation is partially a result of the set of production heuristics that have evolved over the history of filmmaking.

> When discussing storytelling in the Hollywood style, we forego for the moment movements in art and literature, such as Dadaism, that have sought to undermine conventional storytelling requirements.

Since these established animation production workflows support filmmaking economy, as well as film "readability," we can adapt them to support the needs of thoroughly actuality-driven enterprises like science research and scientific communication.

8.4 THE THREE-STAGE WORKFLOW

The animator's initial task is to critically formulate the story idea to be communicated and then explore and refine potential approaches to its expression. This stage is known as preproduction. At the end of this stage, the animator has a solid plan for the execution of the project. Preproduction leads to the production stage. Here, the animator implements the plan generated in preproduction and creates the resources necessary to complete the film. This is generally the longest and most labor-intensive part of the process. Postproduction follows, where the media developed in production are assembled (edited together) and refined into a form suitable for final delivery. This usually takes the form of a film or film segment intended for theatrical release, for television broadcast, release via the web or podcast, presentation at a scientific meeting, or a video game cut scene.

Let's explore this workflow.

8.4.1 Workflow Stage 1: Preproduction

Animation is one of the least direct of the visual arts: the animator works at the drawing table or computer screen, preparing countless images, intending that the arrangement of those images in time will evoke the sense of life that is sought. Preproduction involves all the project initiation steps, as well as the development of a coherent plan for the completion of the film. Effective preproduction helps assure that suitable animations are produced in the fewest possible steps of execution and revision. The key elements of effective preproduction are defining your animation's visual style or "look," the treatment and the script, the storyboard, and the 2D *animatic*.

8.4.1.1 The Animation's "Look"

A cancer animation that depicts the deadly cells as whimsical, anthropomorphic cartoon characters might work well for an audience of young children. However, it might also leave an audience of investment bankers ready to fund a new cancer drug less than impressed. Such qualities of overall visual appearance are often referred to as your film's "look," a subject demanding careful attention right at the start of your project. The message or point of a film can be misunderstood, or lost entirely, if poor decisions are made about its appearance or look.

Let's consider three of the most popular looks for cell science animation. The list is by no means exhaustive; indeed, one of the benefits of working with a 3D program is the possibility of creating entirely new, never-seen-before representations.

8.4.1.1.1 The Photorealistic Look

Photorealism is a term from art criticism which refers to pictures that attempt to emulate the qualities of photographs. As a movement in twentieth century painting, it has been associated with the work of artists like Chuck Close and Mary Pratt. Photorealism consciously imitates the effects of optical lenses and adheres closely to the rules of vanishing point perspective, creating solid, believable images. In addition to the surface qualities of light and texture familiar to us from our experience of the real world, photorealism often includes artifacts of the photographic process, such as depth-of-field effects, motion blur related to shutter speed, compressed dynamic range, and lens flare. One version of the history of computer graphics research would see it as a progressive march toward the goal of seamless, true photo-like rendering (which has, arguably, recently been achieved with unbiased, light simulator-style rendering engines like Maxwell, from Next-Limit Technologies). A broader look at computer graphics would see computer-generated imagery (CGI) encompassing a number of representational styles.

8.4.1.1.2 The Micrographic Look

A substyle of photorealism, devoted to emulating micrography, has emerged over the past several years: this is the micrographic look (the appearance of objects as seen or photographed through microscopes). At the present time in human history, photorealism is a near-universal strategy for depicting the events of our everyday lives in the entertainment and news media. The camera's "eye" is ubiquitous. The conventions of photorealistic depiction have therefore been adapted by artists and scientists to reveal objects and events too large (as in astronomy) or too small (as in cellular medicine) to be seen with the unaided eye. Sometimes, although objects are small, they are still big enough to deflect light rays. Most intact cells are big enough to do this, so with special lenses and other imaging technologies (microscopes) we can magnify their images and take their picture. Other subjects require more exotic preparations and techniques; for instance, researchers have begun to use small fluorescent proteins (such as green fluorescent protein, derived from a jellyfish) to "tag" cellular components they wish to observe. The resulting micrographs are often hauntingly beautiful (Fig. 8.4).

A popular approach for animators working at the cellular and molecular level therefore is to render their models in a style of micrographic photorealism. These can include light microscopy, scanning electron microscopy (SEM) (simulated in Fig. 8.5), phase-contrast microscopy (simulated in Fig. 8.6), confocal microscopy (Fig. 8.4), and transmission electron microscopy (TEM). Each of these approaches produces a signature visual texture, which is imitable in a 3D program like Maya.

8.4.1.1.3 Nonphotorealistic Looks

At the molecular level, the objects of biological interest are at or below the dimensions of the wavelengths of ordinary visible light; ordinary cameras don't work in this world. Here, our everyday intuitions about the nature of light and form break down. We could try to (and scientists do!) use illuminations of shorter wavelength to diffract from those small structures, as in X-ray crystallography and electron microscopy. The resulting photographs hover at the threshold where our sense of visual comprehension departs from the everyday experience. Once we reach the molecules and atoms of biological structure, we are on the doorstep of atomic physics. This is the quantum realm, where matter seems at once wave like and particle like – traits that do not have anything like a photorealistic depiction. Nevertheless, photorealism has, as we shall see in a later project, been used for depicting certain properties of atoms and molecules. These properties are both

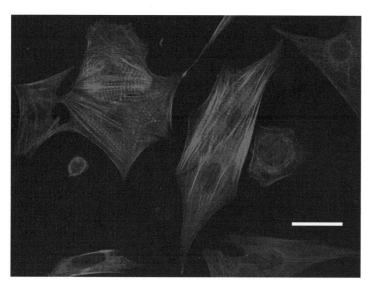

FIGURE 8.4

Cell micrographs can often be appreciated for their intrinsic beauty, quite apart from their obvious utility as scientific objects. This image shows cardiomyocytes (or heart muscle cells) that have been specially stained to make the cellular proteins actin (red) and calreticulin (blue) visible to the microscope under special lighting conditions. Scale bar $\approx 10\,\mu m$ (Images courtesy and copyright © 2006 Sylvia Papp, Institute of Medical Science, University of Toronto and Michal Opas, Department of Laboratory Medicine and Pathobiology, University of Toronto. From research supported by the Canadian Institutes of Health Research (CIHR)).

essential to biological function and well described in terms of the mathematics of NURBS surfaces. But that is just a start: as a result, animation at the cellular and molecular levels is ripe for various kinds of interpretive rendering, which can draw even further on photorealistic effects, or mix them with other nonphotorealistic approaches to represent the molecular fabric of living matter for maximum impact and interpretability.

The term nonphotorealistic rendering (NPR) refers to computer-generated images that either emulate traditional artistic styles (hand-drawn, painted, engraved, etc.) or otherwise represent images in a nonphotoreal way (see Fig. 8.7). As noted above, research in computer graphics, for its first few decades, was consumed primarily with the goal of creating photorealistic images. Before that goal was even accomplished, many questioned why photorealism should be the default end goal of rendering systems [3,4] – after all, artists have, for millennia, made compelling and informative images without cameras (or computers), and there must be something of use in the variety of visual styles toward which they have gravitated. In response, over the last decade or so numerous graphics researchers have explored stylized depiction; the result has been a discipline named (unfortunately) for what it is not, rather than what it is [5].

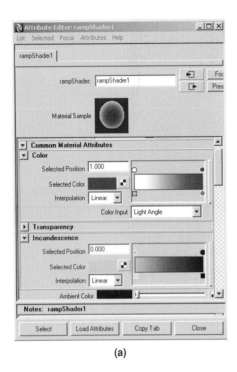

(a)   (b)

FIGURE 8.5

The appearance of objects in a SEM – with their characteristic bright edges and darkened centers – is often emulated in illustrated depictions of cells and molecules. Such a look can be created in Maya using the Ramp shader (a), as was done for the rendering of bacteria (*Clostridium difficile*) in (b). Scale bar ≈ 10 μm (b) (Courtesy Shaftesbury Films and AXS Biomedical Animation Studio; copyright Shaftesbury ReGenesis III Inc.).

Why choose an NPR style to define the look of your animation or film? There are several possible reasons:

■ A number of studies [6,7] have shown that nonphotorealistic representation (especially well-constructed line drawings) is often easier for people to interpret than photographs or continuous tone images. The reason for this has not been fully elucidated, but it may have to do with the necessary simplification of line drawings, their elimination of extraneous detail, and the presegmented nature of the objects in a line drawing. It is worth noting that, despite the ease of acquiring photographs, line drawings are still very common in technical documentation.

■ Photorealistic rendering approaches can be convincing enough that viewers of an animation might mistake what they are looking at as empirical imagery, rather than a simulation, reconstruction, or interpretation. In some cases, this misattribution of veridicality to animated sequences could be problematic.

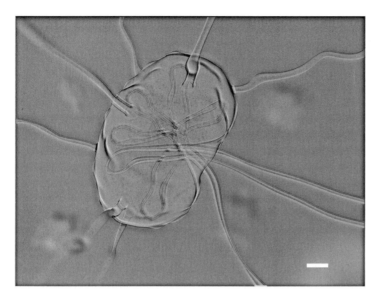

FIGURE 8.6

A Maya rendering of a lymph node, composited in Adobe After Effects to stimulate the appearance of phase-contrast microscopy. Scale bar ≈ 2 mm. (Courtesy and © 2006 Marc Dryer; used with permission).

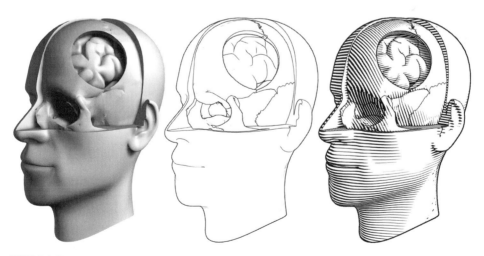

FIGURE 8.7

A 3D model rendered using left: a typical "photorealistic" adaptive scanline render; middle: a pen-and-ink style "nonphotorealistic" (*NPR*) render; and right: an engraving style NPR render.

One could argue that NPR-rendered sequences will usually be understood by viewers as interpretations and would be far less likely to be mistaken for "reality" as captured by a camera.

- NPR approaches tend to communicate the "provisional" or contingent nature of what is being represented, and therefore may be more appropriate when the animation is highly simplified, or when the particular structures or processes being represented are not fully characterized.

- NPR can be used for purely aesthetic reasons. Also, digital pen-and-ink is far less messy than its real-world counterpart and potentially easier to learn.

There has been an explosion of interest during the last few years in stylized depiction, with attendant research groups, conferences, and commercial development. Interestingly, the difficulty of deriving a good line-drawn representation of a 3D model, for instance, has emphasized how little science grasps about the psychology of picture perception. In that sense, many NPR researchers may be helping, from the algorithm upward, to build models of human visual perception.

8.4.1.2 The Treatment and the Script

A film treatment is a short narrative description of what the viewer of the proposed film would see. It is less about the "backstory" of the animation and more about what the experience of watching the film would be like. Treatments are often the first step in the filmmaking process and are often used to gain initial approval and financing for a project.

A script is also a written document, but a far more detailed one which formalizes the proposed film in terms of sequences, scenes, shots, dialog or narration, sound effects, and production notes. There are several standard formats for scripts, which use special text formatting to distinguish these different elements (see Fig. 8.8).

If the film is a live action one, the script is often the final required preproduction document created before shooting can begin. Animation, however, requires a more intensive preproduction phase, and two more elements are usually required before production starts.

8.4.1.3 The Storyboard

A storyboard (Fig. 8.9) takes the production script and breaks it down, shot for shot, into visual form. Salient frames from each shot are rendered in thumbnail form and assembled in sequence. Narration or other scripted elements are often included below or to the side of the rendered frames. Storyboards are a presentation medium and are the focal point of the "pitch," where team members are led through a proposed film sequence.

The storyboard images reflect what the camera would see. Graphic devices, such as arrows and superimposed rectangles, are used to indicate intended camera motion

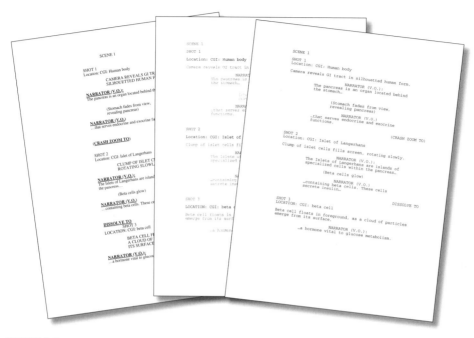

FIGURE 8.8

Examples of script formatting styles: from left to right: BBC, grey-coded, and tombstone.

or change in focal length. The rendering approach used to make storyboard frames should not be "careful" or "finished" since a storyboard is meant to be a working document that, in a successful project, will see numerous revisions as sequences are reworked, new camera angles and movements tested, and shots added or eliminated.

In classical (i.e. Disney-style) animation preproduction, the storyboard can be the principal arena for the definition of the overall narrative, supplanting the script as the source of the story.

8.4.1.4 The 2D Animatic

The 2D animatic is a more recent innovation. It usually involves the transformation of the static storyboard into a piece of motion media, complete with test sound track. Storyboard frames are scanned and assembled in an editing, compositing, or motion graphics software package like Adobe After Effects. These programs allow for the animation of 2D elements over time; thus object and camera movement can be simulated and synchronized with audio. The storyboard images are sometimes separated into foreground, midground, and background elements to better facilitate the creation of object motion and *parallax* effects. The animatic allows the film director to test story flow and timing; since the result is a rudimentary film, it is the first working version of the project. In some studios, an animatic is called a *story reel*. In the

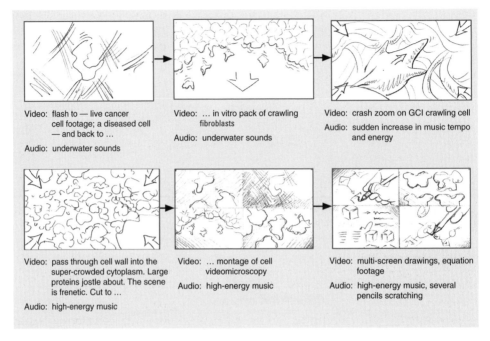

Video: flash to — live cancer cell footage; a diseased cell — and back to ...
Audio: underwater sounds

Video: ... in vitro pack of crawling fibroblasts
Audio: underwater sounds

Video: crash zoom on GCI crawling cell
Audio: sudden increase in music tempo and energy

Video: pass through cell wall into the super-crowded cytoplasm. Large proteins jostle about. The scene is frenetic. Cut to ...
Audio: high-energy music

Video: ... montage of cell videomicroscopy
Audio: high-energy music

Video: multi-screen drawings, equation footage
Audio: high-energy music, several pencils scratching

FIGURE 8.9

Plans for animation, storytelling, and science unite in this storyboard for a film about cancer cell migration. A storyboard is an essential tool in the computer animation workflow.

earliest years of hand-drawn animation, story reels were known as *pencil tests* since the animators' penciled drawings were put on a camera stand and photographed, one by one, as film frames to be projected for review and criticism of the animation.

8.4.2 Workflow Stage 2: Production

In the production stage, the plan developed in the preproduction phase is implemented. Ideally, at this point the story is well defined, and no further narrative changes are anticipated. In most studio settings, animated scenes and films are the creative work of teams of artists and technical specialists who work together in the preproduction, production, or postproduction stages of the workflow. One artist would not normally undertake all of the numerous steps and stages alone. Animation production in Maya and similar top-tier products for 3D computer animation will require your attention to the following elements of the production workflow.

8.4.2.1 The 3D Scene: Your Digital Stage

The term scene has two meanings for animators. Traditionally, it refers to a sequence of events that comprise a distinct element in a story. In Maya, on the other hand, a scene is the 3D environment, including models and animation, contained in one computer file. It is essentially a stage for digital action. Several Maya scenes may be developed to create a single traditional one, or one Maya scene may contain the models, action, cameras, and lights needed to create an entire story comprised many traditional scenes.

For a scientist, this notion of the word scene might seem a hazy or foreign concept. Perhaps the best way to think about it is as a model world, or, more specifically, a specialized apparatus for running an experiment. Just as the cell biologist might have a bank of petri dishes, each growing a different variety of bacteria, the Maya-using researcher might have a range of scene files, comprising various projects, tests, and iterations of particular experimental approaches.

8.4.2.2 Geometry Modeling

The creation of objects and environments in digital 3D space is called modeling. Objects in computer animation are typically modeled as shells with no solid, or volumetric, form to them. There are two main surface types that make up these shells. These are polygonal surfaces, comprised of many interconnected flat polygons and spline surfaces, also called NURBS, that are described by mathematical curves (Fig. 8.10). NURBS modeling generally produces smoother surfaces with geometries limited by the curve properties, whereas polygonal models, comprised of many small facets, can appear coarser but can be built in any conceivable shape, unencumbered by topological limitations. The choice of model type depends on the purpose and desired qualities of the finished model, but often comes down to personal preference.

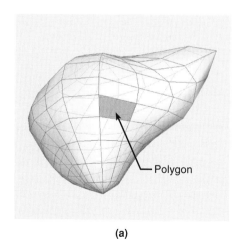
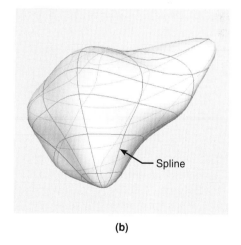

(a) (b)

FIGURE 8.10

Common surface model types. (a) Polygonal surface: composed of interconnected three- or four-sided polygons. (b) NURBS surface: described by parametric curves known as *splines*.

Modeling and animation applications typically offer a suite of tools for model creation and manipulation in addition to a collection of primitives – ready-made models like spheres, cubes, cylinders, cones, and tori that are often the starting point for more complex geometries. Maya has a range of polygon and spline primitives as well as tools for working with both types of model. Once you understand how models are created and manipulated using the standard tools, you can tackle procedural modeling, using a computer program to automate the modeling for you and to simulate the dynamics of their interaction.

As you work on your geometry models in Maya, you may find it necessary to adjust the fidelity of the display to the source geometry (Fig. 8.11). Several preset levels of detail and shading are available, such as smooth shaded, wireframe, point mode, and box. These trade off visual quality for display speed. When models and scenes become complex, it is also handy to be able to selectively hide or reduce detail on specific objects, so your workspace becomes less cluttered.

8.4.2.3 Volumetric Modeling

Mention should be made of volumetric models, which use an approach very different from most commercial 3D modeling applications. Surface models, such as those discussed above, are shells possessing no inherent solidity. Volumetric models, on the other hand, are composed of arrays of cubes inhabiting 3D space called voxels (a word derived from *volume pixels*), or densely sampled point clouds. Voxels encode for some spatially distributed variable, such as luminance, color, temperature, or density. Volumetric models can be derived from serial imaging technologies, like CT, MRI, and confocal microscopy, or produced by computational models of dynamic systems (as in modeling of storm systems). One famous example of volumetric modeling is the Visible Human Project [8], a freely available database of sectional anatomy. In this project,

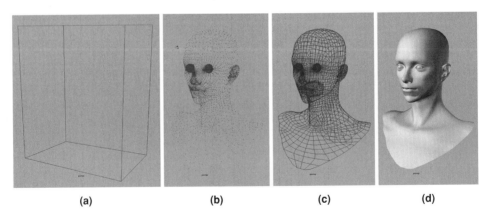

(a)   (b)   (c)   (d)

FIGURE 8.11

3D scenes can often be visualized using different display modes. Shown here from least to most computer intensive are (a) box; (b) points; (c) wireframe; and (d) smooth shaded.

sponsored by the US National Library of Medicine, researchers froze and thin-sliced male and female cadavers taking detailed photographs of the end blocks. This huge serial image database (along with calibrated MRI and CT scans done before the slicing started) can be reconstructed into a highly detailed volumetric model, with the voxels deriving their color from the pixels in the 2D images. This volumetric model is then amenable to various representational approaches (arbitrary slices, selective transparency) that allow for an unprecedented look into the human body.

While voxels are generally arranged in a rectilinear grid, point clouds can be freely arranged, with more densely packed points concentrated at points of detail or interest. Like voxels, point clouds can have color or some other property at each sample location, and can build up interestingly representative displays that are less computationally demanding than voxels.

Maya contains some volumetric tools, in the form of Maya Fluid Effects, and, to some extent, particle tools and Maya Paint Effects. But generally speaking, volumetric modeling comes at some computational cost, and the tools available for the manipulation and *de novo* creation of volumetric models have yet to approach the sophistication of those available for surface models. As tools and algorithms evolve, volumetric animation and simulation approaches will surely move into the mainstream, and therefore developments in the field bear watching.

8.4.2.4 Procedural Modeling

Procedural modeling is the generation of geometry in a 3D program by algorithmic means. Many natural structures, such as plants, landscapes, and circulatory trees, exhibit qualities that are tedious to model by hand but which are amenable to scripted or programmed modeling approaches. Some of these qualities include randomness, high detail, and self-similarity at a number of scales. The key benefit of this approach is that, with a small amount of input (simple equations or formulas, initial parameters), a huge amount of output can be derived (complex models of forests, coastlines, mountains, arteries, and veins).

There are numerous procedural modeling approaches, several of which are built in to Maya.

8.4.2.5 The Frame Rate

It's important to note that, when using 3D software for a simulation, the work doesn't necessarily end when the simulation has run its course. The stunning imagery that makes a program like Maya so attractive to use must be rendered out. Once produced, the final images are played back at a specified rate of display, in *fps*. For example, a 30-frame animation will produce one second of motion when played back at 30 fps. The frame rate determines the quality of perceived motion and varies depending on the requirements of the viewing medium. The slower the frame rate, the less convincing the illusion becomes. Nonetheless, there are practical considerations that may warrant a slower frame rate. Rendering finished frames is a time-intensive, and therefore expensive, endeavor. A slower frame rate is therefore often a cost-saving measure used by animation studios resulting in a trade-off between quality and efficiency.

In the case of animations produced for Internet viewing, a slower frame rate may be used to conform to limited data transfer rates, resulting in uninterrupted viewing but with relatively poor visual persistence.

The intended rate of display should be determined *before* you begin animating items in a scene. A walking figure animated for 30 fps playback will appear in slight slow motion if projected at 24 fps. When using a 3D application for simulation, the frame rate acquires an additional meaning; it becomes the rate at which simulation events are evaluated. When you play a rendering of the simulation at the typical NTSC 30 fps, one second of playback equates to roughly 100 minutes of cell movement! Were you to set the frame rate to 15 fps, one second of playback would represent only 50 minutes of migration. This distinction is important when presenting simulation results to your audience.

8.4.2.6 Animation

Animation, we've seen, is the art of taking otherwise static images and objects and imparting a sense of motion, and life, to them. The property being animated (called an *attribute* in Maya) could be position, scale, shape, or color among others. For example, consider depicting a deflating balloon with a sequence of still images (see Fig. 8.12). As air rushes out, we make the balloon careen in all directions and gradually shrink, so it winds up looking flatter, less bright, and more opaque frame by frame. To achieve this, we have animated, over time, the balloon's position (or translation in Maya), scale, shape, and its color and transparency.

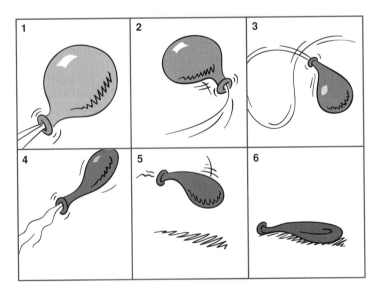

FIGURE 8.12

A deflating balloon represents the concept of animated attributes. Not only do the balloon's position and rotation change over time, but so do its size (scale), and surface appearance (opacity).

Animation software like Maya generally takes two different approaches to creating these changes: *key-framed animation* and *procedural animation*. The concept of animation is inseparable from that of time. The smallest unit of time in film animation is the frame (many physically based calculations within a 3D application can rely on arbitrarily divided subframes for precision, however). Animators use a timeline, a linear scale divided into equal measures of seconds or frames, to locate key moments in the action. Frames containing these key moments are called *keyframes*, for which values are assigned by the animator or by a script to the attribute(s) being animated.

Disney-style animation exemplifies the keyframe approach taken to a highly refined stage of drawing and action timing: the term keyframe comes from hand-drawn animation, where a senior, or "lead," animator would draw only those frames considered "key" to the action being represented – the most dramatically intense moments of the action. Less experienced animators known as animation assistants and (below them) "in-betweeners" would fill in the frames between those keyframes.

In the digital era, the computer acts as our in-betweener, interpolating object qualities from keyframe to keyframe. The interpolation is represented as an *animation curve*, a 2D plot of the attribute in question versus time. In the case of translation through space, the animation curve is a velocity graph. Some applications, including Maya, give animators complete control over the shape of these curves and, therefore, over the nature of the in-between action. The velocity curve, for example, can be manipulated to give a desired acceleration throughout a translation.

Procedural animation is a term for animation that is driven algorithmically, not unlike its cousin procedural modeling. It is far more similar to simulation than animation per se; the animator sets the initial parameters for the objects and then watches to see how the animation evolves over time. In a procedural animation, the animation curves are produced by your computer model.

8.4.2.7 Dynamics

Many 3D applications have dynamic simulation capabilities that utilize a built-in *physics engine*. In this case, natural laws of motion can be applied to a model, which has assigned physical properties, to emulate the effects of various forces acting on it. A simple example is that of a bouncing ball. A gravitational force applied to a ball on a sloped surface makes it roll, drop off the edge, and bounce when it strikes the ground below. Attributes such as mass, elasticity, and friction are input by the user and the physics engine does the rest. A useful time–saver for animators, the robust onboard dynamics capabilities of a program like Maya can prove useful in the type of predictive scientific modeling. Where the modeling requirements go beyond the capabilities of the onboard engines, Maya's programming tools let you develop the model to meet your needs.

8.4.2.8 Lights

Like a real stage, a digital stage is dark until you add lights. Most 3D applications offer a suite of available lights that mimic those found on a movie set or in a photographer's studio. These include spotlights, area lights, point lights, and infinite lights among others, but vary in actual name from application to application. For instance, a light bulb is a *point light* in Maya but an *omni light* in Cinema 4D (another robust 3D animation package developed by MAXON Computer GmbH of Germany). There is usually a default light to provide general illumination before you begin adding lights to a scene. Once lights are added, the default is switched off. You may add as many or as few lights as you wish, as you will see, and place them throughout the 3D space to best illuminate your models to be seen from a given viewpoint. Lights can be colored and assigned a number of attributes that produce special effects such as dappling or a visible beam of light.

Shadows cast by lighted objects in a scene can be a very useful device for conveying realism and for emphasizing spatial relationships within a scene. CGI shadows may have hard or soft edges (as do real-world shadows) and are typically set and adjusted within the controls for a given light.

Good lighting is an art in itself, but a beginner can achieve a reasonably good effect with the standard three-point lighting setup pictured in Fig. 8.13. This configuration, often a starting point for photographers, involves a key light for primary illumination, a fill light to "fill in" the potentially harsh shadows created by the *key light*, and a *back light* to add a high-lit rim to the upper edges of objects and emphasize their contours.

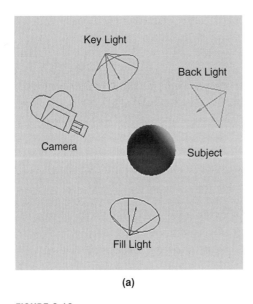
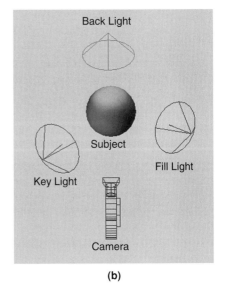

(a)   (b)

FIGURE 8.13

A standard three-point lighting rig involves a *key light*, a *fill light*, and a *back light*. (a) Side view. (b) Top view.

8.4.2.9 Cameras

In everyday life, we use cameras to view and record models and action in our 3D environment. Maya, like many other 3D animation tools, implements the same idea to help you plan how you will depict the events of your 3D virtual world. When you create a new scene in Maya, a default camera provides the view that you see. As you maneuver in the space to get a desired view of the scene, you are actually translating, rotating, and perhaps zooming the Maya virtual camera through which you're looking. 3D cameras provide orthogonal and perspective views and have many of the attributes of real cameras, such as exposure settings, lens angle, and focal length. These attributes, along with the camera's translation and rotation, can be animated and keyed for narrative purposes.

8.4.2.10 Shading

In 3D CGI, shading refers to the combined effects of lighting, surface color, surface texture, and geometry, determining the final rendered appearance of your models. When a Maya object is first created, it is assigned a default shader (also called a material in Maya) with appearance attributes including color, opacity, and surface characteristics like texture or a geometric pattern. Shaders can be created and applied to objects in a number of ways to emulate real-world surfaces and, in some cases, volumes such as glass or fog. Some approaches to shading focus on nonrealistic appearances, such as a pen-and-ink or cartoon (or toon) style (Fig. 8.7).

> In recent years, computer graphics cards have improved to the point where, in certain cases, their output is sufficient for final quality renders. Programs like Maya have embraced this possibility with the option to render scenes using the hardware renderer. Enabling this option uses the power of the hardware in modern graphics cards (sometimes called Graphics Processing Units [GPUs]) to create the final images, often in a fraction of the time a software-based render would take.

8.4.2.11 Rendering

The production of images from a 3D scene is called rendering, a complex subject which combines the effects of lights, cameras, and shading. The images are saved as individual picture files or as a group in one movie file and can then be displayed in succession using a viewing application or passed along for postproduction work. Collectively, rendered images are often referred to as footage, borrowing from film terminology. The image format and pixel resolution of the footage are assigned in the render settings of the 3D application, having been determined by the end purpose of the animation. For example, you would usually require a different format and resolution for a small movie destined to be viewed in an Internet browser, compared to a feature film on a large screen. It is important to know the requirements prior to setting up cameras and rendering, particularly if you're creating an animation for an established format such as NTSC or an existing Web page.

3D applications provide a range of standard formats and resolutions to choose from as well as custom settings.

Render engines support a number of *photorealism* effects that may be of use in developing a look for your animation projects, including

- *Subsurface scattering*, in which light penetrates a surface, scatters, and re-emerges (as in real-world translucent materials such as skin and wax). This can create the impression of translucent, gel-like substances.

- *Ambient occlusion*, which models the decrease of ambient light where surfaces come close together. This is a computationally inexpensive way to add a sense of real-world light interaction and solidity to an object.

- *Global illumination*, which is a computationally expensive way to model real-world illumination, where light bounces diffusely around a scene and the color of one object can "bleed" onto another one nearby. One global illumination algorithm is *radiosity*.

A simple approach to creating a photorealistic look of SEM in Maya, for example, is to apply a material called a Ramp shader, which is controlled by the camera direction. This technique was used to create the image in Fig. 8.5b.

There are currently numerous rendering algorithms available to assist you in creating nonphotorealistic looks for your animations. These NPR tools are available commercial options (built-in to production renderers like mental ray) and as do-it-yourself shader techniques. Many NPR algorithms are designed to emulate traditional cel-based animation (which consisted of pen drawings on transparent acetate "cels," with flat or simply shaded color painted on the back) and are therefore referred to as toon shader (from cartoon) or cel shader techniques.

Whatever approach you choose in terms of the look of your film, you will need an efficient strategy for producing your final renders. This strategy should have two components:

1. **Compositing plan**. A computer animation scene, like the ones you see in films and on television, is rarely rendered as a single entity. Usually, an individual frame is composed of layers, numbering anywhere from two to tens (or even hundreds) of separately rendered images. Sometimes the passes are composed of different image planes (e.g. foreground, midground, and background), sometimes they are of different "characters" (e.g. interacting proteins), and sometimes they are of individual image components (e.g. texture color, shadow, and highlight passes). There are very practical reasons for this: some effects are too difficult or compute-intensive to render directly (e.g. depth-of-field effects) and relatively easy to add at the compositing stage; and changes are easier to make when only one component of a scene needs be re-rendered rather than the whole scene. Also, by rendering elements like lights and shadows in separate passes, they can be easily tweaked for maximum effect. While affording flexibility, rendering multiple passes can be more time-consuming than rendering just one. The choice, therefore, will depend on available time, and the end use.

2. **Data management plan**. Given the huge number of render files generated by the typical animation project and the general practicality of rendering in multiple passes (which can multiply the number of render files many times), it is essential to maintain a sane data management strategy. This has a number of components:

- Project directory hierarchies are used to organize files by type. For example, Maya will, by default, save rendered image files to the Images directory within your current Maya Project folder.

- File naming conventions help you keep track of your work and are important for tracking file versions (e.g. myScene_001, myScene_002, and so on). Naming conventions are especially helpful on larger projects where multiple users are sharing files.

- Multiple backups of essential files: the most important files in the production phase are your Maya animation scene files and the files on which they depend (textures, ASCII data, embedded reference files); these should be redundantly backed up, preferably with an off-site option. Final renderings are also important, but in a crunch, they can be re-rendered from the scene files. In the postproduction phase, your editing/compositing application project files are most important. Losing your footage (render) files means re-rendering lost scenes; annoying and time-consuming, but not tragic. But losing your Maya scene and editing/compositing project files would mean recreating the project from scratch.

Rendering can tax your computer system enormously, with a single frame taking from as little as a few seconds to as long as 30 minutes or more to produce. The time taken is a function of scene complexity, image resolution, available memory (*RAM*), and processor speed among other factors. Commercial animation studios typically employ an array of computers, called a *render farm*, to produce renderings more efficiently. Imagine a 90-minutes animated feature created at 30 fps, with each frame taking an average of 10 minute to render. This translates to 27 000 h or 1125 days on a single computer! That's over three years of nonstop computing, assuming there are no errors and, therefore, a need to re-render some portion. It's easy to see why RAM and processors are at a premium when it comes to producing animated footage. Don't be discouraged, however. We routinely produce high-end rendered animations on modestly powerful desktop PCs and Macs.

> Much of our rendering work to date has been done on PCs equipped with Pentium 4 or AMD Athlon XP2700 processors and typically 1 GB of RAM.

8.4.2.12 The 3D Animatic or Layout

In some 3D animation production workflows, a further refinement of the 2D animatic is completed as an early stage of production. This is called the layout stage, or the 3D animatic. Draft versions of key object geometry and sets are constructed in 3D and camera movement and simple object motions are choreographed. Draft quality renderings are set to a "scratch" (draft) sound track. The result offers another opportunity to confirm the choices made in the earlier stages, or to refine the narrative flow further. An added benefit to the animator is the knowledge of exactly where cameras are to be placed in each scene and the economy that can be realized by only building and refining things that will be seen by those cameras. There is no use building a whole street when you are only going to shoot one side of it.

The 3D animatic is considered part of production since much of the work, especially the camera positioning and animation, will survive in the final version, even though the sets and objects are usually substantially refined or completely replaced.

8.4.3 Workflow Stage 3: Postproduction

It is rare that an animation is in final form when rendered from a program like Maya. More often lengths of footage are produced and combined in an editing application where other elements like sound and titles are added. It is here, in the postprocessing (or just post) stage, that special effects usually are produced. In our workflow, for example, we regularly use Adobe After Effects to composite and enhance the appearance of our footage, and to add special effects, titles, narration, and music. Compositing applications like Adobe After Effects, Discreet's Combustion, and Apple's Shake are well suited to compositing and special effects work for short films and for individual shots within longer films. While also a competent compositor, an application like Apple's Final Cut Pro is more oriented to editing and is well suited to longer films. It is not uncommon to use After Effects to produce segments of effects-heavy footage and then composite all footage in an editor like Final Cut Pro to create the assembled film.

Moreover, it is also common to render components of 3D animated scenes, such as the background and foreground elements, in separate passes to be composited in post. By rendering elements like lights and shadows in separate passes, they can be easily tweaked for maximum effect. If, however, they are rendered together in one pass, they can only be adjusted within the 3D application and then re-rendered. While flexible, rendering multiple passes is more time-consuming than just one and requires competent file organization and management. The choice, therefore, will depend on available time, and the end use.

Regardless of the approach taken, your final animation must be output from the editing application as a sequence of image files or as a self-contained movie file. Since there is considerably less computer processing involved at this stage, the output or "final render" from the editing or compositing stage (not to be confused with the 3D animation rendering discussed above!) takes far less time than an average render from a 3D application.

8.4.4 Putting It All Together

Now that you have a sense of the computer animation workflow, it's time to start Maya and have a closer look at how crucial workflow steps like modeling, animation, and rendering are tackled.

8.5 ANIMATION

An object is composed of nodes, each with a number of attributes. Using the transform tools and the Channel Box in Maya, you can change certain attribute values in order to move, scale, rotate, and change the shape of objects. Here, you will record such changes at different times – called *keyframes* – on the timeline in order to create animation.

The relevant Maya windows, menus, and tools will be introduced in the upcoming tutorials. You will use the Hypergraph to see what happens behind the scenes when attributes are animated and examine how animation is stored within a node. By the end of this chapter you will have learned how to animate a simple object using both manual keyframing techniques and automated *procedural* methods.

What is discussed in the remainder of this chapter is by no means exhaustive; as with modeling, one could easily fill a book or book series with techniques, tips, and tricks on animation with Maya.

8.6 MAYA

In Maya, animation is simply the change over time in the value of an attribute. An attribute that can be animated is said to be *keyable*, in reference to the word *keyframe* (also *key*), which is both a noun and a verb in Maya. As a noun, it means a *frame*, or unit of animation time, at which a value has been recorded, or *set*. As a verb, it refers to the action of setting the value.

While keyframes are a means of recording animation for playback, they are not necessarily a requirement of animation; all that is required is for an attribute to change with time. Keyframes are merely a convenient way to store attribute values at different times, within a Maya file. Alternately, values may be stored in an external file, or they may not need to be stored at all.

Maya stores keyframe data for every animated attribute in a separate animation node. The input for this node is time and its output is an attribute value. This data is in the graphical form of attribute versus time and is visualized in the Graph Editor, a handy Animation Editor you'll meet shortly. Like other nodes in Maya, you can inspect and edit an animation node's values in the Attribute Editor.

8.6.1 Procedural versus Keyframe Animation

Generally speaking, *procedural animation* refers to the use of computer procedures, or algorithms, to change attributes over time. The procedure can be as complicated as an algorithm for DNA replication or as simple as an instruction to make an attribute equal to a constant value; the point is that it uses an instruction or set of instructions, not a recorded value, to determine the attribute value.

The following example illustrates the difference between keyframe and procedural animation. Figure 8.14 shows a cube that moves along the X-axis from

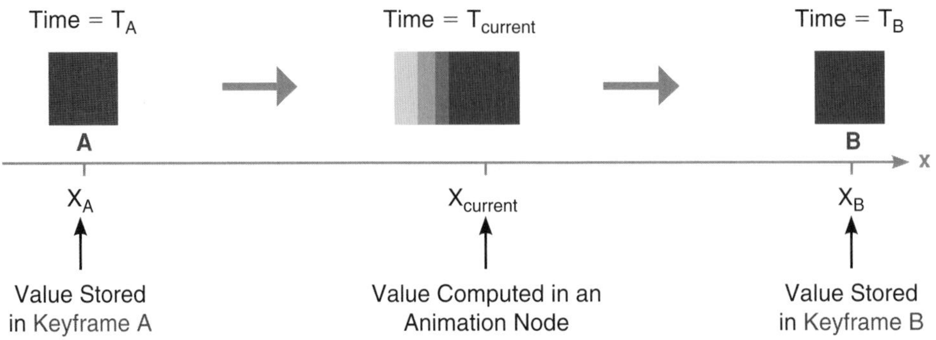

FIGURE 8.14

Animation of a cube's Translate X attribute between keyframes A and B.

point X_A at time T_A, to point X_B at time T_B. The animation here is the change in the Translate X attribute over time. If this action were keyframed, Maya would use the current time, $T_{current}$, to look up $X_{current}$ in the animation node. If instead the action were procedural, Maya would calculate the $X_{current}$ value using a source other than an animation node. This source could be an *animation expression* node, a MEL script, or another type of node, such as a *procedural texture* which calculates its output value using an internal algorithm. We will examine the nodes and connections used in animation through specific examples in the tutorials later in this chapter.

Keyframe and procedural animation need not be exclusive from one another. Keyframes are often used to record the outcome of procedural animation for later playback. Nor is procedural animation limited to the physical properties of objects. Procedural textures are texture nodes that use mathematical procedures to create interesting patterns for shading objects. Similarly, a light can have its attributes animated procedurally to produce interesting effects.

8.6.2 Keyframes and Memory

Each time you set a keyframe, the relevant information is stored in RAM until you save the Maya file, at which time it is written into the file. The more keyframes you set, the larger your file. In a simulation using procedural animation, where you want to record animation for many objects (e.g. interacting molecules) over many time increments, setting keys can eat up RAM and drive your computer to use *virtual memory*, with its associated time penalties. You can use these techniques to record animated attribute values to an external file rather than keyframing them in Maya. Such an approach keeps RAM use down, and Maya file size to a minimum.

> Virtual memory refers to the practice of using a hard drive for storage and retrieval of data once RAM becomes full. Helpful for alleviating low-memory situations, it comes with a heavy time penalty – about an order of magnitude slower than RAM.

8.6.3 The Animation Menu Set

In addition to tools for keyframing, this menu set provides access to ones used to deform and rig objects. Rigging, which is widely used in character animation, is the practice of endowing a model with attributes that deform its shape in a controlled manner. A common example is the rigging of a character, the "skin," with a jointed skeleton. Joints are then rotated, deforming the skin to bend limbs. A skeleton's joints can be animated to make a character walk and talk. Deformers work like joints, changing an object's shape by moving its components.

For our *in silico* work, we have for some projects used rigging techniques to deform motile cells as they locomote through scaffolds (Fig. 8.15). We focus here on the menu items concerned with keyframing. To activate the Animation menu set, use the Status Line pull-down menu at the far left of the Status Line.

8.6.4 Setting Keys

Below are a few ways to set keys for, or *keyframe*, an attribute.

Using the Channel Box (Fig. 8.16)

1. Select the item (object, camera, etc.) for which you want to key an attribute;
2. Select the attribute(s) you wish to key by name in the Channel Box;
3. RMB+click over a selected attribute name. This brings up a context menu;

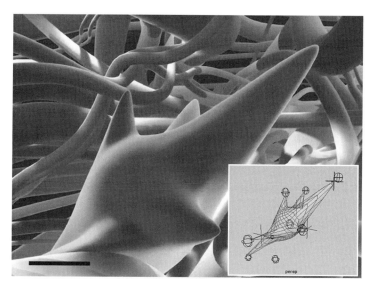

FIGURE 8.15

In this animation of a migrating fibroblast cell, the cell body is rigged to extend and retract appendages called pseudopodia. The rigging uses joints and deformers (inset) to deform the cell surface smoothly as it crawls through its environment. Scale bar ≈ 10 μm.

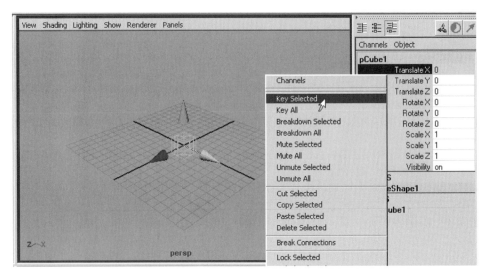

FIGURE 8.16

Using the Channel Box to set a keyframe for the Translate X attribute.

4. Choose **Key Selected** and release the RMB. This will set a key for all selected attributes.

In the Attribute Editor:

1. Select the item for which you want to key an attribute;
2. Open the Attribute Editor (Ctrl+A);
3. RMB+click on the attribute name to key all attributes corresponding to the name (e.g. clicking on **Translate** allows you to set all three (X, Y, and Z) Translate values)
   or
   RMB+click on the attribute field to key only a single attribute name (e.g. Translate X);
4. In the context menu, select **Set Key**.

Using a hotkey:

1. Select the item for which you want to key an attribute;
2. Use one of the hotkeys shown in Table 8.1 to set a keyframe.

8.6.5 Auto Keyframe

When you turn on *auto keyframing*, Maya automatically sets a key every time you change an attribute. For example, if you were to key the position of an object at time 1, move the time indicator ahead to time 2, then drag the object to a new

Table 8.1 Hotkeys to Set Keyframes for Selected Objects

Hotkey	Action
S	Set keys for all transform attributes
Shift + W	Set keys for Translate X, Y, and Z
Shift + E	Set keys for Rotation X, Y, and Z
Shift + R	Set keys for Scale X, Y, and Z

position, Maya would set a key for the new position at time 2. This can certainly speed workflow in some circumstances, but it can also be dangerous because it can lead to setting keys accidentally. This can ruin a carefully arranged animation. To turn auto keyframing on:

1. Choose Window → Settings/Preferences → Preferences. Select Settings → Animation;
2. Under Auto Key, check Auto Key (uncheck to turn off auto keyframing)
   or
   Press the auto keyframe icon ⊶ in the bottom right corner of the user interface (UI).

8.6.6 Graphing Animation

Maya represents animation graphically in two ways, using the *Dope Sheet* and the *Graph Editor*. The Dope Sheet provides a tabular account of keyframes for a selected item (Fig. 8.17). You can use it to edit animation by selecting and moving keys along the timeline. In a traditional animation workflow, the Dope Sheet is used to coordinate event and sound synchronization and timing.

The Graph Editor (Fig. 8.18) is a 2D graph displaying *animation curves* (also called *keysets*). These represent attribute values plotted on the vertical axis against time values plotted on the horizontal axis; they are the *in-between* animation spanning the keys, which are the plot points. Their interpolation through and between keys determines the smoothness of animation. A curve can use *linear* or *spline* (nonlinear) *interpolation*, as shown in Fig. 8.18. Spline curves correspond to smooth acceleration and deceleration in animation. In other software applications, spline interpolation is sometimes called *ease in* and *ease out* (*into* and *out* of a keyframe). This is the opposite of linear interpolation that makes for abrupt changes – instantaneous acceleration – in attribute values at keyframes. This is not to say that spline interpolation can't generate abrupt changes in direction.

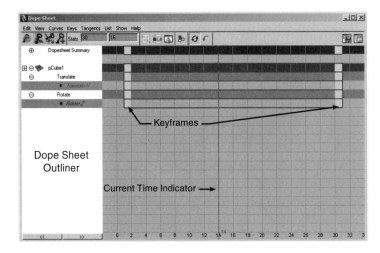

Dope Sheet Outliner

Keyframes

Current Time Indicator ⟶

FIGURE 8.17

The Dope Sheet provides a tabular view of keyframes for a selected object.

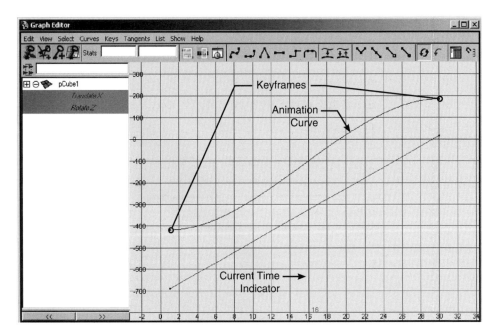

Keyframes

Animation Curve

Current Time ⟶ Indicator

FIGURE 8.18

The Graph Editor. The blue curve, which represents the Rotate Z attribute of pCube1, uses spline interpolation. Its slope approaches zero at either end, making for a gradual increase and decrease in the rate of change of Rotate Z. The red curve represents the Translate X attribute and uses linear interpolation. Its slope is constant, which makes for an instantaneous increase and decrease in the rate of change of Translate X.

In addition to displaying animation curves, the Graph Editor contains tools for adjusting interpolation and for moving and scaling keys. For keyframe animation, we find it to be one of the most useful tools in Maya. You will explore it further, along with animation curve interpolation, in the upcoming tutorial.

Dope Sheet and Graph Editor

Maya Help → Using Maya → Animation, Character Setup, and Deformers → Animation → Animation Windows and Editors → Editors

→ Dope Sheet
→ Graph Editor

8.6.7 Deleting Keys

Once keys are set, they can be deleted in one of the following ways:
  Use the Dope Sheet or the Hypergraph to delete one or more keys for the selected object(s):

Select the keys in the Dope Sheet and hit Delete.
  or
Select the keys in the Hypergraph and hit Delete.

Use the Timeline to delete all keys for the selected object(s) at a specific frame:

1. Select the red key tick mark in the Timeline;
2. RMB+click on the key and select Delete.

Use the Channel Box or Attribute Editor to delete all keys for the selected attribute(s):

1. Select the attribute in the Channel Box or Attribute Editor;
2. RMB+click on the attribute and select Break Connections.

8.6.8 Time Units

Maya lets you determine the working units for time, which are set to 24 fps by default. You can choose from a variety of fps settings, including broadcast standards *PAL* and *NTSC*, and clock settings: hours, minutes, seconds, and milliseconds. A clock setting of "milliseconds" is equivalent to an fps speed of 1000. A setting of seconds is equivalent to 1 fps, and so on for minutes and hours. To access the Time settings,

1. Open the Preferences Window and choose Settings;
2. Under Working Units → Time, select an appropriate playback frame rate. (In North America, it is common to use NTSC (30 fps), which is a television video broadcast standard.)

It is good practice to set your Time working units at the start of a project. Changing units midway will shuffle keyframes along the timeline unless you have **Keep Keys at Current Frames** checked in the Working Units settings.

The Time working units are as important as the speed of the action in a rendered movie. For instance, if an action were to occur in one second as seen by an audience, then you would set the working units in Maya to match those of the viewing technology. Suppose, for example, you were animating the *cell cycle* for a European television audience, and you had one second to show the *cytokinesis* phase. In Maya, you would set the Time working units to PAL (25 fps) (the European television broadcast standard) and animate cytokinesis within 25 frames.

For *in silico* simulations, the working units are generally flexible. Our practice is to use NTSC (30 fps) because we often output movies to video for a North American audience.

8.6.9 Playback Settings

After setting the working units, you can further specify speed of playback in the scene view. This can be the speed you set in Time working units, half or twice that speed, or a different frame rate altogether. Since this determines only how quickly Maya plays frames in the workspace, it does not affect the per-second rate of animation in your scene.

It is not uncommon for a scene to be too complex to play back at the specified fps. In this case, Maya skips frames to keep pace. This is generally fine for keyframed animation, but is a major pitfall for scenes involving dynamics or procedural animation; calculations are missed in the skipped frames, leading to bogus animation results. To prevent this, Maya must be set to play every frame, independent of a desired frame rate:

1. Open the Preferences Window and choose Settings → Timeline.
2. Under Playback, select Play every frame.

Within the Playback settings, Update View determines if Maya will redraw all windows in the workspace during playback or just the active one, which requires less memory and processing. You can also choose whether animation is to play once or loop. Finally, you can skip frames for quicker playback of complex scenes by setting Playback by to a number other than 1; for instance a setting of 3 means Maya will play every third frame. For scenes involving dynamics and procedural animation, this setting should always remain at 1, for the reason mentioned in the previous paragraph.

8.7 TUTORIAL 08.01: A KEYFRAME ANIMATION

This is a quick exercise to become familiar with setting time-dependent attribute values using keyframes. You will animate the Translate X value for a primitive cube. We're starting with this very simple example in order to demonstrate the core concept of animation in Maya: the change of an attribute's value over time. Armed with this understanding and the fact that almost all attributes for all the nodes in a Maya scene can be animated, you will have at your fingertips enormous creative potential for simulations and visualizations of complex biological phenomena. Let's get started.

8.7.1 Preparation

To start, create a polygon cube, then select it in the scene view. Next, you'll set the Time working units, the Playback settings, and the duration of the animation.

1. Choose Create → Polygon Primitives → Cube. If Interactive Creation is turned on in this menu, you'll need to click and drag in the workspace to make the cube.
2. Choose Window → Settings/Preferences → Preferences. Make the following settings:

   a. Settings → Time → Working Units to NTSC (30 fps)
   b. Settings → Animation → Tangents → Default In Tangent and Default Out Tangent both to Linear and check Weighted Tangents.
   c. Settings → Timeline → Playback to Real-time (30 fps), and Looping to oscillate (so that the animation will play back and forth continually until you press Stop in the Playback Controls).

   Hit Save to close the Preferences Window.

3. Set the current time to 1.0 by LMB+clicking on 1 in the Time Slider, or by entering 1 in the Current Time field.
4. Set the Start and End times in the Range Slider to 1.0 and 90.0, respectively (Fig. 8.19).

> Setting Playback to **Real-time** will give you three seconds of animation for 90 frames at 30 fps. This will make the animation easier to watch than would a setting of **Play every frame**. The latter would play back very quickly because this simple animation requires very little computer horsepower to compute and draw each frame.

In Step 2b you set the animation tangents to be linear. We'll explain why shortly.

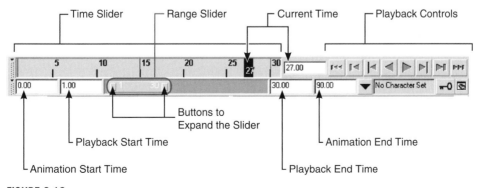

FIGURE 8.19

The Animation Controls.

8.7.2 Set the Keyframes

Now use the Channel Box to record a key for the cube at frame 1.

1. Select the cube.
2. Select the Translate X (not its value field) in the Channel Box.
3. RMB+click over Translate X to bring up a context menu.
4. Choose Key Selected and release the RMB.
5. Repeat steps 2 through 4 for Rotate Z.

> When an attribute has been keyed, its value field in the Channel Box turns from white to orange.

You have just keyed the cube's position at (0, 0, 0) and its rotation at (0, 0, 0). Next, you will change the time, translate and rotate the cube, and set a new key.

1. Enter 90 in the Current Time field or click on 90 in the Timeline to move to frame 90.
2. Hit the W hotkey to activate the Move Tool and drag the cube with the X handle to X = 16.
   or
   Enter 16 in the Translate X field in the Channel Box.
3. Set another key for Translate X at this new time.
4. Enter −720 in the Rotate Z field in the Channel Box.
5. Set another key for Rotate Z.

> You can also key translate values for individual *control vertices* (CVs) in the Channel Box, in the same way you would select and key transform attributes. The resulting animation curve nodes will be connected to the object's shape node, rather than its transform node.

8.7.3 Play, Scrub, and Stop the Animation

Note the red key ticks in the Time Slider, which indicate keyframes (in Preferences, you can change the display size of key ticks in the Time Slider). To play your animation:

1. In the Animation Controls, press the Go To Start button ⬛ to return to the beginning of the playback range.
2. To play the animation, press the Play button ▶ in the Animation Controls.
   or
   Hit the hotkey, Option+V.

You should see the cube roll back and forth across the scene view (Fig. 8.20). To scrub the animation:

LMB+drag in the Time Slider.

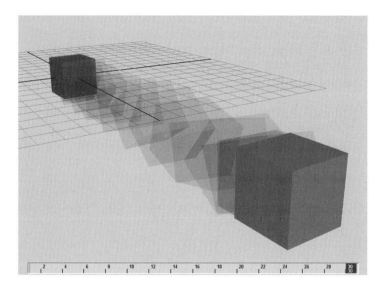

FIGURE 8.20

With its translate and rotate attributes keyed and playback set to Looping: Oscillate, the cube will roll back and forth in the scene view.

To stop playback:

Press the Stop button ▣ in the Animation Controls;
or
Hit the hotkey, Option+V;
or
Hit the ESC key.

8.7.4 Edit the Animation Curves

Notice that during playback the reversal of motion at either end of the cube's trajectory appears abrupt; it appears to instantaneously change direction. This is the result of setting the keyframe interpolation to *linear* in the Animation Tangents Preferences. It's often favorable to have linear versus nonlinear changes in motion when starting to animate, in order to rough in the motion. You can then refine the motion by adjusting the keyframe tangents in the Graph Editor, which is precisely what you will do in a few pages.

> The Graph Editor is a good item to add your custom shelf.

When using procedural animation for *in silico* biology, we often set keys to record the action for later playback in a movie file. By adjusting the interpolation of the resulting animation curves, you can smooth out the motion and make for a more watchable movie in the end. Let's explore the Graph Editor and use it to change the interpolation so that the cube eases into and out of motion.

1. Select the cube.
2. Open the Graph Editor: choose Window → Animation Editors → Graph Editor.
3. In the Graph Editor, choose View → Frame All.
   or
   Hit the hotkey, A, to frame all animation curves for the selected object.

You should see something resembling Fig. 8.21. Note that the curves are color-coordinated with their corresponding attributes.

8.7.5 The Graph Editor Outliner

This panel displays only selected items. Under each one is listed its animation curves (corresponding to its keyed attributes) by name. The curves for **Translate X** and **Rotate Z** appear under the transform node, pCube1. None of the other nodes that make up pCube1 appear here because you did not key their attributes.

8.7.6 The Graph Editor Graph View

When an attribute is selected in the Graph Editor outliner, its animation curve appears in the graph view. Table 8.2 shows hotkeys and key combinations used to adjust this view and work with keys. When you select a key, *Bézier handles* (or *tangents*) appear. Figure 8.22 shows the common types of animation tangents in Maya.

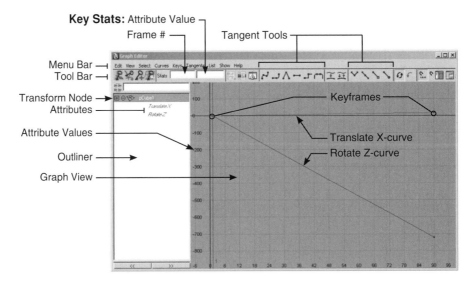

FIGURE 8.21

Features of the Graph Editor. Because of the keyframe settings we used in Preferences, the cube's animation curves are linear – of constant slope – resulting in abrupt changes in direction at the beginning and end of the animation.

Table 8.2 Shortcuts for the Graph Editor Graph View and the Dope Sheet

Hold	Drag	Hotkey	Function
Alt	MMB		Track view
Alt	LMB+MMB		Dolly view
K	MMB		Move current time indicator
	MMB		Move the selected key
Shift	MMB		Move the selected key, constrained to one of the two axes
		A	View all
		F	Frame selected key(s)

Note: To move keys, you must activate one of the Move, Rotate, or Show Manipulator Tools in the main toolbox.

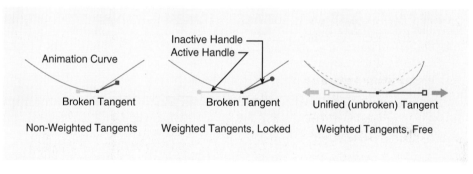

FIGURE 8.22

Different animation curve tangents displayed in the Graph Editor. Free, weighted tangents give you the most control when reshaping an animation curve.

You can MMB+drag a tangent to modify its curve. More control can be gained by weighting the tangents and unlocking their weights.

1. Select the cube.
2. In the Graph Editor, select Curves → Weighted Tangents.
3. Press the Free tangent weight button ↘ in the toolbar.
4. Drag a tangent to distort one of the curves:

    a. Hit the hotkey, W, to active the Move Tool.
    b. LMB+click on a tangent to select it.
    c. MMB+drag the tangent.

Take a moment to modify the curves using their tangents and play the animation back to observe the effect. Don't hesitate to really distort them and see what happens to the animation – you may have to pull your camera back to see the full range of motion in the scene view. Below, you will use the toolbar buttons to reset the curves and then adjust them automatically.

Editing Animation Curve Tangents

Maya Help → Using Maya → Animation, Character Setup, and Deformers → Animation → Keyframe Animation → Edit Tangents

---

8.7.7 The Graph Editor Toolbar

The most commonly used curve editing tools are accessed through the Graph Editor toolbar buttons; several of these are also found in the menu bar.

1. Select the cube.
2. With one of the Select, Lasso, Move, Scale, or Rotate tools active, select both animation curves in the Graph Editor, the same way you would select an object in the scene view.
3. Press the Linear tangents button ∧ in the toolbar. This will return the curves to their original linear state.
4. Press the Flat tangents button ⚊ in the toolbar.

The flat tangents at the start and end of the animation cycle give smooth motion into and out of each translation and rotation direction change. Smooth acceleration is key to natural-looking animations.

8.7.8 Moving Keys

In the Graph Editor you can select, move, or delete keys.

1. Select the cube.
2. Hit the W key to activate the Move Tool.
3. In the Graph Editor, select the two keyframes at frame 90.
4. Hold down the Shift key while you MMB+drag the keys left to frame 30. Then release the mouse.
   or
   Enter "30" in the Frame # field at the top-left of the Graph Editor.

Because you changed only the frame number, and not the attribute values of the selected keys, the cube will now cover the same distance and rotate the same amount in 30 frames as it did previously in 90. Before you hit Play, change the Playback Range to span 1–30 frames to match the animation range, or else you'll spend two seconds watching nothing.

Save your scene as you will need it for the next tutorial.

8.8 ANIMATION NODES IN THE HYPERGRAPH AND ATTRIBUTE EDITOR

Here, you'll employ the Hypergraph, to look at the nodes that were created and/or connected when you keyed the cubes attributes.

1. Select the cube and open the Hypergraph.
2. Choose Graph → Input and Output Connections.

Figure 8.23 shows the nodes composing a polygon cube called `pCube1`. The two new nodes connecting to `pCube1` are animation curve nodes that were created when you keyed the translate and rotate attributes.

Figure 8.24 shows the Translate X animation curve node represented in the Attribute Editor, with which you can edit key values and interpolations.

8.9 TUTORIAL 08.02: A SIMPLE PROCEDURAL ANIMATION

In this exercise, you will add custom procedural animation to the existing keyframe animation on the cube created in the previous tutorial. It will cause the cube to rotate back and forth about its Y-axis, giving the appearance of a wiggle.

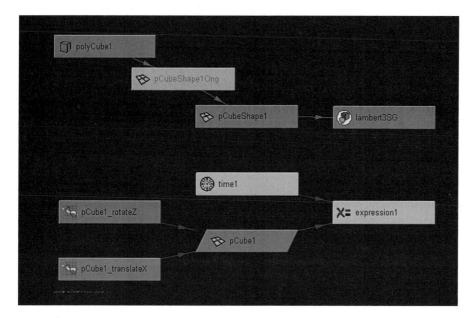

FIGURE 8.23

Maya creates an animation curve node for each attribute you key. Two such nodes are shown here in the Hypergraph for the animated polygon cube. The shape of a node changes from a rectangle to a parallelogram to indicate that it is animated.

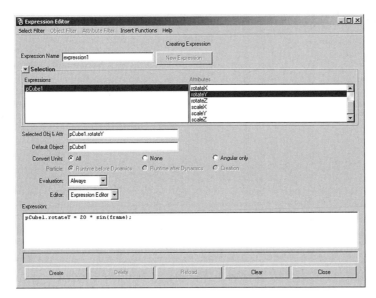

FIGURE 8.24

Animation nodes can be viewed and altered in the Attribute Editor. Here you can edit keyframe times and values as well as set the preinfinity and postinfinity behaviors of the animation curve – that is, how the curve is extended beyond the first and final keyframes.

"What's to come" and "getting ahead of ourselves." This task will require working with the **Expression Editor** and a touch of MEL script. It will demonstrate a strength of the Maya environment: one can make use, quickly and effectively, of procedural animation techniques, involving a host of built-in MEL commands, with little or no prior programming experience.

8.9.1 Animation Expressions in Brief

An animation expression is an instruction or set of instructions, usually invoked to control keyable attributes, which executes in coordination with Maya's timeline. The instructions work much like an animation curve does, telling an attribute what value to assume at a given frame. Rather than go into a lengthy explanation right now, we'll use an example to show you what an animation expression is and what it can do. To start, open the scene file with the animated cube from the previous tutorial.

8.9.2 Create an Animation Expression

1. Select the cube.
2. Select its Rotate Y attribute in the Channel Box.
3. RMB+click on Rotate Y in the Channel Box and select Expressions from the context menu. This will launch the Expression Editor (Fig. 8.25).
4. In the Selected Obj & Attr field, select the text `pCube1.rotateY` and MMB+drag it into the Expression field below.

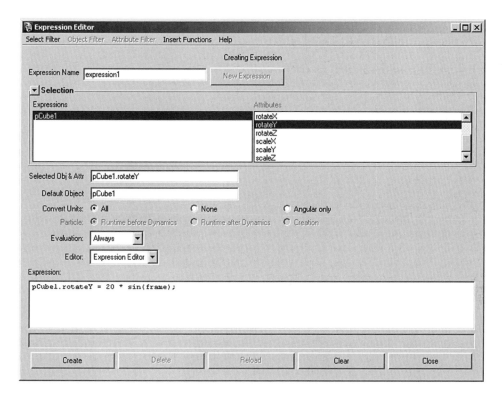

FIGURE 8.25

The Expression Editor displaying an expression created to drive the Rotate Y attribute of the polygon cube. An attribute is referred to in an expression as a node name followed by a period (or *dot*), followed by the attribute name.

This "dot notation" (pCube1 "dot" rotate) is the standard notation for nodes and their attributes in Maya. Here, you will assign the attribute the value of a built-in trigonometric function for the sine of an angle, which is shortened to sin( ) in MEL as in most other programming languages. Trigonometric functions are often advantageous in computer animation because of their cyclic or periodic nature, which can be used to create oscillating motion. You will use sin( ) to give the polygon cube an oscillating rotation about its Y-axis.

Like most functions in Maya, sin( ) requires an argument, which is a number on which to operate. The current frame number makes a suitable argument because it increases steadily as the animation plays. It is therefore a good stand-in for the elapsed time itself. As it increases or decreases, sin( ) will oscillate predictably through a range of positive and negative numbers, which will in turn rotate the cube back and forth about Y. The current frame is represented by a *global variable* called frame. frame is a value that can be queried by its name anywhere with Maya. Let's complete the animation expression:

1. In the expression field of the Expression Editor, type = `sin(frame)` to the right of `pCube1.rotateY`. Your expression so far will look like:

   ```
   pCube1.rotateY = sin(frame);
   ```

2. Press the Create button. This creates a new animation expression.

   > A semicolon is used to separate MEL statements. While its use is not strictly necessary when working with a single statement, it is good programming form.

The name of the new animation expression appears in the Expression Editor under the heading, Selection → Expressions. You can edit an expression at any time by selecting it by name in this field. However, by default the field shows only the expression for selected nodes. To show all expressions in a scene,

Choose Select Filter → By Expression Name

Now play the animation to see the effect on the cube's Y-rotation. You'll notice it's very subtle. To make it more pronounced, increase the amplitude of the `sin()` function.

> When an animation expression has been assigned to an attribute, the attribute's value field turns purple in the Channel Box.

1. In the lower Expression field, type:

   ```
   pCube1.rotateY = 20 * sin(frame)
   ```

2. Press the Edit button to enter the expression.

Now when you hit Play, the magnitude of the Y-rotation will be considerably greater (20 times greater, in fact). Equipped with this understanding of a simple, one-line animation expression, you'll see shortly it's not too great a leap to begin programming more complex instructions to drive attributes in much more complicated models of organic structure and function.

8.9.3 Animation Expression Nodes

Before leaving this example, let's take a quick look in the Hypergraph at the nodes that were created (Fig. 8.26).

1. Select the cube and open the Hypergraph.
2. Choose Graph → Input and Output Connections.

There are two new nodes: an animation expression node and a time node. The time node provides the frame number to the animation expression node, which updates the transform node, `pCube1`.

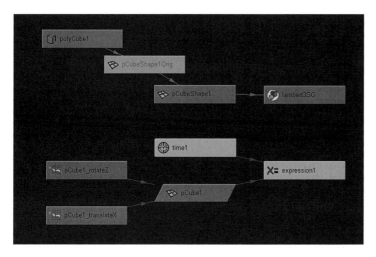

FIGURE 8.26

When you create an expression, you are creating an expression node and a time node, shown here in the Hypergraph.

8.10 SUMMARY

In this chapter you learned that in Maya, animation boils down to the change over time in the value of an attribute. Any attribute that is "keyable" can be animated. Furthermore, an attribute can be animated by keyframing or by using an animation expression. The latter is a type of procedural animation.

Keyframing creates an animation curve dependency graph (DG) node and connects it to the attribute in question. An animation curve spans keyframes and returns a value, at any given frame number, which drives the attribute in question. The shape of a curve, described as its interpolation, is governed by its tangents, which can be manipulated by hand or automatically (i.e. through a procedure). Curve interpolation, in turn, is a measure of the acceleration of animation into and out of keyframes. This acceleration can be gradual or instantaneous and determines the degree to which animation appears smooth or abrupt.

An animation expression is a DG node that contains an instruction or set of instructions that drive the value(s) of one or more attributes. A time node updates the animation expression node at each frame during playback. The expression may be a single line of script, like the example in the last tutorial, or many lines that evaluate equations and use the results to drive attributes, which is the approach we use when simulating behaviors of molecules and cells.

The animation examples in this chapter open the door to powerful concepts. *In silico* simulation methods use keyframing as a way of capturing the results of a simulation, rather than creating animation. The animations are thereby created procedurally using animation expressions and another scripting device called a procedure.

Dynamics is a powerful feature of the Maya environment and is widely used in special effects animation for film and television. For *in silico* biology, we use dynamics in our projects to emulate random motion and collisions in systems of individual molecules and of whole cells.

REFERENCES

[1] I.V. Kerlow, The Art of 3D: Computer Animation and Effects, third ed., John Wiley, Hoboken, NJ, 2003.

[2] J. Anderson, B. Anderson, The myth of persistence of vision revisited, J. Film Video 45 (1993) 3–12.

[3] G. Winkenbach, D.H. Salesin, Computer-generated pen-and-ink illustration, in: Proceedings of the 21st Annual Conference on Computer Graphics and Interactive Techniques. In Computer Graphics; Annual Conference Series, 28 (1994) 91–100.

[4] T. Saito, T. Takahashi, Comprehensible rendering of 3-D shapes. ACM SIGGRAPH Comput. Graph. 24 (1990) 197–206.

[5] B. Gooch, A. Gooch, Non-photorealistic Rendering. AK Peters, Natick, 2001.

[6] T.A. Ryan, C.B. Schwartz, Speed of perception as a function of mode of representation, Am. J. Psychol. 69 (1956) 60–69.

[7] R.M. Newman, N. Bussard, C.J. Richards, Integrating interactive 3-D diagrams into hypermedia documentation, in: Proceedings of the 20th Annual International Conference on Computer Documentation (SIGDOC 2002), ACM Press, 2002, pp. 122–126.

[8] The Visible Human Project (Web site): http://www.nlm.nih.gov/research/visible/visible_human.html (accessed October 14, 2007).

Other Methods

Point-Based Animation

Matthias Müller-Fischer, Mark Pauly, Markus Gross,
Richard Keiser and Martin Wicke

CHAPTER CONTENTS

9.1 INTRODUCTION

Physically based animation using point-sampled representations has emerged recently as a promising alternative to conventional finite element simulation. It is inspired by so-called meshless methods, where the continuum is discretized using unstructured point samples. This chapter will demonstrate that such methods perform for a wide spectrum of material simulations including brittle fracture, elastic and plastic deformations, and fluids. Such physical point representations are combined with high-resolution, point-sampled surface geometry. Section 9.2 gives an introduction to meshless finite elements and demonstrates how they can be utilized to compute elastic and plastic deformations. This method serves as a basis for the simulation of fracture using point-based surface representations in Section 9.3. It will be shown that the surface can be conveniently resampled without the need to restructure it, as is required for triangle meshes. The chapter concludes with a discussion of methods for fluid simulation. The particle nature of fluids makes them ideally suited for point-based methods, but the proper reconstruction and animation of the fluid surface remains a challenge.

9.2 MESHLESS FINITE ELEMENTS

Matthias Müller-Fischer

9.2.1 Overview

In computer graphics, static objects are most often represented by two-dimensional surfaces only while their interior can safely be ignored. In this chapter, however, we will discuss ways to animate deformable objects using points. In order to solve the elasticity equations, the interior of an object needs to be modeled as well. The most popular approaches in computer graphics to simulate volumetric deformable objects are the use of mass-spring systems or finite element meshes [1]. In recent years, meshless point-based approaches have become popular, both in computational sciences [2–4] and in computer graphics [5,6]. On the one hand, points will be used to represent the volume and the elastic properties of the material. As in Müller et al. [6], we call these points *pixels* as an abbreviation for *physics element*. In addition, a different set of points (the *surfels*) can be used to represent the surface of the deformable objects. These surfels passively follow the dynamic motion computed on the pixels (see Section 9.2.9).

In this section, we will present the basic method proposed by Müller et al. [6] for the simulation of elastic and plastic objects. This method is the basis for the simulation of fracturing material described in the next section. In contrast to mass-spring systems, the method is based on continuum elasticity theory. The advantage of continuum-based approaches over simpler methods is the fact that they converge to the continuous solution as the granularity of the discretization goes to zero. In addition, the material stiffness is expressed in terms of Young's modulus E, which can be looked up in textbooks, in contrast to spring constants, which have to be tuned for a specific mesh. Continuum elasticity theory would cover an entire book in itself. Here, we only explain the central ideas necessary to understand the method and refer the interested reader to Chung [7] for more details on elasticity theory.

9.2.2 Continuum Elasticity

Continuum elasticity theory describes the behavior of continuous (three-dimensional) objects. Hereby, the three quantities *displacement, strain*, and *stress* play a major role. In one-dimensional problems, these quantities are all one dimensional and have intuitive interpretations. Figure 9.1 depicts a beam with cross-sectional area A. When a force f_n is applied perpendicular to the cross section, the beam with original length l expands by Δl. The stress σ is the force applied per area f_n/A with unit [N/m²] while the strain ε is the relative elongation of the beam $\Delta l/l$ without unit.

Inside the beam, the displacement u varies linearly. It can be presented by a one-dimensional function $u(x) = x(\Delta l/l)$ as Fig. 9.1 shows. The strain (i.e. the relative elongation of the material) can also be expressed in terms of the displacement function as $\varepsilon_{const} = \dfrac{u(l) - u(0)}{l}$. This *global* expression, however, is only correct for linear displacement functions. For general displacement functions, the strain varies spatially. The strain at location x is then computed *locally* for an infinitesimal element of length dx as $\varepsilon(x) = \dfrac{u(x + dx) - u(x)}{dx}$. This yields the more general expression $\varepsilon(x) = \dfrac{d}{dx} u(x)$ for one-dimensional problems.

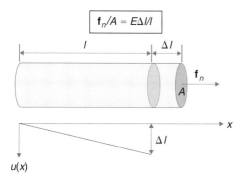

FIGURE 9.1

Hooke's law for a beam. The force per area applied on the cross section of area A (stress) is proportional to the relative elongation of the material (strain). The constant of proportionality E is Young's modulus. The displacement function $u(x)$ defines how far a material point originally at location x is moved to the right.

Hooke's law states that the strain depends linearly on the applied stress (i.e. $f_n/A = E\Delta l/l$ or $\sigma = E\varepsilon$). This law is a good approximation of the behavior of so-called Hookean materials near the equilibrium. The constant of proportionality E is called Young's modulus. For steel, E is in the order of 10^{11} N/m^2, while for rubber, it lies between 10^7 and 10^8 N/m^2. A law that relates strain to stress like Hooke's law is called a *constitutive law*.

In three dimensions, continuum elasticity theory gets a bit more involved mathematically. The concepts, however, are exactly the same as in the one-dimensional case. A three-dimensional deformable object is typically defined by its undeformed shape (also called equilibrium configuration, rest, or initial shape) and by a set of material parameters that define how it deforms under applied forces. If we think of the rest shape as a continuous connected subset Ω of $\mathbb{R}^3$, then the coordinates $\mathbf{x} \in \Omega$ of a point in the object are called *material coordinates* of that point. In the discrete case, Ω is a discrete set of points that sample the rest shape of the object.

When forces are applied, the object deforms and a point originally at location $\mathbf{x}$ (i.e. with material coordinates $\mathbf{x}$) moves to a new location $\mathbf{p}(\mathbf{x})$, the *spatial* or *world coordinates* of that point. Since new locations are defined for all material coordinates $\mathbf{x}$, $\mathbf{p}(\mathbf{x})$ is a vector field defined on Ω. Alternatively, the deformation can also be specified by the *displacement* field, which, in three dimensions, is a vector field $\mathbf{u}(\mathbf{x}) = \mathbf{p}(\mathbf{x}) - \mathbf{x}$ defined on Ω (see Fig. 9.2).

The elastic strain ε is computed from the spatial derivatives of the displacement field $\mathbf{u}(\mathbf{x})$ as in the one-dimensional case. However, in three dimensions, the displacement field has three components $\mathbf{u} = \mathbf{u}(\mathbf{x}) = (u, v, w)^T$ and each component can be derived with respect to one of the three spatial variables x, y, and z. Therefore,

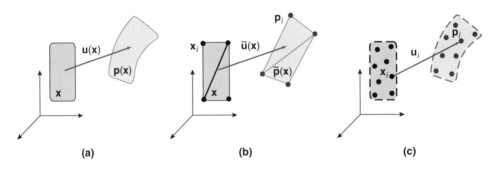

(a)   (b)   (c)

FIGURE 9.2

(a) A deformation is represented mathematically by a continuous vector field $\mathbf{u}(\mathbf{x})$ that describes the displacement of each material point $\mathbf{x}$. A point originally at location $\mathbf{x}$ ends up at location $\mathbf{p}(\mathbf{x}) = \mathbf{x} + \mathbf{u}(\mathbf{x})$ in the deformed shape. (b) In mesh-based approaches, the displacement field $\mathbf{u}(\mathbf{x})$ is approximated within an element by a field $\tilde{\mathbf{u}}(\mathbf{x})$ that interpolates the displacements of the corners of the element. (c) A mesh-free point-based approach represents the displacement field by a set of discrete samples $\mathbf{u}_i$ defined at locations $\mathbf{x}_i$. Displacement vectors between these locations are interpolated (e.g. with the moving least squares approach).

strain cannot be expressed by a single scalar anymore. For example, at a single point inside a three-dimensional object, the material can be stretched in one direction and compressed in another one at the same time. Thus, strain is represented in three dimensions by a symmetric 3×3 tensor:

$$\varepsilon = \begin{bmatrix} \varepsilon_{xx} & \varepsilon_{xy} & \varepsilon_{xz} \\ \varepsilon_{xy} & \varepsilon_{yy} & \varepsilon_{yz} \\ \varepsilon_{xz} & \varepsilon_{yz} & \varepsilon_{zz} \end{bmatrix}. \tag{9.1}$$

In computational sciences, several ways to compute the components of the strain tensor from the spatial derivatives of the displacement field are used. Popular choices in computer graphics are

$$\varepsilon_G = \frac{1}{2}(\nabla \mathbf{u} + [\nabla \mathbf{u}]^T + [\nabla \mathbf{u}]^T \nabla \mathbf{u}), \tag{9.2}$$

and

$$\varepsilon_C = \frac{1}{2}(\nabla \mathbf{u} + [\nabla \mathbf{u}]^T), \tag{9.3}$$

where the symmetric tensor $\varepsilon_G \in \mathbb{R}^{3 \times 3}$ is Green's nonlinear strain tensor (nonlinear in the displacements) and $\varepsilon_C \in \mathbb{R}^{3 \times 3}$ its linearization, Cauchy's linear strain tensor.

The gradient of the displacement field is a 3×3 matrix:

$$\nabla \mathbf{u} = \begin{bmatrix} u,_x & u,_y & u,_z \\ v,_x & v,_y & v,_z \\ w,_x & w,_y & w,_z \end{bmatrix}, \tag{9.4}$$

where the index after the comma represents a spatial derivative.

Now, let us turn to the measurement of stress, the force per unit area applied to a plane. In three dimensions, the force and the orientation of the plane it is applied to are both three-dimensional vectors. The stress relating the two, therefore, is expressed by a symmetric 3×3 tensor:

$$\sigma = \begin{bmatrix} \sigma_{xx} & \sigma_{xy} & \sigma_{xz} \\ \sigma_{xy} & \sigma_{yy} & \sigma_{yz} \\ \sigma_{xz} & \sigma_{yz} & \sigma_{zz} \end{bmatrix}, \tag{9.5}$$

with the following interpretation:

$$\frac{d\mathbf{f}}{dA} = \sigma \cdot \mathbf{n}_A.$$ (9.6)

To get the force per area $\mathbf{f}/A$ with respect to a certain plain with normal $\mathbf{n}_A$, the stress tensor is simply multiplied by $\mathbf{n}_A$.

Hooke's law states that stress and strain are linearly related:

$$\sigma = \mathbf{E}\varepsilon.$$ (9.7)

Both stress and strain are symmetric tensors so they have only six independent coefficients. The quantity $\mathbf{E}$ relating the two can, thus, be expressed by a 6×6-dimensional matrix. For isotropic materials (with equal behavior in all directions), Hooke's law has the following form:

$$
\begin{bmatrix} \sigma_{xx} \\ \sigma_{yy} \\ \sigma_{zz} \\ \sigma_{xy} \\ \sigma_{yz} \\ \sigma_{zx} \end{bmatrix} = \frac{E}{(1+v)(1-2v)}
\begin{bmatrix}
1-v & v & v & 0 & 0 & 0 \\
v & 1-v & v & 0 & 0 & 0 \\
v & v & 1-v & 0 & 0 & 0 \\
0 & 0 & 0 & 1-2v & 0 & 0 \\
0 & 0 & 0 & 0 & 1-2v & 0 \\
0 & 0 & 0 & 0 & 0 & 1-2v
\end{bmatrix}
\begin{bmatrix} \varepsilon_{xx} \\ \varepsilon_{yy} \\ \varepsilon_{zz} \\ \varepsilon_{xy} \\ \varepsilon_{yz} \\ \varepsilon_{zx} \end{bmatrix},
$$ (9.8)

where the scalar E is Young's modulus describing the elastic stiffness and the scalar $v \in \left[0 \ldots \frac{1}{2}\right)$ Poisson's ratio, a material parameter that describes to which amount volume is conserved within the material. Figure 9.3 shows the difference between low- and high-volume conservation modeled *via* the Poisson's ratio.

We now turn to the question of how to simulate a dynamic elastic object. To this end, we apply Newton's second law of motion $\mathbf{f} = m\ddot{\mathbf{p}}$ to each infinitesimal volumetric element dV of the object. Since the mass of an infinitesimal element is not defined, both sides of the equation of motion are divided by the volume $dx \cdot dy \cdot dz$ of the element. This turns mass [kg] into density [kg/m³] and forces [N] into body forces [N/m³]. We get

$$\rho\ddot{\mathbf{p}} = \mathbf{f}(\mathbf{x}),$$ (9.9)

where ρ is the density and $\mathbf{f}(\mathbf{x})$ the body force acting on the element at location $\mathbf{x}$.

Figure 9.4 illustrates the forces that act on an element due to internal stress σ. Only those forces acting on the faces perpendicular to the x-axis are shown. The forces acting on the other faces of the element are computed analogously. According to Eq. (9.6), the forces per unit area acting on the faces with normal $[-1, 0, 0]^T$ and $[1, 0, 0]^T$ are $-\left[\sigma_{xx}, \sigma_{xy}, \sigma_{xz}\right]^T_{x, y, z}$ and $\left[\sigma_{xx}, \sigma_{xy}, \sigma_{xz}\right]^T_{x + dx, y, z}$, respectively. To get forces, we multiply

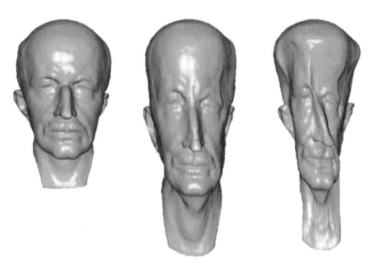

FIGURE 9.3

The effect of Poisson's ratio: the undeformed model (left) is stretched using a Poisson ratio of zero (middle) and 0.49 (right).

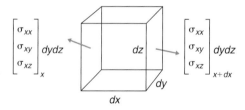

FIGURE 9.4

The elastic forces acting on the faces of an infinitesimal cube due to internal stresses. Only the forces acting on faces perpendicular to the *x*-axis are shown.

by the face area $dy \cdot dz$. Finally, the body forces are the forces divided by $dV = dx \cdot dy \cdot dz$. This yields $\mathbf{f} = \left(\left[\sigma_{xx}, \sigma_{xy}, \sigma_{xz} \right]^T_{x+dx, y, z} - \left[\sigma_{xx}, \sigma_{xy}, \sigma_{xz} \right]^T \right)/dx = \left[\sigma_{xx,x}, \sigma_{xy,x}, \sigma_{xz,x} \right]^T$ for the body forces, where the comma denotes spatial derivatives. If we take the forces acting on the other faces into account as well, we arrive at the final expression for the body forces acting on an infinitesimal element due to internal stresses:

$$\mathbf{f}_{stress} = \nabla \cdot \sigma = \begin{bmatrix} \sigma_{xx,x} + \sigma_{xy,y} + \sigma_{xz,z} \\ \sigma_{yx,x} + \sigma_{yy,y} + \sigma_{yz,z} \\ \sigma_{zx,x} + \sigma_{zy,y} + \sigma_{zz,z} \end{bmatrix}, \tag{9.10}$$

where, again, the commas represent a spatial derivative. We are now ready to write down the entire partial differential equation (PDE) governing dynamic elastic materials:

$$\rho\ddot{\mathbf{p}} = \nabla \cdot \sigma + \mathbf{f}_{\text{ext}}, \tag{9.11}$$

where $\mathbf{f}_{\text{ext}}$ are externally applied body forces such as gravity or collision forces. This hyperbolic PDE describes the evolution of the world coordinates $\mathbf{p}$ of the elastic body since ρ and $\mathbf{f}_{\text{ext}}$ are known quantities, σ depends on ε *via* the constitutive law, and ε, in turn, is a function of the spatial derivatives of the displacements $\mathbf{u}(\mathbf{x})$ and, thus, of the world coordinates $\mathbf{p}(\mathbf{x}) = \mathbf{x} + \mathbf{u}(\mathbf{x})$.

A linear dependency of the stresses on the strains such as in a Hookean material is called *material linearity*. A linear measure of strain such as Cauchy's linear strain tensor defined in Eq. (9.3) is called *geometric linearity*. Only with both assumptions, material and geometric linearity, does Eq. (9.11) become a linear PDE. Linear PDEs are easier to solve because discretizing them *via* finite differences of finite elements yields linear algebraic systems. However, for large deformations, the simplification of geometric linearity causes significant visual artifacts (see [8]).

Linearizing Eq. (9.11) is only useful in connection with *implicit* time integration because in that case, either a linear or a nonlinear system of equations needs to be solved. However, in the explicit case, it does not really matter whether the elastic forces are a linear or nonlinear function of the displacements because they are evaluated explicitly at each time step.

9.2.3 Meshless Discretization

In order to use the governing continuous PDE in a numerical simulation, the volume of an object needs to be discretized into regions of finite size. In mesh-based approaches, such as the finite element method (FEM), the volume is divided into disjoint volumetric primitives such as tetrahedra, which form a mesh. In contrast, in mesh-free methods, the volume is sampled at a finite number of point locations without connectivity information and without the need of generating a volumetric mesh (see Fig. 9.2).

In a point-based mesh-free model, all the simulation quantities, such as location $\mathbf{x}_i$, density ρ_i, deformation $\mathbf{u}_i$, velocity $\mathbf{v}_i$, strain ε_i, stress σ_i, and body force $\mathbf{f}_i$, are carried by the physically simulated points – the pixels. For each simulated pixel, we have a position $\mathbf{x}_i$ in body space, defining what we call the *reference shape*, and their deformed locations $\mathbf{x}_i + \mathbf{u}_i$ the *deformed shape*.

Smoothed particle hydrodynamics (SPH) is a popular method for solving PDEs on point samples without connectivity. It was first proposed in the field of astronomy for the simulation of star clusters [9]. In computer graphics, it has been used to model highly deformable models [5] and fluids [10]. One could also use SPH to solve the governing Eq. (9.11) on the pixels. However, as we will see later, the method is not accurate enough to get stable simulations of highly deforming and freely rotating objects. Still, one important idea can directly be adopted, namely, how volumes and densities are assigned to the pixels. In continuum mechanics, quantities are measured per unit volume. It is, thus, important to know how much volume each pixel represents.

First, each pixel is assigned a fixed mass m_i that does not change through the simulation. This mass is distributed in the neighborhood of the pixel *via* a radially symmetric scalar-kernel function $\omega(r, h)$, where r is the distance from the pixel position and h a cutoff distance after which the kernel is zero. The distance h is also called the *support* of the kernel. In order to properly convert an attribute into a body attribute, the kernel needs to be normalized (i.e. $\int_x \omega(|\mathbf{x} - \mathbf{x}_0|, h)\, d\mathbf{x} = 1$ with unit [1/m³]). Müller et al. [6] propose to use

$$\omega(r, h) = \begin{cases} \dfrac{315}{64\pi h^9}(h^2 - r^2)^3 & \text{if } r < h \\ 0 & \text{otherwise} \end{cases} \tag{9.12}$$

to distribute the masses of the particles. This normalized kernel can be evaluated efficiently because r only appears squared. The density at pixel i can then be computed by smoothing the masses of all the pixels as

$$\rho_i = \sum_j m_j \omega_{ij}, \tag{9.13}$$

where $\omega_{ij} = \omega(|\mathbf{x}_j - \mathbf{x}_i|, h_i)$. Finally, the volume represented by pixel i is simply given by $v_i = m_i/\rho_i$. While the mass represented by a pixel is fixed, the density and volume vary when the reference positions of the pixels change in case of plastic deformation (Section 9.2.10).

The masses m_i and support radii h_i need to be initialized before the simulation starts. Here is a way to finding masses if the pixels irregularly sample the initial volume. For each pixel i, compute the average distance $\bar{r}_i$ to its k (e.g. 10) nearest neighbors. The support radius h_i is chosen to be a multiple of (e.g. three times) $\bar{r}_i$. The masses are initialized as $m_i = s\bar{r}_i^3\rho$, where ρ is the material density and s is the same scaling factor for all pixels, chosen such that the ρ_i resulting from Eq. (9.13) are close to the material density ρ.

9.2.4 Moving Least Squares Interpolation

In order to compute strain, stress, and the elastic body forces, the spatial derivatives of the displacement field $\nabla \mathbf{u}$ are needed [see Eq. (9.2)]. These derivatives can be estimated from the displacement vectors $\mathbf{u}_j$ of nearby pixels.

The approximation of $\nabla \mathbf{u}$ must be first-order accurate in order to guarantee zero elastic forces for rigid body modes (global rotation and translation). Standard SPH approximation does not have this property. A method that is first-order accurate (i.e. that can reconstruct linear functions correctly) is the moving least squares (MLS) formulation [11] with a linear basis. Let us consider the x-component u of the displacement field $\mathbf{u} = (u, v, w)^T$. Using a Taylor approximation, the continuous scalar field $u(\mathbf{x})$ in the neighborhood of $\mathbf{x}_i$ can be approximated as

$$u(\mathbf{x}_i + \Delta\mathbf{x}) = u_i + \nabla u|_{\mathbf{x}_i} \cdot \Delta\mathbf{x} + O(\|\Delta\mathbf{x}\|^2), \tag{9.14}$$

where $\nabla u|_{\mathbf{x}_i} = (u_{,x}, u_{,y}, u_{,z})^T$ at pixel i. Given u_i and the spatial derivatives ∇u at pixel i, the values u_j at close pixels j can be approximated as

$$\tilde{u}_j = u_i + \nabla u|_{\mathbf{x}_i} \cdot \mathbf{x}_{ij} = u_i + \mathbf{x}_{ij}^T \nabla u|_{\mathbf{x}_i}, \tag{9.15}$$

where $\mathbf{x}_{ij} = \mathbf{x}_j - \mathbf{x}_i$. A measure of the error of the approximation is given by the sum of the squared differences between the approximated values $\tilde{u}_j$ and the known values u_j, weighted by the kernel given in Eq. (9.12):

$$e = \sum_j (\tilde{u}_j - u_j)^2 \omega_{ij}. \tag{9.16}$$

The differences are weighted because only pixels in the neighborhood of pixel i should be considered and, additionally, fade in and out smoothly. Substituting Eq. (9.15) into Eq. (9.16) and expanding yields

$$e = \sum_j (u_i + u_{,x}x_{ij} + u_{,y}y_{ij} + u_{,z}z_{ij} - u_j)^2 \omega_{ij}, \tag{9.17}$$

where x_{ij}, y_{ij}, and z_{ij} are the x-, y-, and z-components of $\mathbf{x}_{ij}$, respectively. Given the positions of the pixels $\mathbf{x}_i$ and the sampled values u_i, the best candidates for the derivatives $u_{,x}$, $u_{,y}$, and $u_{,z}$ are the ones that minimize the error e. Setting the derivatives of e with respect to $u_{,x}$, $u_{,y}$, and $u_{,z}$ to zero yields three equations for the three unknowns:

$$\left(\sum_j \mathbf{x}_{ij}\mathbf{x}_{ij}^T \omega_{ij}\right) \nabla u|_{\mathbf{x}_i} = \sum_j (u_j - u_i)\mathbf{x}_{ij}\omega_{ij}. \tag{9.18}$$

The 3×3 system matrix $\mathbf{M} = \sum_j \mathbf{x}_{ij}\mathbf{x}_{ij}^T \omega_{ij}$ (the moment matrix) can be precomputed, inverted, and used for the computation of the derivative of v and w as well. If $\mathbf{M}$ is nonsingular, we have the following formula for the computation of derivatives:

$$\nabla u|_{\mathbf{x}_i} = \mathbf{M}^{-1} \left(\sum_j (u_j - u_i)\mathbf{x}_{ij}\omega_{ij}\right). \tag{9.19}$$

The components $\nabla v|_{\mathbf{x}_i}$ and $\nabla w|_{\mathbf{x}_i}$ are computed analogously using the same moment matrix $\mathbf{M}^{-1}$. If the number of pixels within the support radius b in the neighborhood of pixel i is less than four (including pixel i) or if these pixels are coplanar or colinear, $\mathbf{M}$ is singular and cannot be inverted. This only happens if the sampling of the volume is too coarse. To avoid problems with singular or badly conditioned moment matrices, safe inversion *via* singular value decomposition (SVD) [12] should be used.

9.2.5 Updating Strains and Stresses

With Eq. (9.19), the spatial derivatives of the deformation field at the pixel's location $\mathbf{x}_i$ can be computed based on the displacement vectors $\mathbf{u}_j$ of neighboring pixels j. Using Eqs. (9.2) and (9.7), the gradient of the displacement field, Green's strain ε_i, and the stress σ_i at pixel i can all be computed from these derivatives:

$$\nabla \mathbf{u}_i \leftarrow \begin{bmatrix} \nabla u |_{\mathbf{x}_i}^T \\ \nabla v |_{\mathbf{x}_i}^T \\ \nabla w |_{\mathbf{x}_i}^T \end{bmatrix}, \quad \varepsilon_i = \frac{1}{2} \left(\nabla \mathbf{u} + [\nabla \mathbf{u}]^T + [\nabla \mathbf{u}]^T \nabla \mathbf{u} \right), \quad \sigma_i \leftarrow \mathbf{E} \varepsilon_i. \tag{9.20}$$

9.2.6 Computation of Forces *via* Strain Energy

The last step before the set of pixels can be animated is to derive internal elastic forces for each pixel based on the internal stresses. These forces could be derived from Eq. (9.10) by computing the divergence of the stress components. However, since the stresses σ_i are approximations of the real stresses and only available at the discrete locations of the pixels, the resulting forces would, in general, violate Newton's first law *actio = reactio* (i.e. they would not conserve linear and angular momentum). This, in turn, would introduce so-called *ghost forces* that cause linear and angular accelerations of the entire object.

Another way to derive elastic forces is to compute them as the gradients of the *strain energy*. Such forces automatically conserve both linear and angular momentum. The strain energy is the potential energy stored in a deformed material. The body strain energy (energy per unit volume) can be computed as

$$U = \frac{1}{2} \sigma \cdot \varepsilon, \tag{9.21}$$

where the product $\sigma \cdot \varepsilon$ is the componentwise dot product of all the components of the tensors (i.e. $\sigma \cdot \varepsilon = \sigma_{xx} \cdot \varepsilon_{xx} + \sigma_{xy} \cdot \varepsilon_{xy} + \sigma_{xz} \cdot \varepsilon_{xz} + \ldots$). Intuitively, the strain energy is the energy built up by moving against the stresses along the strains. The unit test reveals stress [N/m²] times strain [2] equals energy per unit volume [Nm/m³].

A pixel i and all its neighbors j that lie within its support radius h_i can be considered a basic unit, analogous to a finite element in FEM (see Fig. 9.5). Based on Eq. (9.21), we estimate the strain energy stored around pixel i as

$$U_i = v_i \frac{1}{2} (\sigma_i \cdot \varepsilon_i), \tag{9.22}$$

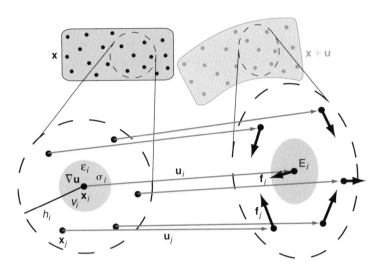

FIGURE 9.5

A basic unit in the point-based approach consists of a pixel at $\mathbf{x}_i$ and its neighbors at $\mathbf{x}_j$ within distance h_i. The gradient of the displacement field $\nabla \mathbf{u}$ is computed from the displacement vectors $\mathbf{u}_i$ and $\mathbf{u}_j$, the strain ϵ_i from $\nabla \mathbf{u}$, the stress σ_i from ϵ_i, the strain energy U_i from ϵ_i, σ_i and the volume v_i, and the elastic forces as the negative gradient of U_i with respect to the displacement vectors.

assuming that strain and stress are constant within the rest volume v_i of pixel i, equivalent to using linear shape functions in FEM. The strain energy is a function of the displacement vector $\mathbf{u}_i$ of pixel i and the displacements $\mathbf{u}_j$ of all its neighbors. Taking the derivative with respect to these displacements yields the forces acting at pixel i and all its neighbors j,

$$\mathbf{f}_j = -\nabla_{\mathbf{u}_j} U_i = -v_i \sigma_i \nabla_{\mathbf{u}_j} \varepsilon_i, \tag{9.23}$$

as Fig. 9.6 illustrates. The force acting on pixel i turns out to be the negative sum of all $\mathbf{f}_j$ acting on its neighbors j. These forces conserve linear and angular momentum. Using Eq. (9.19), this result can be further simplified to the compact form

$$\mathbf{f}_i = -2v_i(\mathbf{I} + \nabla \mathbf{u}_i)\sigma_i \mathbf{d}_i = \mathbf{F}\mathbf{d}_i, \tag{9.24}$$

$$\mathbf{f}_j = -2v_i(\mathbf{I} + \nabla \mathbf{u}_i)\sigma_i \mathbf{d}_j = \mathbf{F}\mathbf{d}_j, \tag{9.25}$$

where

$$\mathbf{d}_i = \mathbf{M}^{-1}\left(-\sum_j \mathbf{x}_{ij} \omega_{ij}\right) \tag{9.26}$$

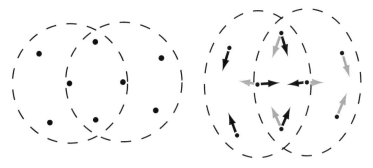

FIGURE 9.6

Each pixel receives one force component from being the center pixel and multiple force components from being a neighbor of other pixels. The image shows the neighborhoods of two pixels in the reference configuration (left) and the deformed configuration (right). The black and gray force components are induced by the left and right neighborhoods, respectively.

$$\mathbf{d}_j = \mathbf{M}^{-1}\left(\mathbf{x}_{ij}\omega_{ij}\right). \tag{9.27}$$

The detailed derivation of these equations can be found in Müller et al. [6]. Using the definition of the vectors $\mathbf{d}_i$ and $\mathbf{d}_j$, we get for the total internal forces:

$$\mathbf{f}_i = \mathbf{F}\mathbf{M}^{-1}\left(-\sum_j \mathbf{x}_{ij}\omega_{ij}\right), \tag{9.28}$$

$$\mathbf{f}_j = \mathbf{F}\mathbf{M}^{-1}\left(\mathbf{x}_{ij}\omega_{ij}\right). \tag{9.29}$$

The matrix product $\mathbf{B} = \mathbf{F}\mathbf{M}^{-1}$ is independent of the individual neighbor j and needs to be computed only once for each pixel i.

9.2.7 Animation of Elastic Objects

We are now ready to write down the entire simulation algorithm. Of course, the Euler integration steps in lines 20–23 could be replaced by any other (higher-order) explicit scheme.

1. **forall** pixels i
2.   initialize $\mathbf{x}_i$, $\mathbf{u}_i = \mathbf{0}$, $\dot{\mathbf{u}}_i = \mathbf{0}$, m_i, ρ_i, v_i,
3.   compute $\mathbf{M}_i^{-1} = \left(\sum_j \mathbf{x}_{ij}\mathbf{x}_{ij}^T\omega_{ij}\right)^{-1}$
4. **endfor**
5. **loop**

6.   **forall** pixels i **do** $\mathbf{f}_i = \mathbf{f}_{ext}(\mathbf{x}_i + \mathbf{u}_i)$

7.   **forall** pixels i

8. $\nabla u_i = \mathbf{M}^{-1}\left(\sum_j (u_j - u_i)\mathbf{x}_{ij}\omega_{ij}\right)$

9. $\nabla v_i = \mathbf{M}^{-1}\left(\sum_j (v_j - v_i)\mathbf{x}_{ij}\omega_{ij}\right)$

10. $\nabla w_i = \mathbf{M}^{-1}\left(\sum_j (w_j - w_i)\mathbf{x}_{ij}\omega_{ij}\right)$

11. $\nabla \mathbf{u}_i = [\nabla u_i, \nabla v_i, \nabla w_i]^T$

12. $\varepsilon_i = \frac{1}{2}\left(\nabla \mathbf{u} + [\nabla \mathbf{u}]^T + [\nabla \mathbf{u}]^T \nabla \mathbf{u}\right)$

13. $\sigma_i = \mathbf{E}\varepsilon_i$

14. $\mathbf{B}_i = -2v_i\left(\nabla \mathbf{u}_i + \mathbf{I}\right)\sigma_i \mathbf{M}_i^{-1}$

15.   **forall** neighboring pixels j

16. $\mathbf{f}_j = \mathbf{f}_j + \mathbf{B}_i(\mathbf{x}_{ij}\omega_{ij})$

17. $\mathbf{f}_i = \mathbf{f}_i - \mathbf{B}_i(\mathbf{x}_{ij}\omega_{ij})$

18.   **endfor**

19.   **endfor**

20.   **forall** pixels i

21. $\dot{\mathbf{u}}_i = \dot{\mathbf{u}}_i + \Delta t \mathbf{f}_i / m_i$

22. $\dot{\mathbf{u}}_i = \dot{\mathbf{u}}_i + \Delta t \dot{\mathbf{u}}_i$

23.   **endfor**

24.   render configuration $\{\mathbf{x}_i + \mathbf{u}_i\}$

25. **endloop**

FIGURE 9.7

The model presented in this chapter represents both the physical volume elements (pixels in yellow) as well as the surface elements (surfels in blue) as point samples. It allows the simulation of elastic, plastic, melting, and solidifying objects (from left to right).

After initialization, in lines 1–4 the simulation loop is started. From the displacement vectors $\mathbf{u}_i$, the nine spatial derivatives of three scalar fields u, v, and w are approximated using the MLS method in lines 8–11. From these derivatives, the strain and stress tensors are derived in lines 12 and 13. The forces acting at the center pixel and all its neighbors are then computed as the negative gradient of the strain energy with respect to the displacements in lines 14–19. Finally, in lines 20–23 explicit Euler integration yields the new velocities and displacements of the pixels.

9.2.8 Plasticity

So far, the set of pixels returns completely to the rest shape (modulo rigid body transformations) if the external forces are released. This way, they simulate a perfectly elastic material. In contrast, a plastic material will store some of the deformation and will remain in a deformed state even if the applied forces are released. An elegant way of simulating plastic behavior is by using strain-state variables [13]. Every pixel i stores a plastic strain tensor $\varepsilon_i^{\text{plastic}}$. The strain considered for elastic forces $\varepsilon_i^{\text{elastic}} = \varepsilon_i - \varepsilon_i^{\text{plastic}}$ is the difference between measured strain ε_i and the plastic strain. Thus, in case the measured strain equals the plastic strain, no forces are generated. Since $\varepsilon_i^{\text{plastic}}$ is considered constant within one time step, the elastoplastic forces are simply computed using Eqs. (9.24) and (9.25) with σ_i replaced by $\sigma_i^{\text{elastic}} = \mathbf{E}\varepsilon_i^{\text{elastic}}$. The plastic strain is initialized with a zero 3×3 tensor. At every time step, it is updated as follows:

$$\varepsilon^{\text{elastic}} \leftarrow \varepsilon - \varepsilon^{\text{plastic}}$$

$$\textbf{if} \left\| \varepsilon^{\text{elastic}} \right\|_2 > c_{\text{yield}} \;\; \textbf{then} \;\; \varepsilon^{\text{plastic}} \leftarrow \varepsilon^{\text{plastic}} + c_{\text{creep}} \cdot \varepsilon^{\text{elastic}}$$

$$\textbf{if} \left\| \varepsilon^{\text{plastic}} \right\|_2 > c_{\text{max}} \;\; \textbf{then} \;\; \varepsilon^{\text{plastic}} \leftarrow \varepsilon^{\text{plastic}} \cdot c_{\text{max}} / \left\| \varepsilon^{\text{plastic}} \right\|_2$$

First, the elastic strain is computed as the deviation of the actual strain from the stored plastic strain. The plasticity model has three scalar parameters c_{yield}, c_{creep}, and c_{max}. If the two-norm of the elastic strain exceeds the threshold c_{yield}, the plastic strain absorbs part of it. If $c_{\text{creep}} \in [0 \ldots 1]$ is one, the elastic strain is immediately and completely absorbed. Small values for c_{creep} yield slow plastic flow in the material. The parameter c_{max} defines the maximum plastic strain an element can store. If the two-norm of the plastic strain exceeds c_{max}, the plastic strain is scaled down accordingly.

In contrast to mesh-based methods, the mesh-free approach is particularly useful when the object deviates far from its original shape in which case the original mesh connectivity is not useful anymore. Using a mesh-free method, the reference shape can easily adapt to the deformed shape. However, changing the reference positions of pixels is dangerous: two pixels from two different objects having reference positions $\mathbf{x}_i$ and $\mathbf{x}_j$ might move within each other's support, even though their actual positions $\mathbf{x}_i + \mathbf{u}_i$ and $\mathbf{x}_j + \mathbf{u}_j$ are far from each other. This large displacement vector difference results in large strains, stresses, and elastic forces, causing the simulation to crash. Therefore, if the reference shape is changed, both reference shape and deformed shape need to be kept close to each other. There is a simple way to achieve this, with which highly plastic materials can be modeled, as well as melting and flow. After each time step, the deformation is completely absorbed by the reference shape while the built-up strains are stored in the plastic strain-state variable:

forall pixels i **do**
$\quad \varepsilon_i^{\text{plastic}} \leftarrow \varepsilon_i^{\text{plastic}} - \varepsilon_i$
$\quad \mathbf{x}_i \leftarrow \mathbf{x}_i + \mathbf{u}_i$
$\quad \mathbf{u}_i \leftarrow 0$
endfor
forall pixels i **do**
$\quad$ update $\rho i, vi$ and $\mathbf{M}_i^{-1}$
endfor

This way, both reference shape and deformed shape are identical after each time step. The strain is not lost but stored in the plastic state variable. However, the original shape information is lost and small errors can sum up over time. Thus, this latter simulation method that changes the reference shape is only recommended for the simulation of highly plastic objects that deviate far from their original shape.

9.2.9 Passive Surfel Advection

Often, a coarse sampling of the volume of an object with pixels is sufficient to capture the object's elastic behavior. However, for rendering, a more detailed surface is needed. If this surface is represented by a set of surfels, the surfels need to be advected along the displacement field of the pixels. To this end, the displacement vector $\mathbf{u}_{sfl}$ at a known surfel position $\mathbf{x}_{sfl}$ is interpolated from the displacements $\mathbf{u}_i$ of nearby pixels as

$$\mathbf{u}_{sfl} = \frac{1}{\sum_i \omega(r_i, b)} \sum_i \omega(r_i, b)\left(\mathbf{u}_i + \nabla \mathbf{u}_i^T (\mathbf{x}_{sfl} - \mathbf{x}_i)\right), \tag{9.30}$$

where $\omega(r_i, b) = \omega(\|\mathbf{x}_{sfl} - \mathbf{x}_i\|, b)$ is the weighting kernel defined in Eq. (9.12). The $\mathbf{u}_i$ are the displacement vectors of pixels at $\mathbf{x}_i$ within a distance b to $\mathbf{x}_{sfl}$.

If displacements are computed not only for the surfel center but also for the tips of the tangent axes, the deformation of the surfel as well as a transformed normal can be derived. Based on the elongations of the tangent axes, a surfel splitting and merging scheme can be applied to maintain a high surface quality in the case of large deformations.

9.2.10 Conclusion

In this introductory section on physics-based animation, the basic concepts of continuum elasticity have been discussed. The equation of motion in the continuous case is a PDE that has to be discretized in order to be solved numerically. In contrast to the FEM where volumes of finite size are used, a meshless method discretizes continuous quantities on randomly distributed point samples (pixels). Elastic forces are computed on those pixels based on their displacements from the rest shape and the elastic properties of the material. Given the elastic forces, the point cloud can be integrated in time like a particle system.

The extension of the state of a pixel by a strain-state variable allows the modeling of plasticity, resulting in objects that do not return to the rest state when external forces are released. Finally, in order to enhance the visual quality of objects, the displacement field of the pixels is used to advect a highly detailed point-based surface.

Section 9.3 discusses extensions to this basic model that allow the simulation of fracturing material.

9.3 ANIMATION OF FRACTURING MATERIAL

Richard Keiser and Mark Pauly

In the previous section, a framework for the animation of elastoplastic materials has been described. Here, we will discuss how this framework can be extended for simulating fracturing solids [14]. Central to the method is a highly dynamic surface- and volume-sampling method that supports arbitrary crack initiation, propagation, and termination, while avoiding many of the stability problems of traditional mesh-based techniques. Advancing crack fronts are modeled explicitly and associated fracture surfaces are embedded in the simulation volume. When cutting through the material, crack fronts directly affect the coupling between pixels, requiring a dynamic adaptation of the nodal shape functions. Complex fracture patterns of interacting and branching cracks are handled using a small set of topological operations for splitting, merging, and terminating crack fronts. This allows continuous propagation of cracks with highly detailed fracture surfaces, independent of the spatial resolution of the pixels, and provides effective mechanisms for controlling fracture paths. The method is applicable for a wide range of materials, from stiff elastic to highly plastic objects that exhibit brittle and/or ductile fracture.

9.3.1 Overview

Physically, fracturing occurs when the internal stresses and the resulting forces are so large that the interatomic bonds cannot hold the material together anymore. Fracturing has been studied extensively in the physics and mechanics literature. However, due to the complexity of the problem, the studies and simulation usually deal only with "simple" fractures, such as the creation or propagation of a single crack. In computer graphics, we often trade physical accuracy for visual realism. By simplifying the physical model, realistic animations of very complex fractures, such as the shattering of glass into hundreds of pieces, can be achieved. However, changing the topology of a simulated object is challenging for both the animation of the volume and the surface. When a solid fractures, the surface needs to adapt to the cracks that propagate through the volume of the solid. To achieve a high degree of visual realism, cracks should be allowed to start anywhere on the surface and move in any direction through the volume. Furthermore, cracks might branch into several cracks or different cracks can merge to a single crack within the solid. While fracturing, not only the topology of the surface changes but also the discontinuities introduced by the cracks in the volume have to be modeled accordingly to achieve physically plausible fracture behavior.

The fracturing characteristics depend on the material. We differentiate between ductile and brittle fracture. While brittle material splits without experiencing significant irreversible deformation (i.e. only elastic deformation), ductile material experience some amount of plastic deformation before fracture [13]. Two examples for brittle and ductile materials are shown in Figs. 9.8 and 9.9. A force acting on the hollow stone sculpture in Fig. 9.8 causes the model to explode. Due to the simulated brittle material, this results in a shattering of the object into pieces. Figure 9.9 shows a ductile fracture of a highly plastic bubblegum-like material that is deformed beyond recognition before splitting along a single complex fracture surface.

Fracturing materials have been simulated using finite difference schemes [15], mass-spring models [16], constraint-based methods [17], finite-element methods (FEM) [18,19], and meshless methods [20]. Meshless methods have several advantages over FEMs. Most importantly, meshless methods avoid complex remeshing operations and the associated problems of element cutting and mesh alignment sensitivity common in FEM. Maintaining a conforming mesh can be a notoriously difficult task when the topology of the simulation domain changes frequently [21]. Repeated remeshing operations can adversely affect the stability and accuracy of the calculations, imposing undesirable restrictions on the time step. Finally, meshless methods are well suited for handling large deformations due to their flexibility when locally refining the sampling resolution.

FIGURE 9.8

Brittle fracture of a hollow stone sculpture. Forces acting on the interior create stresses that cause the model to fracture and explode. Initial/final sampling: 4.3k/6.5k pixels, 249 000/310 000 surfels, 22 s/frame.

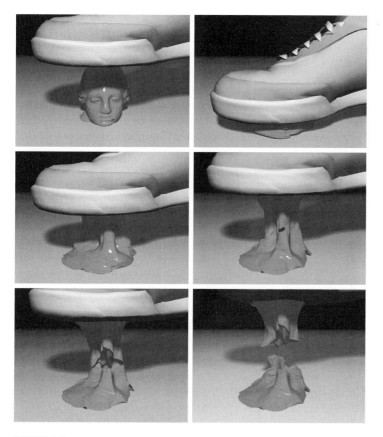

FIGURE 9.9

Highly plastic deformations and ductile fracture. The bubblegum-like material is first deformed beyond recognition. It is then stretched until the stress in the material is too high and it fractures along a complex fracture surface. Initial/final sampling: 2.2*k*/3.3*k* pixels, 134 000/144 000 surfels, 2.4 s/frame.

9.3.2 Historical Background

In this section, we will give a brief overview of fracturing methods in computer graphics. Terzopoulos et al. [22] pioneered physics-based animation of deforming objects using finite difference schemes to solve the underlying elasticity equations. This work has been extended in Terzopoulos and Fleischer [15] to handle plastic materials and fracture effects. Mass-spring models [16] and constraint-based methods [17] have also been popular for modeling fractures in graphics, as they allow for easy control of fracture patterns and relatively simple and fast implementations. Recent efforts have focused on FEMs that directly approximate the equations of continuum mechanics [7]. O'Brien and Hodgins were the first to apply this technique for graphical animation in their seminal paper on brittle fracture [18]. Using element cutting and dynamic remeshing, they adapt the simulation domain to conform with the fracture lines that are derived from the principal stresses. O'Brien et al. [13] introduce strain-state variables to model plastic deformations and ductile fracture effects. Element splitting has also been used in virtual surgery simulation, where Bielser et al. [23] introduced a state machine to model all configurations of how a tetrahedron can be split. Müller et al. [24] and Müller and Gross [8] demonstrate real-time fracturing using an embedded boundary surface to reduce the complexity of the finite element mesh. The virtual node algorithm of Molino et al. [19] combines the ideas of embedding the surface and remeshing the domain. Elements are duplicated and fracture surfaces are embedded in the copied tetrahedra. This allows more flexible fracture paths but avoids the complexity of full remeshing and associated time-stepping restrictions.

9.3.3 Modeling of Discontinuities

We will start by discussing how the discontinuity can be modeled that is introduced by a propagating crack into the domain of a simulated solid. For that, the so-called visibility criterion [25] can be used where pixels are allowed to interact with each other only if they are not separated by a surface. This is done by testing if a ray connecting two pixels intersects the boundary surface, similar to ray tracing.

To see what happens when we use the visibility criterion, we look at the discretization $\tilde{\mathbf{u}}$ of the continuous displacement field $\mathbf{u}$. This is typically approximated as $\mathbf{u}(\mathbf{x}) \approx \sum_i \Phi_i(\mathbf{x}) \mathbf{u}_i$, where $\mathbf{u}_i$ are the displacement vectors at the material coordinates $\{\mathbf{x}_i\}$ of the pixels and Φ_i are shape functions associated with these coordinates. For FEM, the Φ_i are constructed using a tessellation of the simulation domain into nonoverlapping elements. Meshless methods require no such spatial decomposition but instead use techniques such as the MLS approximation [11] to define the shape functions based on the location of the pixels only. Given a complete polynomial basis $\mathbf{b}(\mathbf{x}) = [1 \ \mathbf{x} \ \dots \ \mathbf{x}^n]^T$ of order n and a weight function ω_i, the meshless shape functions can be derived as

$$\Phi_i(\mathbf{x}) = \omega_i(\mathbf{x}, \mathbf{x}_i) \mathbf{b}^T(\mathbf{x}) [\mathbf{M}(\mathbf{x})]^{-1} \mathbf{b}(\mathbf{x}_i), \tag{9.31}$$

where $[\mathbf{M}(\mathbf{x})]^{-1}$ is the inverse of the moment matrix defined as

$$\mathbf{M}(\mathbf{x}) = \sum_i \omega_i(\mathbf{x}, \mathbf{x}_i) \mathbf{b}(\mathbf{x}_i) \mathbf{b}^T(\mathbf{x}_i), \tag{9.32}$$

and $\omega_i(\mathbf{x}, \mathbf{x}_i)$ is the weight function of Eq. (9.12). A detailed account on how to construct shape functions for meshless methods can be found in Fries and Matthies [4].

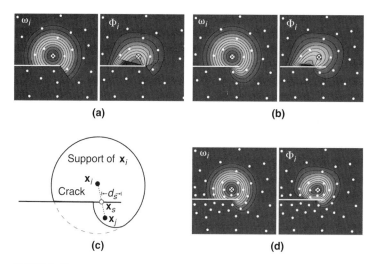

FIGURE 9.10

Comparison of visibility criterion (a) and transparency method (b) for an irregularly sampled 2D domain. The effect of a crack, indicated by the horizontal white line, on weight function ω_i and shape function Φ_i is depicted for pixel $\mathbf{x}_i$ marked by the cross. A schematic view of the transparency method is shown in (c) and the effect of dynamic upsampling is illustrated in (d).

Figure 9.10a shows the weight and shape functions when using the visibility criterion. The crack not only introduces a discontinuity along the crack surface but also undesirable discontinuities of the shape functions within the domain. The transparency method proposed by Organ et al. [26] alleviates potential stability problems due to these discontinuities. The idea is to make the crack more transparent closer to the crack front. This allows partial interaction of pixels in the vicinity of the crack front. Suppose the ray between two pixels $\mathbf{x}_i$ and $\mathbf{x}_j$ intersects a crack surface at a point $\mathbf{x}_s$ (Fig. 9.10c). Then the weight function ω_i (and similarly for ω_j) is adapted to $\omega_i'(\mathbf{x}_i, \mathbf{x}_j) - \omega_i\left(\|\mathbf{x}_i - \mathbf{x}_j\|/b_i + (2d_s/(\kappa b_i))^2\right)$ where d_s is the distance between $\mathbf{x}_s$ and the closest point on the crack front, and κ controls the opacity of the crack surfaces. Effectively, a crack passing between two pixels lengthens the interaction distance of the pixels until eventually, in this adapted distance metric, the pixels will be too far apart to interact. As shown in Fig. 9.10b, this method avoids the discontinuities of the shape functions within the domain and thus leads to increased stability.

9.3.4 Surface Model

Introducing cuts into the model exposes interior parts of the solid that need to be bounded by new surface sheets. Previous approaches based on FEM define fracture surfaces using faces of the tetrahedral elements, which requires complex dynamic remeshing to avoid unnaturally coarse crack surfaces [18]. To simplify the topological complexity and avoid stability problems during the simulation, mesh-based approaches impose restrictions on where and how the material can fracture. These restrictions can be lifted by embedding a surface and explicitly creating new fracture surface sheets whenever the material is cut. Using a point-based representation as the boundary of a 3D solid allows simple and efficient creation of these surface sheets, since no explicit connectivity information needs to be maintained between surfels. Sharp creases and corners are represented implicitly as the intersection of adjacent surface sheets using the constructive solid geometry (CSG) method. The precise location of crease lines is evaluated at render time (see Fig. 9.17 later), avoiding costly surface–surface intersection calculations during simulation.

A crack consists of a crack front and two separate surface sheets that are connected at the front to form a sharp crease. The crack front itself is defined by a linear sequence of crack nodes c_1, ..., c_n that continuously add surfels to the fracture surfaces while propagating through the material. For surface cracks, the end nodes of the front lie on a boundary surface or a fracture surface of a different crack. Interior cracks have circularly connected crack fronts; in other words, the two end nodes c_1 and c_n coincide (see Figs. 9.11 and 9.12).

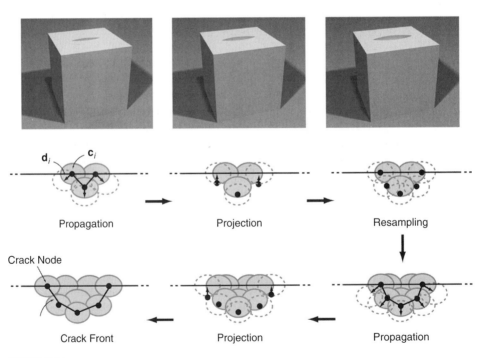

FIGURE 9.11

Front propagation and fracture surface sampling. The *upper row* shows a top view of an opening crack, the *lower part* shows a side view of a single fracture surface. After propagating the crack nodes c_i according to d_i, end nodes are projected onto the surface. If necessary, the front is resampled and new surfels are added to the fracture surface sheets.

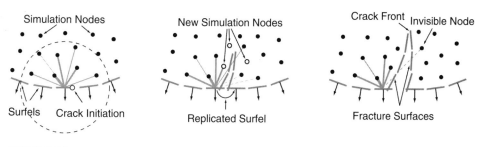

FIGURE 9.12

Transparency weights for embedding surfels in the simulation domain. The thickness of the lines indicates the influence of a pixel on the displacement of a surfel. During crack propagation, new surfels and pixels are created using dynamic resampling.

To animate the boundary surface of the solid, the free-form deformation approach described in Section 9.2.8 is used. To ensure that the displacement field is smooth at the crack front, the transparency weights described above are also used in Eq. (9.30) because as the changes of the transparency weights are localized to a small region around the crack front, only a small fraction of the weights needs to be updated in every time step, leading to an efficient implementation.

9.3.5 Crack Initiation and Propagation

Crack initiation is based on the stress tensor σ [see Eq. (9.8)]. A new crack is created where the maximal eigenvalue of σ exceeds the threshold for tensile fracture (opening mode fracture [27]). This condition is evaluated for all pixels. To allow crack initiation anywhere on the surface or in the interior of the model, a stochastic scheme can be applied to initiate crack fronts. A random set of surface and interior sample points are created and the stress tensor at these points is evaluated using weighted averaging from adjacent pixels. The inherent smoothing is usually desired to improve the stability of the crack propagation. If a crack front is initiated at one of these spatial locations, the fracture thresholds of all neighboring samples are increased to avoid spurious branching.

A new crack is initialized with three crack nodes, each of which carries two surfels with identical position and radius but opposing normals. These surfels form the initial crack surfaces that will grow dynamically as the crack propagates through the solid (Fig. 9.11). Crack propagation is determined by the propagation vectors $\mathbf{d}_i = \alpha_i \lambda_i (\mathbf{e}_i \times \mathbf{t}_i)$, where λ_i is the maximal eigenvalue of the stress tensor at $\mathbf{c}_i$, and $\mathbf{e}_i$ is the corresponding eigenvector. The vector $\mathbf{t}_i$ approximates the tangent of the crack front as $\mathbf{t}_i = (\mathbf{c}_{i+1} - \mathbf{c}_{i-1})/\| \mathbf{c}_{i+1} - \mathbf{c}_{i-1} \|$, where $\mathbf{c}_0 = \mathbf{c}_1$ and $\mathbf{c}_{n+1} = \mathbf{c}_n$ for surface cracks. The parameter α_i depends on the material and can be used to control the speed of propagation. The new position of a crack node $\mathbf{c}_i$ at time $t + \Delta t$ is then computed as $\mathbf{c}_i + \Delta t \mathbf{d}_i$, where Δt is the simulation time step. Additionally, the end nodes of surface cracks are projected back onto the surface that they originated from using the projection method. Since propagation alters the spacing of crack nodes along the front, the sampling resolution of the crack nodes is adjusted dynamically after each propagation step. If two adjacent crack nodes are farther apart than the radius of their associated surfels, a new node is inserted using cubic spline interpolation to determine the new node's position. Redundant crack nodes are removed when the distance to the immediate neighbors becomes too small. Fracture surface sheets are sampled by inserting new surfels if the propagation distance exceeds the surfel radius, indicating that a hole would appear in the surface. This spatially (along the crack front) and temporally (along the propagation vectors) adaptive sampling scheme ensures uniformly sampled and hole-free crack surfaces (see Fig. 9.11).

During crack propagation, the simulation is adjusted automatically to the newly created fracture surfaces by adapting the shape functions using the transparency method described above. The transparency weight $\omega_i'\left(\mathbf{x}_i, \mathbf{x}_j\right)$ for a pair of pixels is adapted by computing the intersection point on the fracture surface of the ray connecting the two pixels (Section 9.3.3). The distance d_s to the crack front is approximated as the shortest Euclidean distance to the line segments defined by adjacent crack nodes. To avoid stability problems with curved fracture surfaces, weights are allowed to only decrease from one time step to the next.

9.3.6 Topology Control

The major challenge when explicitly modeling fracture surfaces is the efficient handling of all events that affect the topology of the boundary surface and the simulation domain. Apart from crack initiation, three fundamental events are sufficient to describe the often intricate constellations that occur during fracturing: *termination*, *splitting*, and *merging* of crack fronts:

- A crack is *terminated* if the crack front has contracted to a single point.

- *Splitting* occurs when a crack front penetrates through a surface as shown in Fig. 9.13a. The signed distance of a crack node to a surface sheet can be estimated. A splitting event is initiated when a sign change occurs from one time step to the next. The front is split at the edges that intersect the surface, discarding all nodes that are outside the solid, except the ones that are connected to an interior node. These nodes become new end nodes by moving them to the intersection point with the surface. As shown on the left in Fig. 9.13a, a surface crack is split into two new crack fronts that share the same crack surfaces (i.e. independently add surfels to the same fracture surface sheets during propagation). An interior crack becomes a surface crack after splitting, as illustrated on the right.

- A *merging* event is triggered when two surface end nodes of two crack fronts meet by creating the appropriate edge connections (Fig. 9.13b). Two surface cracks are merged into a single surface crack (left), while a circular front is created if the two end nodes are from the same crack front (right). Typically, when cracks merge, their fracture surfaces create a sharp corner, so we maintain separate fracture surface sheets that intersect to create a crease.

As can be seen in Fig. 9.13, splitting and merging are dual to each other. The former introduces two new end nodes, while the latter decreases the number of end nodes by

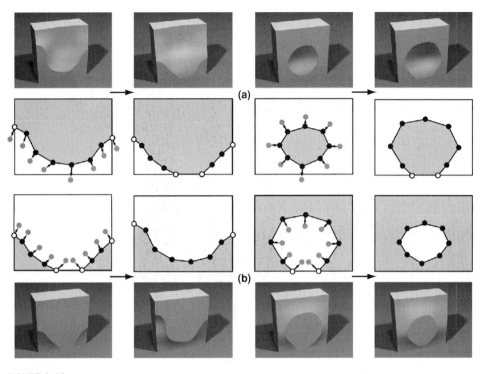

FIGURE 9.13

Topological events during crack propagation: (a) splitting and (b) merging. The *top* and *bottom rows* show a cutaway view with one crack surface exposed. The sketches in the *center rows* show this fracture surface in gray, end nodes of crack fronts are indicated by white dots.

two. Similarly, crack initiation and termination are dual topological operations. Note that the intersection of two crack fronts at interior nodes is handled automatically by first splitting both fronts and then merging the newly created end nodes.

One useful technique to improve the stability of the simulation is *snapping*. Snapping guarantees that problematic small features, such as tiny fragments or thin slivers, do not arise. It works by forcing nodes very near other nodes or very near surfaces to become coincident to ensure that any features present are of size comparable to the local node spacing. Similar methods have been proven to guarantee topological consistency with the ideal geometry in other settings [28]. Specifically, when a front intersects a surface, the crack nodes that are within snapping distance d to the surface are projected onto the surface. This avoids fragmenting the front into small pieces that would be terminated anyway within a few time steps. Furthermore, fronts are merged when the end nodes are within distance d by moving both end nodes to their average position. This avoids the creation of small slivers of material, which would require a significant number of new pixels to be added to the model (see Section 9.3.7). Similarly, the intersection of two crack fronts can lead to multiple splitting and merging events (Fig. 9.14), which are combined into a single

FIGURE 9.14

Crack merging. Four of a total 49 crack fronts merge in the center of the twisted bar to form a circular crack front. Initial/final sampling: 2000/3000 pixels, 29 000/144 000 surfels, 10 s/frame.

event to avoid the overhead of creating and subsequently deleting many small crack fronts. Snapping can also be applied to front termination, where a crack front is deleted when all its nodes are within distance d from each other.

9.3.7 Volumetric Sampling

One of the main advantages of meshless methods lies in the fact that they support simple and efficient sampling schemes. Initially, the volume V bounded by a surface S is discretized by sampling V with pixels as described in Section 9.2.3. Similar to adaptive finite element meshing, we want a higher pixel density close to the boundary surface and fewer pixels toward the interior of the solid.

An appropriate sampling of the pixels can be computed, for example, using a balanced octree hierarchy as shown in Fig. 9.15. Starting from the bounding box of S, a cell of the octree is recursively refined, if it contains parts of S. The final number of pixels is controlled by prescribing a maximum octree level at which the recursive refinement is stopped. Given this adaptive decomposition, a pixel is created at each octree cell center that lies within V. To create a locally, more uniform, distribution, samples are displaced within their octree cell by applying a few iterations of point repulsion.

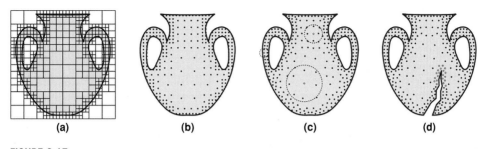

FIGURE 9.15

Volumetric sampling: (a) octree decomposition, (b) initial adaptive octree sampling, (c) sampling after local repulsion, where circles indicate 0.1 isovalue of weight function, and (d) dynamic resampling during fracturing.

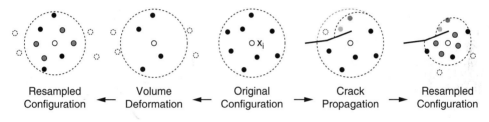

FIGURE 9.16

Dynamic resampling at the pixel $\mathbf{x}_i$ due to strong deformation (left) and fracturing (right).

During simulation, the discretization of the simulation domain needs to be adjusted dynamically. Without dynamic resampling, frequent fracturing would quickly degrade the numerical stability of the simulation even for an initially adequately sampled model. New pixels need to be inserted in the vicinity of the crack surfaces and in particular around the crack front. At the same time, strong deformations of the model can lead to a poor spatial discretization of the simulation volume, which also requires a dynamic adaptation of the sampling resolution. This is particularly important for highly plastic materials, where the deformed shape can deviate significantly from its original configuration.

A simple local criterion can be used to determine undersampling at a pixel $\mathbf{x}_i$. Let $\Omega_i = \sum_j \omega_i'(\mathbf{x}_i, \mathbf{x}_j)/\omega_i(\mathbf{x}_i, \mathbf{x}_j)$ be the normalized sum of transparency weights (see Section 9.3.3). Without visibility constraints, Ω_i is simply the number of pixels in the support of $\mathbf{x}_i$. During simulation, Ω_i decreases, if fewer neighboring pixels are found due to strong deformations, or if the transparency weights become smaller due to a crack front passing through the solid. If Ω_i drops below a threshold Ω_{min}, $[\Omega_{min} - \Omega_i]$ new pixels are inserted within the support radius of $\mathbf{x}_i$ (see Fig. 9.16), similar to Desbrun and Cani [5].

The mass associated with $\mathbf{x}_i$ is distributed evenly among the new pixels and their support radius is adapted to keep the overall material density constant. Note that

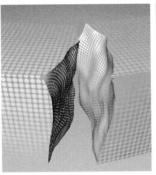

FIGURE 9.17

Surfels are clipped to create sharp creases with dynamically created fracture surfaces, whose visual roughness is controlled using 3D noise functions for bump mapping. The sampling of the simulation domain is shown on the right, where green spheres denote resampled pixels.

mass will not be strictly preserved locally in the sense that the mass distribution of pixels after fracturing will not precisely match the correct distribution according to the separated volumes created by the fracture surface sheets. However, mass will be preserved globally and the local deviations are sufficiently small to not affect the simulation noticeably.

To prevent excessive resampling for pixels very close to a fracture boundary, pixel splitting is restricted by prescribing a minimal pixel support radius. Note that resampling due to fracturing is triggered by the crack nodes passing through the solid, similar to adapting the visibility weights (see Section 9.3.4). Performing these checks comes essentially for free, since all the required spatial queries are already carried out during visibility computation. Figures 9.15d and 9.17 illustrate the dynamic adaptation of the sampling rates when fracturing. The effect on the shape functions is shown in Fig. 9.10d.

9.3.8 Fracture Control

By specifying material properties, the course of the simulation can be influenced. However, often direct control over the fracture behavior is crucial, especially in production environments and interactive applications where the visual effect is usually more important than physical accuracy. By exploiting the explicit point-based representation of the fracture surfaces, the fracture framework can be extended to support precise control of where and how a model fractures. One possibility is to use a painting interface that allows fast prototyping of fracture simulations by prescribing fracture patterns directly on the object boundary. The user can paint arbitrary networks of cracks on the surface and explicitly specify stress thresholds for these cracks. Additionally, a propagation history can be used to control the propagation of cracks through the material. The adjusted propagation vector at time t is computed as the weighted average $\mathbf{d}_i^{-t} = \gamma \mathbf{d}_i^{t-\Delta t} + (1 - \gamma)\mathbf{d}_i^t$, where $\gamma \in [0, 1]$ is the history

FIGURE 9.18

Controlled fracture. While the sphere blows up, it fractures along the prescribed smiley face. Initial/final sampling: 4.6k/5.8k pixels, 49 000/102 000 surfels, 6 s/frame.

factor. A purely stress-based propagation is achieved for $\gamma = 0$, while $\gamma = 1$ yields purely geometric cracks and fracture surfaces. Other possibilities include volumetric textures for adjusting the fracture thresholds within the material, and prescoring techniques, where the stress tensor is modified according to an embedded level set function [19]. Figure 9.18 shows an example of an explicitly controlled fracture, using a combination of crack painting, propagation history, and adaptive fracture thresholds.

9.3.9 Simulation Pipeline

Figure 9.19 shows a high-level overview of the simulation pipeline. An iteration step starts with the detection of collisions between two or several objects. Collision detection is based on the signed distance function of the boundary surfaces. Interpenetrations are resolved by computing an approximate contact surface that is consistent for both models [29]. The objects are separated by computing penalty forces from the contact surface. After resolving collisions and contacts, strains and stresses are computed as described in Section 9.2.2. Given the distribution of stress, new

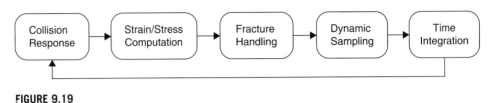

FIGURE 9.19

High-level overview of the meshless simulation pipeline.

crack fronts are initiated and existing cracks propagated, and the spatial sampling of the fracture surfaces is adapted (Section 9.3.5). This stage is followed by the dynamic resampling of the simulation domain (Section 9.3.10). Finally, the forces are integrated (e.g. using an explicit leap-frog scheme) to obtain the new displacements.

9.3.10 Conclusion

With the meshless framework described above, deformable objects with material properties ranging from stiff elastic to highly plastic can be simulated. Extending this framework for fracturing is straightforward and shows several advantages compared to FEM simulation. Instead of maintaining a consistent volumetric mesh using continuous cutting and restructuring of finite elements, the shape functions of the pixels are adjusted dynamically based on simple visibility constraints. The space discretization is continuously adapted using insertions of new pixels. The simplicity of this dynamic resampling of the simulation domain highlights one of the main benefits of meshless methods for physics-based animation. Due to minimal consistency constraints between neighboring nodes, dynamic resampling is efficient and easy to implement, as compared to the far more involved remeshing methods used in FEM simulations. Similarly, a point-based representation is built for the boundary surface, which allows efficient dynamic sampling of fracture surfaces, and facilitates explicit control of the object topology. A general limitation of the meshless approach is that even very small fragments must be sampled sufficiently dense in order to obtain a stable evaluation of the shape functions. This inflates the number of pixels when an object is fractured excessively, which slows down the computations.

9.4 FLUID SIMULATION

Martin Wicke, Richard Keiser, and Markus Gross

9.4.1 Overview

Fluids constitute a large part of our visual surroundings. A fluid is defined as a material that cannot support shear stress in static equilibrium – it flows. This definition spans a wide range of material properties. Smoke and fire, as well as clouds, and other natural phenomena based on the behavior of gases fall in the category of fluid simulation, but also the simulation of liquids such as water, oil, or lava.

While visualization of gaseous fluids is usually performed using volume-rendering techniques, liquids have a surface that needs to be extracted or tracked. The surface of a liquid is highly volatile and subject to frequent changes in topology.

This section presents meshless simulation methods that can be used for fluid simulation and compares those to other established algorithms. One particle method, SPH, will be considered in more detail. We will then turn to the problem of surface tracking and reconstruction.

9.4.2 Simulation Methods

There are two distinct methods to discretize a physics problem in order to simulate it: *Lagrangian* and *Eulerian* methods. While Lagrangian methods discretize the material, Eulerian methods discretize the space in which the material moves. In other words, in a Lagrangian simulation, the simulation elements move with the material, whereas in a Eulerian setting, the material moves through the simulation elements, which are fixed in space. Figure 9.20 illustrates the difference.

All Eulerian methods are mesh-based methods, for example, the finite difference and finite volumes methods [30,31]. The simulation grid is a disjoint set of volume elements that cover the simulation domain. The volume elements do not necessarily form a regular grid, but for implementation and performance issues, this is often the first choice. Since the discretization of space does not depend on the material, it is easy for these algorithms to accommodate large deformations (such as those occurring in flow simulations). Hence, this class of simulation algorithms is well suited for fluid simulation, and they are still dominant in computer graphics (some examples include [32,33,34,35,36]).

Since the discretization of the simulation domain does not change with the material shape, interface tracking and moving boundaries are problematic in Eulerian simulations. Also, mass loss can occur due to numerical dissipation.

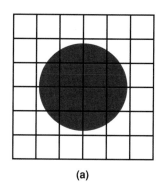 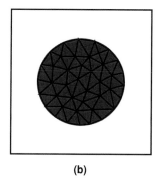 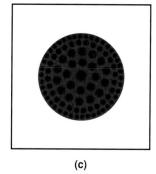

(a) (b) (c)

FIGURE 9.20

A 2D sphere of blue material discretized in a Eulerian mesh (a), Lagrangian mesh (b), and using particles (c). The Lagrangian elements discretize only the material, while the Eulerian elements discretize the embedding space. Only the meshes define a disjoint partitioning of space.

In contrast to the Eulerian approach, Lagrangian methods discretize the material that is simulated, and the discretization moves during the simulation. Since each element of the discretization represents a part of the material, mass loss is not an issue for Lagrangian methods. Also, complex moving boundaries and free surfaces are easier to handle, since the discretization moves along with the material.

Most prominent in this class of algorithms are mesh-based FEMs, which are widely used in continuum mechanics. The numerical accuracy of these methods highly depends on the aspect ratio of the mesh elements used to cover the simulated material (most commonly tetrahedra). If the material undergoes large deformations, the mesh quality degrades and remeshing is needed. Therefore, mesh-based Lagrangian methods are rarely used for fluid simulation in computer graphics.

Particle methods are a Lagrangian discretization that do not require a mesh for simulation. These methods work on a set of samples (particles), without defining nearest-neighbor relationships. In practice, a set of neighbors are computed for each particle in each time step. Strictly speaking, this is only an optimization, exploiting the fact that the interpolation functions used usually have local support, and thus reducing the overall complexity from $O(N^2)$ to $O(N \log N)$ per time step, where N is the number of particles. Although, technically, these neighborhoods define a mesh, this mesh is not a disjoint partitioning of the domain, and explicit neighborhoods need not be stored.

SPH [37,38] was the first particle method and is still the most popular in computer graphics. It was originally invented for astrophysics applications, where the particle metaphor is obvious. In Section 9.4.3, SPH will be discussed in detail.

Other methods include weakly coupled or spatially coupled particle systems. The former are popular methods for a wide range of special effects, like fire, clouds, or other fuzzy gaseous objects [39,40]; waves [41,42]; or even animal flocking behavior [43]. Here, particle behavior is usually determined by a procedural and/or stochastical process. These techniques are fast and easy to control while producing convincing animations for a large class of phenomena. They are, hence, ideally suited for movie productions and especially games.

Spatially coupled particle systems compute forces between pairs of particles in order to animate the particle system [44]. Usually some potential is attached to each particle, defining the occurring interaction forces as the negative gradient of the potential field at each particle's position. Using functions like the Lennard–Jones potential known from molecular dynamics or variations thereof, different material properties can be modeled.

9.4.3 Smoothed Particle Hydrodynamics

The most popular particle method for fluid simulation in computer graphics is SPH. In this section, its basic formulation as a method for function interpolation will be derived. We will then go on to show how this framework can be applied to the problem of fluid simulation. For a more in-depth treatment of the topic, see Monaghan [45] or Liu and Liu [46].

Elements of the SPH method have already been used in the MLS approximation described in Sections 9.2.3 and 9.2.4. SPH approximations are not first-order accurate and thus not suitable for modeling general elasticity. However, this property is less critical for fluid simulation, and SPH is popular for its relatively low computational cost and good controllability.

In SPH, a number of particles represent the material, in our case, the fluid. Each particle carries mass, velocity, and other attributes. A kernel function $\omega_h(d)$ describes the influence of each particle on its surroundings, where the *smoothing length h* is a constant of the particle, and d is the distance from the particle. In almost all cases, the smoothing length is constant over all particles, and does not change during the simulation, yielding equal-sized particles that are much easier to handle algorithmically. The kernel function is generally defined to be a normalized and smooth function with local support, in particular $\omega_h(d) = 0 \ \forall\, d > kh$ for some k.

Using the kernel, a continuous function $A(\mathbf{x})$ can be smoothed to obtain $A'(\mathbf{x})$:

$$A'(\mathbf{x}) = \int w_h(\|\mathbf{x} - \mathbf{x}'\|)A(\mathbf{x}')\mathrm{d}\mathbf{x}'. \tag{9.33}$$

If we turn to the discrete setting, the function $A(\mathbf{x})$ is unknown, and only samples A_j at the particle positions $\mathbf{x}_j$ are accessible. Each particle represents a small volume element V_j, which is related to the particles' mass m_j and density ρ_j by

$$V_j = \frac{m_j}{\rho_j}. \tag{9.34}$$

Thus, the integral in Eq. (9.33) can be approximated by a sum over the particles.

$$\begin{aligned} A'(\mathbf{x}) &\approx \sum_j \omega_h(\|\mathbf{x} - \mathbf{x}_j\|)V_j A_j \\ &= \sum_j \omega_h(\|\mathbf{x} - \mathbf{x}_j\|)\frac{m_j}{\rho_j}A_j = \langle A(\mathbf{x})\rangle. \end{aligned} \tag{9.35}$$

We will call $\langle A \rangle$ the SPH approximation of the function A.

Note that the particle masses m_j are constant during the simulation; however, the densities ρ_j are subject to change. Fortunately, the densities can be approximated by substituting ρ for A in Eq. (9.35):

$$\langle \rho(\mathbf{x})\rangle = \sum_j \omega_h(\|\mathbf{x} - \mathbf{x}_j\|)\rho_j\frac{m_j}{\rho_j} = \sum_j \omega_h(\|\mathbf{x} - \mathbf{x}_j\|)m_j. \tag{9.36}$$

By defining $\rho_j := \langle \rho(\mathbf{p}_j)\rangle$, Eq. (9.35) can be used to interpolate any function from samples at the particle positions.

9.4.3.1 Approximations of Differential Operators in SPH

Differential operators can be directly applied to the SPH approximation $\langle A \rangle$. Since the sample values A_j are constants, we can write

$$\langle \nabla A(\mathbf{x}) \rangle = \sum_j \nabla \omega_b \left(\|\mathbf{x} - \mathbf{x}_j\| \right) \frac{m_j}{\rho_j} A_j, \tag{9.37}$$

where the gradient $\nabla \omega_b \left(\|\mathbf{x} - \mathbf{x}_j\| \right)$ can be rewritten in terms of the kernel derivative:

$$\nabla \omega_b \left(\|\mathbf{x} - \mathbf{x}_j\| \right) = \frac{\mathbf{x} - \mathbf{x}_j}{\|\mathbf{x} - \mathbf{x}_j\|} \omega_b' \left(\|\mathbf{x} - \mathbf{x}_j\| \right). \tag{9.38}$$

Similarly, a Laplace operator for A and a divergence operator for a vector-valued function $\mathbf{A}$ can be defined:

$$\langle \Delta A(x) \rangle = \sum_j \frac{m_j}{\rho_j} \omega_b'' \left(\|\mathbf{x} - \mathbf{x}_j\| \right) A_i \tag{9.39}$$

$$\langle \nabla \cdot \mathbf{A}(\mathbf{x}) \rangle = \sum_j \frac{m_j}{\rho_j} \nabla \omega_b \left(\|\mathbf{x} - \mathbf{x}_j\| \right) \cdot \mathbf{A}_j. \tag{9.40}$$

In a simulation, we mostly need SPH approximations at particle positions. We will therefore introduce the following shorthand notation. For the kernel weight of a particle at $\mathbf{x}_j$ with respect to $\mathbf{x}_i$, we write

$$\omega_{ij} = \omega_b \left(\|\mathbf{x}_i - \mathbf{x}_j\| \right), \tag{9.41}$$

and for any SPH approximation, evaluated at a point $\mathbf{x}_i$,

$$\langle A \rangle_i = \langle A(\mathbf{x}_i) \rangle. \tag{9.42}$$

9.4.3.2 Stability

The above approximations are derived using approximations to the integral in Eq. (9.33). Their accuracy strongly depends on the distribution of particles in the region of interest. In practice, larger values of b provide more sample points and add stability to the simulation. This involves some computational cost and more smoothing, which might not be desirable.

The gradient operator is especially sensitive to a bad distribution of particles. If the distribution is not symmetric, Eq. (9.37) can yield nonzero gradients even if the samples A_i are constant. Noting that the gradient of any function remains unchanged if we subtract a constant function, we can rewrite the gradient approximation at the sample points $\mathbf{x}_i$ and obtain

$$\langle \nabla A \rangle_i = \sum_j \nabla \omega \, \frac{m_i}{\rho_j} (A_j - A_i). \tag{9.43}$$

Note that in order to compute the gradient, the constant field A_i is subtracted everywhere. There are different methods to derive the above result; for a more general derivation, see Monaghan [45]. The same method can be applied to obtain a better approximation to the divergence, yielding

$$\langle \nabla \cdot A \rangle_i = \sum_j \frac{m_i}{\rho_j} \nabla \omega_{ij} \cdot (A_j - A_i). \tag{9.44}$$

The approximations in Eqs. (9.43) and (9.44) are often superior to their counterparts in Eqs. (9.37) and (9.40), especially at the boundaries of the sampled region or in regions with high-density gradients.

The choice of interpolation kernel also influences the stability of the simulation. In the paper introducing SPH, Gingold and Monaghan used Gaussian kernels [38]. These, however, do not have local support and are rarely used nowadays. At the same time, Lucy used spline kernels [37]. A good kernel has local support, is normalized, and has smooth derivatives. Depending on the problem, other properties may be desirable [10]. Higher-order interpolation kernels that have positive and negative regions are problematic when the particles are not equidistant. An example for a (3D) kernel function is given in Eq. (9.12). For use in more or less dimensions than three, the kernel has to be renormalized.

9.4.3.3 Fluid Simulation Using SPH

The motion of a fluid is determined by pressure forces, viscosity forces, and external forces:

$$\dot{\mathbf{v}} = \frac{\mathbf{f}_{\text{pressure}}}{\rho} + \frac{\mathbf{f}_{\text{viscous}}}{\rho} + \frac{\mathbf{f}_{\text{external}}}{\rho}. \tag{9.45}$$

Here, the time derivative $\dot{\mathbf{v}}$ is a material derivative; in other words, the change of $\mathbf{v}$ in time when measuring $\mathbf{v}$ at the same point in the fluid, not the same point in space. In a Lagrangian setting, such as SPH, material derivatives are easy to compute, since the properties attached to the particles move along with the particles.

Pressure forces act against pressure differences:

$$\mathbf{f}_{\text{pressure}} = -\nabla P. \tag{9.46}$$

The direct translation of Eq. (9.46) into an SPH approximation yields a working simulation; however, it cannot be guaranteed that linear and angular momentum are conserved exactly. Especially in computer graphics, where the simulations often use only a few particles to guarantee interactivity, this can be problematic. Several symmetric (and thus momentum-preserving) pressure forces have been proposed.

The derivation from Monaghan [45] shall be presented here. Instead of interpolating the pressure gradient using $\dfrac{\mathbf{f}_{\text{pressure}}}{\rho} = -\dfrac{\langle \nabla P \rangle}{\rho}$, the acceleration is interpolated directly: $\dfrac{\mathbf{f}_{\text{pressure}}}{\rho} = -\left\langle \dfrac{\nabla P}{\rho} \right\rangle$. It can be easily verified that

$$\frac{\nabla P}{\rho} = \nabla\left(\frac{P}{\rho}\right) + \frac{P}{\rho^2}\nabla\rho. \tag{9.47}$$

Approximating this expression in SPH yields a symmetric term for the pressure force at the particles:

$$
\begin{aligned}
\frac{\mathbf{f}_{\text{pressure}}(\mathbf{P}_i)}{\rho_i} &= \left\langle \frac{\nabla P}{\rho} \right\rangle_i = \left\langle \nabla\left(\frac{P}{\rho}\right) + \frac{P}{\rho^2}\nabla\rho \right\rangle_i \\
&= \sum_j \nabla \omega_{ij} m_j \left(\frac{P_j}{\rho_j^2} + \frac{P_i}{\rho_i^2} \right).
\end{aligned}
\tag{9.48}
$$

The pressure is a function of the density and the thermal energy. The latter is often ignored. A common choice for the pressure function is [47]:

$$P = k\left(\left(\frac{\rho}{\rho_0}\right)^\gamma - 1\right). \tag{9.49}$$

The parameter k is a measure for the incompressibility of the fluid. The higher k is, the higher the forces to counteract the density difference will be. Monaghan proposed $\gamma = 7$, whereas in computer graphics, a value of 1 is usually used [5,10]. Low values of gamma make the fluid more compressible. Subtracting 1 in Eq. (9.49) removes artifacts at free boundaries.

High values of k provoke high pressure forces and limit the time step that a simulation can use. The speed of sound in the simulated medium is given by $c = \sqrt{\delta P / \delta \rho}$, and the maximum safe time step for numerical simulation according to the Courant-Friedrichs–Lewy stability criterion is $\Delta t \le \lambda h / c$, where λ is the Courant number. Thus, $\Delta t_{\text{max}} \propto \sqrt{1/k}$. Viscosity further decreases the maximum time step [9,5].

In computer graphics, viscosity effects due to compression are usually neglected. The viscosity force is often modeled after the viscosity term that applies to incompressible fluids [10]:

$$\frac{f_{\text{viscous}}}{\rho} = \mu \nabla^2 \mathbf{v} = \mu \Delta \mathbf{v}. \tag{9.50}$$

This term can again be approximated using SPH:

$$\frac{\mathbf{f}_{\text{viscous}}(\mathbf{x}_i)}{\rho_i} = \mu \langle \Delta \mathbf{v} \rangle_i$$
$$= \mu \sum_j \Delta \omega_{ij} \frac{m_j}{\rho_j}(\mathbf{v}_j - \mathbf{v}_i). \tag{9.51}$$

There are other ways of defining viscosity forces, see, for example, Monaghan [45]. If viscosity is only used for numerical stability, the best approach is sometimes to simulate an inviscid fluid and add *artificial viscosity* later. One type of artificial viscosity is a variation of the XSPH technique [9]. Here, after each time step, the velocity of a particle i is modified in the direction of the average velocity of its neighbors:

$$\Delta \mathbf{v}_i = \xi \sum_j \frac{m_j}{\rho_j} \omega_{ij}(\mathbf{v}_j - \mathbf{v}_i). \tag{9.52}$$

Original XSPH uses the corrected velocities $\hat{\mathbf{v}}_i = \mathbf{v}_i + \Delta \mathbf{v}_i$ only for advection and stores the originally computed velocities for integration. If $\hat{\mathbf{v}}_i$ is also used for integration, the desired viscosity effect is stronger. In Eq. (9.52), $0 \le \xi \le 1$ determines how strong artificial viscosity should be. This leads to better regularization of the particles, at the cost of higher viscosity. Even high values of ξ do not incur stability problems; on the contrary, stability increases as ξ gets closer to 1.

9.4.3.4 Algorithmic Summary

We now have all necessary ingredients to formulate a simple SPH fluid simulation algorithm:

1. **loop**

2.   **forall** particles $i \in \Omega$

3.   find neighboring particles $N_i \leftarrow \{j \in \Omega \,|\, \omega_{ij} > 0\}$

4.   compute density $\rho_i \leftarrow \sum_{j \in N_i} \omega_{ij} m_j$

5.   compute pressure $P_i \leftarrow k\left(\dfrac{\rho_i}{\rho_0} - 1\right)$

6.   **forall** particles $i \in \Omega$

7.   compute acceleration due to pressure forces

$$\mathbf{a}_i^P \leftarrow \sum_{j \in N_i} \nabla \omega_{ij} m_j \left(P_i/\rho_i^2 + P_j/\rho_j^2\right)$$

8.   compute acceleration due to viscosity forces

$$\mathbf{a}_i^v \leftarrow \frac{\mu}{\rho_i}\sum_{j\in N_i}\Delta\omega_{ij}\frac{m_j}{\rho_j}(\mathbf{v}_j - \mathbf{v}_i)$$

9.   **forall** particles $i \in \Omega$

10.   integrate accelerations $\mathbf{v}_i \leftarrow \mathbf{v}_i + \Delta t\left(\mathbf{a}_i^p + \mathbf{a}_i^v\right)$

11.   integrate velocities $\mathbf{x}_i \leftarrow \mathbf{x}_i + \Delta t\mathbf{v}_i$

This algorithm needs three passes over the particles. In the first pass (steps 2–5), all densities and pressures in this time step are computed, which only depend on the particles' positions. The second loop computes the accelerations on the particles (steps 6–8). In the third pass (steps 9–11), the accelerations and velocities are integrated to obtain new positions of the particles. In the above example, the velocity Verlet integration scheme is used. Note that in Verlet integration, velocities and positions are not in sync (i.e. the **v** and **x** that are stored with the particles are half a time step apart). At the end of a time step k, at simulation time $t = k\Delta t$, each particle stores $\mathbf{x}^t$ and $\mathbf{v}^{t-1/2\Delta t}$. Technically, the viscosity force is computed in an inconsistent state (with positions and velocities from different times). In practice, this effect is not noticeable.

In step 3, the *neighbors* of a particle are computed. A particle j is considered a neighbor of i if $\omega_{ij} > 0$. Thus, if the kernels have local support, most of the particles do not have to be considered in the inner loops. If the set of neighbors can be stored with each particle, it does not need to be recomputed for steps 7 and 8. In any case, appropriate acceleration structures such as hash grids or K-d-trees greatly speed up the simulation. Figure 9.21 shows snapshots from a small-scale simulation using the above algorithm.

9.4.4 Surface Representation

So far, only the movement of the particles can be simulated. While this is sufficient for measurements, in the context of computer graphics, the visual appearance of the fluid is of interest.

FIGURE 9.21

Snapshots from a small-scale SPH simulation. The particles are drawn as red spheres. The fluid is pulled into a box by gravity.

For gaseous phenomena such as clouds or smoke, particles are often rendered as semitransparent spheres with a volumetric texture. The texture of the spheres can be chosen depending on density, temperature, or any other value from the underlying simulation (see, for example, [36,48]). For liquids, the interfaces are more interesting. For nontransparent liquids, the interface is the only visible part of the simulation, and for transparent liquids, the surface is important for diffraction and reflection effects.

The easiest way to generate a surface around the particles is to use an implicit surface. Every particle is assigned a potential, and the surface of the fluid is taken to be an isosurface of the superposition of particle potentials [49]. Several variants to this approach have been proposed, for example, Zhu and Bridson [50]. This isosurface can be rendered directly (e.g. using ray tracing) or extracted using the marching cubes algorithm or a variant thereof. The resulting triangle mesh can be rendered with standard rendering algorithms – in the case of transparent liquids, ray tracing is the preferred solution for high-quality images – while hardware rendering can be used for simpler settings. See Fig. 9.22 for an example of a ray-traced extracted surface (from [51]).

Since the particle potentials have no notion of connected components, and the potentials influence also distant particles, these simple isosurfaces do cause problems during topological changes of the surface. See Fig. 9.23 for an illustration.

In order to avoid these problems, level sets are often used [52,34]. Level sets evolve an implicit function according to a velocity field given by the simulation. A PDE is solved on a computational grid in order to animate the surface. In their basic form, level sets suffer from severe volume loss, especially near detailed surface features. *Particle level sets* are a combination of level sets with tracker particles, where the surface computed using level sets is corrected after each time step using tracker particles spawned around the surface [53,54].

(a)　　　　　　　　　　　　　　　(b)

FIGURE 9.22

The particles from a particle simulation (a) and an isosurface of the particle potentials extracted using marching cubes and ray traced (b).

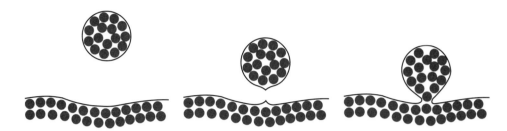

FIGURE 9.23

Artifacts occurring during topological changes using a purely implicit surface representation. Due to the purely spatial influence of the particle's potentials, the surface of the lower part is influenced by the particles in the drop – it anticipates the drop's arrival.

9.4.5 Surface Tracking Using Point Samples

Instead, the surface can be represented by surfels (for a more detailed discussion of this approach, see [55], Section 4). These surfels can then be rendered using either splatting or ray tracing.

By using an explicit surface representation that is only guided by an implicit function, the advantages of explicit and implicit surfaces can be effectively combined. Splitting and merging operations, trivial for an implicit surface representation, remain simple. The unwanted effects of an implicit representation like the artifacts due to long range influence of the particle potentials (see Fig. 9.23) can be avoided. By adding normal displacements of other means of detail encoding to the surface, a highly detailed surface can be represented and maintained. This can be used when modeling melting and freezing, or to reduce simulation complexity when a physical model is used for large-scale movement of the liquid, and a simpler model generates the surface detail.

Initially, the surfels are samples of an implicit surface coating the particles. This implicit surface is an isosurface of a potential function depending on the particle positions alone. This potential function is called the *particle potential function*. Its nature may vary, and good results are obtained using blobbies [49].

In order to animate a surfel s_i, it is first moved using a first-order estimate of the displacement field defined by its neighboring particles j (see also Section 9.2.3):

$$\mathbf{p}_i^{t+1} = \mathbf{p}_i^t + \frac{\sum_j \omega_b\left(\|\mathbf{p}_i^t - \mathbf{x}_j^t\|\right)\left[\mathbf{u}_j^t + \nabla \mathbf{u}_j^t\left(\mathbf{x}_j^t - \mathbf{p}_i^t\right)\right]}{\sum_j \omega_b\left(\|\mathbf{p}_i^t - \mathbf{x}_j^t\|\right)}. \tag{9.53}$$

The gradient of the displacement field $\nabla\mathbf{u}$ is estimated for each particle using an MLS approximation. The surfel normal or tangents axes are also deformed.

9.4.5.1 Surface Potentials

After this first advection step, the surface is additionally deformed by minimizing a number of surface potentials in order to obtain a smooth and well-sampled surface at all times. There are four surface potentials: a guiding potential that pulls surfels toward an implicit function defined by the particles, a smoothing potential that prevents the typical bumpy surface structure of implicit functions, an attracting potential that keeps the surface close to the particles, and a repulsion potential that guarantees a well-sampled surface. Figure 9.24 shows the effect of these potentials. The potentials are weighted and a simple Eulerian integration is used to move the surfels to minimize the weighted sum of potential functions.

9.4.5.1.1 Guiding Potential

Similar to Desbrun and Cani-Gascuel [56], the surfels are attracted to an isosurface of the particle potential function. Given a projection operator that projects onto the implicit function, a surface potential measuring the distance to the implicit function can be defined as

$$\phi_{s_i}^{\text{guiding}} = \frac{1}{2} \left\| \Gamma_I(\mathbf{p}_i) - \mathbf{p}_i \right\|^2.$$ (9.54)

Γ_I is a projection operator that projects onto the isosurface with isovalue I of the particle potential function.

9.4.5.1.2 Smoothing Potential

The implicit surfaces defined in Blinn [49] and similar approaches have the inherent property that the defined surface is "blobby." As the particle-sampling density increases, the blobbiness moves to higher frequencies and eventually becomes unnoticeable. Since the surfels are pulled toward an implicit surface, a smoothing potential to counteract the blobbiness is needed. This potential measures the difference

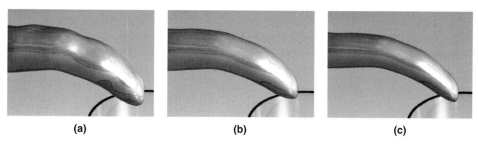

(a)   (b)   (c)

FIGURE 9.24

The effect of the different potential functions on the surface: (a) guiding potential, (b) smoothing potential, and (c) attracting potential.

between the surfel position $\mathbf{p}_i$ and its projection onto the least squares plane defined by its neighbors, $\psi(\mathbf{p}_i)$:

$$\phi_{s_i}^{\text{smoothing}} = \frac{1}{2}\| \psi(\mathbf{p}_i) - \mathbf{p}_i \|^2. \tag{9.55}$$

The forces introduced by this potential are constrained to act only normal to the surface.

9.4.5.1.3 Attracting Potential

Most physical interactions are computed on the particles alone. For a realistic visual impression, it is, therefore, necessary to keep the surface as close to the particles as possible. This is achieved using an attracting force pulling the surfels toward their nearest particles. Writing this as a potential, we obtain

$$\phi_{s_i}^{\text{attracting}} = \frac{\sum_j \omega_b(\| \mathbf{x}_j - \mathbf{p}_i \|) \| \mathbf{x}_j - \mathbf{p}_i \|^2}{2\sum_j \omega_b(\| \mathbf{x}_j - \mathbf{p}_i \|)}. \tag{9.56}$$

9.4.5.1.4 Repulsion Potential

The repulsion potential does not affect the movement of the surface but only the sampling of the surface with surfels. Using repulsive forces between surfels if they are too close, a locally uniform sampling can be achieved. For a given target surfel distance d, the potential is defined as follows:

$$\phi_{s_i}^{\text{sampling}} = \frac{1}{2}\sum_{j \in N(s_i)} (\| \mathbf{p}_i - \mathbf{p}_j \| - d)^2. \tag{9.57}$$

The index j runs over all surfels in the neighborhood of s_i. All these surfels hold $\|\mathbf{p}_i - \mathbf{p}_j\| < d$ so that the forces introduced by this potential are never attracting. The forces introduced by this potential are constrained to act only tangential to the surface. It is easily possible to locally vary d to achieve graded sampling of the surface, for example, for level of detail.

9.4.5.2 Topological Changes

Since our surface representation is not purely implicit, extra handling for topological changes needs to be implemented. Topological changes are characterized by two events: splitting and merging (Fig. 9.25). In a particle setting, splitting occurs when particles are separated by a large enough gap. This criterion carries over to the particle potential function. When splitting between two groups of particles occurs, there is a point between these groups where the potential function is lower than a threshold $I_{\min}$. This minimum isovalue can be used to define which minimum distance

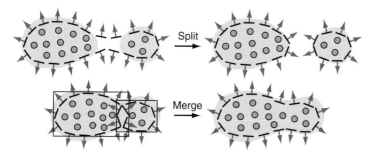

FIGURE 9.25

Splitting: when the isovalue at a surfel position is too low, the surfel is projected onto the mini-mum isovalue. Merging: if the isovalue is too high, the surfel is projected onto the maximum isovalue.

between particles is needed in order to consider them separated. Conversely, if par-ticles are close together, there will be no point between them with a potential lower than a threshold I_{max}.

This can be used to explicitly handle splitting and merging events. If the par-ticle potential at any surfel position is lower than I_{min}, the surfel is reprojected onto the isosurface of the particle potential with isovalue I_{min}: $\mathbf{p}_i \leftarrow \Gamma_{I_{min}}(\mathbf{p}_i)$. For merging events, if the particle potential at the surfel position is too high, the surfel is pro-jected onto the isosurface for isovalue I_{max}: $\mathbf{p}_i \leftarrow \Gamma_{I_{max}}(\mathbf{p}_i)$.

The surfels are free to move within the isorange $[I_{max}, I_{max}]$ of the particle poten-tial, thus giving them the possibility to smooth out the blob artifacts in the isosurface and avoid the anticipating effects seen in purely implicit surface representations.

Since the potential functions rely on surfel and particle neighborhood relations, it is important to keep track of connected components. Flood-fill algorithms can be used to tag connected components. All neighborhoods are then restricted to the same connected component such that different connected components cannot influ-ence each other.

9.4.6 Conclusion

A particle-based fluid simulation has both advantages and disadvantages over alterna-tive approaches, most prominently Eulerian fluid simulation methods.

In general, boundary conditions are easier to enforce in particle-based methods than in Eulerian simulations. Due to the discretization of space, boundary condi-tions in Eulerian simulation have to be aligned with the grid used to represent the simulation domain. For performance reasons, these meshes are usually regular grids, thus leading to artifacts when representing boundaries. Feldman et al. [57] solve the problem by using adaptive meshes to discretize the simulation domain. Guendelman et al. [58] developed a method that couples a Eulerian fluid simulation to thin shells. The same technique could also be used to represent boundary conditions.

In particle-based simulations, the boundary condition can be applied to individual particles. For two-way interaction between fluids and other objects, the forces or impulses used to enforce the boundary conditions on the particles can be applied to the boundary [59].

Another practical difficulty in Eulerian fluid simulations is the surface representation. Usually, the interface is tracked in the velocity field by integration. However, due to integration errors, the total volume of the fluid can change. In practice, this leads to mass loss, especially in thin sheets that cannot be resolved by the simulation grid. In contrast, in an SPH simulation, mass is carried by the particles, thus mass preservation is guaranteed.

A major disadvantage of SPH simulation, especially for fluids like water, is the inherent compressibility of the resulting material. In Eulerian simulations, it is relatively easy to enforce incompressibility by solving a global linear system. An analogous method exists for SPH simulation [60,61]. In practice, methods that use an auxiliary grid to solve for a divergence-free velocity field [62,63,50] are more common.

Fluid simulation using particle methods is a topic of ongoing research. Until now, it has been used mainly in interactive or real-time settings with relatively few particles. Particle methods are relatively easy to implement, and the simple interaction with objects simulated using different simulation methods is an advantage, for example, in computer games. The surface tracking method discussed above, although not suitable for real-time environments, offers tangible advantages over level-set methods. Still, large simulations with photorealistic results have for the most part been left to Eulerian approaches, although recent work has produced results of visual quality comparable to Eulerian simulations [50]. Depending on the application at hand, one should carefully choose which simulation method is most appropriate.

REFERENCES

[1] [NMK+05] Andrew Nealen, Matthias Müller, Richard Keiser, Eddy Boxerman, and Mark Carlson. Physically based deformable models in computer graphics. *Eurographics 2005 State-of-the-Art Report (STAR)*, 2005.

[2] T. Belytschko, Y. Krongauz, D. Organ, M. Fleming, P. Krysl, Meshless methods: an overview and recent developments, Comput. Meth. Appl. Mech. Eng. 139 (1996) 3–47.

[3] G.-R. Liu, Mesh-Free Methods, CRC Press, Boca Raton, FL, 2002.

[4] T.P. Fries, H.G. Matthies, Classification and overview of meshfree methods, Technical report, TU Brunswick, Germany, Nr. 2003-03, 2003.

[5] M. Desbrun, M.-P. Cani, Smoothed particles: a new paradigm for animating highly deformable bodies, 6th Eurographics Workshop on Computer Animation and Simulation 1996, pp. 61–76, 1996.

[6] M. Müller, R. Keiser, A. Nealen, M. Pauly, M. Gross, M. Alexa, Point-based animation of elastic, plastic, and melting objects, pp. 141-151, 2004.

[7] T.J. Chung, Applied Continuum Mechanics, Cambridge University Press, UK, 1996.

[8] M. Müller, M. Gross, Interactive virtual materials, Proceedings of the 2004 Conference on Graphics Interface, pp. 239-246, Canadian Human-Computer Communications Society, 2004.

[9] J.J. Monaghan, Smoothed particle hydrodynamics, Ann. Rev. Astron. Phys. 30 (1992) 543.

[10] M. Müller, D. Charypar, M. Gross, Particle-based fluid simulation for interactive applications, pp. 154-159, 2003.

[11] P. Lancaster, K. Salkauskas, Surfaces generated by moving least squares methods, Math. Comput. 37 (1981) 141-158.

[12] W.H. Press, S.A. Teukolsky, W.T. Vetterling, B.P. Flannery, Numerical Recipes in C: The Art of Scientific Computing, second ed., Cambridge University Press, UK, 1992.

[13] J.F. O'Brien, A.W. Bargteil, J.K. Hodgins, Graphical modeling and animation of ductile fracture, ACM Trans. Graph. (2002) 291-294 (SIGGRAPH 2002 Proceedings).

[14] [PKA+05] Mark Pauly, Richard Keiser, Bart Adams, Philip Dutré, Markus Gross, and Leonidas J. Guibas. Meshless animation of fracturing solids. *ACM Transactions on Graphics*, SIGGRAPH 2005 Proceedings, 24(3):957-964, 2005.

[15] [TF88] Demetri Terzopoulos and Kurt Fleischer. Modeling inelastic deformation: Viscolelasticity, plasticity, fracture. In *Computer Graphics*, SIGGRAPH 1988 Proceedings, pages 269-278. ACM Press, New York, NY, 1988.

[16] K. Hirota, Y. Tanoue, T. Kaneko, Generation of crack patterns with a physical model, Vis. Comput. 14 (1998) 126-137.

[17] [SWB00] Jeffrey Smith, AndrewWitkin, and David Baraff. Fast and controllable simulation of the shattering of brittle objects. In *Graphics Interface*, pages 27-34, May 2000.

[18] J.F. O'Brien, J.K. Hodgins, Graphical modeling and animation of brittle fracture, Computer Graphics, SIGGRAPH 1999, Proceedings, pp. 287-296, ACM Press, 1999.

[19] N. Molino, Z. Bao, R. Fedkiw, A virtual node algorithm for changing mesh topology during simulation, ACM Trans. Graph. 23 (2004) 385-392 (SIGGRAPH 2004 Proceedings).

[20] [BK0+96] Ted Belytschko, Y. Krongauz, D. Organ, Michael Fleming, and Petr Krysl. Meshless methods: An overview and recent developments. *Computer Methods in Applied Mechanics and Engineering*, 139(3):3-47, 1996.

[21] M. Ortiz, A. Pandolfi, Finite-deformation irreversible cohesive elements for three-dimensional crack-propagation analysis, Int. J. Num. Meth. Eng. 44 (1999) 1267-1282.

[22] [TPBF87] Demetri Terzopoulos, John Platt, Alan Barr, and Kurt Fleischer. Elastically deformable models. In *Computer Graphics*, SIGGRAPH 1987 Proceedings, pages 205-214, July 1987.

[23] D. Bielser, P. Glardon, M. Teschner, M. Gross, A state machine for real-time cutting of tetrahedral meshes, Pacific Graphics, pp. 377-386, 2003.

[24] M. Müller, L. McMillan, J. Dorsey, R. Jagnow, Real-time simulation of deformation and fracture of stiff materials, EUROGRAPHICS 2001 Computer Animation and Simulation Workshop, pp. 27-34, 2001.

[25] T. Belytschko, Y. Lu, L. Gu, Element-free Galerkin methods, Int. J. Numer. Meth. Eng. 37 (1994) 229-256.

[26] D. Organ, M. Fleming, T. Terry, T. Belytschko, Continuous meshless approximations for nonconvex bodies by diffraction and transparency, Comput. Mech. 18 (1996) 1-11.

[27] T.L. Anderson, Fracture Mechanics, CRC Press, 1995.

[28] L.J. Guibas, D.H. Marimont, Rounding arrangements dynamically. SCG 1995: Proceedings of the Eleventh Annual Symposium on Computational Geometry, pp. 190-199, ACM Press, New York, NY, 1995.

[29] R. Keiser, M. Müller, B. Heidelberger, M. Teschner, M. Gross, Contact handling for deformable point-based objects. Proceedings of Vision, Modeling, Visualization (VMV) 2004, pp. 339-347, November 2004.

[30] [FW60] George E. Forsythe and Wolfgang R. Warsow. *Finite-difference Methods for Partial Differential Equations*. Dover Publications, 1960.

[31] [And95a] John D. Anderson. *Computational Fluid Dynamics*. McGraw-Hill, 1995.

[32] [FM97] Nick Foster and Dimitri Metaxas. Modeling the motion of hot, turbulent gas. In *Computer Graphics*, SIGGRAPH 1997 Proceedings, pages 181-188, 1997.

[33] J. Stam. Stable fluids. Computer Graphics, SIGGRAPH 1999 Proceedings, pp. 121-128, ACM Press, 1999.

[34] N. Foster, R. Fedkiw, Practical animation of liquids, Computer Graphics, SIGGRAPH 2001 Proceedings, pp. 23-30, 2001.

[35] F. Losasso, F. Gibou, R. Fedkiw, Simulating water and smoke with an octree data structure, ACM Trans. Graph. 23 (2004) 457-462 (SIGGRAPH 2004 Proceedings).

[36] B.E. Feldman, J.F. O'Brien, O. Arikan, Animating suspended particle explosions, ACM Trans. Graph. 22 (2003) 708-715 (SIGGRAPH 2003 Proceedings).

[37] [LuC77] L.B. Lucy. A numerical approach to the testing of the fission hypothesis. *Astronomical Journal*, 82(12):1013-1024, 1977.

[38] [GM77] Robert A. Gingold and Joe J. Monaghan. Smoothed particle hydrodynamics: Theory and application to nonspherical stars. *Monthly Notices of the Royal Astronomical Society*, 181:375-389, 1977.

[39] W.T. Reeves, Particle systems – a technique for modeling a class of fuzzy objects, ACM Trans. Graph. 2 (1983) 91-108.

[40] J. Stam, E. Fiume, Depicting fire and other gaseous phenomena using diffusion processes, Computer Graphics, SIGGRAPH 1995 Proceedings, pp. 129-136, 1995.

[41] D.R. Peachey, Modeling waves and surf, Computer Graphics, SIGGRAPH 1986 Proceedings, pp. 65-74, 1986.

[42] M.E. Goss, Motion simulation: a real-time particle system for display of ship wakes, IEEE Comput. Graph. Appl. 10 (1990) 30-35.

[43] [Rey87] Craig W. Reynolds. Flocks, herds, and schools: A distributed behavioral model. In *Computer Graphics*, SIGGRAPH 1987 Proceedings, pages 25-34, 1987.

[44] D. Tonnesen, Spatially coupled particle systems, SIGGRAPH 1992 Course 16 Notes: Particle System Modeling, Animation, and Physically Based Techniques, pp. 4.1-4.21, 1992.

[45] J.J. Monaghan, Smoothed particle hydrodynamics, Rep. Prog. Phys. 68 (2005) 1703-1759.

[46] G.-R. Liu, M.B. Liu, Smoothed Particle Hydrodynamics, World Scientific, 2003.

[47] J.J. Monaghan, Simulating free surface flows with SPH, J. Comput. Phys. 110 (1994) 399-406.

[48] M. Harris, Real-time cloud simulation and rendering. Ph.D. thesis, The University of North Carolina at Chapel Hill, 2003.

[49] J.F. Blinn, A generalization of algebraic surface drawing, ACM Trans. Graph. 1 (1982) 235–256.

[50] Y. Zhu, R. Bridson, Animating sand as a fluid, ACM Trans. Graph. 24 (2005) 965–972 (SIGGRAPH 2005 Proceedings).

[51] M. Müller, B. Solenthaler, R. Keiser, M. Gross, Particle-based fiuid-fluid interaction, 237–244, 2005.

[52] S. Osher, J.A. Sethian, Fronts propagating with curvature-dependent speed: algorithms based on Hamilton-Jacobi formulations, J. Comput. Phys. 79 (1988) 12–49.

[53] D. Enright, S. Marschner, R. Fedkiw, Animation and rendering of complex water surfaces, ACM Trans. Graph. (2002) 736–744 (SIGGRAPH 2002 Proceedings).

[54] D. Enright, F. Losasso, R. Fedkiw, A fast and accurate semi-Lagrangian particle level set, Comput. Struct. 83 (2005) 479–490.

[55] R. Keiser, B. Adams, D. Gasser, P. Bazzi, P. Dutré, M. Gross, A unified Lagrangian approach to solid-fluid animation, Proceedings of the Eurographics Symposium on Point-based Graphics, pp. 125–148, 2005.

[56] M. Desbrun, M.-P. Cani-Gascuel, Active implicit surface for animation, Proceedings of Graphics Interface, pp. 143–150, 1998.

[57] B.E. Feldman, J.F. O'Brien, B.M. Klingner, Animating gases with hybrid meshes, Proceedings of ACM SIGGRAPH 2003, pp. 904–909, 2005.

[58] E. Guendelman, A. Selle, F. Losasso, R. Fedkiw, Coupling water and smoke to thin deformable and rigid shells, ACM Trans. Graph. 24 (2005) 973–981.

[59] M. Müller, S. Schirm, M. Teschner, B. Heidelberger, M. Gross, Interaction of fluids with deformable solids, Proceedings of Computer Animation and Virtual Worlds, pp. 159–171, 2004.

[60] S. Kochizuka, Y. Oka, Moving particle semi-implicit method for fragmentation of incompressible fluid, Nucl. Sci. Eng. 123 (1996) 421–434.

[61] S. Premoze, T. Tasdizen, J. Bigler, A. Lefohn, R. Whitaker, Particle-based simulation of fluids, Proceedings of Eurographics 2003, pp. 401–410, 2003.

[62] F.H. Harlow, The particle in cell computing methods for fluid dynamics, Meth. Comput. Phys. 3:319–343, 1964.

[63] J.U. Brackbill, H.M. Ruppel, Flip: a method for adaptively zoned, particle-in-cell calculations of fluid flows in two dimensions, J. Comput. Phys. 65 (1986) 314–343.

Animating with MEL for MAYA

Maya Under the Hood

Mark R. Wilkins
Chris Kazmier

CHAPTER CONTENTS

In this chapter, you will learn

- That, to Maya, your scene is nothing more than a collection of nodes and connections, which together compose the dependency graph
- What a dependency graph node is and how it relates to what you see in the 3D viewer
- That the Channel Box and Attribute Editor windows are the Maya interface's most commonly used tools to manipulate the attributes of dependency graph nodes
- That certain nodes, but not all, are part of the transform hierarchy, which establishes spatial relationships among objects
- How to use the Outliner, the Hypergraph, and the Connection Editor to examine how nodes fit into the dependency graph and the transform hierarchy
- How common tasks, such as creating objects, setting animation keyframes, and modeling NURBS surfaces, change the dependency graph and the transform hierarchy
- That Maya's graphic user interface, including menus, toolbars, the timeline, and so on, are built and can be modified with MEL.

10.1 WHY LOOK UNDER THE HOOD?

One reason some animators find MEL scripting tricky to learn is that it requires an understanding of many details of how the pieces of a scene work together, details that the Maya user interface works hard to hide. This chapter opens up many of those details and relates them to what a Maya animator sees in the interface when working without scripting.

Knowing how a Maya scene fits together is important, even when you work entirely without MEL scripting. Thus, if you're an experienced Maya animator, you will already know much of what this chapter describes. However, keeping track of your Maya scene's components and how they fit together becomes critical when developing MEL scripts because, unlike the user interface, MEL forces you to work frequently with your Maya scene at this lower level, doing much less to hide its complexity from you.

10.2 THE DEPENDENCY GRAPH, ATTRIBUTES, AND CONNECTIONS

Internally, every part of a scene, whether it is 3D geometry, animation, an expression relationship, a light, a texture, or the arguments that were used to create an object with history, is represented as one or more nodes, or, more completely, dependency graph or DG nodes. Each node has a set of attributes, each of which stores a characteristic of the thing the node represents. All of these nodes together with all of their connections are called the dependency graph or the scene graph (Fig. 10.1).

One useful source of information about DG nodes is Maya's Node and Attribute Reference, which is available from the Help menu. This document describes most, if not all, of the nodes that are built into Maya, along with their attributes and what function they serve in a scene.

Attributes themselves have characteristics that control how you can manipulate them. Attributes may be locked, which prevents them from being changed. They can be marked keyable, which permits you to animate them by setting keyframes, or nonkeyable, in which case you can't.

Also, each attribute has a data type, which specifies what kind of information the attribute can store. In Maya, attributes can store

- Integer numbers (with no fractional part)
- Floating-point numbers (with a fractional part)
- Strings, which can be a combination of text and numbers
- Boolean values, which are on/off or true/false values
- Enumerated values, which store a value selected from a list of choices defined when the attribute is created
- Also, some attributes store collections of data of the above types, including arrays, vectors, and matrices.

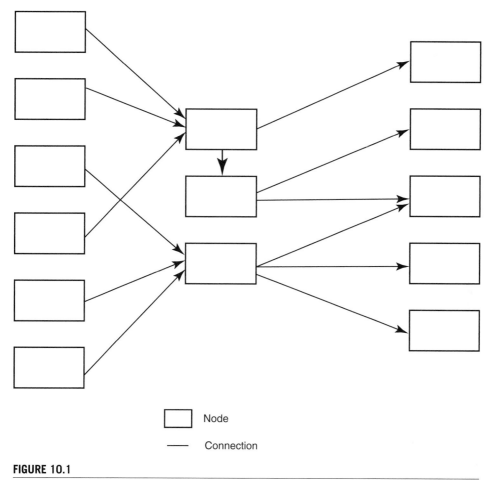

	Node
—	Connection

FIGURE 10.1

The dependency graph.

One important use of MEL is to create and connect DG nodes that create a particular result when your scene is played back. At first, a good way to learn how nodes and connections work to create animation is to animate by hand, then to examine the nodes and connections that Maya has created while you have done so. Later, as we get further into the MEL language, you will learn how to build networks of nodes and attribute connections with scripts. Seeing what Maya does when you animate without scripting can serve as an important source for ideas about how to script complex tasks.

The Channel Box, part of the standard Maya layout, displays the one or more nodes (in this instance `directionalLight1` and `directionalLightShape1`) that make up the selected object (Fig. 10.2).

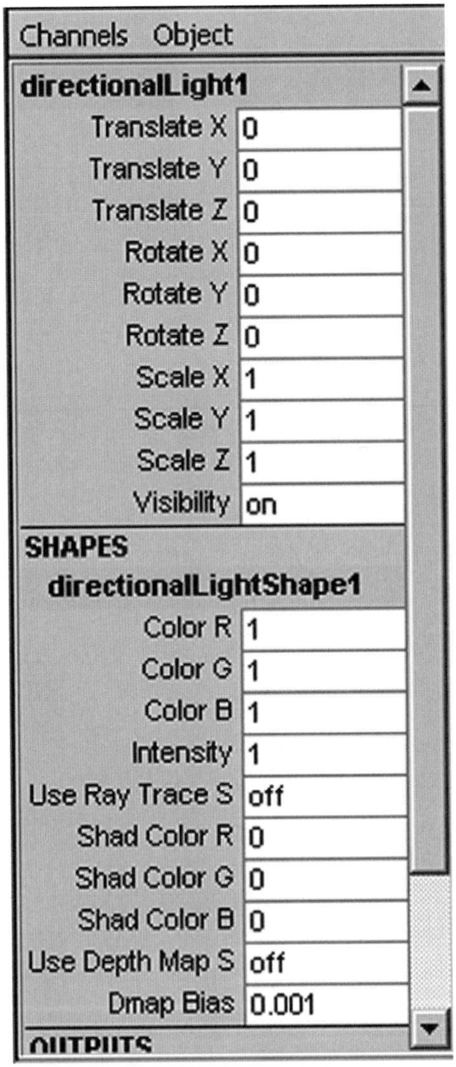

Channels Object	
directionalLight1	▲
Translate X	0
Translate Y	0
Translate Z	0
Rotate X	0
Rotate Y	0
Rotate Z	0
Scale X	1
Scale Y	1
Scale Z	1
Visibility	on
SHAPES	
directionalLightShape1	
Color R	1
Color G	1
Color B	1
Intensity	1
Use Ray Trace S	off
Shad Color R	0
Shad Color G	0
Shad Color B	0
Use Depth Map S	off
Dmap Bias	0.001
OUTPUTS	▼

FIGURE 10.2

The Channel Box.

The Channel Box displays only those attributes that are keyable, because those are the attributes that are most frequently edited while you work. Editing other attributes is usually done through the Attribute Editor (Fig. 10.3). Even the Attribute Editor, though, does not display every attribute. Certain attributes can be manipulated only through MEL scripts and expressions.

The Attribute Editor displays the selected node's attributes as a series of groups that can be expanded by clicking on the arrow button to their left. In the example shown in Fig. 10.3, Directional Light Attributes is one such group. Also, connected nodes appear as tabs at the top of the Attribute Editor to allow you easy access to other nodes related to the one you are editing.

The Attribute Editor allows you to add your own attributes as well, using the choices on the Attributes menu.

A final important characteristic of attributes is that they can be connected to each other. Connecting two attributes forces the value of one attribute to remain the same as the value of another attribute. These connections are directional, meaning, for example, that if you connect one attribute to another you can change the first attribute all you like and the second will follow, but the second attribute cannot be changed because its value is being driven by the connection with the first. You can set up connections between nodes with the Connection Editor (Fig. 10.4).

This characteristic of connection is what gives the dependency graph its name. It's a "graph" because that's a term for a network of connected nodes, and "dependency" refers to the way that each connected node depends on the values of the nodes that connect to it. Nodes whose attribute values connect to the current node are upstream nodes, and nodes that depend on the current node are downstream nodes. The idea of a scene graph like Maya's dependency graph is common in computer animation systems; 3D Studio Max and Softimage, for example, each use scene graph structures.

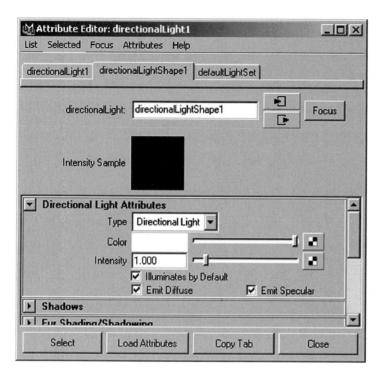

FIGURE 10.3

Attribute Editor.

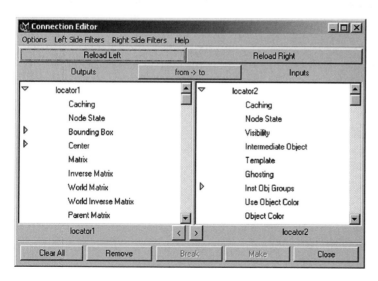

FIGURE 10.4

Connection Editor.

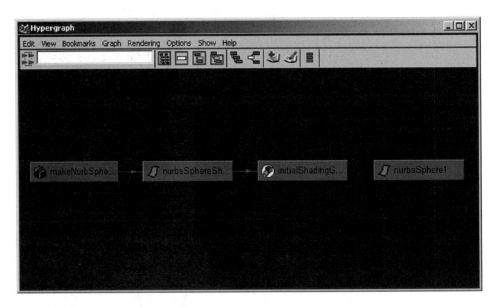

FIGURE 10.5

Viewing connections with the Hypergraph.

The most useful tool for seeing interconnections between multiple nodes is the Hypergraph window (Fig. 10.5), which you can reach by choosing Window > Hypergraph ... from the main menu. With the Hypergraph, you can see the connections that have been made to the selected node by selecting the node and choosing Graph > Up and Downstream Connections from the window's menus.

Note that it is not possible to view the entire scene in Up and Downstream Connections mode. Because there can be so many nodes and connections in even a relatively simple scene, this view in the Hypergraph displays only the connections that lead to the selected object so that working in the Hypergraph remains manageable. While viewing nodes in this mode, you can move the pointer over the arrows that represent connections to see what attributes are connected.

To see how a simple Maya scene is represented as a dependency graph, let's examine what happens when you animate a bouncing ball. For the sake of simplicity, let's assume the ball is only moving along one axis.

As a first pass at animating this ball (Fig. 10.6), you might set three keyframes on the ball's vertical motion at, say, 0 frames, 10 frames, and 20 frames into the animation.

As you work, each action you perform creates nodes and connections behind the scenes. First, as seen in Fig. 10.7, creating the sphere makes three connected nodes.

Then, setting the animation keyframes creates and connects another node (Fig. 10.8), this time an animation curve that drives the `translateY` attribute of `nurbsSphere1`. When you play back the scene, Maya's `time1` node, the scene's clock, tells the animation curve which frame number's value to look up. Then, the animation curve sets the `translateY` attribute to the right value. Finally, Maya draws the sphere where you've placed it.

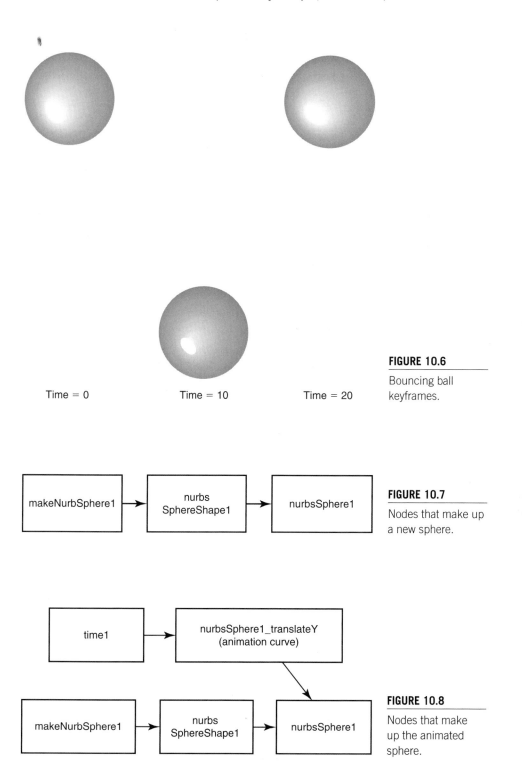

Time = 0   Time = 10   Time = 20

FIGURE 10.6

Bouncing ball keyframes.

| makeNurbSphere1 | → | nurbs SphereShape1 | → | nurbsSphere1 |

FIGURE 10.7

Nodes that make up a new sphere.

| time1 | → | nurbsSphere1_translateY (animation curve) |

| makeNurbSphere1 | → | nurbs SphereShape1 | → | nurbsSphere1 |

FIGURE 10.8

Nodes that make up the animated sphere.

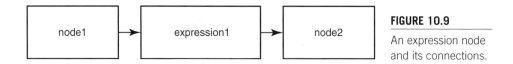

FIGURE 10.9

An expression node and its connections.

As you can tell, simple operations in Maya, such as making a primitive or animating an attribute, have complex implications under the surface. One of the strengths of the MEL language is that it can make it easier to set up large networks of nodes to perform a task.

Maya's concept of an expression is more complex than that of a simple connection between attributes, in that an expression can calculate one attribute from another using mathematical operations or almost any other method that you can script in MEL. A connection simply sets one attribute's value to be the same as another's.

How this works is that creating an expression with the Expression Editor or by typing in the Channel Box makes a new node, an expression node. This node contains the expression script and can calculate the expression's output value from its inputs. If you create an expression that calculates an attribute value for node2 from an attribute value in node1, you get the result shown in Fig. 10.9.

10.3 EXAMPLE 1: USING THE HYPERGRAPH TO EXPLORE THE DEPENDENCY GRAPH

This example demonstrates how to use the Hypergraph to examine how nodes are connected in a scene. First, we'll look at the example, an animated bouncing ball.

1. Make a new scene by choosing File > New Scene from the main menu.
2. Create a sphere by clicking on the Sphere tool or choosing Create > NURBS Primitives > Sphere.
3. Move the sphere up 10 units by typing 10 into the Translate Y field in the Channel Box.
4. Click on the 10 in the Translate Y field of the Channel Box. Then, right-click on the field and choose Key Selected from the menu that appears. The Translate Y field should change color.
5. Click on Frame 10 in the timeline to advance the time. The current time marker should move ahead to Frame 10, leaving behind a red mark indicating a keyframe on Frame 0.
6. Type 0 into the Translate Y field; press Enter to commit the change, and set another keyframe using Key Selected.
7. Click on frame 20 to advance the time, and set a Translate Y keyframe with a value of 10.
8. Rewind and play back the animation.

9. Make sure the sphere is selected, and then choose Window > Hypergraph... . When the Hypergraph window appears, use Alt + MMB to drag the view so that the selected sphere object is in the center. Note the trapezoidal shape, which indicates that the sphere has been animated.
10. Choose Graph > Up and Downstream Connections from the Hypergraph menu. Now, you should be able to see the nodes that make up the sphere as well as several connected nodes, as shown in Fig. 10.10.

In the Hypergraph, you can use the same mouse controls that allow you to move around in perspective and orthographic views. With Alt + LMB + MMB you can zoom in and out, and with Alt + MMB you can track side to side and up and down. Also, as in other views, you can click on a node to select it.

Try moving your pointer over some of the connections. You can see the names of the connected attributes when you do so. If you want to delete a connection, you can click it and press Backspace or Delete. To make a new connection, drag with the middle mouse button from one node to another, and the Connection Editor will pop up with those nodes already loaded, ready to connect attributes.

The colors of the connections indicate whether the arrow represents connected attributes whose data types are a single numeric value (blue), an array (green), or a more complex type of data (pink) such as a matrix or geometry.

In Fig. 10.10, an animation curve called nurbsSphere1_translateY is connected to the trapezoidal nurbsSphere1 node. This node is called a transform node, and

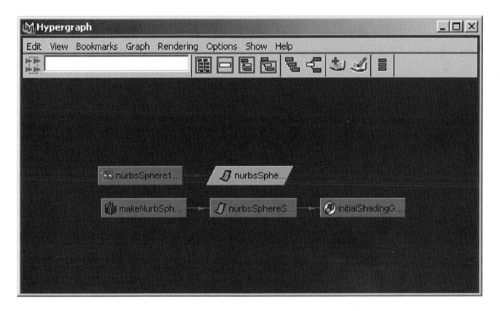

FIGURE 10.10

Up- and down-stream connections for an animated sphere.

the related `nurbsSphereShape1` is called a shape node. The relationship between transform and shape nodes is discussed later in this chapter, but for now it's enough to know that the transform node defines where the ball is in space, and the shape node defines the ball's geometric shape.

Two connections we discussed earlier are not represented in this view in the Hypergraph. First is the connection from the transform node to the shape node, and second is the connection from Maya's scene clock, called time1, to the animation curve. Both of these kinds of connections are hidden by default to reduce clutter, because most animation curves are driven by the current time, and most shapes are connected to the similarly named transform.

Now, let's look at a more complex scene. We will create a series of joints that cause a sphere object to bend, and then look at how the resulting nodes are connected.

1. Make a new scene.
2. Tumble your perspective view so that you're facing the XZ plane; create a sphere.
3. Set Scale X for the new sphere to 3.
4. Select the Joint Tool, make three joints inside your sphere object, and then press Enter to finish.
5. Select the joints and the sphere object, and then choose Skin > Bind Skin > Rigid Bind.
6. Select the middle joint, choose the Rotate Tool, and then rotate the joint to see that the sphere is bound to the joint (Fig. 10.11).
7. Select the sphere and choose Window > Hypergraph from the main menu.
8. Choose Graph > Up and Downstream Connections from the Hypergraph's menus.
9. Choose Show > Show Auxillary Nodes.

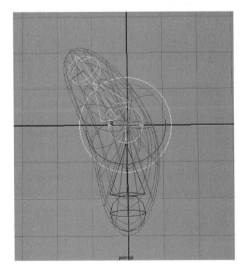

FIGURE 10.11

Scaled sphere bound to three joints.

Results are shown in Fig. 10.12.

In this example, following the pink connections gives you a general idea of how Maya manipulates the geometry as it calculates how the joints have affected the shape of the sphere. On the far left of Fig. 10.12 is the `makeNurbSphere1` history node, connected to the old `nurbsSphereShape1` node, which has been renamed `nurbsSphereShape1Orig` and has been hidden. Hidden nodes appear grayed out in the Hypergraph.

Farther to the right, after a number of tweak, group, and joint cluster nodes that Maya sets up automatically when you choose Rigid Bind, is the new `nurbsSphereShape1` node, which contains the deformed geometry. Finally, the Hypergraph contains some hidden

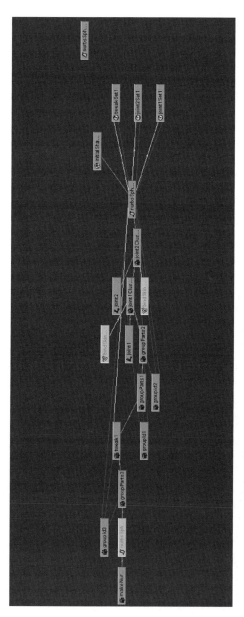

FIGURE 10.12

cluster handles for the clusters of points that each joint controls and some Set nodes that define the sets of points that each joint influences.

10.4 TRANSFORM HIERARCHY AND PARENT/CHILD RELATIONSHIPS

While the dependency graph describes how nodes' attribute values depend on each other, Maya also keeps track of additional geometric relationships among nodes that represent objects in 3D space such as NURBS surfaces, meshes, joints, and locators. These relationships make up a structure called the transform hierarchy, or just the hierarchy. Maya actually also implements the hierarchy as connections between nodes, but the Hypergraph does not display these connections in the connections viewing modes in order to keep the graph free of clutter.

The relationships between nodes that make up the transform hierarchy include grouping and parent/child relationships. In a parent/child relationship, the child's position, rotation, and scaling in world space are the effect of its position, rotation, and scaling attributes, added on to the effect of its parent, and so on. To see how this works, here is an example in which we think of nodes called Grandparent, Parent, and Child. Each node's translate X and translate Y attribute values are shown in Fig. 10.13.

Since each child's translation is added to that of its parent, the translate X and translate Y attributes of the node called Parent add on to those of the Grandparent node (which happen to be zero) to put it at an X position of 1 and a Y location of 2 in world space. The node called Child, when its own local translate X and translate Y values are added on, is at a world space location of $X = 2$ and $Y = 4$.

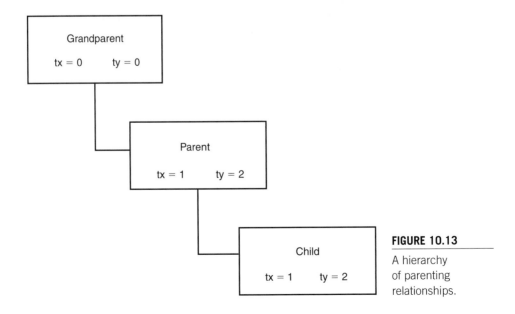

FIGURE 10.13

A hierarchy of parenting relationships.

From the example in Fig. 10.13, you can see some of the rules that govern the geometric relationships represented in the hierarchy. A summary of these rules follows:

- The values of a node's translation, rotation, and scaling attributes do not describe its position in the entire scene's 3D world but only describe its position relative to its parent.
- The translation, rotation, and scaling of a node with respect to the entire scene is the cumulative effect of the node's attributes, and its parent's, and the parent's parent's, and so on.
- A parent can have multiple children.

There's one more rule, though, that may seem not to make sense:

- A child can have multiple parents.

The reason this last rule might seem confusing is that if a child hierarchy node has multiple parents, presumably with their own values for translate, rotate, and scale attributes, it would seem that this would mean that the same object (the child object) would be in two different places. In fact, Maya allows you to do exactly that in its instancing feature. When you instance an object or part of a hierarchy, you make a copy that is linked to the original in that a change to either the copy or the original changes both. In the hierarchy, this is represented as one node having two different parents whose attributes place it in two different places.

The above rules also explain why, when you move a parent, the children move as well: moving the parent changes its translation, rotation, and scaling attributes, which affect the children because the parent's attributes are being added on to the children's attributes to find where the children are in global space.

Some nodes that do not have a meaningful location in 3D space, such as constraints or object sets, are in the hierarchy and can have objects parented underneath them. These objects have no effect on the location in space of their child nodes. In calculating where objects appear in global space, Maya treats them as if their children were parented directly to their parents, and moving them in the hierarchy has no effect on how the objects in the scene appear. They are present in the hierarchy just to allow the animator to place them where they can serve as a meaningful reminder of their function.

10.5 EXAMINING THE HIERARCHY

Maya provides a couple of ways to view the hierarchy that can be useful for different purposes. First, the Hypergraph's Scene Hierarchy view is one way to view the hierarchy. You can reach it by choosing Window > Hypergraph ... from the main menus and then choosing Graph > Scene Hierarchy from the Hypergraph menus.

> **Note:** If the Scene Hierarchy menu item is grayed out, you are probably already viewing in hierarchy mode!

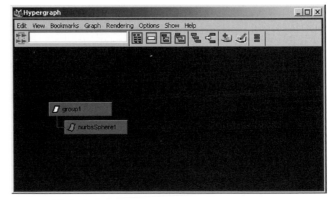

FIGURE 10.14

The same scene in the Outliner and the Hypergraph.

Another common way to view the hierarchy is to open the Outliner window by choosing Window > Outliner... . The Outliner makes it easy to collapse parts of the hierarchy that are of less interest and to expand those that are of more interest by clicking on the [+] buttons to expand and the [−] to collapse parts of the tree (Fig. 10.14).

10.6 TRANSFORM AND SHAPE NODES

At first, it seems that there are many different kinds of nodes that have the basic set of attributes that are needed for a node to make sense in the hierarchy: translation, rotation, scaling, scale pivot point location, rotation pivot point location, and so on.

Actually, most nodes that appear in the Outliner by default are actually a combination of two nodes, a transform node whose attributes store all of the information about where an object is in space and how it's scaled, and a shape node that stores the object's actual geometric shape and properties of its construction and rendering. Looking back at Fig. 10.6, which shows the nodes that are created when you create a NURBS sphere in an empty scene, you'll notice a node called `nurbsSphereShape1` connected to the `nurbsSphere1` that appears in the Outliner. `nurbsSphere1` is a transform node and `nurbsSphereShape` is a NURBS shape node.

There are many kinds of shape nodes (including NURBS surfaces, meshes, lights, cameras, and locators, among others) but only one kind of transform node. One implication of this is that if you have a MEL script that moves or places one kind of object in space, it's easy to adapt it to work with other kinds of objects.

If you want to see the shape nodes in the Outliner window, you can choose Display > Shapes from the window's menus. If you want to see the shape nodes in the Hypergraph, you can choose Options > Display > Shape Nodes from the Hypergraph window's menus.

10.7 EXAMPLE 2: EXPLORING TRANSFORM AND SHAPE NODES, INSTANCING, AND HISTORY

This example shows you how an object you can manipulate in the 3D view is built up of nodes in Maya and how the developers of Maya have implemented common operations, such as instancing and history, as manipulations of the relationships between nodes.

First, create a sphere:

1. Start Maya or choose File > New Scene.
2. Choose Create > NURBS Primitives > Sphere.

A sphere appears, which you can manipulate as a single object. Look in the Channel Box at the top, and you will see the name nurbsSphere1, the object's name. Now, open the Outliner:

3. Choose Window > Outliner … .

and you see your nurbsSphere1 object selected.

So far, there are not many indications that the nurbsSphere1 object is particularly complex. Now, though, we'll turn on Shape display in the Outliner window:

4. In the Outliner window, choose Display > Shapes.

Click on the [+] that expands the nurbsSphere1 entry in the outline. Results are shown in Fig. 10.15.

Now, what had seemed a single object is revealed to be made up of two nodes. The first, nurbsSphere1, is the sphere's transform node, and the second, nurbs-SphereShape1, is the shape node (specifically in this case, a NURBS shape node). Note that when you turn on shape node visibility, the shape node has the NURBS icon, and the transform node that before was represented by the NURBS surface icon acquires the generic transform icon to show you what type of node it is.

Note that when you select the transform node nurbsSphere1, the Channel Box lists the transform node, the shape node, and the history node makeNurbSphere1, while when you select the shape node you only see it and the history node. The Channel Box generally displays related transform and history nodes for easy access to their keyable attributes.

Using the Duplicate command, we can create an instance of the sphere:

1. Select nurbsSphere1 in the Outliner if it is not already selected.
2. Choose Edit > Duplicate > ☐.
3. In the Duplicate window, select the Instance button under Geometry Type.
4. Click Apply.
5. Make sure to select Copy under Geometry Type, and then close the window.

Note: If you do not select Copy before closing the window, then all duplicates you make from now on will be instances until you change this setting back again!

FIGURE 10.15

The `nurbsSphere1` transform node and its shape node in the Outliner.

FIGURE 10.16

Instances of the sphere in the Outliner.

At this point, if you look in the Outliner, you will see a second sphere object, `nurbsSphere2`. So far, so good. Now, expand it by clicking on the [+]. Instead of having its own shape node, the newly instanced sphere shares its shape node with `nurbsSphere1` (Fig. 10.16). By making one shape node with two transform nodes as parents, Maya allows the same geometry, in essence, to be in two places at once, because the transform node determines an object's location and the shape node defines what it is.

To see what this means in practical terms, move one of your spheres away from the origin and pull some points around:

1. Select `nurbsSphere2` in the Outliner and choose the Move tool.
2. Drag one of the arrows to move the sphere away from nurbsSphere1.
3. Click on the Select by Component Type button.
4. Click on one of the vertices of the sphere and drag it around.

You will see that both spheres change shape simultaneously in response to your editing of one sphere. If you're familiar with instancing, this is what you would expect – but if you know that instancing means that two transforms share the same shape, it's obvious why this works.

There is one more node associated with our sphere objects that is not visible in the Outliner.

1. Select the shape object, `nurbsSphereShape1`, in the Outliner.
2. Choose Window > Hypergraph ....
3. Choose Graph > Up and Downstream Connections.

Centered in the Hypergraph window is our `nurbsSphereShape1` node. To the left is the `makeNurbSphere1` node, with an arrow indicating a connection. To the right is the `initialShadingGroup` node.

When you create an object in Maya, by default it is initially created with history. This means that after creation, you can animate or change the parameters (such as sweep angle or number of spans, in the case of a sphere) that were used to build the object. When you select an object and choose Edit > Delete by Type > History, you freeze the current creation parameters in place for that object so that they cannot be modified.

A node such as `makeNurbSphere1` is what Maya uses to store history information. Deleting history for one or more objects deletes these history nodes and stores the creation parameters in the shape object to which they are connected. In the Hypergraph, you can select `makeNurbSphere1` and examine its parameters, as follows:

1. Right-click on `makeNurbSphere1`, and choose Attribute Editor ... from the menu that appears.
2. In the Attribute Editor, you can see all parameters that were used to create the sphere, and you can edit them, if you like.
3. Close the Attribute Editor window.
4. Click on `nurbsSphereShape1` to select it.
5. In the main Maya window, choose Edit > Delete by Type > History, leaving the Hypergraph window open.

In the Hypergraph window, you will notice that the `makeNurbSphere1` history node goes away.

6. Right-click on `nurbsSphereShape1`, and choose Attribute Editor ....

Note that the NURBS Surface History section contains the parameters you used to create the sphere, but they cannot be changed or animated.

10.8 MEL AND MAYA'S USER INTERFACE

Maya's user interface, which includes all buttons and menus around the edge of the work area, is built using MEL. When you pick a menu item, Maya executes a MEL command specific to that menu item. Some of these MEL commands are human-readable scripts that are installed when you install Maya; others are built-in commands that come as part of Maya's executable.

To see the MEL commands being generated by the user interface, open the Script Editor by clicking the Script Editor button next to the timeline or choosing

Window > General Editors > Script Editor ... from the main menu. Choose Script > Echo All Commands from the Script Editor's menu bar. Then, start picking menu items on the main menu bar to see the MEL commands appear in the Script Editor window.

10.9 WHAT TO REMEMBER ABOUT HOW MAYA WORKS BEHIND THE SCENES

- When you work in the Maya interface, Maya implements what you do as collections of nodes whose attributes are connected to one another to implement the behaviors you've set up in the interface. This structure is called the dependency graph.

- One use for MEL is to automate the construction of nodes and connections in the dependency graph so that scenes that are complex to build by hand can be built easily.

- You can use the Hypergraph as a tool to view, establish, and delete connections between nodes with the Upstream, Downstream, and Up and Downstream Connections views.

- Geometric relationships such as parenting and grouping are implemented in the transform hierarchy.

- Transform hierarchy relationships can be viewed in the Outliner or the Hypergraph (in the Scene Hierarchy view). These relationships are implemented as connections between attributes, but these connections are not displayed in the Connections views in the Hypergraph for the sake of clarity.

- Objects that have a position in space are usually implemented as a transform node and a shape node. The one common exception to this is a joint, which is only one node. In the Outliner, you can view shape nodes by choosing Display > Shapes.

- Another important function of MEL is to build Maya's user interface, including its windows, toolbar buttons, and timeline.

MEL Animation

11

David A. D. Gould

CHAPTER CONTENT

11.1 ANIMATION

MEL provides a lot of commands for creating and editing animations. Also, many of the commands can be very useful for automating a lot of the typical animation tasks. While it is usually the task of an animator to define all the keyframes for an object, using MEL, it is also possible to create, edit, and delete keys. By programmatically generating keyframes, you can create complex animations that would be impossible or simply impractical through more traditional methods. It is also possible to use a MEL script that takes a series of hand-animated keyframes and modifies them in some way. MEL can relieve the animator from a lot of the more mundane and tedious tasks, thereby allowing more time for more creative work.

11.1.1 Time

Any discussion of animation must start with an exact definition of time. This is particularly important in Maya, since time can be defined in many different units, including frames, fields, seconds, minutes, and so on. Internally, Maya stores time in seconds, but it can display it in any convenient format. For example, time can be displayed as frames, even though it is being stored internally in seconds.

The current time unit is defined in the Preferences settings. Select **Window | Settings/Preferences | Preferences**.... Click on the **Settings** category. The **Working Units** will be displayed. By default the time unit is **Film[24fps]**. Changing the time unit scales the current animation to match the new unit. For instance, if you had a key on frame 12 when the time unit was **Film[24fps]**, then changed the unit to **NTSC[30fps]**, the key moves to frame 15, since this preserves its relative location in time. At frame 12, using film units, it was at 0.5 s. Under NTSC it has to be moved to frame 15 to ensure that it maintains it location at 0.5 s.

Use the following command to determine what the current time unit is:

```
currentUnit -query -time;
```

To set the current time unit, use

```
currentUnit -time "min"; // Set time unit to minutes
```

By default, Maya adjusts all the keyframes relative to the new unit so that the relative times of keyframes are maintained. To set the current time unit without automatically changing the location of any keys, use the following:

```
currentUnit -time "min" -updateAnimation false;
```

It is important to understand that all MEL commands operate using the current working time unit. If the time unit is set to **Film[24fps]**, the time is specified in frames. If it is set to **milliseconds**, it is specified in milliseconds. When writing MEL scripts, never assume that you know in advance what the working time unit is. The currentTime command is used to set the current time. It does not have the same result if the working time units are different.

```
currentTime 10;
```

If the time unit were set to **Film[24fps]**, this would set the current time to frame 10. If the time unit were in **milliseconds**, this would set the current time to 10 ms. If you need to specify absolute times, irrespective of the current unit, you can append this to the time value. For example, the following command always sets the current time to 2 s:

```
currentTime 2sec;
```

You can use any of the following units after the value: hour, min, sec, millisec, game, film, pal, ntsc, show, palf, ntscf. Setting the current time to 1¼ h can be done as follows:

```
currentTime 1.25hour;
```

The units that don't correspond to standard time value are given in frames per second (fps), as shown in Table 11.1.

To be more precise, NTSC actually plays at 29.97 fps, so rendering at 30 fps requires you to drop frames in the final composite or edit. If outputting to SECAM, simply use the PAL setting, since they both have the same speed.

Table 11.1 Times Units		
Unit	**Description**	**FPS**
game	Games animation speed	15
film	Standard motion picture film	24
pal	PAL video format (frames)	25
ntsc	NTSC video format (frames)	30
show	Show format (frames)	48
palf	PAL video format (fields)	50 (2× frame rate)
ntscf	NTSC video format (fields)	60 (2× frame rate)

When you ask for the value of a given attribute, it will, by default, get the value at the current time.

```
currentTime 5;
getAttr sphere.translateX; // Get attribute at time=5
```

It is possible to use getAttr with an alternative time.

```
currentTime 5;
getAttr -time 10 sphere.translateX; // Get attribute at time=10
```

This feature can be particularly handy when you are getting the values of attributes from different objects at different times. You aren't forced to set the currentTime beforehand. Unfortunately, not all commands provide this. The setAttr command, for instance, allows you to set an attribute's value only at the current time. Since changing the current time causes the entire scene to update, this can be expensive if you just want to change the time, apply some commands, then return to the previous time. Fortunately, it is possible to change the current time without updating the scene. The following example changes the current time, sets a value, then returns to the previous time. Simply use -update false flag to prevent the update of the scene.

```
float $cTime = currentTime -query;  // Get the current time
currentTime -update false 10;  // Go to frame 10 but don't update
                               the scene
setAttr sphere.translateX 23.4;     // Set the attribute value at
                                       frame 10
currentTime -update false $cTime;   // Restore the previous time
```

11.1.2 **Playback**

Maya provides a variety of commands to directly control the playback of the current animation. These options define the playback in Maya's viewports and not the speed of the final animation. This is considered the interactive real-time playback speed, since Maya is calculating the animation at each frame and then displaying it. The speed at which the animation is displayed in the interactive viewports is dependent on many factors including the speed of your machine, the complexity of the scene, and the 3D graphics card used.

1. Open the **SimpleAnimatedSphere.ma** scene.

2. Click on the **Play** button.

   A sphere moves from left to right across the screen.

3. Execute the following in the **Script Editor**:

   ```
   play;
   ```

   The animation is played. The play command is used to play the animation. It is possible to control the direction of playback and other options. Without stopping the playback, complete the following.

4. Execute the following in the **Script Editor**:

   ```
   play -forward false;
   ```

   The animation is now played backwards.

5. Execute the following in the **Script Editor**:

   ```
   play -query -state;
   // Result: 1 //
   ```

   The state of the play command returns 1 if the animation is currently playing and 0 otherwise.

6. Execute the following in the **Script Editor**:

   ```
   play -state off;
   ```

   The animation stops.

The current playback options define the range and speed of playback. Using the playbackOptions command, you can alter these. It is important to understand the difference between the animation range and the playback range. The animation range is the total length of your animation. The playback range can be either the entire animation or a smaller subset. When working on a particular action, it is often best to reduce the playback range to the action while leaving the total animation range untouched.

1. Execute the following in the **Script Editor**:

```
playbackOptions -minTime 12 -maxTime 20;
```

The playback range is set to 12, 20. The animation range remains at 0, 48. Use the `-animationStartTime` and `-animationEndTime` flags to set the animation range.

2. Execute the following in the **Script Editor**:

```
undo;
playbackOptions -loop "oscillate";
play;
```

The animation now oscillates between playing forward and playing backwards.

3. Execute the following in the **Script Editor**:

```
playbackOptions -query -playbackSpeed;
// Result: 1 //
```

The playback speed is at 100%. To play back the animation at half its normal speed, use the following:

```
playbackOptions -playbackSpeed 0.5;
// Result: 0.5 //
```

It is important to understand that the playback speed is just a guide. More often than not, final playback speed won't match the current time unit setting. To see the actual speed at which the animation is being played, you need to display the frame rate in the **Heads Up Display**. To do this, turn on the menu option **Display | Heads Up Display | Frame Rate**. You'll notice that the rate varies. This is because the speed at which Maya can play back the animation is dependent on the complexity of the scene and its animation. If the scene is complex, Maya may have to drop frames in order to maintain the desired frame rate. Because it is continually evaluating and estimating how many frames need to be dropped, the result is an erratic final frame rate.

4. Shrink the current viewport to display all the viewports.

5. Execute the following in the **Script Editor**:

```
playbackOptions -view "all";
```

The animation is played back in all the viewports instead of just the current one. Certain playback options are stored in your preferences and so will be kept between sessions. The playback speed, loop, and view are some of those. To restore them to their default values, use the following:

```
playbackOptions -loop "continuous";
playbackOptions -playbackSpeed 1;
playbackOptions -view "active";
```

6. Click the **Play** button to stop the animation.

The playblast feature can also be controlled using MEL. In a playblast, Maya plays the current animation, storing each frame into an animation file for later playback. Since Maya actually captures the screen at each frame, it is important that the current viewport be exposed during the entire capture period. The following command does a playblast then puts the result in the `test.mov` file.

```
playblast -filename test.mov;
```

11.1.3 Animation Curves

11.1.3.1 Functions

At its most fundamental, animation in Maya is simply the result of an attribute whose value changes over time. As you play back the animation, the value of an attribute is determined at each time instant. If an attribute is animated, its value varies from one time to another. The value that varies is said to depend on time. This relationship between a given time and another value can be defined using a mathematical function. In fact, other packages refer to animation curves as function curves. A function is defined as follows:

$$y = f(x)$$

This notation basically specifies that the function (f) takes an input value (x) and then generates a resulting output value (y). The function itself can be very simple or very complex. For this discussion, it isn't important how the function generates its value. What is important is to understand that the function produces one value given another. Say you had a function that simply added 2 to the x value. This function would be written as follows:

$$y = x + 2$$

Given an arbitrary set of values for x, put them into your function and see what numbers pop out. Given a set of x values (0, 1, 2, 3) the resulting y values are (2, 3, 4, 5). If you put each x value with its resulting y value, you can create a point (x, y). Figure 11.1 shows the result of plotting these points on a graph.

Now if you draw a line through the points, you end up with a straight line. So the function $y = x + 2$ defines a straight line. Depending on the equation for the

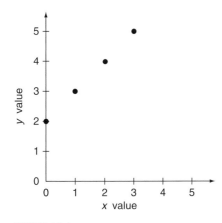

FIGURE 11.1

Plot of the *x* and *y* values.

function, a different set of points will be generated, and when a line is drawn through them, different curves result. For instance, a smooth sine curve results if you set the function to be $y = \sin(x)$.

Now consider the *x* value to be time. As a new time value is put into the function, a different *y* value results. This is precisely how values are animated. By defining a function that takes time as input and pops out a resulting value, you get a series of varying values.

With this understanding, you can see that, conceptually, all of Maya's animation curves can be considered mathematical functions. For a given *x* value, they compute a resulting *y* value. When you create a series of keyframes, you are, in essence, defining a mathematical function. The advantage is that rather than write this as an equation, you can do it visually by adding and manipulating keyframes. Using Expressions, you can actually define your own mathematical functions to animate values.

Another way of expressing this relationship is to consider that mathematical functions define a mapping from one set of values (*x*) to another set of values (*y*). Since animation curves are functions, they also provide this mapping. When creating a time-based animation, you are defining a mapping between time and some attribute's value. If you are animating the **translateX** attribute, for instance, you are defining how values of time are mapping to **translateX** values. A key defines this mapping explicitly. A key has an input and output value:

key = (input value, output value)

For instance, to define a key that, given an input value of 3, you'd like mapped to a value of 2, you'd create the key (3, 2). If you create a key for every input value, you would have directly defined the mapping from *x* to *y*. Alternatively, you could define just a limited number of keys and have the computer determine the mapping where keys don't exist through interpolation. This is exactly how keyframe animation curves work.

In Maya, it is possible to map any value to another. In time-based animation, you'll want to map time to some floating-point value. For instance, when you animate the translation of an object, you are defining a mapping from time to distance. The keys are of the following form:

key = (time, distance)

When animating a rotation, you are defining a mapping from time to angle, so the keys are of the following form:

key = (time, angle)

A *driven key* is simply a mapping from one value to another.

key = (input value, output value)

The driver attribute is fed into the input value and the driven attribute is set to the resulting output value. Understanding that time-based animation and driven animation are conceptually no different opens up a great deal of possibilities. You can map any input to any output. For instance you could map an angle to time. This would produce a given time value for an input angle.

key = (angle, time)

You could then feed this resulting time into some other animation curve that used time as input. There is no limit to the ways you can combine different types of mappings.

11.1.3.2 Keyframing

An animation curve consists of a set of control points (keys) and their associated tangents. The control points define the keys of the animation. The tangents define how values between keys are interpolated. This interpolation can be defined in a variety of ways, including linear, stepped, spline, flat, and so on.

The process of creating an animation curve is greatly simplified by using Maya's various curve editing tools. These tools allow you to create and manipulate the curve points, tangents, and segments interactively. As well as using MEL to create curves interactively, it is also possible to use MEL to create and edit animation curves.

When an attribute is animated using keyframing, Maya automatically creates an animation curve and connects it to the attribute being animated. Animation curves are stored as nodes in the dependency graph. To get a complete list of all the animation curve nodes associated with a given node, use the keyframe command as follows:

```
keyframe -query -name ball;
// Result: nurbsSphere1_translateX ball_scaleX //
```

This shows that the node named **ball** has two animation nodes, **nurbsSpherel_translateX** and **ball_scaleX**. To get the animation curve node for a given attribute, use the following:

```
keyframe -query -name ball.translateX;
// Result: nurbsSphere11_translateX //
```

To determine if a given node is an animation curve, use the `isAnimCurve` command. The following example gets the animation curve node associated with a node's attribute, then determines if it is an animation curve:

```
string $nodes[] = 'keyframe -query -name ball.translateX';
if( isAnimCurve( $nodes[0] ) )
  print( "is animation curve" );
```

To determine if a node is animatable, use the `listAnimatable` command.

```
listAnimatable -type ball;
// Result: transform //
```

Alternatively, you can determine which of a node's attributes can be animated by using the following:

```
listAnimatable ball;
// Result: ball.rotateX ball.rotateY ball.rotateZ ball.scaleX ball.
  scaleY ball.scaleZ ball.translateX ball.visibility //
```

The `listAnimatable` command can be used on the currently selected nodes by not explicitly specifying a node. In the previous examples, simply remove `ball` from the statements.

11.1.3.3 Evaluation

To get the value of an animated attribute, simply use the `getAttr` command. This returns the attribute's value at the current time. This command could indirectly result in any input connections to the animation curve node being updated.

If you'd like to evaluate the animation curve in its current state, then use the following statement:

```
keyframe -time 250 -query -eval ball.translateX;
```

Using the `-eval` flag, you can quickly sample the animation curve at different times without causing the typical dependency graph update on all the curve's input connections. For animation curves that use driven keys, simply use `-float` in place of the `-time` flag.

11.1.3.4 Infinity

The valid range of the animation curve is defined by the first and last keys. If your first key is at frame 10 and your last key is at frame 25, the valid range is 10–25. Any attempt to evaluate the curve outside that range will result in the animation curve's infinity value. A curve has *preinfinity* and *postinfinity* settings. Preinfinity is to the left of the first key and postinfinity is to the right of the last key. They can have one of the following settings:

```
constant, linear, cycle, cycleRelative, oscillate
```

By default all curves have preinfinity and postinfinity set to `constant`. When `constant` is used, the value is that of the next closest key. For preinfinity, this is the value of the first key, and for postinfinity, the value of the last key. To query the current infinity settings, use the `setInfinity` command with either the `-preInfinite` or `-postInfinite` flags.

```
setInfinity -query -preInfinite ball.translateX;
// Result: constant //
```

To set the infinity settings, use the following:

```
setInfinity -preInfinite "cycle" ball.translateX;
setInfinity -postInfinite "linear" ball.translateX;
```

11.1.3.5 Keys

This section covers the creation, editing, and querying of keys on an animation curve.

11.1.3.5.1 Creating

1. Select **File | New Scene**...

2. In the **Script Editor**, execute the following:

```
sphere;
rename ball;
```

You now create some keys for the ball's *x* translation.

3. Execute the following:

```
setKeyframe -time 1 -value -5 ball.translateX;
setKeyframe -time 48 -value 5 ball.translateX;
```

A key is created at frames 1 and 48. When `setKeyframe` is called on an attribute that isn't already animated, an animation curve node is automatically created and connected to the attribute. To see which animation curve node is now controlling the **translateX** attribute, use the following:

```
keyframe -query -name ball.translateX;
// Result: ball_translateX //
```

4. Click the **Play** button.

The ball now moves across the screen.

5. Select **Window | Animation Editors | Graph Editor**...

The animation curve for the ball's **translateX** attribute is shown. You'd like to have the ball's translation control its *x* scaling. To do this you need to create a driven key.

6. Execute the following:

```
setDrivenKeyframe -driverValue 0 -value 0 -currentDriver
    ball.translateX ball.scaleX;
setDrivenKeyframe -driverValue 5 -value 1 ball.scaleX;
```

First, a driven key is created so that the ball's **translateX** becomes the driving attribute and the ball's **scaleX** becomes the driven attribute. At the same time, a key is created so that when the **translateX** value is 0, the **scaleX** value is also 0. Another driven key is then created. This key is set so that when the **translateX** value is 5, the **scaleX** value is 1.

7. Click the **Play** button.

The ball is flat while the *x* translation is less than 0. As the ball moves toward the *x* position 5, it expands gradually. Why does the ball stay flat until it reaches position 0? Since the range of the driven animation curve is from time 0 to 5, when an attempt is made to evaluate the curve outside this range, the preinfinity and postinfinity values are used. Since they are constant by default, the **scaleX** uses the value of the first keyframe, which is 0.

Now delete the driven animation curve.

8. Execute the following:

```
string $nodes[] = 'keyframe -query -name ball.scaleX';
delete $nodes[0];
```

The first statement retrieves the name of the animation curve node. The second deletes it.

Now insert a key in the **translateX** animation curve. Execute the following:

```
setKeyframe -insert -time 24 ball.translateX;
```

A new key is inserted between the two existing ones. Using the `-insert` flag, a new key is inserted without changing the overall shape of the curve.

11.1.3.5.2 Editing

1. Open the **SimpleAnimatedSphere.ma** scene.

2. Select the **ball** object.

3. Select **Window | Animation Editors | Graph Editor**...

The animation curve for the sphere is displayed. Currently only the **translateX** attribute is animated. In Maya, all keyframe animation is stored in an animation curve node. This node holds a list of keys. For time-based animation, each key consists of a time and float value. You will now use MEL to query and edit the keys in the animation curve.

4. Execute the following in the **Script Editor**:

```
keyframe -query -keyframeCount ball.translateX;
// Result: 2 //
```

Using the -keyframeCount flag, you can determine the number of keys in the animation curve.

5. In the **Graph Editor**, select the last key, at frame 48.

6. Execute the following:

```
keyframe -query -selected -keyframeCount ball.translateX;
// Result: 1 //
```

This returns the number of currently selected keys. To determine the time of the selected keys, execute the following:

```
keyframe -query -selected -timeChange ball.translateX;
// Result: 48 //
```

To get the actual value of the selected keys, use this statement:

```
keyframe -query -selected -valueChange ball.translateX;
// Result: 1.64126 //
```

To do the same operations but on all the keys, use the same statements but without the -selected flag. You'll now start moving the keys around. To choose a key to edit, you must specify its time. Execute the following:

```
keyframe -edit -time 48 -timeChange 20 ball.translateX;
```

This moves the key at frame 48 to frame 20. As always, you can specify time using any unit by appending it with the appropriate time-unit specification. For instance, to edit the frame at 1.5s simply use -time 1.5sec. By default, time changes are considered absolute. It is also possible to move keys by relative amounts. Execute the following:

```
keyframe -edit -time 20 -relative -timeChange 5 ball.translateX;
```

This moves the key at frame 20 to the right by five frames. The key is now located at frame 25. Movements to the left can be done by using a negative time change, for example, –5. To change the actual value of a key, execute the following:

```
keyframe -edit -time 25 -valueChange 2 ball.translateX;
```

The ball now moves two units along the *x*-axis at frame 25. As with time changes, it is possible to move a key's value by a relative amount. Using -relative in the previous example would have increased the existing value by 2.

If you don't know the exact time of a given key but do know its relative position in the list of keys, you can use the -index flag. Indices are 0 based, so the first key is at index 0, the second at index 1, and so on. Execute the following to move the first key to the left.

```
keyframe -edit -index 0 -relative -timeChange -5 ball.
    translateX;
```

More than one key can be operated on at a time by specifying multiple keys, using either the -time or -index flag. To move the first and second keys 10 frames to the right, execute the following:

```
keyframe -edit -index 0 -index 1 -relative -timeChange 10
    ball.translateX;
```

It is also possible to apply an operation to a range of keys. The range can be given either in time units or in indices. To increase the value of all keys between time 0 and time 12 by five units, execute the following:

```
keyframe -edit -time "0:12" -relative -valueChange 5 ball.
    translateX;
```

The only key in that time range is the first key. Its value is increased by 5. Using the range notation you can also specify just one of the bounds. To operate on all the keys before time 20, for instance, simply use -time ":20". Since the beginning isn't specified, the first key will be used. Note that the bounds are inclusive, so they include any keys on the range's boundary. Alternatively, to specify a time range starting at time 20 and including all following keys, use -time "20:". It logically follows that to select all keys using this notation, you'd use -time ":". Execute the following to move all the keys three frames to the left:

```
keyframe -edit -time ":" -relative -timeChange 3 ball.
    translateX;
```

This same range notation can be applied to indices. To change all the keys from index 1 to 20, so that they all have a value of 2.5, you'd use the following:

```
keyframe -edit -index "1:20" -valueChange 2.5 ball. translateX;
```

In addition to explicitly setting the time and value of a key, it is possible to scale the values. To scale all the keys' values, execute the following:

```
scaleKey -time ":" -valueScale 0.5 ball.translateX;
```

A key's time can also be scaled using the -timeScale flag. The following scales all the keys' time by half:

```
scaleKey -timeScale 0.5 ball.translateX;
```

Scaling happens about a pivot point. This is the origin used for the scaling. To use a different pivot point for time, use the -timePivot flag. To scale the keys about their center, execute the following:

```
float $times[] = 'keyframe -index 0 -index 1
                         -query -timeChange ball.translateX';
scaleKey -timePivot (($times[0] + $times[1])/2)
         -timeScale 2 ball.translateX;
```

The -valuePivot and -floatPivot flags can be used for using a different value and float origin, respectively. As a result of moving keys around, it is possible that some keys don't fall on exact frame numbers. Currently, the two keys are located at −2.752 and 26.248, in time. To put them back on whole frame numbers, execute the following:

```
snapKey -timeMultiple 1 ball.translateX;
```

The snapKey command can also be applied to individual keys by specifying them explicitly or using a range. The -timeMultiple flag doesn't have to be a whole number. For instance, you may want to have the keys snapped to half-second intervals. In that case simply use -timeMultiple 0.5sec.

11.1.3.6 Breakdown Keys

In Maya, there are two types of keys: normal and breakdown. The difference between the two is that a breakdown key's time is relative to the keys surrounding it. Unlike a normal key, which remains fixed unless you explicitly move it, a breakdown key attempts to maintain its relative time to the surrounding keys if they are moved.

To determine if a key is a breakdown key, use the -query and -breakdown flags.

```
float $isBreakdown[] = 'keyframe -time $keyTime
    -query -breakdown $nodeAttribute';
if( $isBreakdown[0] )
    ... // do something
```

To change a key into a breakdown key, use

```
keyframe -time $keyTime -breakdown true $nodeAttribute;
```

11.1.3.7 Tangents

The direction of the curve as it comes into and out of a key is defined by its *tangent*. Figure 11.2 shows an animation curve with its tangents.

Each key has an *in* and *out tangents*. The in tangent is to the left of the key and the out tangent to its right. Tangents have the following properties: type, angle, weighting, and locking. The type of tangent defines how it interpolates values. Which tangent type is used determines how values are interpolated between keys. A step tangent, for instance, holds a value constant between keys. A spline tangent offers a smoother transition from one key to the next.

The angle of a tangent defines its direction. Weighted tangents allow you to move the endpoints of the tangents to get complete control over the tangents. Tangents support two types of locking. The first is general locking, in which the angle and length of the in and out tangents can't be changed. The tangents can be rotated, but they can't change angles individually. Also, their lengths remain fixed. Tangents also support weight locking. This is when the tangent weights are fixed so the tangent endpoints can't be extended or retracted. The tangents can be rotated however.

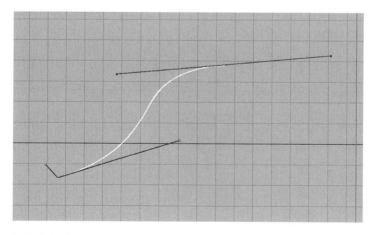

FIGURE 11.2

Example tangent types.

1. Open the **SimpleAnimatedSphere.ma** scene.

2. Select the **ball** object.

3. Select **Window | Animation Editors | Graph Editor**...

4. Press the **f** key in the **Graph Editor** to frame the current animation curve. The current curve is a straight line between the two keys.

5. Execute the following:

```
keyTangent -index 0 -outTangentType flat ball.translateX;
```

If the animation is played, the ball would start out slowly then speed up toward the end. If you want the ball to make a sharp jump from one position to the next, execute the following:

```
keyTangent -index 0 -outTangentType step ball.translateX;
```

The ball stays at its first position, then jumps abruptly to its second position at the end of the animation. Execute the following to restore the tangent to its original type:

```
keyTangent -index 0 -outTangentType spline ball.translateX;
```

The tangents at the first key are broken. Setting some tangent types causes both the in and out tangents to be affected. To change back, it may be necessary to change both tangents. Execute the following:

```
keyTangent -index 0 -inTangentType spline ball.translateX;
```

Now rotate the first tangent to 45°:

```
keyTangent -index 0 -inAngle 45 ball.translateX;
```

All angles are relative to the horizontal x-axis and continue in a counter-clockwise direction. Tangents rotate since they are automatically angle-locked because the "spline" tangent type is being used. Rotations can also be relative.

```
keyTangent -index 0 -relative -inAngle 15 ball.translateX;
```

The in-tangent angle has been increased by 15°. To get the direction of the out tangent as a unit vector (length of 1), use the `-ox` and `-oy` flags.

```
float $dir[] = 'keyTangent -index 0 -query -ox -oy ball.translateX';
print $dir;
```

Result:

```
0.153655
0.988124
```

The same statement, but using `-ix` and `-iy`, gives the in-tangent direction. Now unlock the in and out tangents so they can rotate independently.

```
keyTangent -index 0 -lock false ball.translateX;
```

In the Graph Editor, the two tangents are now drawn in different colors. Rotating the out tangent should no longer affect the in tangent.

```
keyTangent -index 0 -outAngle 15 ball.translateX;
```

In order to give tangents a weighting, the entire animation curve must be converted to use weighted tangents.

```
keyTangent -edit -weightedTangents yes ball.translateX;
```

The curve now has weighted tangents. The tangent endpoints are now displayed differently in the Graph Editor. It is important to know that the curve can become distorted when you convert a curve to use weighted tangents and then attempt to convert them back to unweighted tangents. An unweighted tangent loses its weighting information, so the curve is almost always different. Changing the tangent weighting of the second key can be done as follows:

```
keyTangent -index 1 -inWeight 20 ball.translateX;
```

Since the weights of both tangents are locked by default, you need to unlock them to have them weighted separately. You need to unlock the tangents as well as their weights.

```
keyTangent -index 1 -lock false -weightLock no ball.
    translateX;
```

You can now change the weight of one without affecting the other.

```
keyTangent -index 1 -inWeight 10 ball.translateX;
```

The in tangent's weight has now changed without affecting the out tangent's weight.

When an attribute is first animated, Maya creates an animation curve. As you add keys, the tangent type and weighting are determined automatically by the **Tangents** setting in the **Window | Settings/Preferences | Preferences... | Keys** section.

By changing this, you can ensure that all keys created from then on use the new setting. To query the current settings, use the following:

```
keyTangent -query -global -inTangentType;      // Query in-tangent type
keyTangent -query -global -outTangentType;     // Query out-tangent type
keyTangent -query -global -weightedTangents;   // Query automatic weighting
```

To set the default in tangent, type the following:

```
keyTangent -global -inTangentType flat;
```

To set it so that all new animation curves automatically have weighting, use the following:

```
keyTangent -global -weightedTangents yes;
```

11.1.3.8 Key Clipboard

Keys can be cut, copied, and pasted. Maya has a clipboard into which the cut and copied keys are placed temporarily. From the clipboard, they can be pasted into the same animation curve at a different time or into another animation curve. An entire sequence of keys can be copied to the clipboard.

1. Open the **SimpleAnimatedSphere.ma** scene.
2. Select the **ball** object.
3. Execute the following:

```
copyKey -index 0 ball.translateX;
// Result: 1 //
```

The first key is copied to the clipboard. Now paste it to another time location.

```
pasteKey -time 12 -option insert ball.translateX;
```

The first key is inserted into the curve at frame 12.

The key's value is scaled by half. To remove a key and put it in the clipboard, use the cutKey command.

```
cutKey -index 1 -option keys ball.translateX;
```

To remove a key without putting it into the clipboard, use the cutKey command with the -clear flag.

```
cutKey -index 1 -clear ball.translateX;
```

11.1.3.9 Examples

The next few examples demonstrate how to create and edit keyframe animation curves.

11.1.3.9.1 PrintAnim Script

A common task is to iterate over all the animation curves and get their keys. This script defines the printAnim procedure that prints out the animation information for the currently selected nodes. When asked to print detailed information, it also prints the type of key as well as its tangent information.

```
proc printAnim( int $detailed )
{
print "\nAnimation …";
string $animNodes[];
float $keytimes[];
string $sel[] = 'ls -selection';
for( $node in $sel )
    {
    print ("\nNode: " + $node);
    $animNodes = 'keyframe -query -name $node';
    for($ac in $animNodes )
        {
        print ("\nAnimCurve: " + $ac );
        $keytimes = 'keyframe -query -timeChange $ac';
        print ("\n" + size($keytimes) + " keys: " );
        for( $keyt in $keytimes )
            {
            $keyv = 'keyframe -time $keyt -query -valueChange $ac';
            if( $detailed )
                {
                float $isBd[] = 'keyframe -time $keyt -query -breakdown $ac';
                print ("\n" + ($isBd[0] ? "Breakdown" : "Normal") " Key:" );
                }

            print (" [" + $keyt + ", " + $keyv[0] + "]");

            if( $detailed )
                {
                print ("\nTangent: ");
                $keyinT = 'keyTangent -time $keyt -query -inTangentType $ac';
                $keyoutT = 'keyTangent -time $keyt -query -outTangentType $ac';
                $keyinA = 'keyTangent -time $keyt -query -inAngle $ac';
                $keyoutA = 'keyTangent -time $keyt -query -outAngle $ac';
                print ("("+ $keyinT[0] + " angle=" + $keyinA[0] +
                        ", " + $keyoutT[0] + " angle=" + $keyoutA[0] + ")");
                }
```

```
        }
      }
    }
  }
```

After you've defined the procedure, the first step is to get the list of selected nodes. You then iterate over every node in the list.

```
string $sel[] = 'ls -selection';
for( $node in $sel )
    {
```

Using the keyframe command, you can get a list of all the animation curve nodes associated with a given node. You can then iterate over the animation curves.

```
$animNodes = 'keyframe -query -name $node';
for( $ac in $animNodes )
    {
```

Get a list of all the keys' times for the current animation curve.

```
$keytimes = 'keyframe -query -timeChange $ac';
```

The number of keys is the size of the $keytimes array.

```
print ("\n" + size($keytimes) + " keys: " );
```

With the list of key times, you then iterate over all the keys, since you can index the keys by time. It would also have been possible to index the keys by their order.

```
for( $keyt in $keytimes )
    {
```

Get the value of the current key. It is important that you specify the target key, in this case, using -time $keyt before you use the -query flag. If you don't do it in this order, the command will fail.

```
$keyv = 'keyframe -time $keyt -query -valueChange $ac';
```

When printing out detailed information, you print out the type of key. A key can be either a breakdown or a normal key.

```
if( $detailed )
    {
```

```
float $isBd[] = 'keyframe -time $keyt -query -breakdown $ac';
print ("\n" + ($isBd[0] ? "Breakdown" : "Normal") + " Key:" );
}
```

The time and value of the current key are printed out.

```
print (" [" + $keyt + ", " + $keyv[0] + "]");
```

The tangent information is retrieved using the keyTangent command with the -query flag. Four different properties of the tangent are retrieved: inTangentType, outTangentType, inAngle, outAngle. The tangent types can be any of the following: spline, linear, fast, slow, flat, step, fixed, and clamped. The in and out angles define the angle of the tangents, which in turn define their direction.

```
if( $detailed )
  {
  print ("\nTangent: ");
  $keyinT = 'keyTangent -time $keyt -query -inTangentType $ac';
  $keyoutT = 'keyTangent -time $keyt -query -outTangentType $ac';
  $keyinA = 'keyTangent -time $keyt -query -inAngle $ac';
  $keyoutA = 'keyTangent -time $keyt -query -outAngle $ac';
  print ("("+ $keyinT[0] + " angle=" + $keyinA[0] + ", "
          + $keyoutT[0] + " angle=" + $keyoutA[0] + ")");
  }
```

The following is an example of the output generated by the printAnim procedure:

```
Animation...
Node: ball
AnimCurve: nurbsSphere1_translateX
2 keys:
Normal Key: [1, -5.3210074]
Tangent: (spline angle=8.426138245, spline angle=8.426138245)
Normal Key: [48, 1.641259667]
Tangent: (spline angle=8.426138245, spline angle=8.426138245)
AnimCurve: ball_scaleX
0 keys:
```

11.1.3.9.2 PrintTangentPositions Script

When Maya gives tangent information, it gives it as a direction and weighting. To determine the exact position of a tangent's endpoint, this information needs to be converted to Cartesian coordinates. The following script prints out the end positions of the tangents. It can output the tangents relative to their respective keys or as an absolute position relative to the origin.

```
proc printTangentPostions( string $animCurve, int $absolute )
{
print ("\nTangent Positions...");

float $ktimes[], $kvalues[];
if( $absolute )
   {
   $ktimes = 'keyframe -query -timeChange $animCurve';
   $kvalues = 'keyframe -query -valueChange $animCurve';
   }

float $xcomps[], $ycomps[], $weights[];
int $i, $j;
for( $i=0; $i < 2; $i++ )
   {
   string $xreq, $yreq, $wreq;
   if( $i == 0 )
       {
       $xreq = "-ix";
       $yreq = "-iy";
       $wreq = "-inWeight";
       }
     else
       {
       $xreq = "-ox";
       $yreq = "-oy";
       $wreq = "-outWeight";
       }

    $xcomps = 'keyTangent -query $xreq $animCurve';
    $ycomps = 'keyTangent -query $yreq $animCurve';
    $weights = 'keyTangent -query $wreq $animCurve';
    print("\n");
    for( $j=0; $j < size($xcomps); $j = $j + 1 )
       {
       $xcomps[$j] *= $weights[$j];
       $ycomps[$j] *= $weights[$j];
       if( $absolute )
         {
         $xcomps[$j] += Sktimes[$j];
         $ycomps[$j] += $kvalues[$j];
         }

       print (" [" + $xcomps[$j] + ", " + $ycomps[$j] + "]");
       }
```

```
    }
}

proc testProc()
{
string $animCurves[] = 'keyframe -query -name ball.translateX';
printTangentPostions( $animCurves[0], true );
}

testProc();
```

The printTangentPositions procedure takes the name of the animation curve node ($animCurve) and whether you want to print out the absolute or relative positions of the tangents ($absolute).

```
proc printTangentPostions( string $animCurve, int $absolute )
{
```

If you need absolute tangent positions, you will need the positions of the keys associated with the tangents. All the keys' times and values are retrieved.

```
float $ktimes[], $kvalues[];
if( $absolute )
  {
  $ktimes = 'keyframe -query -timeChange $animCurve';
  $kvalues = 'keyframe -query -valueChange $animCurve';
  }
```

There are two tangents: in tangent and out tangent. You need to iterate over them both.

```
for( $i=0; $i < 2; $i++ )
  {
```

Depending on which tangent you need, you repair the command flags ($xreq, $yreq, $wreq) to retrieve their *x* and *y* vector components, as well as their weights. This could also have been written as a switch statement.

```
string $xreq, $yreq, $wreq;
  if( $i == 0 )
        {
        $xreq = "-ix";
        $yreq = "-iy";
        $wreq = "-inWeight";
        }
```

```
else
    {
    $xreq = "-ox";
    $yreq = "-oy";
    $wreq = "-outWeight";
    }
```

The *x* component, *y* component, and weight of all the tangents are now retrieved.

```
$xcomps = 'keyTangent -query $xreq $animCurve';
$ycomps = 'keyTangent -query $xreq $animCurve';
$weights = 'keyTangent -query $wreq $animCurve';
```

You now iterate over every tangent.

```
for( $j=0; $j < size($xcomps); $j = $j + 1 )
    {
```

The *x* and *y* components make up the unit vector that points in the direction of the tangent. The weight defines the length of the tangent vector. By multiplying the unit vector by the tangent length, you get a vector that has the direction and length of the tangents.

```
$xcomps[$j] *= $weights[$j];
$ycomps[$j] *= $weights[$j];
```

At this point, the vectors are relative to the key, that is, the vector is an offset from the key's position. If you want tangent positions relative to the same origin used for the keys, you need to add the tangent vectors to the key positions.

```
if( $absolute )
    {
    $xcomps[$j] += $ktimes[$j];
    $ycomps[$j] += $kvalues[$j];
    }
```

Print out the final position of the tangent's endpoint.

```
print (" [" + $xcomps[$j] + ", " + $ycomps[$j] + "]");
```

A small testing procedure, testProc, is created to test the printTangentPositions procedure. It prints the absolute tangent positions of the **ball** node's **translateX** animation curve.

```
proc testProc()
{
string $animCurves[] = 'keyframe -query -name ball.translateX';
printTangentPostions( $animCurves[0], true );
}

testProc();
```

Following is an example of the output from the script:

```
Tangent Positions...
[1.009253906, -5.311753494] [60.4534152, 14.09467487]
[32.76284582, 26.44183842] [8113845077, 34.77971043]
```

11.1.4 **Skeletons**

A skeleton is simply a hierarchy of joints. The joints simulate the internal bones of a character. Their hierarchical relationship (parent–child) is what defines the skeleton. By rotating the individual joints, a character can assume a given pose. Typically, the model of a character is attached to the joints. This is done through a process of *skinning,* also known as *enveloping.* Now, when the joints move, the model is affected. Each joint affects a portion of the model and causes it to deform as if the model were muscle and skin wrapped around the bones.

A skeleton is typically created by hand. This is because it is difficult to generate a skeleton for a given model automatically. Depending on the particular needs of the animation, the skeleton may require different joint configurations. For instance, a velociraptor model may need additional joints in the neck that a human model wouldn't.

In the event that you need to generate skeletons using MEL, use the joint command.

1. Select **File | New Scene** ...
2. Activate the **top** viewport and maximize it.
3. In the **Script Editor**, execute the following:

```
joint;
```

A single joint, **joint1**, is created at the origin. Execute the following:

```
joint -position 0 0 10;
```

Another joint is created, **joint2**, and made a child under the first joint, **joint1**. Since the first joint was still selected, calling the joint command automatically adds the new joint as a child. You'd like to insert another joint between the current two:

```
insertJoint joint1;
```

A new joint, **joint3**, is inserted. It is now the child of **joint1** and a parent of **joint2**. The hierarchy of joints is now as follows:

joint1
joint3
joint2

Notice that the new joint is located at the origin. Unfortunately the insert-Joint command doesn't allow the specification of an initial joint position. To edit a joint's position after it is created, use the following:

```
joint -edit -position 0 0 5 joint3;
```

The joint, **joint3**, moved down. Its child, **joint2**, also moved by the same distance. Since joints have a parent–child relationship, wherever the parent moves, the child follows. Reposition the **joint3** node, and the **joint2** node follows. If you'd like to move a joint but not affect its children, then the -component flag can be used. Execute the following:

```
undo;
joint -edit -position 0 0 5 -component joint3;
```

The previous movement is undone, then the **joint3** node is moved but its child joints remain fixed. By default, all positioning is given in world space. It may be more convenient to specify a joint's position relative to its parent. Using the -relative flag enables this.

```
joint -edit -relative -position 5 0 0 joint2;
```

The **joint2** is now positioned five units to the right of its parent, **joint3**. You'll now cover some of the rotation options for joints. By default, a joint is created with three degrees of rotational freedom, that is, the object is free to rotate about the *x*-, *y*-, and *z*-axes. To get the current degrees of freedom, use the following:

```
joint -query -degreeOfFreedom joint1;
```

The result is

```
// Result: xyz //
```

This indicates that the joint is completely free. To reduce the possible rotations to just the *y*-axis, use the following:

```
joint -edit -degreeOfFreedom "y" joint1;
```

The new value for -degreeOfFreedom completely replaces any previous setting. Any attempt to rotate the joint about the *x*- or *z*-axis fails. It is also possible to limit the range of possible rotations on any given axis. By default there is no limit.

```
joint -edit -limitSwitchY yes joint1;
```

The rotational limits, for the *y*-axis, have now been activated. To query what the current limits are, use the following:

```
joint -query -limitY joint1;
```

The result is

```
// Result: -360 360 //
```

Currently, the joint is free to move between −360° and +360°. Limiting the range to 0°–90° can be done as follows:

```
joint -edit -limitY 0deg 90deg joint1;
```

Notice that the deg option was used for specifying the angles. Since you can't know in advance what the current angle unit is, it is best to specify the angle in the exact unit needed. Now rotate the joint beyond its limit:

```
rotate 0 200deg 0 joint1;
```

The joint rotates to a maximum of 90°. To rotate a joint relative to its parent, use the following:

```
joint -edit -angleY 10deg joint3;
```

The **joint3** is rotated 10° about the *y*-axis. It is important to note that all joint rotations using the joint command are relative. Only positioning of joints can be done in absolute coordinates. To query a joint's current rotation, use the following:

```
xform -query -rotation joint3;
```

The result is

```
// Result: 0 10 0 //
```

To delete a joint, use the `removeJoint` command.

```
removeJoint joint3;
```

This command removes the joint, then automatically reparents any orphaned child joints to the deleted joint's parent. If the `delete` command has been used instead, the **joint3** node and all its child joints would have been deleted.

11.1.4.1 Outputjoints Script

This script takes a hierarchy of joints and then outputs the position, rotation, and scale of the joints over a given time range. The output is stored to a file as well as being printed to the Maya window. This script works with skeletons that do and don't use inverse kinematic (IK) handles. As such, this script is particularly useful for exporting joint information to applications that don't support inverse kinematics. The joints' transformation can be output in local or world space.

```
proc writeArray( int $fileHnd, float $array[] )
{
float $v;
for( $v in $array )
    fwrite $fileHnd $v;
}

proc outputJoints( string $rootNode, string $filename,
                   float $startFrame, float $endFrame,
                   int $outputWS )
{
int $fileHnd = 'fopen $filename w';
if( $fileHnd == 0 )
  {
  error ("Unable to open output file " + $filename
                                    + " for writing");
  return;
  }

string $childNodes[] = 'listRelatives -full Path
                        -type joint -allDescendents $rootNode';
string $rn[] = { $rootNode };
string $nodes[] = stringArrayCatenate( $rn, $childNodes );
```

```
float $cTime = 'currentTime -query';

string $spaceFlag = ($outputWS) ? "-worldSpace " : "-objectSpace ";

print "\nOutputting joints...";
float $t;
for( $t = $startFrame; $t <= $endFrame; $t++ )
    {
    currentTime -update false $t;
    fwrite $fileHnd $t;
    print ("\nFrame: " + $t);

  for( $node in $nodes )
     {
     fwrite $fileHnd $node;
     print ("\n Joint: " + $node );

     float $pos[] = 'xform $spaceFlag -query -translation $node';
     float $rot[] = 'xform $spaceFlag -query -rotation $node';
     float $scl[] = 'xform $spaceFlag -query -relative -scale $node';

     writeArray( $fileHnd, $pos );
     writeArray( $fileHnd, $rot );
     writeArray( $fileHnd, $scl );

     print ("\n  pos=[ " + $pos[0] + " "
            + $pos[1] + " " + $pos[2] + " ]");
     print ("\n  rot=[ " + $rot[0] + " "
            + $rot[1] + " " + $rot[2] + " ]");
     print ("\n  scl=[ " + $scl[0] + " "
            + $scl[1] + " " + $scl[2] + " ]");
     }
   }
currentTime -update false $cTime;

fclose $fileHnd;
}
```

Before examining the script, look at it in action.

1. Open the **IKChain.ma** scene.

   The scene consists of a skeleton hierarchy controlled by an IK handle.

2. Click on the **Play** button.

The chain of joints moves from left to right.

3. In the **Script Editor,** enter the preceding script text, then execute it.

4. Execute the following. Substitute another file name if this one won't work on your machine or operating system.

```
outputJoints( "joint1", "c:\\temp\\joints.txt", 1, 10, false );
```

The joint information is output for all frames from frame 1 to frame 10. The transformations are output in object space. Following is the result:

```
Outputting joints...
Frame: 1
   Joint: joint1
      Pos=[ -12.03069362 4.785929251 2.314326079e-007 ]
      rot=[ -2.770645083e-006 -3.756997063e-007 50.410438 ]
      scl=[ 1 1 1 ]
   Joint: |joint1|joint2|joint3|joint4
      pos=[ 7.326328636 8.071497782e-017 7.585667703 ]
      rot=[ 0 0 0 ]
      scl=[ 1 1 1 ]
 . . .
```

This joint information is also written to the given file.

Now look at the script in detail. A simple utility procedure, writeArray, is defined that outputs the given array ($array) to the file ($fileHnd).

```
proc writeArray( int $fileHnd, float $array[] )
{
float $v;
for( $v in $array )
    fwrite $fileHnd $v;
}
```

The outputJoints procedure is then defined. It takes the name of the root joint in the skeleton ($rootNode), as well as the name of the output file ($filename). The range of animation is given by the $startFrame and $endFrame variables. Finally, the $outputWS variable determines whether the transformations are output in world or object space.

```
proc outputJoints( string $rootNode, string $filename,
                   float $startFrame, float $endFrame,
                   int $outputWS )
    {
```

The file is opened using the `fopen` command. It returns a file handle. All subsequent file calls then use this handle.

```
int $fileHnd = 'fopen $filename w';
```

If the returned file handle is zero, then the file opening failed. Notify the user of this, then return.

```
1f( $fileHnd == 0 )
   {
   error ("Unable to open output file " + $filename + " for writing");
   return;
   }
```

Get a list of all the child joints.

```
string $childNodes[] = 'listRelatives -fullPath -type joint
                        -allDescendents $rootNode';
```

Create a list of all the skeleton joints by adding the root node as the first, followed by all the children. Since the `stringArrayCatenate` procedure needs two input arrays, the `$rootNode` node is put into a temporary array, `$rn`.

```
string $rn[] = { $rootNode };
string $nodes[] = stringArrayCatenate( $rn, $childNodes );
```

Store the current time. You'll want to return to it later.

```
float $cTime = 'currentTime -query';
```

The `$spaceFlag` defines in which space you'll retrieve the transformation information.

```
string $spaceFlag = ($outputWS) ? "-worldSpace" : "-objectSpace";
```

You then iterate over every frame in the given range.

```
float $t;
for( $t = $startFrame; $t <= $endFrame; $t++ )
    {
```

The current time is set to time $t. Notice that the scene isn't updated, only the time is set.

```
currentTime -update false $t;
```

The time is output to the file as well as to the screen.

```
fwrite $fileHnd $t;
print ("\nFrame: " + $t);
```

Each joint node is then iterated.

```
for( $node in $nodes )
    {
```

The node's name is output to the file and the screen.

```
fwrite $fileHnd $node;
print ("\n Joint: " + $node );
```

The translation, rotation, and scale are retrieved for the current joint. The request for the scale has to include the -relative flag since you can't get the absolute scaling.

```
float $pos[] = 'xform $spaceFlag -query -translation $node';
float $rot[] = 'xform $spaceFlag -query -rotation $node';
float $scl[] = 'xform $spaceFlag -query -relative -scale $node';
```

The transformation information is written to the file as well as to the screen.

```
writeArray( $fileHnd, $pos );
writeArray( $fileHnd, $rot );
writeArray( $fileHnd, $scl );

print ("\n    pos=[ " + $pos[0] + " "
        + $pos[1] + " " + $pos[2] + " ]");
print ("\n    rot=[ " + $rot[0] + " "
        + $rot[1] + " " + $rot[2] + " ]");
print ("\n    scl=[ " + $scl[0] + " "
        + $scl[1] + " " + $scl[2] + " ]");
    }
}
```

The current time is restored to the previous time.

```
currentTime -update false $cTime;
```

The output file is now closed. It is very important to explicitly close the file when you are finished with it.

```
fclose $fileHnd;
}
```

The `fopen` command is used to open a file in binary mode. It isn't possible to open a file in text mode with this command. It is important to remember this if you intend on reading the file in another application.

11.1.4.2 Scaleskeleton Script

A relatively common task is to take a skeleton and adapt it to a smaller or larger character. Simply doing a scale on a skeleton often won't give the intended result. The problem is that a scale enlarges or reduces the skeleton about the root's origin. What is really needed is that each joint be enlarged or reduced along its bone's direction. Figure 11.3 shows the result of applying a simple scale operation (`scale 0.5 0.5 0.5`) to the original skeleton. It is clear that the proportions haven't been maintained. Using the `scaleSkeleton` script, however, produces the scaling you'd expect.

The `ScaleSkeleton` script is surprisingly small.

```
proc scaleSkeleton( string $rootNode, float $scale )
{
string $childs[] = 'listRelatives -fullPath
                    -type joint -allDescendents $rootNode';
for( $child in $childs )
    {
    float $pos[] = 'joint -query -relative -position $child';
    $pos[0] *= $scale;
```

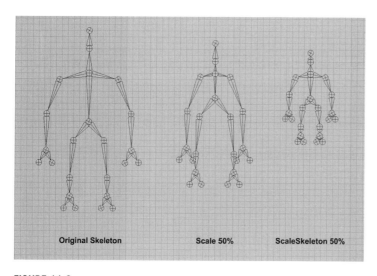

FIGURE 11.3

Incorrect and correct scaling.

```
    $pos[1] *= $scale;
    $pos[2] *= $scale;
    joint -edit -relative -position $pos[0] $pos[1] $pos[2] $child;
    }
}
```

First the scaleSkeleton procedure, which takes the root node of the skeleton ($rootNode) and the scale ($scale), is defined.

```
proc scaleSkeleton( string $rootNode, float $scale )
{
```

A complete list of all the joint nodes under the root node is then created using the listRelatives command. This list includes all descendants and not just the direct children.

```
string $childs[] = 'listRelatives -fullPath
                    -type joint -allDescendents $rootNode';
```

It is very important that the complete path to the children be used. Some of the children have the same name so aren't unique and when used in later statements would cause problems. In fact, Maya would complain that the node name wasn't unique. However, their complete paths (which include their ancestors) are unique, so the complete path is used.

Each of the children is then iterated over.

```
for( $child in $childs )
    {
```

The current position of the joint, relative to its parent, is then retrieved.

```
float $pos[] = 'joint -query -relative -position $child';
```

This position, $pos, is then scaled by the $scale amount. The position is the vector from the parent's center to the joint's center. This vector is therefore pointing in the same direction as the bone between the two joints. By scaling this vector, you effectively move the child joint's center closer to or farther from the parent.

```
$pos[0] *= $scale;
$pos[1] *= $scale;
$pos[2] *= $scale;
```

Finally, the joint's new relative position is set.

```
joint -edit -relative -position $pos[0] $pos[1] $pos[2] $child;
```

For the case of a joint, its center is simple since a node's position relative to its parent is simply its translation.

To see an example of the procedure applied to a skeleton, complete the following:

1. Open the **Skeleton.ma** scene.
2. Define the preceding scaleSkeleton procedure.
3. Execute the following:

```
scaleSkeleton( "rootJoint", 0.5 );
```

The skeleton is now scaled proportionately by 50%.

11.1.4.3 Copyskeletonmotion Script

After you animate a single character, there is often a need to reapply this animation to another character. As long as the two characters share the same skeleton structure, the process of copying the animation from one to the other is relatively simple.

```
proc copySkeletonMotion( string $srcRootNode, string $destRootNode )
{
float $srcPos[] = 'xform -query -worldSpace -translation
                 $srcRootNode':
float $destPos[] = 'xform -query -worldSpace -translation
                 $destRootNode':

string $srcNodes[] = 'listRelatives -full Path
                    -allDescendents $srcRootNode';
$srcNodes[ size($srcNodes) ] = $srcRootNode;

string $destNodes[] = 'listRelatives -fullPath
                     -allDescendents $destRootNode';
$destNodes[ size($destNodes) ] = $destRootNode;

if( size($srcNodes) != size($destNodes) )
   {
   error "Source skeleton and destination skeleton are
          structurely different";
   return;
   }

string $attrs[] = { "translateX", "translateY", "translateZ",
                    "scaleX", "scaleY", "scaleZ",
                    "rotateX", "rotateY", "rotateZ" };
int $i;
for( $i=0; $i < size($srcNodes); $i++ )
```

```
    {
    for( $attr in $attrs )
      {
      string $inPlugs[] = 'listConnections -plugs yes
                              -destination yes
                              ($srcNodes[$i] + "." + $attr)';
      if( size($inPlugs) )
         {
         string $tokens[];
         tokenize $inPlugs[0] "." $tokens;
         string $inNode = $tokens[0];
         string $inAttr = $tokens[1];

         string $dupInNodes[] = 'duplicate -upstreamNodes $inNode';
         connectAttr -force
                     ($dupInNodes[0] + "." + $inAttr)
                     ($destNodes[$i] + "." + $attr);
         }
      else
         {
         $res = 'getAttr ($srcNodes[$i] + "." + $attr)';
         setAttr ($destNodes[$i] + "." + $attr) $res;
         }
      }
    }
string $moveRoot;
string $parentNodes[] = 'listRelatives -parent $destRootNode';
string $found = 'match "_moveSkeleton" $parentNodes[0]';
if( size($found) )
   $moveRoot = $parentNodes[0];
else
   $moveRoot = 'group -name "_moveSkeleton" -world $destRootNode';

move -worldSpace
     ($destPos[0] - $srcPos[0])
     ($destPos[1] - $srcPos[1])
     ($destPos[2] - $srcPos[0]) $moveRoot;
}
```

Before explaining the individual sections of the script, first look at its result.

1. Open the **SkeletonMotion.ma** scene.

   The scene consists of two skeletons. The root nodes of the skeletons are **leadDancer** and **copyDancer**, respectively.

2. Click on the **Play** button.

   The **leadDancer** skeleton has some basic animation applied.

3. In the **Script Editor**, enter the preceding **copySkeletonMotion** script, then execute it.

4. Execute the following:

   ```
   copySkeletonMotion( "leadDancer", "copyDancer" );
   ```

5. Click on the **Play** button.

   The **copyDancer** skeleton now has the same animation as the **leadDancer**. Notice that the **copyDancer** now has a new parent, **_moveSkeleton**. Since the translation values are copied exactly from the **leadDancer** to the **copyDancer**, it follows that they will have the same position. Instead, you'd like the **copyDancer** to move the same as the **leadDancer**, but relative to its initial position. To do this, a new transform, **_moveSkeleton**, was created and translated by the difference in the initial positions of the two skeletons. The **copyDancer** has an exact copy of the **leadDancer's** translations, but the new parent node, **_moveSkeleton**, ensures that it is relative to its initial position.

The copySkeletonMotion procedure is defined to take the source skeleton root node ($srcRootNode) and the destination skeleton root node ($destRootNode). The animation from the source node's hierarchy is copied to the destination node's hierarchy.

```
proc copySkeletonMotion( string $srcRootNode, string $destRootNode )
{
```

The world space positions of the two root nodes are then determined. These are used later to move the new transform parent. Note that the initial position is calculated at the current time. If you'd like the initial position to happen at an absolute time, use currentTime to move to that time beforehand.

```
float $srcPos[] = 'xform -query -worldSpace -translation
                  $srcRootNode';
float $destPos[] = 'xform -query -worldSpace -translation
                   $destRootNode';
```

The complete list of all child joint nodes in the source skeleton is retrieved.

```
string $srcNodes[] = 'listRelatives -fullPath
                     -children -type joint
                     -allDescendents $srcRootNode';
```

The root node is also added to the list. The list now contains all the source joint nodes from the source skeleton.

```
$srcNodes[ size($srcNodes) ] = $srcRootNode;
```

The complete list of all child joint nodes of the destination skeleton is retrieved.

```
string $destNodes[] = 'listRelatives -fullPath
                       -children -type joint
                       -allDescendents $destRootNode';
```

The root node is added to the list.

```
$destNodes[ size($destNodes) ] = $destRootNode;
```

If the size of the two arrays is different, then you have a problem. This indicates that the two skeleton hierarchies are different. In this case, you exit the procedure after displaying an error. Note that this isn't an exhaustive test of whether the two skeletons are structurally the same. When designing your own procedure, do more detailed checking.

```
if( size($srcNodes) != size($destNodes) )
  {
  error "Source skeleton and destination skeleton are structurely
     different";
  return;
  }
```

A list of all the animated parameters you want to copy is then created. If you want to copy other attributes, then simply add them to this list.

```
string $attrs[] = { "translateX", "translateY", "translateZ",
                    "scaleX", "scaleY", "scaleZ",
                    "rotateX", "rotateY", "rotateZ" };
```

You iterate over all the source joint nodes.

```
for( $i=0; $i < size($srcNodes); $i++ )
  {
```

For each joint node, you then iterate over its attributes.

```
for( $attr in $attrs )
  {
```

You retrieve the incoming connection to the current attribute.

```
string $inPlugs[] = 'listConnections -plugs yes
                     -destination yes
                     ($srcNodes[$i] + "." + $attr)';
```

If there is an incoming connection, the attribute is being controlled by another node. In most cases, though not always, this is an animation curve feeding its output into the attribute.

```
if( size($inPlugs) )
   {
```

Since there is a connection, you then take the plug and break it into pieces. A plug is of the form:

```
<node_name>.<attribute_name>
```

For example, sphere.translateX. You want to break the plug into its node name ($inNode) and attribute name ($inAttr). The tokenize command is used to do this.

```
string $tokens[];
tokenize $inPlugs[0] "." $tokens;
string $inNode = $tokens[0];
string $inAttr = $tokens[1];
```

Given the incoming node, you then duplicate it as well as any of its upstream connections. This gives use of a complete duplicate of all nodes that directly, or indirectly, feed into the attribute.

```
string $dupInNodes[] = 'duplicate -upstreamNodes $inNode';
```

Connect the new duplicate node's output attribute to the destination node's attribute.

```
connectAttr -force
            ($dupInNodes[0] + "." + $inAttr)
            ($destNodes[$i] + "." + $attr);
```

If you'd like to have both skeletons *always* to have the same animation, then don't do a duplicate but instead connect the plug directly into the destination node's attribute. This would be done as follows:

```
connectAttr -force
            ($srcNodes[$i] + "." + $inAttr)
            ($destNodes[$i] + "." + $attr);
```

If the attribute doesn't have any input connections, then it mustn't be animated or controlled externally. In that case, simply copy the attribute values from the source node to the destination node.

```
   else
      {
      $res = `getAttr ($srcNodes[$i ] + "." + $lattr)`;
      setAttr ($destNodes[$i] + "." + $attr) $res;
      }
   }
}
```

The destination skeleton now has a duplicate of the source skeleton's animation. The destination skeleton's position will exactly match that of the source skeletons. You'd like to move the destination skeleton to its initial position by adding the **_moveSkeleton** parent. This parent **transform** node's name is stored in the $moveRoot variable.

```
string $moveRoot;
```

Get a list of parents for the destination root node.

```
string $parentNodes[] = `listRelatives -parent $destRootNode`;
```

Determine if the parent is one of the **_moveSkeleton** nodes that this procedure could have created.

```
string $found = `match "_moveSkeleton" $parentNodes[0]`;
```

If it is a **_moveSkeleton** node, then simply set the $moveRoot to the current parent.

```
if( size($found) )
   $moveRoot = $parentNodes[0];
```

If the **_moveSkeleton** node doesn't exist, then create it.

```
else
   $moveRoot = `group -name "_moveSkeleton" -world $destRootNode`;
```

The **_moveSkeleton** node is then moved to the initial position of the destination root node.

```
move -worldSpace
    ($destPos[0] - $srcPos[0])
    ($destPos[1] - $srcPos[1])
    ($destPos[2] - $srcPos[0]) $moveRoot;
}
```

11.1.5 Motion Paths

Rather than set a series of keyframes for the position and rotation of an object, it is often easier to create a curve that an object moves along. The curve defines the path the object follows. By creating a curve on a surface, you can easily set up an animation in which the object moves across the surface. It is also possible to have the object roll into and out of the turns as it moves along the curve.

1. Open the **MotionPathCone.ma** scene.

   The scene consists of a cone and curve. You'd like to set it up so that the cone moves along the path.

2. Execute the following:

   ```
   string $mpNode = 'pathAnimation -curve myCurve myCone';
   // Result: motionPath1 //
   ```

   The cone is moved to the start of the curve. Maya has created a variety of dependency nodes to make this possible.

   While it isn't necessary to know the exact details of these nodes, it is important to understand the general workflow. Since the motion path animation controls the position of the **myCone** object, the **translateX**, **translateY**, and **translateZ** attributes are driven by a **motionPath** node. Figure 11.4 is a diagram of the dependency graph.

   Starting from the left, the **myCurveShape** is the actual curve that the object moves along. The **motionPath1_uValue** is an animation curve node that is used to animate the *u* parameter. Both of these nodes feed into the **motionPath1** node. This node is responsible for calculating the position and rotation of the object at a given parametric position (*u*) along the curve. In this diagram, the output from the **motionPath1** node, the final *x* position, is fed into another node, **addDoubleLinear1**, which then passes it finally to the **myCone's translateX** attribute. A similar flow of data happens for both the **myCone's translateY** and **translateZ** attributes. The **addDoubleLinear** node is a simple node that takes two numbers and adds them together. The result

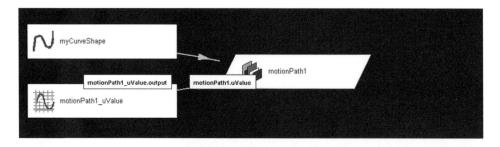

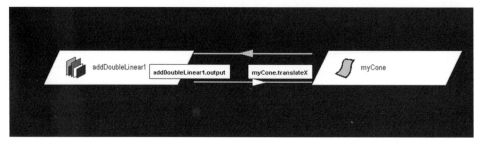

FIGURE 11.4

Dependency graph.

of this addition is then placed in its **output** attribute. In this example, the **addDoubleLinear** node has only one value, so this is output directly.

At the end of the animation range, you'd like the object to be positioned at the end of the curve. To do this, you need to create another key for the *u* parameter. First, the name of the motion path node is needed. Fortunately, the `pathAnimation` command returns the name of the motion path node created. You have stored this in the `$mpNode` variable.

Second, you need to know the parametric range of the curve, that is, the start and end parametric values of the curve's first and last control points. Execute the following to get the curve's maximum *u* extent:

```
float $maxUValue = 'getAttr myCurveShape.minMaxValue.maxValue';
```

Last, you need to know the time at the end of the animation range.

```
float $endTime = 'playbackOptions -query - animationEndTime';
```

With these three pieces of information, you can now create a key.

```
setKeyframe -time $endTime -value $maxUValue -attribute uValue
    $mpNode;
```

This creates a key for the **uValue** attribute of the motion path node (`$mpNode`). The key is created at the end of the animation (`$endTime`), and the value is set to the maximum possible parametric value (`$maxUValue`) for the curve.

3. Click on the **Play** button.

The cone now moves along the curve. It is also possible to create start and end times for the path using the following statement:

```
pathAnimation -startTimeU 0 -endTimeU 48 -curve myCurve myCone;
```

However, the previous method demonstrates how to create keys at any time. You'd now like for the cone to follow the direction of the path.

4. Execute the following:

```
pathAnimation -edit -follow yes myCone;
```

5. Click on the **Play** button.

The cone now moves with its tip pointing in the direction of the path. You'd also like the cone to *bank* along the curve. When an object banks, it rotates into and out of the turns.

6. Execute the following:

```
pathAnimation -edit -bank yes myCone;
```

If you play the animation, it isn't obvious, by looking at the cone, how much it banks. Use one of the other axes to point forward, so you can see the effect of the banking better. Execute the following:

```
pathAnimation -edit -followAxis x myCone;
```

The *x*-axis now points forward, thereby making the point of the cone face outwards. The animation now better shows the effect of the banking. To reduce the amount of banking, execute the following:

```
pathAnimation -edit -bankScale 0.5 myCone;
```

The cone now dips less into and out of the turns. Switch back to having the cone tip face forward by executing the following:

```
pathAnimation -edit -followAxis y myCone;
```

To have the cone change its shape to slither along the path, execute the following:

```
flow myCone;
```

7. Click on the **Play** button.

The cone is now encased in a lattice that deforms the cone as it moves along the path.

Examples Using MEL with Solid Body Dynamics

12

Mark R. Wilkins
Chris Kazmier

CHAPTER CONTENTS

Unlike particles, solid bodies do not have a class of expressions all their own to aid in creating complex animation. However, MEL and expressions are still quite useful in setting up and controlling solid body dynamics systems.

In the following examples, we'll explore how to use MEL to construct scenes that use solid body dynamics and how to use collision events to trigger behaviors both in scenes that only consist of solid bodies and in scenes that combine solid bodies with particles.

12.1 **EXAMPLE 1: PARTICLE COLLISIONS**

In this example, we will look at particles and how they interact with surfaces. We can tell a particle, or particles in a system, to collide and react with a surface or groups of surfaces (Fig. 12.1). These surfaces can be either NURBS or polygon objects.

Let's start off by making a simple collision with a polygon grid and some particles.

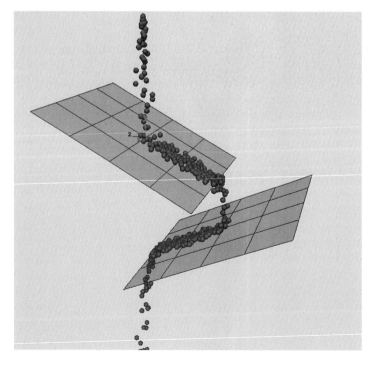

FIGURE 12.1

Particles cascading down two planes.

12.1.1 **Create the Scene**

Select Create > Polygon Primitives > Plane □. This will open the Polygon Plane Options window. Type in the settings for a 4 × 4 plane, as shown in Fig. 12.2.

Or if you like, open the Script Editor (Fig. 12.3) and enter the following MEL command:

```
polyPlane -width 1 -height 1 -subdivisionsX 4
        -subdivisionsY 4 -axis 0 1 0;
```

(Remember to press the Enter key on the numeric keypad to execute the command.)

We need to rename and scale up the plane, so select pPlane1 (it should be selected already), and enter 6 in the scale X, Y, and Z fields in the Channel Box. Now change the name of the plane to Floor in the Channel Box (Fig. 12.4).

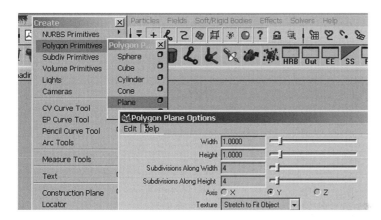

FIGURE 12.2

Polygon Plane Options window.

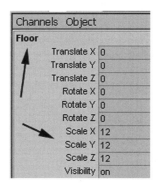

FIGURE 12.4

Renaming and scaling floor plane in Channel Box.

FIGURE 12.3

Script Editor button.

We can do all of this in MEL using the `rename` and `setAttr` commands:

```
rename pPlane1 Floor;
setAttr Floor.scaleX 6;
setAttr Floor.scaleY 6;
setAttr Floor.scaleZ 6;
```

Toggle off the Grid in the Display menu, so we can see our Floor better.

Now let's put in a directional type of emitter and hook up the collisions. First, create the emitter by accessing the Dynamics page and Selecting Particles > Create Emitter ☐ (Fig. 12.5).

Let's change some settings in the options window and add a name to our emitter (Fig. 12.6). Set the Type to Directional, the Rate to 30, and the Directions to X = 0,

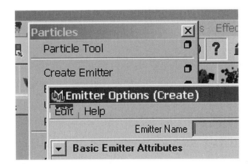

FIGURE 12.5

Creating an emitter with custom options.

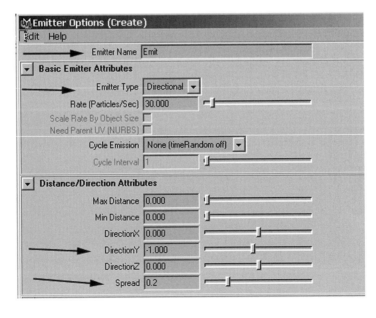

FIGURE 12.6

Emitter options to change.

Y = −1.0, and Z = 0. Also, change the Spread to 0.2. Move the emitter 4 units in Y to give us some time before the emitted particles intersect with the Floor.

Following is the MEL code for the emitter. Now, though, instead of moving the emitter in Y, we just use the -position flag. Let's also create a string array variable that will contain the results of the emitter creation command by using the single quote symbols to enclose the string. By doing this, the string array will contain the names of the nodes that were created. The name Emit will be in array position 0 and its shape node EmitShape will be in array position 1.

```
string $eObject [] = 'emitter -position 0 4 0 -type direction
                     -name Emit -rate 30 -speed 1 -spread 0.2
                     -dx 0 -dy -1.0 -dz 0';
```

When we create an emitter in the Maya interface, it's automatically connected to a particle object. In MEL, we must do this by hand. Here's how to create a particle object and make the connections so that the emitter knows which particle (particle1) to emit. Let's also again store the result name in another string array variable and then use the results in both strings to hook them together with connectDynamic.

```
string $pObject[] = 'particle';
connectDynamic -em $eObject[0] $pObject[0];
```

Now let's change our playback start and end times to a range of 1–500. Then, move the perspective camera to center the scene in its panel and play (Fig. 12.7).

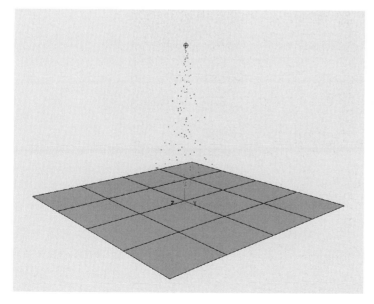

FIGURE 12.7

Directional emitter in action.

To set the start and end times, if you like, you can use the following MEL command:

```
playbackOptions -min 1 -max 500;
```

12.1.2 **Collide the Particles**

Select `particle1`. Then, hold down the Shift key and select `Floor`. Go to the Particles menu and select the Make Collide function (Fig. 12.8).

The MEL code to make the floor a collision object for the particles follows:

```
collision -resilience 1.0 -friction 0.0 Floor;
connectDynamic -collisions Floor particle1;
```

The collision command makes a `geoConnector` node that gives the object `Floor` additional dynamic attributes related to collisions. Then, `connectDynamic` connects the `particle1` object to `Floor` so that particles collide with the floor.

To take a look for yourself, choose Window > Hypergraph and select `Floor` (Fig. 12.9). Now click the Up and DownStream Connections icon (Fig. 12.10). Figure 12.11 shows what you see in the Hypergraph.

Now, play back the scene to see `particle1` bouncing off the floor without going through the floor (Fig. 12.12).

FIGURE 12.8

Make Collide menu item.

FIGURE 12.9

Hypergraph menu item.

FIGURE 12.10

Up and DownStream Connections button.

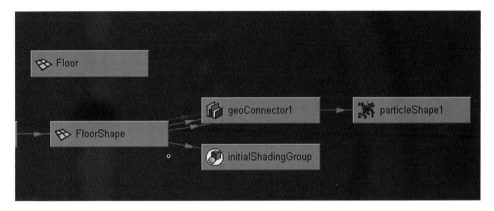

FIGURE 12.11

The geoConnector that implements collisions in Hypergraph.

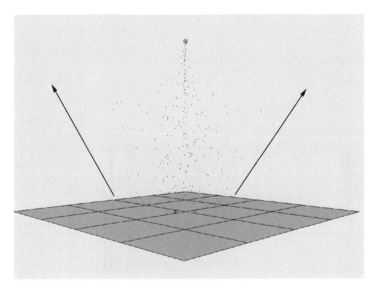

FIGURE 12.12

Particles bouncing off the floor.

12.1.3 Setting Controls for Collisions

Now, we can use MEL to see more details about how the collisions occur. First, let's look at the geoConnector1 that was created. If we select Floor in the Maya interface and look in the Channel Box, we will see the geoConnector1. Once it is selected, we will see an attribute called Tessellation Factor that is set to 200. This is how Floor is being subdivided for the dynamics solver. The higher the tessellation value, the more accurate the collision motion will be. This tessellation attribute controls how the dynamics engine breaks the surface down into triangles when calculating the collision motion (Fig. 12.13).

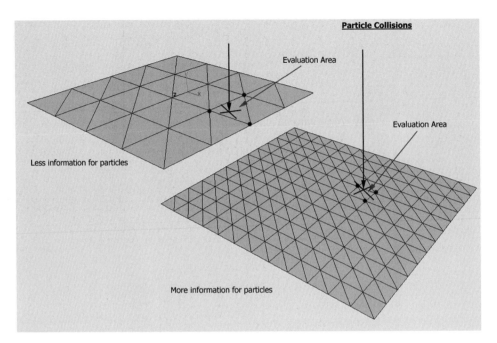

FIGURE 12.13

Effect of increasing the `tessellation factor`.

Also, on the particle object there is a setting called `traceDepth`. The default `traceDepth` is set to 10. If it is set to 0, the particles will pass right through the surface. This setting controls how accurately Maya tracks the positions of the particles as it calculates collisions. You can also set a per-particle attribute called `traceDepthPP` that can control this on an individual particle basis. Changing these attributes can be a solution for problems with particle/surface collisions.

> **Tip:** We have been using a polygon surface for this example, but if we had used a NURBS surface, it would be the same. When you use a NURBS surface, Maya adds an extra step to the collision calculations because Maya will convert the NURBS to polygons.

If you are using production-ready, high-resolution models, it's a good idea to make stand-in polygon objects for use in particle collisions instead of using a high-resolution model when you can. The calculations will be simpler, and you will save some time when you experiment with the scene.

12.1.4 Using Other Controls in geoConnector Node

Other control options that the `geoConnector` node provides are Resilience and Friction. You can think of Resilience as a "bounce" setting and Friction as a "slide" control. If we change the current settings on both of these controls, we can see the difference. Select the Floor object and get a listing for geoConnector1 in the Channel Box. Set Resilience to 0.0 and Friction to 0.5 (Fig. 12.14).

You can set the Resilience and Friction controls in MEL as follows:

```
setAttr geoConnector1.resilience 0.0;
setAttr geoConnector1.friction 0.2;
```

Figure 12.15 shows the results of playback. The particles in particle1 now slide over the surface.

12.1.5 Finish Scene Using MEL

Now let's finish the scene by adding a second Floor object and rotating it so that particle1 particles slide off one floor to the other. We will also add a gravity field to the simulation so that the particles fall downward.

First rotate the Floor object −26.00 in X.

```
xform -rotation -26 0 0 Floor;
```

OUTPUTS
geoConnector1
Tessellation Factor	200
Resilience	0
Friction	0.2

FIGURE 12.14

Dynamic collision settings for geoConnector1 node.

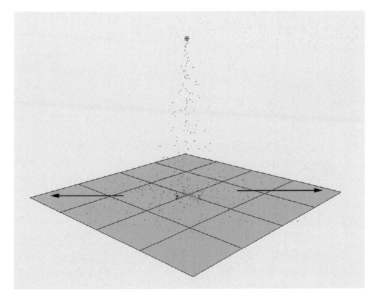

FIGURE 12.15

Particles sliding over surface.

Copy Floor and move it 3.0 units in Z, −3.0 units in Y. Then, rotate it 26.0 units in X.

```
duplicate -name Floor1 Floor;
xform -a translation 0 -3 -3 Floor1;
xform -a rotation 26 0 0 Floor1;
```

We need to make particle1 collide with the new Floor1, so let's add a second geoConnector node and set its Resilience and Friction the same as geoConnector1.

```
collision -resilience 0 -friction 0.2 Floor1;
connectDynamic -collisions Floor1 particle1;
```

Attach a gravity field to particle1 so that it will fall and slide off the Floor objects.

```
gravity -magnitude 3 -attenuation 0.0;
connectDynamic -fields gravityField1 particle1;
```

Finally, make particle1 a sphere type and set its radius to 0.2.

```
setAttr particle1.particleRenderType 4;
addAttr -longName radius -defaultValue 0.2 particleShape1;
```

Figure 12.16 shows the results of playback.

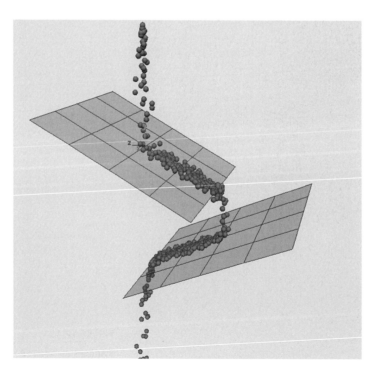

FIGURE 12.16

Resulting particle cascade.

In this example, we have seen how collision objects interact with particle objects and how to set up collision objects in MEL. In the next examples, we will look at how to use MEL to create more complex particle collision effects.

12.2 **EXAMPLE 2: COLLISION EVENTS**

In this example, we will take a look at a method for triggering particle behavior with collisions, called an event. Figure 12.17 shows the results of an event. Events can cause particles to do certain things when a particle collides with a surface, or a number of collisions have taken place. They also can be used to trigger MEL scripts.

Start by loading the example scene. Choose File > Open and find the scene chapter20.ma in the archive on the Web site at http://www.melscripting.com.

The scene has three polygon objects named `bucket1`, `bucket2`, and `bucket3`. These were made by revolving a NURBS curve with the output set to Polygon in the Revolve options (Fig. 12.18).

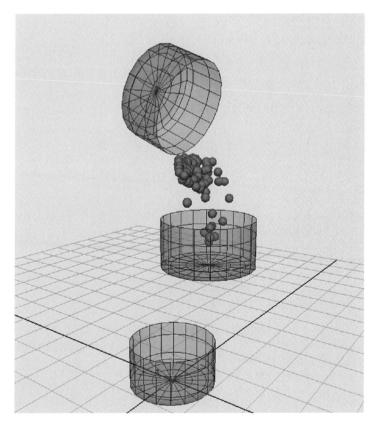

FIGURE 12.17

Particles in buckets.

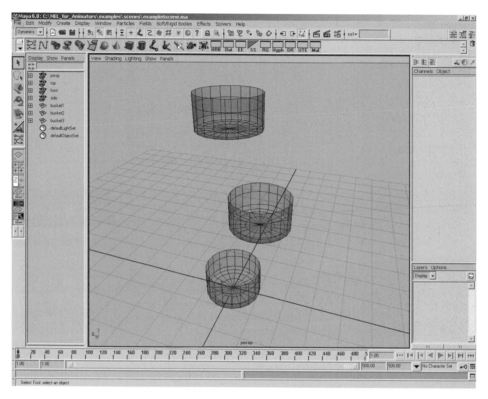

FIGURE 12.18

Contents of chapter12.ma.

12.2.1 **Overview**

We will create an emitter, positioned such that the particles fall into the first bucket, bucket1, and then a collision event will make bucket1 spill the particles into bucket2. Then, another collision event will trigger bucket2 to spill into the last bucket, bucket3. The collision events will call a MEL expression that will make the buckets rotate and spill the particles.

12.2.2 **Add Emitter and Particles**

In the Dynamics page (Fig. 12.19), create an emitter by choosing Particles > Create Emitter ❐. This will be a directional emitter called waterEmit with an emission rate of 100, a direction of −1.0 in Y, and a spread of 0.2 (Fig. 12.20).

In the side view, move the emitter above bucket1, perhaps to X = 0, Y = 9.0, and Z = 0. As before, we can simplify this process using MEL.

FIGURE 12.19

Create Emitter menu item.

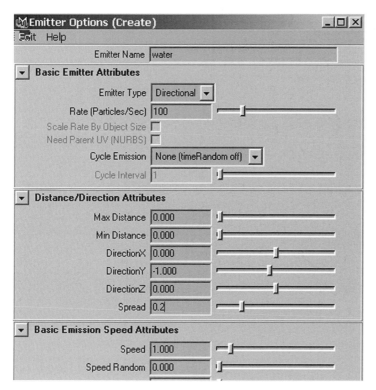

FIGURE 12.20

Emitter options.

Launch the Script Editor and enter the following:

```
string $eObject[] = 'emitter -name waterEmit -position 0 9 0
        -type direction -rate 100
        -spread 0.2 -dx 0 -dy -1.0 -dz 0';
string $pObject [] = 'particle';
connectDynamic -emitter $eObject[0] $pObject[0];
```

Set the start and end frames in the timeline to 1 and 500, respectively, and then play. You should see the particles fall through bucket1 (Fig. 12.21).

Let's make bucket1 a collision object and change the particle render type to sphere. Also, when we add the collision node, let's set the bucket's Resilience to a small bounce and set Friction to 0.

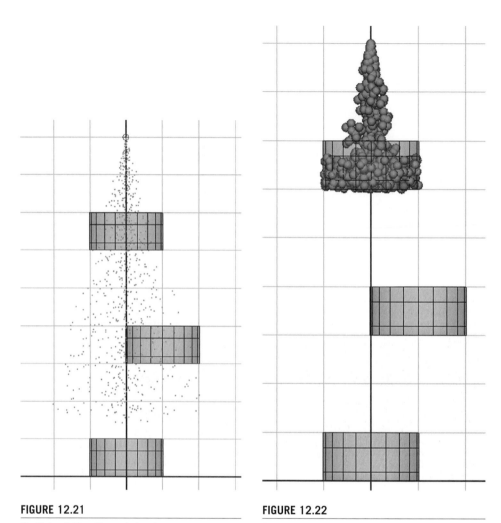

FIGURE 12.21

Particles falling through buckets.

FIGURE 12.22

Particles caught in first bucket.

```
collision -resilience 0.3 -friction 0.0 bucket1;
connectDynamic -collisions bucket1 particle1;
setAttr particle1.particleRenderType 4;
addAttr -longName radius -defaultValue 0.1 particleShape1;
```

Now play. Figure 12.22 shows a side view of what you should see in your scene.

12.2.3 Dynamic Relationships

In Example 1, we saw how the menu item for making collision objects corresponded to MEL commands. Now, let's look at the menu equivalent to the `connectDynamic` command. Choose Window > Relationship Editors > Dynamic Relationships (Fig. 12.23).

Select `particle1` by clicking on its name in the object list. Then, click the Collisions option in the SELECTION MODES area. You will see `bucket1Shape` in the list (Fig. 12.24).

The operations you can perform in this window correspond to the function of the `connectDynamic` MEL command. This window is an interface for organizing and connecting fields, emitters, and collisions.

12.2.4 Limit Number of Particles and Add Gravity

We only want 150 particles to fall into the buckets. To do this, set the Max Count attribute of `particle1` to 150. You will find it in the Channel Box. (By default, this attribute is set to −1, which allows Maya to create an infinite number of particles.) The corresponding MEL command would be

```
setAttr particleShape1.maxCount 150;
```

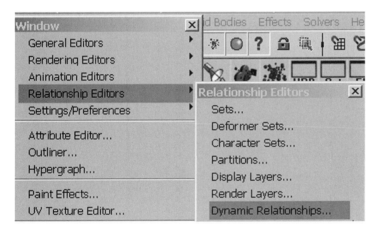

FIGURE 12.23

Dynamic Relationships editor menu item.

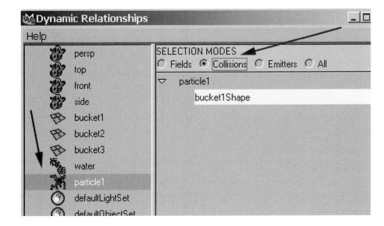

FIGURE 12.24

Creating a collision relationship in Dynamic Relationships editor.

If you prefer to set this attribute in MEL, type the above statement into the Script Editor. Then, add a `gravity` field and connect it to `particle1` by typing the following MEL commands:

```
gravity -magnitude 10 -attenuation 0.3 -dx 0 -dy −1 -dz 0;
connectDynamic -fields gravityField1 particle1;
```

Figure 12.25 shows the results of playback.

Now, only 150 particles will fall into `bucket1`, while the `gravity` field adds some force to `particle1` to keep the particles under control while still retaining a small amount of bounce.

12.2.5 Add Other Collisions

Now, we'll add the other buckets (2 and 3) to the collisions. Let's use the same settings for Resilience and Friction as we did before. Enter the following MEL commands:

```
collision -resilience 0.3 -friction 0.0 bucket2;
collision -resilience 0.3 -friction 0.0 bucket3;
connectDynamic -collisions bucket2 particle1;
connectDynamic -collisions bucket3 particle1;
```

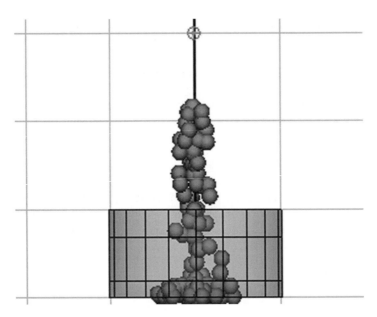

FIGURE 12.25

Smaller number of particles falling into `bucket1`.

The particles in `particle1` will collide with the other buckets as they do with `bucket1`. You won't see this yet, though, because the particles bounce and come to a stop in `bucket1`.

12.2.6 Events

Usually, events are used to split or emit particles when collisions happen. This approach can be used to make splashes from rain particles when they collide with an object. In this example, instead, we will use the `event` command to launch a MEL procedure that will perform a task when an individual particle in the system has a collision with a particular bucket.

We start by creating an event object, which manages what Maya does when an event occurs. When we enter an `event` MEL command to create an event object for `particle1`, we will use the `-proc` flag to designate a MEL procedure that Maya will run when the event occurs. The syntax of the `event` command follows. Do not enter this command just yet.

```
event -name mainEvent -die 0 -count 0
      -proc eventProc particle1;
```

Before creating the object, though, we need to define the `eventProc` MEL script. The `-name` flag designates a name for the event object. The `-die 0` flag establishes that the event should not delete the particles that collide. With a nonzero value, the `-count` flag tells `event` that it should wait for a particular collision, but by setting it to zero we can ensure that the event will take place every time the particle collides with a collision object.

A MEL procedure to be called by an event object, in this case named `event-Proc`, must accept three parameters: first, a string for the particle object name; second, an integer for the particular particle Id; and third, a string for the name of the collision object. Thus, the procedure's definition must look like this:

```
global proc eventProc (string $particle, int $Id,
                        string $geoObj);
```

In a text editor of your choice, enter the code shown in Fig. 12.26. The event will pass the procedure the name of particle system, the particle Id that is colliding, and the object that it is colliding with. This will execute every time a collision takes place.

Instead of defining some complex operation within this procedure that the collision events will trigger, we'll design it to set an attribute on each of the buckets that indicates that a collision has taken place. Then, we will use expressions in the scene to generate the behavior we want when we see that the attribute has been set. Leave your text editor open for now; we will return to the `eventProc` procedure after we have created the buckets' custom trigger attributes.

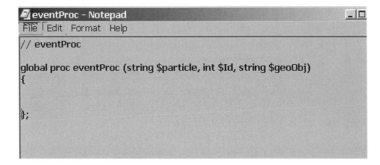

FIGURE 12.26

Shell of an `eventProc` declaration.

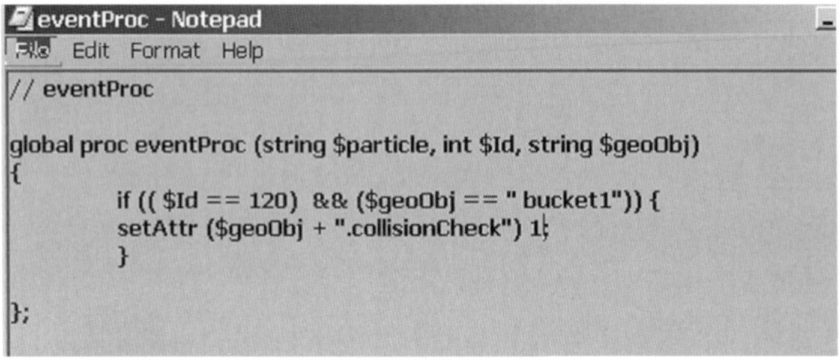

FIGURE 12.27

First bucket's part of the `eventProc` function.

In the Script Editor, type the following statements:

```
addAttr -ln collisionCheck -at long -min 0 -max 1 -keyable 1
        -dv 0 bucket1;
addAttr -ln collisionCheck -at long -min 0 -max 1 -keyable 1
        -dv 0 bucket2;
addAttr -ln collisionCheck -at long -min 0 -max 1 -keyable 1
        -dv 0 bucket3;
```

The above code will add a switch to the buckets that the `eventProc` procedure will change from 0 to 1 when a collision occurs. This will tell the buckets to rotate, making the particles fall into the next bucket. Once you have created these attributes, you will see them in the Channel Box when you select each bucket.

Now, in the `eventProc` procedure, we will add the code that will set the trigger attribute. We'll use an `if` statement that will wait for the particle whose Id is 120 to strike `bucket1`. When this happens, we will change `bucket1.collisionCheck` from 0 to 1. Enter the code in Fig. 12.27 into your `eventProc` procedure.

Note that the `"bucket1"` string has a space after the first double quote and before the word `bucket1`, due to the way the Maya passes arguments to the `eventProc`.

```
if (( $Id == 120) && ($geoObj == " bucket1")) {
    set Attr ($geoObj + ".collisionCheck") 1;
}
```

Now, we can add analogous code for each of the other buckets. Make your eventProc look like the following code block and then save the file in your script directory. Save the file as eventProc.mel since Maya requires that the MEL file be named the same as the global proc you wish to call from your script path. You can find the directories in your script path by typing getenv("MAYA_SCRIPT_PATH") in the Script Editor. Just to make sure that Maya sees the script, we will define it manually, but if you want to have the script defined when you launch Maya, you must place it in the directories that are set in your environment.

```
// eventProc

global proc eventProc (string $particle, int $Id,
                       string $geoObj)
{
   if (( $Id == 120) && ($geoObj == " bucket1")) {
      setAttr ($geoObj + ".collisionCheck") 1;
   }
   if (( $Id == 120) && ($geoObj == " bucket2")) {
      setAttr ($geoObj + ".collisionCheck") 1;
   }
   if (( $Id == 120) && ($geoObj == " bucket3")) {
      setAttr ($geoObj + ".collisionCheck") 1;
   }
};
```

Source the script from the Script Editor menu to define the global procedure eventProc (Fig. 12.28). If you get an error, look over the script to see if you have any syntax problems. The way to source a script with MEL would be to type in the Script Editor:

```
source eventProc.mel;
```

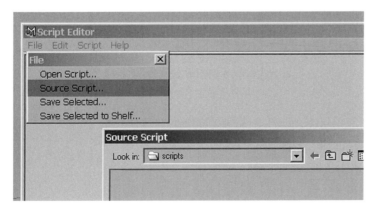

FIGURE 12.28

Source Script menu item.

Now, enter the previously discussed event command in MEL to define the event object that will call the eventProc, as follows:

```
event -name mainEvent -die 0 -count 0
       -proc eventProc particle1;
```

12.2.7 Expression for Buckets

Now that we have created attributes that get set to 1 when particle Id 120 collides with each bucket, we must create expressions to make the buckets tip when this attribute is set. This expression must do a couple of things. First, the expression must make sure to set all the collisionCheck attributes to 0 at frame 1. Without this, once the attribute is triggered there is no way to tell collisionCheck to go back to 0 when we rewind the scene. The second is to tell the bucket rotations to go back to rotation 0 0 0 at frame 1.

Open the Expression Editor by choosing Window > Animation Editors > Expression Editor (Fig. 12.29).

Enter the following code:

```
// Initialize the bucket(1-3).collisionCheck to 0 when on
   frame 1

if (frame == 1) {                    // Check if we're back on frame 1
   setAttr bucket1.collisionCheck 0;
   setAttr bucket2.collisionCheck 0;
   setAttr bucket3.collisionCheck 0;
                              // Set all collisionChecks to 0

}
```

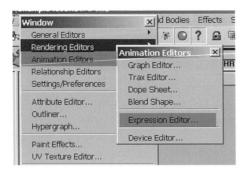

FIGURE 12.29

Opening the Expression Editor.

```
// Initialize the bucket to a rotation of 0 0 0
if (frame == 1) {                  // Check if we're back on frame 1
    bucket1.rotateX = 0;
    bucket2.rotateX = 0;
    bucket3.rotateX = 0;           // Set all rotateX's back to 0
}
```

This part of the expression initializes the collisionCheck and rotate attributes when the animation is rewound. In the same expression, we need now to set up the actions that take place after the event triggers the collisionCheck attribute. Also, notice that we are using a setAttr command for the collisionCheck in order to avoid setting up a connection between the expression node and the collisionCheck attributes, which would make it impossible for the eventProc() callback to set that attribute at runtime. This is why we can't simply use bucket.collisionCheck = 1 syntax in the expression. We will rotate the buckets with a small increment to the rotateX attribute of each bucket when that bucket's collisionCheck attribute is set. The motion will not have any ease in/ease out, but it will suffice for now. In the same expression, after the code above, enter the following:

```
// Set up a triggered rotation with a += to the rotateX attrs
if (bucket1.collisionCheck != 0) {
                           // Check if the attr is not equal 0
    if (bucket1.rotateX > -111) {
                               // If we are not at -111 rotateX
        bucket1.rotateX += -2; // Add the current X -2 each frame
    }
}

if (bucket2.collisionCheck != 0) {   // Same for bucket2,
                                     // only use positive
    if (bucket2.rotateX < 111) {     // numbers for reverse rotation
        bucket2.rotateX += 2;
    }
}

if (bucket3.collisionCheck != 0) {
                                     // Use the same sets as bucket1
    if (bucket3.rotateX > -111) {
        bucket3.rotateX += -2;
    }
}
```

Now, commit the expression by clicking the Create button. Figure 12.30 shows the results of playback.

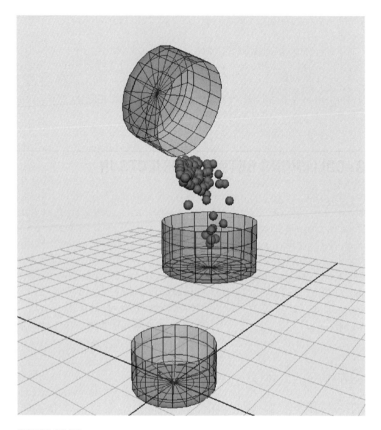

FIGURE 12.30

Finished digital bucket brigade.

12.2.8 Edit Settings to Fix Problems

There are two things that we need to change. The first is to increase the tessellation factor in the `geoConnectors` to 600. We will get better collisions this way since some particles travel through the buckets every once in a while. Use the following statements in MEL:

```
setAttr geoConnector1.tessellationFactor 600;
setAttr geoConnector2.tessellationFactor 600;
setAttr geoConnector3.tessellationFactor 600;
```

We also want to change the friction in `bucket2` to 0.2, so we can cut down on the sliding around in `bucket2`. Input the following statement:

```
setAttr geoConnector2.friction 0.2;
```

12.2.9 **Speed**

As you noticed, the scene does not play back in "real time" because of the collisions, to event, to expression calls. Pick a good camera position and shoot a Playblast movie to see the animation at full speed. If you run into memory problems, lower the Scale settings in the Playblast options. Playblast and its options are available by choosing Windows > Playblast ☐.

12.3 **EXAMPLE 3: COLLISIONS BETWEEN OBJECTS IN SOLID DYNAMICS**

In Example 2, we looked at collisions between particles and objects. Solid dynamics allow similar object interactions but with much more control over how they react to each other. Figure 12.31 shows an example of the solid dynamics approach.

Start by building an array of polygonal planes in a 3 × 3 grid. Select Create > Polygon Primitives > Plane ☐ and make a plane with four subdivisions in width and height. Leave the rest of the Plane options at their default settings (Fig. 12.32).

Rename the pPlane1 object to grid in the Channel Box, and set the X, Y, and Z scale values to 4, 4, and 4, respectively. To do this in the Script Editor, use the following statements:

```
rename pPlane1 grid;
xform -worldSpace -scale 4 4 4 grid;
```

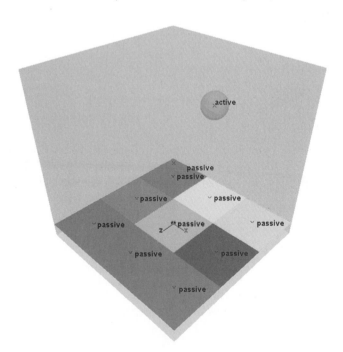

FIGURE 12.31

Bouncing ball made with solid bodies.

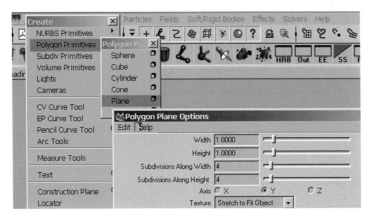

FIGURE 12.32

Polygon Plane Options menu item.

Remember to look in the lower right corner of the screen for the Script Editor button.

> **Note:** We have been using the `xform` command frequently in these examples because this command can complete several functions at once. Otherwise, you might have to make several calls to the `move`, `scale`, and `rotate` commands. In the long run, you will find it more useful to do all at once with `xform`.

In this example, we will assign a shader to `grid`. To attach a `shading-Map` type material to `grid`, choose Windows > Rendering Editors > Hypershade (Fig. 12.33).

Create a `shadingMap` shader from the Create Materials menu by clicking on the Shading Map icon (Fig. 12.34).

Rename `shadingMap1` to `shadingMap` in the Hypershade window by holding down the right mouse button on the shader icon for the rename option. Then, with `grid` selected, select the `shadingMap` icon, hold the right mouse down, and pick Assign Material to Selection. Now `grid` will use `shadingMap` for rendering. Also, each shader has a shading group that defines what objects it shades. Now that we have renamed the shader, rename the corresponding shading group as well.

```
rename shadingMap1SG shadingMapSG;
```

12.3.1 Write Small Duplicate and Position Script

Instead of just duplicating the `grid` eight times so that we get nine grids in the set, we can script it by using an array variable to store the grid positions and move through the array as we duplicate. Our script will duplicate the grid using the array of positions, making a copy of `shadingMap` and assigning it to the new grids, using

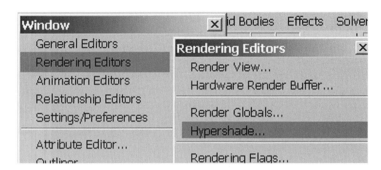

FIGURE 12.33

Hypershade menu item.

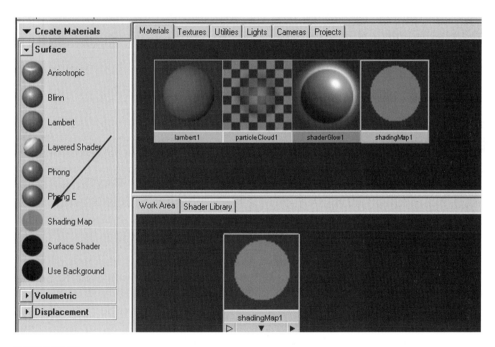

FIGURE 12.34

Shading Map icon in Hypershade window.

string substitutions. This way, each new grid will have its own `shadingMap`. Open your favorite text editor and enter the following header:

```
global proc gridDup () {
```

Now enter the array of positions that we want the other grids to be:

```
$gridArray = {"-4 0 -4", "-4 0 0", "-4 0 4", "0 0 -4",
             "0 0 4", "4 0 -4", "4 0 0", "4 0 4"};
```

We will need to use the `eval` command to assemble a command with the extracted string from `$gridArray` since we cannot use the string of numbers directly in an xform command. Create the for loop that will duplicate the grid and the shading-Map shader and assign the new shaders to the new grids. We are going to let Maya make the names of the new grids that are being duplicated and use them in the loop.

```
for ($i = 0; $i < 8; $i++) {

    // Duplicate grids and transform using array positions
        duplicate -rr grid;
    $cmd = "xform -worldSpace -translation " +
            ($gridArray[$i] + " grid" + ($i + 1) );
    eval($cmd);

    // Duplicate shadingMap shader group and assign to each grid
        duplicate -name ("shadingMap" + $i + "SG")
                    -upstreamNodes shadingMapSG;
    sets -e -forceElement ("shadingMap" + $i + "SG")
                    ("grid" + ($i + 1) );
    }// End loop
};    // End procedure
```

When we make the grid objects, they will be named grid1, grid2, grid3, and so on. Because $i starts at 0, we must use $i + 1 when we refer to the grid objects. The loop starts $i at a 0, which is fine for moving through the array, but we know that the grid names will start with grid1 at the first duplicate. Note that using the variable $i this way in the object name will not affect the actual value of $i.

12.3.2 Common Mistakes in Assembling String Variables

Remember to make sure there is a space before the word "grid" in double quotes.

Save your text file, naming it gridDup.mel. In the Script Editor, source it, using the Source Script menu item (Fig. 12.35). If you get any error messages, go back and check for syntax errors.

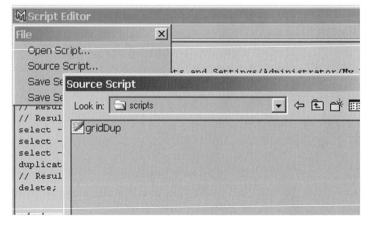

FIGURE 12.35

Source Script menu item.

> **Tip:** This is not really an interactive script that you can use to duplicate any object. Instead, it's a one-time script developed for this particular scene. Later, if you want to modify this script to be more generic, you can alter it to use string parameters in place of the hard-coded strings `grid` and `shadingMap1`.

Now, in the Script Editor, type `gridDup` without `.mel` and press the Enter key on the numeric keypad. This will execute the script and link the new shaders to the new grid objects. Figure 12.36 indicates what you should see in the Maya interface; Fig. 12.37, what you should see in the Hypershade window.

12.3.3 Create Collision Box

Now, we need to create a polygonal box that will surround the grids. In the Script Editor, enter the `polyCube` command, as follows:

```
polyCube -name collisionBox. -w 1 -h 1 -d 1 -sx 1 -sy 1
                             -sz 1 -ax 0 1 0
                             -tx 1 -ch 1;
```

Next, scale and transform the box to surround the grids:

```
xform -worldSpace -scale 12 12 12 collisionBox;
xform -worldSpace -translation 0 5 0 collisionBox;
```

Turn on Shading > Smooth Shade All and Shade Options > WireFrame on Shaded in the persp panel. We can't see through the box, but we can adjust the transparency

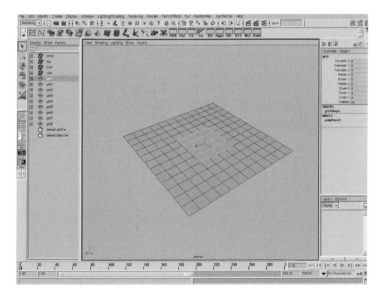

FIGURE 12.36

Grid objects in main window.

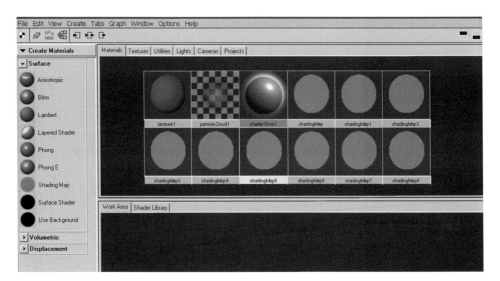

FIGURE 12.37

Grid objects in Hypershade window.

parameter on its shader to fix this. Return to the Hypershade window and adjust the transparency on the `lambert1` shader, which was assigned to the `collisionBox` when it was created. Double-click the `lambert1` icon and move the Transparency slider almost all the way to the right (Fig. 12.38). Figure 12.39 shows what you should see in the persp window.

12.3.4 Flip Normals on collisionBox

Select the `collisionBox` and select the menu item Display > Polygon Components > Normals (Fig. 12.40). From this, you can see that the normals are pointing out. We need them reversed for correct collisions to happen within the box.

Now we can see the normals pointing out in the interface (Fig. 12.41).

Let's flip the normals, using the polynormal command in the Script Editor.

```
polyNormal -normalMode 0 -ch 1 collisionBox.f[0:5];
```

We have to do this for each of the polygon faces; thus, the `collisionBox.f[0:5]`. This statement has changed our selection mode. To change it back to Object mode, click the Select by Object Type icon (Fig. 12.42). Figure 12.43 shows the results of reversing the normals.

You can switch off the normal display by selecting menu item Display > Polygon Components > Normals with `collisionBox` selected.

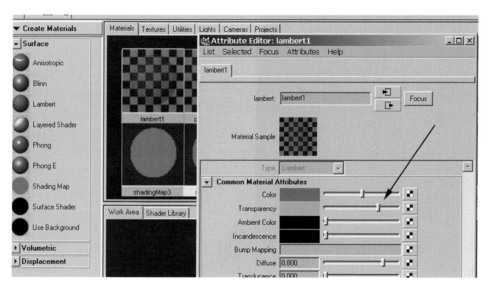

FIGURE 12.38

`lambert1` shader options.

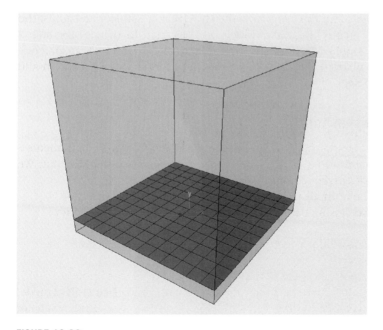

FIGURE 12.39

Semitransparent walls around the floor.

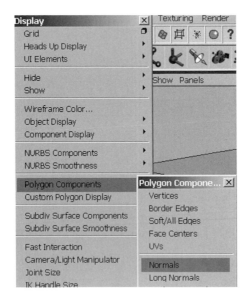

FIGURE 12.40

Normals menu item.

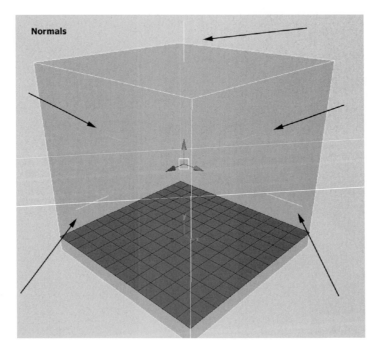

FIGURE 12.41

Normal components as displayed in persp panel.

FIGURE 12.42

Select by Object Type icon.

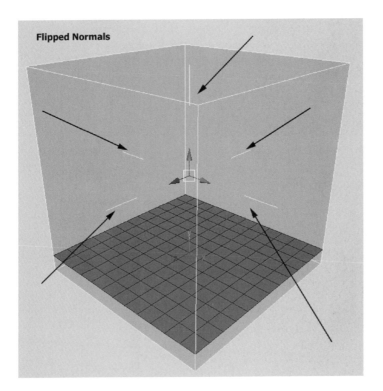

FIGURE 12.43

Reversed normals in persp panel.

12.3.5 **Active and Passive Rigid Bodies**

Now it's time to create a sphere and make it a dynamic object. First, create Ball. In the Script Editor, type the following code:

```
polySphere -name Ball -r 1 -subdivisionsX 12 -subdivisionsY 12
          -ax 0 1 0 -tx 1 -ch 1;
xform -worldSpace -scale 1.0 1.0 1.0;
xform -worldSpace -translation 0 5 0;
```

In the Dynamics menu group, select `Ball` and choose Soft/Rigid Body > Create Active Rigid Body ❏. As you can see, the solid dynamics options for objects are quite extensive. The `Ball` will be an active rigid body while the `collisionBox` will be a passive rigid body. The difference is that an active body acts and reacts to its dynamics and that of others, including active and passive rigid bodies. Passive rigid bodies do not react to active rigid bodies. Passive rigid bodies are instead fixed objects with which active rigid bodies can collide.

Settings for `Ball` are shown in Fig. 12.44. The attributes we are looking for are Static Friction, 0.1; Bounciness, 0.8; and Damping, 0.1.

In the Initial Settings frame, we want to add the settings shown in Fig. 12.45. Specifically, set Initial Spin to 0, 0, and 360, and Initial Velocity to 12, 0, and −12. Then, in Performance Attributes, set Stand In to Sphere (Fig. 12.46).

To set all of the above options, the MEL command statement follows:

```
rigidBody -active -m 1 -dp 0.1 -sf 0.1 -df 0.2 -b 0.8 -l 0
          -tf 600
          -iv 12 0 −12
          -iav 0 0 360 -c 0 -pc 0 -i 0 0 0 -imp 0 0 0
```

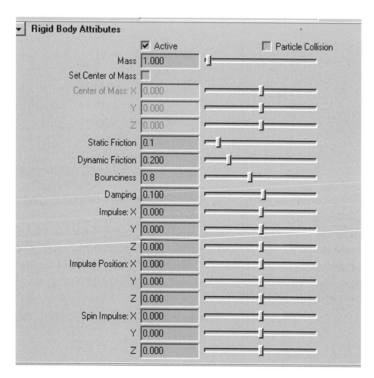

FIGURE 12.44

Rigid Body Attributes for `Ball`.

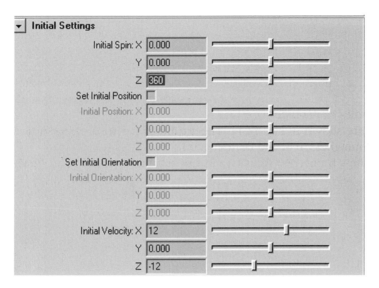

FIGURE 12.45

Initial Settings for `Ball`.

Performance Attributes

Stand In | Sphere ▾
Tessellation Factor | 600
Collision Layer | 0

FIGURE 12.46

Performance Attributes for `Ball`.

```
            -si 0 0 0
            -sio sphere Ball;
```

If we take a look in the Hypergraph, we will see all the connections that setting up rigid bodies creates (Fig. 12.47).

Now we need to make `collisionBox` a passive rigid body. Select the `collision-Box`. From the same menu that we used to make `Ball` an active rigid body, select the menu choice Passive Rigid Body ☐. Make the settings the same as you did for the active rigid body, except set Stand In to none and set all Initial Settings to 0.

The equivalent MEL command follows:

```
rigidBody -passive -m 1 -dp 0.1 -sf 0.2 -df 0.2 -b 0.7 -l 0
            -tf 600 -iv 0 0 0
            -iav 0 0 0 -c 0 -pc 0 -i 0 0 0 -imp 0 0 0 -si 0 0 0
            -sio none collisionBox;
```

Before you play back the scene, add a `gravity` field with a magnitude of 3 and a `turbulenceField` with a magnitude of 20. Both will have an Attenuation of 0 since

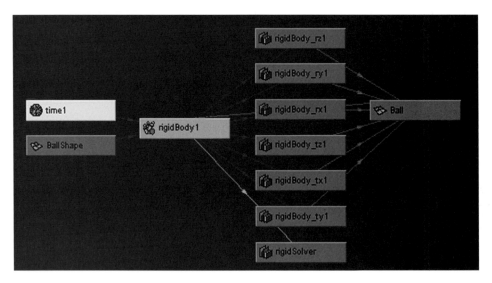

FIGURE 12.47

Rigid body connections in Hypergraph.

we want the effect of these fields to be instant. Following are the MEL commands to do this. (If you choose to use Maya's menus instead, remember to select the Ball first so that the fields will automatically connect to Ball.)

```
gravity -pos 0 0 0 -m 3 -att 0 -dx 0 -dy -1 -dz 0 -mxd -1;
turbulence -pos 0 0 0 -m 20 -att 0 -f 1 -mxd -1;
connectDynamic -f gravityField1 Ball;
connectDynamic -f turbulenceField1 Ball;
```

Now set the playback start and end at 1 and 300, respectively and play.

```
playbackOptions -min 1 -max 300;
```

The playback should resemble a bee-in-a-box animation in which the Ball bounces around in the collisionBox. If you get the following warning message in the Script Editor,

```
// Warning: Cycle on 'Ball.worldMatrix[0]' may not evaluate
as expected. (Use 'cycleCheck -e off' to disable this
warning.) //
```

just type cycleCheck -e off in the Script Editor.
Now, we will make the grids Passive Rigid Bodies for the Ball to collide with.

12.3.6 Make Each Grid a Passive Collision Object

There are two ways in MEL to make the grids passive collision objects for the Ball. The easiest is to select all the grids and run the rigidBody command.

```
select -r grid grid1 grid2 grid3 grid4 grid5 grid6 grid7 grid8;
rigidBody -passive -m 1 -dp 0.1 -sf 0.2 -df 0.2 -b 0.7 -l 0
          -tf 600
          -iv 0 0 0 -iav 0 0 0 -c 0 -pc 0 -i 0 0 0 -imp 0 0 0
          -si 0 0 0 -sio none;
```

The other is to use a for loop, as we did when we duplicated the grids. While using the loop is not as simple in this instance, if you needed to run other MEL commands as you were making each grid a passive collision object, you could place them in the loop to ensure that they are run at the same time.

You have one object named grid and a series named grid1 through grid8, so let's make grid a passive collision object without using a loop, since it does not have a number added at the end of its name. In the Script Editor, type the above rigidBody command, but this time specify the object by name rather than relying on the selection, as follows:

```
rigidBody -passive -m 1 -dp 0.1 -sf 0.2 -df 0.2 -b 0.7 -l 0
          -tf 600
          -iv 0 0 0 -iav 0 0 0 -c 0 -pc 0 -i 0 0 0 -imp 0 0 0
          -si 0 0 0 -sio none grid;
```

Now make the for loop:

```
for ($i = 1; $i < 9; $i++) {

    rigidBody -passive -m 1 -dp 0.1 -sf 0.2 -df 0.2 -b 0.7
              -l 0 -tf 600 -iv 0 0 0
              -iav 0 0 0 -c 0 -pc 0 -i 0 0 0 -imp 0 0 0 -si 0 0 0
              -sio none ("grid" + $i);
}
```

When you play back the above script, the Ball should now bounce off the grids and not the bottom of the collisionBox. If you want, go to the menu Solvers > Rigid Body Solver and turn on the Display Label option. This will tell you which colliders are passive and which are active (Fig. 12.48).

In the persp window, select Shading > Shade Options and turn off the Wireframe on Shaded option (Fig. 12.49).

12.3.7 Turn On Collision Data Options

Since we will be working with collision data, we need to turn on that option in the Attribute Editor for the rigidSolver object. Select Solvers > Rigid Body Solver and click the option Contact Data in the Rigid Solver States section (Fig. 12.50). This is not on by default since it will slow the simulation down from the regular performance. In this simulation, we will not see a difference.

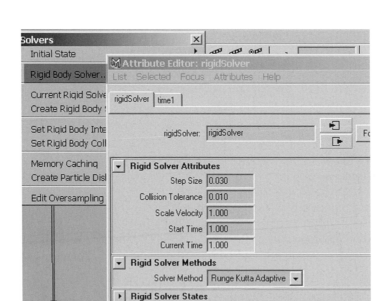

FIGURE 12.48

Rigid Body Solver's Display Label option.

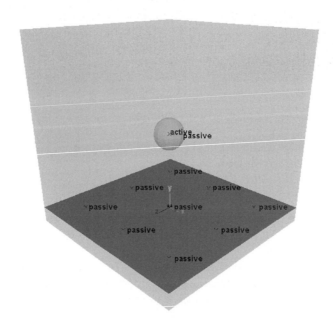

FIGURE 12.49

Scene with Wireframe display turned off.

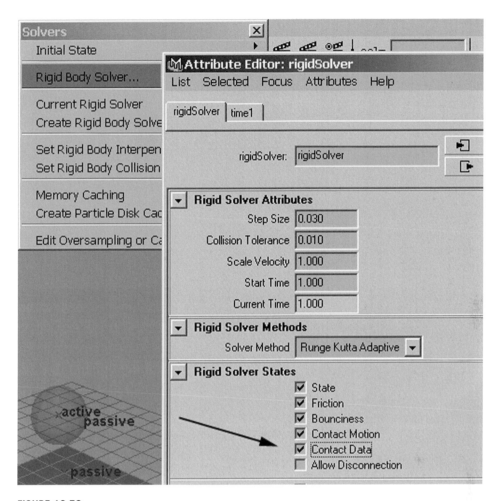

FIGURE 12.50

Contact Data option in Rigid Body Solver attributes.

12.3.8 **Change Color of Grids with Collisions**

Now we'll add an expression that will send a random RGB color to the Ball's shadingMap shader when Ball collides with one of the grids. We will start by adding the expression to grid's rigid body object and then we'll add the expression to the numbered grids' rigid body objects. In other words, we are going to attach the expressions to rigidBody3 through rigidBody11.

With rigidBody3 selected, open the Expression Editor with Windows > Animation Editors > Expression Editor. If you want an easy way to get to rigidBody3, use the Outliner with the Display Shapes option. Then open the + icon to see what is under the selected node (Fig. 12.51).

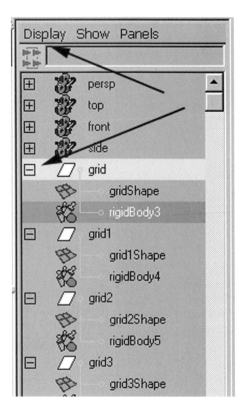

FIGURE 12.51

Using display shapes and expanding the outline to see `rigidBody3`.

In the Expression Editor, type the following code:

```
// Check to see if we are at frame 1 and
// set the color to grey

if (frame == 1) {
   setAttr shadingMap.shadingMapColor -type double3 0.5 0.5 0.5 ;
};

// Check if Ball has hit and capture first collision
// Change color to random RGB value

if (rigidBody3.contactCount > 0) {
   setAttr shadingMap.shadingMapColor -type double3 (rand(0,1))
                                    (rand(0,1)) (rand(0,1));
};
```

The nice thing about a rigid body's `contactCount` attribute is that it will remain 0 until the collision. Then, it will change to 1, then to 2, and so on with each collision. Thus, we only need to check that it's 0 to know that a collision has occurred.

Create the expression by clicking the Create button. Before we click on Play, let's change the initial velocity and spin settings that we gave to the `Ball` and change the magnitude of the turbulence. To do this, type the following code in the Script Editor:

```
setAttr rigidBody1.initialVelocityX 0;
setAttr rigidBody1.initialVelocityZ 0;
setAttr rigidBody1.initialSpinZ 0;
setAttr turbulenceField1.magnitude 0;
```

Then, in the persp window, go to the Shading menu and turn on Hardware Texturing so that we can see the color changes (Fig. 12.52). Also, turn off the grid from the Display > Grid menu so that we can see more clearly. Figure 12.53 shows the results of playback.

The `grid` will now change to a random color each time that `Ball` hits it. Now, we need to make another `for` loop to create the same expression for each of the other grids to control the other `shadingMap` shaders. We can attach this expression to each grid node using a MEL script, by assembling the expression in a variable called `$expstring` and then passing that string to the MEL `expression` command. Remember that we need to start off with `rigidBody4` and end at `rigidBody11`, with each expression manipulating a different `shadingMap` from `shadingMap1` to `shadingMap8`.

FIGURE 12.52

Hardware Texturing menu item.

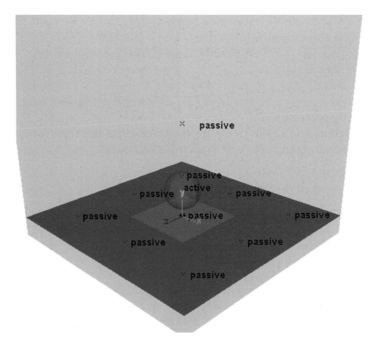

FIGURE 12.53

Playback in the persp Panel.

In the Script Editor, type in this double `for` loop, which increments both $i and $j each time through the loop.

In the Script Editor, type in the following double `for` loop:

```
for ($i = 4, $j = 1; $i < 12, $j < 9; $i++, $j++) {

    $expstring = "\nif (frame == 1) {\n";
    $expstring += "setAttr ";
    $expstring += ("shadingMap" + $j + ".shadingMapColor");
    $expstring += "-type double3 0.5 0.5 0.5;\n";
    $expstring += "};\n";
    $expstring += "if (";
    $expstring += ("rigidBody" + $i + ".contactCount");
    $expstring += "   0) {\n";
    $expstring += "setAttr ";
    $expstring += ("shadingMap" + $j + ".shadingMapColor");
    $expstring += "-type double3 (rand(0,1)) (rand(0,1))
                                 (rand(0,1));\n";
    $expstring += "};";

    // Execute the expressions
    expression -s $expstring -o ("expression" + $j)
               -ae true -uc all;
};
```

If you are assembling strings like the above code, you can test the script first by assembling the string and then printing it to see if it is what you want. To test this, try commenting out the `expression` command by adding a // at the beginning of the line and replace it with

```
print $expstring
```

Enter the command by pressing Enter.

Before you play the scene, set the values for the initial velocities and spins for the `Ball` and also the turbulence magnitude back to their initial values.

```
setAttr rigidBody1.initialVelocityX 12;
setAttr rigidBody1.initialVelocityZ -12;
setAttr rigidBody1.initialSpinZ 360;
setAttr turbulenceField1.magnitude 20;
```

Figure 12.54 shows results of playback. Now, when the ball strikes the grids, their colors change. Try different settings for the ball's `rigidBody1` initial velocities, bounciness, and turbulence magnitude to experiment with variations.

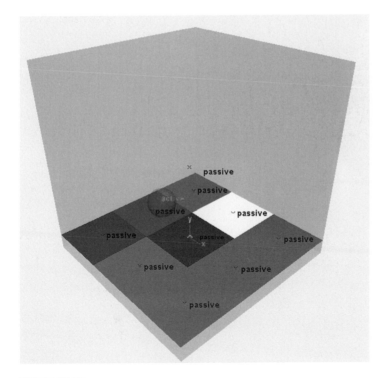

FIGURE 12.54

Changing grid colors in response to bounding ball.

12.4 EXAMPLE 4: SOLID DYNAMICS AND PARTICLES

In this example, we are going to use particle collisions to act on multiple solid bodies with added expressions. Figure 12.55 shows the results of such a strategy. Also, we'll create a small MEL window to control the direction for particle emission.

Let's start by constructing the scene. In the Script Editor, create a NURBS plane, as follows:

```
nurbsPlane -name panel -p 0 0 0 -ax 0 1 0 -w 1 -lr 1 -d 3
          -u 1 -v 1 -ch 1;
xform -worldSpace -scale 20 20 20 panel;
xform -worldSpace -rotation 0 0 -90 panel;
```

These commands will place the panel in the center of the world and point the normals in the positive X direction, which will be important for the collisions.

Now, we need to create a directional emitter called gun. In the Script Editor, type the following:

```
emitter -pos 25 0 0 -type direction -name gun -r 30 -spd 50
        -mxd 0
        -dx -1
        -dy 0 -dz 0 -sp 0;
particle;
connectDynamic -em gun particle1;
```

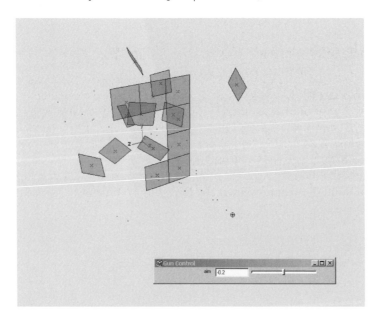

FIGURE 12.55

Particle gun knocks away solid bodies.

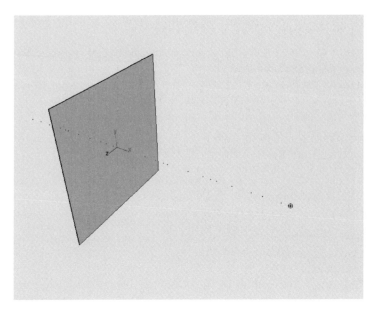

FIGURE 12.56

Directional emitter shooting particles at plane.

Set the timeline's start and end to 1 and 300, respectively, and hit Play. Figure 12.56 shows the result.

12.4.1 Create Interface Window for Aim Control Using MEL

Let's create a floating MEL slider in a window that we will hook up to the gun's Y rotation so that we can control the direction of the particles. First, we have to determine the limits that we want on the rotation. A range of −30 to 30 should be fine since we do not always want the particles to hit the panel throughout the simulation. Also, we want to use floating-point numbers and not integers since the floats will give a smoother transition between −30 and 30.

Open your favorite text editor for MEL scripting. In this editor, we will develop the MEL commands to build the window. Enter the following commands:

```
window -title "Gun Control" -width 400 -height 50;
    columnLayout;
    floatSliderGrp -label "aim" -field true
    -minValue -30.0 -maxValue 30.0 rotY;

connectControl rotY gun.rotateY;
showWindow;
```

After we look at how these commands work, we will paste them into the Script Editor and execute them to see what the window looks like and how it functions.

- `window -title "Gun Control"` is the name of the window as it appears on the interface.
- `-width` and `-height` specify a 400 · 50 pixel window. Although the user can resize it, this will be the default window size.
- `columnLayout` creates the layout of the rest of the settings called after it in a single column.
- `floatSliderGrp` will make a slider and an associated floating-point field.
- `-label` defines the name of the slider.
- `-minValue` and `-maxValue` set the range of the slider.
- `rotY` is the name of the slider that `floatSliderGrp` creates.
- `connectControl rotY gun.rotateY` connects the control `rotY` to the attribute `gun.rotateY` so that dragging the slider changes the attribute.
- `showWindow` displays the window in the Maya interface.

To make the window, select the text in the text editor and cut and paste (Ctrl+C and then Ctrl+V in Windows) into the Script Editor. Press Enter. Figure 12.57 shows the window that you will see.

Now, play back the scene while you move the slider back and forth to see the effect it has on the `gun` emitter (Fig. 12.58).

12.4.2 Add New Window Control to Shelf

We can add the script to make the window we created and put it in Maya's shelf so that it can be executed with the click of a button. In the Script Editor, paste the selected text that you copied from the text editor (it's probably still in the system text buffer). Select the text in the Script Editor and hold down the middle mouse button. With the button held down, drag it into the shelf in the Maya interface (Fig. 12.59).

Close the Gun Control window and click the new MEL icon on the shelf. The window will return. If you want to name the icon, use the Shelf Editor, available from the pop-up menu indicated by the triangle icon at the left side of the shelf.

Save the scene as `ex8start` in your project `scenes` directory (default); we are going to return to it later.

12.4.3 Convert Panel to Polygons and Break Up into Pieces

Later in the example, we will create a script that will convert the panel to polygons and break it into smaller pieces. First, to become familiar with the steps involved, select the panel and choose Modify > Convert > NURBS to Polygons ❑ (Fig. 12.60).

FIGURE 12.57

Gun Control window.

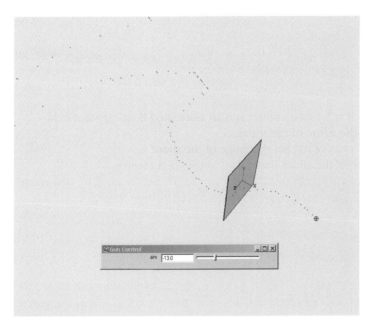

FIGURE 12.58

Erratic spray of particles from rotating gun.

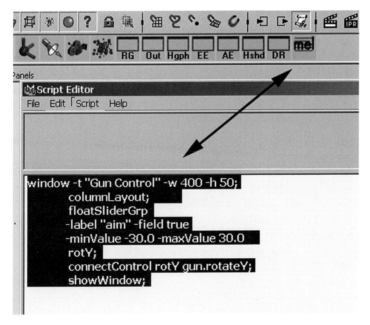

```
window -t "Gun Control" -w 400 -h 50;
        columnLayout;
        floatSliderGrp
        -label "aim" -field true
        -minValue -30.0 -maxValue 30.0
        rotY;
        connectControl rotY gun.rotateY;
        showWindow;
```

FIGURE 12.59

Installing script as MEL shelf button.

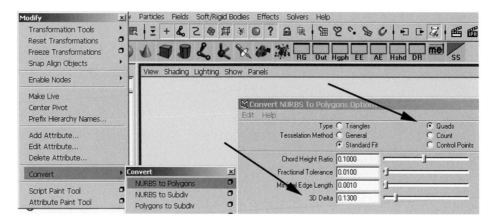

FIGURE 12.60

Converting NURBS to polygons.

Change 3D Delta to 0.13 and Type to Quads and then click Apply. You will end up with a nice polygonal grid with even distribution of square faces. Change the name of the resulting object in the Outliner window to polyPanel. The MEL equivalent follows:

```
nurbsToPoly -name polyPanel -polygonType 1 -delta 0.13 panel;
```

To break the panel into pieces, we need to break it up into individual polygons per face. Hide the original panel by selecting panelL in the Outliner and using the default key mapping Ctrl-H. Or, in the Script Editor, type

```
hide panel;
```

Figure 12.61 shows the results.

To break the panel up, we need to select its faces. Using MEL, we can do this in a way that returns the number of faces that are selected. First, we will use the select command but with "*" wildcard syntax. The following statement will select all the faces in polyPanel.

```
select -r polyPanel.f["*"];
```

Now, we will use the filterExpand command with the -selectionMask 34 flag to get the faces that are selected and store them in a variable called $faceList. filterExpand looks at the selection and returns to your script a list of all of the selected objects of a given type, designated by the selectionMask number. Looking in the MEL Command Reference in the filterExpand page, we can see that a selectionMask of 34 returns selected polygon faces.

```
$faceList = 'filterExpand -sm 34';
```

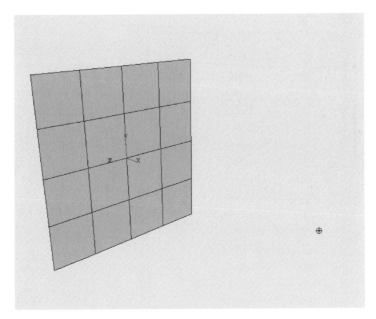

FIGURE 12.61

With the NURBS panel hidden, only the polygon panel remains visible.

Now, we can find the number of faces with the `size( )` function:

```
size($faceList);
```

If you run the above command in the Script Editor, you will see the following:

```
size($faceList);
// Result: 16 //
```

To break up the surface, you will need to know the number of faces in `poly-Panel`. The number of elements in `$faceList` tells us that there are 16 faces, or 0-15 in the `polyPanel.f[]` array. Now that we have the face count, let's extract the faces with the `polyChipOff` command, which makes them individual objects. In the Script Editor, type the following:

```
polyChipOff -keepFacesTogether 0
polyPanel.f[0:(size($faceList) + 1)];
```

Now separate the faces so that each gets its own node. Type in

```
polySeparate -name smPanels polyPanel;
```

You should see each of them under the `polyPanel` node in the Outliner window (Fig. 12.62).

Since the above command leaves the original object, we can delete `smPanels` from the list. We just want the individual, separated polygon objects of `smPanels1` to 16. Use the following command:

```
delete smPanels;
```

FIGURE 12.62

12.4.4 Add Dynamics and Expressions to Pieces

We will use a `for` loop to give `smPanels1` to 16 dynamic properties, to connect them to particle collisions, and then to expressions. Listed below are the actions we want to perform on each piece.

1. Make each a solid body with an initial setting to react to a particle collision.
2. Connect each with `particle1` to enable collisions with its particles.
3. Assign an expression to each piece that will turn off particle collisions once the piece reacts to a particle striking it and that will send the piece in positive X and negative Z to simulate a wind force.

Return to your favorite text editor to assemble the following script so that you can later copy and paste it into the Script Editor. In the text editor enter the following:

```
for ($i = 1; $i <= size($faceList); $i++) {

rigidBody -active -damping 1 -collisions 0 -particleCollision 1
          ("smPanels" + $i);
collision -r 0.2 -f 0.2 ("smPanels" + $i);
connectDynamic -c ("smPanels" + $i) particle1;
```

Note that we have not yet completed the loop. Before we finish, we will add an expression.

The first command turns smPanel + $i into a rigidBody with particle collisions on, and the next command makes it a collision object. Finally, the third command connects the collision object with particle1. We don't want collisions between the smPanels for the sake of speed, so we need to set -collisions to 0, or off, in the rigidBody command.

Now assemble the expression that will give the smPanel piece an impulse if its velocity is less than 0 in X (in the negative X direction). When this happens, our expression will set the impulse velocity in X to 2 and in Z to −2. This will send the piece forward and to the right. We also need to turn the rigid body particle collisions off because the particles will keep hitting the piece and pushing in negative X through dynamics. Once this attribute is turned off, the particles will still bounce off the pieces but not affect the panel's dynamics. And, of course, we need to reset the settings when we rewind to the beginning, frame 1.

Following is the expression as we would type it directly into the Expression Editor. What we will actually do is build this expression in a string and use the expression command to create an expression node connected with the panel object.

```
if (frame == 1) {
    rigidBody1.particleCollision = 1;
    rigidBody1.impulseX = 0;
    rigidBody1.impulseZ = 0;
};

if (rigidBody1.velocityX < 0) {
        rigidBody1.particleCollision = 0;
        rigidBody1.impulseX = 2;
        rigidBody1.impulseZ = -2;
};
```

With the expression written out, we are ready to assemble it in a string. To do this, add the following code segment to the loop that we have been editing.

```
$expstring = "\nif (frame == 1) {\n";
$expstring += ("rigidBody" + $i + ".particleCollision");
$expstring += " = 1;\n";
$expstring += ("rigidBody" + $i + ".impulseX");
$expstring += " = 0;\n";
$expstring += ("rigidBody" + $i + ".impulseZ");
$expstring += " = 0;\n";
$expstring += "};\n";
$expstring += "\nif (";
$expstring += ("rigidBody" + $i + ".velocityX");
$expstring += " < 0) {\n";
$expstring += ("rigidBody" + $i + ".particleCollision");
```

```
$expstring += " = 0;\n";
$expstring += ("rigidBody" + $i + ".impulseX");
$expstring += " = 2;\n";
$expstring += ("rigidBody" + $i + ".impulseZ");
$expstring += " = -2;\n";
$expstring += "};\n";

expression -s $expstring -o ("expression" + $i)
                          -ae true -uc all;
```

Finally, end the loop with a curly bracket and a semicolon:

```
};
```

Now, select the text from the text editor and copy and paste into the Script Editor. Press Enter on the numeric keypad to execute it.

Finally, we need to adjust the life span of `particle1` so that the particles will not live forever in the scene. Type the following:

```
setAttr particleShape1.lifespanMode 1;
```

```
setAttr particleShape1.lifespan 1.0;
```

Access the window that we created earlier by clicking the icon on the shelf. This will bring back the Gun Control slider (Fig. 12.63).

Now, play the scene, moving the slider to the left side so that it reads 30 and then move it to the right (Fig. 12.64).

12.4.5 Create Full MEL Script

Now that we have tested all the parts, let's assemble the full MEL script in the text editor so that we can load the saved scene and run the script on the `panel` object. The full script follows:

```
global proc panelBreakup( ) {
    print "Converting panel to polys\n";
    nurbsToPoly -name polyPanel -polygonType 1 -delta 0.13 panel;

    print "Selecting face and creating individual poly pieces\n";
    select -r polyPanel.f["*"];
    $faceList = 'filterExpand -sm 34';

    polyChipOff -keepFacesTogether 0
                polyPanel.f[0:(size($faceList) + 1)];
    polySeparate -name smPanels polyPanel;

    print "Clean up conversion\n";
    delete smPanels;
```

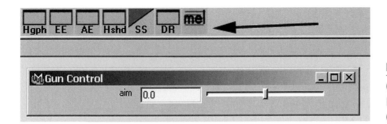

FIGURE 12.63

Clicking on the MEL button reveals Gun Control window.

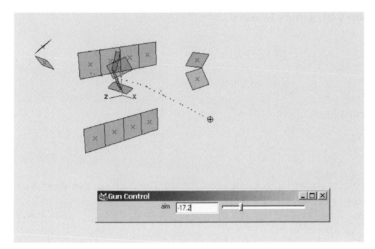

FIGURE 12.64

Knocking away solid bodies with the gun.

```
print "Convert poly pieces to rigidBodies and attach
    expressions\n";
for ($i = 1; $i <= size($faceList); $i++) {

    rigidBody -active -damping 1 -collisions 0 -
            particleCollision 1 ("smPanels" + $i);
    collision -r 0.2 -f 0.2 ("smPanels" + $i);
    connectDynamic -c ("smPanels" + $i) particle1;
    $expstring = "\nif (frame == 1) {\n";
    $expstring += ("rigidBody" + $i + ".particleCollision");
    $expstring += " = 1;\n";
    $expstring += ("rigidBody" + $i + ".impulseX");
    $expstring += " = 0;\n";
    $expstring += ("rigidBody" + $i + ".impulseZ");
    $expstring += " = 0;\n";
    $expstring += "};\n";
    $expstring += "\nif (";
    $expstring += ("rigidBody" + $i + ".velocityX");
```

```
$expstring += " < 0) {\n";
$expstring += ("rigidBody" + $i + ".particleCollision");
$expstring += " = 0;\n";
$expstring += ("rigidBody" + $i + ".impulseX");
$expstring += " = 2;\n";
$expstring += ("rigidBody" + $i + ".impulseZ");
$expstring += " = -2;\n";
$expstring += "};\n";

    expression -s $expstring -o ("expression" + $i) -ae true
            -uc all;
};

print "Set up scene environment\n";
hide panel;
setAttr particleShape1.lifespanMode 1;
setAttr particleShape1.lifespan 1.0;
setAttr gun.spread 0.2; // Adjust gun spread to hit more
pieces
cycleCheck -e off;
playbackOptions -min 1 -max 300 -loop continuous;

print "Call up the Gun Control window and play....\n";
};
```

Save the text file as panelBreakup.mel in your scripts directory and source it by choosing File > Source Script in the Script Editor (Fig. 12.65).

12.4.6 Load in Scene and Run Script

Load the scene ex8start that we saved earlier by choosing the menu item File > Open Scene (Fig. 12.66).

Now open the Script Editor and run the panelBreakup script:

```
panelBreakup;
```

Figure 12.67 shows the results of scene playback.

If you want to change the number of pieces, change the -delta flag in the script's conversion to polygons to a smaller number. This will affect the performance of the playback.

12.4.7 Pass a Float into panelBreakup

You can change the function to accept a float parameter and pass it to the -delta setting. In the panelBreakup function header, add the following:

```
global proc panelBreakup (float $myDelta)
{
```

FIGURE 12.65

Source Script menu item.

FIGURE 12.66

Opening the scene.

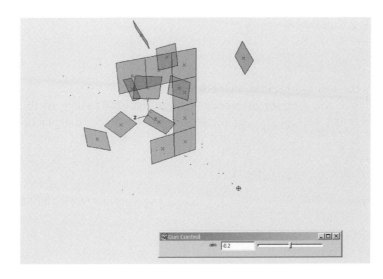

FIGURE 12.67

Results of panel-
Breakup script.

In the script body, add:

```
nurbsToPoly -name polyPanel -polygonType 1 -delta $myDelta
panel;
```

Save the script, and re-source it. If the script is in one of the Maya environment script path directories, you can simply type and execute it in the Script Editor as follows:

```
source panelBreakup;
```

Load the scene ex8start again and type

```
panelBreakup 0.1;
```

You will get an error if you do not give the function a float number after typing panelBreakup.

```
// Error: panelBreakup; //
// Error: Wrong number of arguments on call to panelBreakup. //
```

Examples Using MEL in Character Rigging

13

Mark R. Wilkins,
Chris Kazmier

CHAPTER CONTENTS

Using MEL does not revolutionize character setup, but it can make animating your characters easier by giving you useful tools for working with features of your character setup. Expressions can simplify animation, user interfaces can make manipulating the character easier, and other tools can be developed that will automate common tasks.

In production, many of the most useful MEL scripts and expressions perform simple tasks, such as managing animation curve data, selecting parts of the character,

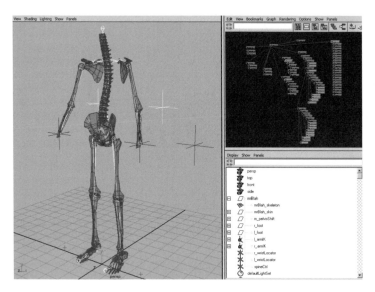

FIGURE 13.1

Example character.

and so on. Almost everything that character-related MEL scripts do can be done by hand in the interface; the advantage of using MEL is that by scripting these tasks they can be repeated and in many cases performed much more quickly.

In the following examples, we'll explore how to use Maya's expression language to create high-level animation controls on a simple skeleton. We will then move on to look at how to create a user interface that eases the animator's interaction with the character rig. These examples are based on the assumption that you are familiar with basic character setup in Maya. Figure 13.1 shows the character developed in the examples.

13.1 EXAMPLE 1: CHARACTER CONTROLS

In this example, we'll look at a setup for a bipedal character based on a human skeleton, and we'll examine how we can add to the character high-level animation controls that use expressions to drive complex motion. In Example 2, we'll add a user interface to simplify animation.

13.1.1 Load Scene

First, load the scene mrBlah.mb. From the File > Open Scene menu, select the scene mrBlah.mb in the archive on the Web site.

Figure 13.2 shows what you should see once the scene loads. Depending on your preferences in Maya, the joints might look different. You can change the size of the joints by choosing Display > Joint Size > 25%.

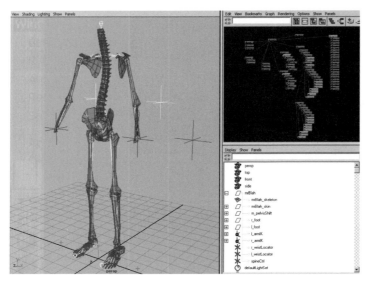

FIGURE 13.2

Contents of
mrBlah.ma.

You can zoom out a little in the Hypergraph panel on the upper right side of the screen to get a better view of the nodes that make up the character.

13.1.2 **Overview of Scene**

The character mrBlah is an example of a biped character that is already equipped with bones and skin. The skin consists of a polygonal skeleton model called mrBlah_ skeleton that was used to lay out the joints for mrBlah. Let's look at the joints alone by going to the persp panel's Show menu and deselecting the Polygon option (Fig. 13.3). This will hide the mrBlah_skeleton model so that you see only the joints, IK handles, and locators.

13.1.3 **Overview of** mrBlah**'s Controls**

Let's start by organizing the character's animation controls. Then, we'll create some custom attributes and expressions for mrBlah that will aid in animating him.

The character has some foot controls that are already set up. Zoom in the persp panel to the right foot area, and look for a locator just to the right of the foot. Select it; then move it up and down and back and forth with the Transform tool to see what it does (Fig. 13.4).

This control can also be found in the Outliner window under the name r_foot. Find it in the Outliner window, and open the entire hierarchy beneath it (Fig. 13.5). (Remember that you can open the entire hierarchy all at once by holding down the Shift key while clicking the + symbol.)

In the r_foot hierarchy, you will see a hidden node called r_toePivot. Select it, and "unhide" it by choosing Display > Show > Show Selection from the menu. The IK relationships that were created in setting up the foot are displayed in Fig. 13.6.

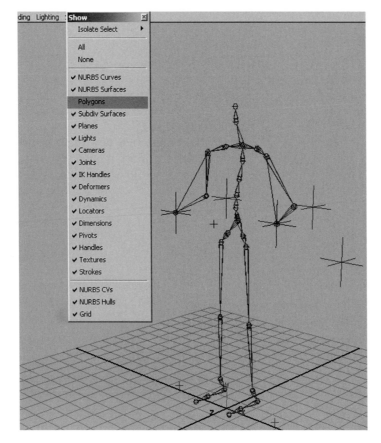

FIGURE 13.3

Hiding the polygon model.

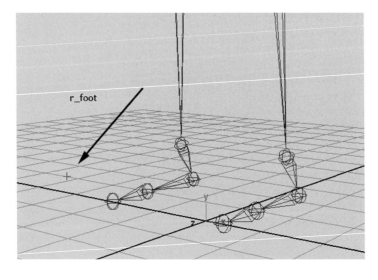

FIGURE 13.4

The `r_foot` handle.

A custom attribute added to the foot's top node r_foot is called Roll. When you select the node r_foot and open the Attribute Editor (Ctrl-a), you will see the attribute Roll under the Extra Attributes tab (Fig. 13.7).

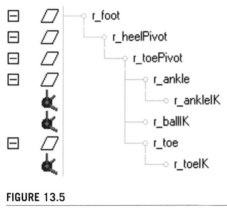

FIGURE 13.5

r_toePivot in Outliner.

The Set Driven Key feature was used to control the rotations of the foot structure by using the Roll attribute in r_foot as an input. Move the slider to see the results (Fig. 13.8).

If you want to view how the Roll attribute drives the foot's motion, open the Graph Editor by selecting Windows > Animation Editors > Graph Editor, and then select the r_heelPivot, r_toePivot, and r_ankle nodes in the Outliner. In the Graph Editor, you'll see the curve values that were used on the RotateX channels for each node(Fig. 13.9).

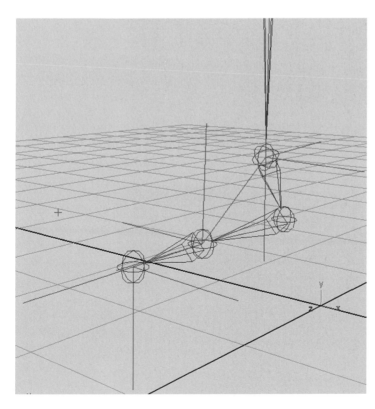

FIGURE 13.6

IK relationships in foot.

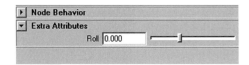

FIGURE 13.7

Roll custom attribute in Attribute Editor.

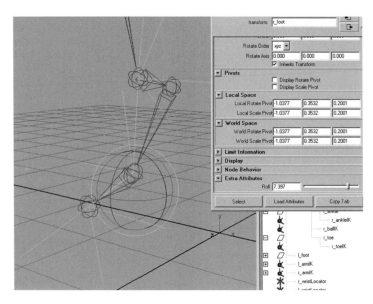

FIGURE 13.8

Effect of Roll attribute.

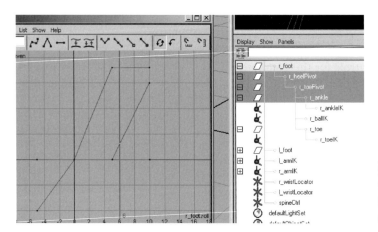

FIGURE 13.9

Curves that allow a Roll attribute to drive rotate attributes.

Set the Roll attribute back to 0; then select the r_toePivot node, and hide it once again (using the Hide Selection menu item or Ctrl-h). The right foot and left foot are set up the same way.

13.1.4 Locking Attributes

Before you close the Attribute Editor for r_foot, note that the Scale channels have been locked to 1.0. This was done to preserve the hierarchy's scale transform by preventing the animator from changing it or setting keys for it. If you look in the Channel Box, you will notice that the Scale channels will not be displayed in the window. Using locking and range of motion limitations can help the animator avoid modifying attributes that will break the character setup.

13.1.5 Arm Controls

The character setup in the example scene features two simple arm controls – wrist control and an elbow control – each of which is manipulated with a locator next to each arm. The locators for the right arm are called r_wristLocator and r_elbowLocator. The r_wristLocator is under the main mrBlah hierarchy, and the r_elbowLocator is under the m_pelvisShift hierarchy. The character was built this way because m_elbowLocator's transform will move with mrBlah's spine and orient itself correctly with respect to his backbone. Move these locators around with the Move tool to see how they work. Make sure that you select r_wristLocator in the Outliner window when you want to move it (Fig. 13.10).

In the Hypergraph window, find the IK node for the right arm, called r_armIK. Select it and you will see the two constraints that are used to control the arm (Fig. 13.11).

This control uses a point constraint and a poleVector constraint to control the arm.

13.1.6 Set Up mrBlah's Backbone Controls

Let's set up some controls for the character's backbone. To do this, we first need to add some custom attributes on a locator that is in the scene. Open the Outliner window, and find the locator called spineCtrl in the Outliner window at the top level of mrBlah's hierarchy at the bottom of the list (Figs 13.12 and 13.13).

In the Script Editor, we'll add the custom attributes using MEL that we will later use in our expressions. Type the following MEL command, and use the Enter key on the numeric keypad to execute it.

```
addAttr -ln Side -at double -keyable 1 |mrBlah|spineCtrl;
```

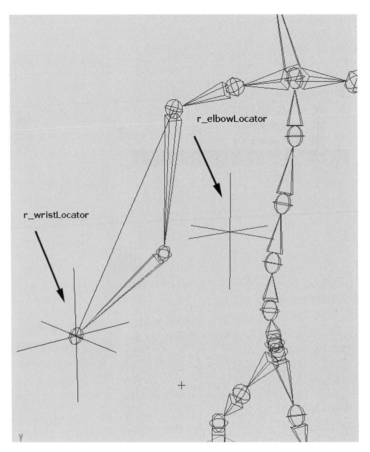

FIGURE 13.10

r_wrist_loca-
tor and r_elbow_
locator.

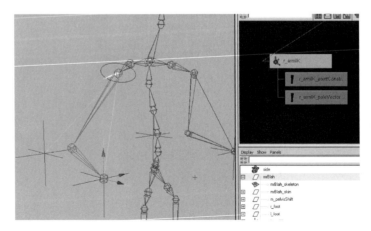

FIGURE 13.11

Constraints used to
limit arm motion.

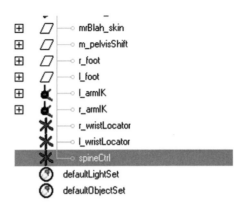

FIGURE 13.12

spineCtrl in Outliner.

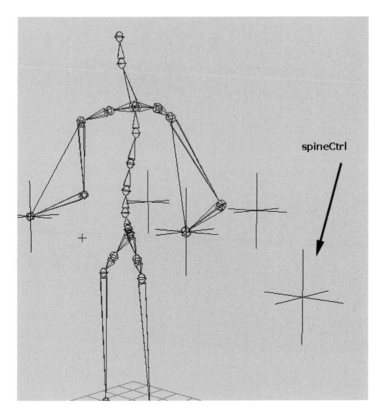

spineCtrl

FIGURE 13.13

spineCtrl in
persp panel.

Note that we use the | symbol to separate the names of the nodes along the way from the top of the hierarchy to the node that we want to manipulate. This is essential if your scene has multiple identically named objects in it but is not necessary if each node is named uniquely.

At this point, we need to add two more attributes that will control twisting and bending of the spine. We are not going to specify minimum and maximum values since we will later create a slider control to these attributes for the animator, and we can place limits on the slider to control the minimum and maximum. In the Script Editor, execute the following commands:

```
addAttr -ln Twist -at double -keyable 1|mrBlah|spineCtrl;
addAttr -ln Bend -at double -keyable 1 |mrBlah|spineCtrl;
```

Select the `spineCtrl` locator in the Attribute Editor, and open the Extra Attributes tab (Fig. 13.14).

Now, we need to enter expressions that allow the attributes to control the backbones. Figure 13.15 shows how the backbones, `m_back0` to `m_back4`, are set up.

We'll need our expression to control the individual rotations of X, Y, and Z for each bone 0–4. Open the Expression Editor by choosing Window > Animation Editors > Expression Editor, and then enter in the following expression:

```
// Control each backbone's rotation with the attrs Side,
// Twist, and Bend
m_back0.rotateZ = -spineCtrl.Bend;
m_back1.rotateZ = -spineCtrl.Bend;
m_back2.rotateZ = -spineCtrl.Bend;
m_back3.rotateZ = -spineCtrl.Bend;
m_back4.rotateZ = -spineCtrl.Bend;

m_back0.rotateX = spineCtrl.Twist;
m_back1.rotateX = spineCtrl.Twist;
m_back2.rotateX = spineCtrl.Twist;
m_back3.rotateX = spineCtrl.Twist;
m_back4.rotateX = spineCtrl.Twist;
```

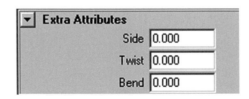

FIGURE 13.14

Side, Bend, and Twist attributes in Attribute Editor.

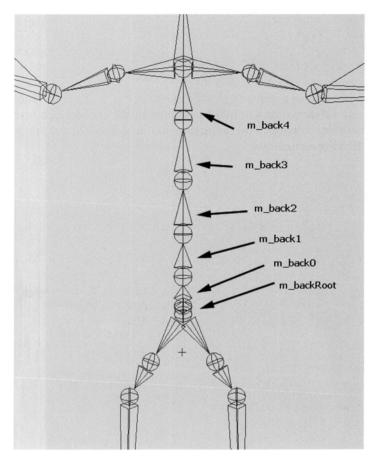

m_back4

m_back3

m_back2

m_back1

m_back0

m_backRoot

FIGURE 13.15

Backbone joints.

```
m_back0.rotateY = -spineCtrl.Side;
m_back1.rotateY = -spineCtrl.Side;
m_back2.rotateY = -spineCtrl.Side;
m_back3.rotateY = -spineCtrl.Side;
m_back4.rotateY = -spineCtrl.Side;
```

Type the name mrBlah_expression into the Expression Name box at the top of the window, and click Create (Fig. 13.16).

Select the spineCtrl locator, and select the Side channel's name (Fig. 13.17). In the persp panel, hold down the middle mouse button, and move the mouse from side to side to emulate a slider control (Fig. 13.18). Try this for the other channels as well.

Let's look at the first part of the expression and see how it adjusts the joints when you modify the Bend attribute.

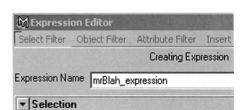

FIGURE 13.16

Creating `mrBlah_expression` in Expression Editor.

spineCtrl	
Side	0
Twist	0
Bend	0
SHAPES	

FIGURE 13.17

Side attribute in Channel Editor.

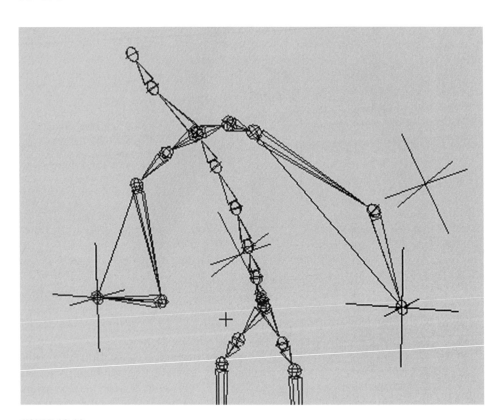

FIGURE 13.18

Effect of Side, Twist, and Bend on spine.

```
m_back0.rotateZ = -spineCtrl.Bend;
m_back1.rotateZ = -spineCtrl.Bend;
m_back2.rotateZ = -spineCtrl.Bend;
m_back3.rotateZ = -spineCtrl.Bend;
m_back4.rotateZ = -spineCtrl.Bend;
```

As you change the value for Bend, it will rotate each of the m_back joints in the negative direction around the Z-axis or counterclockwise as you look in the positive Z direction. As each joint is rotated, the parent–child relationships of the joints add each joint's transform to the joint above, causing a cascading, increasing rotation as you travel up the chain. Twist will do it with a positive value to the X rotation, and Side will do another negative value to the Y. This is a simple expression that does not rely on complex IK to do the trick.

Set the Bend, Twist, and Side attributes back to 0 before moving on.

13.1.7 Create Sway Effect When Picking Up Feet

Let's add a sway expression to mrBlah so that when you pick up either foot, the upper body will shift its weight to the other side. Open the Expression Editor again, and choose Select Filter > By Name. Pick the expression mrBlah_expression (Fig. 13.19).

Now, add the following two lines to the end of the other expression that we entered earlier.

```
// Cause sway when moving feet
m_backRoot.rotateY = (l_foot.translateY * 2)
                     -(r_foot.translateY * 2);
m_backRoot.translateX = (-l_foot.translateY / 4)
                        -(-r_foot.translateY / 4);
```

Click Edit to accept the changes to the expression. Select the r_foot locator; then use the Move tool to move the locator up in Y (Fig. 13.20).

Now, the skeleton sways to its left as we lift the right foot. This happens because when r_foot or l_foot is moved in Y, the expression multiplies each foot's Y translation by 2, and then it subtracts the results to find how far to rotate the root joint in Y. The body tends to rotate away from whichever foot is higher.

The negated Y translations of r_foot and l_foot are then divided by 4, and right is subtracted from left to translate the back away from the foot that's higher. This completes the effect of shifting the character's weight onto the lower foot.

Turn on the skeleton model that we turned off in the beginning by going back to the persp panel and selecting the Polygon option from the Show menu (Fig. 13.21).

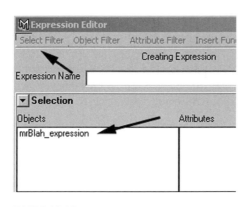

FIGURE 13.19

Selecting mrBlah_expression by name.

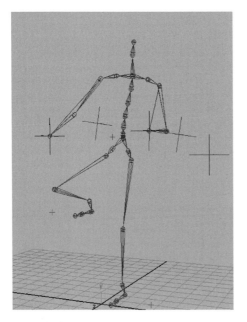

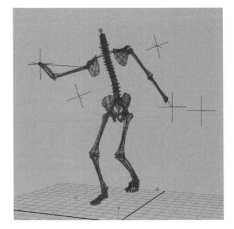

FIGURE 13.20

Raising foot shifts character's balance.

FIGURE 13.21

Get up and dance!

Finally, save the scene in your projects directory so that you have it for the next example. In Example 2, we will build some user interface tools to make animating mrBlah easier.

13.2 EXAMPLE 2: BUILDING A CHARACTER USER INTERFACE

In this example, we'll build on the previous example by adding a user interface to control mrBlah. This user interface will be a window containing sliders (for our high-level Bend, Twist, and Side attributes) and selection buttons (for all of the most-used body part controls). Also, the window will contain display control buttons to allow the user to select whether to display joints only, low-resolution geometry, or high-resolution geometry. Finally, the window will contain controls that allow the user to set keyframes from within the window (Fig. 13.22).

13.2.1 Load Saved mrBlah Scene

From the projects directory into which you saved the mrBlah scene at the end of Example 1, load the scene by selecting File > Load Scene, and then choose mrBlah.ma.

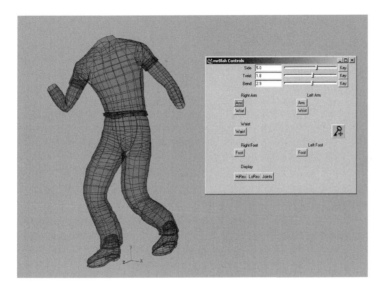

FIGURE 13.22

Finished user interface for character.

Turn off the skeleton polygonal model as before so that you can concentrate on the joints only. This time, we'll hide the model instead of turning off the display for all the polygonal models that might be in the scene. In the Script Editor type

```
hide mrBlah_skeleton;
```

Check to see that all the expressions that you added in Example 1 are there by choosing Windows > Animation Editors > Expression Editor > Select Filter, and then select By Name. You should see `mrBlah_expression` in the list (Fig. 13.23).

13.2.2 **Organize Controls for Users**

If you're developing a character that will be animated by someone else, the first step in developing user interfaces for the character is to meet with your audience and discuss how they would like to control the character. However, since we are setting up this character for ourselves, let's first make a list of what interface options we want. Besides buttons to select control handles and set keyframes, we also will want to allow ourselves to use our user interface window to switch between displaying the two different versions of the model that are already contained in the setup.

Figure 13.24 shows the layout of controls in the character. Following is a map of where we want to place buttons in our user interface window to help manipulate those controls.

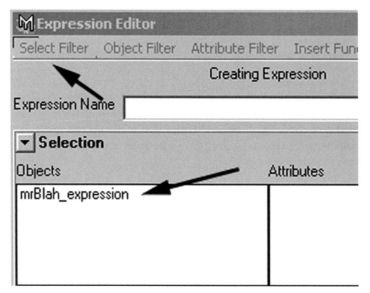

FIGURE 13.23

Selecting mrBlah_
expression by
name.

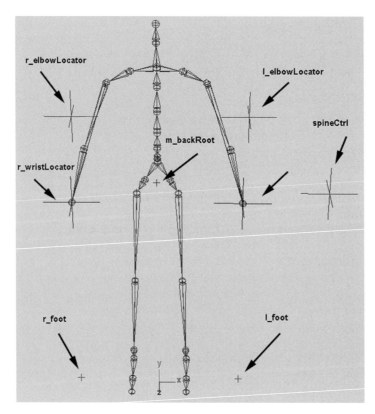

FIGURE 13.24

Overview of
mrBlah controls.

r_wristLocator	move	l_wristLocator	move
r_elbowLocator	move	l_elbowLocator	move
r_foot	move	l_foot	move
m_backRoot	move	spineCtrl	select to display Side, Twist, and Bend controls

A button to select each of these handles or locators will make up the main part of the window. Additionally, we'd like to be able to use buttons in our user interface window to move around among the following:

- HiRes: Display high-resolution NURBS model that is smooth skinned to the joints.
- LoRes: Display low-resolution polygonal pieces that are rigid skinned to the joints, plus the joints themselves.
- Joints: Display joints only.

Finally, we want to include a Key option in the interface window so that the user can directly set keyframes to the items that are selected.

13.2.3 **Create** mrBlah**Controls.mel**

Open your favorite text editing program, and start building the script mrBlah-Controls mel. At the top of the file, start writing the global proc mrBlahControls().

```
global proc mrBlahControls ( ){
    window
        -title "mrBlah Controls"
        -widthHeight 450 450
        MBcontrols;
```

This first command in the mrBlahControls procedure will give us the framework and title for the window.

Now, let's create the static text headings to form sections for the buttons.

```
string $form = 'formLayout';

// Interface text
string $txt1 = 'text -label "Right Arm        Left Arm"';
string $txt2 = 'text -label "Waist"';
string $txt3 = 'text -label "Right Foot       Left Foot"';
string $txt4 = 'text -label "Display"';
```

The string $form will contain the name of the formLayout object that the formLayout command creates. When you enter the text strings containing Right Arm and

Left Arm, make sure that there are 49 spaces between the end of Right Arm and the beginning of Left Arm – spacing is important because we'll be placing buttons precisely to align with those names.

To create the necessary buttons, enter the following code:

```
// Create buttons

// Right arm
string $b1 = 'button -label "Arm"
            -command "select -r r_wristLocator r_elbowLocator"';
string $b2 = 'button -label "Wrist"
            -command "select -r r_wristLocator"';

// Left arm
string $b3 = 'button -label "Arm"
        -command "select -r l_wristLocator l_elbowLocator"';
string $b4 = 'button -label "Wrist"
            -command "select -r l_wristLocator"';

// Waist
string $b5 = 'button -label "Waist" -command "select -r m_backRoot"';

// Right foot
string $b6 = 'button -label "Foot" -command "select -r r_foot"';

// Left foot
string $b7 = 'button -label "Foot" -command "select -r l_foot"';

// Display buttons
string $b8 = 'button -label "HiRes"
            -command "int $dis = 1;displayFunc($dis)"';
string $b9 = 'button -label "LoRes"
            -command "int $dis = 2;displayFunc($dis)"';
string $b10 = 'button -label "Joints"
            -command "int $dis = 3;displayFunc($dis)"';
```

The -command flags in the button creation section set up a select command for each button that will be executed when that button is clicked. The Arm buttons will select both the wrist and the elbow for movement. The display buttons' -command flags introduce a new variable $dis and a function called disp-layFunc. When these buttons are clicked, the variable is given a value of 1, 2, or 3 and then passed to displayFunc.

We have not yet defined this function, so at the top of the file, above the global proc mrBlahControls, enter the following:

```
global proc displayFunc(int $dis) {
int $dis;
switch ($dis) {
```

```
    case 1:
        HideJoints;
        hide "*_stdin";
        select -r mrBlah_skin; showHidden -a; select -d;
    break;
    case 2:
        hide mrBlah_skin;
        select -r "*_stdin";
        showHidden -a; select -d;
    break;
    case 3:
        hide mrBlah_skin;
        hide "*_stdin";
        ShowJoints;
    break;
    default:
    }
}
```

The function passes the value of $dis into a switch function to determine what display mode we have chosen. The case 1 displays high-resolution geometry, hides all joints, and hides all the stand-in objects that are bound to the joints. These are low-resolution polygon objects that help give users an impression of where the high-resolution version of mrBlah's skin will be. We use the wildcard format "*_stdin" to hide all the stand-in objects, because they've all been named to end with _stdin. Then, the last command selects the high-resolution skin, unhides it, and then deselects it.

As you can see, in the other case structures, we use similar commands to swap the displays. case 2 hides the high-resolution geometry and displays the low-resolution geometry, while case 3 hides both high- and low-resolution geometry, leaving only joints displayed.

Under // Display buttons in the main global proc, let's create a Key button that will allow us to keyframe the transforms of the locators that are selected in the window. Following is the MEL code to create this button:

```
// Keyframe button
string $KEYframe = 'symbolButton -image "setKey.xpm"
                    -parent $form
                    -command setkeys';
columnLayout;
```

This new symbolButton type will display the standard Maya key icon, whose picture is in the image file "setKey.xpm" as the button (Fig. 13.25).

FIGURE 13.25

`setKey.xpm` button image.

The file `setKey.xpm` is one of Maya's standard icons used for its interface, so an explicit path is not necessary for Maya to find the file. However, if you prefer, you could substitute your own icon in `xpm` format to replace it.

The button section is closed with the final `columnLayout` call. The keyframe button's `-command` flag tells the button to call a new function `setkeys` when it's clicked. Again, at the top of the script that we've been working on, enter the following `global proc`:

```
global proc setkeys() {
    string $names[ ] ='ls -sl';
        if ($names[0] != "m_backRoot") {
            string $name;
                for ($name in $names) {
                setKeyframe ($name + ".tx");
                setKeyframe ($name + ".ty");
                setKeyframe ($name + ".tz");
                }
            } else {
                setKeyframe m_backRoot.ty;
                setKeyframe m_backRoot.tz;
        }
    }
```

The `setkeys` procedure gets the selected locator from the scene by using `ls -sl` to store the selection list in an array variable called `$names[ ]`. Then, it checks to see whether the locator `m_backRoot` is selected; if it is, the script will not be able to set a keyframe for the X channel.

If `m_backRoot` is not in the first `[0]` position of the array, the script loops through the array by using a `for-in` loop. This `for-in` loop sets a keyframe for the x, y, and z channels of each selected locator. The `setkeys` button needs to loop over a selection list instead of just keying the first selected locator because the Arm selection option that we are putting in the interface selects two locators (both the elbow and the wrist), so we will need to set keyframes for both.

If our test at the beginning found the name `m_backRoot` at the start of the array, it bypasses the loop and skips directly to the last section, where the control gets its y and z channels keyed.

13.2.4 **Create Sliders to Control spinCtrl Attributes**

Let's create a slider interface to control values for the spine's Bend, Key, and Twist attributes. In the area under the last columnLayout call, enter the following:

```
// Sliders for spineCtl

floatSliderButtonGrp -label "Side" -field true
                     -buttonLabel "Key"
                     -buttonCommand
                     "select -r spineCtrl; setKeyframe spineCtrl.Side"
                     -minValue -20.0 -maxValue 20.0
                     -value 0.0 Side;
                     connectControl Side spineCtrl.Side;

floatSliderButtonGrp -label "Twist" -field true
                     -buttonLabel "Key"
                     -buttonCommand
                     "select -r spineCtrl; setKeyframe spineCtrl.Twist"
                     -minValue -20.0 -maxValue 20.0
                     -value 0.0 Twist;
                     connectControl Twist spineCtrl.Twist;

floatSliderButtonGrp -label "Bend" -field true
                     -buttonLabel "Key"
                     -buttonCommand
                     "select -r spineCtrl; setKeyframe spineCtrl.Bend"
                     -minValue -45.0 -maxValue 45.0
                     -value 0.0 Bend;
                     connectControl Bend spineCtrl.Bend;
```

The sliders will each have their own Key button, so they will not need to use the setkeys global procedure. Also, we added a select -r before the setKeyframe command. This selection is not needed to perform the set key; instead, it's there because by selecting it, the user will get visual feedback on the timeline of what frames keys exist at for the selected control (Fig. 13.26).

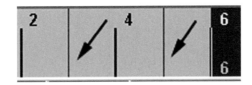

FIGURE 13.26

Keyframes in timeline.

13.2.5 Create Layout for Window Controls

Now, we will add the MEL code that lays out the text and the buttons that will appear in the window. We'll use the `formLayout` layout type, anchoring the items to the "top" and "left" sides to keep the code simple. Under the slider section, add the calls to `formLayout -edit` that will add the text items to the layout, as follows:

```
// Text layouts

formLayout -edit
            -attachForm        $txt1        "top" 80
            -attachForm        $txt1        "left" 100
            -attachForm        $txt2        "top" 160
            -attachForm        $txt2        "left" 100
            -attachForm        $txt3        "top" 220
            -attachForm        $txt3        "left" 100
            -attachForm        $txt4        "top" 280
            -attachForm        $txt4        "left" 100
    $form;
```

In the next section, where we will lay out the buttons, let's create three variables for offsets. We can position some of our buttons by using some of the same positions that we used before for the text but with an added offset. Enter the following code:

```
// Button layouts
int $bOffsetW = 180;
int $bOffsetH1 = 80;
int $bOffsetH2 = 140;

formLayout -edit
            -attachForm        $b1        "top" 98
            -attachForm        $b1        "left" 80
            -attachForm        $b2        "top" 120
            -attachForm        $b2        "left" 80
    $form;

    formLayout -edit
            -attachForm        $b3        "top" 98
            -attachForm        $b3        "left" (80 + $bOffsetW)
            -attachForm        $b4        "top" 120
            -attachForm        $b4        "left" (80 + $bOffsetW)
        $form;
```

```
    formLayout -edit
            -attachForm        $b5        "top" (98 + $bOffsetH1)
            -attachForm        $b5        "left" 80

  $form;

    formLayout -edit
            -attachForm        $b6        "top" (98 + $bOffsetH2)
            -attachForm        $b6        "left" 80

  $form;

    formLayout -edit
            -attachForm        $b7        "top" (98 + $bOffsetH2)
            -attachForm        $b7        "left" (80 + $bOffsetW)

  $form;

    formLayout -edit
            -attachForm        $b8        "top" 305
            -attachForm        $b8        "left" 80
            -attachForm        $b9        "top" 305
            -attachForm        $b9        "left" 118
            -attachForm        $b10       "top" 305
            -attachForm        $b10       "left" 158
  $form;

    formLayout -edit
            -attachForm        $KEYframe        "top" 170
            -attachForm        $KEYframe        "left" 360
  $form;

    showWindow MBcontrols;
}
```

The final command, showWindow, will launch the window. Save the MEL file as mrBlahControls.mel in your default scripts directory so that Maya will know where to look when you source the file.

13.2.6 **Test Window**

In the Script Editor window, source the script and launch the window so that we can see if everything is there and whether it works.

```
source mrBlahControls;
mrBlahControls;
```

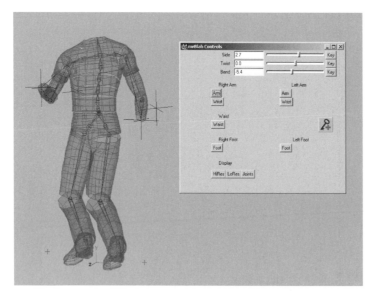

FIGURE 13.27

User interface for
mrBlah.

Figure 13.27 shows what you should see if everything went well.
Try out the buttons and sliders. Use the Move tool to transform what you select in the
window. Also, try the Display buttons and the Key icon button to make sure that everything
is in order. If you are getting errors and need to delete the window, type in

```
deleteUI MBcontrols;
```

13.2.7 Display Only What You Want User to See

Let's hide all the locators, handles, and IK handles in the scene to reduce the temptation
for the user to select them in the interface. We can do this by using the Show
menu in the persp panel. Enlarge the persp panel to full screen by pressing the space
bar with the mouse over the window. Now, go to the Show menu, and turn off the
options shown in Fig. 13.28 by deselecting them from the list.

13.2.8 Create Script Node for Window

We did not put a Close button in the interface because this window was designed to
be open all the time and only "stowed" if the user wants to hide it temporarily. The
window will be automatically launched when the scene is loaded. This will be done
using a scriptNode that the scene will execute as it loads. In the Script Editor, enter
the following command:

```
scriptNode -beforeScript "source mrBlahControls;mrBlahControls;"
    -n Controls;
setAttr Controls.scriptType 2;
```

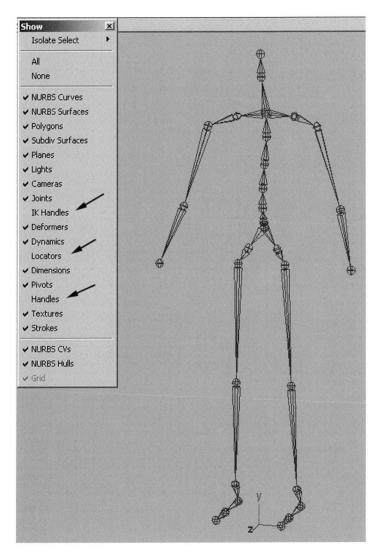

FIGURE 13.28

Turning off extraneous object display.

Setting the `scriptType` to 2 will open the window only when Maya's interface is used to load the scene. It will not execute the script if the scene is batch rendered.

Now choose File > Save Scene As, and call the file `mrBlahAnimation.mb` in the `scenes` directory (Fig. 13.29).

Close the `mrBlah` Controls window, and choose File > New Scene to clear out the scene. Now choose File > Open Scene, and select the `mrBlahAnimation.mb` file. When the scene is loaded, the custom window pops up and the scene is ready to animate.

FIGURE 13.29

Save Scene As...menu item.

13.2.9 Create Shelf Icon to Reopen Window When Closed

To give the user a means to open the window if he or she accidentally closes it, create an icon on the shelf that will reopen it, even if it's just stowed. In the Script Editor, enter the following:

```
if ('window -exists Mbcontrols') deleteUI MBcontrols;
source mrBlahControls;
mrBlahControls;
```

Do not execute the commands now; instead, select the text with the mouse and middle-mouse drag it to the shelf (Fig. 13.30).

13.2.10 Full Text of mrBlah**Controls.mel**

```
global proc setkeys() {
    string $names[] ='ls -sl';
        if ($names[0] != "m_backRoot") {
            string $name;
            for ($name in $names) {
                setKeyframe ($name + ".tx");
                setKeyframe ($name + ".ty");
                setKeyframe ($name + ".tz");
            }
        } else {
            setKeyframe m_backRoot.ty;
            setKeyframe m_backRoot.tz;
        }
    }
global proc displayFunc(int $dis) {
    int $dis;
    switch ($dis) {
```

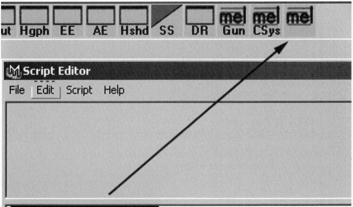

FIGURE 13.30

Making shelf button to open mrBlah user interface.

```
    case 1:
        HideJoints;
        hide "*_stdin";
        select -r mrBlah_skin; showHidden -a;select -d;
    break;

    case 2:
        hide mrBlah_skin;
        select -r "*_stdin";
        showHidden -a; select -d;
    break;

  case 3:
     hide mrBlah_skin;
     hide "*_stdin";
     ShowJoints;
  break;
  default:
  }
}
global proc mrBlahControls ( ){
   window
      -title "mrBlah Controls"
      -widthHeight 450 450
      MBcontrols;
      string $form = 'formLayout';
```

```
// Interface text
string $txt1 = 'text -label "Right Arm        Left Arm"';
string $txt2 = 'text -label "Waist"';
string $txt3 = 'text -label "Right Foot       Left Foot"';
string $txt4 = 'text -label "Display"`;

// Create buttons

// Right arm
string $b1 = 'button -label "Arm" -command
              "select -r r_wristLocator r_elbowLocator"';
string $b2 = 'button -label "Wrist" -command
              "select -r r_wristLocator"';

// Left arm
string $b3 = 'button -label "Arm "-command
              "select -r l_wristLocator l_elbowLocator"';
string $b4 = 'button -label "Wrist" -command
              "select -r l_wristLocator"';

// Waist
string $b5 = 'button -label "Waist" -command "select -r m_backRoot"';

// Right Foot
string $b6 = 'button -label "Foot" -command "select -r r_foot"';

// Left Foot
string $b7 = 'button -label "Foot" -command "select -r l_foot"';

// Display buttons

string $b8 = 'button -label "HiRes" -command
              "int $dis = 1;displayFunc($dis)"';
string $b9 = 'button -label "LoRes" -command
              "int $dis = 2;displayFunc($dis)"';
string $b10 = 'button -label "Joints" -command
              "int $dis = 3;displayFunc($dis)"';

// Keyframe button
string $KEYframe = 'symbolButton -image "setKey.xpm"
                    -parent $form -command setkeys';

columnLayout;

// Sliders for spineCtl
floatSliderButtonGrp -label "Side" -field true -buttonLabel "Key"
  -buttonCommand "select -r spineCtrl; setKeyframe spineCtrl.Side"
  -minValue -20.0 -maxValue 20.0
  -value 0.0 Side;
```

```
    connectControl Side spineCtrl.Side;
floatSliderButtonGrp -label "Twist" -field true -buttonLabel "Key"
    -buttonCommand "select -r spineCtrl; setKeyframe spineCtrl.Twist"
    -minValue -20.0 -maxValue 20.0
    -value 0.0 Twist;
    connectControl Twist spineCtrl.Twist;
floatSliderButtonGrp -label "Bend" -field true -buttonLabel "Key"
    -buttonCommand "select -r spineCtrl; setKeyframe spineCtrl.Bend"
    -minValue -45.0 -maxValue 45.0
    -value 0.0 Bend;
    connectControl Bend spineCtrl.Bend;

    // Text layouts
    formLayout -edit
    -attachForm        $txt1        "top" 80
    -attachForm        $txt1        "left" 100
    -attachForm        $txt2        "top" 160
    -attachForm        $txt2        "left" 100
    -attachForm        $txt3        "top" 220
    -attachForm        $txt3        "left" 100
    -attachForm        $txt4        "top" 280
    -attachForm        $txt4        "left" 100
    $form;

        // Button layouts
        int $bOffsetW = 180;
        int $bOffsetH1 = 80;
        int $bOffsetH2 = 140;

        formLayout -edit
            -attachForm $b1       "top" 98
            -attachForm $b1       "left" 80
            -attachForm $b2       "top" 120
            -attachForm $b2       "left" 80
        $form;

        formLayout -edit
            -attachForm $b3       "top" 98
            -attachForm $b3       "left" (80 + $bOffsetW)
            -attachForm $b4       "top" 120
            -attachForm $b4       "left" (80 + $bOffsetW)
        $form;

        formLayout -edit
            -attachForm $b5       "top" (98 + $bOffsetH1)
            -attachForm $b5       "left" 80
```

```
        $form;

        formLayout -edit
           -attachForm $b6        "top" (98 + $bOffsetH2)
           -attachForm $b6        "left" 80
        $form;

        formLayout -edit
           -attachForm $b7        "top" (98 + $bOffsetH2)
           -attachForm $b7        "left" (80 + $bOffsetW)
        $form;

        formLayout -edit
           -attachForm $b8        "top" 305
           -attachForm $b8        "left" 80
           -attachForm $b9        "top" 305
           -attachForm $b9        "left" 118
           -attachForm $b10       "top" 305
           -attachForm $b10       "left" 158
        $form;

        formLayout -edit
           -attachForm $KEYframe "top" 170
           \attachForm $KEYframe "left" 360
        $form;

           showWindow MBcontrols;
    }
```

Index

Note: Page numbers with "f" refer to figures.